A Gift From My Dad
Hilton W Woods
July, 1979

From The Library Of
Robert H Woods

The
Great Controversy

BY
ASHLEY S. JOHNSON

REVISED AND BROUGHT TO 1939

BY
M. D. BAUMER

ELEVENTH EDITION

★

GOSPEL ADVOCATE COMPANY

NASHVILLE, TENNESSEE

1963

Copyright, 1946
By
F. L. ROWE

GOSPEL ADVOCATE CO., *Owner*
NASHVILLE, TENN.

PREFACE TO THE REVISED EDITION

More than a quarter of a century ago this little volume was one of the most popular books among the disciples of Christ in America. The original author died several years ago and the book fell into disuse. For some time the reviser and publisher have considered revising it and bringing it to date. To this end a large number of denominational books and pamphlets have been studied, three of the sects described in the original text have been discarded because they have almost disappeared and three of the later denominations that have come into existence in the last sixty years have been substituted.

We do not know of any one text that contains so complete a statement and refutation of modern denominationalism as this one. All statements of beliefs have been taken from official sources and can be completely relied on.

M. D. BAUMER, *Reviser.*
F. L. ROWE, *Publisher.*

CONTENTS

Chapter		Page
I.	Methodist Speech	7
II.	Baptist Speech	14
III.	Presbyterian Speech	24
IV.	Episcopalian Speech	32
V.	Lutheran Speech	37
VI.	Roman Catholic Speech	41
VII.	Infidel Speech	46
VIII.	Adventist Speech	50
IX.	Mormon Speech	52
X.	Church of God Speech	57
XI.	Nazarene Speech	62
XII.	Christian Science Speech	66
XIII.	Inquirer Speech	70
XIV.	Inquirer Speech	100
XV.	Iconoclast Speech	116
XVI.	Iconoclast Speech	125
XVII.	Apostolos Speech	135
XVIII.	Business	146
XIX.	Visitor Speech	151
XX.	Visitor Speech	156
XXI.	Visitor Speech	162
XXII.	Peacemaker Speech	168
XXIII.	Peacemaker Speech	193
XXIV.	Peacemaker Speech	221
XXV.	Peacemaker Speech	246

CHAPTER I.

NOTE.—Messrs. Methodist, Baptist, Presbyterian, Episcopalian, Lutheran, Church of God, Roman Catholic, Nazarene, Infidel, Adventist, Mormon, Inquirer, Iconoclast, Apostolos, Business, and Peacemaker meet in convention to examine the Bible and search for the true basis of Christian union. After the usual preliminaries, Methodist advances to the front and addresses the assembly as follows:

METHODIST

I am profoundly glad to meet my friends of the different religious organizations of our age, and especially as we are to investigate our respective Church peculiarities, and search for the true basis of Christian union. This is an opportunity for which we have long prayed; let us, therefore, endeavor to make the best possible use of it. I stand before you today as a representative of one of the largest, grandest, and most influential religious movements of modern times. I could give you statistics showing our educational, financial and ministerial strength; but as these are no evidence that we are right, I regard it as unnecessary. There are different parties in our Church, some of the names of which are as follows: Methodist Episcopal Church, Methodist Episcopal Church South, Reformed Methodist Church, Methodist Protestant Church, Wesleyan Methodist Church, Primitive Methodist Church, Independent Methodist Church, African Methodist Episcopal Church, and African Methodist Episcopal Zion Church; yet it rejoices my heart to feel that we are all Methodists, a grand and glorious brotherhood, engaging in the same blessed cause, and expecting the same reward for our "work of faith and labor of love." We believe in a free salvation, a free church, a free people. I am entirely satisfied with the doctrines and blessings of Methodism. I believe they are broad enough and liberal enough to meet the wants of the whole world, and judging from the way we are increasing, it seems that others are being convinced that we stand upon a safe foundation. We are orthodox, evangelical, what more can you ask? Let it be understood that I am not denying the orthodoxy of my brethren who are present. I am no bigot. I believe there are Godloving, self-sacrificing and consecrated Christians among all the Churches represented in this assembly. We do not claim to be any better than any one else, but we do make great pretensions to doctrinal purity and simplicity of worship. Methodism is a grand power, and I feel that I shall do myself and my people a great injustice if I do not make good use of the present opportunity. I will give you a brief history of our Church and work, and leave you to decide on their merits for yourselves.

Our Church was founded in 1729 by the illustrious Christian and reformer, John Wesley. He was a clergyman in the Church of England. He viewed with an aching heart the religious degeneracy of the times, and set out with a determination to improve them. He organized societies for the promotion of personal holiness. The people were aroused from their sleep. Faith superseded formalism, the practice of religion the mere profession of it, and the influences set in motion caught from heart to heart, from city to city, from continent to continent, and from year to year, until those who are blessed by them are numbered by the million. Some unimportant changes have been introduced since Mr. Wesley's day, yet he is universally recognized as our founder. The Church has become divided on some ordinary matters, but we are still one in reference to the great principles of human redemption.

We have always been sound on the union question. Hear the testimony of our great founder: "I would to God that all party names and unscriptural phrases and forms which have divided the Christian world, were forgotten, and that we might all agree to sit down together as humble, loving disciples at the feet of our common Master, to hear His word, to imbibe His Spirit, and to transcribe His life in our own."—Wesley's

Notes, page 5. I feel sure that this will strike a responsive chord in every Christian heart. Why should it not? We are all brethren. We have the same Bible. We love, honor, and reverence the same Saviour, and we expect to live together in the place He has gone to prepare.

Leaving this department of our inquiry, I will proceed to show further our convictions in reference to the problems of this life, and that which is to come. By turning to our Discipline, page 2, and Art. v., you will find the following fearless and comprehensive enunciation: "The Holy Scriptures contain all things necessary to salvation; so that whatsoever is not found therein, nor may be proved thereby, is not to be required of any man, or be thought requisite or necessary to salvation. In the name of the Holy Scripture, we do understand those canonical books of the Old and New Testament, of whose authority there was never any doubt in the Church." We are willing to print this in burning letters on the banner under which we march. God's revelation is complete, and we are willing to submit to its demands. Divine authority transcends all human authority, and our submission to it lifts us above confusion and the possibility of doubts and fears. I referred to our Discipline; a few words of explanation are necessary. It contains the twenty-five articles of our religion, also an exemplification of our form of church government. These twenty-five articles are fundamental principles in the Methodist Church. We look upon our Discipline as second to no book save the Bible. In its preface you will find the following address to our members: "Far from wishing you to be ignorant of any of our doctrines, or any part of our Discipline, we desire you to read, mark, learn and inwardly digest the whole. You ought, next to the word of God, to procure the articles and canons of the Church to which you belong. We regard our Discipline as being in strict harmony with the word of the Lord, and have arranged these articles of faith and suggestions as to Church government for the sake of convenience. Our Discipline has been tried, and it works well. If it should be adopted by all the religious denominations of modern times, I feel assured that we would speedily come to the end of the sectarian peculiarities which have so long divided the people of God.

By referring to page 17, Art. xiii., you will find our definition of the Church: "The visible Church of Christ is a congregation of faithful men, in which the pure word of God is preached, and the sacraments duly administered, according to Christ's ordinance, in all those things that of necessity are requisite to the same." We hold this definition to be in strict harmony with the Testament of Jesus Christ, and that the Methodist Church contains all the constituents of the Church of the Bible. If it contains these elements, my claims to orthodoxy are no exaggeration, but are in strict harmony with the facts in case. The Church was established in the days of Abel, and has been continued through Abraham, Isaac, Jacob, Moses and the prophets, John the Baptist, and Christ and His apostles. I freely admit that there have been many important changes and developments since Abel's day. The grandest principles revealed before Christ, were embraced in the "Abrahamic covenant." It was to be an everlasting institution, and as the word is not yet exhausted, it must still be in force. Some have inquired with a great deal of impunity: "Where did your infant baptism and membership come from?" It came from an everlasting covenant. Infants were circumcised according to the provisions of this covenant. Baptism, in what we commonly call the New Testament, comes in the room of circumcision. Therefore infants should be admitted to baptism and Church membership. In addition to these incontrovertible facts, Jesus said: "Suffer little children, and forbid them not to come unto me; for of such is the kingdom of heaven," (Matt. 19:14). To my mind this is enough to convince any man not blinded by sectarian bigotry that He baptized them. Surely He would not take them in His arms and "bless them," and deny them the privileges of His gracious institution. In the tenth chapter of John, Jesus speaks of the shepherd, the sheep and the sheepfold. Now suppose Brother Baptist was a shepherd; would he put the old sheep into the fold and leave the tender lambs outside to the mercy of the thieves and wolves? This would be exceedingly foolish, yet it is just as reasonable as to admit the adults to Church membership and protection, and leave the infants out at the mercy of Satan. We also read of the baptism of entire households, and even of nations, as indicated in the last chapter of Matthew, and it is absolutely certain that these contained myriads of infants. The membership of our Church is composed of several classes; some who are "powerfully converted," some who are "hopefully converted," some "probationers," and many who are not "matured in years." These different classes open up desirable fields for the labor of all the public and private members of the Church.

We hold to the word of God in Church organization and in Church government, and while we are devoted to our ways, we do not propose to antagonize our brethren of the other denominations. It is impossible for us all to understand the Bible alike, any way, and in this big world there is room and work enough for all, and there should be no friction. We also believe that Jesus Christ "tasted death for every man;" that He published "life and immortality through the gospel;" and that He sent the Spirit into the world to convict sinners of "sin, righteousness and judgment." We believe that at some time in the sinner's life the Holy Spirit knocks at the door of his heart and demands entrance. He may be far away from home on the "mountains wild," but God will certainly visit him.

Here is our opinion as to justification: "We are accounted righteous before God only for the merit of our Lord and Saviour Jesus Christ, by faith, and not for our own works or deservings; wherefore that we are justified by faith only, is a most wholesome doctrine, and very full of comfort."—Disciplines, Art. ix., pages 14, 15. These are precious words. They are food for the hungry soul. But some one is ready to ask, How does the sinner get in possession of the faith which brings justification, peace and joy? We have our General Conferences, Annual Conferences, District Conferences, Quarterly Conferences, Class Meetings, Love Feasts, Sunday Schools and Revivals; also Bishops, Presiding Elders, Circuit Riders, Local Preachers, Deacons, Stewards, Class Leaders and Exhorters. These meetings and officials are all means of grace. The revivals more especially. They usually come once a year. The preacher in charge is generally assisted by some brother preacher and some godly members of the Church. The preacher delivers a soul-stirring sermon. The brethren exhort, sing, pray and shout. For convenience's sake the penitents are invited to indicate their interest in the prayers of the Church by coming forward to the anxious seat. The Spirit of God moves mightily among them. Broken-hearted, they cry aloud for mercy. They are exhorted to accept Christ, to give up everything, to throw themselves unreservedly at the foot of the cross. God answers the prayers of His people, and souls are born into the kingdom of God. This is justification, sanctification, redemption. These conversions are frequently accompanied by shouts which gladden the hearts of the children of God. These meetings sometimes continue for weeks, after which the different officials of the Church are required to employ themselves in cultivating the new converts. Some people ridicule and denounce what they are pleased to call the "mourner's bench process of conversion," but the more thoughtful and zealous of the community have adopted it, and from every quarter we hear cheering reports from those who are helping us to sustain the practice. So you perceive that Methodist principles are being felt among the other religious denominations.

The last department of my inquiry embraces an

ordinance about which some people have had much to say, and a great deal of it to no purpose. "Baptism is not only a sign of profession, and mark of difference, whereby Christian are distinguished from others that are not baptized; but it is also a sign of regeneration or the new birth. The baptism of young children is to be retained in the Church."—Discipline, Art. xxvii., page 20. What constitutes Scriptural baptism? Some are in favor of sprinkling, others of pouring, and others of immersion. We accept either. In speaking of the person to be baptized, our Discipline, on page 201, says: "The minister shall sprinkle or pour water upon him, or if he shall desire it, shall immerse him in water." We give every one his choice. The mode does not affect the validity of the ordinance. If a man's heart is right it does not matter whether you apply one drop or an ocean of water to him, he will be saved any way. God looks at the heart rather than outward ordinances. We allow plenty of latitude in reference to doctrine, and place great emphasis on righteousness, holiness and liberality. If a man has been baptized with the Holy Ghost we do not reject him, providing he is willing to submit to our Discipline. This is liberality. It is also doctrinally sound. However, if anyone has anything better to present, I am ready to consider it, but candidly, I do not expect to find anything better.

I am satisfied that any intelligent audience can see that there is something in Methodism worth contending for. I have redeemed my promise. I have given you a synopsis of our history and doctrines. Here is the true basis of Christian union. Here we can unite without the sacrifice of truth or conscience. Here is the fountain of life and peace. I must urge my brethren forward. A grand field opens for the dissemination of liberal principles and experimental religion. We will publish the Gospel of Christ from the "rivers to the end of the earth." I am happy. Beyond the existence of sectarian bigotry and strife, I see union, peace, and millennial joy. "Alleluia, the Lord omnipotent reigneth"!

CHAPTER II.

BAPTIST.

I join Brother Methodist in reference to the importance of the occasion. We will doubtless remember it with unusual gratification. If by a free exchange and discussion of views we discover a foundation on which we can unite without the sacrifice of principle, we will bless ourselves and the generations following. Jesus Christ prayed for the unity of His children. Paul commanded the Corinthians to be "perfectly joined together in the same mind and in the same judgment," (I. Cor., 1:10). Good men of all ages have prayed for it. We discuss it and confidently expect it some time in the future. There is a basis on which we can be one, but the question arises: Are we willing to build upon it? Permit me to say at the outset, that Christian union means more than simply to "agree to disagree," and thereby preach, pray, and work together in peace and harmony. It means everything comprehended in the quotation just made from Paul. We must all be members of the "one body."

I will now turn my attention to what was said in the previous address. I can not accept the conclusions of Brother Methodist. He mixes a little too much tradition, human authority, with his religion. The Bible is God's only book. If a man's creed contains more than the Bible, it contains too much. If less than the Bible, it does not contain enough. I have no book of my own to defend. I think I can show his arguments are unscriptural, unreasonable and absurd; that his Discipline contains more humanisms than gospel. He quotes Mr. Wesley and his creed with a manifestation of wonderful confidence, but we will see further on if he will stand by what they teach. He quotes the fifth article of his creed, and almost in the next breath attempts to apoligize for the existence of the book in which he finds it. Now, if the Old Testament and the Testament of Jesus Christ are of Divine authority, and contain all things necessary to salvation, what is the use in scattering these creeds broadcast over the country? Why not invest the same amount in Bibles and give them to the poor? But, perhaps he will say. "We want the people to know our dotcrine." To be sure, but you say your doctrine is in the Bible. If that is true your creed is a superfluous book. It is my honest opinion that he cannot justify its existence either on scriptural or logical grounds. I may appear somewhat severe, but I have no patience with these modern innovations. If Christians ever become united it will not be accomplished by the diffusion of human theories and speculation. The Metholist Church is founded on the Discipline. The Discipline is founded on the "experience of a long series of years." Brother Methodist asserts that the Discipline is founded on the Bible, but the preface of his book disagrees with him. We conclude, therefore, that his theory is founded on "experience," rather than upon the words of eternal truth. The Discipline contains the twenty-five articles of his religion, some of which are as far from the truth as nothing is from Omnipotence. They receive and exclude members according to its provisions. They conduct all their meetings, and in fact every work and ceremony is performed in keeping with its demands. He thinks he has found the true basis of Christian union, and I suggest that he try its merits on his own brethren, for he admits that they are divided, and if he succeed we will consider his claims. A theory or creed that will not unite the factions of the Methodist Church, will never unite the other denominations of modern times. He seems to think if we should all become Methodists, sectarianism would come to an end. I disagree with him. I do not think such steps would improve our spiritual condition, or bring us nearer the great fountain of day. We want something better than humanisms. **Something more enduring than time, that will not need to be changed almost every year to meet the wants of an advancing civilization.** He affirms that the Methodist Church contains all the constituents of the Church of the Bible. Then why call it the Metholist Church? There were no Methodist Churches in apostolic times. He says the Church was established in the days of Abel, and continued through Abraham, Isaac, Jacob, Moses and the prophets, John the Baptist, and Christ and His apostles. This is no excuse for the existence of the Methodist system. If we admit that this theory is correct, it will do him no good. There has not been a day since the smoke of Abel's sacrifice ascended to God that the Divine administration has resembled the Methodist Church. Compare the "Abrahamic covenant," the "Mosaic dispensation," or even the "Fullness of the Gospel" under Christ, and His apostles, with it, and you will be compelled, by the force of inflexible facts, to conclude with Brother Methodist that it was founded by Mr. Wesley and improved by the "experience of a long series of years." Methodism is a human institution. Proof: "As Methodism arose and progressed, when the want of a rule was felt to aid the work, it was adopted. If its practical working was found to be good, it was retained; but if not good, it was modified or abolished. Thus each , prudential regulation has been brought to the test of experience and practical utility, one page of which is worth more than a volume of theory."—Bishop T. A. Morris.

"A more wise or better àrranged system of religious or moral enterprise could not have been conceived. Of course, like all other human institutions, it had its imperfections."—J. L. Inskip.

Mr. Wesley's reference to its origin is as follows:

"On Monday, May 1st, our little society began in London; but it may be observed, that the first rise of Methodism, so called, was in November, 1729, when four of us met together at Oxford. The second rise of Methodism was at Savannah, Georgia, in 1736, when twenty or thirty persons met at my house. The third rise of Methodism was in London, May 1, 1737, when forty or fifty of us agreed to meet together every evening in order to a free conversation, begun and ended with singing and prayer."—Wesley's Works, Vol. 7, page 348.

Again Mr. Wesley says: "I am, under God, the father of the whole family."

Please do not forget that this is Methodist authority of the highest character. We have here presented to us three distinct risings of this system, and a frank admission that it is imperfect, "like all other human institutions."

My friend devises quite an ingenious argument to sustain his practice of sprinkling infants, but when we throw the pure, resplendent light of truth upon it, the deformity and unreasonableness of it can be clearly seen. If he had affirmed that infant baptism is authorized by his creed I should have remained silent, but as he attempts to make the word of God responsible for it, I unhesitatingly enter my emphatic protest. He says "our authority for this practice came from an everlasting covenant." Will he stand by this assertion? I affirm, on the authority of Divine revelation, that this "Abrahamic covenant" does not contain a single blessing for him or any other Gentile. By consulting the seventeenth chapter of Genesis, you will find that the participants in the privileges of this institution are described as "He that is born in thy house and he that is bought with thy money." Can my friends claim membership under either of these provisions? I think not. In the same connection God said to Abraham: "My covenant shall be in your flesh for an everlasting covenant." Brother Methodist did not descend from Abraham according to the flesh. He is not a member of this institution, and it is too late for him to become one. Having assumed this erroneous proposition, it forces him to affirm the identity of the two covenants (Gal., 4:21-31). Two things may be similar, but they cannot be identical. But where do the children come in? Hear his argument: Children were circumcised according to provisions of the "Abrahamic covenant." Baptism comes in the room of circumcision. Therefore children should be baptized. I suggest a very wide difference between the Abrahamic covenant and Methodism. Children were circumcised because they were born in Abraham's house, in the covenant. Brother Methodist baptizes them to bring them into the Church. He may deny this, but if he does, his Discipline will rise up in judgment and sustain my affirmation. But let me state several particulars in which there is a striking dissimilarity. Circumcision was a parental duty (Gen., 17:11-14). Baptism is a personal duty (Acts, 2:37, 38). Circumcision was a permanent mark by which the Jew could always be distinguished (Gen., 17:9-11). Will he say baptism is a substitute for it in this particular? Circumcision was only for the males. (Gen., 17:14), but he baptizes both males and females. Children were circumcised on the eighth day, but my friend will baptize them on any day (Gen., 17:12). Every male child not circumcised was to be cast out (Gen., 17:14). Will he affirm the same of children that are not baptized? "Circumcision in the flesh made by hands," was not typical of baptism, but a circumcised heart (Rom., 2:29). Circumcision was commanded (Gen., 17:9-14), but who can find a command for baptizing infants? Baptism is a burial (Rom., 6:1-4). I should like to know if it is a substitute for circumcision in this respect. The circumcised children had free access to all the privileges and blessings of the covenant, but the Methodist Church does not admit them into full membership by baptism, although its Discipline teaches that this act brings them into the Church. Finally, three thousand Jews were admitted into the Church on the day of Pentecost. They had been circumcised, but Peter, regardless of this, commanded them to "repent and be baptized," (Acts, 2:1-41). This is the most frivolous and preposterous theory every advanced by an intelligent man. There is not an item of Scripture that favors it from Genesis to the Revelation. He next introduces the words of Jesus:

"Suffer little children, and forbid them not, to come unto me; for of such is the kingdom of God," and thinks it is conclusive evidence that He baptized them. But hear the inspired apostle: "Jesus Himself baptized not," (John, 4:2). He may say His disciples did it. Not on this occasion, for they even rebuked the parents who desired to have their children blessed (Mark, 10:13, 14). He next tries his hand on the tenth chapter of John; the shepherd and the sheepfold. He wants to know what I would do with the lambs. I will let the Great Shepherd answer. He informs us that the "sheep hear his voice." Infants can not do this; hence we conclude that in their helpless condition they will be cared for by "Him who doeth all things well." He next tries to sustain his practice by referring to the great commission (Matt., 28:18-20). This proves too much, and therefore proves nothing. He wants to baptize infants because they are a part of the nation. Let us try his method of interpretation on all classes of citizens; thieves, defaulters, idolaters, murderers, heathen; and does nationality qualify them for this solemn ordinance? Surely not. Then the infants must wait until they can understand, believe and obey. He makes his final struggle on the household baptisms. He is absolutely sure that he has found an unanswerable argument. Let us examine the one recorded in Acts, 16:13-15. I admit that they were all baptized, but were there any infants? Brother Methodist, to sustain his unreasonable dogma, makes the following assumption: (1) He assumes that Lydia was married. (2) That she had children. (3) That she had them with her. (4) That some of them were infants. (5) That they were baptized. The jailer's house was composed of believers .(Acts, 16:19-34), and the house of Stephanas was composed of persons who were old enough to minister to the wants of the saints (I Cor., 16:15). No infants! Not even one!

Now this is too much of a guess work for me, and I unhesitatingly pronounce it an imposition and a farce. Brother Methodist, your logic is out of joint.

You take the responsibility of sprinkling a poor, unconscious infant in the sublime name of Father, Son, and Holy Spirit, when the word of God does not contain the slightest authority for the practice. Why not do it in the name of the Methodist Church, or admit that it is unauthorized, and that you do it as a matter of expediency?

Brother Methodist quotes his views on Baptism from the Discipline. He believes in sprinkling and pouring, but rather than lose a "valuable member," he will immerse him. He admits our practice to be right, but endeavors to show that something else will do. Now look at his argument, and you will see that we can not unite upon such a disjointed system as this. He closed with a shout as if he felt that Methodism would revolutionize the world. Not while I live!

Doubtless you want to know by this time who I am, and what I believe. I am a representative of the Baptist Church of Christ, sometimes called the Missionary Baptist Church. I must confess, with my esteemed friend who preceded me, that there are divisions among Baptists. We are called Six Principle Baptists, Seventh-Day Baptists, Anti-Mission Baptists, Missionary Baptists, Regular Baptists, Free-Will Baptists, New Connexion Baptists, and Particular Baptists.

The party to which I belong is by far the most numerous, and the others, I am glad to say, are rapidly dying out. We call ourselves Baptists, because we adhere to and submit to the one baptism—immersion. We hear a great deal about the identity of the covenants, but Christianity is undoubtedly a new institution. It is manifestly superior to the old covenant, and the man whose religion is based upon the old is most evidently living in the dark. The Church founded by John has continued through Christ and His apostles. It has withstood the influences of Roman Catholicism during the dark ages, and it is standing upright in this age as the Church, with no creed but the Bible. We can trace the existence of our Church back to its foundation. History bears testimoney to the fact that the "gates of hell" have not prevailed against the Church. We claim succession from the apostles. We can trace our existence back to its Divine source. If we can not do it the Church is a failure. The honor, power, majesty, glory, and dominion of Jesus Christ depend upon it. Jesus Christ was a Baptist, the apostles were Baptists, the martyrs were Baptists, and there have been Baptists in all ages since the Church began. Hence I feel honored to stand before you in this age of intelligence and claim to be a Baptist; to hold in my hand the chain of historical succession, apostolic succession, which reaches back to the old foundation! We are ready to meet the world on this claim. With it we stand or fall. Now this forever excludes the claims of Brother Methodist or any other modern Church. But let me emphasize my solemn conviction that there are many Christians in all the evangelical denominations. I think the charge that we are uncharitable is false. We admit that they are Christians, but we deny that they are in the Church. We believe they are unbaptized, yet many of them go to heaven every day. We agree with our Methodist brethren that the "anxious seat" is a "means of grace." Yet I think many were converted before its introduction; it is not, therefore, indispensably necessary to salvation. In fact many of our intelligent churches do not use it at all. This is correct, for one of our eminent ministers recently said: "Your knowledge is the measure of your religion."

The Church was fully set up by Jesus while here on earth, This is proven by the fact that He laid down the law for its government, which could not have been done if the Church had not then been in existence. I challenge contradiction of this statement.

Two of our cardinal doctrines are total depravity and salvation by "grace alone." These propositions are worthy of your attention. You cannot be a Baptist and reject them. I do not agree with Brother Methodist's definition of the Church. If he had said "a congregation of immersed believers worshiping God according to the New Testament," we could indorse it without injustice to our principles. We believe in a converted membership; a membership composed of justified men and women. No one is qualified for a position in our Church until he is saved by repentance and faith. We receive persons into the fellowship of our Churches by "experience of grace," and immersion. A preacher in our Church can not receive a member. Our rules demand that the congregation shall hear the candidate's experience and vote on his reception. If it judges him favorably, the preacher is then authorized to immerse him. We believe he is a Christian before this, but in order to Church membership it must be done by a regular Baptist preacher; hence we can not receive into our fellowship any who have been immersed by our religious neighbors. To state the matter plainly, we believe immersion is necessary to Church membership, but not to salvation. I speak of immersion; it was the invariable practice of the Church in the early ages of its existence. Brother Methodist, and those who stand with him, think it is a small matter whether a man is immersed, or has a few drops of water sprinkled or poured upon him. I think it is very important. Paul says there is "one baptism." It cannot be that the action is a matter of indifference, as our opponents try to teach. I have not the slightest doubt that we are on apostolic ground, for no scholar of eminence denies that our practice is in perfect harmony with the practice of the apostles and their immediate successors. Immersion has never been in doubt, but sprinkling and pouring as substitutes for it, have always and will ever be in dispute. A correct translation of the Scriptures will remove every difficulty and bring us back to original ground.

It is charged by our opponents that we make too much of baptism. We deny the charge. We do not make any more of it than the Bible makes of it. We stand by the book! It is a Christian duty. Hence we immerse none but the converted. We deny that it is essential to salvation, or for the remission of sins, or that it changes the state or the relationship, and affirm with all confidence that what it does is figurative or declarative.

I confess that while the Baptist Church possesses all the characteristics of the Apostolic Church, both of a doctrinal and practical nature, it has changed somewhat in its progress through the ages. I claim to stand with Jesus, Paul, Peter, John and the long line of saints who have made their names deathless in the annals of time. There is no call for a new Church. The old is good enough. We claim to stand on the Bible. We call on all contending parties to abandon their man-made creeds, lay down their implements of ecclesiastical warfare, and stand together with us on the old foundation. There never has been any reason for the existence of so many sects. Reason, revelation and experience condemn them and encourage the hope of their early dissolution.

I present to you the gospel of Christ in its purity; its facts, its ordinances as they were delivered from heaven. We can stand together here in the one Church. Here is something on which we can rest from doubts and confusion. I present to you facts of momentous importance; the basis on which we can be one in Christ Jesus. This is important. The salvation of the world, in a great measure, depends upon it. Let us be united in heart, life and work, and the blessings of the pure gospel will be ours for time and eternity. May the presence of God abide with us all.

CHAPTER III.

PRESBYTERIAN

I was unwilling to enter this convention from the very beginning, believing it would degenerate into useless controversy and end in strife and confusion, and that the cause of Christianity would suffer rather than be benefited by our deliberations. I hope no one will understand that my reluctance arose from fear. Quite the contrary; Presbyterianism can not possibly lose anything by honest investigation: "The eternal years of God are hers." It has passed through the persecutions of centuries. It has withstood the assaults of sectarians, infidels, and "false brethren," and now it stands erect amidst the storms, and bids defiance to the powers of earth and hell.

I do not feel disposed to give it up for anything beneath the sun. I do not think it can be improved by human legislation; hence, I see but little use of my presence in this august assembly. As to Christian union, what is it? Are we not united already? Are we not Christians? Do any of the evangelical denominations represented in this convention deny a single one of the essential or fundamental principles of Christianity? Not one. True, we have our differences, our denominational peculiarities, but these are unimportant, and non-essential when compared with the great facts on which we have always been one. Now, shall we lay aside our distinguishing doctrines and attempt to formulate a universal creed to gratify the whims of a few religious enthusiasts? I think not. Jesus Christ justified our separate existence when He said: "He that is not against us is for us," and "I am the vine and ye are the branches." It is absolutely impossible for us to see alike in all things. Jesus knew this, hence the lessons just given. There is work for us all to do. The field is unlimited and I think that we can accomplish more in our present condition than if we were all united upon one creed. As it is now, every man can be pleased. If he does not want to be a Presbyterian, let him be something else. There are many evangelical roads, but they all have the same terminus: "The everlasting city of God." I would much rather give you my hand as a pledge that I am willing to live in peace with my denominational brethren, than to proceed further with this discussion, but as it is insisted upon, and we are commanded to "contend earnestly for the faith once delivered to the saints," I can not refrain. I expect to speak my sentiments plainly, pointedly, and unequivocally; hence I ask my brethren beforehand to treat them with due consideration.

Presbyterians are slightly divided in name, but very closely united in doctrine. They are called American Presbyterians, Northern Presbyterians, Southern Presbyterians, New School Presbyterians, Old School Presbyterians, English Presbyterians, Scotch Presbyterians, Reformed Presbyterians, Associate Presbyterians, or Seceders, Associate Reformed Presbyterians, United Presbyterians, and Cumberland Presbyterians. Our doctrines are based, with a few alterations, upon the Westminister Confession of Faith. See Preface to Confession. The doctrines compiled and published by the Westminster Assembly have been somewhat modified to meet the wants of some of our branches, but these changes are unimportant, and I am glad to say that in the rudimental principles of Christianity we are substantially one.

I think we have the best creed in the world. It was originally compiled by one hundred and twenty-one divines and thirty laymen from England, and five Commissioners from Scotland. The Assembly was engaged more than five years and a half in preparing, discussing, and adopting the Confession of Faith, the Larger and Shorter Catechisms, Directory for Worship, and the form of Church Government. The distinguished Richard Baxter, who was personally acquainted with most of the members, but was not himself one of them, says: "The divines there congregated were men of eminent learning, godliness, ministerial ability and fidelity." Their work was soon approved by the House of Commons, and adopted by the General Assembly of the Church of Scotland. Now, shall he abandon the enunciations of this ancient assembly, or attempt to improve the results of their labors? I answer with an emphatic no! Pardon me, but if you want an universal creed, why do you not adopt this one? If you will insist on Church union, this is most unequivocally the foundation.

But let me give you a more explicit exhibition of our distinctive doctrines. We are willing to be governed by the word of God. It is our guide and counsellor. Our Confession of Faith is in strict accordance with the Bible. You will see by referring to it that we furnish the plain words of Holy Writ to sustain every article of faith and item of practice.

Nearly all our parties are strictly Calvinistic, and that you may understand me more fully, I will give you a brief synopsis of the "five points" of "our theology."

I. *Predestination.*—"As all men have sinned in Adam and have become exposed to the curse and eternal death, God would have done no injustice to any one if He had determined to leave the whole human race under sin and the curse, and to condemn them on the account of sin; according to those words of the apostle, 'all the world is become guilty before God.' "—Scott's Synod of Dort, pages 112-124. Predestination has reference to both angels and men. "By the decree of God for the manifestation of His glory, some men and angels are predestinated into everlasting life, and others foreordained into everlasting death. These angels and men, thus predestinated and foreordained, are patricularly and unchangeably designed; and their number is so certain and definite that it cannot be either increased or diminished."—Confession of Faith, pages 23 and 24. This election did not grow out of foreseen faith, obedience, good disposition, or good qualities of the elect, but out of the sovereign will and wonderful grace of God. These purposes of God are immutable, so He softens the heart of the elect and redeems them from sin, but the others are left alone to reap the fruits of their labors.

At our Annual Convention in 1938, by a vote of 151 to 130, this doctrine was annulled, but as you will perceive, more than 46% of the delegates still considered this ancient and sacred doctrine sufficient for the present century.

II. *The Death of Christ.*—God entered into a covenant with His Son before the foundation of the world. "He willed that Christ, through the blood of the cross, should, out of every people, tribe and language, efficaciously redeem all those, and those only, who were from eternity chosen to salvation, and given to Him by the Father; that He should confer on them the gift of faith."—Scott's Synod of Dort, pages 128-130. Hence you perceive that Christ died for those who were His before the foundation of the world.

III. *Man's Corruption.*—"All men are conceived in sin and born the children of wrath, indisposed to all saving good, propense to evil, dead in sin, and the slaves of sin; without the regenerating grace of the Holy Spirit they neither are willing nor able to return to God to correct their depraved nature, or to dispose themselves to the correction of it."—Scott's Synod, page 125, 126. "Our first parents being seduced by the subtlety and temptation of Satan, sinned in eating the forbidden fruit. This their sin, God was pleased according to His wise and holy council to permit, having proposed to order it to His glory. By this sin they fell from their original righteousness and communion with God, and so became dead in sin, and wholly defiled in all the faculties and parts of soul and body. They being the root of all mankind, the guilt of this sin was imputed and the same death in sin and corrupted nature conveyed to all their posterity, descending from them by ordinary generations."—Confession of Faith, pages 39, 40.

IV. *Grace and freewill.*—"God hath endowed the will of man with natural liberty that it is neither forced nor by absolute necessity of nature, determined to good or evil. Man, in his state of innocency, had freedom and power of will, and to do that which is good and well-pleasing to God, but yet mutably, so that he might fall from it. Man, by his fall into a state of sin, hath wholly lost all ability of will to any spiritual good accompanying salvation; so as a natural man being altogether averse from that good, and dead in sin, is not able by his own strength to convert himself, or to prepare himself thereunto."—Confession of Faith, pages 58-60.

V. *Final Perseverance.*—"God, who is rich in mercy, from His immutable purpose of election, does not wholly take away His Holy Spirit from His own, even in lamentable falls; nor does He permit them to decline, that they should fall from the grace of adoption, and the state of justification; or to commit the sin unto death, or against the Holy Spirit; that being deserted by Him they should cast themselves into headlong destruction; therefore, it is impossible for one of God's elect to fall away and be lost."—Scott's Synod of Dort, page 141.

There are some among us who are rather moderate in their Calvinistic principles, but those who are specially so are just that far removed from the original ground. I believe several of the evangelical denominations in this assembly virtually agree with us in reference to our "five points," though they are not always explicit in their statement. To sum up, we believe a certain portion of the race to have been predestinated to everlasting life; that this part was redeemed by the death of Christ, and that they are called, sanctified, adopted and saved through the Holy Spirit; saved from sin, saved from the possibility of ever falling, saved eternally. I listened very attentively to the addresses of the brethren who preceded me. I heard many things with which I heartily agree, and others which

I cannot conscientiously approve. Of course I do not agree with Brother Methodist's twenty-five articles of faith, and I think he is entirely mistaken as to the practicability of our uniting upon them. I agree with him in reference to the Abrahamic covenant, Infant Baptism, and Church Membership. His definition of the Church will do tolerably well, but is not so explicit as ours. See our Confession, page 124. He admits persons to membership in his Church by sprinkling, pouring, or immersion. We are not quite so liberal as that. Our Confession of Faith, page 146, says: "Dipping of the person into the water is not necessary; but baptism is rightly administered by pouring or sprinkling water upon the person." Dr. Rice, of New York, recently said in reply to Dr. Armitage, of the Baptist Church: "I do not believe immersion is Christian Baptism at all." So you see where we stand, and if we ever unite in one brotherhood, we must not be so particular about "modes."

As to Brother Baptist's speech, I disagree with almost everything he said. I think he is an extremist and exceedingly inconsistent also. He believes in immersion and nothing else. He says we must have a new translation and substitute "immersion" for "baptism." Yet he persists in calling himself a Baptist. According to his theory, John the Baptist must become John the Immerser. "Baptize," must become "immerse." Then the Baptist Church will become the Immerser Church!

The preachers of the different Baptist denominations ridicule us for practicing sprinkling and pouring. Yet they uncompromisingly affirm that their practice is nonessential to salvation; hence, it seems shameful to set it up as a barrier between the children of God. They admit that Methodists, Baptists, Presbyterians, Quakers, etc., are orthodox; that they are Christians, and that they will go to heaven without immersion. Why then do they raise such a confusion in reference to this custom? Immersion is the door into the Baptist Church; hence, according to their theory and practice, it is easier to get into the everlasting city of God than to get into their Church! They denounce Disciplines, Confessions of Faith and Prayer Books with severity. Yet, if you will take the pains to look into their church books throughout the land, you will find written articles of Faith and Rules of Decorum. Also by looking into many of the libraries throughout the country, especially the old ones, you will find copies of the "New Hampshire Confession of Faith," and the "Philadelphia Confession of Faith." "But," says my friend, "we deny these; they are not binding on us now." They used to be authoritative with the Baptists, and they must acknowledge them now or deny their ancesty. Does not this at least "crack" a link in the chain of historical succession? Why do they hide their light under a bushel? I presume it is in order to enable them to raise a cry about what others do.

Brother Baptist assulted Brother Methodist with all the power at his command. He said that "there were no Methodist Churches in Apostolic times." This is confessedly true, but I assure him that in the next verse after the one which speaks of a Baptist Church, he will find a full history of the origin, progress and victories of Methodism.

The Baptist method of receiving members is contrary to Scripture and common sense. A man makes a profession of faith in Christ. He goes before a Baptist Church and tells his experience. The members of the Church compare his experience with theirs, and express by their vote that he has religion, that he is saved, and, therefore, saved eternally. They accept him as a brother, baptize him and admit him to their table. In a few months he falls away. They withdraw their fellowship from him by vote, and by this act declare that he was never converted.

They unite with other religious organizations in revivals, treat them as brethren, Christians, and at the end exclude them from what they call the Lord's table! If I am good enough to work in revivals and go to heaven, I am good enough to go to the Lord's table! But why do they exclude us? Simply because their hands have not conducted us through what they call a "figure, and only a figure," immersion! Let this convention take notice that the Baptist Church makes a test of fellowship of that which they universally and unanimously designate a nonessential.

Brother Baptist professes to be able to trace his existence back to John in the wilderness. I think from the speech he made he has never been out of the wilderness! He enumerated about nine kinds of Baptists. I do not think this is very complimentary to his theory of apostolic succession. I should like to know which branch of his Church can claim historical descent from John. If he can find any distinct order known as the Baptist Church beyond the sixteenth century, I should like to see his evidence. I think he is mistaken, and for his edification I volunteer a little advice: "Those who live in glass houses would do well not to throw stones," and "happy is he that condemneth not himself in the things which he alloweth."

Now, my dear brethren, I have given you a brief outline of our history and principles, but it is sufficient, and when you come to make up your final decision, give them the consideration which their importance and antiquity demand. I feel sure that the results will be satisfactory and beneficial. May the grace of God abide with us all. Amen.

CHAPTER IV.

EPISCOPALIAN.

I stand before you today, not as a representative of a "sect," or a "branch of the Church," but as a minister of the only true and Apostolic Church. It has long been considered as incompatible with the character and dignity of a clergyman in our Church to participate in deliberations of this kind. We know we are right; on the only true foundation, hence, we endeavor to pursue the even tenor of our way, and let other people alone. We have always been ready, however, to disseminate the pure doctrine, to direct inquirers to the right way, to contend earnestly for the primitive gospel, and to give a "reason for the hope that is in us." In compliance with the combined requests of the eminent clargymen of the "religious sects," I am here to direct them to what I consider the fountain of truth, life and peace. First of all, those who are in our Church are one. The true faith and practice destroy sectarianism. We all believe and practice the same doctrines, hence we cannot be divided into factions. I have listened very attentively to the addresses already made. I feel that you have manifested too much of the carnal or partisan spirit. Lay aside these encumbrances and listen, calmly and impartially to the exposition of divine truth which I shall endeavor to make. There are some true propositions on which we all agree. We all believe in the existence of the One Supreme Ruler of heaven and earth; the divinity, mission, death, resurrection and glorious ascension of our Lord Jesus Christ; and that the word of God contains all things necessary to salvation. But you disagree in reference to what constitutes the true Church and the best creed. Do you ask for the true Church? Do you inquire which is the best creed? In answer to the first, I direct your attention to the Protestant Episcopal Church. In answer to the second, I direct your attention to the Book of Common Prayer. Here you find the true Church and the true creed. Here you can find rest from sectarianism and strife. Here you can build and be infallibly safe. Here you can find the true foundation for Christian union and co-operation.

By turning to the third page of our Book of Common Prayer, you will find that it was ratified by the bishops, clergy and laity of our church in the year of our Lord one thousand seven hundred and eighty-nine, or one hundred and fifty years ago. You will further see that it was not only recommended, but absolutely established, as the liturgy of the Church. So you readily perceive that it bears the stamp of age and authority. It is in incessant use in all of our Churches, and is universally acknowledged to be the very foundation of our faith and worship.

Our Church had its origin in England, where it is called the Church of England, and we remember with deep gratitude the long nursing and protection which our English brethren have bestowed upon us. In this country there is no relation between Church and State, and as this is true, some unimportant changes have been introduced to meet the demands of local circumstances.

Our Book of Common Prayer contains the fundamental articles of our religion; thirty-nine in number. I have neither time nor disposition to quote them in full, but I will give you an abridgment of what they contain. The first five articles contain a profession of faith in the Trinity, the incarnation of Jesus Christ, His descent into hell, and His resurrection, the divinity of the Holy Ghost. The three following relate to the canon of Scripture. The eighth article declares a belief in the Apostles' and the Nicene creeds. The ninth and following articles contain the doctrine of original sin, of justification by faith alone, of predestination, etc. The nineteenth, twentieth and twenty-first declare the Church to be the assembly of the faithful; that it can decide nothing except by the Scriptures. The twenty-second rejects the doctrine of purgatory, indulgences, the adoration of images, and the invocation of saints. The twenty-third decides that only those lawfully called shall preach or administer the sacraments. The twenty-fourth requires the liturgy to be in English. The twenty-fifth and twenty-sixth declare the sacraments effectual signs of grace (though administered by evil men) by which God confirms our faith. They are two: Baptism and the Lord's Supper. Baptism, according to the twenty-seventh article, is a sign of regeneration, the seal of our adoption by which faith is confirmed and grace increased. In the Lord's Supper, according to article twenty-eight, the bread is the communion of the body of Christ, the wine the communion of His blood, but only through faith, (Art. xxix); and the communion must be administered in both kinds (Art. xxx). The twenty-eighth article condemns the doctrine of transubstantiation; the thirty-first rejects the sacrifice of mass as blasphemous; the thirty-second permits the marriage of the clergy; the thirty-third maintains the efficacy of excommunication. The remaining articles relate to the authority of the King, the traditions of the church, and the condemnation of Anabaptists, etc.

In addition to these thirty-nine articles, our book gives full, clear and explicit directions for making, ordaining and consecrating bishops, priests and deacons, baptizing infants, baptizing those of riper years, the order of confirmation, the solemnization of matrimony, visiting the sick, the burial of the dead, the forms of morning and evening prayers, administering the holy communion, the litany and suffrages, a selection of psalms and hymns, the order of worship, a catechism, etc.

On page 296 we find a full and Scriptural exposition of infant baptism. "There shall be for every male child to be baptized, when they can be had, two Godfathers and one Godmother; and for every female, one Godfather and two Godmothers; and parents shall be admitted as Sponsors, if desired."

This, I think, is an improvement on the Methodist and Presbyterian plan. The children can not answer for themselves, hence those of mature years do it for them. The entire ceremony is fully described. By this act of the child by its Sponsors, it is brought into the congregation of the Lord.—Page 299. The minister closes with the following prayer, and charge to the Godfathers and Godmothers:

"We yield Thee hearty thanks, most merciful Father, that it has pleased Thee to regenerate *this Infant* with Thy Holy Spirit, to receive *him* for Thine own *Child* by adoption, and to incorporate *him* into Thy holy Church. And humbly we beseech Thee to grant that *he*, being dead unto sin and living unto righteousness, and being buried with Christ in His death, may crucify the old man, and utterly abolish the whole body of sin; and that *he is* made *partaker* of the death of Thy Son, *he* may also be *partaker* of His resurrection; so that finally, with the residue of Thy holy Church, *he* may be *an inheritor* of Thine everlasting kingdom; through Christ our Lord. *Amen.*"

"Forasmuch as *this Child hath* promised by you *his* sureties to renounce the devil and all his works, to believe in God and to serve Him, ye must remember that it is your parts and duties to see that *this Infant* be taught so soon as *he* shall be able to learn, what a solemn vow, promise and profession *he hath* here made by you. And that *he* may know these things the better, ye shall call upon *him* to hear sermons; and chiefly ye shall provide that *he* may learn the Creed, the Lord's Prayer, and the Ten Commandments, and all other things which a Christian ought to know and believe to his soul's health; and that *this Child* may be virtuously brought up to lead a godly and a Christian life; remembering always that Baptism doth represent unto us our profession; which is, to follow the example of our Saviour Christ and to be made like unto Him; that, as He died and rose again for us, so should we, who are baptized, die from sin and rise again unto righteousness; continually mortifying all our evil and corrupt affections, and daily proceeding in all virtue and godliness of living."

"Ye are to take care that *this Child* be brought to the Bishop to be confirmed by him, so soon as *he* can say the Creed, the Lord's Prayer, and the Ten Commandments, and *is* sufficiently instructed in the other parts of the Church Catechism set forth for that purpose."

The Protestant Episcopal Church stands or falls with the principles here enumerated. They cannot fall, for they are in strict harmony with the Testament of Jesus Christ. And His holy apostle says: "The word of the Lord endureth forever." Our Church has a grand record, and it is destined to become the admiration of mankind. It will live when your "Disciplines," "Confession of Faith," and the "Articles of Faith," and "Rules of Decorum," shall have gone to the dark shades of relentless oblivion. If you are really searching for the "old paths," here you can find them and be at rest. It rejoices my heart to offer you a Church and a Creed which will be as enduring as time. Will you abandon the doubtful and accept that which is infallibly sure? Will you renounce the transient and accept the eternal? If so, may the great Head of the Church bless you, strengthen you and bring you to His everlasting kingdom.

CHAPTER V.

LUTHERAN.

I have something better to present to your consideration than the twenty-five articles of Methodism, the fanciful assertions of my friend, Brother Baptist, the Confession of Presbyterianism, or the thirty-nine articles of Episcopalianism. It is the primitive gospel, the pure faith and the true Church wrenched from the grasp of Roman Catholicism by the great Martin Luther. The truth has withstood the trials of ages, and it cannot possibly lose anything by being submitted to the examination of this assembly. I am happy to stand before you as a friend and brother to the great reformer. It matters not how lightly you may esteem it, you are in a great measure indebted to him for the word of God and the great religious privileges you now enjoy. He was born on the 10th of November, 1483, consequently at the time in which the Pope of Rome exercised almost unlimited ecclesiastical and political power. He was taught the Roman Catholic religion from infancy. He became in many respects a sincere and zealous advocate of his religion. He was a great student. In 1508 he became a teacher in the University at Wittemburg. In addition to the duty of hearing his class and preaching, he occasionally heard confessions. Different occurrences led him to a more serious contemplation of the teachings of Romanism. He became involved in a controversy with its authorized representatives. They threatened him and his followers with the horrors of the Inquisition. This did not discourage him, so on the 31st day of October, 1517, he published ninety-five propositions, discussing copiously the doctrines of penance, charity, indulgences, purgatory, etc. A long and tedious discussion followed, in which error suffered and truth triumphed. His enemies burned his books. He retaliated, and as he committed some of the standard Catholic works to the flames, he exclaimed in a loud and triumphant voice: "Because ye have troubled the saints of the Lord, therefore let eternal fire trouble you." He was excommunicated from the Church by the Pope of Rome. He treated him with unreserved contempt, and committed his "Bull of Excommunication" to the fire. His zeal was boundless, his determination unconquerable. In all his mighty contests he came out victor. In April, 1521, he appeared before the Diet at Worms. Several charges were made against him. In reply he emphatically refused to retract anything he had said or written. He closed his defense with these immortal words: "Let me be convinced by the testimony of the Scriptures, or by the clearest arguments; otherwise I can not and will not retract, for it is neither safe nor expedient to act against conscience. Here I take my stand. I can not do otherwise. God help me. Amen." These noble words flashed like lightning through the German and surrounding nations, and Popery trembled from center to circumference. This Reformation has rolled from country to country, and from age to age, and we are enjoying its benefits today. Luther was no ordinary man. He did not labor for self-aggrandizement, but for the good of his fellowmen. He died as he lived, in full confidence of the truth which he preached. These words were among the last he ever uttered: "Oh, my heavenly Father, eternal and merciful God, Thou hast revealed to me Thy Son, our Lord Jesus Christ! I have preached Him. I have confessed Him. I love Him, and I worship Him as my dearest Saviour and Redeemer; Him whom the wicked persecute, accuse and blaspheme."

His words live after him, and eternity alone can give an adequate conception of his life and its results.

I have given you a brief statement of the rise and progress of the Reformation. I will now present a synopsis of our distinctive doctrines. I hold in my hand a little book called the Augsburg Confession of Faith. It contains an invincible system of doctrine. The learned men of Europe have never been able to overthrow it. It was drawn by Luther and Melancthon, and presented to the Emperor Charles V., in 1530, at the Diet of Augsburg. It is divided into two parts, of which the former, containing twenty-one articles, was designed to repesent with truth and perspicuity the religious opinions of the reformers, and the latter, containing seven articles, is employed in pointing out and confuting the seven capital errors which occasioned their separation from the Church of Rome. These were communion in one kind, the forced celibacy of the clergy, private masses, auricular confession, legendary traditions, monastic vows, and the excessive power of the Church. We submit these articles for your investigation. We stand or fall with them.

Martin Luther restored the Bible to the world, and we take it as our guide. We acknowledge that Christ died for all who are partakers of Adam's transgressions, but those only who believe in Him and persevere in their faith to the end will be saved. We do not believe that good works are in anywise meritorious with regard to salvation. As to free will, we deny its power before conversion. We maintain that none are converted but by the prevailing efficacy of grace alone. We acknowledge but two sacraments: the Lord's Supper and Baptism. We deny transubstantiation, the mass, elevation and adoration of the host, the ceremonies and all external worship which the Church of Rome observes with respect to the body and blood of Jesus Christ. We reject the adoration of saints and relics. We endeavor to imitate every good example, but nothing further. We condemn all acts of penance and human expiation, such as solemn vows and pilgrimages, and depend alone on Christ for salvation.

We heartily agree with many things which have been said in this convention. We join the brethren in every expression of reverence for God and the adaptability, simplicity and all-sufficiency of His Word. We believe in the perpetuity of the Abrahamic Covenant, and the baptism of children. It is useless to deny the reasonableness and practicability of this custom. We believe that baptism is necessary to salvation, and that the Church is a permanent institution. Now, my dear friends, do you not feel satisfied that we can harmonize on these principles? I close with the words of an inspired Apostle: "Be perfect; be of good comfort, be of one mind, live in peace, and the God of love and peace shall be with you."

CHAPTER VI.

ROMAN CATHOLIC.

I propose to exhibit for your examination the doctrine of the only true, united and Apostolic Church. I expect to contradict almost everything advanced by this convention. I have heard a wonderful variety of theories, but when we throw the pure and luminous words of God's eternal truth upon them, they appear deformed, out of joint, unreasonable and absurd. The chosen representatives of the Protestant Episcopal and Baptist Churches even have the effrontery to lay claim to an uninterrupted and continuous existence from the apostles down to the present. Admitting that they are each worthy of confidence and respect, how shall we decide which one is right? They both pretend to quote history and Scripture. They seem entirely satisfied, and pretend to be resting on the truth. Can they be right and hold theories so much at variance? I think not. Hence their pretensions amount to nothing. There were no sects in apostolic times. The true Church has never been divided. True, some have become dissatisfied with it and departed from its instruction and protection, but they have generally carried with them enough of the true doctrine to indicate to an absolute certainty their primitive home. Every preacher in this assembly has made positive assertions in reference to his relations to the word of God and the Church of Jesus Christ. These are not Churches of Christ, they are sects originated to gratify the ambitions of men. Some of them are ignorant and erring children, and whenever they renounce their traditions and return home, we will receive them with open arms.

I have said the true Church is and always has been one. By this I mean its members have been united in the belief of the same doctrines of revelation, and in the acknowledgment of the same divinely constituted pastors. Heresy and schism have always been opposed to Christian unity. By heresy a man rejects one or more articles of the Christian faith. By schism he spurns the authority of his spiritual superiors. That the Church has always been one is evident from the teaching of the Holy Scriptures, and from unbroken tradition of the Fathers. The types employed by our Saviour and His inspired Apostles to indicate the distinctive character of His Church, clearly denote the necessity of this unity of faith. Thus it is compared to the human body, and it is even declared to be the body of Christ. 'For as the body is one,' says St. Paul (I. Cor., 13:12), 'and hath many members, and all the members of the body, whereas they are many, yet one body, so is Christ.' The same Apostle says: 'You are the body of Christ, and members one of another.' Now all the members of the human body, must be animated by the same principle of life and joined together so as to feel and move and act together; therefore the members of this Church must be animated by the same principle of life and be so joined together that they may feel, move and act in perfect harmony. Yet how would this be possible, if they were not animated by the same faith, if they were not united in the belief of the same doctrines of revelation, if they were in contradiction among themselves, one believing what another rejects? Our Lord prayed for this unity to be like that which exists between the Father and Himself, that it might be an argument to the world of His Divine mission (John, 17:20-21)."

"In what did this unity consist? St. Cyril, of Alexandria, answers: 'In the common attainment of unity by a mutual consent in all things and an indivisible concord of hearts.' But if the members of Christ's mystical body were not united in the belief of the same revealed truths, but were at war among themselves concerning some of them, could their unity be compared to the one that exists between the Eternal Father and His Divine Son, and could this unity be an argument to the world of the divinity of Jesus Christ? St. Cyprian assures us that 'he who holds not this unity holds not the faith of the Father and the Son; holds not life and salvation. There is one God and one Christ, and His Church one, and the faith one, and the people one, joined into the solid unity of one body by the cement of concord. The great, the good and the learned admit that.' When all hold one faith there is unity."

"Is this unity of faith to be found among our separated brethren? No one who values the truth will dare to assert that it is. In support of this statement we invoke the testimony of one whom his own people consider a Doctor in Israel; he is a professor in a Protestant College, and evidently a man of deep research and thoughtful study; we allude to Dr. Philip Schaff, professor of Biblical literature in the Union Theological Seminary of New York. His work on the 'Creeds of the Evangelical Protestant Churches', (N. Y., Harper, 1877), is a striking truth of the painful and conspicuous absence of that perfect unity in faith, intended by our Lord as a mark of His Church. They do not profess one Creed, but have different Creeds. Hence they do not constitute one Church, but different Churches. This is the reason why Dr. Schaff had to entitle his volume the 'Creeds of the Protestant Evangelical Churches.' In order to form a tolerably accurate idea of their many Creeds, with the numberless variations which they underwent, we refer the reader to Bossuet's 'History of the Protestant Variations.' There he may trace distinctly the truth of the censure contained in Bishop Dudith's letter to Beza: 'What beings are we Protestants, wandering to and fro, and carried about by every wind of doctrine, sometimes to this side, sometimes to that! You may perhaps guess what we believe today; but you will never be able to ascertain what we shall profess tomorrow. In what point of religion do the Churches agree among themselves which have rejected the authority of the See of Rome? Examine them from first to last, you will scarce find any one tenet affirmed or believed by one sect, which is not immediately condemned by another.'—Fletcher's 'Guide to the True Religion,' page 153. London, 1836."

"An English Protestant writer, the learned Dr. Walton, in the preface to his Polyglot (London, 1657), acknowledging this want of unity among Protestants, points out one of the causes to which it may be traced. 'Aristarchus,' he says, 'heretofore could scarcely find seven wise men in Greece; but *among us* so many idiots can without difficulty be found. For all are Doctors, all are divinely learned, there is not so much as the meanest fanatic, or jackpudding, who does not give his *own dreams* for the word of God. . . . . These have filled our cities, villages, camps, houses, nay our Churches and pulpits too, and lead the poor deluded people with them to the pit of perdition.' Rather remarkable testimony considering the source from which it comes."

"In these words the true reason of this want of unity in faith is but faintly outlined. Their rule of faith is the principal cause why Protestants generally 'give their *own dreams* for the word of God.' It is the true reason for the different beliefs that exist among the various Protestant denominations. So long as every one is told that 'he not only has the right, but that it is his duty to interpret the Scriptures for himself,' so long as the private interpretation of the Bible is to settle all religious controversy, so long will religious division be perpetuated, not only among the different sects, but even among the members of the same denomination."

I will now proceed to present a further statement of our origin, doctrines and practice. You perceive from the foregoing that we have no confidence in sectarianism. We are for the primitive plan. The Church was established in the city of Rome by the two most glorious Apostles, Peter and Paul, and has continued uninterruptedly to the present time.

Christ appointed Peter as the visible head or supreme ruler of His Church. The Church did not die with Peter, but was destined to continue to the end of time. Consequently whatever official prerogatives were conferred on him, were not to cease at his death, but were to be handed down to his successors from generation to generation. We believe in the infallibility of the Pope and the Church. We regard the infallibility of the Pope as the guiding star of our work and destiny. "The infallibility of the Church is an extraordinary gift of the Holy Ghost. It is not a new revelation, and is not to be confounded with the gift of inspiration. It is rather a special providence of God, and a particular assistance of the Holy Ghost by which the Church of Christ is preserved from error when believing in a revealed truth, or when explaining the doctrine received from Christ and His Apostles. Hence, Catholic theologians make a distinction between active and passive infallibility—the former being the infallibility of the Church in teaching; the latter her infallibility in believing."—True Faith of our Forefathers, page 88. It is affirmed, therefore, by one of our eminent men, that "the Church has authority from God to teach regarding faith and morals, and in her teaching the special assistance of the Holy Ghost." The Church is, therefore one, Catholic and Apostolic. We believe in the holiness of the Church, as will be seen from our writings. It is also held as an inviolable principle of the Church, that "it is good and useful suppliantly to invoke the saints and to fly to their prayers, aid and assistance, in order to obtain favor from God through His Son Jesus Christ our Lord, who is our only Redeemer and Savior." We believe in the "immaculate conception of Mary, the Mother of God," the use of images in sacred worship, and the seven sacraments, viz.: Baptism, Confirmation, Holy Eucharist, Penance, Extreme Unction, Orders and Matrimony.

I now submit these unimpeachable facts to your consideration. They are unchangeable—eternal. We are one. Protestantism is divided and is becoming more so every year. Remember your obligations to God and the people with whom you live, forsake your sectarianism, and cast your lot with the only true Church.

CHAPTER VII.

INFIDEL.

I appear in this convention because the announcement indicated that it would afford an opportunity for every man, religious and irreligious, to express his sentiments fully and freely. I came because I had a right to do so, and not because I am interested in the Bible or the advancement of the cause of any religious body. I am making the best of this life, and as to the "life to come," of which we hear so much, I shall let it take care of itself. I call myself a free thinker. I am not bound by the chains of legendary "theology," nor the petty prejudices which characterize many of the religious thinkers of the age. I feel that I am infinitely above superstition; that I am in the bright sunlight of independence, enjoying the high privilege of thinking and acting for myself. In other words, I do not believe the Bible, not a word of it. It is a fable from Genesis to Revelation. These declarations seem rather sweeping, nevertheless they are my honest convictions; and perhaps it will entertain some of you to hear my "experience;" the influences which led me to regard religion a myth and the practice of it a farce. I had religious parents. They were pious and devoted to what they believed to be right. They taught me to read the Bible, go to Church, and look with deep reverence upon religious ceremonies. When I grew up to manhood they died and left me alone in the world. Soon after these sad events, I concluded to "change my life," as our "orthodox" brethren term it, but notwithstanding my early training, I had no positive convictions. I felt troubled, and resolved to consult some of the "spiritual counselors" of our city. Accordingly I presented myself at the study of Father Apostolic, of the Catholic Church. He treated me with great kindness, spoke of the Pope, the "visible head of the Church," his infallibility, the infallibility of the Church, the seven sacraments, priestly absolution; gave me some literature and bade me call again. I left without any special feelings of relief. I read the literature, and felt that it was "confusion worse confounded."

Soon after this I made a visit to Dr. Decrees, of the Presbyterian Church. He was a ripe scholar and a most excellent man. I had a long interview with him, which for a short time seemed to be satisfactory. He spoke of the rich provision made for my "salvation and eternal welfare." He exhorted me to trust Christ. This I tried to do, but I had little evidence on which to base a trust. When I departed, I requested the privilege of reading some standard work of the Church. He gave me the "Confession of Faith." I read it with the greatest interest imaginable until I came across this passage: "By the decree of God for the manifestation of His glory, some men and angels are predestinated to everlasting life, and others foreordained to everlasting death, and their number is so certain and definite, that it cannot be either increased or diminished." I was amazed. I thought of what the Doctor had told me, and I concluded that if I were elected I was all right. If not, I was all wrong. I resolved to try again, but not until I had wept and prayed over what I considered my awful condition. Tears did not relieve an aching heart.

Very soon after this I met Mr. Earnest, the successful and popular pastor of the Methodist Church. I laid my case before him. He said I should pray more, and quoted for my consolation, "Blessed are they that mourn; for they shall be comforted." I told him I had prayed. He referred me to his brother, Mr. Junius, who had been a mourner for ten years before the Lord "blessed him." He invited me to attend his services and join his Church on six months' probation. During all this time the old passage of Scripture, "Now is the accepted time, and now is the day of salvation," was ringing in my confused and excited brain.

I had often attended the Baptist Church, and a revival was in progress under the ministration of Mr.

Strictly, the pastor. He was a gentleman of fine educational attainments, and one of the most acceptable pulpit orators in the city. There was a large audience assembled when I went. I determined to hear everything he said, so I took my place on one of the front seats. His text was I. Cor., 1:23. He spoke of the awful condition into which sin has plunged the human race. He taught us that man is totally depraved, that he can do nothing to save himself, that a sinner's tears and prayers do no good, that it is impossible for him to do anything unaided by the "Spirit from on high." At last he brought his remarks to a close by fervently exhorting us to amend our ways. He then invited us to a front seat to engage in an effort to "get religion." He said "God is here. He is ready; ready now." I went. They sang and exhorted. At last they knelt and prayed for God to come. I found no relief. I departed with a thousand conflicting thoughts running through my mind. I did not return. I decided that I could find no consolation in such contradictory statements.

Mr. Historicus, the pastor of the Protestant Episcopal Church, was a man of good reputation, both as a scholar and as a preacher. I had an interview with him. He politely informed me that he represented the true Church, and that the other religious orders with which I had been associated were sects—human organizations. I was encouraged. I thought that surely a preacher would tell the truth! I became interested, and requested the use of one of his standard theological works, and he presented me with the "Book of Common Prayer." I said: "Who wrote this book?" He replied: "Our great men." I then inquired: "What do you mean by our great men; Peter, Paul and the other apostles?" He answered: "I mean our great men who lived over two hundred years ago." I asked, "Were they inspired?" He, of course, admitted that they were not. I then put this question to him: "Can a man be an Episcopalian and disbelieve this creed?" He answered in the negative. I finally inquired: "Were there any Protestant Episcopal Churches in New Testament times, if so, will you please tell me where to find the proof?" He became con.. sed, excited and abrupt, and I left him to his though'.s.

I interviewed nearly all the preachers in the city with similar results. I found they took the Bible for their guide. Yet they differed on the material points of its teaching. They had one book and one destiny, so they said, but they did not fellowship each other on account of some peculiarity. In my extremity I wandered into a book-store and incidentally picked up Tom Paine's Age of Reason. I read it. I found my fears were unfounded. My tears ceased to flow. I ceased to interview preachers, and now it is my solemn conviction that your systems are all impositions on the credulity of mankind. Two of my greatest objections to your systems are your divisions and a want of practice of what little good you preach. I close by saying: Lay aside your theories, shake off your traditions, ascend above your superstitions, and be free and untrammeled in the exercise of your private judgment. As for me, let me be free while I live, and when the end comes, "Environ me with music, sprinkle me with incense and crown me with flowers, that I may pass to my eternal sleep."

CHAPTER VIII.

ADVENTIST.

It is with almost inexpressible joy that I appear today in this great convention with the unrestricted privilege of participating in its deliberations. I recognize this day's work, as a grand forward step toward the fulfillment of prophecy, the evangelization of the race, and the inauguration of the millennium by the personal return of Jesus Christ to earth. For many years we have contemplated the contention of rival sects, and the irresistible conclusion comes down upon us that as long as there are sects there will be sectarians, and as long as there is sectarianism the work of Christ will be hindered and obstructed. Men of learning, character and eloquence have stood before us, and we have listened honestly and patiently, and what is the result? Each man presents his own creed, endorses his own sect, promulgates his own doctrine, and leaves the great question of the hour where he found it. I present no creed, I advance no confession of faith, but simply call you back to the fundamental principles of Christianity. I will mention a few of our cardinal doctrines, and ask you to profoundly consider them: (1) The Divine origin, perpetuity and universal obligation of the Sabbath day. Amen. I see that this proposition strikes a responsive chord, for the majority of the organizations represented in these deliberations teach that the decalogue is still binding on the Church of God, notwithstanding they observe the heathen "first day of the week." Why should it not? The suggestion of Christian union without a return to the observance of the primitive day of rest is the very essence of absurdity and contradiction. (2) The establishment of the Kingdom of Christ, and the inauguration of the millennium at His second coming. (3) The utter unconsciousness of both the sainted and wicked dead from death to the resurrection. (4) The resurrection of all the dead. (5) The destruction, the complete annihilation, of the wicked after judgment. I will not elaborate these propositions. You know they cannot be overthrown, and you also know that to combine them with the truths on which we are all agreed nothing can hinder us in our onward march. I stand pledged to the truths of the sacred scriptures, and to this cause I give my life, looking for the coming of the Lord from heaven. Amen.

CHAPTER IX.

MORMON.

Great opportunities do not come often in this short life. Hence, I esteem it a great privilege to stand in the presence of this august assembly and present for your investigation the doctrines of the Church of Jesus Christ of Latter Day Saints. I shall not waste my valuable time by discussing the theological medley that has been presented for your entertainment, but proceed at once to the presentation for our doctrines and also our history. Our founder was Joseph Smith, who was born in Sharon, Vt., on the 23rd day of December, 1805. When he was fourteen years old, he began to reflect on the importance of preparing for the future state. He attended the Churches around him with most unsatisfactory results; he found nothing but a great clashing of sentiment. At length, disappointed and disguested with what he saw and heard, he began to withdraw to secret places for meditation and prayer. During these times of retirement he received a visit from an angel of the Lord. On the 21st of September, 1823, he received the second supernatural visitation. It seemed to him that the house was filled with "consuming fire," and a personage stood before him "with a countenance like lightning," and visible to the extermities of the body, proclaiming himself to be an angel of God. He distinctly told him that his prayers were heard, that his sins were forgiven, that the ancient convenant which God made with Israel was at hand to be fulfilled, and that the preparatory work for the second coming of the Messiah must be speedily inaugurated; further, that the time was at hand for the proclamation of the gospel in its power and fullness to all nations, and that he was the instrument in the hands of God to bring about these glorious ends. The angel also gave him a brief sketch of the origin, progress, civilization, laws, and government of the original inhabitants of America. The angel appeared to him many times, and after due disciplinary probation, he placed in the hands of the prophet the wonderful plates containing the records of the ancient people that had lived on the American continent. This was September 22nd, 1827. I will describe these plates. They were eight inches long by seven inches wide, a little thinner than tin, and bound together by three strings running through the whole. The entire volume thus formed was about six inches thick, a part of which was sealed. The characters of the unsealed part were beautifully engraved. They were translated by Joseph Smith, the prophet. The angel, in order to enable him to do this, had given him the Urim and Thummim, consisting of two transparent stones. The prophet sat behind a blanket hung across the room to keep the sacred record from profane eyes, and as he translated, Oliver Cowdery wrote it down. The Book of Mormon appeared in the year 1830, with the names of Oliver Cowdery, Martin Harris and David Whitmer appended to a certificate that an angel of heaven had come down. Three competent witnesses to any question of fact ought to be enough, but humanity is prone to hesitate, hence the statement of these three noted saints was subsequently backed up by the testimony of the prophet himself and seven others who had seen the wonderful plates. I pause long enough to propound to this assembly two questions, and demand answers: What object could these men have had in knowingly testifying to a lie? Why can we not believe them as well as Moses, Isaiah and Paul?

Indulge me while I tell you something about the ancient history of this continent. It was originally settled by a colony that came from the Tower of Babel. They were Jaredites, and were a bloody race, and following their warlike instincts they destroyed each other until, at the beginning of the fifth century of the Christian era, silence settled down upon America. In the beginning of the sixth century, however, a new race came to these shores directly from Jerusalem. These people were the ancestors of the North American Indians. The continent was the scene of a constant warfare and unbelief, and darkness prevailed; but before the final night of absolute apostasy set in, God commissioned the prophet Mormon to prepare an abridgment of all their prophecies and histories and hide it in the earth until God should see fit to bring it forth, and unite it with the Bible for the accomplishment of His purposes in the last days of the Christian dispensation. This is the book dug from the earth by our founder under the instruction of the angel of God. We accept it as a Divine revelation, and equal in authority with the Jewish and Christian Scriptures. We stand by Jesus Christ. It is recorded that in the time of Nephi the Second, an awful earthquake announced the crucifixion of the Messiah. Three days subsequent to this, He came down from heaven and showed the Nephites the wounds in His body. He also instructed them for forty days in the truths of Christianity, healed the sick, blessed the children, administered the sacrament, and planted churches, with apostles, prophets, pastors, teachers, evangelists, the same order, the same priesthood, the same ordainances, gifts, powers and blessings that were enjoyed on the eastern continent. I have given you only a brief sketch, for I am admonished that my time is growing short.

In organization, Mormonism is a pure theocracy. Its priesthood, which rules in matters temporal and ecclesiastical, is divided into the various orders, beginning with President. The second office is Patriarch. The third is the Council of the Twelve. The fourth is the Seventies. The fifth is the High Priests. The sixth is the Bishop. The seventh is the Elders. The eighth is the Priests. The ninth is the Teachers and Deacons.

We believe in God, in Jesus Christ and in the Holy Spirit, and hence accept the Old and New Testaments: we believe that men will be punished on account of their personal transgressions, and not for the sins of Adam; we believe that through the atonement of Christ all mankind may be saved by obedience to the laws and ordinances of the gospel; we believe these ordinances to be: first, faith in the Lord Jesus Christ; second, repentance; third, baptism; fourth, imposition of hands and the gift of the Holy Spirit; fifth, the Lord's Supper, administered kneeling; we believe that men must be called to the work of God by inspiration; we believe that the same organization must exist now that existed in the primitive Churches; we believe that miraculous gifts—"discerning of Spirits, prophecy, revelations, visions, healing, tongues"—have not ceased; we believe that the word of God is recorded in the Bible, in the book of Mormon, and all other good books; we believe in all that God has revealed, is revealing or will reveal; we believe in the gathering of Israel, the restoration of the ten lost tribes—the North American Indians—and the establishment of the New Zion on the western continent, the millennial reign of Christ on earth and the transformation of earth into a paradise; we believe in the literal resurrection of the body; we believe in the absolute liberty of private judgment in matters of religion; we believe it is our duty to submit to the laws of the country in which we live, whether it be monarchial or republican; we believe in being honest, true, chaste, temperate, benevolent, virtuous, and upright; and in doing good to all men, and that an idle or lazy person cannot be a Christian or have salvation.

Our doctrines have stood the test of fiery persecution and of time, and have come out of the fire untouched. Our illustrious founder, Joseph Smith, the prophet of last days, was mercilessly ridiculed, bitterly persecuted and malignantly opposed on every side, but he persevered. We have caught his spirit and we are growing in numbers and power, and insist that the saints shall gather on this fair continent. As to our moral influence at home, I quote one who is not of us: "Their streets are clean, their houses bright, their gardens fruitful. Peace reigns in their cities. Harlots and drunkards are unknown among them. They keep up more common schools than any other sect in the United States."

I propose as a foundation for our union, the Bible, the book of Mormon as translated by Joseph Smith, all that God has revealed, all that He is revealing, and all that He may reveal hereafter. Will you accept my proposition?

CHAPTER X.

CHURCH OF GOD.

I am pleased to be able to appear before this assembly to-day. And I am pleased to learn that you are all anxious to bring about the unity of God's people; for this is the purpose of the church to which I belong. I think we all agree that Christian unity is badly needed at the present time and is increasingly desired by devout Christians everywhere. That this desire is inspired by the Holy Spirit is my honest belief. And that there is no organic unity of the whole church of Christ to-day is so patent a fact that it needs no proof. However, God's true people everywhere are looking for light on this church question. Honest Christians will think, and are now thinking, in terms of a universal Christianity. If I therefore can be of service in pointing out Christ's plan and purpose to gather together in one the children of God who are scattered abroad, and also to be instrumental in helping to accomplish this grand work, I shall feel abundantly repaid. Because of this I am pleased to come before this assembly to-day to present the earnest plea of the last and final reformation that God is now using to bring about the restoration of the original church to its apostolic glory.

The Church of God reformation movement is an outgrowth of the holiness agitation of the last century. It had its inception about the year 1880, when Daniel S. Warner and other ministers severed their connection with humanly-organized churches and maintained that the Scriptural, all-sufficient standard for Christians is membership in the body of Christ alone. On this account Brother Warner and his associates made no attempt to organize a church along denominational lines, but made direct appeal to the teaching of Scripture instead, contending that spiritual fellowship with Christ and with each other and devotion to Scriptural ideals constitute a sufficient bond for the followers of Christ.

It may be appropriate at this time to state that the Church of God reformation movement is not to be confused with the Winebrennarian church of God, with Mormonism, Adventism nor with the Pentecostal, or the "tongues movement," whose congregations are sometimes known by the name of "church of God."

We believe that the Bible is the inspired word of God, and the writings therein teach us that it is the express purpose of God to call out of the world a saved people who shall constitute the body or church of God which was built and established upon the foundation of the apostles and prophets, Jesus Christ himself being the chief cornerstone. Therefore we assemble ourselves together for worship, fellowship, counsel and instruction in the word of God and for the exercise of those spiritual gifts and offices provided for in the New Testament.

There are many religious bodies in the world today who are holding aloft a name and a doctrine that have been instituted by man. Thus their origin can only be traced as far back as their uninspired founders. For instance: the Methodists, a religious group that was founded by John Wesley; the Lutheran group originated by Martin Luther; the Presbyterians and others. We who identify ourselves with the church of God do not accept Christianity as taught by John Wesley, John Calvin, John Huss or the Pope of Rome. We accept the Christian teachings as taught by Christ and his apostles. For this reason we rightfully bear the name of the church that was born on the day of Pentecost. "Unto the church of God which is at Corinth, to them that are sanctified in Christ Jesus." I. Corinthians, 1:2; 10:32. The inspired writings describe the New Testament church as the church of God eleven times. Therefore the church that began on Pentecost can only be known as the church of God.

Now let us analyze the Bible and find the principal

doctrines that were taught by the apostles and which should be our only rule of faith and practice.

Man is in a lost condition and must therefore be born again in order to see the Kingdom of God. "Verily, verily I say unto thee, Except a man be born again, he cannot see the kingdom of God." John, 3:3. But one will say, How can we be born again? We know that inasmuch as we are inclined to evil, and evil only; we must seek forgiveness or pardon for our sins. "Let the wicked forsake his way, and the unrighteous man his thoughts." Isaiah, 55:7. "Repent ye therefore, and be converted, that your sins may be blotted out, when the time of refreshing shall come from the presence of the Lord." Acts, 3:19.

Man must be born again, and when he prays through to victory and is accepted by God he is a new creature in Christ Jesus. Every person knows whether he is saved or not, for the saved person was there when the change transpired. The church of God does not teach a guess so salvation or a hope so salvation, but a know so salvation.

Sanctification and baptism with the Holy Ghost is another great Bible doctrine. Sanctification or cleansing is a second work of grace for those who have become brethren. "This is the will of God, even your sanctification." I. Thessalonians, 4:3. The early disciples were commanded to tarry for the Holy Ghost in Jerusalem. "And behold I send the promise of the Father upon you; but tarry ye in the city of Jerusalem until ye be endued with power from on high." Luke, 24:49. Jesus promised the disciples when the Comforter, the Holy Ghost, is come he would testify of him when they received him. "But when the Comforter is come . . . . he shall testify of me." John, 15:26. In I. Corinthians, second chapter, we are taught that no one can understand the scriptures without the aid of the Holy Ghost.

Another great Bible doctrine is water baptism. This is a gospel ordinance which shows forth the death, burial and resurrection of our Lord Jesus Christ. There is only one mode that commemorates this; viz.

baptism by immersion. This is the mode followed by Jesus and the church of God in the beginning. In baptism public testimony is given that we have been crucified with Christ, buried with him and raised with him to walk in newness of life by the answer of a good concience toward God. I. Peter, 3:21.

A baptism with the Holy Ghost is a grand and glorious possibility provided for every man and woman. It is an experience that our great, loving God has planned and provided. No greater gift is possible than the gift of the Holy Ghost.

There are two other ordinances that should be practiced by all Christians. They are the Lord's Supper and Washing the Saint's Feet. We are taught to observe all things that Jesus has taught us in his word. Washing the saints' feet w s instituted by the Lord who said, "If I then, your Lord and Master, have washed your feet, ye also ought to wash one anothers feet."

The Church of God supports their ministry and missions by paying tithes. Abraham who is our father, paid tithes under the priesthood of Melchisedec and Christ was made a priest after the order of Melchisedec. Thus it is only logical to conclude that God's people should pay tithes to Jesus.

Divine Healing is another Bible teaching that must be accepted by all followers of Christ because there is nothing in the Bible to indicate that the spiritual gifts mentioned in First Corinthians are not for the church to-day as well as then.

We believe in living a life of holiness, for the Bible teaches us to "Follow after peace and holiness without which no man shall see the Lord."

We do not "join the church" because that term is not in the Bible. They were added to the church daily as they would be saved, Acts, 2:47.

There are certain forms of government set forth in the New Testament that the church as a whole is to be governed by through the local congregations or assemblies. Bishops, or elders, were provided for to act as overseers of the flock. (These are also called pastors) Evangelists were sent out to preach the gospel to the unsaved. But in no case have the officers a right to become a legislative group. All the officers are for is to see that God's will is carried out.

The church is a spiritual creation. It includes all of the redeemed in heaven and earth; and Christ is head of the body, the church. It is true that the Bible mentions various local churches, but they were not denominations. They were all parts of the same body.

No man can open or shut the door of the church. "He that openeth, and no man shutteth, and shutteth, and no man openeth." Revelation, 3:7.

The final reformation is on. "Final", I say because it leaves nothing to be restored as regards either doctrine, practice or spirit. Will you not come with us in this movement of God?

CHAPTER XI.

NAZARENE

It is always a pleasure for me to appear before an appreciative audience and present the great truths of the church of the Nazarene. We are not a schism or branch from any other denomination. We are not raised up to advocate any particular ordinance or to propagate any special form of church government, but we do exist in response to a demand for an organization to conserve the work done by holiness pastors and evangelists in preaching the doctrine and experience of entire sanctification.

Our beginnings are of interest to every child of God. Toward the close of the nineteenth century there was a revival of the preaching of the doctrine of entire sanctification as taught by John Wesley. Between 1885 and 1901 a number of missions and churches were organized with this doctrine in view. During this time several of these groups united under various names. In response to memorials from thirty-five District assemblies the name was finally changed to Church of the Nazarene, a name which belongs first and pre-eminently to One who came and dwelt at Nazareth. From a small number of congregations this church has spread until now there are organizations in every state of the Union, in Canada, the British isles and foreign fields.

Our Manual has been formed by representative bodies of consecrated men and women, elected by the people, sitting in general assembly, who have carefully and prayerfully sought to promote the kingdom of God without personal interests. Our people are urged sincerely to read and study this Manual because it contains a brief history of the church and the doctrines and laws of the church. We urge loyalty to our principles, interests and institutions, and consider it important that our members acquaint themselves thoroughly with the laws of their church.

We believe in the Triune God, Father, Son and Holy Spirit.

We believe in the plenary inspiration of the Holy Scriptures and that whatever is not contained therein is not to be enjoined as an article of faith.

We believe that believers are to be sanctified wholly, subsequent to conversion, through faith in the Lord Jesus Christ.

We believe that the Holy Spirit bears witness to the new birth and also to the entire sanctification of believers.

Our distinguishing doctrine is the tenet of entire sanctification as a second work of grace wrought in the hearts of believers by faith.

The church of the Nazarene practices, in common with most Protestant churches, the two ordinances of baptism and the Lord's Supper. Baptism is administered either by affusion or immersion, according to the election of the candidate.

The ecclesiastical organization of our church is representative throughout, having a General Assembly which meets every four years, forty-four district assemblies which meet annually, and local congregations in charge of regularly elected pastors. There are General Superintendants, District Superintendants, Pastors, Evangelists, Young People's Societies, Junior Societies, Women's Missionary Societies, etc.

Justification, regeneration and adoption are gracious acts of God and are simultaneous in the experience of seekers after God and are obtained upon the condition of faith, preceded by repentance, and to this work and state of grace the Holy Spirit bears witness.

Entire sanctification is that act of God, subsequent to regeneration, by which believers are made free from original sin, or depravity, and brought into a state of entire devotement to God, and the holy obedience of love made perfect. It is wrought by the baptism with the Holy Spirit and comprehends in one experience the cleansing of the heart from sin and the abiding, indwelling presence of the Holy Spirit, empowering the believer for life and service.

Entire sanctification is provided by the blood of Jesus, is wrought instantaneously by faith, preceded by entire consecration; and to this work and state of grace the Holy Spirit bears witness.

We believe in prevailing prayer, or the prayer that goes clear through. To be able to pray through is more to be desired than wealth, knowledge or eloquence.

Three things are necessary to praying through:

First, a burden.
Second, persistance.
Third, a witness of faith.

He who would pray through must first familiarize himself with the word of God.

We have the assurance already and when we pray through, we have the seal of the Spirit in our hearts.

We believe in the Bible doctrine of divine healing and urge our people to offer the prayer of faith for the healing of the sick. Providential means and agencies when deemed necessary should not be refused.

We believe that the Holy Spirit bears witness to the new birth, and also to the entire sanctification of believers.

The Baptism with the Holy Spirit is emphasized by Jesus as the most needful experience for this age. It is interesting to note the terms used in the Acts of the Apostles relative to this work of grace. They are: "baptized," "filled", "poured out", "gifts of", "received", etc. John Wesley used at least twenty-five phrases to indicate this state of grace. The one hundred and twenty who had tarried for the outpouring of the Holy Spirit were on the day of Pentecost "filled" with the Holy Ghost. Pentecost, or the experience of the baptism with the Holy Spirit, "purified their hearts by faith". The experience described in the second chapter of Acts is the sanctifying and energizing baptism with the Holy Spirit and fire which is the heritage of all believers.

The provisions of our Constitution may be repealed

or amended when concurred in by a two-thirds vote of all the members of the General Assembly.

The Church of the Nazarene has an evident and well defined commission from God, namely, to propogate the gospel throughout the world, seeking the conversion of sinners, the reclamation of backsliders and the sanctification of believers. I therefore respectfully ask you to consider our work and faith and join in with us in our great objects.

CHAPTER XII.

CHRISTIAN SCIENCE.

It is with pleasure that I appear before this august assembly to present the claims of our organization. The clarity of Mrs. Mary Baker Eddy's teachings leaves one in no doubt as to the availability of an armor of protection from the evils of mortal existence. In perfect consonance with the lessons in Holy Writ she describes this armor, and spiritually illumines and reinforces the teachings of the Bible.

Mrs. Eddy, the founder, or if you prefer, the discoverer of Christian Science, was a remarkable woman. From a very early age her striking character and endowments showed themselves. When she was about eight years old, a strange incident occurred, which repeated itself again and again during the space of a year. The child would hear a voice calling her distinctly by name, three times in an ascending scale. One evening in November of the same year, little Mary begged her mother to let her go out to comfort the pigs which she heard squealing in their sty. At first her mother refused, but later she consented. Little Mary ran out of the house to the pigsty and sang a lullaby to the pigs who responded to her kind thought and settled down comfortably to sleep.

In Mrs. Eddy's Message to the Mother Church in 1901 she writes: "What I have given to the world on the subject of metaphysical or Christian Science is the result of my own observation, experience and final discovery quite independent of all other authors except the Bible." The discovery of Christian Science was made in 1886 so the experiments to which she refers must have begun about 1846.

Homoeapathy was first brought to her notice by her cousin when she was eighteen years old. As she had been benefited by it she determined to study the subject. As it is known, homoeapathy attenuates or dilutes the drug to be used. High attenuations were in great favor. The making of these occupied much time and attention. The preparation was shaken 30 times at each attenuation, and every time it was shaken the thought naturally presented itself that by this process the remedy was being made more powerful. Thus it was plainly mind action and not matter which affected the cure. After her experiments with homoeapathy she became interested in spiritualism. After her first investigation of spiritualism, though she did not attribute the phenomena in every case to tricks, she became convinced that there was nothing scientific about it and nothing spiritual. It was not till after her discovery of Christian Science that the matter became clear to her. "When I learned how mind produces disease on the body, I learned how it produces the manifestations ignorantly imputed to spirits." she wrote. Why is it more difficult to see a thought than to feel one? Education alone determines the difference.

It is not yet eighty years since the discovery of Christian Science, yet during this time it has gained adherents in every quarter of the globe and has produced a profound and ever-increasing effect on the medical and religious views of large numbers of those outside the movement.

In Mrs. Eddy's own words, "God is infinite, the only Life substance, Spirit, or Soul, the only intelligence of the universe, including man." "Jesus," she defines as "The highest human corporeal concept of the divine idea, rebuking and destroying error and bringing to light man's immortality." By the autumn of 1866. Mrs. Eddy had gained the conviction that ."all causation was Mind, and every effect a mental phenomenon." God, the first cause or Principle of the universe, is Mind, and this Mind expresses itself in ideas which naturally partake of the nature of Mind and are made in God's image. In the second chapter of Genesis we are presented with an account of the creation which is at all points the antithesis of that set forth in the first chapter. Christian Science explains this as an allegory. It begins with a mist, a dream; everything is represented as evolved from lower forms of matter; a sense of evil appears, a delusion, disobedience, fear follows, a sense of separation from God, toil, pain, difficulty, and finally the deluge. This Adam dream lasted down the ages till our Lord came and proved the reality of Spirit and the unreality of matter.

Christian Science teaches that God is the only cause. He is therefore the source of all supply; man is his image and reflection; he therefore reflects the abundance of God. Thus the disease called poverty can be healed by the "renewing of mind".

Shortly before her marriage to Mr. Eddy in 1877 she saw that the church of Christ, Scientist, must be founded in Boston. This accordingly was accomplished and a charter received from the state. The constitution and by-laws of this church were formed by Mrs. Eddy and adopted by her followers. Christian Scientists regard the Manual of The Mother Church, the volume which contains the Church by-laws, as a divinely inspired guide by which they can safely navigate the stormy waters of human experience.

Christian Science teaches that death is a part of the belief in material life and therefore as unreal in the strict meaning of the word. It maintains that there is a probationary and progressive state beyond the grave, but that eventually every prodigal will find his way home, every wandering sheep find the fold, and man be satisfied, when he awakes from these dreams, with God's likeness.

At the time the church was organized, its rules and by-laws were adopted, three years later personal preaching was abolished and the Bible and *Science and Health* ordained as Pastor. Lesson-sermons which consist entirely of passages from the Bible and *Science and Health* are read. The lesson-sermon is read by the first and second readers, one of whom shall be a man and the other a woman.

Christian Science accepts as actual facts the **virgin**

birth, the resurrection and ascension, but it does not regard them as miraculous occurrences. It holds them to be manifestations of spiritual laws which eventually will be understood by all. The communion which we hold, commemorates the morning meal which our Lord prepared for his disciples on the shores of the Lake of Galilee during those wonderful forty days between the resurrection and the ascension. Baptism, according to Christian Science, is nothing less than a purification from all error. It is not, therefore, a brief ceremony to be performed; it is an object to the attainment of which the whole energy of man must be devoted. If people to whom we mention the subject of Christian Science show no interest in it, we leave them lovingly alone, we never enter into controversy.

As Christian Science satisfies our intelligence and reason, so too, it satisfies the heart. It opens the door of expectation and receptivity and brings us in touch with the inexpressible tenderness of the divine Mind. The practical living conciousness of God's nearness, of his infinite care, of the beauty and radiance of his Love, embracing, supporting, with more than a mother's tenderness or rather a father's strength, makes the waste places of the heart blossom as the rose.

CHAPTER XIII.
INQUIRER.

I stand before you not as a preacher, or as a representative of an "Apostolic Church," but as a representative of a large class in every community who are inclined to be religious, but have never been able to find a resting place. When I heard of this convention I was very highly gratified, as it seemed to me that such an august assembly of divines as this could direct an inquiring and troubled sinner to the fountain of life and peace. I have listened attentively, prayerfully and honestly to every address which has been made, and now, instead of hope and joy, I find myself disappointed, confused and disgusted. All the speakers professed to believe in the all-sufficiency of the word of God. Each one believes he is guided by the special direction of the Holy Spirit. I should like to know if the word of God is responsible for the contradictions to which I have listened. Is the Holy Spirit the author of confusion and speculation? I had almost come to Mr. Infidel's conclusion, and this convention would have confirmed me, had I not appealed to the Bible instead of the modern preachers who set themselves up as its interpreters. Jesus Christ said, "Search the Scriptures." This I have done sufficiently to believe that they are of Divine origin, but I am not sure that I know my duty. I came here expecting to get some additional light, but I am further away than when I came. I am an inquirer. I am in deep earnest. I am searching for the "old paths." I want to know what I must do to be saved from my past sins. Here is what perplexes me: Brother Methodist proposes to take me through his theological process and bring me out a Methodist; Brother Baptist proposes to take me through his theological process and bring me out a Baptist; Brother Presbyterian proposes to take me through his theological process and bring me out a Presbyterian; Brother Episcopalian proposes to take me through his theological process and bring me out an Episcopalian; Brother Lutheran proposes to take me through his theological process and bring me out a Lutheran, and so on through the entire catalogue. If there are no divisions among you, if all of you are orthodox, why am I not a Baptist when I pass through the Methodist theological process, or a Methodist when I pass through the Baptist theological process? If there are many ways to heaven and one is as good as another, why is a Baptist offended if called an Episcopalian, or an Episcopalian if called a Baptist? It appears, from my point of vision, that each order entertains something peculiar to itself indicated by its name and creed, and that this is what makes denominations, and therefore sectarians. I have a question that I desire, in all respect, to submit to this convention, and I demand an answer. Is there not a process revealed in the Scriptures through which, if I pass, I may become a Christian, live a Christian and die a Christian, and will the process make me anything but a Christian, and will any deviations from this process justify the hope of infallible safety and security for this life or the next, and will the New Testament, "as it is written," make a Baptist, Methodist, Presbyterian, Lutheran, Nazarene, Christian Scientist, or Mormon? If so, proof! I pause for reply.

Again, if a man may be a Christian in spite of the existence of organization utterly unknown to the New Testament, why may not all denominational Christianity be relegated to oblivion so that Christianity may run and be glorified without hindrance? I want to be a Christian only; only a Christian.

I hold in my hand a little book called the New Testament. I read from its pages the following from the lips of Jesus: "If any man shall say unto you, Lo, here is Christ, or there; believe it not. For there shall arise false Christs, and false prophets, and shall shew great signs and wonders, insomuch that, if it were possible, they shall deceive the very elect. Behold,

I have told you before. Wherefore, if they shall say unto you, Behold, he is in the desert; go not forth: behold, he is in the secret chambers; believe it not" (Matt., 24:23-26). I lift my eyes and behold this convention: Nine kinds of Methodists are each saying: "Lo, here is Christ." Nine kinds of Baptists are each saying: "Here is the true and living way." Twelve kinds of Presbyterians are each saying: "Here is the truth in its purity." The Protestant Episcopal Church opens wide its portals and says: "Behold the only true, the Apostolic Church." The Lutheran Church offers me instruction and consolation. The Roman Catholic, with hands dripping with the blood of martyrs, says: "I represent the true Church, all others are miserable sects." Mr. Infidel says: "Religion is a myth, and the practice of it a farce." I turn again to the word of God, and I find that, "There is one body, and one Spirit, even as ye are called in one hope of your calling" (Eph., 4:4). Do all the sects represented in this assembly constitute one body? Is the Bible responsible for all these contradictions and the confusion which they produce? Does it authorize the multiplication of sects and creeds to gratify the whims of ungrateful men? These questions, as professed ministers of Jesus Christ, you are bound to answer. I desire to be a Christian, but I can never be until these discrepancies are satisfactorily explained. If you refuse to do it, you will be held accountable in the judgment of the great day. I have read the Bible, and if you will hear me patiently, I will present some of my observations and conclusions. I turn to the pages of inspired prophecy: "Thus saith the Lord, Stand ye in the ways, and see, ask for the old paths, where is the good way, and walk therein, and ye shall find rest for your souls" (Jer., 6:16). The prophet doubtless had an eye on this convention! Here are nine Methodist ways, nine Baptists ways, twelve Presbyterian ways, the Protestant Episcopal way, the Lutheran way, the Roman Catholic way, and the Infidel way. I turn to the revelation and I find this is called "Babylon," confusion, and God's people are invited to come out (Rev., 17:2). I thank God that I have never been in it. I propose a further examination, so I lay down a rule, the justice of which can not be denied by the most extreme sectarian.

"All Scripture is given by inspiration of God, and is profitable for doctrine, for reproof, for correction for instruction in righteousness: that the man of God may be perfect, throughly furnished unto all good works" (II. Tim., 3:16, 17). "The prophet that hath a dream, let him tell a dream; and he that hath my word, let him speak my word faithfully. What is the chaff to the wheat? saith the Lord. Is not my word like as a fire? saith the Lord; and like a hammer that breaketh the rock in pieces" (Jer., 23:28, 29)?

These passages indicate the character of my remarks. I intend to try you by the "Bible and the Bible alone." Human creeds and speculations will be rejected. It does not matter who taught you, nor how much you hate a "turn-coat," your opinion will be unconditionally excluded. Our constant inquiry will be, "What saith the Lord?"

I will refer to the addresses in the order they were made:

I do not read in the word of God of the Methodist Episcopal Church, or of the Methodist Episcopal Church South, or of any other kind of a Methodist Church. This, to my mind, is a sufficient reason to condemn the entire system. I do not read anything of General Conferences, Annual Conferences, Quarterly Conferences, Love Feasts or Class Meetings. I do not read of Bishops of the Methodist character, Presiding Elders, Circuit riders or Class leaders. I do not read of the twenty-five articles of the Discipline, and as to the baptism of unconscious babes in the sublime name of Father, Son and Holy Spirit, the Bible is as silent as the grave. The General Conference of 1808 declared the twenty-five articles of the Discipline infallible; that is to say, no change could be made by any General Conference in the future. This seems to me like an echo from Rome. The General Conference of the Methodist Episcopal Church South in 1882, found it necessary to *revise* the Discipline. It seems that they get things a little mixed. In the advertisement of the new work, I find these words: "Let every preacher see to it that his Church is supplied. A copy should be placed in every family. How can our membership be expected to know our doctrines or keep our rules without the Discipline?" This is a clear admission that the doctrines of Methodism are not in the Bible. I do not read of the "anxious seat," or "mourner's beench," process of conversion in New Testament times. I do not find where the early ministers of Jesus Christ prayed for God to baptize "mourners" with the "Holy Ghost and with fire." I do not read where any of the apostles ever encouraged inquirers by quoting, "Blessed are they that mourn; for they shall be comforted." I do not find a single instance where any one went away mourning, seeking or inquiring; but under the Methodist system mourners go away mourning, seekers go away seeking, and inquirers go away inquiring. There were no failures in apostolic times, and there will be none in our times, it seems to me, if men will preach and practice no more, nor no less, than what is found in the Holy Scriptures. Methodism affirms that baptism is a substitute for circumcision. The Bible does not intimate this. It is merely an opinion. Methodists advocate many things which are clearly taught in the word of God, but this does not prove the divinity of the system that makes Methodists. John Wesley was the author of it, and not a vestige of it is sustained by the volume of inspiration. Methodism was born of the apostasy. It is the grand-daughter of the church of Rome. It has many features of its maternal ancestor. I prefer it to Romanism, both in faith and practice, yet that which is distinctly Methodistic had its origin in Rome, and not in Jerusalem. I do not find where water was carried into the house and sprinkled or poured upon the people, but I do read of "baptizing in Enon near to Salim, because there was much water there" (John, 3:23). Baptizing in the Jordan (Mark, 1:5). Buried in Baptism (Rom., 6:4). Going down into the water and coming up out of it (Acts, 8:38,

39). How does this correspond with the doctrines and practices of Methodism?

I do not read of justification by "faith only," but I read that men are justified by many things. I will enumerate: (1) By grace (Rom., 3:24). (2) By the blood of Christ (Rom., 5:9). (3) By the resurrection of Christ (Rom., 4:25). (4) By knowledge (Isa., 53:11). (5) By faith (Rom., 5:1). (6) In the name of the Lord Jesus, and by the Spirit of our God (I. Cor., 6:11). (7) By works (Jas., 2:24). (8) By the Lord (Rom., 8:33). Who will affirm that any item in this list may be omitted or compromised? As long as these mighty truths stand in the word of God, as long as the authority is maintained in the heavens that placed them there, the fundamental doctrines of Methodism will be undeniably, unexceptionally, and delusively false.

One argument introduced by Brother Methodist was simply astounding. In an attempt to justify divisions among the people of God he declared that we can not all understand the Bible in the same way. I beg permission to disagree with him. I should say, we can not all *misunderstand* the Bible alike, but as there is only one way to *understand* it, all who understand it must, in the very nature of things, understand it the same way. Demonstrate to me, by incontestible facts, that two men can *understand* one proposition differently, and I will take pleasure in withdrawing this argument. Where is the man who will undertake the task?

I am glad to say things are improving among Methodists. Some of their advanced thinkers are crying in the great wilderness of confusion and doubt for a return to the doctrines of the apostles. One of their great evangelists recently said: "The world will never be saved by the preachers, and God is powerless to save a person from hell without some man or woman to help Him to save the poor fellow. How many heathen were saved before we sent our missionaries to India or China? I am not saying God could not have fixed it up in some other way, but I am talking about how He has fixed it up."

My objections to Methodism may be summed up in a few words: (1) Its name is unknown to the New Testament. (2) Its Discipline virtually implies the insufficiency of the word of God as a rule of faith and practice. (3) Its officers and offices are not authorized by the word of God. (4) It teaches that the two covenants are identical. (5) It teaches that baptism comes in the room of circumcision. (6) It teaches that pouring and sprinkling may be substituted for the apostolic "buried in baptism." (7) It advocates the baptism of unbelievers—infants. (8) It accepts members on "six months' probation," in positive opposition to the New Testament. (9) It introduced and perpetuates the "mourner's bench" process of conversion. (10) Its doctrine of justification by "faith only" contradicts the teaching of the inspired apostles. (11) It is divided into contending factions. (12) It began too late in the gospel dispensation, 1729. (13) It began at Oxford, and not at Jerusalem. (14) It was founded by John Wesley, and not by Jesus Christ. (15) It justifies divisions, and therefore retards the union of God's people upon the "Bible and the Bible alone."

Brother Baptist was the next speaker. When I turn to the Scriptures, I am forced to put him in the same category with Brother Methodist, for I do not read anything of a Baptist Church, or of a Baptist Church of Christ; yet my friend makes very positive claims to "apostolic succession;" proposing to trace his existence back to John, the forerunner of Christ. Mr. Webster defines "apostolic succession in theology," as "the regular and uninterrupted transmission of ministerial authority by a succession of bishops, from the apostles to any subsequent period." The Protestant Episcopal and Roman Catholic Church make similar pretensions. Someone is wrong. Who is it? Suppose either one of these institutions could trace its existence back to the death of the last surviving apostle, would this afford the least ground imaginable that it is right, if its teachings are not in harmony with the preaching of the apostles? Surely not. The Church of Christ was established in the city of Jerusalem immediately after the ascension of Christ. Nearly two thousand years have rolled away into the dark past, and if the aforesaid parties attempt to verify their assertions, for part of the distance, I fear they, at least some of them, will have to travel the same road. They will wander back through the winding streams and mists of ecclesiastical tradition, through the dark ages, and when the task is done, each will think he has an unanswerable argument that he represents the Church of Christ, and that the other two are miserable sects. Here are three organizations claiming descent from the apostles, and not one of them can find its name in the Bible! Is it not time for intelligent men to begin to think and act? There is a much shorter and clearer route to the apostles. The chain which binds the Church of the twentieth century to the primitive Church is not an unbroken succession in ministry; it is not the uninterrupted administration of an ordinance; it is not merely a succession of regenerate souls. It is the acknowledgment of the same divine authority. Paul says, 'Be followers of me, even as I am of Christ.' The New Testament contains the creed, laws, organization, discipline and order of worship in the primitive Church. Now if a religious body is governed exclusively by the same authority, accepts the same creed, obeys the same laws, is called by the same name, has the same officers with the same powers, practices the same ordinances, uses the same means for the conversion of the world, receives members in the same way and adopts the same worship, it is the same organism, the same Church. But neither of the orders referred to can do this, hence their claims are failures. I do not read in the Bible that the Church of Christ ever borrowed its ordinances from human institutions. Brother Baptist will not deny that his brethren borrowed the "mourner's bench" from the Methodists.

On this practice J. R. Graves testifies as follows:
"As to the special 'mourning-bench' in protracted meetings, about which the Campbellites make so much ado, because they have no mourning for sin in their

religion, we have no defense to offer. Every bench in the meeting house should be a true mourning-bench and place of prayer. We think as they have been used since borrowed from the Methodists, they have worked an immense injury to our Church and Christianity. They have been exalted by revivalists into sacraments of religion—almost essential means of getting religion. Sinners have almost come to believe that they cannot get religion without the revival and 'mourner's-bench,' or 'altar of prayer,' with the loud and confused praying and singing and shouting all together, that usually accompany the successful use of the 'bench' or the 'altar' or 'straw-pen.' Multitudes are tremendously excited, mentally excited, nervously excited, mesmerically excited, and made to profess a change of feeling, and in this state hurried into the Church; but the vast majority of these cases, when they cool off, find themselves back just where they were before the excitement and profession, and, after going through this process once or twice more, they become thoroughly disgusted with what has been palmed off on them for religion, and are thus prepared to become obstinate infidels. We are satisfied that nine-tenths of all the infidels and Universalists of this country have become so through the influence of those 'benches' and 'altars' and 'straw-pens,' having passed through them, or witnessed the workings, and result in the lives of the converts made by them. We should think Baptists had seen enough of their bitter fruit—that they bear little else than the apples of Sodom—to adjure them altogether."

Still the Baptist church continues the practice and affirms that Methodism is a human institution, from beginning to end!

Brother Baptist and his brethren are very severe in their denunciations of creeds, "human innovations." I hold in my hand a little book, on the title page of which I find the following: "A Confession of Faith put forth by the elders and brethren of many congregations of Christians (baptized upon profession of their faith), in London and in the country. Adopted by the

Baptist Association met at Philadelphia, Sept. 25, 1724." These lines occur in the preface: "Which Confession we own, as containing the doctrine of our faith and practice; and do desire that the members of our Churches respectively do furnish themselves therewith." Brother Baptist says this creed is not authoritative with his brethren now. Then they have changed! This breaks one link in their chain of apostolic succession. This creed is Calvinistic to the core. It declares on the seventh page that the elect and the nonelect "are particularly and unchangeably designed, and their number so certain and definite that it cannot be increased or diminished." This work contains a full exposition of the Baptist faith in the eighteenth century. It contains thirty-four chapters, discussing copiously the propositions usually discussed in works of similar character. It is explicit in reference to the acceptance of new members. It positively says on page ten, that the Church is to judge the applicants. I am glad to see the Baptists improving, but I am sorry to hear them denying their ancestry. I do not read that converts to Christ, in apostolic times, were required to give a "Christian experience," or an "experience of grace" before baptism, but upon an open confession of faith in the Lord Jesus Christ they were admitted to this solemn ordinance, and consequently "translated into the kingdom of God's dear Son." But the Baptist Church examines its converts and admits them to baptism by a vote of the Church. This experience-telling was born of the great apostasy. Did each of the three thousand converts on the day of Penecost give a "Christian experience" before they were baptized? There is not a precept or an example in the New Testament sustaining this practice. A farmer can give a farmer's experience. A mechanic can give a mechanic's experience. A Jew can give a Jew's experience. An infidel can give an infidel's experience. A Christian can give a Christian's experience. The experience grows out of the life. To require a man to relate a Christian experience who is just starting in the Christian race is as absurd as to require a man to give a preacher's experience who has never delivered a sermon; or to require a man to give a soldier's experience who has never been in war; or to require a man to give a farmer's experience who has never been out of a city. I do not read of baptism as a "Christian duty," but as an obligation resting alone upon the penitent believer. Jesus said: "He that believeth and is baptized shall be saved" (Mark, 16:15, 16). Brother Baptist baptizes him because he is saved. A slight discrepancy!

Brother Baptist said "that Jesus Christ was a Baptist, the apostles were Baptists, the martyrs were Baptists." Talk is cheap, gratuitous assertions are worthless; if they were, let him take the New Testament and turn to the place where it is so stated. I have been laboring under the impression that the apostles and early Christians were followers of Christ, and not of John the Baptist!

John the Baptist did not found the Church. After his head was cut off (Matt., 14:1-12), Jesus said: "I will build my Church (Matt., 16:18)." John the Baptist was only a *voice* crying in the wilderness (Isaiah, 40:1-8; Matt., 3:1-7)." "Voice," unquestionably signifies that his ministry was temporary. He was not in the kingdom; he died before it began (Matt., 11:11). He came in the spirit and power of Elijah (Luke, 1:17). He preached a coming Redeemer (Matt., 3:11). He decreased as Jesus increased (John, 3:30). His light shone but for a season (John, 6:33-35). His work was confined to the Jews, Abraham's descendants (Matt., 3:1-9; Acts, 13:46).

Brother Baptist affirms that men are "totally depraved," and that salvation is by "grace alone." He can not find either of these expressions in the Bible. Will he affirm that the thought is there, when the words are not? If so, he must also affirm that the New Testament was not written in as forcible language as he is now able to command! Both of these phrases contradict the word of God! The fact that men are exhorted to save themselves (Acts, 2:40), is an eternal contradition of the first, and the New Testament teaches that men are saved by twelve different things, thus forever destroying the second. Do you ask for the proof? Listen: (1) By grace (Eph., 2:4-8). (2) By Jesus Christ (Mat., 1:21; Luke, 19:10). (3) By His blood (Rom., 5:9). (4) By His resurrection (Rom., 4:25). (5) By His life (Rom., 5:10). (6) By the gospel (Rom., 1:16; I. Cor., 15:1-5). (7) By Faith (Acts, 16:31). (8) By repentance (Luke, 13:1-5; Acts, 17:30, 31; II. Pet., 3:9). (9) By confessing Christ (Matt., 10:32; Rom., 10:9, 10). (10) By calling on the name of the Lord (Acts, 22:16; Rom., 10:13). (11) By baptism (Mark, 16:15, 16; I. Pet., 3:20, 21). By works (Phil., 2:12; Jas., 2:24). Will my friend affirm that any one of them in this list may be omitted? Will he affirm that one item is non-essential? Will he affirm that one item is more important than another? Will he affirm that each one of these items does not have a place, an important place, in the salvation of every sinner? Have I not as good a right to claim that men are saved by "faith alone," or "baptism alone," as he has to declare that it is done by "grace alone?" The fact is, this "alone" business is the most consummate fraud ever perpetrated by man!

Brother Baptist said that in view of the fact that the Lord Jesus gave a rule for the government of His Church (Matt., 18:15-17) the Church was already set up. Not necessarily. God gave a law for the government of the kings of Israel three hundred and fifty years before Saul was crowned king (Deut., 17:14-20; I. Sam., 10:17-25).

Brother Baptist denies the "identity" of the two covenants, but shows his inconsistency by placing the Church in the wilderness with John the Baptist before the death of Christ, and before the abolishment of the "first covenant," and before Jesus purchased the Church with His blood (I. Cor., 6:20; Eph., 5:23-25; Heb., 8:1-13).

I submit the following questions to Brother Baptist, and through him to all the other denominations represented here. I take the liberty to say that to correctly and honestly answer these questions is to undermine the whole denominational fabric and let it down to eternal ruin! If you doubt my word, try it.

1. Where is the proof that Jesus established a Baptist Church, or the Baptist Church?

2. Where is the proof that the apostlss were members of a Baptist Church?

3. Where is the proof that the Church began before Jesus died?

4. Where is the proof that the apostles taught that men are totally depraved?

5. Where is the proof that the apostles taught that men are saved by grace alone?

6. Where is the proof that the apostles set out a mourner's-bench and invited men to it?

7. Where is the proof that converts had to tell an experience before baptism?

8. Where is the proof that the apostles required the Church to vote on the reception of new members?

9. Where is the proof that the early Christians celebrated the Lord's supper once a month, once a quarter, twice a year?

10. Where is the proof that the early Christians said at the Lord's table: "We invite those of like faith and order?"

11. Where is the proof that any apostle called himself a Baptist?

12. Where is the proof that any apostle called the Church a Baptist Church?

13. Where is the proof that any apostle called the Church the Baptist Church of Christ?

14. Where is the proof that the apostles taught that a sinner cannot do anything to save himself?

15. Where is the proof that the apostles baptized men because they were saved?

16. Where did any apostle ever ask a convert how he felt; and what convert described his feelings?

17. If a man whom you knew to be sincere, were to come to you and confess his faith in Christ, and ask you to baptize him on that confession, assuring you

that he would wear no name but Christian, would you baptize him?

18. Why do you refuse to affiliate with immersed believers outside of your organization, when their lives prove that they have the spirit of Christ and are therefore the children of *your* Father, particularly as you assert that baptism is non-essential to salvation?

19. If you were preaching Christ, and people were to cry out as on Pentecost, would you give them Peter's answer (Acts, 2:1-42)?

20. If you were preaching to a man on the highway and he were to confess his faith and demand baptism of you as the Eunuch did under the preaching of Philip, would you baptize him (Acts, 8:26-39)?

21. If you had been called to a man who had been praying three days like Saul, would you give him the answer Ananias gave (Acts, 22:1-16)?

22. If a man were to ask you, under such circumstances as the jailer addressed Paul and Silas, what to do, would you tell him to *believe* first, or *repent* first (Acts, 16:23-40?

23. Will you define Christian unity (John, 17:20, 21)?

24. Are we married to Christ (Rom., 7:4)? If so, whose name should we wear? When is the marriage ceremony complete? When does the bride lose her identity in the bridgroom and take his name?

25. What process makes man a Christian? What process makes man a Baptist? Is the process the same? If you answer *yes*, you affirm that a man can not be a Christian without baptism, for he cannot be a Baptist without it. If you answer *no*, you make the Church higher and better than heaven.

26. Would you accept a Six-Principle, Primitive, Free will, Seventh Day, Old Connexion, New Connexion, Regular or Particular Baptist without re-baptizing him?

27. Did Jesus have a people in reality before He purchased them with His death? If *yes*, why was it necessary that He should die? If *no*, why do you set up the Church before His death?

28. Is prayer limited to God's promises? If *yes*, where has He promised to save sinners at the mourner's bench? If *no*, to what shall we appeal?

29. Is God willing to save the sinner? If you answer *yes*, how do you account for the large number of persons who go away from your revivals mourning, seeking, inquiring, seeing all are equally dead according to your theory? If you answer *no*, what will make Him willing?

30. What is heartfelt religion? If a man will believe in Christ with all his heart and obey Him, will he have it?

31. Is the plan of salvation revealed in the New Testament? If *yes*, why have the mourner's bench? If *no*, where is the plan of salvation?

32. Is salvation conditional? If you answer *yes*, what are the conditions, and how can a helpless, dead sinner perform them? If you answer *no*, who is responsible for the damned?

33. At what point is the penitent pardoned, and what are his evidences of it?

34. Would you accept a man into your fellowship who persistently teaches that baptism is for the remission of sins? If *no*, on what ground do you claim to be apostolic, seeing Peter preached it with the approval of all the other apostles on Pentecost? If *yes*, why do you not preach it?

35. What part of redemption is the work of the Lord? What part is the work of the sinner? If you say the sinner has nothing to do, I have driven you to Universalism. If you say he can and must do what is commanded and trust God for the result, I have driven you to baptism for the remission of sins.

36. Do hearing, faith and repentance merit anything on the part of the sinner? If not, why not take the same view of baptism, seeing faith, repentance and baptism are all found in the Great Commission and in the apostolic answers, and say that all derive their strength from the fact, and that alone, that they are the appointments of the King?

37. Do you believe that the prayers of the Church

can in any way influence the Lord to save a man who has not obeyed the gospel as laid down by the twelve on the day of Pentecost? If *yes*, why can not the Church, by prayer, save the whole world, seeing all are equally dead according to your theory? If *no*, why do you have the mourner's bench?

38. Is the command to be baptized the word of God? If *yes*, baptism is a part of the new birth, for we are born of the word of God. If *no*, why do you practice it (I. Pet., 1:23)?

39. How do you explain Peter's statement that those to whom he wrote had purified their souls in obeying the truth (I. Pet., 1:22)? When did this process of purification begin? If not with the sinner's first step toward God, please locate the time?

40. In view of the fact that man lost all by sin, that he could not without Divine aid reinstate himself in the favor of God, and in view of the fact that salvation is the act and gift of God, is it any less salvation by grace if He sees fit to impose conditions in order to obtain it? If *no*, how do you account for the damnation of a large part of the human race?

41. How do you explain Paul's statement to the Romans that they had obeyed from the heart the form of doctrine delivered them at which time they were made free from sin (Rom., 6:17, 18)?

42. When does the sinner become totally depraved? Either he is born so, or he becomes so. If he becomes so at the commission of his first sin, how do you explain Paul's statement that evil men and seducers wax worse and worse (II. Tim., 3:13)? If not when he commits his first sin, there are sinners who are not totally depraved, and your favorite doctrine, the mudsill of your denominational fabric, is broken into a thousand pieces.

43. Is there any salvation out of Christ? Is it not a fact that we believe into, repent into, confess into and are baptized into Christ (Mark, 16:15, 16; Acts, 2:38; Rom., 10:9, 10)?

44. How do you explain John's statement that the Spirit, water and blood agree in one, in view of the fact

that you claim to "receive the Spirit" and to have "the blood applied" before baptism (I. John, 5:8)?

45. How do you, in view of your doctrine that apostasy is impossible, explain the two hundred passages in the epistolary writings that make the Christian's eternal salvation conditional, to say nothing about the great number of passages in the Gospels and Acts that do the same?

46. In view of the facts; (a) That the Divine side of redemption was finished when Jesus sent the Holy Spirit down (John, 14:26); (b) that faith comes by hearing (Rom., 10:17); (c) that faith purifies the heart (Acts, 15:9); (d) that obedience purifies the soul (I. Pet., 1:22); is it not true that the sinner must place himself in such a relation to the Divine government that he may be forgiven without violence to the same?

47. Admitting for argument's sake that the Baptist Church is the true Church of Christ, how is the inquirer to decide between the great number of organizations claiming to be the true Baptist Church, seeing that not one of them is mentioned in the Book?

48. What is the washing of regeneration mentioned by Paul in his letter to Titus (Titus, 3:5)? If not baptism and its antecedents, what is it?

49. If a man believes in Christ, repents of his sins and is baptized in obedience to the law of Christ, will he be regenerated or born again? If not, what shall we say of those whose conversion is recorded in Acts, seeing this book does not mention directly either the new birth or regeneration? If *yes*, why do you pray for outside power?

50. How do you account for Paul's action in bursting up the Baptist Church that he found at Ephesus, seeing it is the only one of which we have any account in the Book (Acts, 19:1-7)

51. Can a man be a Christian without being a Baptist? If *yes*, on what ground do you claim that it is necessary to be a Baptist? If *no*, bring the proof!

52. If, after a convert gives his experience and is received as a candidate for baptism, he should *refuse*

to be baptized, do you think he could be saved? What would you do with him? You could not turn him out because he was not a member, and you could not baptize him because he would not let you!

53. What is the first step in the salvation of a sinner, and who must take it?

54. Do you not think that baptism for the remission of sins is much more attractive to a man of intelligence than the mourner's bench, with its confusion, for the remission of sins? What is there in one of your revivals to attract a man who reads and thinks?

55. Will sinners be damned on the account of personal neglect of the requirements of the Gospel? If *yes*, what becomes of the mudsill of your doctrine—total depravity and helplessness? If *no*, on what ground will they be damned?

56. Did the three thousand converts on Pentecost each give an experience similar to what is required by Baptist churches now? If *yes*, how did the apostles succeed in accomplishing so much in one day, and where is the proof? If *no*, on what ground do you claim that the custom is apostolic?

57. Why do you vote persons into the church? You hear their experiences, compare their experiences with yours instead of the word of God, and vote them in, declaring by this act that they are saved eternally, and in a short time vote them out for sin, thus declaring that they were never saved!

58. Does not the experience grow out of the life—the storms, cares and duties that confront us? If *yes*, why do you ask a person just beginning a Christian life to give a "Christian experience?" If *no*, bring the proof that the apostles require it.

59. If baptism, with its antecedents, is not "for the remission of sins," what is it for? Everything has its design. What is the design of baptism? Explain the Commission in the light of your answer.

60. What constitutes baptism? It is not simply an immersion, for one might fall into the water and thus be "buried." Is it not a fact that the action, person and design all play a part? If *yes*, on what ground do

you criticize sprinklers for abandoning the apostolic action, seeing you abandon the design? If *no*, why not leave out the person, or the action?

61. Do you endorse the Philadelphia Confession of Faith? If not, do you endorse the Baptists who endorse it? Which is worse, to have a creed, or endorse your ancestors and their creeds? Is it not a fact that nothing, however small in heaven, earth or hell can be identified in fact, in truth, in history, without a name? If *yes*, how do you establish the fact that the Baptist Church is apostolic, seeing it is not named in the New Testament? If *no*, please identify something that has no name ! ! !

62. If a man can be a Christian only, only a Christian, on what ground do you claim that it is necessary to be anything else? In other words, if he can be a Christian without being a Baptist, is it not a fact that Baptistism is sectarianism of the most malignant type? Why are you not content with Christianity unmixed with tradition? Is it not time for a reformation even in the Baptist Church?

My objections to the doctrine and practice of the Baptist Church are: (1) It has an unscriptural name. No institution that wears a name unknown to the apostles can be "apostolic in doctrine and practice." (2) It has a human creed. In proof of this declaration I present to the Convention the "Philadelphia Confession of Faith," adopted by the Baptists in 1724. (3) It is unscriptural in organization. In apostolic times the Churches of Christ had each a plurality of elders (Acts, 20:17; Titus, 1:5). These Churches were not *Baptist* Churches, for Baptist Churches have usually one elder to four congregations. (4) It has an unscriptural language. In the Baptist Church they use such expressions as "get religion," "get through," "regenerated and born again," and "mourners," and they call their preachers "Reverends" and "Doctors of Divinity." (5) It teaches that salvation comes by praying—prayers of the Church. This is the only legitimate explanation of the mourner's bench system in all its variations. (6) It teaches that sinners can please God without faith by placing repentance first. There are only two motives that lead men to repentance: (a) The fear of Judgment (Acts, 17:30, 31). (b) The goodness of God (Rom., 2:4). Compare Rom., 1:16; Heb., 11:6. The Baptists place repentance before faith and therefore before godly sorrow. (7) It teaches that men can repent without Christ by affirming that faith in Him follows repentance, thus making the Cross of Christ of none effect. Repentance is "toward"—in the direction of God (Acts, 20:21). Jesus declares that He is the way and the truth and the life, and that men can only approach the Father through Him (John, 14:6), and Paul affirms that He is the Mediator—"one who stands between parties at variance"—between God and man (I. Tim., 2:5). Now if a man can repent toward God without faith in Jesus as the only Saviour and intercessor, we might as well go back to Judaism and worship Jehovah without reference to His only begotten Son. The Cross of Christ stands between the sinner and his God (I. Cor., 1:18), and to deny the power of the Cross is to nullify the gospel and make repentance a farce or an impossibility. (8) It calls upon its converts to confess their feelings instead of Christ. Every applicant for Church membership must tell how he feels (Matt., 10:32, 33; Acts, 8:35-38; 19:18; Rom., 10:9, 10; I. Tim., 6:12, 13). (9) It votes upon the reception of new members. Bring the chapter and verse where any apostle ever practiced this or commanded this to be done! If you cannot do it you must acknowledge your defeat. (10) It preaches salvation by works—the mourner's bench. Not one word of Scripture can be introduced to sustain this practice, but if the Church has the keys of the kingdom, it is infallible and can change the ordinances! (11) It neglects the weekly observance of the Lord's Supper (Acts, 20:7). (12) It neglects the weekly contribution (I. Cor., 16:1, 2). (13) It teaches the impossibility of apostasy. I introduce one million, one hundred and ninety-nine thousand, nine hundred and ninety-eight arguments against this assumption. They are the graves of those who fell in the wilderness

(600,000 men and a woman for every man), between the Red Sea and Canaan (Ex., 12:37; Num., 13:1-33; 14:1-35; 26:63-65; I. Cor., 10:1-12). (14) Its theory of conversion tends to produce unbelief in the word of God. As long as men are taught that they must do what God says and yet wait for a power they cannot control or influence to enable them to do it, infidelity will walk triumphantly through the land. (15) It baptizes dead sinners after they come to life! In Paul's day they were baptized and "raised up" in order to walk in newness of life" (Rom., 6:1-5). (16) It excludes part of those whom it recognizes as God's children from the Lord's table on the ground that they have not been baptized, and then designates baptism a non-essential and only a figure. It sets up a "figure" as a "wall of separation" between the children of God! It *works* with Methodists, Presbyterians and others, many of whom have been immersed, but it will not *eat* with them because, and for no other reason, it has not "figured" on them! (17) It sets the Church up at the wrong place. They set it upon the banks of the Jordan or at Cesarea Philippi, and all this simply to avoid the necessity of fellowshipping Simon Peter in his teaching that baptism is for the remission of sins. (18) It makes too much of baptism. It makes baptism its standard; calls itself for it, and rallies around it. It is baptism from Dan to Beersheba, and baptism in the mountains of Lebanon north of Dan, further than any one has ever gone, and baptism south of Beersheba in the land of Idumea, further than any one has ever penetrated. (19) It makes too little of baptism. At the vital point: *"He that believeth and is baptized shall be saved"* (Mark, 16:15, 16), it throws it overboard as a non-essential. (20) It sets up one plan for salvation and another for Church membership. In apostolic times the *Lord* added to the Church those that "were being saved" (Acts, 2:47; Rom., 15:7; I. Cor., 12:18), but the Baptists have one process to make a man a Christian and another to get him into the Church. They get a man into Christ by preaching Christ, mixed with predestination, total depravity and regeneration as the result of the prayers of the Church. They get him into the Church by experience, vote of the Church and baptism. (21) It teaches that men are saved out of Christ. In other words, before they are in the body (I. Cor., 12:13; Gal., 3:26, 27). (22) It teaches that men are saved outside of the name of Father, Son and Holy Spirit. They are saved according to Baptist theology before baptism (Matt. 28:18-20). (23) It perverts the Great Commission in teaching that men have the promise of salvation without obedience to the command of Christ to be baptized (Mark, 16:15, 16). (24) It teaches the total depravity of the human race (Luke, 8:15). (25) It makes God a tyrant—responsible for the damned. The Baptist theory in brief is: (a) All men are totally depraved and therefore unable to do anything to save themselves. (b) Regeneration is the first step in the sinner's return to God, and it must be taken by the Holy Spirit. Now if He never comes it is because the Lord does not send Him, and the sinner is damned for failing to do that which he cannot do. (26) It teaches that baptism is because of remission: "Then Peter said unto them, Repent and be baptized every one of you in the name of Jesus Christ, *for the remission of sins*, and ye shall receive the gift of the Holy Ghost" (Acts, 2:38). (27) It will not give the apostolic answer to inquirers (Acts, 2:38; 8:37; 22:16). (28) It teaches that baptism is the *answer* instead of the *seeking* of a good conscience, as the best scholars agree (I. Pet., 3:21). (29) Its teachings tend to confusion— Missionary Baptists, Primitive Baptists, Seventh Day Baptists, Regular Baptists, Free-will Baptists, Old Connexion Baptists, New Connexion Baptists, Particular Baptists, Six-Principle Baptists, Two seed Baptists, no two kinds alike and no fellowship among them. (30) It makes *non-essential* the institution of Christ (Matt., 28:18-20; Mark, 16:15, 16; Acts, 2:38). (31) It teaches that salvation is by grace alone. (32) It teaches that salvation is a dry-land matter (John, 3:5). (33) It denies the doctrine of James the Apostle (Jas., 2:1-26). (34) It misues the name Baptist. A

Baptist is one who baptizes, and no one else can appropriately wear the name. (35) It requires converts to give an experience. There is absolutely no proof of this custom in the apostolic writings, and no Church requiring it is apostolic either in doctrine or practice. (36) It perverts the gospel by teaching that sinners are converted outside of it.

I do not read of any kind of a Presbyterian Church in the word of God, and I am surprised that men of such culture fail to see that they are propagating human institutions. Brother Presbyterian endeavored to apologize for the existence of modern denominations. Let him examine the names worn by the different orders, their creeds, their infant sprinkling, their controversies, and the general character of their work, and decide if they constitute the "one body of Christ." I do not read in the Scriptures of the Presbyterian Confession of Faith, either for the uncompromising Calvinist or the more liberally disposed. But the speaker says it is in harmony with the word of God, and that the proof texts are submitted along with the articles of faith. So all the creed-makers affirm. They can not all be right, for they contradict each other. I think many of the quotations are palpable misapplications of the truth. For example, certain passages are quoted to sustain the practice of sprinkling infants, but not one of them intimates this practice in apostolic times. My friend gives us a full exposition of Calvinism. He presents his "five points" with a grace worthy of a better cause. Now, suppose these "five points" are true, it is immaterial whether I believe them or not. If I am predestinated unto everlasting life I will be saved whether I believe in Presbyterianism or not. If I am a reprobate or a non-elect, my efforts will be unavailing. The first proposition of Calvinism makes the number of the saved and the lost so definite that they can neither be increased nor diminished. If any man in this convention ever read such a statement in the Bible as this, let him arise and make it known. How could it be affirmed by an inspired apostle that "God is no respecter of persons" (Acts, 10:34) if He is willing to save some and unwilling to save others? How could He have said to Abraham, that in him should all families of the earth be blessed (Gen., 12:1-3), if a part were foreordained from all eternity to be saved and a part to be lost? How could the angel sing and shout to the shepherds on the hills of Judea: "I bring you good tidings of great joy, which shall be unto all people" (Luke, 2:10) if this fundamental principle of Presbyterianism is true? How could God be just, holy and merciful if He predestinated me to an eternal hell centuries before I was born? I begin to have a good idea why the different sects do not fellowship each other. It is to a great extent attributable to dogmatic assertions in their creeds. He passes on to the death of Christ and affirms that He died only for those who were His from all eternity. This is a positive and unequivocal contradiction of the word of God, for Paul says that He tasted death for every man (Heb., 2:9). According to the word of God a very large part of the human race, on account of disobedience, will be lost. Satan will get these. A small portion, through faith and obedience will be saved. Jesus will get these. Now, according to Presbyterianism, God virtually said: "Son, I will make man, he will sin, and with an innumerable host of his descendants plunge into condemnation. If you will depart from heaven and become a missionary among the lost and die upon the cross to purchase them, I will give you a small portion of the race, but the remainder I will give to the devil." Bible reader, what do you think of this? Is it consistent? Is it reasonable? Is it in harmony with the word of God? Is it not enough to drive thinking men into doubts, and even into positive infidelity?

Man's corruption is taught in the word of God, but not to the degree which Presbyterianism affirms, for Jesus taught that notwithstanding man's alienation from God, there are still *honest and good hearts* (Luke, 8:15). Presbyterianism teaches that absolute corruption of the human race. Please behold the contrast! Presbyterianism teaches that by the fall man lost "all ability or will," hence regeneration must be a work of naked omnipotence. Is man "wholly defiled in all the faculties and parts of the soul and body?" Is he "utterly disposed, disabled and opposite to all good, and wholly inclined to evil?" I know I am a sinner—out of Christ—without hope, but I have inclinations—strong yearnings to know God and obey His holy will. My experience may not be considered applicable, so I will turn to the word of God. Can a sinner do anything to save himself? An inspired apostle teaches that he can: "Save yourselves" (Acts, 2:40). The Presbyterian creed teaches that he cannot. Can a sinner accept the call of Jesus? The New Testament teaches that he can: "Come unto me, all ye that labor and are heavy laden, and I will give you rest" (Matt., 11:28-30). The Presbyterian creed teaches that he can not. Can the sinner believe the gospel when he hears it? Jesus Christ teaches that he can: "If ye believe not that I am He, ye shall die in your sins" (John, 8:24). The Presbyterian creed teaches that he can not. Can a sinner repent when he hears the gospel? Jesus teaches that he can: "Except ye repent, ye shall all likewise perish" (Luke, 13:3). The Presbyterian creed teaches that he can not. Presbyterianism is not alone in this. The Baptists hold to the dogma of "total depravity," hence they must bear the same criticism. This theory has been an impediment to the advancement of the cause of Christ. Convince a man that he can not do anything to save himself and he will sit down, fold his arms and wait for "power from on high." The gospel is an unlovely exhibition when its obligations are made binding, and the sinner is boldly informed that he can not move in obedience to its requirements. The gospel has its facts to be believed, and its commandments to be obeyed. The sinner is left to choose for himself. It offers eternal life to the obedient, and eternal death of the disobedient. "Choose you this day whom ye will serve." Every theory to the contrary is a delusion, a deception, a cheat. "Final perseverance" is a phrase not found in the New Testament, hence I conclude that the thought which it contains is not there. Paul says: "Let him that thinketh that he standeth take heed lest he fall" (I. Cor., 10:12). It therefore behooves us to "watch and pray" and "continue steadfast unto the end."

Brother Presbyterian attempted to defend Brother Methodist. He said concerning the remarks of Brother Baptist: "I assure him that in the next verse after the one that speaks of a Baptist Church you will find a full history of the rise, progress and victories of Methodism." I presume that in the next verse he will find a history of the rise and progress of Presbyterianism! Consistency must indeed be a jewel!

My objections to Presbyterianism are: (1) Its name is not mentioned in the New Testament. (2) Its creed was compiled by uninspired men. (3) They are divided among themselves; it is affirmed that there are forty-two kinds in all! (4) Their Calvinism is contrary to Scripture. (5) They teach the identity of the two covenants. (6) They teach that Baptism comes in the room of circumcision. (7) They substitute sprinkling and pouring for immersion, contrary to the voices of history and revelation. (8) They sprinkle unconscious infants without finding authority for it in the Bible, either by precept or example. (9) It began too far this side of Jerusalem. (10) They teach that the gospel of Christ is a "dead letter." (11) They teach that the conversion of sinners is miraculous. (12) They prevent the union of God's people in "one body" by justifying divisions.

The Protestant Episcopal preacher does not entertain a single doubt that he represents the true Apostolic Church, and that the Book of Common Prayer, with its thirty-nine articles of faith, is the best basis for Christian union that can be found. I turn to the Scriptures, and I do not find anything said about this institution, or the creed upon which its founded. I do not find where any were commanded to present their children at the "font," nor where older persons were required to present themselves there to have water sprinkled upon them. I do not read anything about

"God-fathers," or "God-mothers." Of this custom in the Church of England the Bishop of Salisbury said:

"I must candidly and broadly state my conviction that there is no one passage nor word in Scripture which directly proves it; not one word, the undeniable and logical power of which can be adduced to prove, either in any way of fact, that, in the scriptural age, infants were baptized, or of doctrine that they ought to be baptized. Nor, I believe, is there any such direct statement to be found in any writings of the fathers of the Church before the latter end of the second century after Christ."

In the face of this frank and unequivocal admission, the Protestant Episcopal Church continues its practice! They take the unconscious infants and bind them to a human creed before they know good from evil. They then bind themselves to bring them up in this creed, and bring them to the bishop for confirmation as soon as they can repeat a human catechism and a creed. This reverses the Divine order. In fact it completely nullifies it. Children are brought into this institution by *water alone,* and precious little water at that! I do not find where any of the converts to Christ in primitive times were confirmed by the imposition of the bishop's hands, but I do read that they were confirmed by Paul and Barnabas, who exhorted them to continue in the faith (Acts, 14:21, 22). Hence I affirm that Episcopal confirmation is a relic of the superstitions of ages gone by. But where did this so-called "Apostolic Church" come from? My friend says from the New Testament. If this is true, why does not the New Testament say something about it? The first Episcopal Church ever in existence was not organized until about fourteen hundred years after the death of the last surviving apostle. That Church is the English Episcopal Church. How can an institution, the origin of which is known to be fourteen hundred years after the apostolic age, claim an uninterrupted succession of bishops from the apostles down to this day? How did this sect originate? Henry VIII. was king of England. He was a devout Roman Catholic. He defended his religion against the assaults of the illustrious Martin Luther. The Pope gave him the title, "Defender of the Faith." He wanted a divorce from one of his wives. The Pope refused to grant it. He withdrew from the Church of Rome on this account, with the Catholic Churches of his country, and became head of what is now known as the Church of England, or the Protestant Episcopal Church. This looks like apostolic succession, does it not? Henry VIII. was a corrupt tyrant, and the chief business of his life seemed to be selecting and marrying new queens, making room for each succeeding one by discarding, divorcing or beheading her predecessor. There were six of them in all, and with one exception the history of each one is a distinct, separate and dreadful tragedy. This man originated the Episcopal Church. How unlike the character of an apostle! They may trace their existence back to King Henry, but for the balance of the journey they must travel the same line with the Roman Catholics. Yet they profess to be Protestants!

Brother Episcopalian said: "First of all, those who are in our Church are one. The true faith destroys sectarianism." If this is true, what is meant by "High Church," and "Low Church?" Do not these appellations show that one faction of the Protestant Episcopal Church leans a little more toward Roman Catholicism than the other? Does not one love the pomp and ceremony of Rome more than the other? If not this, will he please tell us what they do mean? When he answers this we will be ready to hear him preach on the unity of the Church.

My objections to the Episcopal Church are: (1) Its name can not be found in the Bible. (2) Their creed is a human production. (3) It began fourteen hundred years after apostolic times. (4) It was founded by Henry VIII. and not by Christ. (5) It is a daughter of Roman Catholicism. (6) It borrowed sprinkling from the apostasy. (7) It teaches justification by "faith only." (8) It binds infants to a human creed before they know good from evil. (9) It binds parents to teach their children tradition. (10) Its creed, containing thirty-nine articles, implies the insufficiency of the Bible as a rule of faith and practice. (11) Its system of confirmation is not found in the New Testament. (12) It calls the Lord's supper and Baptism sacraments, thus perpetutaing the language of Rome. (13) It hinders the progress of Christian union by making its creed a test of fellowship.

Brother Lutheran comes before us with a great deal of confidence in the righteousness of his cause, and I entertain a high degree of admiration for the reformatory work of Martin Luther, but God never commissioned him to found a Church. He gave Roman Catholicism many blows, from which it has never recovered: For this I shall ever cherish a grateful remembrance of his name. But did he fully shake off the chains of the papacy and return to the old foundation? Let the word of God decide. I turn to its pages and I do not find anything concerning an "Evangelical Lutheran Church." I do not find anything concerning the Augsburg Confession of Faith, on which it is established. I do not find in the Scriptures that baptism is necessary to the salvation of infants, yet Lutheranism teaches this (Confession, Article 9). They deny the Roman Catholic dogma of transubstantiation, but teach that the "body and blood of Christ are truly present and are communicated to those who eat the Lord's Supper." What is the difference? Will my friend rise up and explain? The Confession, Article 11 contains the following: "Concerning confession, they teach that private absolution be retained in the Church, though enumeration is not necessary." Who ever read such a statement in the word of God? How far is it from priestly forgiveness in the Roman Catholic Church? The word of God says nothing about the mass, but Brother Lutheran says: "It is retained among us and celebrated with great reverence." Martin Luther did not, in my humble opinion, intend to establish an institution to perpetuate his name. I think he was actuated by higher and purer motives. When his friends said "Luther forever," he said: "No, no! Christ forever. Do not call yourselves Lutherans, call yourselves Christians." My objections to Lutheranism are: (1) Its name can not be found in the word of God. (2) Its confession of faith was formulated by human hands. (3) It began at Wittenburg and not at Jerusalem. (4) It teaches the identity of the two covenants. (5) It practices sprinkling and pouring. (6) It sprinkles infants. (7) It borders too near transubstantiation in reference to the loaf and the cup. (8) It echoes some of the principles of Catholicism. (9) They call themselves Lutherans contrary to the wishes of Luther. (10) Its doctrine of justification by faith only is not true. (11) They are divided among themselves. (12) They prevent real union among the people of God by exalting human standards into tests of fellowship.

CHAPTER XIV.

INQUIRER.

I am continuing my inquiries into the things I have heard here to-day. I am still an inquirer seeking for light and truth, but so far I have been unable to find either.

Roman Catholic comes before the convention with characteristic audacity, attempting to convince us that he is an exponent of the truth. I propose to try "the rule" on his pretensions. I acknowledge all he says about the Church in apostolic times, but let him remember that it was called the Church of Christ. It had neither Roman nor Catholic attached to it. He misrepresents the apostles Paul and Peter when he makes them responsible for the establishment of his system. I do not think he can show, by reliable authority, that Peter was ever in the city of Rome; and Paul says concerning this corrupt and deceptive institution, that it is the "mystery of iniquity;" "the man of sin," "the son of perdition." He describes it more fully in the following language: "Who opposeth and exalteth himself above all that is called God, or that is worshipped; so that he as God sitteth in the temple of God, showing himself that he is God" (II. Thess., 2:1-2). This gives a good idea of Paul's opinion of this abomination. True to this prediction, the Pope styles himself the "Vicar of Christ," the "visible Head of the Church." John says: "He is anti-Christ, that denieth the Father and the Son" (I. John, 2:22). Does not the papacy virtually deny the authority of Jesus Christ in substituting human legislation and tradition for divine revelation? This institution is called the beast with seven heads and ten horns (Rev., 13:1-18). Again this description is given by the Spirit of inspiration centuries before Roman Catholicism reached the zenith of its power: "I saw a woman sit upon a scarlet-colored beast, full of the names of blasphemy, having seven heads and ten horns. And the woman was arrayed in purple and scarlet color, and decked with gold and precious stones and pearls, having a golden cup in her hand full of abominations and filthiness of her fornication; and upon her forehead was a name written, MYSTERY, BABYLON THE GREAT, THE MOTHER OF HARLOTS AND ABOMINATIONS OF THE EARTH" (Rev., 17:3-5). And still Mr. Catholic claims to represent the Church of Christ! I do not read anything in the word of God of Popes nor their infallibility. Neither is there a single intimation as to infallibility of the Church. This may do for Romanism, but is incompatible with the teachings of the New Testament. The speaker made very strong pretensions as to the holiness of his Church, but look at the Christians they have burned at the stake, the Bibles they have destroyed, and the corruptions they have perpetrated in the name of religion; and decide how these comport with Roman Catholic holiness! He makes Rome his beginning point, but I assure him that the Church of Christ began at Jerusalem (Isaiah, 2:1-3; Luke, 24:47; Acts, 8:1, 2) He tells us that the "official prerogatives conferred upon Peter were to be transmitted to his successors through all ages. The Bible says nothing about transmitting any power or authority from an Apostle to a Pope; hence I conclude that this is another imposition. He says we must "invoke the saints," thus denying the words of Paul, in which he commands us to do all things in the name of Jesus Christ (Col., 3:17). The Bible says nothing about the "immaculate conception of Mary, the mother of God," the use of images, or of "seven sacraments." It does not intimate such a thing as priestly absolution, but teaches us to consider our personal relation to Jesus Christ our Lord. Roman Catholicism is an engine of destruction, the center of universal corruption, and the culmination of Satan's scheme to deceive a dying race.

While the entire system is false, I will sum up a few of the worst features: (1) Its name is unknown in the New Testament. (2) It makes tradition equal to revelation. (3) It makes a sinful man its head. (4) It teaches the infallibility of the Pope. (5) It teaches infallibility of the Church. (6) It teaches priestly forgiveness. (7) It originated sprinkling as a substitute for immersion. (8) It opposes private investigation of the Scriptures. (9) It has burned Bibles to prevent the people from reading them. (10) It combines itself with human government—anything for power. (11) It has slain thousands for protesting against its corruptions. (12) Its officials, from the Pope down, are unknown to the word of God. (13) It is "the mother of harlots and abominations of the earth."

As to Mr. Infidel's criticism, I have but little to say. He virtually acknowledges that he has never investigated the evidences of Christianity. I think he has formed his opinion from the divided state of the religious denominations of the age, rather than from the fountain—the pure word of God. There is a wide difference between Christianity traditionized and sectarianized, and Christianity in its primitive purity. The Bible is a consistent, harmonious and reasonable book. Sectarianism is contradictory and inconsistent in its teaching. Mr. Infidel wants to destroy the Bible and the Christian hope, because some professors are not as true as they should be. If the Bible is true, he will lose everything; if it is false, the Christian will not lose anything by practicing its great demands; for it makes a better husband, a better wife, a better son, a better daughter, a better neighbor, a better citizen. The whole question can be summed up in a few words: Mr. Infidel wants to destroy the Bible, the Church, the hope, without giving anything in their stead. Until something better can be offered, it would be foolish—preposterous—to throw them away. Chrsitianity, pure and unmixed with tradition, has withstood the bitter persecutions of the Jews; the superstitions of idolatry; the degeneracy of political governments; the missiles of infidelity; the contraditions of sectarianism; the glowing eloquence of human philosophy; the glittering periods of "science, falsely so called;" and though it has gone through many battles, its Author still lives, stands erect amidst the storms and bids defiance to all opposition. I hope Mr. Infidel will change his "creed" accept the only book which throws any light upon the problem of human life here and hereafter. I think this convention may learn a lesson from Mr. Infidel's speech. Who can answer it? Who an deny that sectarianism makes infidels?

Brother Adventist has a plaster to cover all theological ailments, but I noticed that it is not large enough to cover several Biblical truths that seem to have entirely escaped his attention; however, I must confess that the part of his speech referring to the keeping of the Sabbath affected part of his audience in a way that is utterly astonishing to me. Why did not Brother Methodist arise in his place and reply to this energetic speech? Manifestly because he, too, is under the law of Moses in doctrine, and he can not do it without completely overturning his position that the Church was established in the days of Abel, enlarged in the days of Moses, and continued uninterruptedly through the old dispensation. Why did that fervent "Amen" arise from the Presbyterian delegation and meet such an emphatic reverberation from the Episcopal representation? Undeniably because Presbyterians and Episcopalians are, doctrinally, under the law just as much as Brother Adventist—or any other Jew! Why did not Brother Baptist, earnest, aggressive and apostolic in pretensions, arise, start his theological mill and grind this doctrine to powder? Unquestionably because he, too, is a Jew in doctrine; he can not distinguish between the Law of Moses and the Gospel of Christ, and he can not do it without forever abandoning his position that the Church was established on the banks of the Jordan or at Cesarea Phillippi, before the Law was nailed to the cross?

I desire to ask Brother Adventist a few questions, and if he will answer them fully, honestly and Scripturally, I will accept his position and join my destiny with his. He must be aware of the fact that nothing but Scripture will move me. I must be convinced by the word of God or I will be an "inquirer" until I die.

1. Where is the proof that any man ever kept the seventh day, except by special commandment, prior to the proclamation of the ten commandments at Mt. Sinai (Gen., 2:2, 3; Ex., 16:1-30; 19:1-25; 20:1-17)?

2. If Christians are required to keep the seventh day, why do you depart from your dwelling on that day, seeing those to whom the law was given were plainly commanded not to do so (Ex., 16:29)?

3. If you keep one Sabbath—the seventh day—why not keep them all, the seventh year and the year of Jubilee? Who authorized you to make distinction in favor of the seventh day (Lev., 25:1-22)?

4. If Christians are required to keep the Sabbath, how are they to live in cold climates (Ex., 35:1-3)?

5. Is it the duty of Christians to put to death those who desecrate the seventh day (Num., 15:32-36)? If *yes,* who will be the public executioner? If *no,* what will you do with the law (Ex., 35:2)? If you say the penalties are abolished, I answer that the same passages that you use to prove this, establish beyond the shadow of a doubt that the law, too, is abolished. If you admit that the penalties are still in force, and the proof that they are is unanswerable and invincible, if the law is in force, there is not an Adventist on top of the green earth who an escape the vengeance of the broken law! It seems, from my point of view, in contemplating the great question of Christian union, that you have only to carry out the principles of Adventism to their legitimate conclusion to eliminate one troublesome element from the earth!

6. If Christians are under obligations to observe the seventh day, why did Jesus declare that all law and prophecy hang on *love* instead of the Sabbath, seeing the command to keep it is the one on which *you hang* your everlasting all (Matt., 22:34-40; Rom., 13:8-10)?

7. Why did Jesus not require the young ruler to keep the Sabbath, when enumerating the commandments (Matt., 19:16-20; Mark, 10:17-22; Luke, 18:18-24)?

8. If Christians are to keep the law of Moses—the Sabbath, why did the apostles and elders who met at

Jerusalem leave it out of their address to the churches (Acts, 15:1-29)? This case finds, in some respects, a parallel in your theorizing. Judaizing teachers had gone forth declaring to the brethren that unless they would submit to circumcision and keep the law of Moses, they could not saved. The apostles said. "We gave no such commandment."

9. If Christians are required to keep the Sabbath, how are we to account for the open violation of the law by Jesus Christ, who is our example, unless by saying that the power that made the law can take it away, and that He did it (Matt., 12:1-8; John, 7:22, 23)?

10. If you keep the Sabbath because, as you think, it was kept before the law of Moses, why do you not practice circumcision, seeing it is plainly commanded in these ages (Gen., 17:1-14; Gal., 5:1-6)?

11. When did patriarch, prophet or apostle, or anybody else, command any Gentile to keep the law of Moses? No dodging here. Proof! Proof!! Proof!!!

12. Paul says the ministration of death written and engraven in stone (Ex., 20:1-17; 31:18; 32:15, 16; 34:1-28) was done away (II. Cor., 3:1-18). When, where and by whom was it brought back into force? Name the day, the age, the authority, and give proof from the book! If your doctrine is true, the great apostle of the Gentiles stands convicted of a mistake!

13. If the early Christians kept the Sabbath day, why did they break bread on the first day of the week (Acts, 20:7)?

14. If Christians are to keep the Sabbath day, how do you account for the fact that the apostles preached the gospel in Jerusalem, Samaria, to Cornelius the Gentile, and to many others without commanding a single individual to keep it? Did they, under the inspiration of the Holy Spirit, fail to properly instruct their converts (Acts, 2:1-47; 8:1-40; 10:1-48; 16:1-40)?

15. Is it not a fact, according to the book of Acts, that the thing done was of more importance than the day (Acts, 20:7)?

16. Can you demonstrate that the day you keep is

really the seventh day or Sabbath coming down in regular succession from the day on which God rested? If not, your day is no better than any other day? Admitting for argument's sake that the Law of Moses is still in force, and that the fourth commandment is binding on the whole human race, will you affirm that it is possible for all men to keep the same day? If so, how do you explain the fact that the traveler who starts out to go around the earth, gains, say, if going east, one hour for every thousand miles traveled, or if going west loses an hour for every thousand miles traveled? How far would he go before he lost the count? Do you not see how he would inevitably be behind or in advance? Further, how do you explain the fact that far away toward the extremes of the earth, traveling from the equator, there are periods of six months night and six months day from age to age? Do you not see that it is a geographical impossibility for all men to keep the same day, and that the Law was only intended for one people, one country and one age?

17. Do *you* keep the Sabbath day? No dodging; do you? Do you *rest*, or put in the day promulgating your doctrines? Do you not eat food on that day prepared by work on a fire kindled in violation of the Law (Ex., 20:8-11; 35:1-3)? Do you offer the burnt offering required by law (Num., 28:3-10)? Do you remain in your house during the day? If you do not keep the day according to the Law, you do not keep it at all. If you admit that any part of the Law concerning the Sabbath is done away, you are driven to the inevitable and irresistible conclusion that it is all done away! If you deny that any part of it is done away, you condemn yourself, for you do not keep it! Which way will you take?

18. If the kingdom of Christ is now not an established institution, or if it will not be set up until after the millennium, how do you explain: (*a*) the declaration of John the Baptist that the kingdom was, in his day, at hand (Matt., 3:2); (*b*) Paul's statement to the Colossians that they had been translated into the king-

dom (Col., 1:13); or his statement that he and his contemporaries had received a kingdom that could not be moved (Heb., 12:28); and (c) John's statement that he was in the kingdom (Rev., 1:9)?

19. If all men are unconscious between death and the resurrection, on what ground do you claim that man is superior to the brute, or that there will be a resurrection? What will be raised up? Is it not really a new creation from your point of vision?

20. If Jesus Christ is to come at the beginning of the millennium, and reign in person over the children of men, who will be the priest before the Father's throne?

21. If hell is not eternal, how long will heaven last (Matt., 25:46)?

When these questions are answered by the Book, I will consider Brother Adventist's claims. Until then I shall look upon him as an adventurer and a deceiver.

Brother Mormon's modesty is phenomenal. In the face of the record of his predecessors for nearly seventy-five years, written in blood and prostitution, he asks us to accept him as a real representative of the real Church of Jesus Christ of the Latter Day Saints. I propose to put his claims to a severe test, by turning on them the light of history, Scripture and reason, and in order to help you to follow me successful, I will number my propositions and discuss them separately.

I. *The Character of the Founder of Mormonism.* Who founded Mormonism? I answer, Joseph Smith, of the United States of America. What kind of a man was he? I answer that he was both an ignoramus and a scoundrel. He and his family were noted for avoiding honest labor; they were intemperate, untruthful, and accused by their neighbors of stealing sheep. While the Mormons try to deny these accusations, it is a fact that Joe Smith himself partly admitted them, and in extenuation claimed that he had never done anything as bad as was reported of King David, who was a man after God's own heart. If you will compare Smith's character with the character of Jesus Christ, Peter, Paul, John, Polycarp, Wycliffe, Luther, Wesley,

Spurgeon, or Campbell, you can easily decide that a pure revelation or a genuine reformation could not proceed out of such a source. I wish to propound to Brother Mormon a question in reference to Joe Smith's character in the words of the Scripture: "Doth a fountain send forth at the same place sweet water and bitter? Can a fig tree, my brethren, bear olive berries? either a vine, figs? So can no fountain both yield salt water and fresh" (Jas., 3:11, 12).

II. *The Book of Mormon.* Smith claims to have discovered this book, by the help of an angel of God. In what language was the book written? They claim that it was the "reformed Egyptian;" probably the "language in which Adam courted Eve!" How did the false prophet translate these wonderful hieroglyphics? That is easy to answer. Along with the records he found the Urim and Thummim, consisting of two transparent stones set in the rim of a bow fastened to a breastplate. By these stone spectacles God helped him to translate the book of Mormon into the humble English that he used, it being his vernacular. Smith hung a blanket across the room to keep the sacred record from the gaze of profane eyes, and as he read, Oliver Cowdery wrote it down. What became of these plates? Let Mormons answer. Who saw these plates? Only Joe Smith and eleven of his followers. This stamps the whole thing a fraud. If Joe Smith had made such a discovery no sane man doubts that those plates would have been preserved. The book appeared from the press in the year 1830. I should like to know why the world, with eyes profane, could look upon the printed translation and not upon the original copy! The work attracted some attention, and as a matter of course controversy followed. It was proven that excepting certain illiterate and ungrammatical interpolations, the whole thing was stolen from a MS. of romancer Solomon Spaulding, who died in 1816. The contents of the book present strong evidence of this. It has the flavor of the New World and not of the Old. While it does not name Calvinism, Universalism, Methodism, Millenarianism and Roman Catholicism, it discusses them, thus showing that the man who wrote it was but an echo of the prevailing controversies in the villages of western New York in those days. The book condemns polygamy, free-masonry and infant baptism!

III. *The Doctrines of Mormonism.* Mormons claim to have restored or reorganized the Church of Jesus as it was in the days of the apostles. Have they done it? Take his speech and read his list of officials, and then ask him to find their names in the New Testament. If he cannot do it, and you know he cannot, I brand the whole scheme as a fraud.

IV. *The Fruits of Mormonism.* Jesus Christ gives one infallible, universal and unchangeable test: "Wherefore by their fruits ye shall know them" (Matt., 7:20). I propose to try Mormonism by this rule. In the first place, I affirm that the system tends to fanaticism. They began early in their history to proclaim that the Millennium was near at hand, that the Indians would soon be converted, and that the new Jerusalem—the final gathering place of the saints—was to be somewhere in the heart of the American continent. Not only this, but they openly proclaimed that the more wives and children a man has in this world, the purer, higher and grander he will be in the next; that wives, children and property will not only be restored, but doubled, at the resurrection of the dead. They claim the power to speak with tongues, cast out devils, cure the sick and heal the lame and the halt. They claim that they have a Prophet and Revelator who holds the keys of the Kingdom, and that through him alone can access be had. They hold to the Bible, but explain it to suit themselves, and hold it subject to new revelation, which they claim, takes the place of the old. They claim that God was once a man, who was gradually developed into His present power, and that in the future, good Mormons will become gods. They teach the shedding of blood for the remission of sins; in other words, if a Mormon departs from the faith, they believe in cutting his throat. Proof? Here it is the words of Brigham Young himself: "I could refer you to plenty of instances where men have been righteously slain in order to atone for their sins." In the next place, their distinguished leaders were dishonest. In about the year 1837 or 1838, the bank at Kirkland, Ohio, suspended, and action was taken against the prophet and his associates for swindling. How did he answer the charge? Did he pay up like a real prophet, or even an ordinary man of God? No. He received a "revelation" to depart for the State of Missouri, which he did immediately, to the great chagin of his creditors and the great replenishment of his exchequer, no doubt. In the next place, the system is responsible for some of the most atrocious murders in the annals of savagery and crime. If any man doubts this, let me remind him of Mountain Meadows and Jno. D. Lee. A contemporary historian describes that terrible butchery in the following language: "The Mountain Meadows massacre stands without a parallel amongst the crimes that stain the pages of American history. It was a crime committed without cause or justification of any kind to relieve it of its fearful character. Over one hundred and twenty men, women and children were surrounder by Indians, and more cruel whites, and kept under constant fire from hundreds of unerring rifles, for five days and nights, during all of which time the emigrants were famishing for water. When nearly exhausted from fatigue and thirst, they were approached by white men with a flag of truce, and induced to surrender their arms, under the most solemn promises of protection. They were then murdered in cold blood, and left nude and mangled upon the plain. All this was done by a band of fanatics, who had no cause of complaint against the emigrant, except that the authorities of the Mormon church had decided that all the emigrants who were old enough to talk, should die—revenge for alleged insults to Brigham Young, and the booty of the train being the inciting cause of the massacre." John D. Lee was arrested, tried and executed for this crime, and beyond a doubt Brigham Young was as bad as he. Hence there is no ground on which to deny this charge, or to assert that the Mormons were not the guilty party. In the next place, the system of polygamy inaugurated by Mormons is, for deep-dyed corruption, beastly passion, unbridled and satanic cunning, without a parrallel, or even an imitation in the history of civilization. Think of a man with twenty wives, or a man, under the guise of piety and in the name of religion raising children by two sisters, or a mother and her daughter at the same time! It is enough to bring a blush to the cheek of the devil himself. But Mormons will say polygamy has been abolished. Certainly it has, but by whom? By the Mormons? No indeed. It was done by the government of the United States. Hence it turns out that the Mormons have more fear of the law than they have respect for the new revelations about which they have so much to say. You may think I am bitter in the denunciation of polygamy. I am bitter. I have no language sufficient to express my contempt for a people who practiced it for years, and who would be doing it yet if it were not for the laws of the country. What have the leaders of Mormonism to say concerning woman: Let them speak for themselves. President J. M. Grant, in a sermon delivered September 21, 1856, reported in the *Deseret News* (Vol. 6, p. 235), said:

"And we have women here who like anything but the celestial law of God; and, if they could, would break asunder the cable of the Church of Christ; there is scarcely a mother in Israel but would do it this day. And they talk it to their husbands, to their daughters, and to their neighbors, and say that they have not seen a week's happiness since they became acquainted with that law, or since their husbands took a second wife. They want to break up the Church of God, and to break it from their husbands and from their family connections."

President Brigham Young, in a sermon delivered the same day, reported in the same paper, said:

"Now for my proposition; it is more particularly for my sisters, as it is frequently happening that women say that they are unhappy. Men will say, 'My wife, though a most excellent woman, has not seen a happy day since I took my second wife; no, not a happy day for a year!' It is said that women are tied down and abused; that they are misused, and have not the liberty they ought to have; that many of them are wading through a perfect flood of tears, because of the conduct of some men, together with their own folly.

"I wish my women to understand that what I am going to say is for them as well as all others, and I want those who are here to tell their sisters, yes, all the women of this community, and then write it back to the States, and do as you please with it. I am going to give you from this time to the 6th day of October next for reflection, that you may determine whether you wish to stay with your husbands or not, and then I am going to set every woman at liberty, and say to them, 'Now go your own way, my women with the rest; go your way.' And my wives have got to do one of two things; either round up their shoulders to endure the afflictions of this world, and live their religion, or they may leave, for I will not have them about me. I will go into Heaven alone, rather than have scratching and fighting around me. I will set all at liberty. 'What, first wife, too?' Yes, I will liberate you all.

"I know what my women will say; they will say, 'you can have as many women as you please, 'Brigham.' But I want to go somewhere and do something to get rid of the whiners; I do not want them to receive a part of the truth and spurn the rest out of doors.

"Let every man thus treat his wives, keeping raiment enough to clothe his body; and say to your wives, take all that I have and be set at liberty; but if you stay with me you shall comply with the law of God, and that, too, without any murmuring and whining. You must fulfill the law of God in every respect, and round up your shoulders to walk up to the mark without any grunting.

"Now, recollect, that two weeks from tomorrow I am going to set you all at liberty. But the first wife will say, 'it is hard, for I have lived with my husband twenty years, or thirty, and have raised a family of children for him, and it is a great trial to me for him to have more women that will bear children.' If my wife had borne me all the children that she ever would bear, the celestial law would teach me to take young women that would have children. Sisters, I am not joking; I do not throw out my proposition to banter your feelings, or to see whether you will leave your husbands, all or any of you. But, I do know that there is no cessation to the everlasting whinings of many of the women of this Territory. And if the women will turn from the commandments of God and continue to despise the order of Heaven, I will pray that the curse of the Almighty may be close to their heels, and that it may be following them all the day long. And those that enter into and are faithful, I will promise them that they shall be queens in heaven and rulers for all eternity."

President Heber C. Kimball, in a discourse delivered in the Tabernacle, November 9, 1856 (*Deseret News*, Vol. 6, p. 291), said:

"I have no wife or child that has any right to rebel against me. If they violate my laws and rebel against me, they will get into trouble just as quickly as though they transgressed the counsels and teachings of Brother Brigham. Does it give a woman a right to sin against me because she is my wife? No, but it is her duty to do my will as I do the will of my Father and my God. It is the duty of a woman to be obedient to her husband, and unless she is, I would not give a damn for all her queenly right and authority, nor for her either, if she will quarrel and lie about the works of God, and the principles for plurality. A disregard of plain and correct teachings is the reason why so many are dead and damned, and twice plucked up by the roots, and I would as soon baptize the devil as some of you."

In the language of Caiaphas: "What further need have we of witnesses?"

My address up to the present moment will give you a good idea of modern Christianity as beheld by an inquiring outsider. The more I look into its contradictions and absurdities, the more fully I am convinced that the world can never be brought to Christ until there are some radical changes.

"Why are many good people so much divided in their views of Scripture, seeing they have but one Bible, and all read it in the same language? Because they belong to different sects and have different systems, and they rather make the Bible bow to their system, than make their system bow to the Bible; or in other words, each man too generally views the Bible through the medium of his system; and of course, it will appear to him to favor it. Just as if A., B. and C. should each put on different-colored glasses; A. puts on green spectacles, B. yellow, and C. blue. Each of them, through his own glasses, looks at the Bible. To A. it appears green, B. yellow, and C. blue. They begin to debate on its color. It is impossible for any one of them to convince another that he is wrong. Each one feels a conviction, next to absolute certainty, that his opinion is right. But D., who has no spectacles, and who is standing by during the contest, very well knows that they are all wrong. He sees the spectacles on each man's nose and easily accounts for the difference."

Thus, it seems that one man reads the Bible to get proof to sustain Methodist doctrine; another to sustain Baptist doctrine, and so on throughout the entire catalogue of contending sects. This is wrong. The Bible is divine, and was given to be obeyed, and not to be "spiritualized," mutilated, warped or interpreted to gratify the preferences of men.

I feel that I have been benefited by this investigation. As I have advanced in the study of the Scriptures, my mind has been enlightened, and now I think I see my way clearly. A man may be a Christian and repudiate every human creed in Christiandom. Christ is supreme. If a man obeys him, every sect represented in this assembly will admit his infallible safety. If he does not obey Christ, every sect in this convention, will admit the impossibility of his salvation. Human creeds do no good. They do harm by keeping good people in continual strife. Let every man purge the sectarian spirit from his heart, tongue and life, and bury it in the dust of oblivion, and mark upon its tomb in undying colors: "NO RESURRECTION." After this, nothing remains to be done but to unite the zeal of the Methodists, the independence of the Baptists, the order of the Presbyterians, the devotion of the Episcopalians, the steadfastness of the Lutherans, the determination of the Roman Catholics, the aggressiveness of the Mormons, the activity of the Nazarenes and the Church of God with the name of Jesus Christ and the pure gospel, and go forward to conquer the world!

CHAPTER XV.

ICONOCLAST.

I am interested in the great subject of Christian Union. Hence I appear in this convention, for it is impossible for the people of God to become one until the Baals, Ashtoreths, Chemoshes, Molechs, and Milcoms now dividing them are broken to pieces and ground to dust. I shall direct my attention to the mourner's bench, or anxious seat, process of conversion, and I ask your atttention, and challenge you to meet my arguments. I declare my unfaltering and uncompromising enmity to the whole system. I propose to submit incontestable facts in justification of my position. I am aware of the fact that I have been adversely criticised by some of the members of this convention on account of my antagonism to this custom. I now take pleasure in looking you in the face and declaring war on this idol and all others. I am aware of the fact that I would be more popular, and the apparent results of my preaching greater, if I would use the anxious seat in my work. I can readily understand how you feel about it, but reflecting that you believe in it and that you think that I am not doing my duty as a preacher in refusing to adopt a custom that to your minds is right, and the use of which you think would result in the glory of God. I give you credit for sincerity in this matter, and claim that much for myself. You do not know my reasons for not having an anxious seat; therefore, in selfdefense I propose to give them, and then if you do not modify your feelings and criticisms you will at least know my reasons for my failure to do that which you consider my Christian duty. But to the reasons. Here is the first one: When I started out to preach years ago, I made up my mind that God helping me I never would believe, preach, or practice anything for which I could not find plain and full authority in the word of God. When I began to preach I began to "search the Scriptures" (John, 5:39). I have been searching ever since. It is my business; it is my daily occupation; it is my life-work. I have never yet found where Jesus Christ, Peter, Paul, James, John, or any other apostles or prophet ever used an anxious seat or mourner's bench as a means of advancing the salvation of men. If it is taught in the Book, some one ought to know where it is. If it is there and you can not find it, I will furnish the money to pay for the telegram, and go with you, and you can telegraph to any preacher, editor, or member in the world, and if any one can show ten words, five words, yea, one word in favor of the practice, I will inaugurate it immediately, abandon my life-work and hold revivals to the end of my life. There is only one question to ask: Is it authorized by the Bible? If it is, show it. If it is not, stop criticising me for not practicing it. The responsibility lies upon you; the gauntlet lies at your feet. You can not ask me to forsake what I have done in the past without proof, indisputable, invincible proof that I am not doing my duty. "Here I stand, my conscience is bound in God's word, I can not do otherwise, so help me God, amen." If there is no Scripture for the mourner's bench; if Jesus did not authorize it; if the apostles did not use it; if the New Testament does not approve it, it is clearly an invention of men. What does God say about the inventions of men? "Lo, this only have I found, that God hath made man upright; but they have sought out many inventions" (Ecc., 7:29). What does He say about the prophet who presumes to speak in His name? "But the prophet, which shall presume to speak a word in my name, which I have not commanded him to speak or that shall speak in the name of other gods, even that prophet shall die" (Deut., 18:20). What does He say about adding to His words? "Ye shall not add unto the word which I command you, neither shall ye diminish aught from it, that ye may keep the commandments of the Lord your God which I command you" (Deut., 4:2). "Add thou not unto his words lest he reprove thee, and thou be found a liar" (Prov., 30:6). "For I testify unto every man that heareth the words of the prophecy of this book, if any man shall add unto these things, God shall add unto him the plagues that are written in this book: and if any man shall take away from the words of the book of this prophecy, God shall take away his part out of the book of life, and out of the holy city, and from the things which are written in this book" (Rev., 22:18, 19). "But though we, or an angel from heaven, preach any other gospel unto you than that which we have preached unto you, let him be accursed" (Gal., 1:8).

The anxious seat or mourner's bench system of conversion proceeds upon the supposition that the plan of salvation is not revealed in the Scriptures. If it is revealed in the Scriptures, and the mourner's bench must be added, what became of the thousands, millions, who lived and died before the system was first thought of over one hundred years ago? Is the gospel the power of God unto salvation (Rom., 1:16)? If so, what is the use of doing something that is not taught either by precept, example or allusion in the gospel? Is the way of salvation plainly and fully revealed in the New Testament (Matt., 28:19, 20; Mark, 16:15, 16; Luke, 24:46, 47; John, 20:21-23)? If so, why ask people to do something that is not revealed? Is the New Testament a complete revelation of God's will? If so, why inaugurate an unauthorized practice and try to add to its completeness?

If the Bible does not tell us, all, everything to the smallest detail, that we must do in order to salvation, then it is not the will of God, the complete will, the way to heaven. If it does, the anxious seat and its attendant excitement are not required, are not of God, are not of heaven, are not necessary to salvation, and they are hindrances to truth and to the obedience it requires. Here are your alternatives, which will you take? Here is where I stand: The Bible contains the will of God concerning us; what it requires we must do or be lost; what it does not require we must not place between the sinner and his salvation, his God, the Church, the hope of heaven. I make you a fair proposition: Find the authority for the mourner's bench and I will use it. If you can not find it, you can afford to give it up and quit criticising me. Do you believe the Bible contains the full revelation of the will of God? If you answer *yes*, you must abandon the mourner's bench. If you answer *no*, you must forsake the Bible. Which will you take? Do you believe the man who hears, believes, obeys and lives up to the requirements of the New Testament is pardoned, is a Christian, is a member of the body of Christ, is an heir of heaven? If you answer *yes*, you must give up the anxious seat; if you answer *no*, you must give up the Bible. Which will you do?

The anxious seat and its atttendant exercises are based upon the supposition that salvation comes in answer to prayer alone. I believe in praying; but not in prayer alone. Why do people come to the anxious seat? Because they are taught that salvation, forgiveness, or the gift of the Holy Spirit comes in answer to the prayers of the Church. What is the difference between this custom and the confessional, and priestly absolution in the Catholic Church? I confess that I can not see any. The priest does not forgive sin. No good Catholic claims this so far as I know. Here is what they claim: The priest is a holy man; they confess their sins to him, and in answer to his prayer God forgives. Here is what the anxious seat business amounts to: Men and women come forward, bound hand and foot, utterly unable to do anything, and in answer to the prayers of the Church, God forgives. What is the difference? There is only one redeeming feature, and the Catholics have it; they teach that the sinner can confess his sins and that he must do it in order to salvation. The other makes salvation come in answer to prayer alone. The sinner, it is affirmed, can do nothing in order to salvation. Nothing means nothing! He can not possibly do anything. He can not believe. He can not repent. He can not be penitent. He can not pray an acceptable prayer. He can not think. He can not obey. He is utterly dead and helpless. If he can not do anything he is dependent upon prayer, and prayer only, and the prayers of others at that! Admit that the sinner can do one thing, however small; if he can think one good thought, pray one good prayer, accept one fact of the gospel, obey one command or be penitent for one sin, the entire mourner's bench system falls to the ground, for all the advocates of the process claim that the sinner can not do anything pleasing to God in obedience to His word, and we can only suppose that the mourner's bench is set up so that the prayers of the Church may come to the rescue in his awful and lost condition! But does salvation come in answer to the prayers of the priest or Church member, however good? Now do not misunderstand me. I believe God hears the prayers of His people when they ask for what He has promised to give. Mark this declaration. Now a question: Where has God promised to save the alien in answer to the prayers of the Church? If that is His law of pardon, what is the use of the gospel? Again, if the Church can pray salvation down, and the evidence of it for one sinner, why can not it do it for all the world, Why delay? Why not pray it down on all the world, and let all nations awake in the light of God at the rising of the morning sun? You say that it is impossible because all the world is not willing. Listen; that makes no difference, for according to the advocates of the mourner's bench and its attendant practices, the sinner can not do anything! I hold you to your theory. If he can not do anything, he can not do one thing, and that is the end of it. If he can do even the smallest thing, the theory is false, all false. If he can not do anything, his salvation is dependent on prayer alone, and the prayer that will save one will save the world! Which will you take? The two ways are before you. You must choose. If the sinner can do one thing, he can do anything, if he can not do one thing, he can not do anything, and if you are consistent you must consider yourself responsible for the world's damnation. I put you to the test. If you can pray salvation down on one mourner who can not do anything, according to your theory, you can pray it down on the whole world, for your theory is that all are helpless, and one can not be more helpless than another; that all are dead, and one can not be more dead than another! If you can not pray pardon down on the helpless, dead world, you can not pray it down on one helpless, dead mourner. Come to judgment, the facts are before you. How are you going to meet them? If you can not meet them you can not afford to practice that which you can not prove or successfully defend. Brother, do not criticise me until you can answer this argument and show that you are consistent in your claim.

The anxious seat process of conversion makes feelings an evidence of pardon. "But," you say, "we do not think there is anything meritorious, or any other special good about the bench." I know you do not. I am not talking simply about the bench or seat; I am talking about the practice. The plan is all contrary to the word of God, whether at a special bench or elsewhere. The whole system is based upon the supposition that God has not fully told the sinner what to do in the Bible. Do you deny it? If so, produce the passage that says that there should be an anxious seat, or that a man must feel that he is pardoned, or that the Church must pray for salvation. If you do not deny it you are bound to abandon the practice, and return to the practice of the primitive church. But you insist that feelings are an evidence of pardon. Let us put it to the test. Here is a man who claims that he is pardoned, and that he knows it because he feels it. Let us interrogate him. Question: "Are you pardoned?" Answer: "I am pardoned." Question: "How do you know that you are pardoned?" Answer: "I know that I am pardoned because I feel it in my soul." Question: "Where you ever pardoned before?" Answer: "I never was pardoned before." Question: "If you were never pardoned before and you take your feelings as an evidence, how do you know how a man ought to feel when he is pardoned; by what standard are you to judge yourself, seeing you never experienced this feeling before?" He answers not. There is not a man beneath the circle of the sun who adheres to the theory of conversion outside of the gospel, who can answer it. There is not a promise in the word of God based on feelings. It is do! do!! do!!! from the beginning to the end. Do not misunderstand me. I have good feelings always when I do good, and in no other way. Do you know any better way than this? If so, give me the book, chapter and verse, and I am ready to accept it! I am looking for the truth. If you have it and I have it not, I am ready to go along with you.

The anxious seat is a positive hindrance to the gospel. It sets up a man-made custom between the penitent believer and his salvation. This is a fact. Do you deny it? Bring your proof that the anxious seat is of God? Why do men and women go to the anxious seat? Because they are believers in Christ; because they are penitent on account of sin; because they are ready, if properly instructed, to obey the gospel of Christ. My sympathies are all with the mourners. I believe they are honest; I believe they are sincere. I believe they are tired of sin; I believe they trust Christ. I believe they are ready to obey the Lord. If not, why do they come up to the anxious seat? Why not tell them what Peter told the Jews on the day of Pentecost (Acts, 2:37, 38)? Why teach them to tarry? Why teach them to wait? What is in the way? Nothing under the sun but the unauthorized agonies at the mourner's bench and a preacher, who on the account of prejudice, pelf or ignorance, will not give the apostolic answer. The anxious-seat plan of salvation makes God a respecter of persons (Acts, 10:34, 35). Do you deny it? Well, here is the proof: You first tell the sinner he can not do anything to save himself and you do your best to prove it. When the sinner cries for mercy you invite him forward. Thirty persons come. You must admit that all are equally earnest and honest, and according to your theory, equally dead. Songs are sung; prayers are offered. Some profess to be converted, and some do not. If all are equally sinful, helpless, dead, how do you account for the conversion of some while others are not converted, except on the ground that God is a respecter of persons? Perish the thought! It is not on account of the prayers, for the same prayers are offered for all. How can we account for it? Simply on the ground that the impressible, the excitable ones, are persuaded under the excitement that they have experienced pardon, while the cold, calculating, thinking ones do not, and that is the end of it. We often read of revivals in which twenty were converted and fifteen went away inquiring. How do you account for this? Did you ever read in the New Testament that seekers went away seeking, or mourners went away mourning? No, a thousand times no! Why not! The simple reason is they had no mourner's bench, the preachers of those blessed days knew what to tell inquirers and they did it, and every one who mourned was made glad, and every one who sought the Lord found Him in peace. The Lord revealed the way, and the apostles preached it, and the people accepted it, and that was all there was of it. The way is open. God invites. The gospel invites. There is no difference. All have the same chance. The Lord Jesus Christ is ready, and if you are tired of sin you can have the promise of salvation, the gift of the Holy Spirit, by yielding to Him and doing what He says, no more, no less (Mark, 16:16, 17; Acts, 2:38; 5:32). I sum up my reasons and leave the subject with you and your God.

1. The anxious seat is not once mentioned in the Bible, and if the Bible is a complete revelation of the will of God, the system is purely an invention of man.

2. It nullifies the gospel and practically says that what is written in the Bible will not save without something else.

3. It puts Protestanism on the same basis with Roman Catholicism, and makes the salvation of the world dependent upon the prayers of others.

4. It makes uncertain and delusive feelings the evidence of pardon, and exalts human experience above the law of pardon laid down in the New Testament.

5. It keeps honest, sincere and anxious persons from obedience to the gospel by leading them to believe that conversion is a miracle, and that they must wait for evidence of pardon utterly unknown in the Book of God.

6. It is salvation by works in the very worst sense. It is an attempt to "work" the way to heaven on a purely human plan. It is not of faith, for faith comes by hearing (Rom., 10:17), and the word of God says nothing whatever about it; and whatever is not of faith is sin (Rom., 14:23).

CHAPTER XVI.

ICONOCLAST.

I appear again before this convention for the purpose of breaking idols.

"And such trust have we through Christ to Godward; not that we are sufficient of ourselves to think anything as of ourselves; but our sufficiency is of God; who also hath made us able ministers of the New Testament; not of the letter, but of the spirit: for the letter killeth, but the spirit giveth life" (II. Cor., 3:4-6).

"And for this cause he is the mediator of the new testament, that by means of death for the redemption of the transgressions that were under the first testament, they which are called might receive the promise of eternal inheritance; for where a testament is, there must, also of necessity be the death of the testator. For a testament is of force after men are dead; otherwise it is of no strength at all while the testator liveth" (Heb., 11:15-17.

When I survey the vast assemblage before me, and my ear catches the echo of the confusion that exists throughout the world, my indignation rises, and I feel that the time has come to break all the idols worshipped by the people of God, bury them by the wayside, and then march on with the triumphant hosts to the conquest of the world. The great idol, the father of all the smaller ones, is compounded of equal parts of the law of Moses, human tradition and the gospel of Christ. It is generally "called the identity of the two covenants," but the name is changed and varied according to the temple in which it is worshipped, and the high priest who presides over the homage that is paid to it. It is an easy task to break this idol. Paul speaks in unmistakable terms of the two covenants (Gal., 4:24), and no process of logic or ecclesiastical legerdemain can make them one! He also declares that the first has been abolished or done away (II. Cor., 3:1-8; Heb., 8:1-13), and no power in the universe can bring it back into force! Where now are the scattered fragments of your beloved idol? Echo, borne upon the cold and pulseless wind, answers, "Where!"

It being settled by incontestable testimony that there is only one covenant or testament in existence, and that it is a new covenant, we can proceed to the examination of it. We may legitimately ask, Who is the author of this testament? What does it embrace? When and where did it begin?

Before proceeding to answer these questions, I propose to settle another important point. It is this: What is the meaning of the word testament, or covenant? Many people speak of the New Testament without comprehending what it is or what it offers. A testament is simply a will; the words will and testament may be used interchangeably. This is easy enough for any one to understand. The New Testament is, therefore, the will of God concerning men. You will notice that Paul declares that in order to enforce the provisions of a will or testament, the death of the testator must be brought in or declared. There are some peculiarities about wills or testaments with which all intelligent persons are familiar. It is a fact that I wish to state with all possible emphasis, that every important characteristic of a human will or testament may, also, be seen in the divine will. God adapts Himself to us, and speaks to us in language suited to our comprehension. There are many things we know concerning testaments, testators and administrators, for they touch us in every day business life. Our constitution, our laws and our customs unite in guaranteeing to every man the right to make a will or testament, and thus determine what shall be done with his earthly possessions after he shall have gone to the grave. They guarantee to him the incontestable and inalienable right to begin at the age of twenty-one and make as many wills or testaments as his fancy or judgment may suggest. They guarantee to him, in spite of this, the right to use his possessions as he pleases after making his will. They guarantee him the right to make any changes in his will, or to supplement it in any way he chooses. They guarantee to him the right to make his will conditional or unconditional. They decree that a testament cannot be enforced until the death of the person who makes it, and that after this only, can it be probated and executed according to his desire. They further guarantee that no power can make any changes in a will after the death of its author. If he places conditions between the legacy and the legatee, no earthly power can legitimately remove them. If he does not place conditions in his will, no earthly power can legally introduce them and require submission to them. You know these statements to be true in the affairs of this life. Why may they not be true in reference to the things that pertain to the life beyond the grave? It is a fact that you can not and will not deny, that a testament may be changed repeatedly during life. Neither can you deny that after death it must stand without change, supplement, amendment, and must be executed to the letter!

In order to make a testament that will stand in law, certain things are absolutely necessary. I will name them: (1) The testator must be of proper age. (2) He must be in his right mind. (3) He must have something to give. (4) He must be explicit; leaving no room for doubt; making it conditional or unconditional as his desire may dictate. (5) There must be competent witnesses. (6) It must, after his death, be admitted to probate. (7) If there are conditions they must be performed in the precise manner required. A person of improper age can not make a will or testament. A person of an unsound mind can not make a will or testament. A testament without a consideration is not worth the paper on which it is written. A will that is obscure can not stand the fire of antagonism, and therefore can not be executed. A will without a sufficient number of competent witnesses is null and void. A testament is prophetic; it relates to what shall be after the death of the person making it. He can therefore, at pleasure, make changes in it, or make gifts entirely independent of it; or if he chooses, make an entirely new one. The right to make gifts independent of the will lasts until death, but the moment the testator dies the will is forever sealed, and must therefore stand. A will can not be probated without witnesses, and when once probated it can not be changed or abolished: it must stand forever! All these things are true in reference to the testaments of men. They are equally true in reference to the testament of our Lord and Savior Jesus Christ.

I affirmed that a testament must stand, after the testator's death, just as it is written, and that if there are conditions added to its provisions they must be performed without addition or subtraction. Allow me to illustrate: I own ten acres of land. Law says it is mine. Custom says it is mine. I have the power to control it during my natural life, and also to say to whom it shall go at my death. I sit down in the presence of competent witnesses to write my will. I have the power to make it conditional or unconditional. I choose to make it conditional. I decide what the conditions shall be: (1) A wire fence six feet high on the north side. (2) An iron picket fence six feet high on the west side. (3) An oak plank fence six feet high on the south side. (4) A common rail fence six feet high on the east side. (5) At the completion of the fence according to the specifications, the legatee is to take possession, and it is specified that he shall have, own and control the land as long as he keeps the fence in good repair and the land in a good state of cultivation. Now, who will affirm that the legatee can be brought into possession and control of the land without the exact performance of the conditions? Who will affirm that he could complete three sides of the fence according to the requirements, and then take possession of the land? Who will affirm that he can maintain his right to the land without the performance of all the conditions laid down in the will through his entire life?

It is an established fact that Jesus, while making His will, lived under the "first covenant," and that it continued in force until the ratification of the New Testament by His death on the cross (Col., 2:11-14; Heb., 8:1-13).

Jesus was of proper age to make a testament (Luke 3:23). He also had the power to do whatever He desired (John, 10:17, 18). Did he have anything to give? If so, what? Did He have enough to meet the wants of all men in all ages? Let Him speak for Himself: "Even as the Son of Man came not to be ministered unto, but to minister and to give his life a ranson for many" (Matt., 20:28). Again, "And ye will not come to me, that ye might have life" (John, 5:40). "The thief cometh not, but for to steal and to kill, and to destroy; I am come that they might have life, and that they might have it more abundantly" (John, 10:10). He came with the riches of heaven to the poor and needy of earth. Hear the triumphant refrain of the great Apostle to the Gentiles: "For ye know the grace of our Lord Jesus Christ, that, though he was rich, yet for your sakes he became poor, that ye through his poverty might be rich" (II. Cor., 8:9). Hear him again: "This is a faithful saying, and worthy of all acceptation, that Christ Jesus came into the world to save sinners; of whom I am chief" (I. Tim., 1:15). Jesus Christ brought these things for you; they are incorporated in His will; He calls on you to accept and perform the conditions today; will you do it? He is plain, full and explicit in His requirements, and there is absolutely no excuse. There are competent witnesses to the will or testament of Jesus Christ. Both the Old and New records unite in declaring that the testimony of two or three witnesses is sufficient to establish any question of fact (Deut., 17:6; II. Cor., 13:1). Jesus, the Christ, came as the last, yea, the final remedy for sin, hence in order to make His testimony overwhelmingly convincing, He chose twelve competent witnesses (Matt., 10:1-15). Hear His word concerning them: "Ye have not chosen me, but I have chosen you, and ordained you, that ye should go and bring forth fruit, and that your fruit should remain; that whatsoever ye shall ask of the Father in my name, he may give it you" (John, 15:16). Again: "As thou has sent me into the world, even so have I also sent them into the world" (John, 17:18). After His resurrection He said to them, after having given them their commission: "And ye are witnesses of these things" (Luke, 24:45-48). On the day of Pentecost, after having preached to the people, they triumphantly proclaimed: "This Jesus hath God raised up whereof we are all witnesses" (Acts, 2:1-32). Again, at Solomon's porch, Peter declared that God had raised up Jesus: "Whereof we are witnesses" (Acts, 3:15). It is a fact that can not be successfully contradicted that after the death of the testator everything depends on the witnesses. Human law recognizes this, universally. Jesus also recognized it. He called the twelve apostles. He taught them during His entire life. They knew His will. They knew His manner of life, but He did not leave them alone. He sent power from God upon them that they might be inspired, illuminated, taught, until it was absolutely impossible for them to make a mistake. Their words were truly, undeniably, incontestably the words of God, of Christ, of the Holy Spirit! Who will deny it? Who will dare to tread so close to the great loving heart of Divinity and even doubt or question? Away with your doubts! Away with your questions! Away with the crumbling remains of your idols! God has spoken, Jesus Christ, the Great Testator, has spoken, the witnesses have spoken, let human kind listen, believe and obey! Do you call for proof? Listen: "For it is not ye that speak, but the Spirit of your Father which speaketh in you" (Matt., 10:20). Again: "But the Comforter, which is the Holy Spirit, whom the Father will send in my name, he shall teach you all things, and bring all things to your remembrance, whatsoever I have said unto you" (John, 14:26). Again: "But when the Comforter is come, whom I will send unto you from the Father, even the Spirit of truth which proceedeth from the Father, he shall testify of me: and ye also shall bear witness because ye have been with me from the beginning" (John, 15:26, 27). Again: "But ye shall receive power, after that the Holy Spirit is come upon you; and ye shall be witnesses unto me both in Jerusalem, and in all Judea, and in Samaria, and unto the uttermost part of the earth" (Acts, 1:8). Again: "And they were all filled with the Holy Spirit, and began to speak with other tongues, as the Spirit gave them utterance" (Acts, 2:4). In the face of this testimony who will affirm that the twelve witnesses made any mistake? Who will affirm that they failed to unfold the provisions of the will or testament of Jesus Christ? Who will affirm that it is safe to disregard their testimony and seek elsewhere for the way of salvation? Did Jesus put conditions in His will? If not, and God is no respector of persons, it is a decree and not a will! If it has no conditions, what necessity was there for the apostles? If there were no conditions, what necessity was there for the Church? In order to settle the matter beyond dispute I appeal to the record. Let the Master speak: "Not every one that saith unto me, Lord, Lord, shall enter into the kingdom of heaven; but he that doeth the will of my Father which is in heaven" (Matt., 7:21). Hear the apostle Peter: "Of a truth I perceive that God is no respecter of persons: but in every nation he that feareth him, and worketh righteousness, is accepted with him" (Acts, 10:34, 35). Hear the apostle Paul: "Though he were a Son, yet learned he obedience by the things which he suffered; and being made perfect, he became the author of eternal salvation unto all them that obey him" (Heb., 5:8, 9). Hear the apostle John: "Blessed are they that do his commandments, that they may have right to the tree of life, and may enter in through the gates into the city" (Rev., 22:14). This settles, settles fully, settles forever, the question of conditions in the will of Christ. No man can deny it without denying the plain and unequivocal statements of the record.

What were the conditions? This is an important question. Indeed it transcends all others, and when compared to it, they are as nothing. Before proceeding with the answer, I wish to submit a few preliminary considerations that will assist in properly understanding it. Returning to our fence illustration, I remark that many different parts or pieces enter into the different sides, and many details enter into it in order to its completion according to the specifications, but when it is completed, it, in brief, comprehends the four sides designated. It is so with the plan of redemption developed in the testament of Jesus Christ. Many things enter into it; the goodness and love of God, the gift of Jesus Christ, preaching penitence, the fear of punishment; yet it can all be successfully summed up in four conditions. What are they? Let the Bible answer! What is the first condition? "I said therefore unto you, that ye shall die in your sins: for if ye believe not that I am he ye shall die in your sins" (John, 8:21-24). What is the second condition? "Except ye repent, ye shall all likewise perish" (Luke, 13:1-5). What is the third condition? "Whosoever therefore shall confess me before men, him will I confess also before my Father which is in heaven. But whosoever shall deny me before men, him will I also deny before my Father which is in heaven" (Matt., 10:32, 33). What is the fourth condition? "Jesus answered, Verily, verily I say unto thee, except a man be born of water and of the Spirit, he can not enter into the kingdom of God" (John, 3:5). Who is the author of these statements? Jesus the Christ. Who were the witnesses that He made them? The twelve apostles. Where are they found? In the will or testament of the Son of God recorded by Matthew, Mark, Luke and John. Is one condition more important than another? Is one side of the fence more important than another? Where is the man who will affirm it? Bring him out, I want to look him in the face!

When did Jesus Christ make His will? During His life on earth. He began with His ministry and continued unto His death. During His public ministry He dispensed rich gifts, as He clearly had a right to do. He also imposed such conditions as the immediate circumstances required. He said to the impotent man: "Rise, take up thy bed and walk" (John, 5:1-8). He said to the man sick of the palsy: "Son, be of good cheer; thy sins be forgiven thee" (Matt., 9:1, 2). He said to the sinful woman: "Thy faith hath saved thee; go in peace" (Luke, 7:36-50). He said to the penitent thief on the cross: "Today shalt thou be with me in paradise" (Luke, 23:39-43). Who will affirm that these incidents are precedents for us, seeing they were never so used by the apsotles? Who will affirm that Jesus intended to have us consider these as examples of conversion recorded for our guidance? If I begin to write my will today and continue to write for three years, I will have a perfect right to make any gifts that I desire to make, and this would form no precedent for my executors to bestow similar gifts under similar circumstances. What the testator does himself, and what he directs his executors to do, are absolutely and unalterably different. We must not appeal simply to what Jesus did, but what He commanded the witnesses to do. The testator personally controls everything until his death. The moment he expires his personal acts sink into insignificance, and the executors must deal only with what is expressed as his will. This will or testament of Jesus was not and could not be executed during His life. This is stated as plainly as language can make it: "For where a testament is, there must also of necessity be the death of the testator" (Heb., 9:16).

Jesus continued His work through His life, gradually unfolding the provisions of His will to His chosen witnesses. He was constantly engaged in preparing them to take charge of His work after His departure from them. At last those whom He came to save nailed Him to the cross, and He yielded up His life in order to the world's redemption. The moment He expired His testament was sealed and could only be opened by His chosen representatives. They were confined to what He had commanded them to do. The conditions were in the testament when the testator expired; they were so recognized by His executors, and they must remain until the end of time. There is no power on earth or in heaven that will remove the obligations and bring the man into his legacy who has never done his part.

The testator is king, and he demands a strict compliance with all the requirements. The person to whom I gave the land, on the conditions, knew when he had completed the fence according to the requirements that the property was his, and that no earthly power could deprive him of it so long as he kept the fence in good repair and the land in a good state of cultivation, and we know that when we comply with the requirements of the gospel we receive the remission of sins, and if we continue in the faith there is no power that can separate us from the love of God.

The apostles were the witnesses of the testament of Jesus Christ. They began in Jerusalem and carried out its provisions. This you can find by reading the record of their labors in the book of Acts. Their works sustain me in all I have proclaimed. Search and see!

My task is done. My promise is fulfilled. I am ready to bid you adieu. Truth is prevailing. Idols are crumbling. Time-honored customs are passing away. Creeds are losing their grasp on the minds of intelligent people, and soon they will be remembered as the Shibboleths of others days. The world is moving toward Christ. The Bible is cutting its way. Light is breaking. The morning is approaching, and faith is chasing away the dark clouds that have so long hung their black drapery over the straight and narrow way. I am glad to be able to bear some part in this mighty revolution, and I join you in a fervent prayer to Almighty God to hasten the day when the knowledge and glory of God shall cover the whole earth, and His will be done on earth as it is done in the courts of heaven!

CHAPTER XVII.

APOSTOLOS.

I appear in this convention in order to uphold and represent the apostles of the Lord Jesus Christ. At first thought it appears that in a Christian assemblage like this, they would not need such support, but I think by your indulgent attention I can abundantly prove that they do. Their call, mission and authority are wofully misunderstood. Each speaker has suggested a remedy for the alarming and widespread denominational difficulties and contradictions that afflict us. I have a remedy. Indeed it is a panacea. Do you ask what it is? I answer, Restore the apostles of Jesus, not their successors in office, for they have none, to their rightful places as proclaimers and interpreters of the terms of salvation made known by the Lord of earth and sky. Allow me to state and emphasize a few elementary facts. It took God four thousand years to prepare the children of men for the full revelation of His will. The complete revelation of the way of salvation, therefore, did not come with Adam. It did not come with Abraham. It did not come with Moses. It did not come with Elijah. It did not come with the prophets. It did not come with John the Baptizer. It did not come with Jesus of Nazareth. It came—it came fully—with the glorious descent of the Holy Spirit on the day of Pentecost in the city of Jerusalem after Jesus became Lord, King and Priest. We may refer to Adam, to Abraham, to Moses, to Elijah, to the prophets, to John, to Jesus of Nazareth, but our last appeal must be made to the apostles as they sit upon thrones proclaiming the gospel as the Holy Spirit gave them utterance. Every act and word from Adam forward looked to apostolic times. From this there can no appeal. Adam, and the saints and prophets who have made themselves illustrious in the annals of time, looked for something to come. To them the gospel was an unrevealed and inexplicable mystery. Not so with the apostles. They saw and revealed the truth as God intended that it should be known to the end of time. I verily believe that Christianity, as interpreted by the orders represented here, in a large measure dethrones the apostles who testified of Jesus, and forever established their claims to sincerity by sealing their testimony with their blood. I am aware that this is a grave charge, but who will dare arise and put it to the test by the word of God? If I can not sustain it, let it fall. If I can, denominationalism must adjust itself to the truth. In order to enable you to follow me with care, I shall state my points distinctly and clearly:

I. *The meaning of the word apostle.* Open your lexicons and dictionaries. What does it mean? Brother Baptist, you may answer: "Literally: one sent forth, a messenger. Specifically, one of the twelve disciples of Christ, specially chosen as His companions and witnesses, and sent forth to preach the gospel." That is sufficient. The fact that Jesus sent them is all important. He always acts wisely, always for the best, always in the interest of mankind. He manifestly had an object in sending them. Can we find out what this object was?

II. *The sanctity of their mission.* I can not be too emphatic on this point. He not only sent them to do a great and enduring work, but He forever made their mission sacred by putting it on the same basis as His own. In that wondrous prayer that has so greatly stirred this convention, He said to them, addressing His Father: "As thou hast sent me into the world, even so have I also sent them into the world" (John, 17:18). The only possible interpretation of this declaration is that the work of the apostles had the endorsement of Jesus, just as His work had the sanction of the Father. Whoever therefore rejects the word, work and authority of the twelve apostles, disregards the authority of Jesus Christ who sent them.

III. *Their selection and education.* Jesus selected His witnesses from among His own countrymen, men who were the best product of the Jewish religion and civilization. Allow me to digress long enough here to remark that if the modern theory of the identity of the two covenants is true, Jesus would doubtless have confined His selections to the priests, for they were by Divine legislation and hoary tradition, the only safe and lawful interpreters of the law of Moses (Deut., 17:8-13), but He turned to the people, the plain people, thus proclaiming that priestly caste and function among men would play no part in the day that He should become King. The men chosen doubtless knew both the Hebrew and Greek languages. They had also been taught the law of Moses from their childhood. Jesus immediately began their new education. He spoke to them as one who had come from God. He spoke with authority. He assured them that He would supersede Moses in all things (Matt., 5:17-19). He secretly confided to them the wonders of His coming kingdom (Matt., 10:26, 27), but charged them to keep them secret until after He should rise from the dead (Matt., 16:20). The fact that He led them, tolerated their follies, met their unbelief, made them His personal friends for three years, places additional emphasis on the fact that He had something important for them to do.

IV. *Their ordination.* The word ordain is significant. Jesus used it in connection with the sending forth of the apostles. "Hear ye Him." "Ye have not chosen me, but I have chosen you, and ordained you, that ye should go and bring forth fruit, and that your fruit should remain, that whatsoever ye shall ask of the Father in my name, he may give it you" (John, 15:16). Note these truths and let their emphasis startle you. Their "fruit" was to remain. God was to hear and answer them. Such things are not affirmed of any one else "from the beginning" to the close of God's revelation.

V. *Their authority.* Jesus Christ sent them. This should be enough to satisfy us. They had His authority and power back of them. Does this not make them practically irresistible? Who can appeal from their decision? Who can despise their mission? Do you ask for proof of their authority? Here it is: "Then answered Peter and said unto him, Behold, we have forsaken all and followed thee; what shall we have therefore? And Jesus said unto them, Verily I say unto you, That ye which have followed me, in the regeneration when the Son of Man shall sit in the throne of his glory, ye also shall sit upon twelve thrones, judging the twelve tribes of Israel" (Matt., 19:27, 28). This is unquestionably a reference to the time that the apostles should begin to preach in the name of the glorified Redeemer. Brother Methodist, why did Jesus come to earth? Answer: "In order to set up His kingdom." Correct. Brother Presbyterian, did the Lord provide for the translation of men and women into His kingdom? Answer: "He did." Correct. Brother Episcopalian, to whom did Jesus give the keys of His kingdom—the authority to make known the conditions of pardon? Answer: "To the apostles." Correct. See Matt., 16:18; 18:18. Now a question to the whole convention: If Jesus gave the keys of His kingdom to His apostles, if they made known the terms or conditions of pardon, and if the New Testament contains the record of these things, who has a right to offer pardon on fewer, or on other terms? I re-emphasize the authority and perpetuity of the Lord's apostles.

VI. *The Lord's promise to them.* Jesus not only gave His apostles personal instructions, but He promised them the miraculous guidance and infallible direction of the Holy Spirit. They doubtless had good memories, but the work was too important to be trusted to the treacherous and uncertain memory of mortal man, hence He said to them: "For it is not ye that speak, but the Spirit of your Father which speaketh in you" (Matt., 10:20). Again: "But tarry ye in the city of Jerusalem, until ye be endued with power from on high" (Luke, 24:49). Again: "But the Comforter, which is the Holy Spirit, whom the Father will send in my name, he shall teach you all things, and bring all things to your remembrance, whatsoever I have said unto you" (John, 14:26). This promise was literally fulfilled (Acts, 2:1-15). Who will dare affirm now that the apostles were not authorized to expound the gospel for all generations?

VII. *Their commission.* Jesus taught the apostles personally, and in order to prevent mistakes promised them the guidance of the "Spirit of truth." He also gave them a world-wide and age-lasting commission. See Matt., 28:18-20; Mark, 16:15, 16; Luke, 24:45, 49; John, 20:22, 23. This was a new commission, new in every respect. This commission limited the twelve apostles to what it embraced. They could not go back of it. They could not go beyond it. They could not abrogate any of its conditions. Indeed they could not change it or deviate from it in the least. Let all the preachers in this assemblage take this commission and follow it out as developed in the book of Acts, and proclaim it without change, and a revolution would inevitably follow. Whenever a man goes back to this commission, or attempts to find salvation save in the provisions it contains, he disregards Jesus who gave it, because "all authority" in heaven and in earth had been given unto Him.

VIII. *Their beginning and guidance.* The apostles were divinely commanded to begin at Jerusalem (Acts, 1:1-8). If the kingdom of heaven had been fully set up, if the gospel had been fully preached, if the Church of Christ had been started on its way to victory previously, why this commission, why the descent of the Holy Spirit, why make a new beginning at Jerusalem? Let me emphasize the fact that they were to begin something, not to resume something previously begun, but something new! Brother Baptist, please tell this convention what they began from the standpoint of your theory, of the inauguration or establishment of the Church on the banks of the Jordan, or at Cesarea Phillippi. "Daniel, come to judgment!" They began a new work. I ask this august assembly what it was. No one answers, and no wonder! Let me answer: They began to unfold the provisions of the Great Commission and proclaim terms of pardon hitherto unknown because unrevealed, and in order that they might give an infallible interpretation of all that had gone before, the power of God came upon them and they "began to speak with other tongues, as the Spirit gave them utterance" (Acts, 2:1-4). Surely this ought to bring us to the knowledge of the conditions of pardon, and a sure haven where we shall be tossed by the storms of doubt and uncertainty no more. Are you in doubt on any question of faith or practice? Ask the apostles—turn to the book of Acts, and to their epistles—for they are the last, the final, the only authorized interpreters of Moses, of the prophets, of John the Baptizer, of Jesus the Christ, for Jesus called them, taught them, commissioned them and inspired them for this purpose, and this purpose only. Brother Methodist objects. That is his privilege. He asks: "Are not the other books good, inspired, and profitable?" Certainly, who said they were not? Genesis had its place, Isaiah had his place, John had his place, Jesus had His place, but they all looked to the future and talked of the good time to come; Jesus declaring of Himself, looking to His glorification at God's right hand: "And I, if I be lifted up from the earth, will draw all men unto me" (John, 12:32). But the apostles in a few words gave the essence of the transactions of four thousand years of the world's history, and thus began a new work in the history of time—the proclamation of the completed and universal plan of redemption. I would not under any circumstances decrease your respect and admiration for the Old Testament and the men who have made the world's history worth reading, but I greatly desire to drive away the mists, uncertainties and traditions with which the eyes of many have been blinded, so we may find "the beginning" and learn to respect the apostles as the real and only representatives of Jesus Christ our Saviour, since His ascension.

IX. *Their doctrine.* The apostles had clear conceptions of the person of Jesus, and the burden of their preaching was that He is God's only begotten and well-beloved Son, and the only Saviour of sinful men. Christ was the center of all apostolic thought and preaching. The things they required of men were in the nature of tests of faith and means of bringing them to Him, where they might know Him and the power of His resurrection, the forgiveness of sins, and the glory of His coming in the clouds of heaven.

X. *The emphasis they placed on their work.* Jesus repeatedly told the apostles that they would bear witness of Him (Luke, 24:48; John, 15:27; Acts, 1:4-8). This they proclaimed everywhere; in Jerusalem, in Samaria, and among the Gentiles (Acts, 2:32; 8:1-12; 10:1-48), without fear, without hesitancy, and in the face of stripes, stones, prisons and death, and it is a fact that their most malignant enemies conceded that they spoke for Christ, in His name, by His authority, even when they spurned them and the message they brought (Acts, 4:13-22). Paul boldly affirms that "the ministry of reconciliation," or "word of reconciliation," had been delivered unto them, that they were the ambassadors of Christ, and that they besought men in Christ's stead to be reconciled to God (II. Cor., 5:18-20). I can not see how language could be any stronger than this. Hear ye the apostles, "the sent" of Jesus!

XI. *The perpetuity of their work.* In closing the great commission, Jesus promised to be with the apostles to the end of the world (Matt., 28:18-20). This was in perfect harmony with the assurance that they had previously received from Him that whatever they bound on earth should be bound in heaven, and whatever they loosed on earth should be loosed in heaven (Matt., 16:19; 18:18; John, 20:22, 23). If Jesus is still with the apostles—and who doubts or denies it?—if their interpretations, decisions and proclamations have never been repealed, I am bold to affirm that whoever wilfully and knowingly rejects their authority does it at his present and everlasting peril. The apostles are still preaching and judging, and they will continue to do so until "the end."

XII. *The greatness of their work.* Moses did a great

work in bringing Israel out of bondage and in receiving and making known God's law. The prophets did a great work in calling their countrymen back to the law from which they had departed, in waking the harp to Jehovah's praise during the long night of Israel's apostasy and rebellion, and climbing to the mountain tops and shouting to the multitudes below that the "Son of Righteousness," "the light of the world," was rising beyond them. John did a great work by announcing to his fellow-citizens that the reign of Heaven was at hand. Jesus did a great work by teaching men how to live, how to die, and how to break the chains of death's cruel bondage, but His apostles, in doing His work, in honoring His name, in proclaiming His authority and glory, did a work that is without parallel in the annals of the world. Addressing them He said: "Verily, verily, I say unto you, he that believeth on me, the works that I do shall he do also; and greater works than these shall he do; because I go unto my Father" (John, 14:12). It was a great work to redeem the human race; it was a greater work to make known the terms of pardon for all time.

XIII. *Our dependence upon them.* The apostles saw the Lord after He arose again. They handled Him (I. John, 1:1-4). They went forth to preach, backed by all authority or power in heaven and in earth (Matt., 28:11-20). They were absolutely confined to this commission. No one else was authorized to open its provisions, and there is no escape from the conclusion that we must hear them and obey the Lord as they preached Him or perish. Lord, help this convention!

XIV. *Some startling facts.* God sent Jesus. Whoever received Him or His word received His Father. Whoever rejects Him or His word rejects His Father. Jesus sent the twelve. Whoever recives them and their message receives Him. Whoever rejects them and their message rejects Him. This is indeed startling. Do you desire the proof? It is abundant and irresistible. Jesus said to them: "He that receiveth you receiveth me; and he that receiveth me receiveth him that sent me"

(Matt., 10:40). Again: "He that heareth you heareth me; and he that despiseth you despiseth me; and he that despiseth me despiseth him that sent me" (Luke, 10:16). Jesus, the Father, and the Apostles, so far as authority is concerned, are absolutely upon the same basis—if you reject the one you thereby reject the others.

In view of these weighty considerations I desire to propound some questions to this convention. A proper answer to them, will, I am sure, help greatly toward the solution of the mighty problems that come down upon us, and in attempting to answer them I earnestly ask you to keep in mind the arguments previously adduced:

1. Where did the apostles express any doubt as to the Mosaic authority of the books usually attributed to him?

2. Where did the apostles preach on or attempt to establish the theory of the identity of the "two covenants?"

3. Where did the apostles declare that baptism comes in the room of circumcision, or anything from which this can be inferred?

4. Where did the apostles preach that we are required to keep the Sabbath as required by the law of Moses?

5. Where did the apostles place Moses and his authority on an equal footing with Jesus and His authority?

6. Where did the apostles refer to the Church as having begun in the days of Abel or Moses?

7. Where did the apostles refer to the establishment of the Church by John, or during the life of Jesus?

8. Where did the apostles teach the doctrine of the universal hereditary total depravity of the human race?

9. Where did the apostles teach predestination as taught by the Presbyterian and Baptist creeds?

10. Where did the apostles teach a limited atonement, that is, that Jesus died only for the elect?

11. Where did the apostles teach the doctrine of "effectual calling"—the calling only of the elect?

THE GREAT CONTROVERSY.

12. Where did the apostles teach the doctrine of "final perseverance of the saints," as taught in modern times?

13. Where did the apostles teach that a sinner can not do anything to save himself from sin and its consequences?

14. Where did the apostles teach that regeneration is a miracle accomplished without the sinner's co-operation?

15. Where did the apostles teach that salvation comes in answer to the sinner's prayer before obedience?

16. Where did the apostles teach that salvation comes, in answer to the prayers of the Church, upon disobedient sinners?

17. Where did the apostles set up a mourner's bench and invite sinners to it, and sing and pray and shout over them?

18. Where did the apostles exhort sinners to "accept Christ" and then let them go without requiring them to obey Him?

19. Where did the apostles hold "revival services" and mutually agree to let the "converts" join "whatever church they preferred?"

20. Where did the apostles proclaim that the gospel of Jesus Christ was a "dead letter," thus making it appear that it is without inherent power?

21. Where did the apostles declare that the gospel of Jesus is "the mere word," and that it is powerless unless "accompanied by the Spirit?"

22. Where did the apostles preach that there must be a direct and therefore irresistible work of the Holy Spirit in conversion?

23. Where did the apostles pray for God to baptize sinners in the Holy Spirit, or teach that this baptism of the Holy Spirit was given to change the moral character or to convert men?

24. Where did the apostles teach that men are saved by faith alone, grace alone, or anything else alone?

25. Where did the apostles baptize infants, or do

anything from which it can be logically inferred that this was and is the will of God?

26. Where did the apostles have water carried into a house and use it in sprinkling it upon men in the name of Jesus Christ?

27. Where did the apostles teach that one command of the gospel is more essential or necessary than another, or that baptism is because of remission of sins?

28. Where did the apostles preach that one church is as good as another, or thank God for denominational divisions in order to suit every one's taste?

29. Where did the apostles give the Church a sectarian name, or authorize any one else to do it?

30. Where did the apostles set up the office of Pope, Cardinal, Archbishop, Bishop, or Priest, or hint that they were to have successors in office?

31. Where did the apostles authorize men to compile a creed as a test of fellowship among Christians, or to substitute sprinkling for baptism, or any other humanism for the command of the Lord?

CHAPTER XVIII.

BUSINESS.

I appear in this convention because I was invited to come as a business man and give my opinion of Christian union, simply as a matter of practical every-day business. In doing this, I shall not enter into the merits or demerits of the Biblical historical and theological distinctions to which you have so long and patiently listened. I want to make an effort to find out if the ideas that prevail in the world of commerce would, if carried into practical use in the domain of the religious, tend to its betterment. The writers of the Bible certainly had some business ideas. Hear Solomon the Wise: "Seest thou a man diligent in his business? he shall stand before kings; he shall not stand before mean men" (Prov., 22:29). Hear Paul the Apostle: "Not slothful in business; fervent in spirit; serving the Lord" (Rom., 12:11). Men do business on account of the money there is in it. With them it is a practical thing. A new firm proposing to enter upon a commercial career must first decide on a name under which to do business; second, invest money without stint; third, have a plan of business on which all the members can and do agree; fourth, be permeated with the feeling of the necessity for economy of time and money; fifth, locate in a place where there is, or where there can be created, a demand for that which they propose to sell. It is impossible to do business without a firm name on which all the members fully agree. James Jones, Thos. Johnson, and John Smith form a copartnership with the design of selling dry goods, and it is decided that the firm shall be known as the Union Dry Goods Company. The business opens auspiciously. Customers pour in from every direction. The newspapers and the people unite in commending the enterprise of the new house. Things move on successfully for a time, but after awhile it is noted that things have changed about the store. Customers are scarce, and there is an air of dilapidation about everything. What is the cause of it? The members of the firm have disagreed as to the firm name. Jones insisted that the firm name should be changed to James Jones & Co. Johnson contended that the style of the firm should be Thos. Johnson Company. Smith declared that he would never be satisfied until the name read Smith, Jones & Johnson. While this contention was going on, their competitors across the street were pushing ahead and getting the trade. The firm lost time, money and public confidence, and finally reached a state of absolute bankruptcy. This is no fanciful picture. It might become a reality in any school, store, bank, or railroad office in the country. You will please note that the contention arose about a matter of no importance whatever, and also that personal pride and personal preference played the chief part in this serio-comedy.

I was born sixty-four years ago in eastern New York, near what was then a small but promising village. My parents were moral people, but not church members, although they were frequent attendants on the services of the neighborhood church. When I was a small boy there was no church in the village, but as it began to grow quite rapidly, a young man came from a Presbyterian theological seminary and announced his desire to start a school and organize a church, and the people showed a willingness that was commendable, with the result that a flourishing school was started, which was followed by the organization of a Presbyterian Church. It prospered in many directions. A comfortable and commodious meeting-house was soon erected. The following year an earnest and successful Methodist preacher came and rented a hall and began to preach. The Presbyterians did not like it. They thought that they owned the town. The beginning of the new church was the cause of much neighborhood talk. Both churches grew, but I observed that the two did not gain as fast as the one had previously done. However, there was but little rivalry. Things continued in this way for three or four years, when a young Baptist preacher came to the town and began to preach in the court-house. Then the war began in earnest. The Methodist and Presbyterian Churches each began, or tried to begin a revival. Finally they united, and the attractions they offered just about balanced those at the court-house. Much excitement prevailed. Much bitterness was engendered. Many friends were alienated. Many sinners were hardened. Religion was misused, yea, murdered in the house of its friends. The revivals closed, and a Baptist Church was organized with about fifty members. They at once proceeded to build a meeting-house. They were not able to do it, and the Methodists and Presbyterians would not help them, hence they sent out solicitors who, by extraordinary persistence, succeeded in raising money enough in cash and promises, to build the finest meeting-house in the place. The population of the village at this time was seven hundred. I tried to figure out the matter according to ordinary business principles. I was working in a store at the time, and had excellent opportunities for observations. The Presbyterian Church had cost two thousand five hundred dollars, and at the time of which I speak, had a membership of one hundred and eighty. The church-house, however, had a seating capacity of fully three hundred and fifty, and a regular weekly attendance of about ninety, including outsiders. The Methodist Church had cost a little less than the Presbyterian Church, but it furnished accommodation for over four hundred, and had a weekly attendance of not less than one hundred and twenty-five, including outsiders. The membership numbered nearly one hundred. The Baptist Church was more costly than either of the others, although the membership was much smaller. The house was large enough to accommodate every church member in town, and leave ample room for outsiders. I looked upon this rivalry as a waste of money. Each Church kept and supported, in a way, its own pastor, when one man could easily have done all of the work if it had been delivered from its denominational peculiarities and reduced to the simple proclamation and practice of Christian precepts. Denominationalism built the houses, employed the preachers, took the glory, and Christianity had to foot the bill. This state of affairs continued for several years. In the meantime our village grew into a city. The Roman Catholics, Lutherans, Congregationalists, Episcopalians, and Jews erected costly houses. The so-called Free Thinkers also erected a costly temple. The simple preaching of the gospel gave way to the modern Sunday show. The Churches do not co-operate to any extent in any work. Occasionally some of them unite in what is supposed to be "a revival," but after the expiration of a few months things move on just as before the "union revival" began. Today there are in that city, by actual count, thirty-nine churches and one hundred and ninety-five saloons. Do the churches stand together even on moral questions? It pains me to say they do not. What about the saloons? They stand together, for it is a matter of business with them. On the question of policy there is only one saloon in the town! But there are thirty-nine churches!! This is a sad commentary on humanity as revealed through denominational peculiarities, and it is costly experiment. But it is only one of ten thousand, for the same farce has, in some degree, been enacted in every village, town and city where denominationalism is known. Millions multiplied over and over again have been squandered by men who think they are doing the Lord's work. If a dollar possessed by a Christian is a Christian dollar, what right has he to spend it save for Christianity alone? The money spent in the last century to build churches, colleges, seminaries, print books and papers, and support men to propagate and defend Methodism, Baptistism, Presbyterianism, Episcopalianism, Lutheranism, Roman Catholicism and other sects would, if turned into the simple work of propagating Christianity, "turn the world upside down." Oh! the carelessness, Oh! the waste, Oh! the fearful responsibility of those who have thus wasted the money that was the Lord's while millions of those for whom He died have gone down to death without one ray of hope to cheer their closing hours! These are cold facts. Say what you will it still remains true that money must and does play an important part in the extension of the kingdom of Christ, and money spent to build up rival sects is worse than wasted. It may be said in reply that rivalry is a good thing in business and religion, too. I deny this most emphatically. It is, so far as the facts show, good for neither. The business house, the railroad, the manufactory that makes an extraordinary success, does it on the union principle. The tendency is more and more, in business circles, toward the confederation and co-operation of firms that do the same kind of business. This you can not deny. Does it pay? Ask the big merchant, the big railroader, the big ship company, the big mining company, or the big farmer. I will not stop here, I assert that if the time, enegry and money that have been spent during the last century to maintain denominational peculiarities, and foster sectarian rivalry, had been turned into non-sectarian channels, it would have dotted the whole earth—"the continents and the islands beyond them"—with hospitals and orphanages, and the churches, running simply along Christian lines, would have done infinitely more for themselves and the territory adjacent to them. Sectarianism is a failure in every respect. It has and does waste an astounding amount of the Lord's money. I suggest no remedy. I write no prescription. I attempt no further diagnosis. The facts are before you. Treated simply as a matter of dollars and cents, denominationalism is a failure. Yes, it is worse than a failure; it is an imposition, a delusion, an insatiable monster that swallows up millions anually that should go to the cause of uncorrupted—New Testament—Christianity!

CHAPTER XIX.

VISITOR.

I endorse most heartily the speeches of Apostolos and Business Man. I am appearing before you to-day only as a visitor. I am not a clergyman, but I am one of a large company who are vitally concerned about the great question of religion as it exists in our day. And I have been very much interested in the different phases of the subject as presented by the several speakers on this occasion. Therefore the criticisms I offer are my honest views and can in no wise be interpreted as prejudice or mere opposition.

My friend of the Church of God brought out quite a few splendid thoughts in regard to the attitude of his church, but so have all the other speakers. And while I agree with most of his remarks, I must dissent with others. Consequently I cannot recognize his denomination as the church described in the Bible. He uses the name Church of God in a sectarian sense, that is, he uses it to distinguish his church group from all others. The name Church of God is not the only Biblical name for the people of God, and it is never used to distinguish one denomination from another; in fact, there were no denominations in the days of the earliest church. If you will consult your Bibles you will read of "My church", Matthew, 16:18; "The church," Matthew, 18:17; Acts, 2:47; 5:11; and more than a dozen other places; "Church of the Lord", Acts, 20:28; (Revised version); "Churches of Christ", Romans, 16:16; and "Church of the firstborn", Hebrews, 12:23.

My friend's stricture about the time and place of the beginnings of other denominations is just as true about the Church of God as it is about the other churches. According to his statements his denomination began about the year 1880, and was started by Daniel S. Warner and other ministers of that day. This is centuries later than the beginning on the Pentecost after the resurrection of the Lord.

Your assembling yourselves together for worship fellowship, counsel and instructions in the word of God is not like that of the New Testament. In those days the singing was with the spirit and the understanding, I. Corinthians, 14:15; by those who offered up a sacrifice of praise to God, that is, the fruit of the lips which make confession of his name. Hebrews, 13:15. And they made melody with their hearts to the Lord. Ephesians, 5:19. I have attended a number of your meetings and you not only made melody on musical instruments when they accompanied your voices, but frequently the instrument was used alone. There is no warrant in the New Testament for the use of instrumental music in the assemblies of the saints. It is supposed that at Alexandria some accompanied the singing with a flute, but Clement of Alexandria in 190 A. D. forbade this as too worldly. It (instrumental music) could not have been used in the fourth century or Ambrose, Basil or Chrysostom, 330-407 A. D. would have mentioned it in their description of church music. Your prayers, especially during a revival, were noisy and confusing. Sometimes several were praying at once and the "Amens" seldom fitted the petitions. Many of the shouts and other confusion had but little to do with the wording of the prayers. And I never saw "the breaking of bread" which was a weekly custom of the New Testament church. See Acts, 20:7.

It is certainly true that a man must be born again, but it is nowhere taught that he must pray through to be reborn. Your methods of conversion and sanctification are merely the old mourners' bench or anxious seat method of bygone years. You call penitents to the "Altar" and when they have prayed through, as you call it, you claim that they are converted. Then at a later date you call them up again and go through the same process; now you claim they have been sanctified or received the second blessing. One of your church publications advertises a pamphlet for those seeking holiness with the statement "anyone *who feels the need* of a spirit-filled life should read the book." It plainly teaches that it is a matter of feeling instead of faith and that it is something to be sought at the mourners' bench. Nothing was known of this practice before 1795. I quote from *The Life And Labors Of James Quin* by John Wright: "The first I ever saw or heard of it was in 1795 or 1796 at a meeting held at the home of that mother in our Israel, the widow Henthorn, near Uniontown, Pennsylvania. The person who conducted the meeting was Reverend Valentine Cook. . . . The sermon closed with an almost overwhelming exhortation which appeared as if it would carry all before it. Then came the invitation to the mourners to come to the vacated seats to be prayed with and for. I think this was perfectly new, for the people seemed panic stricken."

If you will carefully read Luke 24:49 and its accompanying verses, 45 to 53, and Acts 1:1-5, 12, 13; you will learn that the baptism of the Holy Ghost was promised only to the eleven who were with him and who would be witnesses of his teaching. People to-day can only testify to what they believe; those who were baptized in the Holy Ghost were to testify of the things they saw and knew. You demand more than the word of God for your evidence of conversion and sanctification. You are demanding an assurance of feeling and knowledge instead of an assurance of faith. Hebrews, 10:22. These early disciples always testified of Christ. I have heard a number of your so-called testimonies, and I do not recollect a single one that did this or that agreed with the word of God. And may I suggest that neither myself nor you or any one else in this century has heard those who claim Holy Ghost baptism speak in other tongues—languages—unless he has learned them some where by natural methods. When you can address an audience in such a manner that people speaking fourteen or fifteen different languages can hear everyone in his own language wherein he was born (Acts, 2:7, 8); or if you will speak in foreign languages without being educated in them as occurred in the house of Cornelius, Acts, 10:45, 46, then we will accept your statement, but until you can do that we will be compelled to relegate your remarks to the realm of human opinion.

Footwashing is not mentioned in the New Testament as a church ordinance. The inspired writers certainly knew the teaching of Jesus, and they have no record of footwashing after the beginning of the church on Pentecost except as an act of humility and kindness among brethren, I. Timothy, 5:10.

Paying tithes is a Jewish custom that was never officially used in the early church. Even when the early church was wholly Jewish, there is no record of using tithes. It is part of the first covenant which was done away in Christ. If your church demands paying of tithes because Abraham gave tithes, then to be consistant, you should also circumcise because Abraham also circumcised, Genesis, 17:10, 11. There were three sorts of tithes to be paid; 1. To the Levites, Numbers, 18:21, 24. 2. For the Lord's feasts and sacrifices, Deuteronomy, 14:22-24. 3. Every third year a tithe for the poor, Deuteronomy, 14:28, 29. Your church does not follow these commands. In fact, like other denominations, you accept such parts of the scriptures as attract you· and neglect the remainder.

Another thing I have noticed in the statements concerning the Church of God—and may I say, it is common among denominational expressions. You all use the words teachings, doctrines, truths in the plural number, this is never done by the inspired writers when they discuss the Lord's work. They do use the plural when they mention men's and demon's works.

People are frequently misled in regard to churches as well as to other things. If a large number of doctrines or practices of a certain church resemble the New Testament teaching or practice, many jump to the conclusion that that church is apostolic. They usually miss important discrepancies because they do not carefully examine every point of doctrine or practice. To illustrate: A young man leaves his home on an extended visit. After some time both the mother and the father die. A search is then made for the missing heir that the estate may be settled. After some days a young man appears in the community and claims to be the missing son. He bears the correct name, is of the right height and has a number of the same characteristics of the missing son. The resemblance is so close that the neighbors decide that he is the heir and advise the executor to give him the estate. About this time an old friend of the family appears and after studying the young man a little while says: This is not the son. The neighbors begin to explain the resemblances, but the old friend persists, This is not the son; he has brown eyes, this man has gray eyes. So it is with the church of God; it has a number of resemblances, but there are also a number of differences.

I am concluding because of these discrepancies between the Church of God and the New Testament church that we must look elsewhere for a church in which all can worship the Lord in spirit and in truth, John, 4:24.

CHAPTER XX.

VISITOR.

It is interesting to notice the similarities and dissimilarities among the different denominations. Many of their doctrines are based on the Bible, and in these they invariably agree. Others are based on the opinions of their leading men, and in these they invariably disagree. You will notice therefore that their disagreements are not about what the Bible teaches, but about the opinions of their leaders who tell them what they think the Bible teaches.

My friend of the Church of the Nazarene tells us that they are not a schism or a branch of any other denomination. The fact that he says, any other denomination, shows plainly that he considers his church one of them. Webster defines schism: Formal division or separation in the Christian church. The history of the Church of the Nazarene as given in their Manual shows plainly that most of them left other denominations for this one. My friend's opening statement also hints this.

This church, like all other denominations, began centuries too late to be the original church of the Lord. It began in America instead of Jerusalem; in 1885 instead of 33 A. D. and instead of one beginning it had several beginnings and is a combination of several "Holiness" sects.

I would like to ask a few questions:

Why do you consider it important that your members acquaint themselves thoroughly with the laws of their church unless it is to uphold another division in modern Christianity?

If the scriptures contain all things necessary to our salvation, of what use is your Manual or church constitution?

What do you mean by "original sin," and where in the Bible is it taught?

The scriptures nowhere mention a Church of the Nazarene. Your Bible will tell you that the name is not "that worthy name by which ye are called", James, 2:7. Again, if the word was translated into English, you would not wear it. The prophecy mentioned in Matthew, 2:23 cannot be found in either the English or American Bibles. The Hebrew word *Netzer* from which the words *Nazarene* and *Nazareth* are obtained is the word *branch*. Isaiah, 11:1; Jeremiah, 23:5.

You believe that conversion depends on faith preceded by repentance and that sanctification comes to the believer through faith.

Is this latter a second faith or a different kind of faith?

If a sinner accepts the Lord Jesus Christ as his Savior why is he not justified and made holy in doing so?

How can one repent without faith when the scripture says, without faith it is impossible to please God, Hebrews, 11:6?

Where in the Bible is your doctrine of entire sanctification, subsequent to conversion, through faith, taught?

Your doctrine of conversion or as you like to call it, regeneration, is contrary to the scriptures which nowhere tell you that if any one prays through to victory and is accepted of God he is a new creature. Your very expression contains a doubt. If one prays through is he or is he not accepted by God?

How can you know when one has prayed through?

Where does the Bible say anything about praying through?

What evidence have you that any one praying through is accepted of God? Is this evidence feeling or faith? If faith, then tell us: faith in what?

You say, the Holy Spirit is witness *to* the new birth and also *to* the sanctification of believers. I do not read anything like that in the Bible.

In what manner does the Holy Spirit bear witness to your converts?

Does the Spirit have a different testimony for the new birth than it does for entire sanctification?

What evidence have you that it is the witness of the Holy Spirit?

Have you tried the spirits whether they be of God, I. John, 4:1; and what method did you use?

The only way I can tell whether a person has the Holy Spirit or not is to learn if he has obeyed from the heart that form of doctrine which was delivered to the early Christians, Romans, 6:17, and shows the fruit of the Spirit in his life, Galatians, 5:22. Self-boasting without scriptural reasons is worthless. Jesus said, If I bear witness of myself, my witness is not true, John, 5:31. Nothing like this witness theory appears in the Bible. But it is recorded that the Spirit is given to all who become Christians and that the world cannot receive him, John, 14:16, 17; Galatians, 4:6. It is also recorded that the Spirit is not given until we have been baptized, Acts, 2:38; 5:32.

If you mean by your "distinguishing doctrine" that your doctrine of entire sanctification is peculiar to your denomination, you are badly mistaken. That doctrine is common to all Holiness sects and to others who use the mourners' bench. You preach the gospel of holiness whereas the early preachers preached the gospel of God and of the kingdom, the everlasting gospel.

Your ordinance of baptism differs very much from the New Testament ordinance. There was no affusion in those days and, so far as I can learn, there was none taught till about 120 A. D. *The Didache* or *Teaching Of The Apostles,* a series of tracts of about 120 A. D. has the folowing: "And touching baptism, thus baptize; having first declared all these things, baptize in the name of the Father, and of the Son and of the Holy Spirit, in living (that is running) water. But if thou have not living water, baptize in other water; and if thou canst not in cold, then in warm. But if thou have neither, pour on the head water thrice." Please notice that the writer uses the word *pour* instead of *baptize* when he can't find any water. Also, your baptism is according to the wishes of the candidate and not to the honor of the Lord. You also teach and practice "The baptism of infants" which is nowhere found in the scriptures. When you do this, it becomes an ordinance without faith and therefore not pleasing to God, Hebrews, 11:6.

The early disciples met every first day of the week to break bread, that is, to observe the Lord's Supper. The scriptures say, For *as often as* ye eat this bread and drink this cup. You say, *As seldom as* you eat and drink.

Your ecclesiastical organization is based on the old Methodist organization, not on the New Testament. I do not read in my Bible of General Superintendants, District Superintendants, District assemblies, Young people's Societies, etc. You also have female elders— the very opposite of the New Testament which expressly states that an elder, or bishop, must be the husband of one wife. Female elders and female evangelists are no part of New Testament teaching.

You connect the baptism with the Holy Spirit with several things that are not so taught in the scriptures. Baptism in the Holy Spirit was a special gift to prove the plea of the apostles and was never given after apostolic days. It was accompanied by signs and wonders that are entirely missing to-day. You who claim to be baptized with the Holy Spirit never give any evidence of your baptism. In fact, it has been my experience through a number of years that those who claimed this baptism never follow the New Testament teaching on a number of subjects. The Bible nowhere suggests that the baptism with the Holy Spirit is emphasized by Jesus as the most needful experience for this age. You cannot find any such expression in the gospels. Jesus never promised the baptism in the Holy Spirit to the multitude of Christians during this age. The terms you mention are not synonyms of the baptism, and John Wesley's many phrases are only his opinions and not Bible teaching.

Your instances of "Divine Healing" can be duplicated by Silent Unity, New Thought, Christian Science, and other cults. The New Testament nowhere presents an account of sick or injured persons being brought to the platform in an annual campmeeting to be prayed for by a group of men and women, and the Testament nowhere presents an account of men and women meeting in a sick or injured person's home to pray him to health. Again, your method of healing is not a success. Your pamphlet, *"Why Some Are Not Healed"*, gives thirty-eight reasons why some are not healed, and not one of these is a satisfactory Bible reason or reply.

The whole structure of the Church of the Nazarene fails because it is not permanent. Your Manual, and you also, say that the provisions of your Constitution can be amended. No one can amend the teaching of God's word.

In your teaching of "Divine Healing" you admit that it is wise to obey the law of vaccination and that broken bones should be set. Also diet, change of climate, sanitation and surgery are recommended.

Before I close my remarks I want to ask my friend some questions which, I hope he will be able to answer.

Why do those who claim the Baptism and witness of the Spirit not know how to rightly divide the word?

Is there no life or service in Christ without your method of sanctification? If there is, of what use is your theory, if not, where is the Bible proof?

The scriptures say that he who has the Son has life, I. John, 5:12. If one accepts Christ and obeys him does he have life seeing he has accepted the Son?

What part of God's word should one familiarize himself with in order to seek sanctification seeing the scriptures say nothing about such seeking?

Where is there any evidence that you have a seal of God different than the one mentioned by Paul in II. Timothy, 2:19?

How can anyone consecrate himself to anything in which he does not believe, or if you please, in which he has no faith?

If all Christians are to be baptized, that is, immersed in fire, why does the New Testament not clearly say so?

If baptism is immersion, how can tongues *like as of fire* appearing on the heads of people be a baptism?

How can the Spirit give to all who repent the gracious help of penitence of heart that they may believe, seeing that without faith we cannot please God?

What is the difference between repentance and penitence? (Penitence is a Roman Catholic word, not a Bible word).

If repentance is a change of mind in regard to sin, an *is Demanded of all sinners,* how can the Holy Spirit give it seeing that it is a demand, not a gift?

Is believing unto pardon and spiritual life different than believing in Christ; if different is it not a faith based on human opinions?

What is a witness of faith? Is it a witness by someone about faith or does faith in some manner witness to something? Where do the scriptures say anything about it?

In conclusion let me say to all: Know ye not that to whom ye yield yourselves servants to obey, his servants ye are to whom ye obey. Do you serve Luther, or Calvin, or Wesley, or Bresee, or Warner, or any other human leader in your distinguishing doctrines or do you serve Christ. No man can serve two masters, therefore I beg of you to leave all and follow the Lord.

CHAPTER XXI.

VISITOR.

The nineteenth century saw the rise of a philosophy and religion that has attracted considerable attention. Mrs. Christian Science has told this assembly something about it and its discoverer. Like all other modern sects, it has many things against it. It began in New England instead of Jerusalem, and it began in the nineteenth century instead of the first. According to the speaker's statement, the experiments which led to its discovery began about 1846, but the discovery came several years later. Christianity is divine, Christian Science is human. Again and again in their journals you will find the expression, "Mary Baker Eddy, the Discoverer and Founder of Christian Science."

Christian Science was founded by a divorced and remarried woman. This is contrary to the very essence of Christianity. Mrs. Mary Baker Glover Patterson Eddy cannot be the founder of an inspired organization even though her followers regard the Manual of the Mother church as a divinely inspired guide. There are too many foolish things in their religion to mark it anything but human. No book on earth can equal the Bible. The inspired writer of Revelation says: I testify unto every man that heareth the words of the prophecy of this book, If any man shall add unto them, God shall add unto him the plagues which are written in this book. Revelation, 22:18.

Mrs. Eddy added a whole book to what she claims is God's message when, in 1876, she published the first edition of *Science And Health.* On page 453 of the edition which I possess, Mrs. Eddy says: "A Christian Scientist requires my work on Science and Health for his text book, and so do all his students and patients."

I think all who are here to-day know that a Christian needs only the Bible to learn God's will.

Her definition of God and Jesus do not in any way agree with the Holy Scriptures. Jesus is not man only, but the only begotten Son of God. If God is Good, and God or Good is Mind, then Jesus did not exist. The speaker's statement about the Adam dream stultifies the Bible statement of creation and the reference of Jesus to Genesis: Matthew, 19:4, 5; Mark, 10:8. And her references to Mary Baker's childhood days are puerile. Did those pigs have unusual intelligence or was it just natural for them to quiet down at the sound of a human voice? Surely the speaker does not want us to believe that they were Christian Scientifically healed of some ailment!

Christian Scientists continually mention Mrs. Eddy's fine spirit, but they seldom tell that one of her husbands, Dr. Patterson "would have liked to resume life with his wife, but she could not consent, and later obtained a divorce.

Like other female founders of sects, Mrs. Eddy became a pastor. She accepted the call from her students and was ordained in 1881. Now a pastor in New Testament usage is a bishop or elder and must be the husband of one wife. I think I need not comment on this.

In Mrs. Eddy's Message to the Mother Church in 1901 she writes: "What I have given to the world on the subject of metaphysical healing or Christian Science is the result of my own observation." Metaphysics is that division of Philosophy which includes the science of being, and the theory of knowledge. I leave it to you, my friends; Is that any kind of a definition or description of Christianity?

Mrs. Christian Science told us that if people show no interest in their theories, they leave them lovingly alone, they never enter into controversy. I have written several articles against this philosophy, and invariably the day the paper was put into the mails, a member of their organization was in the office demanding that we publish a long reply.

Our speaker told us that their communion commemorated the morning meal which our Lord prepared for his disciples on the shore of Lake Galilee during his forty days sojourn on earth after his resurrection. Matthew, Mark and Luke tell us that it originated at the last passover before his crucifixion, and that he took bread and wine and gave them to his disciples telling them do partake in memory of him. The morning meal referred to was fish and bread. See John, 21:9. Paul, in I. Corinthians, 11:20, says; When ye come together therefore into one place, this is not to eat the Lord's Supper. It is the Lord's Supper, not the Lord's breakfast.

Let me ask a few questions:

If death is only a part of the belief in material life and is but a dream, as unreal as the dreams we have in sleep, where is Mrs. Eddy and why don't she awake? She passed away in December, 1910, thus making it a rather long dream.

If the disease of poverty can be healed by the renewing of the mind, why are there so many poor Christian Scientists?

If God is the one and only mind, and men do not possess private separate minds of their own, why do men do so much thinking contrary to God's will?

If sin punishes itself and as we get rid of sin we get rid of the suffering it brings, why is it that so many rich rascals are healthy and so many good Christians physically ill and financially poor?

If from mortal mind comes reproduction of the species and that union of the sexes is not necessary for procreation, and that gender is mental, not material, why was Mrs. Eddy's son, George Glover, not born that way?

A moment ago, I remarked that some things in Christian Science sounded foolish to me. Well, here are some of them. "Divide the name Adam into two syllables and it reads A-dam or obstruction. This suggests the thought of something fluid, of mortal mind in solution." Discord is the nothingness named error; harmony is the somethingness named truth." "Burial.— Corporeality and Physical sense put out of sight and hearing." But let me ask this: If there is no such thing as corporeality or physical sense, and I understand you so teach, how can nothing get into sight or hearing or be put out of it? "The recognition of the fact that God is mind, and that the real and spiritual man lives within this mind, leaves no room for a mortal, material, sick and sinful man, yet we have the problem of materiality with its sickness and woes to deal with." In other words Christian Scientists must deal with things that *do not exist* because they *do exist*. "Man is neither young nor old. He has neither birth nor death. He is not a beast, a vegetable, or a migratory mind." Yet all Christian Scientists must admit that man is here and they should tell us how they came. Every tottering gray haired old gentleman or lady shouts opposition to this statement.

Now please notice these statements from *"Science And Health* published in 1875, and revised in 1905. "Sin, sickness, death, is a belief only. Death is an illusion, for there is no death." But in another place Mrs. Eddy says, "Salvation is life, truth and love understood and demonstrated as supreme over all sin, sickness and death destroyed." May I ask again, There being none of these things, how can they be destroyed?

In *Scence And Health* (1875) Mrs. Eddy says, "The Holy Ghost is divine science." In (1905) "The Comforter, I understand to be divine science." Again, "Holy Ghost, divine science, the developement of eternal life, truth and love." And again, "The spiritual essence of blood is sacrifice. The material blood of Jesus was no more efficacious to cleanse from sin when it was shed upon the accursed tree than when it was flowing in his veins as he went about his Father's business." "Devil: a lie, error, neither corporeality nor mind;

the opposite of truth; a belief in sin, sickness and death, animal magnetism, lust of the flesh." "Angels are pure thoughts, not messengers. Angels—God's thoughts passing to man. Spiritual intuitions, pure and perfect."

If Christian Science is the teaching of Jesus, how could Mrs. Eddy be the founder centuries later?

If Christian Science is true, why did Mrs. Eddy's sister-in-law suffer from cancer for seven years and die from that disease? Why did not Mrs. Eddy heal her own husband who died of heart-disease in her home?

I might continue thus for a long time, but I think I have shown you that we cannot accept this philosophy or metaphysics as the basis of the unity of all Christians. There is no truth but God's truth that we can follow and be safe. Let us then prayerfully turn unto Jehovah who will abundantly pardon.

Our task is done. Our appeal has been, is, and evermore will be, to the word of God as it is translated by the unbiased, unsectarian and unprejudiced scholarship of the world. Who will affirm that this is not the key that will unlock the hearts of the people of God and lead to the solution of the problem of the world's evangelization? Who will affirm that there is any other solution of the mighty problems that come rushing down upon us? Who will affirm that there is any other answer to the innumerable voices that come from around us and beyond the seas asking for the bread of life? Who will affirm that there is any other remedy for the sins that have left their foul blots upon every land beneath the circle of the sun? Who will affirm that anything less will satisfy the demands of the King: Men of Israel, to the work! Sons of the living God, arise! Reapers of the harvest of the world, thrust the sickle into the golden grain! Army of the living God, unfurl the banner of peace, and march on to victory!

The world still waits for His law. Forward, ye conquering host! The King in tenderness still calls, for

"Large are the mansions in thy Father's dwelling,
    Glad are the homes that sorrows never dim:
Sweet are the harps in holy music swelling.
    Soft are the tones which raise the heavenly hymn,
Come unto Him, all ye who droop in sadness,
    Come unto Him, and he will give you rest."

CHAPTER XXII.

PEACEMAKER

"Is Christ divided" (I. Cor., 1:13).

"Can two walk together, except they be agreed" (Amos, 3:3)?

"Behold, how good and how pleasant it is for brethren to dwell together in unity" (Ps., 133:1)!

"Neither pray I for these alone, but for them also which shall believe on me through their word; that they may all be one; as thou, Father, art in me, and I in thee, that they also may be one in us; that the world may believe that thou hast sent me" (John, 17:20, 21).

"He that hath my commandments and keepeth them, he it is that loveth me" (John, 14:21).

"We have the mind of Christ" (I. Cor., 2:16).

I am very glad to have heard the three short talks by Visitor, who confined his criticism to the people known as the Church of God, also the Church of the Nazarene, and I am glad he gave vigorous attention to the Christian Science people. This latter group I consider least entitled to the term "Christian" of any sect in the world, and I know them to be the most unreasonable. If you try to talk to them and give them a chance to defend their doctrine, they will leave you with the remark, "I can do you more good by praying for you".

But in my Bible I find we are urged to "contend earnestly for the faith, once for all delivered to the saints," and I also find the apostle Peter says we should "be ready to give a reason of the hope that is in us," but you cannot get these Christian Scientists to discuss anything Bible with you. The other two groups Visitor handled in very nice style and with courtesy. I will now confine my speech to the other groups, and so I appear in this convention as a Peacemaker, using the words of Jesus: "Blessed are the peacemakers; for they shall be called the children of God" (Matt., 5:9). I am amazed at the divisions which exist among those who profess to follow in the footprints of Jesus Christ, and His chosen apostles. One speaker professed to see ample authority in the word of God for the existence of the Methodist system. Another regards the Baptist system as being in strict harmony with the Divine model, and is, therefore, led to condemn all other religious orders as sects, and their devotees as heretics. Another plants himself down upon the Presbyterian system, and announces to the world that he has found the truth. Another advances to the front with the Episcopalian system, claiming to represent "the only Apostolic Church." Another advocates the Lutheran system, because he thinks Martin Luther restored the principles of Christianity in practice when he renounced Popery and restored the Bible to the world. Another finds abundant reason for being an infidel because, he says forsooth, the preachers of "modern orthodoxy" teach contradictory doctrines, yet professing to be guided by the Bible. Glancing over what I have heard, and giving each of you credit for integrity and truthfulness, I conclude that all the religious denominations believe every word of the Bible, from Genesis to Revelation, and practice it in spots—at long intervals! Christian union is the grandest theme that ever demanded the attention of religious people. It is universally admitted to be right; positively demanded by the gospel of Christ, but there seems to be a difference of opinion as to what it is. Some think there is no need of a more intimate union than now exists. They even thank God that there are divisions, so that sinners may be without excuse. This is poor logic. There are more sects now than in any other age of the world. Still, there is more unbelief, more sin, more rebellion against God. Surely, "the legs of the lame are not equal." In order to justify sectarianism, Brother Presbyterian referred to the oft-quoted passages: "He that is not against us is for us" (Luke, 9:50), and "I am the vine, ye are the branches" (John, 15:5). He should remember that Jesus also said: "He that is not with me is against me; and he that gathered not with me scattereth abroad" (Matt., 12:30), and "Every plant which my heavenly Father hath not planted shall be rooted up" (Matt., 15:13). It can not be shown from the Scriptures that God planted the numberless institutions now in existence, claiming to be the Church of Christ, or branches of it. "With me," evidently means in the "one body," the Church. When Jesus spoke of the vine and the branches there were no denominations; hence, He must have been speaking to His individual followers. "We are already united!" is echoed from hill to hill by many modern preachers. Each one feels absolutely certain, however, that if a more intimate relation is to be established, his creed is the only reliable basis. One thing, if no more, has been developed by this investigation, viz.: the partisan spirit growing out of human creeds, and the utter impossibility of uniting upon them. For example: The Episcopalians and Methodists do not recognize or affiliate with each other. Why is this? Do they not worship the same God, and accept the same Bible? Certainly. What then keeps them apart? The Episcopal creed, containing thirty-nine articles, is an addition to the Bible, and the Methodists do not believe it. The Methodist creed, containing twenty-five articles, is an addition to the Bible, and the Episcopalians do not believe it. The warfare is not so much about the Bible as their respective creeds. These institutions are built upon their creed. Their existence will be parallel with their creeds. Abolish the creed, and you abolish the sect. Perpetuate the creed and you perpetuate sect. The union characteristic of the Church in apostolic times will never be restored until creeds are buried in the dust of eternal forgetfulness, and every good man becomes willing to comply with all the requirements of the word of God, and take it as his only rule of faith and practice. Again, Methodists, Baptists, Presbyterians, Lutherans frequently combine their efforts in what they call a "union meeting." It is generally considered a success until the participants begin to divide the converts!

Brother Methodist preaches a sermon in which he endeavors to show the practicability of his system. Brother Baptist proves that baptism is an immersion of the whole body, and that pouring and sprinkling are human inventions to gratfy the whims of those who are too proud to be "buried in baptism." Brother Presbyterian replies to it, and convinces his brethren that "the mode does not affect the validity of the ordinance." Brother Lutheran preaches a glowing sermon, presenting his plea in a manner which is very convincing to his own brethren, but no one else. The excitement becomes intense. Men are seen upon the public highways, disputing about some proposition advanced during the controversy. When the excitement dies away it is found that the real cause of Christianity has suffered immeasurably by the contest, that many of the most intelligent people in the community have become doubters, and that many of the "converts" are worse than before the meeting began. These denominations profess to recognize each other as Christians, but they will not work together in peace and harmony. They agree to preach Christ together for awhile, and at last they return to their old theories without benefiting themselves or any one else. Is this Christian union? With an open Bible before me, I am bound to declare that there is absolutely no union in it. Jesus said: "By this shall all men know that ye are my disciples, if ye have love one to another" John, 13:35). Do such meetings as these manifest brotherly love, indicate that those who engage in them are one as Christ and His Father are one, or prove the divinity of the Saviour's mission? Let this convention answer. An anxious world is waiting for the response.

Divisions among people professing to be Christians have been a greater disadvantage to the cause of Christ than Judaism, Roman Catholicism and infidelity combined. Is there any remedy? There must be, for Jesus Christ would not have prayed so fervently for the oneness of His people without furnishing a basis on which it can be accomplished. Whatever makes a man a sectarian is useless, and may, therefore, be laid aside. Can a man be saved and not believe in Methodism? Methodists themselves admit that he can. Methodism is not the gospel, for "He that believeth not shall be damned" (Mark, 16:16). Can a man be saved and not believe in Baptist doctrine? Baptists themselves admit that he can. Baptist doctrine is not the gospel, for "He that believeth not shall be damned." Can a man be saved and not believe in Presbyterianism? Presbyterians themselves admit that he can. Presbyterianism is not the gospel, for "He that believeth not shall be damned." The same argument may be applied to many of the religious orders in Christiandom with the same results in every particular, hence I conclude that a man may be a Christian—be a follower of Christ—be saved and reject all systems of human opinion. In order to be a Christian a man must believe in Christ and obey the gospel. In order to be a sectarian—a Methodist, Baptist, Presbyterian—a man must accept something in addition to the divine system.

"The Bible, and the Bible alone, is the religion of the Protestants."—*Chillingworth.*

"In my judgment, it is about time for the truly Christian people to begin to look the matter of denominationalism square in the face, as being themselves morally wrong before God, and to cease from expecting real Christian union without Church oneness."—*Dorus Clarke, D. D.*

"The gospel can not accomplish its great triumphs and collect the redeemed from every land until the law of Christ be fulfilled by these Protestant sects—until they become one."—*Richard Baxter.*

"If the Protestant world were as zealous and faithful in giving the gospel to Italy as Rome in spreading her religiou over the earth, the victory might be ours. O! for a union among Protestants, spiritual, visible, cordial union in effort to give the simple gospel to all who are perishing for want of it. I would rejoice to hear of another Luther, or Savonarola, or Calvin, or Wesley, or Whitfield, to call for the wind to blow on the bones in this great plain; but far more would I rejoice to know that party names in the Church of God had been forgotten, and Christ's people *were,* and were called *only Christians,* as at Antioch."—*Dr. Prime.*

"That they, and all that believe through their word, may be one body, united by one Spirit to me their living head. The union which Christ recommends here, and prays for, is so complete and glorious, as to be fitly represented by that union which subsists between the Father and the Son."—*Dr. Adam Clarke, on John,* 17:21.

"This prayer (that they all may be one) was literally answered in the *first* believers, who were all of *one heart* and of *one soul.* And why is it that believers are not in the same spirit now? Because they neither attend to the example, nor to the truth of Christ."—*Adam Clarke.*

"The members of the Church of God should labor to be of the same mind, and speak the same thing, in order to prevent divisions, which may hinder the work of God."—*Adam Clarke, on I. Cor.,* 1:10.

"Christian union, what is it? Ah! that is a delightful question. There were no sects in the Apostolic Church; therefore, we want no union of sects, for that would be the sum total of sectarianism. But we want a union of Christians. The prayer of Jesus is that those who 'believe on me may be one, as thou Father are in me and I in thee, that they may also be one in us.' Not 'one' as men may be one in one ecclesiastical body, but 'one in us.' Jesus says to the Father, 'one,' 'as we are one.' Now, who would speak of the Trinity as a union, yet all may speak of the Godhead as unity. Then for what does Jesus pray? That all His followers may be one precisely as He and His Father are one—not that they form a union, but that they constitute a unity. Then His prayer contemplates that **believers** attain a oneness of mind in faith, **and not** merely a oneness of feeling—a oneness of heart in the obedience which they offer, and a oneness of effort in the work which they do.

And then Jesus measures this Christian unity by the standard of the Divine nature: 'One as we are one.' If this unity among Christians consists in mere heart-kindness, there is no visible appositeness in this tremendous petition. The Father and the Son are one in feeling, action, counsel, name. Therefore, the prayer means that Christians are to be one in the same sense—that is, one in feeling, action, counsel, name. So completely are the Father and the Son one, that the same acts are ascribed to both, and the same purposes are formed by both. Such is their identity in these respects, that the eye of the keenest archangel can not see a shade of variation. This is the real picture of Christian unity, as Jesus hung it upon the supper chamber. Perfect unity must subsist among the people of God, and their unity must agree in agreeing, and not in differing, just as the unity of the Father and the Son agrees. We are told to hold the same affections, the same doctrines, and the same ordinances, and we are to hold to them as Jesus held to them, or else our union is a counterfeit and a pretension. This is Christian unity, as Jesus prays for it, and it seems to me, with the open Bible before me, that nothing else is. Who would suppose that the Father holds one form of truth, and the Son another, but for the sake of peace they 'agree to disagree'—that is, they mutually agree to suppress the varying expressions of their mind, and they call this being at one? The very thought is offensive. Christ was exclusively one with the Father in doing His will, and our unity must be like the unity of the Father and the Son. In other words, Christian unity must be Scriptural, or it is unreal, it is nothing. Therefore, nothing but a return of all those who love the Savior to the naked teachings of the Bible, as the Father and the Son avowed those teachings, can ever result in Christian unity. Christian bodies may declare an armistice and be peaceable, but it is one thing to be peaceable and another to be united. It is a shame that one man should denounce another as exclusive, because that other more literally and fully obeys the word of God than himself. God has expressed His will in the broadness of infinite thought, and that man who does not scruple to obey every part of it, is the most catholic believer. His exclusiveness is exclusive oneness with Christ in obeying His will, and therefore he partakes of the catholicity of God. But no man can obey that will without sympathy with the catholic God. Hence David prays, not when thou shalt contract, but 'when thou shalt enlarge my heart, I will run in the way of thy commandments.'

I take it, then, that the only way in which we Christians can be united, is to agree that we will mutually obey whatever is positively enjoined in the New Testament, and to insist upon nothing beyond that. Let each man appeal to the Bible only, and he will need to ask for no concession from his brethren. Opinion will then give place to faith; convenience, and preference, and expediency to Divine authority. How common it is for Christians to retain their distinct peculiarities, because they are not forbidden in the word of God. This is a dangerous principle—it is one of the rocks on which Christian sects split. The things that are especially required are the things that are to be done, and not the things that are especially forbidden. Luther fell into this trap. Carstadt demanded of him, 'Where has Christ commanded us to elevate the host?' 'Where has He forbidden it?' Luther retorted. Our trouble springs largely from this false position. We should only ask that each other's tastes and preferences should yield to God's word, and we shall soon begin to respect each other's views of it, and begin to grow in real unity. Do you wonder that when a man asserts, for instance, that my views of baptism are Scriptural and Apostolic, and adds that, for some reason aside from their Scripturalness, he prefers something else, and then requires me to give up my views in order to accommodate him, that he may unite with me—do you wonder that I resent it as an insult to my convictions?

I am tempted to say: 'Rather give up what is a matter of indifference to you, be baptized with what you confess to be Bible baptism, and we are one in a moment.'

These are my views of Christian union, and the method of attaining it. I can see no other in harmony with the word of God. And if this be Christian union, its profound sanctity overwhelms me, its infinite tenderness moves my whole being. The delicious conception of its purity, and preciousness, and power, makes me tremble with holy awe from head to foot. I remember that when my Redeemer bowed beneath the ponderous load of my sin, this holy thought soothed His bleeding heart, and just before the purple blood-drops forced their passage through every pore of His body, He breathed out this intercession for every ransomed disciple and for me—'That they all may be one, that the world may believe that thou hast sent me.'"—*Dr. T. Armitage.*

"Unless you have investigated for yourself, you have no idea into what a multitude of fragments the Church is split. The Baptists divided into, first, regular; second, Disciples; third, Dunkards; fourth, Free Will; fifth, Anti-Mission; sixth, Winnebrennarian; seventh, Seventh Day; eighth, Six Principle; ninth, General; tenth, Mennonites. The Methodist Church is divided into, first, Methodist Episcopal Church; second, Methodist Episcopal Church South; third, African Methodist Episcopal Church; fourth, Methodist Episcopal Zion Church; fifth, Colored Methodist Church; sixth, African Methodist Church; seventh, Union American Methodist Episcopal Church; eighth, Congregational Methodist; ninth, Primitive Methodists; tenth, Independent Methodists; eleventh, Free Methodists; twelfth, Welsh Calvanistic Methodists; thirteenth, Wesleyan Methodist Connection; fourteenth, Methodist Evangelical Association; fifteenth, Methodist Protestant; sixteenth, United Brethren of Christ. The Adventists are divided into, first, Second Adventists; second, Seventh Day Adventists; third, Evangelical Adventists; fourth, Non-Resurrection Adventists; fifth, Age to Come Adventists. The Quakers are divided into, first, Orthodox; second,

Hicksite; third, Wilbur, or Friends on Original Principle; fourth, Kingsites; fifth, Lambornites; sixth, Progressives. The Presbyterians are divided into the Northern Presbyterians, Southern Presbyterians, Cumberland Presbyterians, United Presbyterians, Reformed Presbyterians, Associate Reformed Presbyterians, and many other denominations, more in number than I have mentioned, are more or less absurdly cut up into a great ecclesiastical hash, with enough salt of real grace to keep it, and enough pepper of biting controversy to spice it, but, nevertheless, hash. With some it is a question of robes; with some, a question of days; with some, a question about non-essentials, so small that the theologian has to get his dictionary to find them. The mere recital of their names shows the necessity that something be done for their combination. If this world is ever taken for God, and its sins overthrown, it will be by forgetfulness of unimportant differences and the marching of all the hosts of God in solid column to attack it. The sixteen kinds of Methodists will come under one wing, the ten kinds of Baptists must come under still another wing, and the seven kinds of Presbyterians under still another wing. After all the branches of each denomination have united, then the great denominations nearest akin will unite, and this absorption shall go on until there shall be one great millennial Church, divided only for convenience into geographical sections, and as of old it was the Church of Laodicea, the Church of Philadelphia, and the Church of Thyatira, so it shall be the Church of America, and the Church of Africa, and the Church of Australia. Of the world-wide Church there will be only one article of creed—Christ, first, Christ last, and Christ forever."—*T. DeWit Talmage in the Christian Herald and Signs of Our Times.*

These extracts give a good idea of Christian union as viewed by prominent Methodist, Baptist and Presbyterian theologians. They emphasize the necessity of forsaking "party names and unscriptural phrases," and returning to the "naked teachings" of the New Testament. This, I think, is the only reliable solution of the greatest question that ever demanded the attention of students of the sacred oracles. If each denomination will ask no more and accept no less than the full authority of Christ, the work can be accomplished without further delay. But if each one continues to make its creed a test of fellowship, divisions will be multiplied, and the salvation of the world impeded. Oh, for a full appreciation of the maxim of immortal Chillingworth: "The Bible, and the Bible alone, is the religion of the Protestants!" There was a day in which there were no "Christian sects." The followers of Jesus were all members of one Church; one in mind, sentiment, aim, judgment and destiny. Jesus prayed for this just before He suffered (John, 17:20-26). Luke describes this unity: "The multitude of them that believed were of one heart and one soul" (Acts, 4:32). Do the religious organizations represented in this assembly manifest this oneness? Paul wrote to the Church of God at Corinth: "Now I beseech you, brethren, by the name of our Lord Jesus Christ, that ye all speak the same thing, and that there be no divisions among you; but that ye be perfectly joined together in the same mind and in the same judgment" (I. Cor., 1:10). Do all the preachers in this convention "speak the same thing?" Are there no divisions among them? Are they "perfectly joined together in the same mind and the same julgment?" Listen: "Now the God of patience and consolation grant you to be like-minded one toward another according to (literally, after the example of) Jesus Christ. That ye may with one mind and one mouth glorify God, even the Father of our Lord Jesus Christ" (Rom., 15:5, 6). Do the denominations of modern times glorify God with "one mind and one mouth after the example of Jesus Christ?" "I, therefore, the prisoner of the Lord beseech you that ye walk worthy of the vocation wherewith ye are called, with all lowliness and meekness, with long suffering, forbearing one another in love, endeavoring to keep the unity of the spirit in the bond of peace; there is one body, and one Spirit, even as ye are called in one hope of your calling, one Lord, one faith, one baptism, one God and Father of all, who is above all, and through all, and in you all" (Eph., 4:1-6). Here are seven units. Do the religious denominations of this age endeavor to "keep the unity of the spirit in the bond of peace?" Do they constitute but "one body?" Do they have the same faith? Do they practice the "one baptism?" Does Paul reason correctly? Did God hear the prayer of Jesus? Will it ever be answered? "As we have therefore opportunity, let us do good unto all men, especially unto them who are of the household of faith" (Gal., 6:10). In all candor, I desire to know if the sects represented in this convention constitute "the household of faith?" "Christ also loved the church, and gave himself for it; that he might sanctify and cleanse it with the washing of water by the word, that he might present it to himself a glorious church, not having spot or wrinkle, or any such thing; but that it should be holy and without blemish" (Eph., 5:25-27). Do such battles as this controversy exhibit a Church without blemish, spot or wrinkle? Can Christ be the head of all these institutions? He is represented as the bridegroom, the Church as the bride (Matt., 25:1-15). "Let us be glad and rejoice, and give honor to him; for the marriage of the Lamb is come, and his wife hath made herself ready; and to her was granted that she should be arrayed in fine linen, clean and white; for the fine linen is the righteousness of saints" (Rev., 19:7, 8). Do the denominations of this age, representing an inexhaustible variety of opinions, constitute the bride of Christ? Bible reader, answer the question! Many are running "to and fro" and asking for the "old paths." There is so much controversy about human standards that men are saying, "Where is the Church of Christ? How may I enter it? How may I know that I am a member of it?" Let us forget the condition of religious society at present, and go back beyond nineteen centuries to Jerusalem, take our position at the old beginning corner and survey the world. The founder of the Church put unchangeable marks upon it, by which it is to be known during all the ages. But before presenting the cardinal principles of the institution, I will endeavor to show what it is not:

I. *It is not a political institution.* "In the days of these kings shall the God of heaven set up a kingdom which shall never be destroyed: and the kingdom shall not be left to other people, but it shall break in pieces and consume all these kingdoms, and it shall stand forever" (Dan., 2:44). Jesus answered, "My kingdom is not of this world" (John, 18:36). "The kingdoms of this world are become the kingdoms of our Lord and of his Christ: and he shall reign forever and ever" (Rev., 11:15).

II. *It is not the "old covenant."* There are two covenants (Gal., 4:24). Human argument can never make them one. When Paul went to Rome, the people said, "We desire to hear of thee what thou thinkest: for as concerning this sect, we know that everywhere it is spoken against" (Acts, 28:22). The Jews were all members of the old covenant, born in it (Gen., 17:5-14). They were the enemies of the Church of Christ. They persecuted its members with burning bitterness. If the old covenant and the Church of Christ are identical, the Jews persecuted their own interests. Paul was born a Jew, in the covenant, yet he wrote: "Salute Andronicus and Junia, my kinsmen and my fellow-prisoners, who are of note among the apostles, who also were in Christ before me" (Rom., 16:7). If the old covenant and the Church of Christ are identical, there never was a time in Paul's life in which he was not "in Christ." Nicodemus was a Jew, born in the covenant. Jesus informed him that in order to enter the kingdom of heaven, the Church, he must be born again (John, 3:1-12). If the covenant and the Church of Christ are identical, Christ taught him to be "born again," to enter an institution of which he had always been a member. The prophet Jeremiah, long after the death of Abraham and Moses, predicted the establishment of "a new covenant" (Jer., 33:31-34). If the old covenant and Church of Christ are identical, it is strange that such language as this should be used by the Lord's representative! Jesus said: "There be some of them that stand here, which shall not taste death till they have seen the kingdom of God come with power" (Mark, 9:1). The kingdom and the Church are the same (Matt., 16:18, 19). If the old covenant and the Church of Christ are identical, he would have said: "The kingdom came in the days of Abraham, over nineteen hundred years ago, or it came in the days of Moses, over fifteen hundred years ago." Paul said: "He taketh away the first, that he may establish the second" (Heb., 10:9). If the old covenant and the Church of Christ are identical, he would have said: "There is but one covenant. It began in the days of Abraham. Christ confirmed it." Paul says: "Cast out the bond-woman and her son; for the son of the bond-woman shall not be heir with the son of the free-woman" (Gal., 4:30). Three thousand members of the Abrahamic covenant were brought into the Church on the day of Pentecost in the city of Jerusalem. If the old covenant and the Church of Christ are identical, the apostles misapplied their time and talent. They should have preached to some who were born outside of the covenant.

Now, brethren of the convention, by your permission I will take the Bible in my hand and "Walk about Zion and go around about her." I will "mark well her bulwarks" and "consider her palaces," that we may "tell it to the generations following." Please bear in mind that the distinctive principles which are here presented are not recent discoveries. They have lived upon the pages of Divine history for more than eighteen centuries. They will live until our Redeemer comes again. I proceed to submit the following propositions to your impartial investigation. Examine them in the light of God's eternal truth, with unprejudiced minds, and I shall be satisfied. Examine them at once, for our union and co-operation are absolutely dependent upon them:

I. *The Founder of the Church was born at Bethlehem:* "And thou Bethlehem, in the land of Juda, are not the least among the princes of Juda: for out of thee shall come a Governor, that shall rule my people Israel" (Mic., 5:2; Matt., 2:6). A person born at any other place could not found the Church of Christ, or a branch of it.

II. *Jesus of Nazareth is the Founder of the Church:* "Thou art Peter, and upon this rock I will build my church; and the gates of hell (hades) shall not prevail against it" (Matt., 16:18). "Let no man glory in men" (I. Cor., 3:21). John Wesley founded Methodism; Henry VIII., Episcopalianism; John Knox, Presbyterianism; John Calvin, Calvinism; Martin Luther, Lutheranism.

III. *Jesus Christ is the Foundation of the Church:* "For other foundation can no man lay than that is laid, which is Jesus Christ" (I. Cor., 3:11). An institution built upon any other foundation is not the Church of Christ. Methodism is built upon the twenty-five articles of the Discipline; Baptistism is built upon Baptism; Pesbyterianism is built on the Confession of Faith; Episcopalianism is built upon the thirty-nine articles of the Prayer Book; Lutheranism is built upon the twenty-eight articles of the Augsburg Confession of Faith; Roman Catholicism is built upon tradition; The Church of God was started by Daniel S. Warner. The Church of the Nazarene began in 1885, and Christian Science is a product of Mary Baker Eddy's fertile mind.

IV. *Jesus Christ is the Only Head of the Church:* "He is the Head of the Body, the church: who is the beginning, the first-born from the dead; that in all things he might have the pre-eminence" (Col., 1:18). An institution having any other head is not the Church of Christ. The Pope of Rome is the head of Roman Catholicism.

V. *Jerusalem is the beginning corner:* "And it shall come to pass in the last days, that the mountain of the Lord's house shall be established in the top of the mountains, and shall be exalted above the hills, and all nations shall flow unto it. And many people shall go and say, Come ye, and let us go up to the mountain of the Lord, to the house of the God of Jacob; and he will teach us of his ways, and we will walk in his paths: for out of Zion shall go forth the law, and the word of the Lord from Jerusalem" (Isaiah, 2:1-3). This prediction was made seven hundred and sixty years before the advent of the Messiah. Just before He returned to his Father He commanded His apostles to begin at Jerusalem, and preach repentance and remission of sins in His name (Luke, 24:47). Paul says: "Jerusalem which is above is free, which is the mother of us all" (Gal., 4:26). An institution which began at any other place is not the Church of Christ. Methodism began at Oxford. Baptistism, as a distinct institution, is little more than three hundred years old. Presbyterianism began in Scotland. Episcopalianism began in London. Lutheranism began in Wittenberg. Roman Catholicism began at Rome. Calvinism began at Geneva. The Church of Christ began in the year 33. Methodism began about the year 1729. Baptistism about the year 1611. Presbyterianism about the year 1587. Episcopalianism about the year 1521. Lutheranism about the year 1521. Cumberland Presbyterianism about the year 1815. I can not given the exact date of the beginning of Romanism, but it is certain it did not assume an organic form until several centuries after the inauguration of the Christian era.

VI. *The primitive Church was one body:* "There is one body and one Spirit" (Eph., 4:4). "For as we have many members in one body, and all members have not the same office: so we, being many, are one body in Christ, and every one members one of another" (Rom., 12:4, 5). "For we are members of his body, of his flesh, and of his bones" (Eph., 5:30). "The Churches of Christ salute you" (Rom., 16:16). Paul sent his salutations to the saints at Rome from the Churches of Christ. He gave Christ the glory. This is in harmony with all Divine revelation. He is the founder, foundation, head and life of this institution, hence it must bear His name, and it alone. He purchased it (Eph., 5:25). Do not endeavor to rob Him of His well-earned honor!

An institution composed of many bodies or sects is not the Church of Christ; Methodists, Baptists, Presbyterians, Episcopalian, and Lutherans are divided among themselves.

VII. *There was a well-defined law of admission into the Church:* "He that entereth not by the door into the sheepfold, but climbeth up some other way, the same is a thief and a robber" (John, 10:1). "Go ye therefore, and teach all nations, baptizing them in the name of the Father, and of the Son, and of the Holy Spirit; teaching them to observe all things whatsoever I have commanded you: and lo, I am with you alway, even unto the end of the world" (Matt., 28:19, 20). Repent, and be baptized every one of you in the name of Jesus Christ for the remission of sins, and you shall receive the gift of the Holy Spirit" (Acts, 2:38). "For the law of the Spirit of life in Christ Jesus hath made me free from the law of sin and death" (Rom., 8:2). "But whoso looketh into the perfect law of liberty, and continueth therein, he being not a forgetful hearer, but a doer of the work, this man shall be blessed in his deed" (Jas., 1:25). The great commission unfolds "the law of the Spirit." "The perfect law of liberty" demands of those who desire to enter the Church, faith in Christ and obedience to His demands. Every denomination in modern times has a law of admission peculiar to itself. The Methodists admit members according to the Discipline. The Baptists admit them by an experience of grace, which generally contradicts the apostolic answer to the convicted Pentecostans, a vote of the Church and immersion. The Presbyterians admit them according to the Confession of Faith. The Episcopalians admit them according to the Prayer Book. The Lutherans admit them according to the Augsburg Confession of Faith. The Methodists will not admit people into membership who deny the twenty-five articles of the Discipline, even if they believe every other creed in Christendom. The Episcopalians will not admit a member who denies the thirty-nine articles of the Prayer Book, it matters not how great his pretentions to "orthodoxy" may be. The

Baptists will not admit a member from the Methodists even if he has been immersed. These orders do not believe each other's creeds, recognize each other's membrs or meet together and worship the Lord in peace and harmony. Yet they profess to recognize each other as Christians, and many of them profess to belong to "branches of the same Church," but what Church is that? Not the Church of Christ, I am sure, for it is not composed of branch institutions. It is one body. It is safe to affirm that an order which has a law of admission unknown to the New Testament is not the Church of Christ.

VIII. *The followers of Christ were distinguished by a divinely-given name:* "The Gentiles shall see thy righteousness, and all kings thy glory; and thou shalt be called by a new name, which the mouth of the Lord shall name" (Isaiah, 62:2). Soon after the Gentiles were brought into the kingdom of Christ, Luke informs us that "the disciples were called Christians first in Antioch" (Acts, 11:26). "Almost thou persuadest me to be a Christian" (Acts, 26:28). "Yet if any man suffer as a Christian, let him not be ashamed; but let him glorify God on this behalf (literally in this name)" (I. Pet., 4:16). "A name which is above every name" (Phil., 2:9). "Ye shall be hated of all men for my name's sake" (Matt., 10:22). "Thou holdest fast my name" (Rev., 2:13). "Do they not blaspheme that worthy name by which ye are called" (Jas., 2:7). "Neither is there salvation in any other; for there is none other name under heaven given among men, whereby we must be saved" (Acts, 4:12). "It seemed good unto us, being assembled with one accord, to send chosen men unto you with our beloved Barnabas and Paul, men who have hazarded their lives for the name of our Lord Jesus Christ" (Acts, 15:25, 26). "And whatsoever ye do in word or deed, do all in the name of the Lord Jesus, giving thanks to God and the Father by him" (Col., 3:17). "For this cause I bow my knees unto the Father of our Lord Jesus Christ, of whom the whole family in heaven and earth is named" (Eph., 3:14, 15). "Justified in the name of the Lord

Jesus, and by the Spirit of our God" (I. Cor., 6:11). "I write unto you, little children, because your sins are forgiven you for his name's sake" (I. John, 2:12). "The name of the Lord is a strong tower: the righteous runneth into it and is safe" (Prov., 18:10). "We will walk in the name of the Lord our God forever and ever" (Mic., 4:5). "And the Lord shall be king over all the earth: in that day there shall be one Lord, and his name one" (Zech., 14:9). "We will rejoice in thy salvation, and in the name of our God we will set up our banners" (Ps., 20:5). "And ye shall leave your name for a curse unto my chosen: for the Lord God shall slay thee, and call his servants by another name" (Isa., 65:15).

In the face of this testimony, this convention has decided that there is nothing in a name. Is there anything in the great names of history? What name is sufficient to awaken the deepest emotions in every believer's heart? The name of Paul the apostle! What name rekindles the fires of patriotism in the heart of every true American? The name of George Washington! To what name does Protestantism pay the tribute of a grateful remembrance? The name of the unconquerable hero, Martin Luther! To what name does Methodism bow in holy awe? The name of the illustrious John Wesley! To what name will all the nations of the earth and the angels in heaven bow in humble reverence? The name of our Lord Jesus Christ (Phil., 2:10)! There is something in the names recognized by the denominations of modern times, for Methodists are not Baptists, and Baptists are not Methodists; Presbyterians are not Episcopalians, and Episcopalians are not Presbyterians. The name of Christ—Christian—is the grandest name known among the children of men. It identifies those who wear it without any explanation. Not so with sectarian names. They imply historical associations which the generality of mankind know but little about. Paul informs us that Christians are married to Christ (Rom., 7:4). Brides, to be respected, must wear their husband's name. When the same apostle wrote to the Church at Ephesus, in the year 64, he informed them that the "whole family in heaven and in earth," recognized and honored the name of Christ. Peter declares that there is salvation in the name of our King, and John endorses it by informing us that our sins are forgiven "for His name's sake." Every blessing of the new institution comes through the name of Jesus Christ. When the apostles began their labors, immediately after the ascension, their first answer to penitent inquirers embraced this name, and whatever is done in this or any other age, in the name of Him, by His authority, as He directs, will be recognized in heaven. It is dangerous to be anything more or less than a Christian. True, the followers of Christ, in primitive times, were known as disciples, saints, or brethren, but the term Christian embraces all of these. At the rollcall of Eternity, it will not be asked whether I am a Methodist, Baptist, Presbyterian, Episcopalian, Lutheran, or a Roman Catholic, but whether I am a Christian: "a follower of the Lamb." If God cursed the Jews who refused to wear the name which He gave them, what, think you, will be the destiny of those who wear the names of men in preference to the name of His Son?

"But," says Brother Methodist, "there is nothing in a name!" If not, why do you wear the name Methodist in preference to the name Baptist, or Presbyterian, or Roman Catholic, or Infidel, or Mormon, or Know-Nothing, or Beelzebub?

We can harmonize on the name Christian, for it expresses our highest conception of what every man desires to be, but we can never unite on any human name. If a man is a Christian, why should he hide his light under a bushel of human titles or names? Let him look to Christ. He "leadeth them out;" out of fog, doubt, ignorance, into the light of life!

IX. *The primitive Churches or congregations had but one system of government* "And he gave some, apostles; and some, prophets; and some, evangelists; and some, pastors and teachers; for the perfecting of the saints, for the work of the ministry, for the edifying of the body of Christ" (Eph., 4:11, 12). The apostles and prophets had no successors. The Bishops, Pastors, Elders or Overseers, had no jurisdiction outside of the congregations to which they belonged. Peter informs us that they were required to "feed the flock of God" (I. Pet., 5:1, 2). The deacons were servants of the Church (Acts, 6:1-5; I. Tim., 3:8-13). The evangelists were the public proclaimers of the word of life (II. Tim., 4:5). An instituition having any other system of Church organization or government is not apostolic. The Scriptures do not say anything about Popes, Archbishops, Presiding Elders ,Class Leaders, Rt. Reverends or Doctors of Divinity, nor of Bishops possessing the authority now claimed by officials of that name among Methodists, Episcopalians and Roman Catholics.

X. *The members of the Churches of Christ in primitive times, assembled regularly on the "first day of the week" to "break bread;" to remember the Lord in the institution which he ordained:* "Not forsaking the assembling of ourselves together, as the manner of some is, but exhorting one another, and so much the more as ye see the day approaching" (Heb., 10:25). "And upon the first day of the week, when the disciples came together to break bread, Paul preached unto them" (Acts, 20:7). That weekly communion was the custom in ancient times is sustained by the testimony of history and the acknowledgments of the leading orders represented in this convention. An institution, however pure in teaching, which fails in this particular, is not apostolic. Do the denominations represented in the speeches made before this convention, with all their pretensions to "apostolic succession," and purity of doctrine, respect the example of the first followers of the Lord Jesus Christ?

XI. *The primitive Christians had but one bond of union, faith in Christ and obedience to his law; one tie of affiliation, love to God and one another; one mission, the conversion of the world to Christ; one destiny, the everlasting city of our God.* Lift up your eyes and survey the religious field. Every religious order in Christendom has a system or doctrine peculiar to itself. Whatever is taught and held sacred by one is immediately denied by another. I hope I shall not be misunderstood. I am not endeavoring to unchristianize any one. I am simply applying the invincible "logic of facts" to sectarians and sectarianism. Whatever truth any man holds and practices, I endorse and practice, too. I am trying to show the God-loving and God-fearing of all religious orders, that there is a foundation on which we can unite without sacrificing truth or conscience. Christ made the triumphs of His cause dependent upon the efforts of His people. There are efforts, but they are in a great measure failures, because professing people are exhausting their means in fighting among themselves, while attempting to evangelize the world. This is contrary to the spirit of Christianity, and it can not succeed.

"But," says Brother Presbyterian, "we can not all see the same way." If not, why did Jesus pray for it, and compare it with the oneness which subsists between the Father and Himself? Why did He establish but one Church and why did the apostles consecrate their lives to this work? In what way is this unity to be produced? Not by formulating a new creed, for they have long since proven themselves to be insufficient. Not by justifying divisions, for this would be sinful. Not by a new revelation, for the one we have is universally acknowledged to be sufficient, as a rule of faith and practice. Not by adopting what is known in modern times as "liberal Christianity," for this would be an insult to the wisdom of our King. Not by forsaking the plain ordinances of the gospel, for this would pave the way to the abandonment of the entire system. Not by attempting to justify ourselves in following the dictates of our imaginations, for this would imply that opinion is equal to revelation. Not by agreeing to disagree; for this would imply that we are unwilling to concede the wisdom of that for which our Redeemer prayed, and for which His apostles labored. Not by giving up the Bible altogether, for this would involve the destruction of our brightest hopes. Not by casting our lot with the Church of Rome, for this would involve the endorsement of a system which is unknown to the New Testament. Not by forsaking the right of private investigation, for this would be disobedience to the command of Jesus: "Search the scriptures" (John, 5:39). Not by interpreting the Bible so as to make it appear to favor our opinions, for this would be treason. Not by bending the word of God to our professions, for this would encourage the introduction of new creeds and sects. Not by expecting the Holy Spirit to guide us independently of the Word of God, for this world deny its authority and concede that sectarianism is encouraged by the great Head of the Church. Not by folding our hands and waiting for the Lord to come, for "woe to them which are at ease in Zion." What then must be done? Simply abandon sectarianism and go back to original ground. There was but one foundation in the olden time: "Thou art the Christ, the Son of the living God" (Matt., 16:16). There was but one Church, the Church of God, of Christ (Rom., 16:16; I. Cor., 1:2). The Church had but one head, Jesus the Christ (Col., 1:18). There was but one beginning place, Jerusalem (Acts, 1:8). There was but one law of admission into the Church, the gospel of Christ (Rom., 1:16). There was but one Spirit, the Spirit of truth (John, 14:17). There was a divinely given name by which the followers of Christ were known; the name of Christ (Acts, 11:26). There was but one hope, the hope of everlasting life (Rom., 8:24). There was but one Lord, the King of kings, and the Lord of lords (Eph., 4:5). There was but one faith, trust in God through the Son of His love (Heb., 11:1). There was but one baptism, immersion (Rom., 6:1-4; Eph., 4:5). There was recognized but one God, the Father of our Lord Jesus Christ (Eph., 4:6). There was but one bond of union, the authority of Jesus Christ (Matt., 28:16-20). There was but one destiny for the people of God, the everlasting kingdom of our Lord and Saviour Jesus Christ (II. Peter, 1:11). The early Christians labored together in peace and with constant success. They were "fitly framed together;" builded together for a habitation of God through the Spirit; "joined together and compacted" (Eph., 2:19-22; 4:15, 16). The world could not stand before the united Church of the early ages. The opposition of the Jews and Romans melted away before it as the snow dissolves before the rays of the morning sun. They did not waste their time, talent, energies and money in fighting among themselves or in chasing imaginary enemies. In obedience to the command of Jesus they "went everywhere preaching the word." We can harmonize on the same principles, labor in the same cause, and enjoy the same results. No opposition will be sufficiently strong to confuse our triumphant army. Before our undivided host, infidelity in all its forms will bow its head in shame and disappear forever. Divided as we are, we can never successfully combat it, but united as Jesus demands, it will die of its own accord. Divided as we are, we can never convert the world, but united as the early Christians were, our victory will be sure. Of one thing I am fully satisfied, we can never have Christian union without Church oneness!

When I survey this convention, its talents, its divisions, its creds, I am amazed. There are divisions, but thanks to our heavenly Father, there is an unfailing remedy. We can give up everything for Christ. We can substitute faith for speculation, love for variance, and devotion for formalism. We can find and walk in the "old paths." We can live for Christ and the publication of the pure gospel. Nothing short of "one body," "one spirit," "one hope," "one Lord," "one faith," "one baptism," "one God and Father," and one name, will settle us on the old foundation. The signs of the times are full of encouragement, for sectarianism is slowly but surely dying. The Lord is preparing His army for the coming triumph. I unfurl His banner today. Upon its shining folds are written letters of fire: "THE BIBLE, AND THE BIBLE ALONE." Good men everywhere are rallying to this infallible standard, and as the light rolls in beauty across the storm, I catch the inspiration and shout: "On to victory!"

Our union will be the herald of the brighter day. Missionary work, home and foreign, will be increased a thousand fold. The "glad tidings" of peace will flow like a gentle river to "earth's remotest bounds." The race will accept Jesus Christ as its last and greatest hope. Darkness will flee away into "uncreated night," and the "millennial trumpet" will announce the universal brotherhood of man. Asia, for centuries under the reign of heathen darkness, will shake off its slumber and proclaim in triumphant tones: "There is no king but Jesus!" Africa, long under the reign of an unbroken night, will break its chains and respond: "Glory to God in the highest!" Europe, long under the reign of formalism, will awake and say: "Allelulia, for the Lord omnipotent reigneth!" America, "the land of the free and the home of the brave," long under the reign of sectarianism, will rise to see the better day, and shout as it rises: "Glory, honor and power to Him that sitteth upon the throne and unto the lamb forever!' The far-off isles of the sea will join the chorus of "Peace on earth and good will to men," and the angels around the eternal throne will take up the immortal strain and shout it back to earth again, and the universe will be thrilled with unusual joy.

> "Party names then lay aside,
>   And cast away your broken cistern;
> Christ the Lamb, the Church, the Bride;
>   Then take no other name but Christian.

> "Brides, they take the husband's name;
>   Nor would he sanction any other;
> Why should we not do the same?
>   What do you say, contending brother?"

CHAPTER XXIII.

PEACEMAKER

"Glorious things are spoken of thee, O city of God" (Ps., 87:3).

"Walk about Zion, and go around about her: tell the towers thereof. Mark ye well her bulwarks, consider her palaces, that ye may tell it to the generation following" (Ps., 48:12, 13).

"For out of Zion shall go forth the law, and the word of the Lord from Jerusalem" (Isa., 2:3).

"Thou art Peter, and upon this rock I will build my church; and the gates of hell shall not prevail against it" (Matt., 16:18).

"The church which was at Jerusalem" (Acts, 8:1).

"Jerusalem which is above is free, which is the mother of us all" (Gal., 4:26).

"They shall ask the way to Zion, with their faces thitherward, saying, Come, and let us join ourselves to the Lord in a perpetual covenant that shall not be forgotten" (Jer., 50:5).

"And the ransomed of the Lord shall return and come to Zion with songs and everlasting joy upon their heads: they shall obtain joy and gladness, and sorrow and sighing shall flee away" (Isa., 35:10).

It is absolutely impossible to overestimate the importance of beginning at the right place and in the right way. The surveyor must find the *beginning corner* before he can make a survey. The child must learn the twenty-six letters of the alphabet before it can go to college and study the higher branches. We must find the beginning *place* and *time* of the "dispensation of grace" before we can understand the demands of Jesus Christ. Where did the gospel, in fact, begin? When did the Church of Christ assume an organic form? When did Christ inaugurate His reign on earth? These are interesting questions, and I propose to answer them in the light of divine truth. My answer to them will contradict some of the theories advanced during this convention, but I ask for my arguments a calm and impartial examination. If they are based upon the truth, no opposition will be sufficient to crush them. If they are not, they will come to nought (Acts, 5:33-39). The Church of Christ is presented to us in different places in the New Testament, under various descriptive terms. It is called a testament, or covenant (Heb., 8:1-13). It is called the Church of God (I. Cor., 1:2). It is called the Church of the first born (Heb., 12:23). It is called one body (Rom., 12:4, 5; Eph., 4:4). It is called *one new* man (Eph., 2:15). It is called the kingdom of heaven (Matt., 3:2). It is called the kingdom of God (John, 3:5). It is called the kingdom of God's dear Son (Col., 1:13). It is called a fold (John, 10:16). It is called the household of God (Eph., 2:19). It is called the habitation of God (Eph., 2:22). It is called the household of faith (Gal., 6:10). It is called the temple of God (I. Cor., 3:16). It is called the pillar and support of the truth (I. Tim., 3:45). It is called the house of Christ (Heb., 3:6). It is called the new and the living way (Heb., 10:20). It is never called the Methodist Church, Baptist Church, Presbyterian Church, Episcopal Church, Lutheran Church, Roman Catholic Church, or Church of the Latter Day Saints.

It is evident from the testimony of both the Old and New Testaments that the Church was not established immediately after first disobedience. The plan of salvation was gradually unfolded from man's banishment from the garden of Eden to the cross of our Lord Jesus Christ; thence to the day of Pentecost at Jerusalem. Jesus taught this in His parables: "For the earth bringeth forth fruit of herself, first the blade, then the ear, after that the full corn in the ear" (Mark, 4:28). "And he said, Whereunto shall we liken the kingdom of God? or with what comparison shall we compare it? It is like a grain of mustard seed, which, when it is sown in the earth, is less than all the seeds that be in the earth; but when it is sown, it groweth up, and becometh greater than all herbs, and shooteth out great branches; so that the fowls of the air may lodge under the shadow of it" (Mark, 4:30-32). God revealed His will as man was able to understand and obey it. I find several departments in the gradual development of the scheme of redemption, under each of which man was held responsible for the performance of such duties as were made binding upon him. Duties increased with the light, until he became able to understand the fullness of the gospel. We have

I. *The Gospel in Purpose.* "According to the eternal purpose which he purposed in Christ Jesus our Lord" (Eph., 3:11). This purpose looked down the ages to the "better testament," the authority of Christ in heaven and earth and the salvation of men through His name.

II. *The Gospel in Intimation and Promise.* The first intimation of redemption was embraced in the sentence which the Lord pronounced upon Satan: "I will put enmity between thee and the woman, and between thy seed and her seed; it shall bruise thy head, and thou shalt bruise his heel" (Gen., 3:14, 15). An apostle informs us that "the Son of God was manifested to destroy the works of the devil" (I. John, 3:8). The same idea was subsequently embodied in the promise made to Abraham, afterwards renewed to Isaac, then to Jacob (Gen., 12:1-3; 26:1-5; 28:10-14). Paul says: "Now to Abraham and his seed were the promises made. He saith not, And to seeds, as of many; but as of one, And to thy seed, which is Christ" (Gal., 3:16).

III. *The Gospel in Prophecy.* This includes a long period of time. Hear Jacob: "The sceptre shall not depart from Judah, nor a lawgiver from between his feet, until Shiloh come; and unto him shall the gathering of the people be" (Gen., 49:10). This was entirely prophetic. Paul says: "It is evident that our Lord sprang out of Judah" (Heb., 7:14). Hear Peter: "Of which salvation the prophets' have inquired and searched diligently, who prophesied of the grace that should come unto you; searching what, or what manner of time the Spirit of Christ which was in them did signify, when it testified beforehand the sufferings of

Christ, and the glory that should follow" (I. Pet., 1:10, 11).

IV. *The Gospel in Preparation.* This department embraces the period of time from the beginning of John's work to the day of Pentecost. You can not grasp the great truths of the gospel without comprehending the mighty principles embraced in this proposition. Now, in order to bring the matter fully before you, I will be very speciffc: (1) The mission of John. There are some things which John did, and some things he did not and could not do. Let us look at the things recorded concerning him. The prophets of the Lord had predicted his coming. They saw the necessity for his reformation in the almost helpless condition of their countrymen. Hear Isaiah: "The voice of him that crieth in the wilderness, Prepare ye the way of the Lord, make straight in the desert a highway for our God. Every valley shall be exalted, and every mountain and hill shall be made low; and the crooked shall be made straight, and the rough places plain; and the glory of God shall be revealed, and all flesh shall see it together, for the mouth of the Lord hath spoken it" (Isa., 40:3-5). Hear Malachi: "Behold I will send my messenger, and he shall prepare the way before me; and the Lord, whom ye seek, shall suddenly come to his temple, even the messenger of the covenant, whom ye delight in: behold he shall come saith the Lord of hosts" (Mal., 3:1). Again: "Behold, I will send you Elijah the prophet before the coming of the great and dreadful day of the Lord; and he shall turn the heart of the fathers to the children, and the heart of the children to their fathers, lest I come and smite the earth with a curse" (Mal., 4:5, 6). Hear the New Testament concerning John: "And he shall go before him in the spirit and power of Elias, to turn the hearts of the fathers to their children, and the disobedient to the wisdom of the just; to make ready a people prepared for the Lord" (Luke, 1:17). John the Baptist was "sent from God," as a messenger to His people; the children of Israel (John, 1:6). Take a view of the history of these people from Solomon's apostasy, down the ages through the kingdoms of Israel and Judah, and their history is the history of continual apostasy. They forgot God. They departed from the law of Moses, their schoolmaster (Gal., 3:24). Hence they were not ready for the messenger of "the covenant" to come to His people, and it was necessary for the voice to "cry in the wilderness" for the people to prepare for the coming Lord. It is a notable fact that John came in the "spirit and power of Elijah?" What was the spirit of Elijah? Manifestly the spirit of a reformer. His countrymen had departed from the law of Moses. Idolatry held high carnival over the crumbling remains of the altar of God. The nation had descended into the lowest depths of degradation and shame. Elijah's voice broke the silence and stirred the conscience of the people. He was the most distinguished reformer of his generation (I. Kings, 17:1-24; 18:1-46). He inaugurated no new covenant. He proclaimed no new law. He simply called the people back to their covenant with God, and "repaired the altar of the Lord that was broken down" (I. Kings, 18:30). John found the people in a similar condition. He was a reformer. He, like Elijah, lived and died under the law of Moses. John was the harbinger of Jesus Christ. He introduced Jesus to the people of Israel, saying: "Behold the Lamb of God, which taketh away the sin of the world" (John, 1:29). Immediately John's sun began to decline (John, 3:27-30), indeed, his work was done. The word of God is clear in reference to John, and it may all be summed up in the brief sentence: "Prepare ye the way of the Lord." It is well for you to note that during the life of John, the law of Moses was in full force, and that he did not attempt to inaugurate a new institution, but he called the Jews back to their Law, their Lord, and their King! (2) The mission of Jesus Christ. He was sent by His Father to do His will (John, 17:18). Hear His own words: "Thy will be done" (Matt., 6:10). "I am come in my Father's name" (John, 5:43). These passages indicate the design of His mission. Follow Him through His earth-life, even down to the last, and the great burden upon His great and loving heart was: "Nevertheless, not my will, but thine, be done" (Luke, 22:42). His personal ministry was limited. Do you ask for proof? Hear His own words: "I am not sent but unto the lost sheep of the house of Israel" (Matt., 15:24). (3) The work of the apostles under the first commission (Matt., 10:1-7). Their work may be summed up in a few sentences. It was confined to "the lost sheep of the house of Israel." They were simply and only to announce that the kingdom of heaven was at hand. After this, when the powers of darkness were gathering about the Lord, He charged His disciples to keep His divinity a secret (Matt., 16:20)! Do you call this a full and complete gospel? If so, on what ground? It is safe to affirm that during this period the apostles of Jesus, His most intimate friends, did not understand His doctrine or the design and scope of His approaching reign. The resurrection of the dead is the foundation on which everything must rest. If the dead rise not, Jesus did not rise; if He did not rise the apostles were false teachers, the disciples believed a lie and the "dead in Christ" have perished (I. Cor., 15:1-21). Yet the apostles, while carrying out their first commission, did not know "what the rising from the dead should mean" (Mark, 9:1-10). They "disputed among themselves, who should be the greatest" (Mark, 9:34). They did not believe that Jesus would rise from the dead, and the reports to that effect after His resurrection "seemed to them as idle tales, and they believed them not" (Luke, 24:11). Thomas declared: "Except I shall see in his hands the print of the nails, and put my finger into the print of the nails, and thrust my hand into his side, I will not believe" (John, 20:24, 25). He was with "the twelve" after the resurrection forty days (Acts, 1:3). Notwithstanding His instructions, they were still ignorant, and just before He departed they asked Him to restore again the kingdom of Israel (Acts, 1:6). Where is the man who will risk his reputation as a scholar on the affirmation that these men understood their mission, and that they were competent to preach the gospel in its fullness? Where is the man who will affirm that during this period the followers of Jesus did not expect Him to enter Jerusalem and reestablish the throne of David, or that the apostles had any higher conception of their work than the occupancy of exalted positions in the new government. If any man is disposed to doubt this argument, let him consider: (a) Their spiritual condition (Luke, 9:54, 55). (b) They tried by force to make him a king (John, 6:15). (c) His entrance into Jerusalem (Mark, 11:1-11). (d) The necessity for the coming of the Holy Spirit upon them (John, 14:26; Acts, 1:8).

V. *The Gospel in its Fullness.* The promise of redemption embraced "all families of the earth" (Gen., 12:1-3). But the promise could not be fulfilled until Jesus broke down the middle wall of partition and abolished the law of Moses by nailing it to His cross (Eph., 2:14-16; Col., 2:14-17). After the resurrection of Jesus and just before His ascension, He gave the apostles a world-wide and age-lasting commission. I challenge the world to produce any law or commission before this that comprehends all nations and all ages. We can not go back of this commission and find the way of salvation fully revealed. We can not appeal from it, for it is the highest court in the revelation of God to man. This commission embraced in brief all that came before it. It is the accumulated and concentrated wisdom and power of forty centuries. It is fire from the burning altar of God. It is the final, the culminating message of Jesus the Christ to the perishing race. Behold the circumstances under which it was given. Give wings to thy imagination. Stand with Jesus and His apostles upon the sacred mountain in the land of His nativity. The hour for His departure has come. The pain of separation shows itself in every face. There is silence on earth. Hark! The same voice that awoke sleeping Lazarus and stilled the turbulent waves of the sea, sounds again. See Him move His hand! He draws the veil that enwraps the unborn ages; see the mighty hosts of men pass in solemn review before Him! There is silence in Heaven. Angels, cherubim and seraphim, crowd toward the gates of the city, and to the tops of its turrets, and towers, and battlements. In heaven all eyes are turned toward earth; on earth all eyes are turned toward heaven. The universe with its innumerable hosts, stops to listen. The chariot of fire, drawn by fleet-footed steeds, rolls down the sky. The time has come to say farewell. Listen, oh ye saints. Listen, oh ye dying sinners. Listen, oh ye angels of God. But He is going, listen to His farewell: "All power is given unto me in heaven and in earth: Go ye therefore, and teach all nations, baptizing them in the name of the Father, and of the Son, of the Holy Spirit: teaching them to observe all things whatsoever I have commanded you: and, lo, I am with you alway, even unto the end of the world" (Matt., 28:18-20). "And He said unto them: Go ye into all the world and preach the gospel to every creature. He that believeth and is baptized shall be saved; but he that believeth not shall be damned" (Mark, 16:15, 16). "Thus it is written, and thus it behooved Christ to suffer, and to rise from the dead the third day: and that repentance and remission of sins should be preached in His name among all nations, beginning at Jerusalem, and ye are witnesses of these things, and, behold, I send the promise of my Father upon you: but tarry ye in the city of Jerusalem, until ye be endued with power from on high" (Luke, 24:46-49).

The sum of this commission is,"go teach," or "preach the gospel," "believeth," "repentance," "baptism," "remission of sins, beginning at Jerusalem." It will be observed that this is all based upon the death of Christ and His authority. The development of this commission, under the apostles, embraces the law of remission for all men and all ages. This, to us, is very significant. It is the completion of God's plan to save. It is the "full corn in the ear" (Mark, 4:28). It is the "faith which was once," once for all time and all men, "delivered unto the saints" (Jude, 3). "The faith," the divine system of government, was delivered by Jesus Christ to the apostles, and they afterward unfolded it as the "Spirit gave them utterance" (Acts, 2:1-47). This is the law that Jeremiah predicted would be written in the hearts or minds of men (Jer., 31:31-34). It is the law that Isaiah and Micah predicted would go forth out of Zion (Isaiah, 2:2, 3; Micah, 4:1, 2). It is the law of which Isaiah said: "He shall not fail nor be discouraged, till he have set judgment in the earth: and the isles shall wait for his law" (Isaiah, 42:4). Paul calls it, "The law of the Spirit of life in Christ Jesus" (Rom., 8:2). James calls it "The perfect law of liberty" (Jas., 1:25).

Paul said: "I determined not to know anything among you, save Jesus Christ and him crucified" (I. Cor., 2:2). He also teaches that the gospel is the death, burial and resurrection of Christ (I. Cor., 15:1-5). The patriarchs and prophets believed in a coming Redeemer. No man ever announced authoritatively His death, burial and resurrenction, from the first disobedience to the day of Pentecost. If these propositions constitute the gospel, it was never preached in its fullness until that day. If a man prefers the "full corn in the ear" to "the blade," he must accept the injunction of Jesus to His disciples just before He left them, "tarry ye in the city of Jerusalem." That is to say, "walk about Zion, go around about her," and "mark well" the transactions of the first Pentecost after the ascension.

I will now turn to the leading feature of this investigation; the time and place of the establishment of the Church of Jesus Christ. "When Jesus came into the coasts of Cesarea Philippi, he asked his disciples, saying, Whom do men say that I, the Son of Man, am? And they said, Some say that thou art John the Baptist; some Elias; and others, Jeremias, or one of the prophets. He saith unto them, But whom say ye that I am? And Simon Peter answered and said Thou art the Christ, the Son of the living God. And Jesus answered and said unto him, Blessed art thou, Simon Bar-jona: for flesh and blood hath not revealed it unto thee, but my Father which is in heaven. And I say also unto thee, That thou art Peter, and upon this rock I will build my Church; and the gates of hell (hades) shall not prevail against it. And I will give unto thee the keys of the kingdom of heaven: and whatsoever thou shalt bind on earth shall be bound in heaven; and whatsoever thou shalt loose on earth shall be loosed in heaven" (Matt., 16:13-19). This interview is the foundation of my present discourse. It should be remembered that Jesus was on earth with His disciples. He desired to know what opinions were entertained by the people concerning Himself and His mission. Opinion said He was John the Baptist; opinion said He was Jeremias; opinion said He was Elias; opinion said He was one of the prophets. Peter said, by faith: "Thou art the Christ, the Son of the living God." Please observe the vast distinction between opinions and faith. On which foundation did Jesus build the Church, the opinions of men or the truth? Unquestionably upon the truth. Mark you, He said, "I will build." If the Church had been built before this time, is it not remarkably strange that He did not say "the Church was built in Abraham's day," or "John set up the Church in the wilderness," or "I have built my Church," or "I am building my Church?" What of the foundation on which this institution rests? Some people assert that it is built upon Peter, a mortal man. Let us see: "Thou art Peter, and upon this rock I will build my Church." "Thou," refers to the apostle. "This," refers to Christ, or the truth which Peter had just confessed. To settle this matter beyond doubt or controversy, I turn to the testimony of the prophet: "Therefore thus saith the Lord God, Behold I lay in Zion for a foundation a stone, a tried stone, a percious corner stone, a sure foundation; he that believeth shall not make haste" (Isa., 28:16). Paul and Peter refer to this stone and teach that it is Christ (Rom., 9:33; I. Pet., 2:5-8). If Peter were the foundation of the Church, he did not leave anything in his sermons or writings indicating that he knew it, for in every word he spoke, and in every line he wrote, the supreme authority of Christ is the leading idea. Paul settles the question, once for all, when he says: "For other foundation can no man lay than that is laid, which is Jesus Christ" (I. Cor., 3:11). The Church is not built upon human opinions, frail man or the prejudices of men, but alone on the divinity and Lordship of the Son of God. The prophet declared that the foundation laid in Zion would be a "tried stone." When was this done? What does it mean? Jesus said of this foundation, "the gates of hell (hades)—the unseen world—shall not prevail against it." Death was victorious in his conquests for over forty centuries. Now, if Jesus died and rose again, He demonstrated His supreme power over death and the grave. If He died and revived not, the "gates of hell" prevailed. He arose triumphantly. By this act the foundation stone was tried. There are conflicting opinions in reference to the time and place of the actual organization of the Church. It is asserted that the Church was organized in the days of Abel. If it can be shown by the word of God that the foundation was tried at this particular period in man's history, it will be admitted that the Church was then and there established. It is asserted by others that the Church of Christ dates from the partiarch Abraham, and that he was one of its first members. If the foundation were tried when God made a covenant with Abraham, it will be admitted that the Church of Christ was then and there established. It is asserted by others that John the Baptist organized the Church in the wilderness of Judea. If it can be shown from the testimony of John or any other messenger from God that the foundation was tried when John began to call the Jews to repentance, it will be admitted that the Church of Christ was there established. But who can show it? This is not a question of power, but of fact. The word of God is the only tribunal to which we may safely appeal. Jesus asserted that He was superior to death: "Therefore doth my Father love me, because I lay down my life that I may take it again. No man taketh it from me, but I lay it down of myself. I have power to lay it down and I have power to take it again" (John, 10:17, 18). Jesus was recognized by His Father when He was immersed by John in Jordan (Matt., 3:13-17); also upon the mount of transfiguration (Mark, 9:1-7). He went about doing good. God proved Him by "miracles, wonders and signs." He finished His earthly ministry. He was betrayed and denied. He made the "good confession" before Pontius Pilate. He was mocked, condemned and crucified. He died upon the cross, and His friends took His body down and buried it in the rock tomb in the garden. His disciples were disappointed and turned sorrowfully away. Their brightest hopes went down in tears and gloom when he dropped His head upon His blood-stained and heaving breast, and said: "It is finished." The grave, to the doubting disciple, enveloped everything, with no ray of light beyond it. All is disappointment. Not a friendly star rolled in view from the thunder's home to guide the weary pilgrims of earth. Not a word of hope came from the home beyond the river, to bring consolation to the broken-hearted. Not a being on earth could wipe away the falling tear, or say to the troubled spirit: "Peace, be still." Wicked men rejoiced, believing that the "gates of hell" were victorious. He rested in the grave until the dawn of the first day of the week. An angel descended from heaven and rolled back the mighty stone from the door of the sepulcher, saying by his radiant face: "Roll back, roll back, ye mighty clouds of sin, death and darkness, and let the conquering one arise." The earth trembled. The soldiers became as dead men. Death yielded up her prey. The "gates of hell" were overcome. Satan was vanquished—conquered—on his own battlefield. Life was purchased for a dying race!

Joy to the world, the Lord revived! Joy to the poor, for He brings them "unsearchable riches;" joy to the rich, for He teaches them to use their riches for His glory; joy to the suffering, for He whispers "Peace, be still;" joy to the thirsty, for the "water of life" flows in beauty from the summit of Calvary; joy to the hungry, for He brings them the "bread of life;" joy to the captives, for He offers liberty; joy to the dying, for He has abolished death and brought life and immortality to light through the gospel; joy to the homeless, for He promises an eternal home beyond the shadows; joy to the heathens, for the wilderness shall blossom as the rose; joy to the "desert places" in human life, for His love is as boundless as His mercy, and its crystal tides will flow on forever; joy to the whole earth, for the sun will never set on the advancing columns of His victorious army; joy to all nations, tribes and tongues, for the scheme finished by His resurrection is as deep as the stains of sin, as wide as the demands of our sinful condition, and as high as the eternal throne; joy to the angels of heaven, for they shall worship Him in the presence of the Father; joy to us, for He shall come again and bring an eternal benediction to those who love and serve Him!

The Christian foundation has stood the test. It is stronger than death, Satan or the grave. The claims of Jesus are now established. He is all that He claimed to be. Paul teaches that Christ was "declared to be the Son of God with power, according to the Spirit of holiness, by the resurrection from the dead" (Rom., 1:4). When he arose again He assumed "all power in heaven and in earth" (Matt., 28:18). After this event He said to John: "Fear not, I am the first and the last; I am he that liveth and was dead; and behold I am alive forevermore, Amen; and have the keys of hell and of death" (Rev., 1:17, 18). Jesus is the foundation of the Church. This foundation was tried when He arose from the dead. The foundation was laid in Zion, the city of Jerusalem. Wherever the foundation is laid the building must begin and go forward to completion. It would be a mistake, to say the least of it, to lay the foundation in Zion, which is Jerusalem, and erect the building on "the banks of the Jordan," in Rome, in London, in Oxford, or anywhere else. Jesus said: "I will build my Church." This was before His death. After His glorification, Luke says: "Great fear came upon all the Church" (Acts, 5:11). Jesus referred to the Church as something in the future. Luke spoke of it as an actual institution. Taking the Savior's promise and the testimony of Luke, we naturally conclude that the Church was established between the two given points. But where was the Church first built in fulfillment of the promise of Jesus? Let inspiration answer and mortal man be silent: "The Church which was at Jerusalem" (Acts, 8:1). If the Church were established in Jerusalem, it was not established in the days of Abel, Abraham or John the Baptist, nor in Rome, London, Oxford, Geneva or Wittenburg.

The scheme of redemption, as we have seen, was unfolded as man was able to comprehend it. God proceeded with reference to His will and man's condition. The beginning, time and place, was announced centuries before the advent of Christ. "It shall come to pass in the last days, that the mountain of the Lord's house shall be established in the top of the mountains, and shall be exalted above the hills; and all nations shall flow unto it. And many people shall go and say, Come ye, and let us go up to the mountain of the Lord, to the house of the God of Jacob: and he will teach us of his ways, and we will walk in his paths; for out of Zion (Zion is another name for Jerusalem) shall go forth the law, and the word of the Lord from Jerusalem" (Isa., 2:1-3; Mic., 4:1-3). This prediction was made by Isaiah 760 years before Christ. Micah repeated it 710 years before Christ. Hear David: "The Lord said unto my Lord, Sit thou at my right hand until I make thine enemies thy footstool. The Lord shall send the rod of thy strength out of Zion: rule thou in the midst of thine enemies" (Ps., 110:1, 2). Hear Zechariah: "And it shall be in that day, that living waters shall go out from Jerusalem; half of them toward the former sea, and half of them toward the hinder sea; in summer and winter it shall be, and the Lord shall be King over all the earth: in that day shall there be one Lord, and his name one" (Zech., 14:8, 9).

After Jesus arose from the dead He appeared unto His disciples frequently. Just before He ascended to the Father He gave them authority to "go into all the world and preach the gospel to every creature." One of the disciples who had every opportunity to see, hear and know, gives us the following report of what He did and said just before He departed: "Then opened he their understanding, that they might understand the Scriptures, and said unto them: Thus it is written, and thus it behooved Christ to suffer, and to rise from the dead the third day; and that repentance and remission of sins should be preached in his name among all nations, beginning at Jerusalem. And ye are witnesses of these things, and, behold, I send the promises of My Father upon you: but tarry ye in the city of Jerusalem, until ye be endued with power from on high" (Luke, 24:45-49). In obedience to His word they "returned to Jerusalem." Here Jesus marks Jerusalem as the "beginning corner." He commanded His apostles to remain in Jerusalem, promising to send the Holy Spirit to guide them; after which they were to testify of Him "in Jerusalem and in all Judea and in Samaria, and unto the uttermost parts of the earth" (Acts, 1:1-8). Peter, the apostle, recognized Jerusalem as the beginning of his official labors (Acts, 2:1-10; 11:15). Paul says: "Jerusalem which is above is free, which is the mother of us all" (Gal., 4:26). How many of the religious orders represented in this assembly acknowledge this? Again he says: "Ye are come unto Mount Sion (Jerusalem), and unto the city of the living God, the heavenly Jerusalem, and to an innumerable company of angels, to the general assembly and church of the first-born, which are written in heaven, and to God the Judge of all, and to the spirits of just men made perfect, and to Jesus, the mediator of the new covenant (testament), and to the blood of sprinkling, that speaketh better things than that of Abel" (Heb., 12:22-24).

"The fact that the day of Pentecost is the birthday of the Church has always been recognized."—*Lechler, in Lange's Com. on Acts,* 2:4, p. 53.

"The history of the distinctively *Christian Church* commences with the first great act of the risen and glorified Redeemer; the outpouring of the Holy Spirit on the day of Pentecost."—*Guericke's Ch. Hist.,* p. 43.

"The first of all the Christian Churches founded by the apostles was that of Jerusalem; and after the form and model of this, all the others of that age were constituted."—*Mosheim Ec. Hist., Harper's ed.,* 1 p. 46.

"On this day the new festival of Pentecost (the joyful, happy, and blessed kingdom of Christ, which is full of gladness, courage, and security) was founded."—*Lechler, in Lange's Com. on Acts, 2:4.*

"This book (Acts) is, therefore, a witness of apostolic doctrine and primitive Christianity; a rule and guide for the government, discipline, and the order of the Church; an army which furnishes the Church with weapons in its conflict with antichrist; a repository that offers a remedy for every soul- destroying disease engendered by errors in the faith and offences in the life and conduct of men; a storehouse which abundantly nourishes faith, patience and hope; a mirror and a stimulus, promoting love and its appropriate works; a treasury abounding in learning and sound doctrine."—*Starke, quoted in Lange's Acts, Int., p. 2.*

"This Church at Jerusalem was composed of those only who "gladly received the word and were baptized." Their *unity of spirit* was their *beauty of holiness*. This Church, so constituted, is the acknowledged pattern or model by which other Christian Churches were formed (I. Thess., 2:14), since the law was to go forth from Zion, and the word of the Lord from Jerusalem. This community of Christians was also the arbitrator in spiritual affairs during apostolic days, and must be allowed still to be the standard of doctrine and practice of every Christian Church, aided as it was by all the wisdom of inspired teachers; and particularly since no promise is found in the Scriptures allowing us to expect those extraordinary aids to qualify any man in forming any other Church than the New Testament presents. This Christian assembly, as it was the first, so is it the mother-church in the Christian dispensation."—*Orchard's Hist. Baptist, 1:6, 7.*

"That the heralds of Divine grace should begin at Jerusalem, was appointed both graciously and wisely; *graciously*, as it encouraged the greatest sinners to repent, when they saw that even the murderers of Christ were not excepted from mercy; and *wisely*, as hereby Christianity was more abundantly attested, the facts being published first on the very spot where they happened."—*Benson's Commentaries on Luke,* 24:47.

In the Book of Acts we see how the Church of Christ was formed and settled. * * * As far as any Church can show that it has followed this model, so far it is *holy* and *apostolic.* And when *all* churches or congregations of people, professing Christianity, shall be founded and regulated according to the *doctrines* and *discipline* laid down in the Book of Acts of the Apostles, then the *aggregate* body may be justly called *the* Holy *Apostolic and Catholic Church."—Adam Clark, Preface to Commentary on Acts.*

"'Beginning at Jerusalem.' This was the dwelling of His murderers, and it shows His readiness to forgive the vilest sinners. It was the holy place of the temple, the habitation of God, the place of the solemnities of the ancient dispensation, to which the Messiah came, and it was proper that pardon should first be proclaimed there." See Acts 2.—*Barnes' Notes on Luke,* 24:47.

Before proceeding further with my argument, allow me for a few moments to contrast the two institutions. It is only by contrast that the glory of the latter can be seen. Therefore I indulge the hope that you follow me honestly and criticise me unsparingly.

The Bible naturally divides itself into two distinct parts, the Old Testament and the New Testament. What is the difference betwen them? Is the New Testament a continuation of the Old Testament, or is it a new and separate institution? A Scriptural answer to these questions will help us to reach satisfactory conclusions in reference to our duty under the mediation of Christ and the authority of the apostles. Both Testaments came by Divine authority, and one is just as perfect as the other for the accomplishment of the purpose of the Lord. The moon is as perfect as the sun, yet it can not be denied that the sun is the source of light and heat. The Old Testament was limited in its application. It was intended for only a very small part of the world, Abraham and his descendants. If you will read the seventeenth chapter of Genesis, you will find a full description of the covenant and the people who are to receive and enjoy its blessings. Two classes of people were to participate in its privileges and honors. (1) Those who were born in Abraham's house. (2) Those who were bought with his money. You can not claim membership under either of these provisions; hence you can never become a member of the Abrahamic covenants. This institution was not developed until the days of Moses. Indeed, it extended from the promise made to Abraham unto the death of Christ. You have observed that God gave him two promises (Gen., 12:1-3). The development and fulfillment of the first included the Jews as a nation, the Levitical priesthood, and the most remarkable people in the world. The unfolding and accomplishment of the second embraces the gospel of Jesus Christ, or the good news of God manifested to all the world. The development of the first promise belonged to the administration of the law of Moses. The development of the second was "through the blood of the everlasting covenant;" in other words, the New Testament dedicated or sealed by the blood of Christ (Heb., 13:20). The old covenant was intended for one nation, the Jews (Gen., 17:1-13); the new covenant is intended for all nations and all ages (Matt., 28:18-20). The old covenant was dedicated by the blood of animals (Heb., 9:19); the gospel is sanctified by the precious blood of Christ, as of a lamb without blemish and without spot (I. Pet., 1:19). The old covenant was administered by a priesthood composed of frail men (Heb., 7:11); the new covenant is administered by the everlasting priest, Jesus the Christ (Heb., 7:28). The old covenant sacrifices were offered "year by year continually" (Heb., 10:1); the new covenant sacrifice was offered when Jesus gave Himself "a ransom for all" (I. Tim., 2:5, 6). Circumcision in the flesh and made by hands (Eph., 2:11) was the distinctive feature of the first covenant; circumcision in the heart and character are distinctive features of the second covenant (Rom., 2:29; Col., 2:11). The Bible answers all legitimate questions concerning our deliverance from the thraldom of sin. It is the word of God.

It separates God's methods of revealing Himself into the two Testaments, and you can not confound them unless you do it at your peril. It is a dangerous thing to interfere with the book of God, or to mix things which He has made distinct.

Looking backward to that which was accomplished through the old covenant or the law of Moses, the apostle Paul, with the gospel in his heart and the light of heaven shining around his path, made a number of delarations concerning the first covenant that ought to attract the attention of every man who desires to be saved: (1) The law was only a shadow of the good things to come: "Who serve unto the example and shadow of heavenly things, as Moses was admonished of God when he was about to make the tabernacle; for see, saith He, that thou make all things according to the pattern showed to thee in the mount" (Heb., 8:5). (2) It could not produce righteousness: "I do not frustrate the grace of God; for if righteousness come by the law, then Christ is dead in vain" (Gal., 2:21). (3) It could not produce perfection: "For the law made nothing perfect, but the bringing in of a better hope did; by the which we draw nigh unto God" (Heb., 7:19). (4) It could not produce life: "Is the law then against the promise of God? God forbid; if there had been a law given which could have given life, verily righteousness should have been by the law" (Gal., 3:21). (5) It could not give a good conscience: "Which was a figure for the time then present, in which were offered both gifts and sacrifices, that could not make him that did the service perfect, as pertaining to the conscience" (Heb., 9:9). (6) It could not justify the people: "By him all that believe are justified from all things, from which ye could not be justified by the law of Moses" (Acts, 13:39). (7) The law was ended when Christ died upon the cross: "For Christ is the end of the law for righteousness to every one that believeth" (Rom., 10:4). (8) It is abolished or done away: "But if the ministration of death, written and engraved in stones, was glorious, so that the children of Israel could not steadfastly behold the face of Moses for the glory of his countenance; which glory was to be done away; how shall not the ministration of the Spirit be rather glorious? For if the ministration of condemnation be glory, much more doth the ministration of righteousness exceed in glory. For even that which was made glorious had no glory in this respect, by reason of the glory that excelleth. For if that which was done away was glorious, much more that which remaineth is glorious" (II. Cor., 3:7-11). (9) It has been taken away: "He taketh away the first, that he may establish the second" (Heb., 10:9). (10) It was fulfilled by Jesus Christ: "I am not come to destroy, but to fulfill" (Matt., 5:17). (11) It was nailed to the cross: "Blotting out the handwriting of ordinances that was against us; which was contrary to us, and took it out of the way, nailing it to his cross" (Col., 2:14). (12) We are not under the law: "For sin shall not have dominion over you, for ye are not under the law but under grace" (Rom., 6:14). You can not seek for or obtain pardon under the law, for it is abolished. Therefore in your attempts to divide the word of truth, and find the beginning corner, you should make a careful discrimination between the law of Moses and the gospel of Christ.

What is the new testament or covenant? Where did it begin? What does it embrace? The Bible answers: "For finding fault with them, He saith, Behold, the days come, saith the Lord, when I shall make a new covenant with the house of Israel and with the house of Judah; not according to the covenant that I made with their fathers, in the day when I took them by the hand to lead them out of the land of Egypt; because they continued not in my covenant, and I regarded them not, saith the Lord. For this is the covenant that I will make with the house of Israel after those days, saith the Lord; I will put my laws into their mind and write them in their hearts; and I will be to them a God, and they shall be to me a people; and they shall not teach every man his neighbor and every man his brother, saying, Know the Lord: for all shall know me, from the least to the greatest.

For I will be merciful to their unrighteousness, and their sins and their iniquities will I remember no more. In that he saith, A new covenant, he hath made the first old. Now that which decayeth and waxeth old is ready to vanish away" (Jer., 31:31-34; Heb., 8:8-13). This is a significant passage. Observe: (1) That God found fault with the old covenant. (2) He declared that He would make another. (3) That it was to be unlike the old one. (4) That He would write His law in the minds and hearts of the people, and not upon tables of stone. (5) That all should know the Lord, from the least unto the greatest. (6) That sins should be forgiven, and therefore remembered no more. (7) The first covenant waxed old and passed away. If there is a doubt lingering in your minds in reference to the new covenant, this plain and comprehensive statement ought to destroy it forever: "But now hath he obtained a more excellent ministry, by how much also he is the mediator of a better covenant, which was established upon better promises" (Heb., 8:6).

Jesus Christ is the testator of the new testament, the apostles are the witnesses, and the patrimony is eternal life: "For where a testament is, there must also of necessity be the death of the testator. For a testament is of force after men are dead: otherwise it is of no strength at all while the testator liveth" (Heb., 9:16, 17). A testament is no more nor no less than a will. The New Testament is the will of Christ. No will or testament can be enforced before the death of the testator. Therefore, the new testament was not enforced during the natural life of Jesus. The cross of Jesus is the dividing line. The law of Moses was in full force until "the veil of the temple was rent in twain from top to bottom" (Mark, 15:38). Jesus Christ observed the law and commanded His disciples to do likewise (Matt., 23:1-3). During the three years of His ministry He was submitting the principles of His will to His chosen witnesses. When He died upon the cross He sealed forever the lessons He taught them. When did they bear witness to His life, works and words? Not until the day of Pentecost. It was impossible for them to begin before that time. The law began at Mount Sinai, and the gospel in the city of Jerusalem after Jesus went up on high (Ex., 20:1-17; Isa., 2:1-3).

The gospel of Christ is deeper, more positive and more extensive in its demands than the law of Moses was. Do you ask for proof? Here it is. The law of Moses said: "Thou shalt not take the name of the Lord thy God in vain" (Ex., 20:7). The New Testament says: "Let your communications be, Yea, yea; nay, nay; for whatsoever is more than these cometh of evil" (Matt., 5:37). The law of Moses said: "Thou shalt not kill" (Ex., 20:13). The New Testament says: "Whosoever hateth his brother is a murderer: and ye know that no murderer hath eternal life abiding in him" (I. John, 3:15). The law of Moses said: "Thou shalt not steal" (Ex., 20:15). The New Testament says: "Let him that stole steal no more; but rather let him labor, working with his hands the thing which is good, that he may have to give to him that needeth" (Eph., 4:28). The law of Moses said: "Thou shalt not bear false witness against thy neighbor" (Ex., 20:61). The New Testament says: "But speaking the truth in love, may grow up into him in all things, which is the head, even Christ" (Eph., 4:15). The law of Moses said: "Thou shalt not covet" (Ex., 20:17). The New Testament says: "Love worketh no ill to his neighbor, therefore love is the fulfilling of the law" (Rom., 13:10).

It is assumed by this convention that the Church was established before the day of Pentecost. Let us see:

1. If it were established before the death of Christ and the authoritative announcement of it on Pentecost, it was established under the law of Moses; *Jesus took away the first that He might establish the second* (Heb., 10:9). See Matt., 23:1-3; Rom., 1:4; Eph. 2:14, 15; Col., 2:14.

2. If it were established before the death of Christ and the authoritative announcement of it on Pentecost,

it was established before the foundation was *tried* (Isa., 28:16; I. Cor., 3:10, 11; Rev., 1:17, 18).

3. If it were established before the death of Christ and the authoritative announcement of it on Pentecost, it was established before the death of the testator, which is contrary to custom, law and reason (Heb., 9:15, 17).

4. If it were established before the death of Christ and the authoritative announcement of it on Pentecost, it was established under a limited commission (Matt., 10:2-7).

5. If it were established before the death of Christ and the authoritative announcement of it on Pentecost, it was established before the resurrection of the dead became a settled fact, and therefore before its members had any certain knowledge of the future life (Mark, 9:1-9; I. Cor., 15:12-19).

6. If it were established before the death of Christ and the authoritative announcement of it on Pentecost, it was established before the atonement (Matt., 20:28; 26:28; John, 10:11; Rom., 5:8-11; I. Cor., 6:20; Heb., 9:12).

7. If it were established before the death of Christ and the authoritative announcement of it on Pentecost, it was established before Jesus became the head of the Church (Eph., 18:1-23; Col., 1:18).

8. If it were established before the death of Christ and the authoritative announcement of it on Pentecost, it was established before Jesus was recognized as King (John, 6:15; Acts, 2:36).

9. If it were established before the death of Christ and the authoritative announcement of it on Pentecost, it was established before the gift of the Holy Spirit, and was therefore a dead body (John, 7:38, 39; Jas., 2:26).

10. If it were established before the death of Christ and the authoritative announcement of it on Pentecost, it was established before Jesus became Priest, and therefore its members, having no Mediator, could not approach the Father (Heb., 7:28; 8:4).

11. If it were established before the death of Christ and the authoritative announcement of it on Pentecost, it was established before Jesus became the Intercessor (Heb., 7:25, 26).

12. If it were established before the death of Christ and the authoritative announcement of it on Pentecost, it was established before the Gospel could be preached in full, and it did not have any Cross in it (I. Cor., 15:1-4; Gal., 6:14).

13. If it were established before the death of Christ and the authoritative announcement of it on Pentecost, it was established before the completion of the Divine side of Redemption (John, 19:30).

14. If it were established before the death of Christ and the authoritative announcement of it on Pentecost, it was established before His friends understood and believed Him (Matt., 18:1-3; Mark, 9:31, 32; Luke, 24:11; John, 20:24, 25).

15. If it were established before the death of Christ and the authoritative announcement of it on Pentecost, it was established before they were at liberty to proclaim Christ (Matt., 16:20).

Beginning with the first flickering uncertain ray of hope that fell athwart the crumbling walls of Eden lost, we have traced its unfolding through the majestic march of forty centuries, listening as we advance to the heartrending wail of the dying sinner, the triumphant acclaim of the dying saint, the joyous notes of prophet's lyre ringing in harmony with the higher hopes of man, until at last, upon Golgotha's rugged heights, the cross, with its arms outstretched to embrace the world, the dying Saviour burst upon our enraptured vision!

Calvary passed, on to Pentecost! The first Pentecost after the ascension of Jesus was the highest, brightest, grandest day in the world's history. All lines of history, past and present, converge there.

I. *It was the first time the disciples heard from Jesus after He bade them farewell at Bethany* (Luke, 24:45-53; Acts, 2:1-21). He was condemned as unworthy to live among men, and crucified by those whom He came to save. He told His disciples to tarry at Jerusalem. He wafted to them a farewell benediction, and appealed His cause to the righteous Judge on high. They returned to the place appointed and waited patiently for about a week. "When the day of Pentecost was fully come," they learned that Jesus had been received in heaven as the "mediator between God and man."

II. *The Holy Spirit came into the world to abide forever.* Jesus promised this comforter to His disciples before He left them (John, 16:7-11; Acts, 2:1-21). The Spirit's mission was two-fold: (1) He was to comfort the disciples during the absence of their Teacher and Friend. (2) He was to convict the world of sin, righteousness and judgment. They could not preach until the Holy Spirit brought to their remembrance the things spoken and commanded by the Lord (John, 14:26; I. Pet., 1:12).

III. *The prophecies of David, Isaiah, Micah, Joel and Zechariah were fulfilled* (Ps., 110:1-5; Isa., 2:1-3; Micah, 4:1-2; Joel, 2:28-32; Zech., 14:1-9; Acts, 2:1-41). Centuries before, these "holy men of God" had looked down the dusty pathway of time to the coronation of the Christ as the King of heaven and earth, and predicted the beginning and triumphs of His succeeding reign. If their predictions were not fulfilled on the day of Pentecost, they remain unfulfilled to this day.

IV. *The apostles, for the first time, used the keys of the Kingdom* (Matt., 16:19; 18:18, 19; John, 20:21-23; Acts, 2:1-41). They began on this day to unfold the Great Commission. Their words and actions were ratified in heaven. They spoke as Christ's representatives, and if we desire to know His will, we have only to appeal to the record. Every transaction in apostolic times corresponds with the facts, commandments and promises here submitted. Every religious transaction in this age which deviates from the teaching of Peter and his associates is wrong in proportion to its distance from what they taught.

V. *The first law of remission was proclaimed in the*

name of Jesus Christ. He had previously preached and worked in His Father's name (John, 5:43; Heb., 10:7). To the believing Jews, Peter said: "Repent and be baptized every one of you in the name of Jesus Christ for the remission of sins, and ye shall receive the gift of the Holy Spirit" (Acts, 2:38). Paul says: "Whatsoever ye do in word or deed, do all in the name of the Lord Jesus" (Col., 3:17).

VI. *The first additions were made to the Church.* Jesus said at Cesarea Philippi, "I will build my Church" (Matt., 16:13-19). After making this promise "he charged his disciples that they should tell no man that he was Jesus Christ" (Matt., 16:20). They could not make additions to the Church and keep this charge. In fact His apostles themselves did not understand the nature of His work until after His resurrection. All the while they expected Him to re-establish the throne of David in Jerusalem, and begin to reign over the Jewish people. Peter rebelled when informed that his Jesus would be slain (Matt., 16:21-23). After He arose again they desired Him to restore again the kingdom to Israel (Acts, 1:6). The Holy Spirit enlightened their minds; after which they understood their mission. The result of their first day's labor is summed up by Luke: "Then they that gladly received his word were baptized; and the same day there were added unto them about three thousand souls" (Acts, 2:41).

VII. *The law of remission of sins published at the beginning was to continue to the end of time* (Matt., 28:18-20; Acts, 2:1-41). The day of Pentecost was the introduction of the grandest era that ever dawned upon a sinful race; a day to be remembered by all generations. It is literally the fountain of pure Christianity. The record of it left for us is remarkable for its brevity, simplicity and comprehensiveness. The apostles waited until they received authority from on high. When it came they began to preach. It is worthy of observation that they did not discuss such questions as "hereditary total depravity," "effectual calling" or "final perseverance of the saints." The sermon was full of Christ from one end to the other. The following points are developed: (1) The introduction, consisting of a brief reference to the immediate surroundings and the prophecies that were then being fulfilled. (2) God sent His Son Jesus Christ into the world. (3) He proved Him by miracles, wonders and signs. (4) The Jews crucified and slew Him. (5) God raised Him from the dead. (6) The apostles were witnesses of these facts. (7) He is glorified in heaven. (8) The wonderful demonstrations which they beheld were from Him. (9) He is both Lord and Christ. (10) The people were cut to the heart and inquired what to do. (11) They were told what to do. (12) They did it and were saved; added to the Church. (13) There were no failures; not one went away seeking, inquiring, or mourning.

Thus the gospel began according to "the determinate counsel and foreknowledge of God," and thus it continued uncorrupted for many years. If men had continued to drink at the fountain instead of the corrupted stream, the sects represented in this convention would have been unknown to history. Not one of them can find its name in the Bible. Not one of them, excepting Roman Catholic, can trace its existence to history beyond the sixteenth century, and Roman Catholicism is as far from the Bible as heaven is from earth. The Church established in Jerusalem in the year 33 was universally recognized as "one body," all members of which entered into it the same way. There were different congregations in the land of Judea, but in the aggregate they constituted the body of Christ. They were united by truth and brotherly love. They had a single mission—the conversion of the world to Christ. I am in favor of going back to Jerusalem, and this means a return to apostolic Christianity in letter and spirit. How many of you are in favor of this? Are your faces turned toward Zion? Are you willing to abandon your creeds and walk in the "old paths?" Are you willing to be simply members of the Church of Christ —Christians? Are you willing to be guided by the Scriptures in faith and practice? Will you unite with me upon the "Bible and the Bible alone?" We need not formulate a new creed. We must go back beyond Rome, from whence came Roman Catholicism; back beyond London, from whence came Episcopalianism; back beyond Oxford, from whence came Methodism; back beyond Geneva, from whence came Calvinism; back beyond Wittenburg, from whence came Lutheranism; back beyond England, back beyond Scotland, from whence came Presbyterianism; back beyond America, from whence came Mormonism; *back*, BACK, BACK to the old foundation at Jerusalem: "Thou art the Christ, the Son of the living God!"

CHAPTER XXIV.

PEACEMAKER

"For it is not ye that speak but the Spirit of your Father which speaketh in you" (Matt., 10:20).

"It is the spirit that quickeneth; the flesh profiteth nothing; the words that I speak unto you, they are spirit, and they are life" (John, 6:63).

"But the natural man receiveth not the things of the Spirit of God; for they are foolishness unto him; neither can he know them, because they are spiritually discerned" (I. Cor., 2:14).

"Unto whom it was revealed, that not unto themselves, but unto us they did minister the things, which are now reported unto you by them that have preached the gospel unto you with the Holy Spirit sent down from heaven; which things the angels desire to look into" (I. Pet., 1:12).

Our friend, Inquirer, raised a question which must be clearly answered before we can even approximate the unity in heart and work which the New Testament requires, viz.: How does the Holy Spirit operate upon the hearts of men in order to their enlightenment and redemption? It is universally admitted among religious people that the Bible contains the grandest principles that ever demanded the attention of a sinful race; that it contains the only reliable history of man's origin, condition, duty and destiny; that it is the only revelation God has ever made to His rebellious creatures; that it spans all time, and rests upon eternity past and eternity to come; that it tells of man as he was in his primeval home in the delightful Eden, man as he is since the disobedience, and man as he will be when the probation of life is over; that it unfolds to the mind the gradual development of the plan of salvation, from the banishment of our ancestors to the crucifixion of Christ; that it shows how God dealt with Patriarchs and prophets under former dispensations; and how He deals with us under the "dispensation of grace;" that it is "profitable for teaching, for reproof, for correction, for instruction in righteousness;" that it thoroughly furnishes the Christian unto every good work. All the denominations represented in this convention unite in one grand and triumphant declaration that the word of God is sufficient in matters of faith and practice; yet we frequently hear them use such expressions as "apply the word," "send home to the word," "back the word," "render the word effectual," "Pentecostal showers," and "accompany the word," thus indicating that they believe that something in addition to the word of God is necessary to render it effectual. "What power," they sometimes inquire, "is there in the mere word? Can ink and paper awaken the dead sinner and give him spiritual life!" Jesus said: "It is the Spirit that quickeneth; the flesh profiteth nothing; the words which I speak unto you, they are the spirit and they are the life" (John, 6:63). The word of God certainly is not a "dead letter," and I suggest to my friends who use those expressions that the power is not simply in the "ink and paper," but in the Divine intelligence communicated in words adapted to the human understanding. When a man reads or hears the word of God, his Creator is literally addressing him. Glancing backward over the ages, taking the Bible as our telescope, we find to our satisfaction that God has embodied His will in human language under all dispensations, Patriarchal, Jewish and Christian, and I do not think that there is embraced in all the literature of all the centuries a single spiritual thought that is not traceable, either directly or indirectly, to this Divine source. It is to the spiritual universe what the sun is to the natural universe. If we are in darkness, it is our light-house. If we are weak, it is our strength. If we are ignorant, it is our instructor. If we are in trouble, it is our everlasting consolation. God has spoken to man by His own voice! through the holy prophets; His Son our Lord Jesus Christ; and finally the gospel was preached by the apostles "with the Holy Spirit sent down from heaven;" but every message has been presented in words; living, instructive, elevating, burning, everlasting words, and when the last book of the New Testament was written, He placed the seal upon it, and from that day forward no additional revelation has been made, and for all time to come men will be absolutely dependent upon the "Bible, and the Bible alone." It is perfect. It can not be improved. If men refuse to hear it they would refuse a messenger from the dead (Luke, 16:31).

Before Jesus ascended to the Father He promised His apostles that He would not leave them comfortless. He said: "Nevertheless I tell you the truth; it is expedient for you that I go away: for if I go not away, the Comforter will not come unto you; but if I depart, I will send him unto you, and when he is come, he will reprove (convict) the word of sin and of righteousness, and of judgment of sin, because they believe not on me; of righteousness, because I go to my Father, and ye see me no more; of judgment, because the prince of this world is judged" (John, 16:7-11). "But the Comforter, which is the Holy Spirit, whom the Father will send in my name, he shall teach you all things, and bring all things to your remembrance, whatsoever I have said unto you" (John, 14:26). "But when the Comforter is come, whom I will send unto you from the Father, even the Spirit of truth, which proceedeth from the Father, he shall testify of me, and ye shall bear witness, because ye have been with me from the beginning" (John, 15:26, 27). "If ye love me, keep my commandments, and I will pray the Father, and he shall give you another Comforter, that he may abide with you forever; even the Spirit of truth; whom the world can not receive, because it seeth him not, neither knoweth him; but ye know him; for he dwelleth with you and shall be in you. I will not leave you comfortless (orphans): I will come to you" (John, 14:15-18). "For it is not ye that speak, but the Spirit of your Father which speaketh in you" (Matt., 10:20). Luke describes the scene which followed the fulfillment of those promises in the following language: "And when the day of Pentecost was fully come, they were all with one accord in one place, and suddenly there came a sound from heaven as of a rushing mighty wind, and it filled all the house where they were sitting. And there appeared unto them cloven tongues like as of fire, and it sat upon each of them, and they were all filled with the Holy Spirit, and began to speak with other tongues, as the Spirit gave them utterance" (Acts, 2:1-4). No one who accepts the Bible as an inspired revelation will deny that God works in the hearts of men by the Holy Spirit; that He is to comfort the Church and convict the world. But the question arises: What means does He use, and how are His power and presence known? For example, will the Holy Spirit make the white man black, or the black man white? Evidently he will not. Will the Holy Spirit make the ignorant man wise, or enlighten the mind of the sinner? Unquestionably He will. If these statements are true, and they will not be denied, the Holy Spirit does not work upon the physical body, the "natural man," or the "heart of flesh," but upon the "inner man," the "hidden man of the heart." What is man? What are constitutional parts?

Man is a being in whom spirit and matter, heaven and earth, and time and eternity are associated. His body, "our earthly house of this tabernacle," comes from the earth, and to the bosom of the earth it must return. His spirit, "the immortal part," comes from God and to Him it must return (Ecc., 12:7; Heb., 12:9). "But," says Inquirer, "I should like to hear a little more Scripture bearing on the creation of man—his elementary parts." Well, to the Scriptures let us turn: "And the Lord God formed man of the dust of the ground, and breathed into his nostrils the breath of life, and man became a living soul" (Gen., 2:7). "Then shall the dust return to the earth as it was; and the spirit shall return unto God who gave it" (Ecc., 12:7). "For he that soweth to his flesh shall of the flesh reap corruption; but he that soweth to the Spirit shall of the Spirit reap life everlasting" (Gal., 6:8). "The flesh profiteth nothing" (John, 6:63). "If ye live after the flesh, ye shall die" (Rom., 8:13). "The natural man" (I. Cor., 2:14). The "outward man" and the "inward man" (II. Cor., 4:16). "The hidden man of the heart," "that which is not corruptible," a "meek and quiet spirit" (I. Pet., 3:4). "Reprobate minds," or "minds devoid of judgment" (Rom., 1:28). "Blinded the minds" (II. Cor., 4:4). "The pure in heart" (Matt., 5:8). "Pure in mind" (II. Peter, 3:1). "Our heart is enlarged" (II. Cor., 6:11). "To open their eyes, and to turn them from darkness to light, and from the power of Satan unto God" (Acts, 26:18). "The eyes of your understanding being enlightened" (Eph., 1:18). "With the heart man believeth unto righteousness" (Rom., 10:10). "So then with the mind I myself serve the law of God; but with the flesh the law of sin" (Rom., 7:25). These passages are sufficient to inform us in reference to our constituent elements, their condition in sin and their respective relations to the work of redemption. They indicate to an unerring certainty that the Spirit does not operate upon our natural bodies like heat, cold or electricity, but upon our minds; that the faculties of the "inner man" are enlightened and elevated. The feelings of the flesh are delusive. We can not decide by them whether we are influenced by the "spirit of truth" or the "spirit of error." A man may be honestly mistaken and still be happy, but if he is led by the words of the Spirit as they are presented to us in the New Testament, he can not be mistaken, neither can he fall into gloom and doubt. The work of redemption begins by planting the "story of the cross" in the heart, mind, and it is to be carried on until it subjugates the whole man to the will of God.

Jesus promised His disciples that the Holy Spirit, the Spirit of Truth, the Comforter, the Spirit of the Father, should come into the world and abide forever (John, 14:16). In the face of this undeniable testimony I hear people, who are doubtless sincere in doing so, pray to God to "send the Spirit from on high;" "pour out thy Spirit upon us;" "baptize us with the Holy Spirit and with fire;" or "send some means of thine own appointing to convert these sinners," or "come, dear Lord, and bless these mourners;" or affirm with confidence that men are saved by a "direct putting forth of the Spirit from the throne of God, or that "God saves men independently of the word." The entire mourner's bech," or "anxious seat" practice, so prevalent among Methodists and Baptists, especially in the less enlightened communities, is based upon the supposition that salvation is obtainable through other means than those ordained of God: faith in Christ through the words of the gospel; and obedience to His law. If God converts men by the words of the Spirit, the New Testament, the petitions and practices just described are wrong. If God converts the sinner independently of His word, it is absolutely a "dead letter." Did any man in this convention ever hear of the conversion of a sinner who had not, in some way become acquainted with the gospel of Christ? If God converts sinners independently of His word in this country, He will do it in all countries, and I should be glad to know why so many of the "evangelical denominations" send missionaries to preach the gospel in foreign lands—among the heathen. If He does the work here, He will do it there without the assistance of our feeble efforts. If there is a "direct putting forth of the Spirit," the work of the ministry is useless. The money we sepnd for books, tracts and religious newspapers, should be appropriated to something else. Human accountability is at an end if a sinner must wait for what is called God's "own good time." Says Brother Baptist: "A man must experience something in addition to the assurances of the mere word." Suppose we admit that this is true, by what standard is he to decide his acceptance? "He must feel it." Feelings are not reliable, for "the flesh profiteth nothing." He might experience too much or too little. Or he might experience the influence of "an evil spirit." The feelings which are supposed to result from the so-called conversion of many do not last. When the excitement is over the good feelings depart, and the person at once begins to doubt. We must "live by faith," making our trust in Christ translated into living deeds, with the promises of the gospel our assurance of everlasting life. The man who reads the Bible, meditates upon its precepts, obeys its commands, and lives in sight of the cross, will be "strong in the Lord and the power of his might," but the man who does not appreciate these means will be a moral weakling, to say the least of it. Bear in mind I do not deny that there is a Holy Spirit, nor that He is instrumental in the conversion of the world, but I do assert in all confidence that He operates through the word of God, and it alone. If this is true, it is indispensably necessary to send missionaries to respond to the "Macedonian cry." It is necessary to "preach the gospel to every creature." It is necessary to publish the truth through the instrumentality of books, tracts and newspapers. Most of my friends in this assembly virtually admit that this argument is correct, for when a revival is proposed among them, they endeavor to procure the most talented, eloquent and magnetic preacher attainable, thus indicating that they believe that there is power in the spoken word. When they buy books, papers or tracts, they get the best. "But," urges Brother Presbyterian, "the Spirit accompanies the word." Where is the chapter and verse in the Bible which says so? If the minister rehearses the words of Jesus, "they are spirit and they are life." If he preaches his opinions or uses such arguments as will excite rather than enlighten, there is no "spirit of truth" about them. Look at these additional facts: The spirit was to "speak," "teach," "testify," "comfort," "convict." In the second and third chapters of the Revelation, I find the following statement seven times: "He that hath an ear, let him hear what the Spirit saith unto the Churches." The last invitation in the New Testament is embraced in the following language: "And the Spirit and the bride say, Come. And let him that heareth say, Come. And let him that is athirst come. And whosoever will, let him take the water of life freely" (Rev., 22:17).

Many centuries have gone to dwell with the years beyond the flood since this invitation was given, but the Divine Spirit is still calling to the weary and disappointed ones of earth to come and drink at "the fountain free," drink and never thirst, obey and never die.

My next argument is based upon the fact that in the work of redemption, whatever is ascribed to the office work of the Holy Spirit is ascribed to the gospel: "That which is born of the flesh is flesh; and that which is born of the Spirit is spirit" (John, 3:6). "Seeing ye have purified your souls in obeying the truth through the Spirit unto unfeigned love of the brethren, see that ye love one another with a pure heart fervently; being born again, not of corruptible seed, but of incorruptible, by the word of God, which liveth and abideth forever" (I. Peter, 1:22, 23). "Elect according to the foreknowledge of God the Father, though sanctification of the Spirit, unto obedience and sprinkling of the blood of Jesus Christ" (I. Peter, 1:2). "But we are bound to give thanks always to God for you, brethren beloved of the Lord, because God hath from the beginning chosen you to salvation through sanctification of the Spirit and belief of the truth" (II. Thess., 2:13). "Sanctify them through thy truth: thy word is truth" (John, 17:17). "The Spirit of grace" (Heb., 10:29). "The word of his grace" (Acts, 20:32). "Quicken your mortal bodies by his Spirit that dwelleth in you" (Rom., 8:11). "My soul cleaveth unto the dust, quicken thou me according to thy word" (Ps., 119:25). "Thou gavest also thy good Spirit to instruct them, and withheldest not thy manna from their mouth, and gavest them water for their thirst" (Neh., 9:20). All Scripture is given by inspiration of God, and is profitable for doctrine, for reproof, for correction, for instruction in righteousness, that the man of God may be perfect, throughly furnished unto all good works" (II. Tim., 3:16, 17).

I glean the following from these quotations: Born of the word, born of the Spirit; sanctified through the Spirit, sanctified through the truth; the Spirit of grace, the word of grace; quickened by the Spirit, quickened by the word; instructed by the Spirit, instructed by the Scriptures.

Paul says: "For the preaching of the cross is to them

that perish, foolishness; but unto us which are saved it is the power of God" (I. Cor., 1:18). Please examine this passage carefully, especially the phrases "the preaching of the cross" and "the power of God." How could the apostle have made this statement if there is "an immediate power" or "putting forth the Spirit" in conversion? "For I determined not to know anything among you, save Jesus Christ, and him crucified" (I. Cor., 2:2). If there is a power to convert outside of "Jesus Christ and him crucified," the apostle was determined not to "know" it among the Corinthians. "But God forbid that I should glory, save in the cross of our Lord Jesus Christ, by whom the world is crucified unto me, and I unto the world" (Gal., 6:14). If the commonly accepted theory of spiritual influence is true, the apostle refused to glory in it. "For I am not ashamed of the gospel of Christ; for it is the power of God unto salvation to every one that believeth; to the Jew first, and also to the Greek" (Rom., 1:16). Observe, the apostle uses a definite article before the word gospel, and also before the word power. He does not say, "a power" or "some power," but *"the* power." He does not say anything about the gospel being a dead letter, or the necessity of the Spirit accompanying it in order to render it effectual. This argument is unmistakably plain. Hence I conclude that the same apostle spoke an important truth when he said: "The sword of the Spirit, which is the word of God" (Eph., 6:17).

Jesus said: "Behold, a sower went forth to sow; and when he sowed, some seeds fell by the wayside, and the fowls came and devoured them up; some fell upon stony places, where they had not much earth, and forthwith they sprung up because they had no deepness of earth, and when the sun was up, they were scorched, and because they had no root, they withered away; and some fell among thorns, and the thorns sprung up, and choked them: but others fell into good ground, and brought forth fruit, some a hundredfold, some sixtyfold, some thirtyfold. Who hath ears to hear, let him hear" (Matt., 13:3-9). The disciples did not understand this parable, hence the great Teacher explained it to them. (1) The sower is the Son of man, the Son of God (Matt., 13:37). (2) The field is the world, all mankind (Matt., 13:38). (3) The seed is the word of God, the glad tidings of Christ (Luke, 8:11). (4) The wayside represents persons who hear the word and understand it not. The devil, who understands the power of good seed, the word of God, comes and steals it out of their hearts, lest they should believe it and be saved (Luke, 8:12). (5) The stony ground represents a person who hears the word and receives it with joy: "Yet hath not root in himself but dureth for a while; for when tribulation or persecution ariseth because of the word, by and by he is offended" (Matt., 13:20, 21). (6) The thorny ground represents persons who receive the "seed of the kingdom," but failing to cultivate it, the cares of the world, the deceitfulness of riches, the allurements of sin, the dreams of ambition, choke it, overcome it, and it brings forth no perfect fruit (Mark, 4:18, 19). (7) The good ground represents persons who possess "good and honest hearts;" who hear the word of God and understand it, and bring forth fruit to perfection; some thirty, some sixty and some one hundred fold. There are six grades of people (character) in this parable; the bad, worse and worst; the good, better and best. It is shown here, in unmistakable simplicity, that in order to spiritual life, spiritual seed must be sown in the rich soil of a "good and honest heart;" not by some mysterious, supernatural or irresistible power, but by the persuasive proclamation of the cross; the death, burial and resurrection of Jesus Christ. Since creation's dawning, there is not an instance in all history where a tree or a cornstalk has grown to perfection without the planting and subsequent cultivation which nature has ordained, and since the inauguration of the gospel dispensation, there is no proof that any one has been converted in the absence of the words of eternal truth. Every one of the six characters in this parable received the seed, but only three of them produced perfect fruit. The first one permitted the devil to steal the word out of his heart. If he had obeyed the apostolic injunction: "Resist the devil" (Jas., 4:7), the result would have been different. The second one became offended because the word was not popular with his associates, and he could not endure their persecutions. The third one received the word, but he loved "this present world," and therefore neglected to attend to his spiritual and eternal interests. The three last received the word and cultivated it, and produced fruit according to talent. It is believed by many who are considered "orthodox Christians," that all men are "totally depraved;" that their minds strive against the influence of the Holy Spirit until they are overpowered and brought into submission. Now, if this is true, I affirm that, as God is omnipotent, every person to whom the Spirit comes will be converted, whether he is willing or not, and the "parable of the sower," the persuasion, conviction and conversion process is not applicable to the situation. Peter, the apostle, doubtless understood this, for he said: "Being born again, not of corruptible seed, but of incorruptible, by the word of God, which liveth and abideth forever. For all flesh is as grass, and all the glory of man as the flower of grass. The grass withereth, and the flower thereof falleth away; but the word of the Lord endureth forever, and this is the word which by the gospel is preached unto you" (I. Pet., 1:23-25). He teaches that spiritual growth is produced by the "sincere milk of the word," and using the means ordained of God he informs the brethren that they may become a "spiritual house," a "holy priesthood, to offer up spiritual sacrifices acceptable to God by Jesus Christ" (I. Pet., 2:1-5). John said: "Many other signs truly did Jesus in the presence of his disciples, which are not written in this book; but these are written, that ye might believe that Jesus is the Christ, the Son of God; and that believing ye might have life through his name" (John, 20:30, 31). For what purpose did John write? That men might believe that Jesus Christ is the Son of God, and believing, they may receive life through His name. Paul said: "For after that in the wisdom of God the world by wisdom knew not God, it pleased God by the foolishness of preaching to save them that believe" (I. Cor., 1:21). He does not say that it pleases God to save where there is no preaching. Jesus said: "Now ye are clean through the word which I have spoken unto you" (John, 15:3). Mark you, Brother Quaker, Jesus cleansed the hearts of His disciples through the spoken word! God said: "Is not my word like as a fire? saith the Lord; and like a hammer that breaketh the rock in pieces" (Jer., 23:29)? Is the sinner's heart filled with trash? Introduce the word of God and it will consume it. Is his heart hard like a rock? Introduce the word of God and it will break it in pieces. Jesus said: "Verily, verily, I say unto you, He that heareth my word and believeth on him that sent me, hath everlasting life, and shall not come into condemnation; but is passed from death unto life. Verily, verily, I say unto you, The hour is coming and now is, when the dead shall hear the voice of the Son of God; and they that hear shall live" (John, 5:24, 25). Is the sinner "dead in trespasses and sins?" Let him hear the word of God and he "shall live." James said: "Of his own will begat he us with the word of truth, that we should be a kind of first-fruits of his creatures. * * Wherefore lay apart all filthiness and superfluity of naughtness, and receive with meekness the engrafted word, which is able to save your souls" (Jas., 1:18-21). Is the sinner lost? Announce to him that the "engrafted word" is able to save his soul. Paul said: "For though ye have ten thousand instructors in Christ, yet have ye not many fathers: for in Christ Jesus I have begotten you through the gospel" (I. Cor., 4:15). The Corinthians were made believers through the gospel of Christ. Paul said: "So then faith cometh by hearing, and hearing by the word of God" (Rom., 10:17). Solomon said: "He that turneth away his ear from hearing the law, even his prayer shall be abomination" (Prov., 28:9). These passages exclude everything but the word of the Lord. All faith is based upon testimony. I am aware that some may say that believing evidence is merely a historical faith. There is one faith (Eph. 4:5), and it comes by hearing the gospel. All religion is based upon history, facts. Is there a man in this convention who knows or believes anything concerning Moses or Jesus Christ, which he did not get from the Bible? The Divine arrangement is fact, testimony, faith. Where there is no testimony there is no faith. Where testimony begins faith begins, and where testimony ends faith ends. A man's faith may fall below the full measure of the facts and testimony of the gospel, but it can never rise above it. To sustain these assertions beyond the possibility of doubt or contradiction. I appeal to the history of the work of the inspired apostles. There is not a single example given that even intimates that the work was done by supernatural agents, excepting as the Holy Spirit spoke through them, or in the absence of the second party, the preacher of the word: (1) The ambassadors of Jesus began their work in the city of Jerusalem. On the day of Pentecost they preached the gospel to the astonished Jews. They were cut to the heart, and inquired what to do. The apostles had a clear and well-defined plan by which to operate. They told them what to do. Result: "Then they that gladly received his word were baptized; and the same day there were added unto them about there thousand souls" (Acts, 2:1-41). (2) Peter and John went up into the temple at the hour of prayer. The lame man who was laid at the "Beautiful Gate" of the temple was healed. The people were astonished. They ran together in "Solomon's porch." Peter explained the power by which the miracle was performed, and rehearsed his argument delivered on the day of Pentecost. Result: "Howbeit may of them which heard the word believed; and the number of the men was about five thousand" (Acts, 4:4). (3) Stephen was a man of God; "full of faith and the Holy Spirit." He preached to the Jews in the city of Jerusalem. They resisted the Holy Spirit by stopping their ears and refusing to listen to his arguments. Their fathers had done this before them (Neh., 9:30). Result: They "cast him out of the city, and stoned him" (Acts, 7:1-60). Please contrast this with the record of the apostolic labor on the day of Pentecost. If there is a direct operation of the Holy Spirit, if God comes as many prayers seem to indicate, I do not think He could be resisted by stopping the ears. (4) Philip introduced the gospel in the city of Samaria. Results: "When they believed Philip preaching the things concerning the kingdom of God, and the name of Jesus Christ, they were baptized, both men and women" (Acts, 8:12). (5) The same evangelist preached Jesus to the Ethiopian officer. Result: They came to a "certain water," and the officer commanded the chariot to stand still: "and they went down both into the water, both Philip and the eunuch; and he baptized him, and when they were come up out of the water the Spirit of the Lord caught away Philip, that the eunuch saw him no more; and he went on his way rejoicing" (Acts, 8:38, 39). (6) Saul of Tarsus persecuted the Church of Christ. He procured authority from the high priest to bind its members and cast them into prison. On his way to Damascus the Lord called to him from heaven, saying: "Saul, Saul, why persecutest thou me?" He inquired what to do. The Lord directed him to go into the city, saying: "It shall be told thee what thou must do." He went. Annanias approached him. Result: "And immediately there fell from his eyes as it had been scales: and he received sight forthwith, and arose, and was baptized" (Acts, 9:18). (7) Cornelius, the centurion, was a devout man, and one who feared God, with all his house, and gave much alms to the people, and prayed to God always. He saw an angel in his house, which stood and said unto him, "Send men to Joppa, and call for Simon, whose surname is Peter, who shall tell thee the words whereby thou and all thy house shall be saved" (Acts 11:13, 14). They were saved by words. This is sustained by the testimony of the angel, the two servants and the soldier, Cornelius himself and the apostle Peter. Cornelius and his household were saved like all others, precisely as they were on the day of Pentecost. Peter preached Christ. The people heard, believed, repented, and were baptized. The outpouring of the Holy Spirit was accompanied by supernatural demonstrations which have not been repeated since the close of the apostolic age. These miraculous demonstrations were not conditions of salvation. If they had been they doubtless would have been repeated in all ages. If the Spirit is poured out in our day as on this household, men would be able to "speak with tongues," as they did. These manifestations were rather intended to convince Peter and the rest of the Jewish brethren, "That the Gentiles should be fellow heirs, and of the same body, and partakers of his promise in Christ by the gospel" (Eph., 3:6). The Holy Spirit did not come on this occasion in answer to prayer, and it is a notable fact that He fell on those who heard the word, and those alone. (8) Lydia was a worshipper of God. She heard Paul preach the gospel. God thereby opened her heart. Result: "She attended unto the things which were spoken of Paul," and "was baptized" (Acts, 16:14, 15). (9) Paul and Silas were in prison at Philippi for preaching the gospel and casting out evil spirits. At midnight they prayed and sang praises to God. The prisoners heard them. An earthquake shook the prison's foundation, opened its doors and loosed the bands of the prisoners. The jailer awoke and attempted to kill himself. Paul assured him that the prisoners had not escaped. He inquired what to do to be saved. Paul preached unto him the word of the Lord. Results: He and his believing household were baptized "the same hour of the night" (Acts, 16:25-34). (10) Paul preached at Athens, "in the midst of Mar's Hill. Result: "Certain men clave unto him, and believed" (Acts, 17:16-34). (11) He preached at Corinth. Result: "Crispus, the chief ruler of the synagogue, believed on the Lord with all his house; and many of the Corinthians hearing believed, and were baptized" (Acts, 18:8). (12) He preached in the city of Rome. Result: "Some believed the things which were spoken, and some believed not" (Acts, 28:16-24).

I now proceed to sum up my argument, and submit to you some transcendently important propositions. I challenge your attention and invite your investigation:

1. God has never in any age or any country, by patriarch, priest, prophet, or apostle, promised the Holy Spirit to any person in unbelief or disobedience.

2. The Bible furnishes no record of any person in any age who received the Holy Spirit in unbelief and disobedience.

3. The Bible does not furnish the record of any sinner being commanded in any age to pray for, or expect, the gift of the Holy Spirit.

4. The Bible furnishes no command to the Church to pray for the Holy Spirit to come upon a man in unbelief and disobedience.

5. The advocates of the abstract work of the Holy Spirit can not present one thought concerning redemption, and demonstrate it to be true, that can not be found in the Bible.

6. Every operation that comes within the domain of the human mind is inseparably, in some form, connected with language. Man can not act without thinking; he can not think without words. Let the man who denies it, bring the proof to the contrary.

7. If the Holy Spirit works independently of the words on the minds of sinners, and God is no respecter of persons, why are there no believers where missionaries have not gone?

8. In every example of conversion recorded in the book of Acts, the preacher was present and the gospel was preached.

9. If the Holy Spirit works independently of the word, how is the sinner to distinguish His work from the work of other spirits, seeing there are many spirits in the world (I. John, 4:1-3)?

10. Throughout the record, whatever is attributed to the word is also attributed to the Spirit. This proves that they work together in bringing men to Christ.

11. If the Holy Spirit works independently of the word, what is the use of preaching? Why is one preacher more successful than another?

12. If the Holy Spirit works independently of the word, on what are His operations dependent? If on

preaching, the theory falls to the ground. If not on preaching, the gospel falls to the ground.

13. If the Holy Spirit works independently of the word, how does He do it? If not through the eye or ear, how?

14. If the Holy Spirit works independently of the word, why is it that all are not converted who come under His power? Men can resist argument, appeal, exhortation, but naked Omnipotence, never!

15. If the Holy Spirit is not in the gospel, it is not of God, for the Holy Spirit is God. If He is in it, there is no need of additional power.

16. If the Holy Spirit works independently of the gospel, how can the gospel be the power of God unto salvation, as Paul affirms (Rom., 1:16)?

17. Throughout the New Testament the Holy Spirit is described as speaking; if He spoke then, why does He not speak now? When, where and under what circumstances did He stop speaking, and adopt another method?

18. I challenge this assembly to produce one individual who has been operated on by the Holy Spirit independently of the gospel, and demonstrate how it was done by the testimony of inspired men!

19. If the Holy Spirit works independenty of the word, how are we to explain the passages that teach that men are cleansed by the word, made alive by the word (John, 5:25; 15:3)?

20. If the Holy Spirit works independently of the word, how are we to explain the declaration that the preaching of the cross is the power of God (I. Cor., 1:21-24)?

21. If the Holy Spirit works independently of the word, why did Jesus Christ say that He would give the keys of the kingdom to the apostles (Matt., 16:17-19)? If the sinner is dead, and helpless, and the gospel as preached by the apostles will not bring him to life without the outside work of the Holy Spirit, He has the keys of the kingdom, and not the apostles!

22. If a man reads the New Testament, believes it, obeys it, lives up to its requirements, will he have the

Holy Spirit, will he be a Christian? If not, what use have we for it?

23. If the Holy Spirit works independently of the word, what necessity is there for printed Bibles, newspapers, tracts, books, preachers, missionaries?

24. The New Testament promises the gift of the Holy Spirit only to the obedient. If you deny it, produce a proof or example to the contrary.

25. If the Holy Spirit works independently of the word, what motive does He use? Man can not act in the right direction without a good motive. Can the Holy Spirit, by abstract operation, introduce any stronger motive than the Cross? Can He introduce a stronger motive than the love of God manifested in Christ? Are not the arguments, entreaties, exhortations and commands of the Holy Spirit given in the New Testament complete, perfect and all-sufficient? If not, point out what is lacking.

26. If the Holy Spirit works independently of the word, how are we to explain the great number of passages that plainly teach that redemption involves the human understanding (Luke, 24:45; Acts, 8:30; Eph., 1:18). The advocates of the direct work of the Holy Spirit teach and believe that His work and His operations can not be explained or understood. Human mind can only grasp, comprehend or understand that which comes in language.

27. If the Holy Spirit works independently of the word, what seed does He plant? Nothing can be produced without seed. This is true in the vegetable kingdom, the animal kingdom, and in the kingdom of Christ. If the Holy Spirit, by direct contact with the sinner's mind, plants different seed from that furnished in the gospel, the gospel falls to the ground. If He plants the same seed, the theory falls to the ground.

28. If the Holy Spirit works independently of the word, by whose authority does He do it? Jesus commanded the apostles to go and disciple all nations. They either could or could not do this. If they could do it through the aid of the Holy Spirit, there was no need of abstract operation. If they could not there was

no use of the apostles. Did the Holy Spirit, immediately after His descent, supersede the apostles? If not then, did He ever do it? If so, when? If He superseded the apostles, their work falls to the ground. If He co-operated with them, inspired their words, the theory of the direct work of the Holy Spirit falls to the ground. If one person, representing any age since the day of Pentecost, can be produced who was converted without the aid of what the apostles preached, the Great Commission forever falls to the dust. If one person can not be produced, the theory is forever false!

29. The Old Testament was a type of the New Testament (Heb., 10:1). If the Holy Spirit operates on the sinner's mind now in order to conversion, it must be shown that He operated without language before the coming of Christ. Let the advocates of miraculous conversion bring the proof, and bring it now!

30. If the Holy Spirit works on the sinner's mind in order to conversion, independently of the word, how are we begotten by the word or gospel (I. Cor., 4:15; James, 1:18; I. Pet., 1:23)?

31. If the Holy Spirit works on the sinner's mind in order to conversion, independently of the word, how are men to be saved by obeying the form of doctrine (Rom., 6:16-18), or how do men purify their souls in obeying the truth (I. Pet., 1:22)?

32. If the Holy Spirit works independently of the word in the redemption of men, in what sense were the apostles ambassadors of Christ (II. Cor., 5:17-21)? An ambassador is one who represents or does work in the name or by the authority of another. What necessity was there for Peter, James, John, Paul and other preachers, if the Holy Spirit did the work without them?

33. If the Holy Spirit works where the gospel has never been preached, or if the preaching of the gospel is unnecessary to His operations, why was the "ministry of reconciliation" committed to the apostles (II. Cor., 5:18, 19), and why did they in turn commit it to

others and assure them that it was sufficient in all things (I. Tim., 4:14-16; II. Tim., 2:2; 3:14-16)?

34. If the Holy Spirit works independently of the word, and feelings are an evidence of pardon, by what is man to know whether or not he has been operated upon? If by the Bible, the theory falls. If not by the Bible to what shall appeal be made?

35. If the Holy Spirit works independently of the word, what design did the Master have in giving the Great Commission (Matt., 28:18-20; Mark, 16:15, 16; Luke, 24:45-49). He charged them to teach, preach, and baptize. If the Holy Spirit does the work, the apostles were superfluous, and their efforts absolutely unnecessary.

36. If the Holy Spirit works independently of the word, how are we to explain Paul's statement that he gloried only in the cross of Christ, proclaiming that by it he was crucified unto the world, and the world unto him (Gal., 6:14)?

37. If the Holy Spirit works on the minds of sinners in order to their conversion, independently of the word, how are we to explain the plain statement of Jesus Christ that the world can not receive Him (John 14:15-18)?

38. If the Holy Spirit works on the mind of an unconverted man, independently of the word of God, which is equivalent to a naked spirit on a naked mind, how are we to explain the statement of John that the Spirit, water and blood agree in one (I. John, 5:8)?

39. If the Holy Spirit works independently of the word, and if He were sent to work and convert men without the aid of the preacher, why did wicked men antagonize the apostles, seeing they could do nothing without the abstract agency of the Spirit (Matt., 10:16-25; Acts, 5:12-18; II. Cor., 23:33)?

40. If the Holy Spirit works independently of the revealed word of God on the mind of the sinner, how can he be judged by the word, as Jesus declared (John, 12:48, 49)? Does God set up one plan for salvation, and another for judgment?

41. If the Holy Spirit works independenty of the word, a sinner can not do anything until He comes, and if He never comes, who is responsible for the damnation of those who are never influenced by Him?

42. If the Holy Spirit works independenty of the word, and God is no respecter of persons (Acts, 10:34, 35), how are we to explain the statement that the wicked shall be sent to hell (Matt., 25:31-36)?

43. If the Holy Spirit works independently of the word, and all who claim this are really under His direction, how are we to account for the divisions among the people of God? There is one Spirit (Eph., 4:1-6). Does He lead one man to be a Baptist, another a Methodist, and another a Presbyterian, and another a Quaker? If He does He contradicts and condemns Himself, for these orders differ fundamentally. If not, how are we to prove that He does anything outside of God's revealed plan? Those who claim the abstract operation of the Holy Spirit are forced to endorse everything claimed by its advocates, notwithstanding the unmistakable contradictions among them.

44. If the Holy Spirit works independently of the word, how are we to explain the teaching of Jesus that His words are spirit and life (John, 6:63)? Can a man received more than spirit and life?

45. If the Holy Spirit works independently of the word, what becomes of the conditions of the gospel (Matt., 7:21)?

46. If the Holy Spirit works independently of the word, how are we to explain the doctrine of John and Paul that faith comes by reading or hearing the word of God (John, 20:30, 31; Rom., 10:5-17)? There is one faith (Eph., 4:4, 5). If the Holy Spirit plants it in the unconverted man's heart without the word of truth, John and Paul forever fall to the ground!

47. If the Holy Spirit works on the sinner's mind independently of the word, why did Jesus pray for those who believe on Him through the apostles's word (John, 17:11-21)? And why did Peter declare that God made choice of him that the Gentiles should hear

"the word of the gospel" by his mouth and believe (Acts, 15:7)? Are there two ways of believing, one by the word and the other by the independent work of the Holy Spirit?

48. If the Holy Spirit works independently of the word, how can it be true that the grace of God that bringing salvation to all men hath appeared, seeing that a majority of the human race is still out of Christ (Titus, 2:11)?

49. If the Holy Spirit works independently of the word, and God gives Him to the sinner in disobedience, how are we to explain the fact that the Holy Spirit was not sent upon Jesus until He was baptized (Matt., 3:13-17)?

50. If the Holy Spirit works independently of the gospel, and if the gospel as preached and recorded by the apostles is insufficient to save, what did Paul commit to Timothy (I. Tim., 4:13-16; II. Tim., 2:2; 3:16, 17)?

51 If the Holy Spirit works independently of the gospel, and thereby accomplishes the work of regeneration, why was "necessity laid upon" Paul to preach (I. Cor., 9:16)? Will some one rise and explain the necessity of preaching?

52. If the Holy Spirit works independently of the word, and saves men by these operations, how are men saved by the gospel (I. Cor., 15:1-4)?

53. If the Holy Spirit works in dependently of the word, who obeyes the law of God (Acts, 6:7; Jas., 1:25)? Listen, oh ye contending sects! God gave us a law; that law was revealed and recorded in the New Testament. It declares that men must believe, must repent, must confess Christ, must be baptized in order to salvation (Matt., 28:18-20; Mark, 16:15, 16; Acts, 2:38; Rom., 10:8-10). Now, if the Holy Spirit comes to the sinner outside of this law, and gives him salvation, God obeys the law and the sinner does not. The advocates of abstract spiritual operations stand before the intelligence of the present decade of the twentieth

century, and proclaim by their acts that **God makes a law,** adds the promise of salvation, and the threat of eternal damnation, obeys His own law and lets the sinners go free!

54. If the Holy Spirit works on the mind of the sinners independently of the word of God, how are we to explain the principle that underlies all revelation, that when God designs to reach and influence the people by the Holy Spirit, He always sends Him to one of His servants who delivers His message, and that those who receive this message receive also the Holy Spirit? When He desired to rescue His people from the King of Mesopotamia, He sent the Spirit upon Othniel (Judg., 3:10). When He desired to redeem them from the oppression of the Midianites, He sent the Spirit upon Gideon (Judg., 6:34). When He desired to deliver them from the vindictive Ammonites, He sent the Spirit upon Jephthah (Judg., 11:29). When he desired to break the galling yoke of the Philistines, He sent the Spirit upon Samson (Judg., 13:24, 25). When He designed to teach, comfort and warn them, He sent the Spirit to the prophets, and through them addressed the minds of the people (II. Kings, 17:13; II. Chron., 36:13-16; Neh., 9:30; Jer., 7:25; 25:4; Acts, 7:51; I. Peter, 1:11, 12; II. Peter, 1:21). When He desired to send salvation to the ends of the earth, He sent His Son as the great missionary, and gave not the Spirit by measure unto Him (Isa., 61:1-3; Matt., 3:16, 17; John, 3:34). When Jesus departed from earth, He sent the Holy Spirit to the apostles that they might proclaim an infallible gospel to the whole creation (Matt., 10:16-20; John, 14:15-17, 26; 16:7-11; Acts, 1:6-8; 2:1-4). I challenge the world to produce one example of the Holy Spirit being sent directly or miraculously to any one where the good of others, and ability to teach or warn them, was not involved, except where God sent Him in judgment on the ungodly (Lev., 10:1, 2; Num., 16:35; I. Sam., 25:38; II. Sam., 6:6-8; II. Chron., 13:20; Acts, 5:1-10; 12:21-25).

55. If the Holy Spirit works on the sinner's mind independently of the word in order to conversion, how are we to explain the statement of Jude that "the faith" was once for all delivered to the saints (Jude, 3)?

56. If the Holy Spirit works on the sinner's mind, in conversion, independently of the word, what part has the Church in bringing the world to Christ? If the Holy Spirit works in answer to the prayers of the Church, and if all unconverted men are dead, passive or helpless in conversion, why can the Church not bring Him down upon the world, and thus make short work of the evangelization of the human race? If the Church can by intercession bring the Holy Spirit down upon one man, the same faith and intercession will bring Him down on the whole human family. If the Church can not bring Him down on the whole human family, it can not bring him down on a single man. No man who reads the Bible can deny that the Church has a work to do. It remains for the advocates of abstract spiritual operation to define the relation and the responsibility of the Church in the salvation of men. Either the Holy Spirit comes and brings coverting power in answer to prayer, and thus leaves the Church responsible for the damnation of millions who have died out of Christ, when they could have been saved by prayer without any faith, desire, or work on their part, or the Church must see that the gospel is preached to "every creature," and recognize a truth that the world can not overturn; that the gospel of Christ, dictated to the apostles by the Holy Spirit sent down from heaven, is God's power, only power to save men from sin (Rom., 1:16; I. Peter, 1:12)!

57. If the Holy Spirit works on the sinner's mind independently of the word, how are we to account for the declaration of the prophet (Isa., 54:13), endorsed by Jesus Christ, that men are to be taught of God (John, 6:44, 45)? Man is to be drawn to Christ by something taught and learned. Can a man be more than drawn to Christ?

58. If the Holy Spirit works on the sinner's mind independently of the world in order to conversion, man is a mere machine. He has neither volition nor the ability to resist. He can not act until the "power" is applied, and he can in no way influence the Spirit in His work! When the Spirit comes, he is powerless to resist; he must be converted whether he desires it or not. I challenge you to bring any proof to the contrary. If man is absolutely dead, helpless or passive in conversion, he is no more than a lump of clay. If the Holy Spirit comes and converts him, he is saved; if not, he is damned. Who is accountable in either case?

You have heard my propositions. Can you meet them? Nay, verily! How much longer will you delude men with the belief that salvation is a miracle, and that they can do nothing until God sees proper to perform it? Oh ye blind guides, come to judgment! Are you ready for the conclusions? Here it is: "And we are his witnesses of these things; and so is also the Holy Spirit, whom God hath given to them that obey him" (Acts, 5:32).

CHAPTER XXV.

PEACEMAKER.

"Men and brethren, what shall we do?" (Acts, 2:37).
"Lord, what wilt thou have me to do?" (Acts, 9:6)
"Sirs, what must I do to be saved?" (Acts, 16:30).

These passages are presented as a basis for an examination of the gospel plan of salvation; in other words, the law of admission into the kingdom of God. This is unquestionably the greatest subject that ever demanded the attention of sinful man. Upon the proper understanding and appreciation of it, his eternal welfare is suspended. I propose to examine it in the light of the New Testament, permitting it to be its own interpreter. The gospel is God's only remedy for sin. There is one God, one Saviour, one Spirit, and one scheme of redemption for accountable creatures. Whatever released men from sin in the days of apostolic labor will release them now. There are different forms of speech used in the New Testament to convey the same idea. For example: The change from sin to righteousness; from darkness to light; from the power of Satan unto the power of God, is called salvation (Mark, 16:16). It is called reconciliation (II. Cor., 5:17, 18). It is called redemption (Col., 1:14). It is called regeneration (Titus, 3:5). It is called conversion (Matt., 18:3; Acts, 3:19). It is called a birth of water and of the Spirit (John, 3:5). It is called sanctification (John, 17:17; I. Cor., 1:2). It is called translation into the kingdom of God's dear Son (Col., 1:13). It is called a death and resurrection (Rom., 6:1-6). It is called passing from death unto life (II. Cor., 5:17; I. John, 3:14). It is called adoption (Gal., 4:5, 6). It is called putting on Christ (Gal., 3:26, 27). These expressions substantially embrace the same principles, and when taken together they exhibit to an amazing degree the beauty, symmetry and harmony of the will of God to man.

Before entering into an investigation of the conditions of the gospel, I propose to settle beyond the possibility of cavil or contradiction one very important proposition: Can a sinner do anything to save himself? Some of the leading denominations represented in this convention assert that "doing is a deadly thing;" that man is utterly passive and helpless in regeneration. Is this true? Is it in harmony with the word of God? I assert that it is not. Jesus said: "Not every one that saith unto me, Lord, Lord, shall enter into the kingdom of heaven; but he that doeth the will of my Father which is in heaven" (Matt., 7:21). Entering into the "kingdom of heaven" is here suspended upon doing the Father's will. Peter said: "Of a truth I perceive that God is no respecter of persons; but in every nation he that feareth him, and worketh righteousness, is accepted with him" (Acts, 10:34, 35). How are men to gain acceptance with God? By fearing Him and working righteousness. John said: "The world passeth away, and the lust thereof: but he that doeth the will of God abideth forever" (I. John, 2:17). When thousands of convicted sinners on the day of Pentecost cried out in their great anguish: "Men and brethren, what shall we do?" the apostle did not say "doing is a deadly thing," but proceeded to inform them what they were required to do. When the convicted and astonished Saul of Tarsus Said: "Lord, what wilt thou have me to do?" the Lord did not say, "you are helpless and passive," but said: "Arise and go into the city, and it shall be told thee what thou must do" (Acts, 9:6). When the distressed jailer at Philippi said to Paul and Silas: "Sirs, what must I do to be saved?" they did not say, "regeneration is a miracle," "you must wait for a blessing from on high," or "come forward to this anxious seat and get religion," but without hesitation, they proceeded to show him that salvation was within his reach.

Jesus, in closing the Great Commission, said: "He that believeth not shall be damned" (Mark, 16:16).

This indicates the Redeemer's determination to condemn the unbelievers of all ages. Has man the power to believe the gospel of Christ? If he has the power to believe it, and refuses to do so, he is responsible for the failure. If he has not the power to believe it he is not responsible, and a righteous and merciful God can not condemn him for failing. The same rule may be applied to repentance, confession and baptism. They are obligations of the gospel. If a man can perform them he is responsible. If he can not he is not responsible. Ability and responsibility are inseparably connected. It will therefore be admitted by all reasonable men that the obligation to act is laid upon the sinner, and his Creator can, and will, hold him accountable for the performance of such requirements as are revealed in the gospel.

It is asserted on good human authority that all men are "totally depraved," "wholly corrupted in body and soul." They attempt to prove this by referring to the first chapter of the prophecy of Isaiah, and sixth verse. This, I think, is a perversion of the word of God, for a careful examination of the entire chapter will convince any impartial observer that it has reference to the corruptions of the Jewish government. In the "parable of the sower," Jesus declared that the "seed of the kingdom" falls into "good ground"—"honest and good hearts" (Luke, 8:15). Paul said: "Evil men and seducers shall wax worse and worse, deceiving and being deceived" (II. Tim., 3:13). Now, if all men are "totally depraved" how can some of them possess "honest and good hearts?" How can others "wax worse and worse?"

There is no doubt that men are wicked, depraved, but the Bible does not say that they are "totally depraved," and I do not understand how devout students of it can affirm that they are. It is asserted that the unconverted are "dead in trespasses and in sins" (Eph., 2:1). This is true, but in what sense are they dead? What does the word "dead" mean when applied to living men? Examine the following passages: "She that liveth in pleasure is dead while she liveth" (I. Tim., 5:6). "Let the dead bury their dead" (Matt., 8:22). "How shall we, that are dead to sin, live any longer therein" (Rom., 6:2)? "For ye are dead, and your life is hid with Christ in God" (Col., 3:3). "For he that is dead is free (justified) from sin" (Rom., 6:7). "The dead shall hear the voice of the Son of God, and they that hear shall live" (John, 5:25). "The wages of sin is death" (Rom., 6:23). Death, in these passages, evidently means separation. The sinner is dead to or separated from the love and practice of the "truth as it is in Jesus." The Christian is dead to or separated from the love of and practices of sin. The sinner is guilty and condemned. His mind is filled with wicked and unholy thoughts. His life presents many contradictions and inconsistencies. His sensibilities are enfeebled by long and constant indulgence in that which is evil. Notwithstanding these things, he still has a heart, a judgment, and a will; a heart to receive the truth, a judgment to weigh it, and a will to put in practice the demands of his King.

The theory of "hereditary total depravity" has exerted a very bad influence upon the minds of many. The sinner is frequently taught that he is responsible for his acts; that if he remains in sin he will be lost, and then he is informed of his utter helplessness—that he can not "obey the truth" until after he is regenerated, and that this must be done by a "power from on high." The order of nearly all the denominations represented here is: The "Adamic sin," "hereditary total depravity," the gospel a "dead letter," a "direct putting forth of the Holy Spirit," and the "absolute passiveness of the sinner in regeneration." This is not the gospel of Christ. The gospel makes us responsible for our own sins. It proclaims the conditions of pardon, and holds us responsible for the performance of duty. It presents to our contemplation the Divine part and the human part; in other words, what God has done for us, and what we are required to do for ourselves. He knew the demands of His sinful creatures, hence

He adapted the gospel scheme to their necessities. He did for us what we could not do for ourselves. Man could not furnish a sin-offering adequate to meet the demands of Divine justice. This God graciously did for him in giving His Son to taste death for every man.

Man was a prisoner of death. Darkness and gloom gathered in awful clouds around his dying hours. He was "without strength." He could not see the bright elysian fields "beyond the swelling flood." Jesus broke the chains of death, scattered the night, destroyed the gloom, "abolished death and brought life and immortality to light through the gospel."

Man was not able to frame a system which would purify his heart, elevate his character, save a perishing race and bring it into communion with God. This has been done for him in the "glad tidings" of Jesus Christ. God has opened a fountain for sin and uncleanness, but it is quite another thing to be cleansed therein and made "whiter than snow." He has broken the "bread of life" and laid it at our door. We can eat it and be satisfied, or refuse it and hunger forever. The Kingdom of Christ has been established on earth. We can enter into it and be saved, or refuse and be lost. The turning point in man's redemption is submission. He is responsible for every act of his life. Every thought, word or deed will tell in the coming judgment. God therefore says to him: "Choose you this day whom you will serve" (Josh., 24:15). Surely, He would not make such demands if man is unable to choose or serve! Jesus said: "Come unto me, all ye that labor and are heavy laden, and I will give you rest" (Matt., 11:28). Strange, Jesus would invite the "weary and heavy laden" to come to Him and find rest if they are too sinful to heed His blessed invitation!

I will now return to the question presented at the beginning of this discourse. What are the conditions on which the Lord has promised remission of sins to gospel subjects? This great question is answered in clear terms in the New Testament by the apostles of Jesus Christ. I do not propose to search for a new answer to it, but I propose to rehearse the answer given by them. God is the great fountain from whom the gospel flows (Rom., 1:1). Jesus is the mediator between God and man (I. Tim., 2:5). The Holy Spirit came into the world to guide the apostles into all truth, and bring to their remembrance the saying of Jesus, or to preach the gospel through them, and therefore to convict the world of sin, righteousness and judgment. Men heard the sweet story of redeeming love. They believed it with all their hearts (Acts, 8:37). They were sorry for sin (II. Cor., 7:10). Godly sorrow led them to repentance (Rom., 2:4). They confessed their faith in Christ (Rom., 10:10). They were baptized into Christ and raised up to walk in newness of life (Rom., 6:1-5).

I. *Faith.* The first thing that must be done by the sinner is to hear the gospel; the proclamation of mercy to a sinful race. "Hear, O heaven, and give ear, O earth! for the Lord hath spoken" (Isa., 1:2). "Incline your ear, and come unto me; hear, and your soul shall live" (Isa., 55:3). "He that turneth away his ear from hearing the law, even his prayer shall be abomination" (Prov., 28:9). "Who hath ears to hear, let him hear" (Matt., 13:9). "So then faith cometh by hearing, and hearing by the word of God" (Rom., 10:17). When he hears it he must believe it. If he does not, he will be condemned. God does not require a man to believe the gospel unless he hears or reads it. There is some confusion on this point. It is argued by some that faith is a direct gift from God; that it is planted in the heart, by the immediate touches of the Holy Spirit. This argument excludes Paul's testimony that it comes by hearing the word of God. It is asserted that Paul teaches that faith is the gift of God when he says: "For by grace are ye saved, through faith; and that not of yourselves: it is the gift of God; not of works, lest any man should boast" (Eph., 2:8, 9). Salvation and faith are not the same. Salvation is the gift of God. Faith is the act of the creature. This view of the question is sustained by the apostle himself, for he says,

"Man believeth" (Rom., 10:10; Phil., 1:29). The ninth verse is often quoted to prove that a sinner is not saved by works. This evidently has reference to the works of the law of Moses, for Jesus said: "This is the work of God, that ye believe on him whom he hath sent" (John, 6:29). Jesus said to the Jews: "If ye believe not that I am he, ye shall die in your sins" (John, 8:24). David said: "The law of the Lord is perfect, converting (restoring) the soul; the testimony of the Lord is sure, making wise the simple" (Ps., 19:7). Paul said: "For the law of the Spirit of life in Christ Jesus hath made me free from the law of sins and death" (Rom. 8:20). James said: "So speak ye, and so do, as they that shall be judged by the law of liberty" (Jas., 2:12). Laws demand the obedience of those to whom they are given. The "law of the Lord" is given to the children of men. It says, believe! Now, if the Lord gives the sinner faith independent of the law, it is a "dead letter," and God is the one who obeys the law, and not the sinner! Faith comes through the word of God. It is trust in God through the gospel of His Son. It is not a bare assent of the mind, but a believing, trusting, or confiding with all the heart. It is a trust that will always take God at His word and ask no questions. Paul said: "Now faith is the substance (ground or confidence) of things hoped for, the evidence of things not seen" (Heb., 11:1).

This is the most important proposition. We can not exaggerate its importance unless, by endeavoring to make it conspicuous, we neglect some other obligation of the gospel. Paul said: "But without faith it is impossible to please him; for he that cometh to God must believe that he is, and that he is a rewarder of them that diligently seek him" (Heb., 11:6). "Whatsoever is not of faith is sin" (Rom., 14:23). "Therefore, being justified by faith, we have peace with God through our Lord Jesus Christ" (Rom., 5:1). Peter said: "And put no difference between us and them, purifying their hearts by faith" (Acts, 15:9). Faith is a wonderful word; without it all is dark and dreary. It connects us with the years that are gone. It makes the great facts of history sparkle into undying realities before our enraptured vision. It brings heaven and earth so near together that we can almost see the tree of life, the crystal river, and hear the music as it rolls in swelling strains over the flowery hills of the better country. It carries us back over the centuries to the cross of Jesus. We see Him as He dies for us. We follow Him to the resurrection morning, the summit of Olivet, and up to His Father's throne, where He lives as the mediator between God and man. Faith purifies the heart. It changes the affections and establishes the kingdom of heaven in the minds of men. Faith is a long word. It covered the whole transaction of the erection of Abel's altar and the presentation of his sacrifice. It stretched itself over all the years in which Noah was building the ark. It embraced the entire journey of Abraham from his father's house to the land which the Lord promised for an inheritance for his descendants. It has been connected with every act of righteousness since the creation of man. It has enduring prominence in our salvation. It reaches from the proclamation of the gospel to the everlasting city of God. By it we live, and by it we press onward to the rest that remaineth for the people of God. By it we look unto Jesus and endure the temptations and trials of life. By it we bear the cross and despise the shame, and by it we will "enter in through the gates into the city." There is nothing said about "historical faith," "faith of miracles, "faith of devils," "temporary and enduring faith," or "saving faith." The Bible recognizes but "one faith," but it may be great or weak, according to the testimony and the opportunities of the individual.

There is nothing said in the Holy Scriptures about salvation by "faith only," although it has been asserted in this convention that "justification by faith only is a wholesome doctrine and very full of comfort." This may be comforting to those who do not understand the other obligations of the gospel, but to the man who does, there is no comfort outside of a full surrender to the demands of Christ. The "faith only" doctrine is false, for James says: "The devils also believe and tremble" (Jas., 2:19). Can a man be saved by an imperfect faith? Certainly not. Faith is made perfect by works (Jas., 2:22). Can a man be saved by a dead faith? Unquestionably he can not. "Faith without works is dead" (Jas., 2:26).

II. *Repentance.* "Except ye repent, ye shall all likewise perish" (Luke, 13:3). "And that repentance and remission of sins should be preached in his name among all nations, beginning at Jerusalem" (Luke, 24:47). "And the times of this ignorance God winked at; but now commandeth all men everywhere to repent: because he hath appointed a day in the which he will judge the world in righteousness by that man whom he hath ordained, whereof he hath given assurance unto all men, in that he hath raised him from the dead" (Acts, 17:30, 31). "Or despiseth thou the riches of his goodness and forbearing and long suffering, not knowing that the goodness of God leadeth thee to repentance" (Rom., 2:4)? "The Lord is not slack concerning his promise, as some men count slackness; but is long suffering to usward, not willing that any should perish, but that all should come to repentance" (II. Peter, 3:9).

What is repentance? "Godly sorrow for sin," says a man. "Salvation," says another. "Religion," says another. "I am trying to learn," says Inquirer.

Does the word of God define this important word? It surely does, "for all men everywhere" are commanded to repent, and the Redeemer lays down the emphatic and startling proposition: "Repent or perish," and in His last commission to the apostles declares, that "repentance and remission of sins should be preached in His name among all nations, beginning at Jerusalem."

Godly sorrow worketh repentance unto salvation (II. Cor., 7:10). But it is not repentance. It only leads to it. "Godly sorrow" is the cause; repentance is the effect. We may grasp the solemn significance of this great gospel appointment by looking into the condition of those to whom the commandment is given. The sinner lives by the gratification of his body; forms his own plans, executes his own schemes, "loves this present world," disobeys his Creator, disregards the "wisdom of God," and follows in the instruction of the "wisdom of the world." His mind is "filled with all unrighteousness," and the "prince of the power of the air" presides over his actions as he pursues his downward journey. He loves the ways of sin and despises the ways of God. He lives for the present and boldly proclaims that "the future will take care of itself."

He hears the gospel of Christ. He believes it. His mind glides backward over the ages past to the crucifixion of his Redeemer, and forward over the ages to come to the day in which God will judge the world. He stands between the divine charms of the one, and the awful horrors of the other. He sees "sorrow and love flow mingled down," and the gathering clouds of eternal vengeance. He realizes the magnitude of his crimes, ingratitude, unbelief. His stubborn will is broken, his stony heart is melted. He is deeply penitent on account of his sins. He is ready to do anything the Lord requires. He changes his mind or purpose, forsakes his sins, reforms his life, and amends his ways and turns his footsteps heavenward.

Repentance involves sorrow for sin, but it is more than this. It is the actual change of mind—purpose—inclination—the amendment of one's way or reformation of his life, and a turning to God with a full purpose of heart and a sincere inclination to "walk humbly" in all His commandments. It involves a full surrender to the authority of the Lord Jesus Christ.

A repentance that does not produce a "new man," is not recognized by the King of Heaven.

This view is sustained by the testimony of the Old as well as the New Testament: "Cease to do evil; learn to do well" (Isa., 1:16, 17). "Let the wicked forsake his way, and the unrighteous man his thoughts;

and let him return unto the Lord, and he will have mercy upon him; and unto our God, for he will abundantly pardon" (Isa., 55:7). "Thus saith the Lord of hosts, the God of Israel, Amend your ways and your doings" (Jer. 7:3). "When the wicked man turneth away from all his wickedness that he hath committed, and does that which is lawful and right, he shall save his soul alive. Because he considereth and turneth away from his transgressions that he hath committed he shall surely live, he shall not die. Yet saith the house of Israel, The way of the Lord is not equal. O house of Israel, are not my ways equal? are not your ways unequal? Therefore I will judge you, O house of Israel, every one according to his ways, saith the Lord God. Repent and turn yourselves from all your transgressions; so iniquity shall not be your ruin. Cast away from you all your transgressions, whereby ye have transgressed: and make you a new heart and a new spirit: for why will ye die, O house of Israel? For I have no pleasure in the death of him that dieth, saith the Lord God: wherefore turn yourselves, and live ye" (Ezek., 18:27-32). "Return unto me, and I will return unto you, saith the Lord of hosts" (Mal., 3:7). Brother Baptist says: "I take the position that repentance precedes faith; that is the first step a sinner must take in order to salvation." If so, what produces repentance? He replies: "Godly sorrow?" What produces "Godly sorrow?" He can not tell, nor can any other man who asserts that faith is second in the gospel order. A sinner must realize his guilt before he will be inclined to repent. He must believe in God and that he is a rebel in His government before he can realize his guilt. Therefore, in the gospel order faith precedes repentance.

Brother Baptist, does it please God for a sinner to repent? He replies: "God has no pleasure in the death of him that dieth." Paul affirms that "Without faith it is impossible to please him" (Heb., 11:6); also "Whatsoever is not of faith is in" (Rom., 14:23).

In the Great Commission, Jesus commanded His

apostles to go and "teach," or "preach the gospel to every creature." This was the first thing that He required them to do, and no man can affirm that repentance is the first requirement of the gospel without doing injustice to the last words of Jesus Christ. This is sustained by the record of the labors of the apostles. They preached the gospel of Christ. After men heard and believed it they commanded them to repent, change their minds, reform their lives.

There are presented in the gospel only two motives to induce men to repent, the goodness of God and the coming judgment. Now if a man neither believes the one nor fears the other, how can he be expected to repent? Let my Baptist friend answer the question!

Certain passages are supposed to contradict these arguments. For example: "Repent ye, and believe the gospel" (Mark, 1:15). This is begging the question, for this command was to the Jews; believers in the true and living God. They departed from the law of Moses and rejected the Messiah. Hence they were commanded to repent of their transgressions and accept the "glad tidings" of Jesus Christ.

The obligation to repent is laid upon the sinner. God requires this of him, and if he fails he will be punished. Now is God's time. Do you hear His voice? Do you believe His word? If you do, "turn yourselves, and live ye."

III. *Confessing Christ.* What does this mean? How is it done? Paul said: "With the heart man believeth unto righteousness; and with the mouth confession is made unto salvation" (Rom., 10:10). Examine the following: "This is my beloved Son, in whom I am well pleased" (Matt., 3:17). "I saw and bear record that this is the Son of God" (John, 1:34). "Thou art the Son of God; thou art the King of Israel" (John, 1:49). "This is indeed the Christ, the Saviour of the world" (John, 4:42). "I believe that thou art the Christ, the Son of God, which should come unto the world" (John, 11:27). "Thou art the Christ, the Son of the living

God" (Matt., 16:16). "Whosoever therefore shall confess me before men, him will I also confess before my Father which is in heaven" (Matt., 10:32). "Among the chief rulers also many believed in him: but because of the Pharisees they did not confess him, lest they should be put out of the synagogue" (John, 12:42). "Art thou the Christ, the Son of the Blessed? And Jesus said, I am" (Mark, 14:61, 62). "And many that believed came and confessed, and showed their deeds" (Acts, 19:18). "Fight the good fight of faith, lay hold on eternal life, whereunto thou art also called, and hast professed a good profession before many witnesses. I give thee charge in the sight of God, who quickeneth all things, and before Jesus Christ who before Pontius Pilate witnessed a good confession" (I. Tim., 6:12, 13).

Jesus Christ is the center, life and power of the Christian system. He is the fountain of eternal life. Whatever there is in the New Testament to make men pure, holy, just and good, is traceable directly to Him. Remove His name and presence from it, and the entire system will be dead. With me Christ is "the same yesterday, today and forever." To confess Him is the grandest work of the human tongue. To obey Him is the grandest work to which a man can devote his life. Would to God I could write this thought upon the hearts of the generation for whose salvation I labor and pray! A penitent believer is not required to confess more or less than that he believes with all his heart, that Jesus Christ is the Son of the living God, and and the Saviour of the world!

All the regeneration the heart can know is to learn to trust Christ, accept His sacrifice, learn His will, and bow to His demands.

It is asserted by some of the people of this convention that this is insufficient, that a man must believe something more than that Jesus Christ is the Son of God, that every sinner in the community believes this. I think this is a mistake. I can prove by the sinners themselves that they do not. Mr. A., do you believe that Jesus Christ is the Son of God? "Yes, sir!" Are you born or begotten of God? "I am not". The New Testament says: "Whosoever believeth that Jesus is the Christ is born (begotten) of God" (I. John, 5:1). Mr. B., do you believe that Jesus Christ is the Son of God? "Yes, sir!" Have you overcome the word? "I have not." The New Testament asks: "Who is he that overcometh the world, but he that believeth that Jesus is the Son of God" (I. John, 5:5). Mr. C., do you believe that Jesus Christ is the Son of God? "Yes, sir!" Have you the witness in yourself? "I have not." The New Testament says: "He that believeth on the Son of God hath the witness in himself" (I. John, 5:10). Mr. D., do you believe that Jesus Christ is the Son of God? "Yes, sir!" Do you keep His commandments? "I do not." The New Testament says: "He that saith, I know him, and keepeth not his commandments, is a lair, and the truth is not in him" (I. John, 2:4). Believing in Christ is more than a bare assent of the mind. It is a confidence in Him which accepts His word and obeys His will. If we apply this rule to the professing people of this age, I fear that we will be forced to conclude that many of them are not believers, for I find many who profess to know Him who make a greater effort to explain away certain passages which condemn their profession than they do to obey them.

In the apostolic age they preached Christ; His divine nature, His glorious mission, His wonderful words, His tragic death, His triumphant resurrection, His ascension to God and His coronation as "King of kings and Lord of lords" in the presence of angels of heaven! When men believed this sufficiently to abandon sin, they confessed it and were baptized; after which they were taught to obey every requirement of the gospel. This statement is sustained by the testimony of all the leading writers of the dispensation of Christ.

IV. *Baptism.* How is it performed? There is "one baptism" (Eph., 4:5). This is universally admitted, but it is affirmed that there are "different modes of the one baptism." This is purely an opinion, for the New Testament says nothing about "modes" of doing the Divine will. Some say the one baptism may be administered either by pouring, sprinkling, or immersion. Others say "water baptism" belonged to an "inferior dispensation," and therefore exclude it from their catalogue of gospel appointments. Let us look into the practice of the people of God in the New Testament times. The question for us to decide is, not whether sprinkling or pouring is regarded by men as sufficient, but whether either was practiced or recognized in the early ages of the Church. I affirm that there is not the slightest trace of either during the lives of the apostles, or for many years afterwards.

"John did baptize in the wilderness, and preach the baptism of repentance for the remission of sins. And there went out unto him all the land of Judea, and they of Jerusalem, and were all baptized of him in the river of Jordan, confessing their sins" (Mark, 1:4, 5). This is the first baptism of which we have a divine record. It was performed in a river, and if any man in this convention can show that they simply had a few drops of water poured or sprinkled upon them, let him proceed to the task! "And John also was baptizing in Enon near to Salim, because there was much water there; and they came and were baptized" (John, 3:23). Brother Episcopalian, do you baptize where there is "much water?" You do not, for your creed directs your applicants to present themselves at "the font," which contains little water at best. But does not Mark say John "baptized with water?" Yes, but the *Revised Testament* informs us that this means "*in* water."

"And it came to pass in those days, that Jesus came from Nazareth to Galilee, and was baptized of John in Jordan, and straightway coming up out of the water, he saw the heavens opened, and the Spirit like a dove descending upon him; and there came a voice from heaven saying, Thou art my beloved Son, in whom I am well pleased" (Mark, 1:9-11). Brother Presbyterian, do you believe that Jesus had only a few drops of water sprinkled or poured upon him? Jesus was immersed; buried. Paul says: "Buried with him by baptism into death" (Rom., 6:4). Dr. Carson said: "There is not, there never was in existence a great scholar who would deny that Jesus was immersed in Jordan." Dr. Macnight said: "Jesus submitted to be baptized, that is, buried under the water, by John, and to be raised out of it again, as an emblem of His future death and resurrection." What does "buried in baptism" mean? John Wesley, commenting on Rom., 6:4, says: "Buried with Him, alluding to the ancient practice of baptizing by immersion." Brother Methodist, do you imitate the example of Jesus, and follow the wisdom of your founder in this particular? This is a most serious question. Are we better than our Lord? Can we not "follow in His steps?" Listen to His words: "He that taketh not his cross and followeth after me, is not worthy of me" (Matt., 10:38). "If any man will come after me, let him denty himself, and take up his cross, and follow me" (Matt., 16:24). "They came to a certain water." Brother Lutheran, do you proceed to the water with your candidates? "They went down both (preacher and convert) into the water." Brother Quaker, do you take your converts "down into the water?" "And when they were come up out of the water" (Acts, 8:36-40). Mr. Roman Catholic, do you bring your converts "up out of the water?" Mr. Catholic replies: "We do not. The Church has a right to change the ordinances. Immersion was the original practice. The Church is infallible and has substituted sprinkling for immersion, and the Protestant sects borrowed the practice from us."

Sprinkling and pouring will not harmonize with the facts presented in reference to "in water," "in the Jordan," "much water," going "down into the water," "up out of the water," "buried in baptism," and no human argument can make them do so. No man who believes the Bible doubts that immersion is authorized, but no man can find a single verse indicating that sprinkling or pouring will gain the approval of Jesus Christ. The man who submissively bows to the plain teaching of the New Testament will be safest in time and eternity.

Baptize, immerse, sprinkle, pour. Here are four words. Do they all mean the same thing? They do not, is the universal response. Baptize means to immerse; some contend that it means to sprinkle and pour also. I have in my possession the testimony of the most eminent lexicographers or writers of the Greek language, none of them immersionists in practice. They are unanimous in teaching that baptize and baptism means immerse and immersion. I do not find the word sprinkle in the catalogue a single time. Immerse means to "plunge into a fluid." Sprinkle means to "scatter in small drops;" pour means "to cause to flow in a stream."

Now, according to these definitions and the place which "baptize" occupies in the passage of the New Testament, I affirm that it is a physical impossibility to sprinkle or pour a man. I will introduce a few passages, but the truth is the same in every place where the word baptize occurs: "Go ye therefore, and teach all nations, baptizing them" (Matt., 28:19). Go ye therefore, and teach all nations, "scattering them in small drops." Go ye therefore, and teach all nations, causing them to "flow in a stream." Go ye therefore, and teach all nations, "plunging them into a fluid." Try another: "Buried with him by baptism" (Rom., 6:4). Buried with Him by being "scattered in small drops." Buried with Him by being caused to "flow in a stream." Buried with Him by being "plunged into a fluid." Comment is unnecessary. The distinguished American scholar and preacher, Dr. Philip Schaff, testifies that: "On strictly exegetical and historical grounds, baptism must be immersion. Without prejudice, no other interpretation would ever have been given to Bible baptism. It is the most natural interpretation, and such we must always give. Immersion is natural and historical; sprinkling is artificial and an, expedient for convenience's sake. All the symbolism of the text (Rom., 6:3, 4), and everywhere in the

Bible, demands the going under water and coming up out of it. Sprinkling has no suggestion of burial to sin and resurrection to holiness. In order to be true to its original meaning, and its vital relation to redemption through Christ Jesus, baptism must be immersion. Why do you wish to get rid of it? Eminent theologians have wasted their learning attempting to defend infant sprinkling. Imposition is not exposition. All the early defenders of Christianity taught that nothing but immersion was baptism, and all the Greek and Oriental churches continue to immerse to this day."

Prof. A Diomedes Kyriacos, Professor of Church History in the University of Athens, Greece, a native and learned Greek, is an important witness as to the meaning of the original Greek word. Some times since C. D. Jones, of Lynchburg, Va., wrote a letter to Prof. Kyriacos, making inquiry as to the meaning of the word *baptizo*. The following letter was received in reply:

"ATHENS, August, 1890.

"DEAR SIR:—The verb *baptizo* in the Greek language *never has the meaning of to sprinkle or to pour, but invariably that of to dip*. In the Greek Church, both in its earliest times and in our days, to baptize has meant to dip. It is through this process that our church baptizes and always has baptized both infants belonging to Christian families and adults turning from any other religion to Christianity—that is, by dipping them into water. Thus, also (meaning by dipping), used the apostles to baptize. Were it not so, St. Paul could not have compared baptizing to the death of Christ, saying that in baptism we are buried with Christ and are risen with Him—that is the old man in us has been buried, and the new man fashioned according to the likeness of Christ risen again. Since baptism, therefore, represents the cleansing of the soul, this idea can only be clearly represented by the *entire dipping of the body into water and not by sprinkling or pouring.*

> Yours truly, etc.,
>
> Dr. A. Diomedes Kyriacos,
>
> Professor."

A few years since, Prof. J. N. Johnson, of Morton's Gap, Kentucky, addressed the following letters to five professors of Greek in five of the leading universities or colleges of the United States:

"Dear Sir:—I desire a favor of you. Will you please to write to me the name and publishers of at least one standard Greek-English Lexicon that gives sprinkle or pour as one of the meanings of *baptizo?* If there is no such standard Lexicon, please state the fact to me.

With much respect, yours truly,

> J. N. Johnson."

1. Prof. W. S. Tyler, of Amhert College, Massachusetts wrote:

"I do not know of any good Lexicon which gives sprinkle as a rendering for *baptizo.* Liddell and Scott, which is now the standard Lexicon for classic Greek, gives 'pour upon' as one of the meanings, and the Lexicons generally give 'wash' and 'bathe,' together with 'dip,' 'immerse,' 'sink' and 'dye' among its meanings. The primitive meaning of the word was probably dip, indeed the root *bap*, like our word *dip*, seems to represent dipping in its very sound."

2. Prof. L. R. Packard, of Yale College, New Haven, Conn., wrote:

"Liddel and Scott, American edition, gives 'pour how upon' as one of the meanings of *baptizo.* I do not know how it is with other English-Greek Lexions, except that the last English edition of Liddell and Scott omits the above definition."

3. Pro. M. L. D'Ooge, Colby University, of Michigan, wrote:

"There is no standard Greek-English Lexicon that gives either sprinkle or pour as one of the meanings of the Greek verb, *baptizo*."

4. Prof. Isaac Flagg, Cornell University, of New York, wrote:

"I know of no Lexicon which gives the meanings you speak of for *baptizo* (that is sprinkle or pour), not even the Lexicon of the Roman and Byzantine periods, by Prof. E. A. Sophocles."

5. Pro. Milton W. Humphreys, of Vanderbilt University, of Tennessee, a noted Methodist institution of learning, wrote:

"Although some Lexicons give pour or sprinkle as meanings of *baptizo*, there is no standard Greek English Lexicon that does."

You can take your choice; be immersed according to the demands of God, or have a little water sprinkled or poured upon you, according to the traditions of men!

Before dismissing this phase of the subject allow me to suggest that immersion is "union ground." No respectable scholar—I repeat respectable!—doubts or denies it. We can never unite on anything else, for we must have Christian union on Christian principles, or nothing.

What character of persons are to be admitted to the benefits of Christian baptism? Those and those only who have been changed in heart and life by faith and repentance; penitent believers. As to infant baptism, no one can show either by a command of Christ, or the practice of the apostles, that it is of divine origin. It was originated by man, and its practice in my judgment is a sin, for it proposes to perform an act in the name of divinity which has no foundation in Scripture or common sense.

What is baptism for? Every institution has a design peculiar to itself. What, therefore, is the design of this command of the gospel of Christ? One man teaches that it is the "sign of an inward work." Another that it is "the seal of pardon." Another that it is "the door into the Church." Another that it is "essential to Church membership and admission to the Lord's supper, but nonessential to salvation." Surely these theories are not very harmonious!

In order to bring the subject fully before the convention, I will introduce all of the most important passages of the inspired volume embracing the idea: (1) "John did baptize in the wilderness, and preach the baptism of repentance for the remission of sins" (Mark, 1:4). (2) The people of Judea and Jerusalem "were all baptized of him in the river of Jordan, confessing their sins" (Mark, 1:3). (3) "And he came into all the country about Jordan, preaching the baptism of repentance for the remission of sins" (Luke, 3:3). (4) Jesus answered, Verily, verily, I say unto thee, "Except a man be born of water and of the Spirit, he can not enter into the kingdom of God" (John, 3:5). (5) "Go ye therefore and teach all nations, baptizing them in (into) the name of the Father, and of the Son, and of the Holy Spirit" (Matt., 28:19). (6) "He that believeth and is baptized shall be saved" (Mark, 16:16). (7) "Repent and be baptized every one of you in the name of Jesus Christ for the remission of sins, and ye shall receive the gift of the Holy Spirit" (Acts, 2:38). (8) "And he commanded them to be baptized in the name of the Lord" (Acts, 10:48). (9) "And he took them the same hour of the night, and washed their stripes; and was baptized, he and all his, straightway" (Acts, 16:33). (10) "Many of the Corinthians hearing, believed and were baptized" (Acts, 18:8). (11) "Arise and be baptized, and wash away thy sins, calling on the name of the Lord" (Acts, 22:16). (12) "Know ye not that so many of us as were baptized into Jesus Christ were baptized into his death" (Rom., 6:3). (13) "For by one Spirit are we all baptized into one body" (I. Cor., 12:13). (14) "For as many of you as have been baptized into Christ have put on Christ" (Gal., 3:27). (15) "One Lord, one faith, one baptism" (Eph., 4:5). (16) "The like figure whereunto even baptism doth also now save us, (not the putting away of the filth of the flesh, but the answer of a good conscience toward God), by the resurrection of Jesus Christ" (I. Pet., 3:21). (17) "And there are three that bear witness in earth, the spirit, and the water, and the blood; and these three agree in one" (I. John, 5:8). Examine this list of seventeen passages and decide whether or not baptism is a "non-essential," "a mere Church ordinance!"

It is plainly stated that John, the forerunner of Christ, "preached the baptism of repentance for (Dr. J. R. Graves says 'into') the remission of sins." Strange that he would baptize the repenting Jews "into" the remission of sins if their pardon had been secured when they believed! Stranger still that the Baptist denominations take John as their founder, and persist in denying one of the most important feautres of his work!

Jesus said: "Except a man be born of water and of the Spirit, he can not enter into the kingdom of God" (John, 3:5). This is a broad declaration. A man must be in the kingdom of God on earth in order to enter the kingdom of God triumphant. In order to enter the kingdom of God on earth he must be born again; born of water and of the Spirit, born of the will of God, born of the incorruptible seed, the word of God (John, 1:13; I. Pet., 1:23). Brother Methodist says: "Born of water does not mean baptism." This passage is so quoted and applied in the Methodist Discipline, the Presbyterian Confession, and the Episcopalian Prayer Book! The illustrous George Whitfield, (Methodist), says concerning this passage: "Does not this verse urge the absolute necessity of baptism? Yes, when it can be had."—*Works, vol. iv., page* 353. Albert Barnes, the great Presbyterian commentator, says: "Born of water —by water here is evidently signified baptism; thus the word is used in" (Eph., 5:26; Titus, 3:5). Timothy Dwight, one of the leading theologians of the age, says: "To be born of water here means baptism, and in my view it is as necessary to our admission in the visible Church, as to be born of the Spirit is to our admission into the invisible kingdom. It is to be observed that he who understands the authority of this institution, and refuses to obey it, will never enter into the visible or the invisible kingdom." The distinguished Dr. Wall says: "There is not any one Christian writer of any antiquity in any language, but what understands it of baptism; and if it be not so understood, it is as difficult to give an account how a person is born of water any more than born of wood." John Wesley, the great reformer and advocate of personal holiness, says: "Except a man be born of water and the Spirit—except he experience that great inward change by the Spirit and be baptized (wherever it can be had) as the outward sign and means of it."—*Wesley's Notes on John*, 3:5. Whoever affirms that "born of water" does not mean baptism, does so in opposition to the principal creed of this age and the learning of the greatest men who have lived since the inauguration of the gospel dispensation. It is an established law in the kingdom of nature that anything brought into the enjoyment of life by birth, is smaller than that of which it is born. It is therefore a physical impossibility for "a man" to be "born of" a few drops of water. This being true, is any man, however good he may be, in the kingdom of God if he has never been "buried" in baptism?

In Matthew's report of the great commission I find the following: "Go ye therefore, and teach all nations, baptizing them in the name of the Father, and of the Son, and of the Holy Spirit" (Matt., 28:16-20). The *Revised Testament* says, "Go ye therefore, and make disciples of all the nations, baptizing them into the name of the Father, and of the Son and of the Holy Spirit." You will observe that he did not command them to baptize any save the taught, the disciples. These characters were to enter into the name of Father, Son and Holy Spirit by being baptized. By this act they were to be brought into all the enjoyments and privileges of the "reign of Christ." In the former dispensation the Lord made the following promise to the children of Israel: "IN ALL PLACES WHERE I RECORD MY NAME I WILL COME UNTO THEE, AND I WILL BLESS THEE" Ex., 20:24). Under the dispensation of favor, God has recorded His name in the ordinance of Christian baptism. No man can claim the approbation of the Father, Son and Holy Spirit until he is baptized. Peter commanded the Jews on the day of Pentecost to "Repent and be baptized in the name of Jesus Christ" (Acts, 2:38). He declares that that is salvation in the name of Jesus Christ (Acts, 4:12). Paul teaches that men are "justified in the name of the Lord Jesus" (I. Cor., 6:11).

Mark's report of the commission embraces the same principles: "Go ye into all the world, and preach the gospel to every creature. He that believeth and is baptized shall be saved; but he that believeth not shall be damned" (Mark, 16:15, 16). The promise of salvation is placed after both faith and baptism. The conclusion of this part of the commission has been variously interpreted. In order to correspond with Baptist doctrine it should read, "He that believeth and is saved shall be baptized; but he that believeth not shall be damned." In order to correspond with Methodist, Presbyterian, Episcopalian or Lutheran doctrine it should read: "He that is baptized and believeth shall be saved; but he that believeth not shall be damned," for their infant sprinkling virtually says: "Baptize them in infancy and teach them to believe when they grow up." In order to correspond with Quaker doctrine it should read: "He that believeth shall be saved; but he that believeth not shall be damned." In order to correspond with Universalism it should read: "He that believeth and is baptized shall be saved; but he that believeth not shall be saved also." In order to correspond with Restorationism it should read: "He that believeth and is baptized shall be saved; but he that believeth not shall be saved when he is punished as much as he deserves." Says Brother Baptist: "If baptism is necessary to salvation Jesus would have said:

'He that believeth not, and is not baptized, shall be damned.'" I think not. The unbeliever is "condemned already" (John, 3:18). Unbelief alone will condemn a man, but it takes both faith and obedience to save him.

On the day of Pentecost, thousands of convicted Jews who had participated in the crucifixion of the Son of God, cried out in their great distress: "Men and brethren, what shall we do?" The preaching of the apostles had convinced them that they had committed an awful crime, and that they were guilty before God. They believed in Jesus Christ and were endeavoring to learn the way of salvation. Peter's answer is one of infinite importance. It is an answer to penitent believers in all generations. Had some of the preachers of this convention been present, the answer would have been: "Brethren, vacate these front seats and let these mourners come forward and pray and be prayed for, and 'get religion,' and then be baptized with any mode of baptism they think proper!" Peter was speaking by inspiration; binding and loosing in the name of the King, hence he said: "Repent and be baptized every one of you in the name of Jesus Christ for the remission of sins, and ye shall receive the gift of the Holy Spirit" (Acts, 2:38).

What does the passage, especially the phrase "For the remission of sins," signify? In order to have something definite before us, I affirm that it means "in order to obtain the remission of sins." This can be proven by a common sense view of the entire passage. No one who is considered orthodox doubts for a moment that repentance was commanded "in order to the remission of sins." Examine the passage and you will find that the two commands, "repent," and "be baptized," are inseparably connected, and that they bear the same logical and grammatical relation to the end in view—the remission of sins. They therefore stand or fall together. What does the term "repent" signify? "Be sorry," says Brother Presbyterian. What does "for" mean? "Because of," says Brother Baptist. "What is the use of baptism?" "It is a non-essential," responds the "orthodox world." I will revise the passage according to these suggestions, and possibly we can get nearer its meaning. It now reads: "Be sorry every one of you in the name of Jesus Christ because of the remission of sins, and you shall receive the gift of the Holy Spirit." This is absurd. When a man's sins are forgiven he should rejoice. I will replace the word "repent." It now reads: "Repent every one of you in the name of Jesus Christ because of the remission of sins, and you shall receive the gift of the Holy Spirit." This commands them to repent because their sins are remitted. I will replace the phrase "be baptized." It now reads: "Repent and be baptized every one of you in the name of Jesus Christ because of the remission of sins, and ye shall receive the gift of the Holy Spirit." This commands them to both repent and be baptized because their sins are remitted. This will not do, for it is certain that they had not received the remission of sins when they inquired what they must do. I will again omit the phrase "be baptized," and substitute "in order to" for "because of." It now reads: "Repent every one of you in the name of Jesus Christ in order to the remission of sins, and you shall receive the gift of the Holy Spirit." This commands them to repent in order to the remission of sins. I will replace the phrase "be baptized." It now reads: "Repent and be baptized every one of you in name of Jesus Christ in order to the remission of sins, and you shall receive the gift of the Holy Spirit." This commands them to do two things; perform two distinct acts, repent, and be baptized "in order to the remission of sins."

In view of the fact that Jesus gave the keys of His Kingdom to the apostles (Matt., 16:13-20; 18:18), and commissioned them to make disciples of all nations (Matt., 28:18-20), it is infinitely important for us to know how they answered inquirers, and what they required them to do. Peter's answer on the day of Pentecost was the first answer ever given after Jesus ascended up on high. From the argument already presented, it will be seen: (1) That the world's salvation depends on Peter's answer. (2) That the meaning of the answer turns on the little word "for." Take this word out of the passage, and you at once destroy the whole force and meaning. What does it mean? I am willing to submit the question to the unbiased scholarship of the world, but before introducing the testimony I want to lay down a proposition. It is this: "For" is prophetic, prospective; it describes motion toward an ultimatum; it looks to the end of an action; it never takes cognizance of what is past, but unexceptionally, unequivocally, and undeniably looks to the completion of an action for its full measure of meaning and power. I now proceed to examine my witnesses: Call Noah Webster, LL. D., who, on the roll of fame, stands at the head of the world's lexicographers. Mr. Webster, what is the meaning of the word "for?" Answer: "In the most general sense, it indicates that in consideration of, in view of, or with reference to, which anything is done or takes place." Will you be specific? Answer: "Indicating the antecedent cause or occasion of an action; the motive or inducement accompanying and prompting to an act or state; the reason of anything; that on account of which a thing is or is done." "Indicating the remoter and indirect object of an act; the end or final cause with reference to which anything is, acts, serves, or is done." "Indicating that toward which the action of anything is directed, or the point toward which motion is made; intending to go to." The word "for" in Peter's answer shows the relation bewteen the commands "repent" and "be baptized" and the remission of sins. Wherever the word follows words expressing action, it indicates the end of the action, or the destination of the action, its ultimatum, or the purpose of it. I therefore affirm before this convention, without the fear even of an effort to contradict me, that repentance and baptism in Peter's answer sustain the same logical and grammatical relation to the remission of sins. Call John Groves, author of the Greek and English dictionary. Mr. Groves, what is the meaning of the preposition (*eis*) for? Answer: "In, into, unto, towards, for, in order to, to the end that, so that." Try these definitions in Peter's answer: "Repent and be baptized every one of you in the name of Jesus Christ towards the remission of sins." "Repent and be baptized every one of you in the name of Jesus Christ to the end that you may receive the remission of sins." Repent and be baptized every one of you, in the name of Jesus Christ, so that you may receive the remission of sins. I affirm that it is impossible to translate this passage so that remission of sins does not depend on both repentance and baptism. Is there a scholar in this convention who will undertake the task? Let us pass to the original. Let scholarship testify. Call J. R. Graves, LL.D., of the Baptist Church. Doctor, what is the meaning of Greek word *eis* in Acts, 2:38? "In the original the preposition is *eis*, the natural significance of which is unto." "Repent and be baptized every one of you in the name of Jesus Christ into the remission of sins." It is simply impossible to baptize a man "into" a thing if he has already entered into by some other act or acts! Who will deny it? Call Jacob Ditzler, D. D., of the Methodist Church. Doctor, what is the significance of *eis?* Answer: *"Eis* is always prospectice, and never retrospective" (Louisville Debate, page 307). Call Prof. J. R. Boise, of the Baptist Church. Professor, what is the meaning of *eis?* Answer: "I render *eis* with the following accusative case into (rather than unto) the remission is sins; the clause denoting the end in view, and the result attained." Call Liddell and Scott, the eminent Greek scholars and lexicographers. What is the meaning of *eis?* Answer: "Direction toward, motion to, on, into." Call W. D. McLaughlin, Professor of Greek in Cumberland University. Professor, what is the meaning of *eis?* Answer: "End of purpose." Call Wilford Saulkins, Professor of Greek in the East Tennessee Wesleyan University. Professor, what is the force of *eis* in the original of the phrase, "for the remission of sins?" Answer: "In order to obtain the remission of sins."

When Jesus presented the cup to His disciples He

said: "For this is my blood of the New Testament, which is shed for many for the remission of sins" (Matt., 26:28). Why did Jesus shed His blood? In order that we might receive the remission of sins. No one will deny this. If not, the design of baptism is forever settled. The expression "for the remission of sins" in the passage relating to repentance and baptism is the same both in English and in the original. Does this settle the controversy? If not, why? I desire to settle it forever, and if you are not ready to acknowledge the truth I am ready to continue the argument until "the last armed foe expires." During the convention I wrote the following letter to many eminent Greek scholars. Their answers ought to be final. These scholars represent nearly all of the denominations participating in these deliberations. The original communications are in my possession, and I will take pleasure in exhibiting them to all who are interested in the great question involved:

KIMBERLIN HEIGHTS, TENN., June 13, 1891.

Dear Sir:—Will you please give me what you consider a literal translation of Matt., 26:28, and Acts, 2:38? Is the expression "for the remission of sins" from the same Greek words in both passages? What is the meaning of the word from which "for" is taken? I ask you to answer these questions simply as a Greek scholar, without reference to theological tenet or dogma.

With much respect, I remain, faithfully yours,

ASHLEY S. JOHNSON.

To this letter I received thirty-one replies. The answers received are from men who have gained distinction in their chosen fields. They declare that the phrase *"for the remission of sins"* is the same in the English and Greek of both passages, and that the significance of "for" is the same in both places. I quote from the letters the matter only that comes under the scope of my questions. I submit it to your candid consideration and ask, How can any unprejudiced mind hesitate to accept the conclusion that baptism under the reign of grace, to the individual qualified by faith and repentance to receive it, is for, with a view to, in order to, or in order to obtain the remission of sins? How can any man go away from this convention and affirm that baptism is not essential to salvation, and stigmatize those who stand with the apostles of Jesus Christ and the unbiased scholarship of the ages as "water salvationists," "baptismal regenerationists?" But here are the letters. They speak for themselves, and in thunder tones:

The Professor of Greek, University of Virginia, Charlottesville, Va., says: "The expression 'for the remission of sins' is the same in both passages. The preposition (*eis*) rendered 'for,' like most prepositions in Greek, require various terms to express it in English. Its *local* sense is 'into,' but from this spring many applications which must be determined by the nature of the subject-matter, and by the context." He gives a number of renderings, and then concludes as follows: "It is quite obvious, therefore, that a Greek scholar can not offer a literal translation of the passages you name, without considering the theological import of his words; and I have found it best not to express any views, when the subject of baptism is involved."

The Professor of Greek, University of Mississippi, University P. O., Miss., says: "Matt., 26:28, 'Drink ye all out of it (i. e., all of you must drink out of the cup); for this is my blood, the (blood) of the New Testament (or covenant), the (blood) poured out for [1]many for [2](the) sending off of sins.' [1]The preposition used here is *peri;* its common significance is *about, concerning, in regard to.* [2]The word rendered 'for' before 'remission', is the regular word for *into*, but a frequent meaning is *with a view to.* Acts, 2:38, 'And (or but) Peter said to them: Repent, and let each one of you be baptized in [1]the name of Jesus Christ for ²sending off of sins; and ye shall receive the gift of the Holy Spirit.' ¹The Authorized Version's text has the preposition that means *upon;* and has the dative case. The Revised Version's text has the literal word for *in.* ²The text is precisely the same as regards the words used for 'for the remission of sins.'"

The Professor of Greek, University of Boston, Mass., says: "The words translated 'for the remission' are identical in the two passages. The word rendered 'for' means literally 'into,' and is given in the Revised Version. So far as I can see, however, 'for' gives a sufficiently accurate sense in the connection in which it is here used."

The Professor of Greek (John A. Broadus), Southern Baptist Theological Seminary, Louisville, Ky., says: "The Greek phrase is certainly the same in Matthew, 26:28, and Acts, 2:38. The Greek preposition in its local sense commonly signifies 'into;' in figurative uses it is commonly represented by 'unto.' Frequently, though not always, it introduces the design or object of the previous action. It certainly has this sense in Matthew, 26:28, and would very readily have the same sense in Acts, 2:38. But it sometimes introduces a variety of other ideas, which may be summed up under the general notion of 'in reference to,' or 'as regards.'"

The Professor of Greek, Knox College (Presbyterian), Toronto, Canada, says: "I would translate Matt., 26:28, thus: 'For this is my blood of the (new) covenant which is shed (poured out) for many unto (*eis*— in order to, with reference to) the remission of sins.' Acts, 2:38. 'But Peter said unto them, Repent ye, and let each one of you be baptized in (upon) the name of Jesus Christ unto (in order to) remission of sins, and ye shall receive the gift of the Holy Spirit.' The Greek, 'for the remission of sins' is the same in both passages."

The Professor of Greek, University of Michigan, Ann Arbor, Mich., says: "The expression 'for the remission of sins' in Matthew, 26:28, and Acts, 2:38, is taken from the same Greek word in each instance. The word 'for' is the translation of the Greek preposition *eis,* and is more commonly translated by our word *into* or *unto,* as indicating *unto* or *into which* anything is or is done, *i e.,* the *purpose, end* or *object.*"

The Professor of Greek, University of Cincinnati, Cincinnati, Ohio, says: "Using Westcott & Hort's edition of the New Testament, I translate Matt., 26:28, thus: 'Drink ye all out of it, for this is my blood of the disposal, which is being poured out concerning many unto a remission of errors.' Acts, 2:38, is translated thus, 'Repent ye, and let each of you be baptized in the name of Jesus Christ unto a remission of your errors.' The phrase 'for the remission of sins' is the same in both passages. The Greek preposition meaning 'for', is here *eis*. It denotes the purpose, or end in view, the goal reached by an action or figurative motion or transition."

The Professor of Greek, Victoria University (Methodist), Coburg, Canada, says: "Matthew, 26:28, 'Drink ye all of it; for this is my blood, that of the New Testament, that is shed for many for the remission of sins.' Acts, 2:38, 'And Peter said to them, Repent and be baptized each one of you in the name of Jesus Christ for the remission of sins. The expression 'for the remission of sins' is the same in each passage. The word *eis,* which is translated 'for,' means properly *to* or *into,* being used, I think, primarily of local relations. Here, I think, it designates the object of the action in question."

Professor Frank M. Bronson, Cornell University, Ithaca, N. Y., a specialist in New Testament Greek, says: "Matt., 26:28, 'Drink (out) of it all of you, for this is my blood of the covenant, which is shed for many unto letting-go sins.' Acts, 2:38, 'Repent ye, and be immersed each of you in the name of Jesus Christ unto letting-go your sins, and ye will (shall) receive the gift of the Holy Spirit.' The phrase rendered 'letting-go sins' might (taken by itself) mean a letting-go on the part of the *sinner*. The phrase, however, seems always to be used of letting-go on the part of the *Judge* or *person sinned against*. Hence, *remission* or *forgiveness* is a better translation than the more literal one."

The Professor of Greek, University College, Toronto, Canada, says: "Matthew, 26:28, is literally as in the Authorized Version—'For this is my blood of the New Testament which is (being) shed for many for the remission of sins.' Acts, 2:38, 'Peter said unto them, Repent and let each one be baptized in (or 'after' or 'according to' or 'in the strength of) the name of Jesus Christ for the remission of sins, and ye shall receive the gift of the Holy Spirit.' The words for 'for the remission of sins' are identical in the two passages; *eis* translated 'for,' means 'into' primarily, but is used very generally in classical, as well as later Greek, to mean for the purpose of."

The Professor of Greek, Washington and Lee University, Lexington, Va., says: "The translation of Matt., 26:28, and Acts, 2:38, both in the Old and New Versions, are as good as I can make them, the only variation at all material is the preposition *eis* rendered 'unto' remission of sins instead of 'for,' etc., the New Version having 'unto,' which is perhaps better. The Greek text is the same in both passages, and means the same in both, the preposition *eis* used in both, and translated 'for' in the Old Version, 'unto' in the New, expresses *end, aim, purpose* to be attained, i. e., very generally *with a view to, to the end that,* a use that is constantly in classic Greek. The passage in Acts, 2:38, may be rendered, 'Repent and let every one of you be baptized in the name of Jesus Christ, *that your sins may be remitted, or gotten rid of.*'"

The Professor of Greek, University of Kansas, Lawrence, Kan., says: "A literal translation of Matt., 26:28, I make, 'Drink of it, all of you; for this is my blood of the covenant which is being shed for many, unto remission of sins;' or absolutely literal, 'concerning many into remission of sins.' Acts, 2:38, reads: 'And Peter said to them, Repent, and let each one of you be baptized in the name of Jesus Christ unto (perfectly literal-into) remission of your sins and you will receive the gift of the Holy Spirit.' The expressions 'unto remission of sins' and 'unto remission of your sins,' are in Greek precisely the same, excepting the addition in the latter case of the word 'your.' The Greek word which you translate by 'for,' and the new revision by 'unto' means literally 'into.'"

The Professor of Greek, Amherst College, Amhert, Mass., says: "You ask me to give you a literal translation of Matt., 26:28, and Acts, 2:38, and also to answer two or three questions touching certain Greek words contained in the original. The translation of both passages in the *Revised Version* is as literal as can be given in the English language. I should not depart from it in any respect in giving a literal translation of my own. The expression 'for the remission of sins' is the same in both passages. The word *eis* which is rendered 'for' in the Authorized Version, and 'unto' in the Revised Version, literally means 'into,' but must frequently be rendered 'unto,' 'to' or 'for' in translating into English the Greek, both of the classics and of the New Testament. It denotes the *end of motion* or *action, bodily* or *mentally*, the end *arrived at* or the *end in view*, according to the connection in which it is used."

The Professor of Greek, Trinity College (Episcopal), Hartford, Conn., says: "The Revised Version seems to me to give the exactly literal translation of the passages in question. The Greek word, *eis*, translated *for* in the Authorized Version, and *unto*, in the Revised Version, indicates the aim, end or purpose with which a thing is done. In Matt., 26:28, it makes the purpose in the shedding of the blood. In Acts, 2:38, the purpose of those addressed in repentance and baptism. The word translated *remission* means, *a letting go, a dismissal*, or *quittance*, as in case of a *person* acquitted in court —then it is used of things, such as debts, a *passing over*, as if they had not been, a *forgiveness*, as in Matt.,

18:32, 'I *forgive* thee all that debt.' The Greek phrases translated 'for the remission of sins' are precisely the same in both passages, excepting the use of the articles and the pronoun, as indicated in the Revised Version."

The Professor of Greek, DePauw University (Methodist), Greencastle, Ind., says: "A literal translation of the passages named, 'For this is my blood, the (blood) shed for many for (the) remission of sins,' 'And Peter said unto them, Repent ye and let each of you be baptized in the name of Jesus Christ for the remission of sins, and ye shall receive the gift of the Holy Spirit.' The expression 'for (the) remission of sins' is the same in both places. The word translated 'for' (in the expression 'for the remission of sins') is the preposition *eis*, used only with the accusative case—its radical meaning is *to*, in the sense of direction or motion towards, and is employed here with the idea of *end* or *purpose*."

The Professor of Greek, McMaster Hall (Baptist), Toronto, Canada, failed to translate Acts, 2:38. He says: "I think the following would be a literal translation of Matt., 26:28, 'Drink of it all for this is my blood of the covenant which is shed (being shed) for many for or unto the remission of sins.' Yes, the expression 'for the remission of sins' is the same both in Matt., 26:28, and Atcs, 2:38, with this exception, that the word 'you' occurs in Acts, 2:38. The preposition from which 'for' is taken is *eis*, and is correctly rendered in these passages by 'for' or 'unto.' The preposition has, of course, other meanings, but the prevailing meaning is 'into.' I might here add that the expression in this place (Matt., 26:28) denotes the 'end or purpose' for which the blood is shed."

The Professor of Greek, University of Georgia, Athens, Ga., says: "I must say 1st, that for a literal rendering of Matthew, 26:28, and Acts, 2:38, I can not improve upon the Revised translation of 1884. 2nd. The 'for' of the Authorized Version is a translation of the final *eis* of the original—into, unto, for the purpose of, for, etc. 3. The Greek for 'for the remission of sins' is the same in both places. I must add that there is no *the* in the Greek though it is used io the Revised translation of Acts, 2:38, inconsistenly with the translation of Matt., 26:28, 'Unto remission' would do for both passages."

Professor William R. Harper, the celebrated Baptist scholar, Chicago University, says: "Matthew, 26:28, 'Drink ye of it all, for this is my blood, of the covenant, that shed for many into remission of sins.' Acts, 2:38, 'Repent and be baptized each of you in the name of Jesus Christ into remission of your sins, and ye shall receive the gift of the Holy Spirit,' etc. Questions: (1) Is the expression 'for the remission of sins' from the same Greek words in both passages? Yes, precisely the same, except that in the latter passage the article is used with the word of 'sins.' (2) What is the meaning of the word from which 'for' is taken? It means *into*, is used where a *verb of motion* is either expressed or implied—here the latter; a paraphrase would be '*entering into the sphere of the remission of sins*,' the precise meaning of which would be determined by the context.

The Professor of Greek, Emory College (Methodist), Oxford, Ga., says: "The words used 'for the remission of sins' are the same in Matthew, 26:28, and in Acts, 2:38. In the former passage, reference is made to the blood which is *pouring* out into the remission of sins. In Acts, the command is, 'Repent and be baptized each of you in the name of Jesus Christ *into the remission of sins*. The word translated 'for' is *eis*, into, which has here its ordinary meaning of *induction* or coming into."

The Professor of Greek, Lane Theological Seminary (Presbyterian), Cincinnati, Ohio, says: "The literal translation of Matthew, 26:28, would be: 'Drink ye all of it: for this is my blood of the covenant, which is poured out for (or, on account of) many unto (or, in order to) remission of sins.' Of Acts, 2:38: 'And Peter (said) unto them, Repent ye, and be baptized each one of you in the name of Jesus Christ unto (or, in order to) the remission of your sins.' The Greek of the clause—'unto remission,' etc., is the same in both passages. The preposition translated 'unto' admits of various rendering, as 'unto,' 'into,' 'among,' 'towards,' 'as far as,' 'for,' 'for the benefit of,' 'against,' etc. The precise shade of meaning has to be determined by the connection. The somewhat analogous uses of 'for' in English may illustrate the variations of the Greek word."

The Professor of Greek, Andover Theological Seminary (Congregationalist), Andover, Mass., says: "Matt., 26:28, 'Do ye all drink of it; for this is my blood of the covenant the (blood) poured out for (viz.: for the sake of) many unto remission of sins.' Acts, 2:38, 'But Peter (said) to them: 'Repent ye, and let each of you be baptized in the name of Jesus Christ unto remission of your sins; and ye shall receive the gift of the Holy Spirit.' I have translated from Westcott & Hort's critical edition of the Greek Testament, which differs somewhat from the common text, but not at the point to which you refer in your letter. The only differences are that in Acts the definite article *'the'* and the personal pronoun *'your'* are found. The preposition *eis,* translated in the Old Version *'for,'* in the Revised Version unto, means, *to, into,* or *unto.* It follows verbs of motion, and when connected with a verb denoting a mental or moral act, it expresses the end aimed at or the end hoped for, or intended result of the action. In Matthew it means that Christ's blood was shed *to secure* remission of sins, and in Acts that this is the aim of repentance and baptism."

The Professor of Greek, Davidson College (Presbyterian), Davidson College, N. C., says: "The Authorized Version of Matthew, 26:28, and Acts, 2:38, is correct. The expression 'for the remission of sins' is the same in Matthew and in Acts. The 'for' (*eis*) is literally 'to,' 'into;' in Matthew *purpose,* in Acts purpose shading into *result.* But it is impossible to get a correct idea of the word apart from the context, and without a comparison of the phrases with similar ones in other passages."

The Professor of Greek, Union Theological Seminary

(Presbyterian), New York, N. Y., says: "Matthew, 26:28, literally translated reads: 'For this is my blood of the covenant which is being shed for many with a view to the remission of sins.' Acts, 2:38, 'And Peter said unto them, Repent, and be baptized in the name of Jesus Christ with a view to the remission of your sins, and ye shall receive the gift of the Holy Spirit.' The phrase 'for the remission of sins,' is the same in the Greek of both passages. In Matthew it is general, 'the remission of sins:' in Luke *special*, 'the remission of *your* sins.' The preposition *eis* (A. V. *for*), in both cases signifies *destination*, 'unto,' 'with a view to,' 'in order to,' i. e., *in order that your sins may be forgiven*. This, of course, does not imply that the *mere act of* baptism effects forgiveness; but that, as a divinely ordained sacrament, typical of the cleansing by the Holy Spirit, *it points to, conduces to, has in view, is in the direction of*—forgiveness of sins, which can not be effected without the agency of the Divine Spirit. Forgiveness may take place *in* baptism, or *through* baptism, but not by baptism. Hence baptism, *points to*, and is *with a view* to forgiveness. *In itself* as a symbol it *means* forgiveness. That intent may be nullified by the subject's unbelief, by his receiving the right as a mere form; but that unbelief does not affect the divine meaning of the rite itself."

The Professor of Greek, Trinity College (Church of England), Toronto, Canada, says: "For this is my blood, that of the new covenant, that which is being shed concerning many FOR the remission of sins." 'Here *eis*—lit. *into, unto, with a view to*.' Repent and let every one of you be baptized on (the condition implied by) the Name of Jesus Christ *for* (with a view to leading up to) remission of sins; and ye shall receive the gift of the Holy Spirit.' Here again the word is EIS."

The Professor of Greek, Williams College, Williamstown, Mass., says: "In reply to your inquiries, I will say that the translation of Matthew, 26:28, and Acts, 2:38, in the Revised Version are literal. I can not render them more literally. Secondly, the expression 'for the remission of sins' is from the same Greek expression in both passages, except that in the Greek, from which the Revised Version of Acts, 2:38, is taken, 'the' and 'your' are added, making 'the remission of your sins.' Thirdly, the Greek word *eis* rendered 'for' in the A. V., and 'unto' in the R. V., means *unto*, or *towards;* sometimes *in respect to.*"

The Professor of Greek, Yale College, New Haven, Conn., says: "I would say that the expression 'for the remission of sins' is found both in Matthew, 26:28, and Acts, 2:38. The Greek word which is here translated *for*, generally means *into* or *to*. It may mean *to the end* that sins may be forgiven, or simply *with reference to* the forgiveness of sins. This sense seems about the same to me either way."

The Porfessor of Greek, Trinity College, Dublin, Ireland, says: "The authorized version is quite literal. In both passages the expression for *for the remission of sins* is the same in Greek. The word for *for* is *eis*, which the Revised Version renders *unto*. The word *eis* can only mean *for—with a view to produce, or unto—with a tendency to result in*, i. e., *eis*—indicates (1) end regarded solely as end, (2) end regarded as purpose or object."

The Professor of Greek, University of Aberdeen, Aberdeen, Scotland, says: "The expression Englished by 'for the remission of sins' is identical in Matthew, 26:28, and Acts, 2:38. So far as I can discover, there is no variant reading in the MSS. The word Englished 'for' is *eis*, which means 'to,' 'into,' here 'with a view to,' rather than 'resulting in,' as some seem to take it."

The Professor of Greek, University of Edinburgh, Edinburgh, Scotland, says: "The literal translation of Matt., 26:28, is—'For this is my blood of the covenant which is shed for many unto remission of sins.' The best manuscripts have not the word 'new' before 'covenant,' and the phrase 'blood of the covenant' is verbally the same as the words used in the Septuagint version of Exodus, 24:8. The word translated 'testament' in the Authorized Version is regularly used in the Greek translation of the Old Testament in the sense of 'covenant,' and this is its use also in other late Greek writings, though in classical Greek it very rarely means anything but a *will* or testamentary disposition. The literal rendering of Acts, 2:38, is—'Repent ye and be baptized each one of you in the name of Jesus Christ and unto the remission of sins, and ye shall receive the gift of the Holy Ghost.' The expression 'unto the remission of sins' is precisely the same in each passage. The 'unto,' or 'for,' as it is in the Authorized Version, denotes the *end* or *result aimed at*."

The Junior Professor of Greek, University of Minnesota, Minneapolis, Minn., says: "The two passages in question can scarcely be more literally translated than they are in the Revised Version. The expression 'unto the remission of sins' is the same in both passages. There is this difference only, that, in the Westcott & Hort's Revised Greek Text, Acts, 2:38, reads, 'unto the remission of *your* sins,' while the old Greek text reads simply, 'unto remission of sins,' as in Matthew."

"The word rendered 'for,' in the Old Version, more accurately 'unto,' in the Revised Version, is the preposition 'into,' which as early even as Homer's time expressed not only 'time' and 'place,' but also 'purpose,' as may be easily seen by reference to the Iliad."

Here is another letter, and an answer to it. It comes from a Professor in the University of Athens, Athens, Greece. This comes from the home of Greek! Surely this distinguished Professor knows his language. Surely we can afford to listen to such testimony. Surely there is no appeal from such authority:

KIMBERLIN HEIGHTS, KNOX CO., U. S.,
June 13, 1891.

Dr. A. Diomedes Kyriacos, Professor,

Athens, Greece:

My Dear Sir—Will you give me what you consider a literal translation of Matt., 26:28, and Acts, 2:38? Is the expression "for the remission of sins" from the same Greek words in both cases? What is the significance of the preposition "for" in the original of these two passages? What is the meaning of the expression: "The answer of a good conscience toward God" in I. Pet., 3:21? I ask you these questions without reference to theological distinctions. *I desire that you answer them simply as a Greek scholar.* I will be glad if you will put your letter in English. Hoping that you will oblige me, I am,

With much respect, faithfully yours,

Ashley S. J.ohnson.

Athens, the 15th of July, 1891.

Dear Sir—With great pleasure I answer to your questions. The expression *"of the remission of sins"* has the same significance in both passages, Matt., 26:28, and Acts, 2:38.

The preposition *"for"* means in both cases the design. The first passage says that receiving the communication we ought to remember the death of our Lord, who suffered for us, in order to get the remission of our sins, to regenerate and to be saved.

The second passage says that whosoever wishes to be saved and to get the remission of his sins, he ought to repent and believe in Christ and be baptized in the name of Christ.

The meaning of the expression *"the answer of a good conscience toward God,"* I. Pet., 3:21, is that the baptism (because it refers to that in this passage) is not the simple cleanliness of the flesh, but the acquisition of a good, quiet and serene conscience, which finds the baptized, who during the baptism is asked and confesses his belief to God and to the Saviour.

It was the custom in the ancient church of asking the baptized if he believes and confesses his faith to God the Father, His Son and Saviour, and the Holy Ghost.

It is to that question that refers this passage of Peter's I. epistle.

Receive, Sir, the assurance of my esteem.

Yours truly,

PROF. A. DIOMEDES KYRIACOS,

Library of
Davidson College

JOSCELYN III
AND THE FALL OF THE
CRUSADER STATES
1134-1199

JOSCELYN III AND THE FALL OF THE CRUSADER STATES

1134-1199

BY

ROBERT LAWRENCE NICHOLSON

LEIDEN
E. J. BRILL
1973

ISBN 90 04 03676 8

Copyright 1973 by E. J. Brill, Leiden, Netherlands

All rights reserved. No part of this book may be reproduced or translated in any form, by print, photoprint, microfilm, microfiche or any other means without written permission from the publisher

PRINTED IN THE NETHERLANDS

To the memory of my beloved parents
and
my master, Professor Einar Joranson

CONTENTS

Preface IX
1. Boyhood and Adolescence. 1134?-1151 1
2. Recovery, Restoration, and Disaster. 1151-1164 28
3. Imprisonment and Release 1164-1176. The Moslem Renaissance 37
4. The Rise of Saladin............................... 59
5. Frankish Developments 1143-1174. The Opening of the Reign of Baldwin IV (1174-1185). The Reappearance of Raymond III and Joscelyn III. The Courtenay Chieftain's Waxing Political and Economic Power as Seneschal.... 66
6. The Appearance of Foreign Princes and Adventurers in the Kingdom of Jerusalem. Saladin's Challenge 80
7. The Rise of Rival Political Parties in the Kingdom of Jerusalem: Northern Nobles vs. the Court Party. Saladin's Waxing Power 1180-1182 88
8. The Further Burgeoning and Consolidation of Joscelyn III's Rôle as a Political and Territorial Magnate 1180-1183 97
9. The Consolidation of Saladin's Moslem Empire 1180-1183 103
10. The Frankish Response to Saladin's Challenge: The Damascus, Red Sea, and Ṣaffūrīyah Campaigns and Limited Economic and Military Defense Measures..... 111
11. The Triumph of the Native Nobles: The Fall of Guy of Lusignan and the Rise of Raymond of Tripoli 118
12. Resumption of Franco-Moslem Conflict and an Ensuing Truce 1184-1185 128
13. Revolution in the Kingdom of Jerusalem: The *Coup d'État* of Joscelyn III and the Court Party. 1185-1186.......... 132
14. Franco-Moslem Developments 1185-1187: The Final Consolidation of Saladin's Power. The Sundering of the Franco-Moslem Truce. Reconciliation of the Warring Parties in the Kingdom of Jerusalem. The Campaign of Hattin.. 147
15. Joscelyn III Surrenders Acre and Loses His Seigneury. The Ensuing Virtual Liquidation of the Frankish Power in the Holy Land 164
16. The Fall of Jerusalem 170

17. The Turning of the Tide: The Franks Retain Tyre 176
18. The Inception of the Contest Between Conrad of Montferrat
    and Guy of Lusignan 180
19. The Further Turning of the Tide: The Frankish Investment
    and Capture of Acre............................. 184
20. The Closing Years and Death 1191-1200?............. 195

Epilogue 199

Appendix A... 204

Appendix B... 207

Appendix C... 212

Bibliography 216

Index 223

PREFACE

This study is an outgrowth of a long cherished desire to present the increasingly interlocked Frankish-Selchük-Byzantine political and military relationships during the 1134-1199 period from a standpoint differing in varying degrees from the views appearing in the standard histories relative to this period of Near Eastern history. It also seeks to fill a lacuna in the list of biographies of crusading leaders of the middle and later twelfth century. My interest in the history of the Syrian-Palestinian branch of the House of Courtenay, of which Joscelyn III was the last male member, was aroused during the course of writing my doctoral dissertation *Tancred: A Study of His Career and Work in their Relation to the First Crusade and the Establishment of the Latin States in Syria and Palestine*. I continued my studies of this family in a subsequent book entitled *Joscelyn I, Prince of Edessa*, which was published in 1954. Hence this study also seeks to show the involvement of Joscelyn III in the aforementioned military and political developments in general and the fall of the crusader states in particular and, in the course of so doing, solve and settle a number of controversies relating to his career.

Special thanks are owed to the staffs of the several libraries of the University of Chicago, my Alma Mater, who aided me in innumerable ways in my researches in this twofold project, and to Professor Claude Cahen of the University of Strassburg for his courtesy in providing me with translations of pertinent passages in Ibn al-Furat's *Târikh ad-douwal wa'l-mouloûk*.

University of Illinois   ROBERT LAWRENCE NICHOLSON
Chicago, Illinois
1973

CHAPTER ONE

BOYHOOD AND ADOLESCENCE
1134?-1151

Joscelyn III, with whose career the decline and fall of the crusaders' political establishment in the Holy Land were intimately interlocked, began his life amidst events of shortsighted strategy and partisan bickering strangely paralleling those at the close of his stormy career.

As was even more true in the case of his grandfather, Joscelyn I, the records of Joscelyn III's boyhood and early career are singularly scanty.[1] He was related to important French and Armenian nobiliary houses, for his father, Joscelyn II, the son of the first Count of Edessa, Joscelyn I of Courtenay, and a sister of Leo the Armenian, had married a woman of noble birth but of still more noble character, Beatrice of Saone, the widow of William of Saone, lord of Saone and/or Zardanā, in 1132.[2] Although the sources are entirely silent on

---

[1] John L. La Monte ("The rise and decline of a Frankish Seigneury in Syria in the time of the Crusades," *Revue Historique du Sud-Est Européen* [Bucarest, 1938], XV, Nos. 10-12, p. 305) supports my view in his observations that "Joscelyn III is first mentioned in history as *filius impuber* at the time of his father's capture." And this event occurred in 1150, about sixteen years after the birth of our subject.

[2] William of Tyre, *Historia rerum partibus transmarinis gestarum*, Bk. XIV, chap. iii and Bk. XIX, chap. iv, in *Recueil des historiens des croisades: historiens occidentaux* (Paris, 1844), I, 610 and 889. (Henceforth references to his subdivision of the *Recueil* will be cited as *Rec. his. occ.*); Ibn al-Qalānisī, *The Damascus Chronicle of the Crusades*, trans. and ed. by H. A. R. Gibb (London, 1932), p. 215; *Les Lignages d'Outremer*, chap. xxviii, *Rec. his. occ.*; *Lois* (Paris, 1843) II, 464. Claude Cahen in an article entitled "Note sur les seigneurs de Saone et de Zerdana," *Syria* [Paris, 1931], XII, 154-59) maintains that the late husband of the widowed Beatrice was the lord of Zardanā rather than the lord of Saone and states in the genealogical chart contained in the article that William of Saone died in 1132. René Grousset (*Histoire des croisades et du royaume franc de Jérusalem* [Paris, 1935], II, 9, n.2), however, avers that William could have been lord of both Saone and Zardanā. Steven Runciman seemingly regards William as simply the lord of Saone in his *The Families of Outremer* (London, 1960), p. 9, n.1 in his observation that "The only marriages between members of the ruling houses and vassals in the twelfth century were those of Joscelin II, Count of Edessa with Beatrice, widow of William, lord of Sahyun, in 1132..." But in his earlier work, *A History of the Crusades* (Cambridge, 1952), II, 190 and 362-63, n. 1 this same scholar's statement that "... Joscelin promptly married his [William of Saone] widow Beatrice, who probably brought him Zerdana as her dower." suggests that he partly supports Grousset's view on this matter. (Henceforth this second work of Runciman will be differentiated from the first by the addition of *History*; the former work will be cited as *The Families*). Although Runciman (*History*, p. 190, n.1) seemingly disavows his dating of 1132 as the time of

the exact date of the birth of Joscelyn III, two pieces of evidence indicate that it probably occurred in the middle 1130's. The most likely year is 1134. The statement by Ibn al-Qalānisī[3] that the lord of Zardanā was killed during the Moslem year A. H. 527 (November 12, 1132 to October 31, 1133) together with Joscelyn II's confirmation to the Hospitallers of Jerusalem in 1141 with the permission and consent of his wife Beatrice and son Joscelyn III of the donation of the village of Cisembourg which had been made earlier by Baldwin II, King of Jerusalem,[4] suggest that our subject was at the age of discretion and had reached the age of seven years.[5]

---

the death of William of Saone in his observation "But Ibn al-Qalanisi (p. 215) says that William was killed early in 1133," the dating of the Moslem year 527 (November 12, 1132 to October 31, 1133) does not rule out his death during the closing weeks of 1132. And this same scholar dates his death as occurring in 1132 later on in this same work (*History*, pp. 362-63, n. 1) in his observation that "Agnes [the sister of Joscelyn III] was probably born in 1133—her mother Beatrice's first husband died in 1132, and she married Joscelin of Edessa very soon afterwards." Moreover, the military dangers inherent in the presence of a helpless widow in charge of a fief made an early marriage on her part imperative. The dating of the account rendered by Kamāl al-Dīn (*Extraits de la chronique d'Alep* in Recueil des croisades: *historiens orientaux* [Paris, 1884] III, 664) to the effect that "Pendant le cours de cette même année (526 = November 23, 1131-November 11, 1132) la discorde et la guerre éclatèrent parmi les Francs (the civil war between the supporters of Alice, the daughter of Baldwin II, and Baldwin II. See William of Tyre, Bk. XIV, chaps. iv-v, *op. cit.*, pp. 611-14 and *Chronique de Michel Le Syrien* trans. and ed. J.-B. Chabot (Paris, 1905), Vol. III, Bk. XVI, chap. v, p. 233) et coutèrent la vie du seigneur de Zerdaña" may be ruled out on the ground that Kamāl al-Dīn was not born until December, 1192 (*Recueil des historiens des croisades: historiens orientaux*, III, 573), whereas William of Tyre and Ibn al-Qalānisī were contemporaries of and well informed about the events in their respective Frankish and Moslem bailiwicks during the 1130's. (Henceforth references to volumes in the *Recueil des historiens des croisades: historiens orientaux* will be cited as *Rec. his. or.* and references to *Chronique de Michel Le Syrien* will be cited as Michael the Syrian). See Robin Fedden *Chronique de Michel Le Syrien* will be cited as Michael the Syrian). See Robin Fedden and John Thomson, *Crusader Castles* (London, 1957), pp. 79-84 for a sketch of the history of the Saone family in the Holy Land as well as a description of the castle of Saone.

[3] Ibn al-Qalānisī, *loc. cit.*

[4] Joseph Marie Antoine Delaville Le Roulx, *Cartulaire général de l'ordre des Hospitaliers de S. Jean de Jérusalem (1100-1310)* (Paris, 1894), I, No. 137, p. 112; Reinhold Röhricht, *Regesta Regni Hierosolymitani (MXCVII–MCCXCI)* (Oeniponti, 1893), No. 206, p. 51. (Future references to these works will be cited as *Cartulaire* and *Regesta* respectively).

[5] Emmanuel Guillaume Rey (*Les colonies franques de Syrie aux XIIme et XIIIme siècles* [Paris, 1883], p. 16) declares that "... Béatrice, veuve de Guillaume, seigneur de Saône, épousa en secondes noces, vers 1140, Joscelyn II, comte d'Édesse." This renders quite unintelligible Joscelyn III's permission and consent in 1141 to his father's donation of the village of Cisembourg. Therefore Rey's dating can be ruled out. In the light of the observations of Runciman (*History, loc. cit.*) concerning the date of Agnes' birth that she "... was probably born in 1133...", the probability is that Joscelyn III was the second

The childhood and early adolescence of Joscelyn III during the 1130's and 1140's were passed among increasingly ominous portents for the Syrian Franks in general and Joscelyn III in particular, because the full development of these warnings in the middle and later 1140's involved the loss of the latter's patrimony, the County of Edessa. The endemic Moslem factionalism, which had contributed markedly to the success of the First Crusade and the ensuing consolidation of Frankish power in the Holy Land from 1100 to 1118, had been replaced during the 1120's by a growing tide of Moslem reaction and a painful groping toward Moslem union under İl-Ghāzī, Belek, and Aksungur. Although still impeded by the continuation of internecine quarrels among various Moslem cliques, the trend toward unity had nevertheless continued and assumed in 1127 a menacing guise in the hands of the crafty Moslem leader Zengi who, newly entrusted by the Sultan with the function of commissioner in Iraq and the principalities of Mosul and Aleppo in recognition of his manifest abilities,[6] had pursued an astute policy of becoming the master of all Moslem Syria and, in the course of so doing, of studiously refraining from serious attack on the several Latin states. This program gave, to be sure, a respite to the harried Frankish forces. But when Zengi finally effected the consolidation of his power, the respite proved to be meaningless, for Zengi's work served to stop the advance of Frankish power and to lead to the loss of the County of Edessa.[7]

Worse still was the growing policy of isolationism prevailing between the leaders of the Kingdom of Jerusalem, the County of Edessa, and the Principality of Antioch. Fulk, the King of Jerusalem

---

child of Beatrice's second marriage and that he was a year younger than Agnes. This view is fortified by the tone of the several sources dealing with Agnes' policies towards her brother Joscelyn III, which leave the strong impression that they are the usual ones followed by a sister towards a younger brother. La Monte (*op. cit.*, p. 304) tends to support this view in his reference to the rôle of Agnes in 1176 (see *infra*, p. 73) "... Agnes de Courtenay had for her young brother Joscelyn that ambitious affection which caused her to push his interests at every occasion and to secure for him his great position in Jerusalem."

[6] Ibn al-Qalānisī, *op. cit.*, pp. 235-36; Ibn al-Athīr, al-Athīr, *Extrait de la chronique intitulée Kamel-Altevarykh* in *Rec. his. or.* (Paris, 1872), I, 373, 376, and 380; Kamāl al-Dīn, *op. cit.*, pp. 656-57; *The Chronography of Abû'l Faraj (Bar Hebraeus)*, trans. Ernest A. Wallis Budge (London, 1932), I, 253. (Henceforth the last cited reference will be referred to as *The Chronography of Bar Hebraeus*).

[7] William Barron Stevenson, *The Crusaders in the East* (Cambridge, 1907), pp. 123-24. See Sir Hamilton A. R. Gibb, "Zengi and the Fall of Edessa," *A History of the Crusades. The First Hundred Years* (Philadelphia, 1955), I, 449-462 for a detailed narrative of the career of Zengi.

(1131-1143), guarded the immediate interests of the Kingdom and, more particularly, the southern ones by a defensive policy of the military *status quo* on all frontiers and a construction of fortresses to protect the southern reaches of the Kingdom against attack by the Moslem forces entrenched in Ascalon. Raymond, Prince of Antioch, and Joscelyn II, the drunken and slothful Count of Edessa, openly opposed one another and felt no responsibility for the safety of each other's state. Furthermore, Joscelyn II, blind to vital matters of security and preferring the greater opportunities for pleasure and leisure provided by Tell Bashir, had departed from the city of Edessa on the exposed eastern frontier of the County.[8] Lastly he, a Latin Christian, had antagonized important Syrian church circles in Edessa by three very injudicious actions: (1) pillaging of the convent of Mar Bar

---

[8] William of Tyre, Bk. XV, chaps. xxi and xxiv and Bk. XVI, chap. iv, *op. cit.*, pp. 692, 696-97 and 708-09. Cf. Stevenson, *op. cit.*, p. 146. *A History of Deeds Done Beyond the Seas by William Archbishop of Tyre*, trans. and ed. by Emily A. Babcock and A.C. Krey (New York, 1943), II, 141, n. 10 maintains that "The basis for this trouble [the feud between Joscelyn II and Raymond of Antioch] probably lay, first, in the fact that Joscelin was a vassal of the prince of Antioch for some of his land and, secondly, that Raymond was a relative newcomer whereas Joscelin had been born in the East and was half Armenian in blood. Prejudice and political rivalry were at the bottom of their antagonism." (Future references to his work will be cited as Babcock and Krey). Grousset (*op. cit.*, pp. 174-75), on the other hand, sees in the continuation of the quarrel a weakness in the Jerusalemite royal authority. "Seul un suzerain respecté, un Baudouin II, un Foulque, eût pu obliger les deux grands vassaux du nord à se réconcilier devant l'ennemi. Mais les institutions monarchiques qui avaient si longtemps assuré le salut de la Syrie franque étaient, du fait de la mort de Foulque et de la minorité de Baudouin III, comme en sommeil. Le lien fédérateur que constituait entre les barons la royauté hiérosolymitaine se trouvait pour cinq ans distendu, car ce n'etait pas la régente Mélisende avec ses intrigues et son tempérament de demi-levantine qui pouvait, quoi qu'en pense Guillaume de Tyr, maintenir la tradition royale. Non seulement la royauté, tombée pour quelques années en quenouille, était incapable, de réconcilier entre eux les grands vassaux, mais, en cas d'invasion turque sur le territoire d'Édesse ou d'Antioche, il n'y avait plus à compter sur l'intervention, si souvent salvatrice, du roi de Jérusalem. Tous les malheurs qui vont suivre jusqu'à la majorité de Baudouin III proviendront de cette seule cause: l'absence momentanée de la royauté." Continuing in the same vein, Grousset (*op. cit.*, pp. 182-83), in the course of commenting on Raymond's refusal to aid Joscelyn II—"L'insensé, en effet, ne se rendait pas compte qu'Édesse une fois tombée entre les mains des Zengides, la principauté d'Antioche, déjà amputée d'une partie de son territoire d'Outre-Oronte, aurait à supporter seule le poids de leurs attaques"—observes that "C'est ici que l'absence d'un roi de Jérusalem, capable d'imposer la concorde à ses grands vassaux, se faisait cruellement sentir. Rappelons-nous les deux premiers Baudouin et Foulque intervenant sans cesse pour obliger le comte de Tripoli, le prince d'Antioche et le comte d'Édesse à s'unir malgré leurs querelles, chaque fois que surgissait le péril turc. Il suffit que, du fait d'une minorité, l'institution monarchique fût pendant quelques années en sommeil pour qu'aussitôt l'anarchie féodale reparût et que la Syrie franque perdît d'un seul coup sous l'invasion turque le quart de son territoire." Cf. Bernhard Kugler, *Studien zur Geschichte des zweiten Kreuzzüges* (Stuttgart, 1866), p. 78.

Cauma, (2) intervention in a dispute over the election of Patriarch Athanasius of Antioch and a subsequent refusal to recognize him as the rightful incumbent, and (3) designation of Basilius Bar Soumana as the bishop of Edessa without prior consultation with and approval of Patriarch Athanasius. Only belatedly did he elect to reconcile himself with the Patriarch and all the other bishops and return the property stolen from the convent of Mar Bar Cauma.[9]

Meanwhile, having reduced the power of his Moslem rivals and having concluded his quarrels with them in 1143, Zengi resumed his war with the Franks and invaded the County of Edessa. Despite the clear warnings provided by Zengi's conquest of several castles and ensuing garrisoning of them with his own troops and his later seizure of Frankish merchants and their military escort during the Autumn of 1144,[10] Joscelyn II was not disturbed by the accompanying and subsequent mobilization of the Moslem forces. Accordingly, he left his trans-Euphratean holdings including the city of Edessa and, passing over to his western or cis-Euphratean holdings,[11] withdrew to Antioch with most of his forces.[12] True enough, in response to the pleas of the Artukid princes for help, who were at the moment losing their lands to Zengi's steady aggressions, he agreed to lend it, and the princes, in

---

[9] Michael the Syrian, chap. x and Bk. XII, chap. i, *op. cit.*, pp. 255-56 and 259-60. René Grousset (*L'empire du Levant* [Paris, 1946], p. 300) speaks of Joscelyn II at this time as follows: "Fils d'une Arménienne, c'est le type du baron créole, préférant à la société des Francs celle des Arméniens et des Syriens et se mêlant des querelles théologiques syriaques ..." (Henceforth references to Grousset's *Histoire des croisades et du royaume franc de Jérusalem* will be cited as *Histoire* to differentiate them from those identified with his *L'empire du Levant*. References to the latter work will be cited as *L'empire*). Also see Claude Cahen, *La Syrie du nord à l'époque des croisades et la principauté franque d'Antioche* (Paris, 1940), p. 352. (Future references to this work of Cahen will be cited as *La Syrie* to differentiate them from those in this scholar's article in *Syria*).

[10] Kamāl-al-Dīn, *op. cit.*, p. 685; Ibn al-Athīr, *op. cit.*, pp. 442-43; Ibn al-Qalānisī, *op. cit.*, pp. 265-66; Stevenson, *op. cit.*, p. 150, n. 3. Gertrude Slaughter (*Saladin 1138-1193* [New York, 1955] p. 28) believes that the interference with the trade routes between Syria and Iraq provided by the County of Edessa caused Zengi to fight for it.

[11] Ibn al-Athīr, *op. cit.*, pp. 434-44.

[12] *The Chronography of Bar Hebraeus*, p. 268. It is true, as Stevenson (*op. cit.*, p. 149) relying on Kamāl-al-Dīn, *op. cit.*, p. 686, points out, that "It was at the instigation of the emir of Ḥarran that he [Zengi] finally attacked Edessa. But for his persuasion, so Zanki himself acknowledged, the attack would not have been made. In any case the opportunity was rightly judged. Although Edessa was strongly fortified the population was chiefly Armenian and Syrian and the Latin garrison was small. Joscelin was absent in Antioch at the time, for no danger was anticipated." However, Zengi's bellicose activities in the County of Edessa itself ought to have warned the Edessan leader of the great risk he was taking in his departure from the city of Edessa itself.

turn, had given him the fortress of Bibol situated ten miles northeast of the town of Gargar. But this alliance proved to be short-lived, for Zengi made peace with his Artukid foemen, who were unconvinced of Joscelyn II's real ability to aid them.[13]

Soon apprised by the Moslem citizenry of Harran and more particularly by his spies in that city, chief of whom was a certain Fadl-Allâh ibn Ja'far, of Edessa's resulting plight and urged on by Harran's governor to capture Edessa, Zengi resolved to seize that Frankish bastion whose hour of doom now seemed assured with the reception of a new report anent the bickering between Raymond and Joscelyn II. The Moslem leader, having assembled a big infantry and cavalry force, moved on Edessa on the pretext that Joscelyn II had aided his foe, Kara Arslan, the sultan of Iconium. Now supported by numerous Moslem leaders, Zengi invested the city closely on November 28, 1144. Joscelyn II sent envoys to Raymond of Antioch and Queen Melisend of Jerusalem and implored their help. The former, engrossed in altercations with Manuel, the new Byzantine emperor, refused, but the latter immediately sent a relieving force, which arrived, however, too late to relieve the besieged Edessans. Meanwhile, Zengi's peace overtures and demands for their surrender were defiantly met by the bravely fighting but outnumbered defenders, most of whom were civilians lacking military training. The Frankish, Syrian, and Armenian bishops of Edessa assumed the city's defense energetically, and the single overture for a truce at length initiated by the Syrian bishop proved abortive. Yet superior force ultimately prevailed, and the Moslems, unceasingly investing the city, captured it on December 23, 1144 with vast slaughter.

Zengi soon completed his victory over Edessa by a triumphant westward march through the trans-Euphratean part of the County, capturing Sarūj and other strongholds. A succouring army of Franks (apparently identified with Raymond's command), which soon gathered at Antioch to help the hapless citizenry of Edessa, was also annihilated en route to Edessa by one of Zengi's corps of Turkmens. Only Bira on the eastern bank of the Euphrates temporarily escaped capture. News of the assassination on May 2, 1145 of Zengi's lieutenant in Mosul, the emir Jaqar b. Ya'qub, led him to fear that his

---

[13] "The First and Second Crusades from an Anonymous Syriac Chronicle," trans. by A. S. Tritton, with notes by H. A. R. Gibb, *Journal of the Royal Asiatic Society* (London, 1933), p. 280. (Henceforth this source will be cited as *Anon. Syriac Chronicle*). *A History of the Crusades. The First Hundred Years* (Philadelphia, 1955), I, 627.

hold on his eastern province was in danger and hence caused Zengi to abandon the siege of Bira. But the Frankish defenders of Bira, apprehensive over the return of Nūr-ad-Dīn, the son of Zengi, and discouraged over the failure of a rescue mission headed by Robert the Fat, were joined in their view by Joscelyn II, who considered the situation an untenable one. Hence the Franks surrendered Bira to the Moslem ruler of Mardin, an enemy of Zengi.[14]

---

[14] William of Tyre, Bk. XVI, chaps. iv-v, *op. cit.*, pp. 709-12; Kamāl al-Dīn, *op. cit.*, pp. 685-87; *The Chronography of Bar Hebraeus*, pp. 268-70; *Anon. Syriac Chronicle*, pp. 281-88; Ibn al-Qalānisī, *op. cit.*, pp. 266-69; Michael the Syrian, Bk. XVII, chap. ii, *op. cit.*, pp. 260-63; Abou Chamah, *Le Livre des deux Jardins, ou histoire des deux règnes* in *Rec. his. or.* (Paris, 1898)., IV, 47; Abū'l-Fidā, *Resumé de l'histoire des croisades* in *Rec. his. or.* (Paris, 1872), I, 26; Abū'l-Mahāsin Yūsuf, *Extraits de Nodjoûm Ez-Zahireh* in *Rec. his. or.* (Paris, 1884), III, 503; Ibn al-Athīr, *op. cit.*, pp. 444-45 and 446-48; Ibn al-Athīr, *Histoire des Atabecs de Mosul* in *Rec. his. or.* (Paris, 1887), II, 118-23 and 126; J.-B. Chabot, "Un épisode inédit de l'histoire des Croisades (le siège de Birta, 1145)," *Comptes rendus des Séances de l'Académie des Inscriptions et Belles-Lettres* (Paris, 1917), pp. 77-84; Grégoire Le Prêtre, *Chronique de Grégoire Le Prêtre* in *Recueil des historiens des croisades: documents arméniens* (Paris, 1869), I, chap. cvii, 157-59. (Henceforth references to the two works of Ibn al-Athīr will be cited as *K.-A.* and *Atabecs* respectively to differentiate them. References to volumes in the Armenian subdivision of the *Recueil* will be cited as *Rec. his. arm.* and references to the *Chronique de Grégoire Le Prêtre* will be cited as Grégoire Le Prêtre). William of Newburgh (*Historia Rerum Anglicarum*, ed. Richard Howlett [London, 1884], I, 59) declares that the fall of Edessa to Zengi resulted from its betrayal on the part of an outraged citizen seeking to avenge the ravishment of his daughter by Joscelyn II. Howlett, the editor of William of Newburgh, seemingly casts doubt (*loc. cit.*, n. 2) on this account in his observation that "William of Tyre (lib. xvi, c. 4) makes no reference to this story. He tells of the usual siege processes: the walls were undermined and fell, and the city was taken by storm." Annie Herzog (*Die Frau auf den Fürstenthronen der Kreuzfahrerstaaten* [Berlin, 1919], p. 62), after referring to this account, casts even more doubt on it, in her observation that "However, it is certain that this eastern stronghold [Edessa] of Christianity, which interrupted with its forts and castles the continuity of the Mohammedan empire, was the strategic objective of its military leaders for a long time already." In extenuation of Raymond's failure to answer Joscelyn II's plea at once, Babcock and Krey (*op. cit.*, p. 144, n. 14) maintain that "William has overlooked the fact that Raymond was involved in difficulties with the new emperor, Manuel. He sought to free himself from the vassalage to the Greeks when he heard of the death of John. But his efforts to extend his sway in Cilicia brought swift retribution from Manuel. There was actual warfare between Raymond and the Greeks (1143-1144), and Raymond was not in a position to give any real aid to Joscelin (see F. Chalandon, *Les Comnène*, II, 241-43)." Grousset (*Histoire*, p. 175) sees in the geographical position of the city of Edessa the basis of Zengi's plan to capture it. "Décision fort judicieuse. Des quatre États francs, celui d'Édesse, aventuré en pleine Jazîra, aux marches du Kurdistan, était le plus "en l'air." Cette baronnie d'avantgarde, en partie séparée par l'Euphrate du reste des possessions latines, se trouvait, dès sa fondation, encerclée sur trois côtés par les Turcs. De ce fait, d'ailleurs, c'était celle dont la présence était la plus insupportable aux Turcs; un coin enfoncé dans la chair de l'Islam. D'Édesse en effet les Francs pouvaient contrôler les caravanes entre Mossoul et Alep, entre Baghdâd et l'Anatolie seljûqide." Dana C. Munro (*The

Still all was not lost for the Courtenays. The cis-Euphratean

---

Kingdom of the Crusaders [New York, 1935], p. 133) apparently considers Zengi's pressure on the Artukid princes just before his assault on Edessa to be a diversionary move, for he states that "By a stratagem he [Zengi] induced the unsuspecting count to leave the city with his troops." Runciman (*History*, pp. 235-36) seems to me, in light of all the considerations advanced above, to be entirely too generous in his observations on Joscelyn II's conduct at this time. "The historian William of Tyre cruelly criticizes him for sloth and cowardice for refusing to go to his capital's rescue. But his army was not strong enough to risk a battle with Zengi's. He had confidence that the great fortifications of Edessa could hold out for some time. At Turbessel he could interrupt any reinforcements that Zengi might summon from Aleppo; and he counted on help from his Frankish neighbours. He had sent at once to Antioch and to Jerusalem. At Jerusalem Queen Melisende held a Council and was authorized to gather an army, which she dispatched under Manasses the Constable, Philip of Nablus and Elinand of Bures, prince of Galilee. But at Antioch Raymond would do nothing. All Joscelin's appeals to him as his overlord were in vain. Without his help Joscelin dared not attack Zengi. He waited at Turbessel for the arrival of the Queen's army." All this overlooks the fact that Joscelyn II left the city of Edessa with the full knowledge that the defenders of the city, by reason of his withdrawal of his military forces, would necessarily have to be, in terms of the commanding officer personnel as well as the soldiery itself, made up primarily of citizens unskilled in military matters. Such a move was certainly a risky one, even if one agrees with the observations of Runciman (*History*, p. 235) that Joscelyn II, in defense of the Artukids, "... marched out of Edessa with the bulk of his army down to the Euphrates, apparently to cut off Zengi's communications with Aleppo." Furthermore, Joscelyn II's religious policies had alienated a considerable part of this civilian body and therefore made distinctly possible, in the event of a Moslem investment, a division of effort and loyalty in the defense. Luckily for him and as a result of no wisdom on his part, the citizen defenders, with the notable exception of the Syrian bishop, rose above their mutual religious animosities and fought bravely side by side against the same religious as well as military foe. Grousset (*L'empire*, pp. 224 and 300-01), Gustave Schlumberger (*Numismatique de l'Orient latin* [Graz, 1954], pp. 14-15), La Monte (*op. cit.*, p. 303), and Stanley Lane-Poole (*Saladin and the Fall of the Kingdom of Jerusalem* [London, 1926], p. 56) support my estimate of Joscelyn II at this time of supreme peril. Cf. Cahen, *La Syrie*, p. 369. Luckily for the Edessan count, the loss of Bira to the Moslems was only temporary. Gibb (*op. cit.*, p. 461, n. 14) points out "... but as this [Bira] was one of the towns ceded by Beatrice to Manuel in 1150 ... this suzerainty must have been merely nominal." See *infra*, p. 24. Grousset (*Histoire*, pp. 192, 194 and 195) raises a question about Zengi's tactics following his capture of Edessa and answers it as follows: "D'où vient que Zengî n'ait pas profité de la démoralisation produite chez les Francs par la chute d'Édesse pour conquérir du même coup les terres situées à l'ouest de l'Euphrate?" .... "De cette suite d'événements deux conclusions se dégagent, indispensables pour comprendre l'enchaînement de cette histoire. D'une part l'anarchie musulmane rendait encore impossible la contre-croisade." .... "Ce regroupement en Syrie des forces musulmanes—et c'est la seconde conclusion des événements de 1144—, les Francs avaient assez d'esprit politique pour en avoir compris les dangers. A l'alliance damasquine dans le Sud, ils ajoutaient maintenant dans le Nord l'alliance avec les Ortoqides de Mârdîn, vieille dynastie turque locale, assagie et conservatrice, qui avait autant d'intérêt que les chrétiens à arrêter les progrès foudroyants de Zengî. La remise d'al-Bîra aux Ortoqides, venant après la conquête de Panéas avec le concours des Damasquins, montre chez les Francs, par delà les défaillances individuelles, une politique musulmane souple et réaliste."

portions of the County of Edessa were still in their hands[15] and from these a counterattack might well eventually ensue. Furthermore, there seemed to be a real possibility of a rebuilding of a Byzantine-Antiochian alliance against Zengi, for Raymond of Antioch now repented of his unsuccessful invasion of Cilicia in 1143, following the refusal of the new emperor Manuel to restore that Byzantine province to his principality,[16] and repaired to Constantinople in quest of the Emperor's forgiveness and aid against Zengi. This plea, after initial coolness on Manuel's part, was answered by the Emperor's promise of a future expedition to relieve the Christian forces.[17] Still more encouraging was Zengi's relaxation of pressure on the weakened Christian position. Aware that the new entente between Antioch and Constantinople counterbalanced the favorable trends provided by the continuation of hostile relationships between Raymond and Joscelyn II, Zengi turned his attention from the northern Frankish theatre to that of Damascus whose several atabegs (regents or stadtholders), namely Tāj-al-Mulūk Böri, Shams-al-Mulūk Ismāʿīl, Shihāb-ad-Dīn-Maḥmūd and the mamluk Muʿīn-ad-Dīn Unur had intermittently known his hostility and that of his able lieutenant Sevar ever since 1128.[18] Moreover, the city of Edessa itself showed itself restive under the rule of Zengi's governor, ʿAlī Küchük, for its Armenian population plotted in the Spring of 1146 to oust the Moslems and restore Joscelyn II. Although this promising development was soon to be dashed by ʿAlī Küchük's quashing of the plot and by Zengi's ensuing retaliatory policies of execution of the ringleaders and of banishment of part of the Armenian population, and their replacement by three hundred

---

[15] Runciman (*History*, p. 238, n. 1) enumerates the specific areas and strongholds as comprising "... the territory from Samosata, through Marash (held by his [Joscelyn II's] vassal Baldwin) south to Birejik, Aintab, Ravendal and Turbessel."

[16] John Cinnamus, *Epitome rerum ab Ioanne et Alexio Comnenis Gestarum*, Bk. II, in *Corpus Scriptorum Historiae Byzantinae* (Bonn, 1836), XXVI, 33-34).

[17] *Ibid.*, p. 35; Michael the Syrian, chap. iv, *op, cit.*, p. 267.

[18] Ibn al-Athīr, *K.-A.*, pp. 386-87, 404-05, 420-21, 431-32, and 435-37; Kamāl al-Dīn, *op. cit.*, pp. 659-60, 669, 681, and 682; *Anon. Syriac Chronicle*, p. 274; Ibn al-Qalānisī, *op. cit.*, pp. 183-84, 200-02, 233-35, 242, 244, 254, 262 and n. 1; Abūʾl-Fidā, *op. cit.*, p. 18; Sibṭ Ibn al—Jauzī, *Extraits du Mirât ez-Zèmân* in *Rec. his. or.* (Paris, 1884), III, 568-69; Matthew of Edessa, *Extraits de la chronique de Matthieu d'Édesse* in *Rec. his. arm.* (Paris, 1869), I, 148 and n. 3. Ernest Barker (*The Crusades* [London, 1925], p. 33) observes that "The atabegs formed a number of dynasties, which displaced the descendants of the Seljukian amirs in their various principalities. These dynasties were founded by emancipated mamelukes, who had held high office at court and in camp under powerful amirs, and who, on their death, first became stadtholders for their descendants, and then usurped the throne of their masters."

anti-Christian and pro-Moslem Jewish families,[19] the likelihood of the continuation of the Moslem hold on the city of Edessa and the trans-Euphratean division of the County of Edessa was soon to be questioned. The redoubtable champion of Islam, Zengi himself, was assassinated on September 14, 1146 during the course of siege operations of Qalʿat Jaʿbar by a disgruntled eunuch.[20]

The Edessan count, who was now residing in Tell Bashir, and his conquered subjects in Edessa were of one mind on the import of Zengi's passing. The erstwhile ruler, calculating that the death of Zengi would lead to such strife among his Moslem followers aspiring to the purple of power as to cause them to be careless in respect to Edessan matters,[21] dispatched a spy to Edessa to urge the citizenry to take up arms against their conquerors and to open the city gates to the Franks. The response was favorable and a date of attack was agreed upon.[22] Meanwhile, the Edessans themselves had not been idle, for they had apprised Joscelyn II of the scanty Turkish defenses in the city.[23] Since Nūr-ad-Dīn, Zengi's second son and successor in the principality of Aleppo,[24] was now detained in Mosul by the question of the succession to his father's dominions and had left only a few retainers in Edessa, the Edessans urged Joscelyn II to come to Edessa with an army and to receive it from the cooperating citizenry. The Edessan count readily agreed and presently a strong cavalry and infantry force headed by the count and his powerful vassal, Baldwin, the lord of Marash, advanced from Duluk in late October, 1146 and appeared before the city. Under cover of nightfall they rapidly effected an entrance, thanks to the slothfulness of the Turkish guards and the cooperation of the Edessan citizenry, who let down ropes and ladders to the succouring forces.[25]

---

[19] Ibn al-Qalānisī, *op. cit.*, p. 270; Michael the Syrian, chap. iii, *op. cit.*, pp. 266-67; Ibn al-Furat, *Târikh ad-douwal wa'l-mouloûk*, An 540, 156v°; *Anon. Syriac Chronicle*, p. 291.

[20] William of Tyre, chap. vii, *op. cit.*, p. 714; *Anon. Syriac Chronicle, loc. cit.*; Michael the Syrian, chap. iv, *op. cit.*, p. 268; Kamāl al-Dīn, *op. cit.*, p. 688; Ibn al-Qalānisī, *op. cit.*, p. 271; *The Chronography of Bar Hebraeus*, pp. 270 and 271; Ibn al-Athīr, *K.-A.*, p. 453; Abou Chamah, *loc. cit.*; Grégoire Le Prêtre, *op. cit.*, pp. 159-60; Ibn al-Athīr, *Atabecs*, p. 132; Babcock and Krey, *op. cit.*, p. 146, n. 18.

[21] *Anon. Syriac Chronicle*, p. 292; Ibn al-Athīr, *K.-A.*, p. 457 and *Atabecs*, p. 156.

[22] Ibn al-Athīr, *K.-A., loc. cit.* and *Atabecs, loc. cit.*; Kamal-Ad-Dîn, *Histoire d'Alep*, ed. and trans. by Edgar Blochet in *Revue de l'orient latin* (Paris, 1895), III, 514-15 (Henceforth references to passages in this edition of Kamal-Ad-Dîn will be cited as *Histoire*).

[23] William of Tyre, chap. xiv, *op. cit.*, p. 728.

[24] Ibn al-Athīr, *K.-A.*, pp. 455-56; *Anon. Syriac Chronicle*, pp. 291-92

[25] William of Tyre, *op. cit.*, pp. 728-29; *Anon. Syriac Chronicle*, pp. 292-93; Ibn

Soon the entire city, save for the strongly defended citadel into which the surviving Turkish defenders retreated, was in the hands of the rescue force, which now issued appeals to other Frankish leaders for aid in the retention of the recaptured city. The failure to capture the citadel, the successful investment of which proved impossible, because of the absence of siege machinery and material for its construction,[26] was to contribute greatly to the eventual Frankish defeat and the second loss of the city.

Meanwhile, Nūr-ad-Dīn, upon learning of the turn of events, effected a *levée en masse* from all parts of the Orient and, proceeding from Aleppo, presently established a tight investment around Edessa with his forces. Caught between the hammer of Nūr-ad-Dīn's besieging forces and the anvil of the counterattacking Turkish garrison in the city itself, the Frankish relief force decided that departure was the only reasonable course to follow, for the alternative, a siege, could end only in death by the sword or in capitulation through starvation. The citizenry of Edessa, despite initial dismay over the grim choice, elected to leave with their rescuers rather than face the sure death which awaited them as collaborators with the Franks. Accordingly, the fighting men and the noncombatant citizenry repaired to the now opened gates but to no avail. The Turkish investing forces, together with those now descending from the citadel, caught the retreating Franks in the narrow gateways and a terrible slaughter ensued. The remnant of the defenders of Edessa retreated to the fort called the

---

al-Qalānisī, *op. cit.*, p. 274; Ibn al-Athīr, *K.-A.*, *loc. cit.* and *Atabecs*, *loc. cit.*; Michael the Syrian, chap. v, *op. cit.*, p. 270; Kamal-Ad-Dîn, *Histoire*, p. 515; *The Chronography of Bar Hebraeus*, p. 273; Abou Chamah, *op. cit.*, pp. 50-51. *Anon. Syriac Chronicle* (p. 292) observes that Raymond of Antioch "... neglected to help as he was enraged with both of them [Joscelyn II and Baldwin, the lord of Marash] for not acknowledging him as their overlord." See Ibn al-Athīr, *Atabecs*, pp. 296-318 and *K.-A.*, pp. 604-05, Runciman, *History*, p. 398, Stevenson, *op. cit.*, pp. 155-56, and Sir Hamilton A. R. Gibb. "The Career of Nūr-ad-Dīn," *A History of the Crusades. The First Hundred Years* (Philadelphia, 1955), I, 513-27 and "The Achievement of Saladin," *Studies on the Civilization of Islam* (Boston, 1962), p. 94 for detailed accounts, encomiums, and estimates of the career of Nūr-ad-Dīn. (Henceforth references to the two works of Gibb cited above will be cited as "Nūr-ad-Dīn" and "The Achievement of Saladin" to differentiate them from his work on Zengi, which will be cited henceforth as "Zengi.")

[26] William of Tyre, *op. cit.*, p. 729; Ibn al-Athīr, *K.-A.*, p. 457 and *Atabecs*, *loc. cit.*; Grégoire Le Prêtre, chap. cviii, *op. cit.*, p. 160. *Anon. Syriac Chronicle* (p. 293) observes, not implausibly, that the invading Franks erred in their policy of discontinuing "mopping up" operations on the remaining Moslem defenders and of allowing them to retreat to the citadel while they (the Franks) resorted to plundering operations. The Frankish victors then compounded their error by failing to guard the walls, thereby permitting many Moslems to escape to Harran without pursuit.

Water-Tower where Joscelyn II and twenty of his knights held forth. But to no avail! This bastion also fell, with Joscelyn II and his companions effecting their escape secretly. Those Franks who succeeded in securing their escape fled to the Euphrates River, fourteen miles distant. On the following day Joscelyn II foolishly counterattacked Nūr-ad-Dīn's pursuing forces on the west and Baldwin of Marash did likewise on the east. Most of the Franks including Baldwin of Marash perished. The Turks effected a disastrous repulse of the Franks on their rear and a Frankish rout ensued. Joscelyn II, despite a wound in his side from an arrow, managed to escape to Samosata. The Turks were now masters of Edessa for the second time in December, 1146.[27]

---

[27] William of Tyre, chaps. xv-xvi, *op. cit.*, pp. 729-32; *Anon. Syriac Chronicle*, pp. 294-97; Ibn al-Qalānisī, *op. cit.*, pp. 274-75; Kamal-Ad-Dîn, *Histoire, loc. cit.*; Grégoire Le Prêtre, *loc. cit.*, Abou Chamah, *op. cit.*, p. 51; Ibn al-Athīr, *K. —A., loc. cit.* and *Atabecs, loc. cit.*; Michael the Syrian, *op. cit.*, pp. 270-72; *The Chronography of Bar Hebraeus, loc. cit. Anon. Syriac Chronicle* (p. 294) and Michael the Syrian (*op. cit.*, p. 270) aver respectively that (1) the retreat was undertaken without consultation with the Edessan citizenry with the result that the citizenry was left to its fate and (2) the retreat of the Frankish soldiery from Edessa was coupled with forcible measures to persuade the Edessan citizens to accompany them. The implications of the tale of *The Chronography of Bar Hebraeus* support the account of Michael the Syrian. The story is as follows: "And when the FRANKS had remained in EDESSA six days, NÛR AD-DÎN with ten thousand TURKS, burst out upon them. Then JOSCELYN harassed the wretched people of EDESSA, and he seized men, and women, and youths, and maidens, and expelled them with violence at the second hour of the night." The former statement hardly seems plausible in view of the consideration that the Frankish leaders in general and Joscelyn II in particular knew full well that the sharp criticism already directed at them over the first capture of Edessa would be as nothing, if they allowed the Christian population of Edessa to fall again into Turkish power. And the latter allegation overlooks the hopelessness, militarily speaking, facing the Edessan citizenry as well as soldiery who were certain to be denounced as collaborators irrespective of their particular Christian faith following their inevitable reimprisonment. What did they have to lose by an attempt to escape? Munro (*op. cit.*, p. 134) supports my view in his observation: "Joscelyn evacuated the city in the night, and the inhabitants, fearing the vengeance of the Turks, went with him." James Cotter Morison (*The Life and Times of Saint Bernard, Abbot of Clairvaux* [London, 1889], p. 364) does likewise in his contention that "The Armenians, conscious of their complicity in the recapture of Edessa, had as much reason to fear the Turks as Joscelyn and his knights." Grousset (*Histoire*, pp. 202-03 and 885-86) on the other hand, gives credence to charges made by both Syrian accounts in the following passages: "Si les malheureux Arméniens, qui se voyaient compromis dans la tentative de restauration franque, s'associèrent spontanément au hasardeux exode de Joscelin II, il semble bien que l'élément syriaque ait eu des sentiments assez différents: n'ayant assisté qu'à regret à la restauration franque, il ne s'associa que contraint et forcé à l'exode des Francs et des Arméniens, maudissant les Francs qui l'avaient impliqué dans cette catastrophe. Les regrets des Syriens devaient être d'autant plus amers que la tolerance de Zengî les avait fait participer à l'administration urbaine, avantage que la malheureuse équipée de Jocelin II leur faisait perdre en les compromettant comme chrétiens aux yeux

Nūr-ad-Dīn's continued pressure on the rump County of Edessa as well as the Principality of Antioch precluded any rôle on the part of Raymond of Antioch or Joscelyn II in the ensuing Second Crusade of 1146-1149[28] and obliged both Frankish chieftains to mount guard on their respective exposed positions now bereft of the city of Edessa which had isolated Aleppo by its geographical position between that city and the emirate of Mesopotamia. Indeed, so great was Nūr-ad-Dīn's new power resulting from the fall of Edessa and the later sundering of the Franco-Damascene alliance subsequent to the Franks' mistaken decision to attack Damascus rather than Aleppo that he was

---

de leurs protecteurs turcs et en les entraînant dans la débâcle générale."... "Tel est le récit plein d'amertume que l'Anonyme syriaque, comme le patriarche Michel, donne du drame édessenien de 1146. Certes son parti pris contre la domination franque est, dès le début, évident et, par moment, sa sympathie pour les Turcs révèle chez lui un véritable esprit de trahison envers la chrétienté. Mais il faut reconnaître que des actes comme la folle réoccupation d'Édesse par Jocelin II devaient provoquer bien des haines. Amener les Chrétiens d'Orient à se solidariser publiquement avec l'Occident, leur faire "trahir" leur maître turc, les compromettre irrémédiablement aux yeux de celui-ci, puis, quand la partie devient décidément trop difficile, les abandonner brusquement et sans défense à toutes les représailles et à tous les massacres, comment qualifier une criminelle légèreté?" For the reasons cited above, I do not believe that the Frankish leaders engaged in tactics indicated by the words "... les abandonner brusquement et sans défense à toutes les représailles et à tous les massacres..." and "... il [the Syriac element] ne s'associa que contraint et forcé à l'exode des Francs et des Arméniens..." Reiterating his theme of the central weakness of the Jerusalemite kingship in the events of the later 1140's, Grousset (*Histoire*, p. 208) also observes that "Mais, si la responsabilité directe de l'échec [the failure of the Franks to recapture Edessa in 1146] incombe tout d'arbord au mauvais prince qu'était Jocelin II, il y a lieu d'incriminer aussi la carence de l'institution monarchique, pratiquement mise en sommeil durant la régence de Mélisende. C'est parce qu'il n'y avait pas de roi à Jérusalem que Jocelin II entreprit seul sa folle équipée sur Édesse, sans s'être assuré au préalable d'une diversion partie de Jérusalem et d'Antioche pour menacer Alep et empêcher Nûr al-Dîn d'intervenir. Pendant ce sommeil de la royauté hiérosolymitaine, aucune discipline commune ne féderait les quatre États francs de Syrie. Une tentative aussi importante que la reprise d'Édesse était conduite isolément, avec une criminelle légèreté, par Jocelin II, sans que rien ait été organisé en temps utile pour coordonner son action à celle des barons d'Antioche, de Jérusalem et de Tripoli. Grave leçon pour les Francs. Dès que la royauté des Baudouin subissait une éclipse, la Syrie franque tombait dans l'anarchie et la reconquête musulmane progressait dangereusement." Babcock and Krey (*op. cit.*, p. 161, n. 28) place the recapture and second loss of Edessa late in 1146 (November-December).

[28] Full accounts of the Second Crusade are provided by Runciman, *History*, pp. 247-88, Thomas Andrew Archer and Charles L. Kingsford, *The Crusades* (New York, 1902), pp. 207-21, Virginia G. Berry "The Second Crusade," *A History of the Crusades. The First Hundred Years* (Philadelphia, 1955), I, 463-512, Grousset, *Histoire*, pp. 225-70, Bernhard Kugler, *op. cit.*, Cahen, *La Syrie*, pp. 379-89, and Reinhold Röhricht, *Geschichte des Königreichs Jerusalem, 1100-1291* (Innsbruck, 1898), pp. 230-58. (Henceforth this work of Röhricht will be differentiated from his *Regesta* by the additional word *Geschichte*).

able, while Damascus was facing the Christian forces, to send his raiders from Aleppo into both Frankish states.[29] Nūr-ad-Dīn himself, shortly after his arrival in power in Aleppo, subjected ʿAzāz, which was then being defended by Joscelyn II, to vigorous assaults for eight days in late November and early December, 1146 and then, having captured and destroyed Hisn Sînâb, Hisn S. r. r. (b?), and Hisn Tell R.mân, returned to Aleppo with great numbers of prisoners and booty.[30] The common peril confronting the entire north Frankish political establishment could be effectively met only if (1) Raymond of Antioch should drop his attitude of hostility toward his Edessan rival and develop with him a solid entente and alliance reflecting a *politique de longue vue* towards Nūr-ad-Dīn's aspirations and if (2) this policy should be buttressed by the adhesion of Raymond II, Count of Tripoli, whose territories abutted upon the southern boundary of the Principality of Antioch. The fate of all three states was of common concern to all three rulers.[31]

But such unified policy never materialized. An example of this failure was provided by the unilateral action of Joscelyn II's search for strictly personal safety and relief from the Moslems' attacks during the course of the Moslem year 543 (May 22, 1148-May 10, 1149). Upon the receipt of news that Nūr-ad-Dīn had departed from Aleppo to recapture Hisn. H. r. sh. r. (r.) which the Franks had seized, this Frankish leader besought Nūr-ad-Dīn's clemency by a personal visit to his camp under a flag of truce. The latter granted his plea and

---

[29] See Runciman, *History*, pp. 281 and 325 and Stevenson, *op. cit.*, pp. 154-55 for discerning comments on the folly of the Crusaders' attack on Damascus and their failure to attack Aleppo.

[30] Ibn al-Furat, *op. cit.*, An 541, 158 r°-v°.

[31] That this *politique de longue vue* was absolutely essential may be seen in still another consideration advanced by Stevenson, *op. cit.*, pp. 163-64. "After the failure of such an effort [the Second Crusade] there seemed no reason to fear anything that Europe might ever attempt again. Besides the effort had expended itself and only the Syrian Latins remained to be dealt with. On the other side the discord and suspicion which had been aroused between Syrians and Westerns showed its effect at once. The hope of another crusade was indefinitely postponed and the annual stream of pilgrims which brought money and men and arms to the holy land was seriously checked and diminished. Louis [Louis VII, king of France 1137-1180] indeed remained loyal to the cause, but it was never in his power to send another crusade. The popes, on their part, were wholly engaged, during the next forty years, by their contest with the German emperors. Even the feeling of bitterness against the Greek emperor roused, or rather stirred into fresh life, in Europe by the incidents of the crusade, had its effect later on the fortunes of the Latins. The contest with Nureddin had now to be fought out with little help from Europe."

bestowed on him a robe of honor at about the time of the arrival of the Crusaders in southern Syria.[32]

Still another example of such shortsightedness was revealed by the tactics of Raymond II, Count of Tripoli, in this same Moslem year. Enraged by the seizure of the castle of al-ʿArīmah in the County of Tripoli by his kinsman Bertram, a grandson of Raymond of Toulouse, and his manifest intentions of seizing the rest of the County, he besought the aid of Unur, the ruler of Damascus, and Nūr-ad-Dīn, who were in conference in Baalbek, in the recovery of the castle. The Moslem leaders readily agreed and summoned Saif-ad-Dīn, Nūr-ad-Dīn's brother, to aid them. The latter dispatched an army to assist his fellow princes. A tight investment was soon established, the walls were pierced, and the Frankish defenders were obliged to capitulate. The entire citizenry along with Bertram fell into Moslem captivity, the military stores of the castle became a Moslem prize, and the castle itself was dismantled.[33] Another diminution of the already weakened Frankish power had occurred. But still greater losses impended!

Emboldened by this success and perceiving the unlikelihood of succour to the Frankish territories, Nūr-ad-Dīn assembled a large army with contingents supplied by Unur, invaded the Principality of Antioch, and subjected the fortress of Inab to siege. Prince Raymond of Antioch rashly advanced from Antioch with a few followers but without the cavalry escort he had called up. Nūr-ad-Dīn, fearful that Raymond intended to bring in a larger force later, abandoned the siege of Inab and withdrew to a secure spot where he proceeded to collect intelligence reports concerning the Franks' strength. Meanwhile Raymond mistakenly decided not to withdraw to his adjacent fortresses and elected to meet Nūr-ad-Dīn in the open plain. Apprised that his Frankish foeman had received no additional aid, Nūr-ad-Dīn encircled the Frankish forces under cover of darkness. Battle was joined at dawn. Raymond's greatly outnumbered forces fled and he, together with Reginald, who was the lord of Marash and the son-in-law of Joscelyn II and the husband of the latter's daughter Agnes, perished in this battle on June 29, 1149.[34]

---

[32] Ibn al-Furat, *op. cit.*, An 543, 189 r°

[33] Ibn al-Qalānisī, *op. cit.*, pp. 287-88; Ibn al-Athīr, *K.-A.*, pp. 470-71 and *Atabecs*, pp. 162-63; Abou Chamah, *op. cit.*, pp. 59-60; Kamal-Ad-Dîn, *Histoire*, p. 517.

[34] William of Tyre, Bk. XVII, chap. ix, *op. cit.*, pp. 771-73; Cinnamus, *op. cit.*, pp. 122-23; *The Chronography of Bar Hebraeus*, p. 275; Michael the Syrian, chap. x, *op.*

The triumphant Moslem then turned westward and led his forces to the sea where, in token of his triumph, he bathed in the presence of his troops. During the course of his return march he seized the fortress of Ḥārim as well as all the villages around Ḥārim only ten miles from Antioch and proceeded to equip Ḥārim strongly with soldiers, food, and weapons. Artāḥ also suffered conquest. His ensuing investment of the city of Antioch, it is true, did not result in its capture, but the truce granted by him to the defenders provided a recognition on their part of his mastery of the Aleppan area. Far worse than these psychological blows was Nūr-ad-Dīn's collection of vast booty from the fortresses and castles around Antioch. This impairment of the fighting capacity of the Principality was soon worsened by Nūr-ad-Dīn's sweep into the southern reaches of the Principality and his gaining of the capitulation of the important Frankish bastion of Apamea on July 26.[35] The Principality of Antioch, the western neighbor and therefore western defense of the truncated County of Edessa, had been greatly weakened by the loss of its illustrious chieftain Raymond, by the penetration of Moslem arms to its very capital, and by the loss of its stronghold of Apamea. Hence with Moslem military power threatening to envelop the County of Edessa simultaneously from the Moslem held areas on the east and southeast and through the slackly held northern districts of the Frankish Principality of Antioch, the future of the County of Edessa was grim indeed. Only Joscelyn II remained of the prominent north Frankish leaders for the time to safeguard the interests of the

---

cit., pp. 288-89 and n.4, p. 289; *Anon. Syriac Chronicle*, pp. 300-01; Abou Chamah, *op. cit.*, pp. 61-62 and n. 1, p. 62; Grégoire Le Prêtre, chap. cix, *op. cit.*, p. 161; Ibn al-Qalānisī, *op. cit.*, pp. 291-92; Kamal-Ad-Dîn, *Histoire*, pp. 521-22; *Chronique de Matthieu d'Édesse (962-1136) Avec La Continuation de Grégoire Le Prêtre Jusqu'en 1162* trans. Edouard Dulaurier (Paris, 1858), chap. cclix, p. 329. (Henceforth this edition of Grégoire Le Prêtre will be differentiated from that in the *Recueil* by the addition of the word *Continuation*. The *Recueil* edition will be cited as *Chronique*); Ibn al-Furat, *op. cit.*, An 544, III 6 r°; *Epistola A Dapiferi Militiae Templi* in *Recueil des historiens des Gaules et de la France.* Edited by M. Bouquet and others (Paris, 1878) XV, 540. (Henceforth this source will be cited as *Epistola A Dapiferi*); Babcock and Krey, *op. cit.*, p. 198, n. 20; Kugler (*op. cit.*, p. 212) believes Reginald of Marash perhaps flung himself with intentional foolhardiness at the enemy, since, in view of recent events, he could hardly hope for anything else than an honorable death.

[35] Abou Chamah, *op. cit.*, pp. 62-3; Michael the Syrian, *op. cit.*, p. 289; William of Tyre, chap. x, *op. cit.*, pp. 774-75; Kamal-Ad-Dîn, *Histoire*, pp. 522-23; Ibn al-Qalānisī, *op. cit.*, pp. 293-94; Ibn al-Athīr, *Atabecs*, p. 180, *Anon. Syriac Chronicle, loc. cit.*; Babcock and Krey, *loc. cit.* Cahen (*La Syrie*, p. 384 and n. 12) designates the villages around Ḥārim as "... Tell-Kachfahân Arzghân, Bezmechân, bref tout le passage de l'Oronte au Roûdj, puis ... 'Imm, Salqîn, Tell 'Ammâr..."

House of Courtenay in the rump County of Edessa as well as those of his fellow Franks in northern Syria.[36]

But that this leader would prove to be an effective guardian of his own interests and those of his young son Joscelyn III seemed highly questionable, for, preferring the continuation of his recently won peace with Nūr-ad-Dīn in 1148,[37] he had done nothing to aid the stricken Principality of Antioch in its recent and still present hour of peril. The Edessan count still nursed a grievance against Raymond of Antioch because the latter had not aided him during Edessa's recent hour of need.[38] Then, at the very moment when unity of all religious groups within the diminished County of Edessa was essential for its survival, he demonstrated that he had learned nothing from his former mistaken policies towards the Syrian Christians by his second pillaging in June, 1148 of the Convent of Mar Bar Cauma and his placing of the monastery in the hands of a group of Armenians, bitter foes of the Syrian Christians.[39] Although the first effect of this whole episode was one of inspiring in Daulah, the neighboring Turkish ruler, of a belief that the monks had delivered their monastery to Joscelyn II because of their resentment over the tribute which Ghazi, Daulah's father, had imposed on them, he soon abandoned his initial policy of reprisal against them as traitors. Refugee monks from the plundered monastery apprised him of the true facts. The resulting new situation was seen in Daulah's remission of the tribute for that year from the monastery of Mar Bar Cauma and in his scornful and insulting refusal to accept the Edessan prince's offer of an exchange of the convent of Mar Bar Cauma for the convents of Zabar recently seized by Daulah. His rejection, so Daulah averred, rested on the belief that Joscelyn II's recent action belied his Christian faith and raised the question as to whether he was a Jew or a pagan.[40]

Still additional evidence of the folly of Joscelyn II was seen in the following August when Kara Arslan's invasion of the country around Gargar caused a general flight of the natives to the monastery of Mar Bar Cauma in search of protection. Upon his arrival at the monastery

---

[36] Grégoire Le Prêtre, *Continuation*, pp. 329-30 and *Chronique*, p. 162.

[37] Michael the Syrian, chap. viii, *op. cit.* p. 282.

[38] *Idem*

[39] *Ibid.*, chap. ix, pp. 283-85; *Anon. Syriac Chronicle*, p. 300. Grousset *Histoire*, p. 285) believes that "L'excuse invoquée pour ce brigandage était la sympathie avérée que, par hostilité envers les Arméniens, alliés des Francs, les communautés jacobites professaient pour les Turcs."

[40] Michael the Syrian, *op. cit.*, pp. 286-88; *Anon. Syriac Chronicle*, p. 299.

Kara Arslan made plausible promises to honor the saint identified with the convent, to spare the convent and its residents, and to release the prisoners he already had, provided that the refugees were surrendered to him. This move provoked a wide division of opinion in the monastery's population, with some favoring acceptance and others favoring rejection of the offer. Finally one of the elders accompanied by representatives of both views sought out Kara Arslan with the proposal that the Turks appoint representatives to meet with the Christians to confirm Kara Arslan's promise of allowing the monastery's population to remain free. The Turks then dropped their masks and revealed their true intention of enslaving it. With the issue clearly drawn and the monastery's population insisting on a policy of no surrender to Kara Arslan, the latter proceeded to devastate the monastery's environs and to seize booty and prisoners. But he soon repented and restored the plunder as well as his prisoners to the monastery.[41] The actions of both Daulah and Kara Arslan towards the Christian populations, although marred by ineptitudes and gaucheries, were clearly designed to widen the split between the Latin and Syrian Christians. And Joscelyn II, failing to see the course of events, not only soon broke his promise made shortly thereafter to three Syrian soldiers to release the Syrian monks he still held captive, but also insisted on full payment of the money fine imposed on the Syrian Christians.[42] Only belatedly did he recognize the error of his ways in his agreement to return the plundered saint's hand as well as money to the monastery.[43]

The stupidity of all these shortsighted policies soon became apparent, for Mas'ūd I, the sultan of the Selchük state of Rūm bordering on the western frontiers of the Principality of Antioch, upon hearing of Raymond's death, invaded the Principality in September, 1149. Employing false promises of kindly treatment, he persuaded many Christian fortress populations to open their gates to him. Thereupon he enslaved or slew them. Many fortresses and cities were captured. Marash fell victim to the joint investment of Mas'ūd I and his father Kîlîj Arslan I. His appetite thus whetted, the former then invaded the southern sectors of the County of Edessa itself and invested Tell Bashir and its defenders including the luckless Count Joscelyn II, his wife, and his children. Fortunately for the Count, King

---

[41] Michael the Syrian, chap. x, *op. cit.*, pp. 290-91
[42] *Ibid.*, p. 292.
[43] *Ibid.*, chap. xi, pp. 294 and 295-96.

Baldwin III sent a force of sixty knights under the Constable Humphrey to the nearby city of ʿAzāz to prevent its capture by the Moslems. The distinct possibility that this succouring force might proceed from ʿAzāz to the relief of Tell Bashir itself together with the decision of Nūr-ad-Dīn to act as a mediator very probably figured in the decision of Masʿūd I to raise the siege and to depart to his own country, having concluded peace with his Frankish foeman. The Courtenay chieftain was obliged to surrender all of Masʿūd I's subjects whom he had imprisoned and to give Masʿūd I twelve suits of armor. Furthermore, he was obliged to recognize the latter's suzerainty.[44] Moslem invasion from the northwest was soon followed by Moslem

---

[44] *Ibid.*, chaps. x and xi, pp. 290 and 294; *The Chronography of Bar Hebraeus, loc. cit.*; *Epistola A Dapiferi, loc. cit.*; Grégoire Le Prêtre, *Chronique*, pp. 162-63 and *Continuation*, p. 330; Ibn al-Furat, *loc. cit.*; William of Tyre, *op. cit.*, p. 775. William of Tyre, after narrating the fact that Masʿūd I laid siege to Tell Bashir, immediately observes, that "Rex vero Henfredum constabularium, cum sexaginta militibus, ad tuendum Hasart, intera dirigit, ne a Turcis occupetur." I do not believe that this immediate juxtaposition of this sentence is accidental but rather deliberate. Runciman (*History*, p. 327) believes that, since Nūr-ad-Dīn had no desire to see Joscelyn II, who was still his client, lose his lands to the Selchüks, Masʿūd I found it wise to retire. Grousset (*Histoire*, p. 290) supports my belief that the decision of Masʿūd I to abandon the siege of Tell Bashir resulted at least in part from the action of the young King of Jerusalem, Baldwin III. "Il convient d'ajouter que l'intervention du roi de Jérusalem avait joué indirectement un rôle décisif dans la délivrance de Turbessel. En effet, dès la nouvelle de l'invasion seljûqide de ce côté, Baudouin III, qui se trouvait alors à Antioche, envoya en hâte le connétable de Jérusalem, Onfroi (II) de Toron, avec soixante chevaliers, pour renforcer la garnison du château de 'Azâz (Hasart), forteresse-frontière de la principauté d'Antioche par rapport au comté d'Édesse. Bien que cette démonstration eût pour but immédiat de couvrir la principauté contre une invasion éventuelle, il est certain qu'elle ne fut pas étrangère à la brusque décision de Masʿûd d'accepter les propositions de Jocelin II et de lever le siège de Turbessel." ... "Avec ce souverain [Baldwin III] de dix-huit ans la royauté hiérosolymitaine avait continué sa mission historique. En apparaissant en temps utile sur l'Oronte, il avait sauvé à la fois la principauté d'Antioche et les débris du comte d'Édesse." Cahen (*La Syrie*, p. 385) implies that Joscelin II's gaining of peace with Masʿūd I resulted in part from the latter's apprehension over the King's actions and also declares that Nūr-ad-Dīn played a mediatory rôle in this matter. "Joscelin cette fois put l'écarter [Masʿūd I] par un tribut, parce que Baudouin III envoyait en hâte, sous son connétable Onfroi de Toron, un renfort vers Tell-Bâchir, et surtout sans doute parce que Noûr ad-dîn agit en médiateur." In behalf of Cahen's first observation is the close proximity of ʿAzāz to Tell Bashir. See map in Runciman, *History*, p. 109. Cahen (*La Syrie, loc. cit.*) further observes that "Les rapports de ce dernier [Nūr-ad-Dīn] avec Masʿoûd sont un jeu savant: de Mar'ach, le Seldjouqide avait demandé l'aide de Noûr ad-dîn, qui, ne pouvant refuser de secourir un musulman contre des chrétiens sans désavouer toute sa politique, lui envoya Chîrkoûh; et certes il ne pouvait que gagner à l'affaiblissement des Francs sur leur frontière nord. Mais on conçoit qu'il n'en tenait pas moins à éviter l'installation de Masʿoûd en Syrie et soit à l'éloigner de conquêtes plus méridionales soit à les opérer avant lui. D'où sa médiation à Tell-Bâchir."

invasion from the northeast with the overrunning of the area around Gargar and neighbouring towns by Kara Arslan. Joscelyn II tried to succour Prince Basil, the Armenian leader in the area, with his own remaining forces and supplies, but the combined Franco-Armenian force was speedily defeated and Prince Basil was captured.[45] Not even the clement treatment accorded to Basil and the other defeated Christians by Kara Arslan[46] could conceal the loss of still more

---

[45] Michael the Syrian, chap. xi, *op. cit.*, p. 294; Grégoire Le Prêtre, *Chronique*, p. 163 and *Continuation*, pp. 330-31.

[46] Michael the Syrian, *op. cit.*, pp. 294-95; Grégoire Le Prêtre, *Chronique*, pp. 163-64 and *Continuation*, p. 331. Ibn al-Athīr, *Atabecs*, pp. 181-82 and *K.-A.*, pp. 480-81 and Abū'l-Fidā, *op. cit.*, p. 29 are in agreement that Joscelyn II inflicted a signal defeat on Nūr-ad-Dīn, following the latter's blow at Tell Bashir, Aintab and ʿAzāz. Thereupon the Edessan chieftain, in a moment of intemperate rejoicing, sent the captured Moslem arms to Masʿūd I with the promise of new gifts to him gained from Nūr-ad-Dīn. All three accounts agree on the time of this episode, which is the Moslem year 546 (April 20, 1151 to April 7, 1152) and indicate that Nūr-ad-Dīn had married Masʿūd's daughter. The accounts are respectively "Voici les armes du mari de ta fille," "Je vous envoie les armes de votre gendre," and "Voici les armes du mari de votre fille." Kamal-Ad-Dîn, *Histoire*, p. 523, narrates the same events with the observation "Voici les armes du mari de ta fille," but assigns them to the Moslem year 545 (April 30, 1150 to April 19, 1151). The chronology of the first three accounts is clearly erroneous, for Joscelyn II was captured in May, 1150. Abou Chamah, *op. cit.*, p. 60, speaks of the defeat inflicted on Nūr-ad-Dīn by Joscelyn II, but says nothing about the alleged insult uttered by Joscelyn II and the son-in-law relationship of Nūr-ad-Dīn to Masʿūd I. This authority places the defeat of Nūr-ad-Dīn by Joscelyn II as occurring in the Moslem year 543 (May 22, 1148-May 10, 1149). Lastly, Michael the Syrian, *Chronique*, p. 297, says under the heading of the year 1150 that "Le sultan [Masʿūd I] lui [Nūr-ad-Dīn] donna sa fille ... et Nour ed-Dîn l'épousa." This marriage is dated as occurring *after* the capture of Joscelyn II. In the light of all these varying datings of these events I am inclined to believe that the clash between Joscelyn II and Nūr-ad-Dīn and the ensuing tendering of an insult by the former to the latter occurred considerably earlier than the winter of 1149-1150, the time which is assigned to these events by Cahen (*La Syrie, loc. cit.*) with considerable doubt on his part. "Dans l'hiver 1149-1150, Joscelin remporta peut-être un succès sur Noûr ad-Dîn mais sans lendemain." This scholar's doubt is further shown (*La Syrie*, pp. 385-86, n. 15) as follows: "Il [Joscelyn II] aurait capturé le porte-drapeau de Noûr ad-Dîn et l'aurait envoyé à Masoûd. Cet épisode, qui ne figure que dans I.A. At. 181, K. 100 H 480, est suspect; seul Michel connaît des hostilités, mais défavorables à Joscelin (294); on peut supposer une autre date, peut-être antérieure à 1149, mais I.A. dit Noûr ad-dîn, gendre de Masoûd, ce qu'il ne devint qu'en 1150." Stevenson (*op. cit.*, p. 167, n.4) supports my views relating to a still earlier time than the winter of 1140-1150 in his observation that "a victory of Joscelin's related as if just preceding his capture (I.A. ii. 181, Kem Blochet 15 = iii. 523) if over Nureddin in person, must have been some time previously." In the light of these considerations, I am inclined to accept the dating given by Abou Chamah. The editor of Ibn al-Athīr's *Atabecs* erroneously states (p. 181, n. 1) that "Le Josselin dont il s'agit ici était le troisième du nom et petit-fils du grand Josselin." Chabot, the editor of Michael the Syrian (*Chronique*, p. 297, n. 1), in commenting on Michael the Syrian's statement that Nūr-ad-Dīn married Masʿūd I's daughter *after* the capture of Joscelyn II, observes as follows: "Selon Ibn el-Athir (*Hist. or. des Crois.* II, 181) Nour ed-Dîn avait épousé la fille du sultan avant la prise de Josselin. Il est probable

cis-Euphratean areas of the already sadly shrunken County of Edessa to the Moslem enemy.

But the military disasters and territorial losses of the closing months of 1149 were soon to be augmented, for Nur-ad-Dīn sundered his truce with Joscelyn II in the winter of 1149-1150. The last reed of protection afforded to the moribund County of Edessa now disappeared. Nūr-ad-Dīn and Masʿūd I now joined forces, with the former's troops striking the County of Edessa from Aleppo on the southeast and those of the latter invading the County on the northwest. Truly the Edessa Franks, as William of Tyre[47] so graphically observes, were figuratively ground between two millstones.

But a still greater disaster was soon to be the lot of the Edessan Franks, for their leader, Joscelyn II, was to fall into Turkish hands in the mid-Spring of 1150. Summoned to Antioch by Patriarch Aimery, who had meantime played the rôle of protector of the weakened Principality of Antioch and Raymond's widow Constance and four children,[48] the Edessan leader left for Antioch in early May, 1150 attended by an escort to assume the regency of the Principality. When the former separated from his escort, he was captured by Turks on May 5 who thereupon took him to Aleppo. When his identity became known, he was led to Nūr-ad-Dīn, who proceeded to blind and imprison him in chains. The luckless Count remained in his Aleppan prison loyal to his Christian faith despite punishments, threats, and blandishments designed to make him a convert to Islam until his death in May, 1159. Denied permission to receive the services of a Latin or Armenian chaplain, he received the last sacraments from Ignace, the Jacobite metropolitan of Aleppo.[49]

---

que l'anecdote contée ici se rapporte à une tentative contre Tell Bašer, peut-être à celle dont-il est question du chap. précédent." Kamal-Ad-Dîn also declares that the marriage had taken place before Joscelyn II's capture. In summary, the alleged rash behavior of Joscelyn II toward Nūr-ad-Dīn occurred *before* his visit to the latter's camp in search of clemency. See *supra*, p. 14. The Edessan leader's quest for clemency apparently resulted from a belated recognition of the folly of his dispatch of Nūr-ad-Dīn's arms to Masʿūd I.

[47] William of Tyre, chap. xvi, *op. cit.*, pp. 784-85.
[48] *Ibid.*, chap. x, p. 775.
[49] *Ibid.*, chap. xi, p. 776; *Anon. Syriac Chronicle*, p. 301; Ibn al-Qalānisī, *op. cit.*, p. 300; Abou Chamah, *op. cit.*, p. 67; *The Chronography of Bar Hebraeus*, pp. 276-77 and 285; Grégoire Le Prêtre, *Continuation*, pp. 331-32 and *Chronique*, p. 164; Ibn al-Furat, *op. cit.*, An 545, 31 v° and 553, 118 r°; Ibn al-Athīr, *K.-A.*, p. 481 and *Atabecs*, pp. 182-83; Kamal-Ad-Dîn, *Histoire*, pp. 523-24; Abū'l-Fidā, *loc. cit.*; Michael the Syrian, *op. cit.*, p. 295 and nn. 1 and 4 and p. 297 and Bk. XVIII, chap. v, p. 315; *Extrait de la chronique de Michel Le Syrien* in *Rec. his. arm.* (Paris, 1869), I, 342-43 and 353.

The psychological and military results of the capture of Joscelyn II were tremendous. The Moslem forces, near and far, were filled with unspeakable joy while the Christian communities were profoundly dejected over the loss of their warrior leader.[50] Beatrice, Joscelyn II's wife, bravely tried to meet the menacing situation with the assistance of the principal men still left in the Kingdom of Jerusalem by a policy of strengthening her fortresses with fresh supplies of arms, men, and food.[51] Her Frankish supporters in Tell Bashir raised her young son, Joscelyn III, to take his father's place.[52] All this, however, was of little avail. Masʿūd I invaded in late May, 1150 the northwestern districts of the County of Edessa adjacent to his own territories and succeeded in securing the surrender of all the Frankish cities and fortresses in return for his pledge of unimpeded and safe conduct to their populations to Tell Bashir, the permanent residence of Joscelyn II after the loss of the

---

(Henceforth this edition of Michael the Syrian will be differentiated from that of the Chabot edition by the addition of the word *Extrait* after Michael the Syrian, whereas the Chabot edition will be differentiated by the addition of the word *Chronique*). See Appendix A for discussion of the sources pertinent to the capture and imprisonment of Joscelyn II. Galust Ter-Grigorian Iskanderian (*Die Kreuzfahrer und ihre Beziehungen zu den armenischen Nachbarfürsten bis zum Untergange der Grafschaft Edessa* [Wieda in Th., 1915], p. 105) believes that Joscelyn II was blinded probably because of his unwillingness to become a convert to Mohammedanism.

[50] Grégoire Le Prêtre, *Chronique, loc. cit.* and *Continuation*, p. 332; Abou Chamah *loc. cit.*; Ibn al-Athīr, *K.-A.*, pp. 481-82 and *Atabecs*, p. 183; Abū'l-Fidā, *loc. cit.*; William of Tyre, *op. cit.*, p. 777. Hans Prutz (*Kulturgeschichte der Kreuzzüge* [Berlin, 1883], p. 163) erroneously states that Ibn al-Athīr believes that Joscelyn III was full of astuteness and treachery and ever ready to forget his oaths and break his engagements. Furthermore, he made solemn peace treaties with Nūr-ad-Dīn, but as soon as he felt he had thereby extricated himself from danger, he soon betrayed his promises. Ibn al-Athīr (*Atabecs, loc. cit.*), writing under the date of the Moslem year 546 (1151-1152 in the western chronology), does make such a charge, but it is made against Joscelyn II, *not* Joscelyn III. I may add that Stevenson (*op. cit.*, p. 150 and n. 2) observes that "Joscelin's [II] personal courage and military capacity are praised by the Moslem historians." [2] "Cf. I. A. i. 433. [sic] But there may be confusion with Joscelin I." This reference to Ibn al-Athīr's *K.-A.*, which actually appears on p. 443 and is listed under the Moslem year 539 (1144-1145 in the western chronology), refers to "... Josselin, grâce à sa bravoure et à son esprit de ruse, était l'âme des conseils des Francs et le chef de leurs armées." Since this language resembles markedly Ibn al-Athīrs's *Atabecs* reference (*loc. cit.*) to Joscelyn II: "Cet homme [Joscelyn II] était rempli de ruse et de perfidie..." it may not even apply to Joscelyn I, but rather is pertinent to Joscelyn II. *Both* references of Ibn-al-Athīr to Joscelyn are chronologically long *after* the death of Joscelyn I in 1131. Hence it seems to me that the Stevenson observation, namely "But there may be confusion with Joscelin I," is erroneous. In any event, Ibn al-Athīr's references have no relevance whatsoever to Joscelyn III.

[51] William of Tyre, *loc. cit.*

[52] *The Chronography of Bar Hebraeus*, p. 277; Michael the Syrian, Bk. XVII, chap. xii, *Chronique*, p. 296.

city of Edessa.⁵³ Kesoun, Raban, Behesni, and Marzban fell into Mas'ūd I's hands and Tell Bashir itself suffered investment. The citizenry of Kesoun, terrified by Mas'ūd I's military power, surrendered their city after their spokesman, Bishop Iwannis, received a promise from Mas'ūd I that the Franks resident in Kesoun could depart in peace to Aintab.⁵⁴ The spirited defense of Tell Bashir made by the young Joscelyn III, his father's soldiery, and the citizen population finally obliged Mas'ūd I to withdraw into his own country. But still, on balance, his invasion was successful, for he now turned over the conquered areas to Kîlîj Arslan II, his son and heir to the sultanate.⁵⁵

Meanwhile, the Byzantine emperor, Manuel, having been apprised of the desperate condition of the County of Edessa, dispatched a large military force with an offer to Countess Beatrice of a fixed annual revenue large enough to allow her and her children a respectable living, if she, by way of compensation, would turn over to him the fortresses she still retained.⁵⁶ King Baldwin III of the Kingdom of Jerusalem, who had recently journeyed north to Antioch with the Count of Tripoli, the Constable Humphrey II, and Guy, the lord of Beirut, to protect the now leaderless Principality of Antioch and County of Edessa,⁵⁷ decided that, because the prior requirements of his own state prevented him from tarrying very long in the north and because his own military forces were insufficient to permit him to rule two provinces so distant from one another, it would be best to accept the Emperor's offer. If disaster must come to the County of Edessa, it would be preferable to have the onus of this eventuality devolve upon the emperor rather than upon himself. Accordingly, a new treaty embodying the emperor's proposals was concluded with the consent of Countess Beatrice and her children. In addition, both parties fixed a day for King Baldwin's entrance into the County of Edessa to effect the surrender of the

---

⁵³ William of Tyre, chap. xv, *op. cit.*, p. 784.

⁵⁴ *The Chronography of Bar Hebraeus*, *loc. cit.*; Ibn al-Qalānisī, *op. cit.*, pp. 300-01; Michael the Syrian, *Chronique*, *loc. cit.*; Grégoire Le Prêtre, chap. cxi, *Chronique*, p. 165 and chap. cclxi, *Continuation*, p. 332; Ibn al-Furat, *op. cit.*, An 545, 32 v° and 33 v°. Grousset (*Histoire*, p. 296) considers the sending of Bishop Iwannis to Mas'ūd to be an example of the Turcophile viewpoints of the Syriac Christian population of Kesoun and observes that "... il est difficile de ne pas y voir un ralliement spontané de la communauté syriaque à la restauration turque."

⁵⁵ Grégoire Le Prêtre, *Chronique*, pp. 165-66 and *Continuation*, pp. 332-33; Ibn al-Qalānisī, *op. cit.*, p. 301; Ibn al-Furat, *op. cit.*, An 545, 32 v°. Runciman (*History*, p. 330) believes that Mas'ūd I had designated Tell Bashir as his daughter's dowry. Cahen (*La Syrie*, p. 387) speaks of Joscelyn III at this time as "encore enfant."

⁵⁶ William of Tyre, chap. xvi, *op. cit.*, pp. 784-85

⁵⁷ *Ibid.*, chap. xv, pp. 783-84; Michael the Syrian, *Chronique*, p. 297

fortresses still under Frankish control and to place Manuel's men in possession. The transfer arrangement was executed as planned, with King Baldwin III taking under his protection Countess Beatrice and her children and all others both Latins and Armenians desiring to leave. The Emperor's forces now took over all the Countess's remaining fortresses in August, 1150, namely Tell Bashir, Aintab, Ravendan, Bira, and Samosata,[58] save for Qaʻlat ar-Rūm which she retained briefly and

---

[58] William of Tyre, chap. xvi, *op. cit.*, pp. 785-86; *The Chronography of Bar Hebraeus, loc. cit.*; Michael the Syrian *Chronique, loc. cit.*; Babcock and Krey: *op. cit.*, p. 208, n. 30) observe that "Emperor Manuel's attention had been aroused by the events of 1149. The situation seemed to offer an unusual opportunity to realize ancestral claims upon the region. He not only reinforced his army in the neighborhood, but also prepared to extend his interests in both Edessa and Antioch. The transactions here recorded must be dated in 1150 (see F. Chalandon, *Les Comnène*, II, 424-25)." Writing in similar vein, Runciman (*History, loc. cit.*), while stating that the reason for the Emperor's decision to purchase the remainder of the County of Edessa from the Franks is uncertain, discounts the belief of the Franks that "... in his [the Emperor's] pride he thought that he could hold them. [the territories ceded by the Franks to Manuel] It is unlikely that he was so badly misinformed. Rather, he was looking ahead. He hoped before long to come in force to Syria. If he lost them now he could recover them then; and his claim would be beyond dispute." Cahen (*La Syrie, loc. cit.*) suggests that Emperor Manuel's program—"Loin de renoncer aux visées syriennes de son [Manuel's] père (il intervenait au même moment en Cilicie), il vit dans la triste condition des Francs une occasion de réaliser des progrès de leur côté"—afforded Constance, the widowed ruler of Antioch, a chance to continue her husband's policies vis-à-vis the Kingdom of Jerusalem: "Constance d'Antioche, restée veuve avec deux fils en bas âge, cherchait déjà, semble-t-il, comme plus nettement plus tard après la captivité de son second mari Renaud, à s'appuyer, en partie pour échapper à la tutelle jérusalemite, sur Manuel Comnène, prolongeant en somme la politique des dernières années de Raymond." Charles Diehl ("The Byzantine Empire and the Crusades," *Essays on the Crusades* [Burlington, Vermont, 1903], pp. 113-14) comments in similar vein on Emperor Manuel's long-run strategy in respect to the County of Edessa. In respect to the question of the respective views of Emperor Manuel and the Edessans on the political relationship of the County of Edessa toward the Byzantine Empire and the Kingdom of Jerusalem, John L. La Monte ("To What Extent was the Byzantine Empire the Suzerain of the Latin Crusading States?", *Byzantion* [Paris, 1932], VII, 256) observes that "Edessa, which was feudally dependent upon Jerusalem and Antioch, seems to have been considered by the Byzantines to have formed a part of the Empire, and ... there can be little doubt as to the Imperial pretentions over the county. That the Edessans recognized these claims does not seem probable. Though Edessan troops served together with the Antiochene in the army of the Emperor John it was in all probability as vassals of Antioch rather than as direct vassals of Byzantium. And when the Emperor Manuel purchased the territories which remained after the fall of Edessa from Beatrice, the wife of the imprisoned Count Joscelin, King Baldwin of Jerusalem, as her suzerain, carried out the transfer of the lands to the Basileus. The counts of Edessa were liegemen of the kings of Jerusalem and of the princes of Antioch, but I cannot find any definite acceptance of the suzerainty of the Byzantine Emperors." Both Runciman (*History*, p. 329) and Marshall Baldwin ("The Latin States under Baldwin III and Amalric I, 1143-1174," *A History of the Crusades. The First Hundred Years* [Philadelphia, 1955], I, 534) state that Beatrice surrendered Duluk to the Greeks. But none of the sources dealing with Beatrice's cessions to the

then gave to the Catholicos (vicar), Gregory III, the head of the Armenian church, with the stipulation that he would return it to her son, Joscelyn III, if he should ever return to power. The Catholicos agreed and, assuming the rule of Qal'at ar-Rūm, made it the seat of the Armenian Catholicos. Joscelyn III, agreeing with his mother's views on the impossibility of holding the fortress in the midst of the surrounding Turkish sea and persuaded by a money gift, confirmed the arrangements.[59] The Countess and her children, having been taken

---

Greeks mentions Duluk. Furthermore, as Runciman's own map (*History*, p. 109) shows, Duluk was situated within the northeastern corner of the Principality of Antioch rather than within the boundaries of the County of Edessa. If Beatrice had actual possession of Duluk as of the time of the cession of the other towns, it had been for only a brief time and as a result of the recent misfortunes of the Principality of Antioch (*supra*, pp. 15-17) which, in turn, created a power vacuum which Beatrice in the closely adjacent County of Edessa was able to fill. William of Tyre (*op. cit.*, p. 786) speaks of "et fortasse alia quaedam" after his listing of the six towns ceded to the Greeks by Beatrice namely "...Turbessel, Hamtab, Ravendel, Ranculat, Bile, Samosatum..." Duluk *may* have been one of these "et fortasse alia quaedam." But the evidence will not support the proposition that Duluk *was* ceded by Beatrice to the Greeks. (Henceforth Baldwin's chapter will be cited as "The Latin States.")

[59] Michael the Syrian, *Extrait*, p. 343; Guiragos de Kantzag, *Extrait de l'histoire d'Arménie* in *Rec. his. arm.* (Paris, 1869), I, 415; Behâ Ed-Dîn Abu El-Mehâsan Yûsuf, 'Saladin'; *Or What Befell Sultan Yûsuf (Salâh Ed-Dîn) (1137-1193 A. D.)* Palestine Pilgrims Text Society (London, 1897), XIII, 185, n. 1 and p. 189; (Henceforth this last source will be cited as Behâ Ed-Dîn, *Saladin*); Sěmpad, *Chronique du royaume de la Petite Arménie* in *Rec. his. arm.* (Paris, 1869), I, 618; Vartan Le Grand, *loc. cit.* Michael the Syrian (*Chronique, loc. cit.*) affords a variant version of this transfer. Following the imprisonment of Joscelyn II a certain Michael, who had been established in power at Qal'at ar-Rūm by the now imprisoned Count, ordered Beatrice and Joscelyn III to call upon Gregory to journey to Qal'at ar-Rūm and render assistance to Michael. Gregory complied with the request, but soon seized Michael's person by knavery, drove him out of the fortress, and seized it for himself. I agree with editor Dulaurier's views set forth on this version in his footnote. (Grégoire Le Prêtre, *Chronique*, p. 154, n. 4) "...conte qui lui a été suggéré par la haine qu'en sa qualité de Syrien et de Jacobite il avait vouée aux Arméniens, et dont il fait preuve en maints passages de son livre." Since *The Chronography of Bar Hebraeus* (*loc. cit.*) tells essentially the same story as that recounted in this edition of Michael the Syrian, the same criticism obtains here as well. Cahen (*La Syrie*, pp. 336-37) considers Countess Beatrice's decision to cede Qal'at ar-Rūm to the Armenian Catholicos to be in harmony with the excellent relations maintained by Joscelyn I and Joscelyn II with the Armenians in earlier times. Sirarpie Der Nersessian ("The Kingdom of Cilician Armenia," *A History of the Crusades. The Later Crusades 1189-1311* [Philadelphia, 1962], II, 641-42) observes that "Hromgla [Qal'at ar-Rūm] seems to have been given at first "in trust", [by Beatrice] but later the catholicus purchased it from Joscelyn III for 15,000 tahegans; the official deed of transfer was kept in the archives of Hromgla so that—adds the Cilician Chronicle—no member of the Courtenay family should ever claim the castle." Ter Grigorian Iskanderian (*op. cit.*, p. 106) differs in his emphasis, stating that "Als aber nach einigen Jahren Joscelin III. nach Romkla kam, wurde er mit einer Geldsumme abgefunden, da er einsah, dass die Burg nicht zu halten war."

under the protection of King Baldwin III, then repaired to the security of Jerusalem.[60]

The years 1149 and 1150 had been unfortunate ones for the House of Courtenay and, in particular, its imprisoned ruler and his now landless son, Joscelyn III. But still even after the departure of the Countess and her children there seemed to be the possibility of an eventual recovery of at least a portion of the County of Edessa for the Franks, if for no other reason than that some of it was in the hands of schismatic Greeks who might in time change their generally hostile policies towards the Latin Franks and elect to cooperate once more against their common Moslem foes. However, even this faint hope was soon extinguished with the decision of Mas'ūd I and Nūr-ad-Dīn in the Spring of 1151 once more to join forces and to invade the County of Edessa which was now bereft of its former Frankish protectors. Timurtash, the Artukid ruler of Mardin, and Kara Arslan joined in the kill. The Greek garrisons were unable to withstand the quadruple attacks and soon Timurtash ruled in Bira, Samosata, Cafersoud, Khourous, and Qal'at ar-Rūm, Mas'ūd in Aintab and Duluk, and Nūr-ad-Dīn in 'Azāz, Cyrrhus, Krak des Chevaliers, Tall-Khālid, Ravendan, Hisn Kerzin, and Nahr al-Djauz. Other towns falling into the Moslem net were Burj-ar-risas and Kafarlāthā. Tell Bashir surrendered through starvation to Ḥassān, the governor of Manbij and Nūr-ad-Dīn's lieutenant, in July, 1151.[61]

---

[60] Michael the Syrian, *Chronique*, *loc. cit.*; William of Tyre, *loc. cit.*; *The Chronography of Bar Hebraeus*, *loc. cit.* Runciman (*History*, p. 329, n. 1) states that "The Byzantine historians make no mention of the transaction" between Emperor Manuel and the Franks. Cahen (*La Syrie*, p. 388, n. 23), on the other hand, maintains that Kinnamos, IV, 17 does have material relevant to his matter. However, the reference to Cinnamus in *Recueil des historiens des croisades: historiens grecs* (Paris, 1875), I, 270, which is listed as "Cinna. IV, #17, p. 103," dates the material as pertinent to the year 1159 and relevant to "Manuelis iter in Ciliciam et Syriam." The 1159 expedition of Manuel is, of course, entirely distinct and different from that of 1150.

[61] Ibn al-Qalānisī, *op. cit.*, pp. 300-01 and 309; William of Tyre, chap. xvii, *op. cit.*, p. 789; Ibn al-Furat, *op. cit.*, An 545, 33 v°, An 546, 35 r° and An 547, 42 r°; *The Chronography of Bar Hebraeus*, *loc. cit.*: Ibn al-Athīr, *Atabecs*, *loc. cit.* and *K.-A.*, p. 481; Kamal-ad-Dīn, *Histoire*, pp. 524-26; Abū'l-Fidā, *loc. cit.*; Michael the Syrian, *Chronique*, pp. 296-97 and *Extrait*, p. 342; Grégoire Le Prêtre, *Chronique*, pp. 165-66 and *Continuation*, p. 333. The account provided by Kamal-ad-Dîn states that Nūr-ad-Dîn's gains in 1150 comprised merely 'Azāz, Tell Bashir, and Tall Khālid and that it was not until 1155 that he gained Aintab, Cyrrhus, Ravenden, Burj-ar-risas, Bira, Cafersoud, Marash, and Nahr al—Djauz. This account is superseded by the more contemporary Latin, Arabic, and Syriac accounts. It is because of these considerations that I reject Stevenson's observation (*op. cit.*, p. 169), which is apparently based on Kamal-ad-Dîn's *Histoire*. "Nureddin's first share was small. His chief acquisitions were made in the year

1155, at the expense of Mas'ud's son." Cahen (*La Syrie*, p. 387) finds the critical situation of the northern Franks in the fact that "... il n'était plus possible de communiquer avec Antioche que par la route détournée de Aïntâb et Marrî, et combien de temps cette route même, menacée au nord et au sud, résisterait-elle?" Cf. Stevenson, *op. cit.*, p. 168. Grousset (*Histoire*, p. 307) summarizes the total import of the disappearance of the County of Edessa as a Frankish entity as follows: "La liquidation du comté d'Édesse, pour douloureuse qu'elle fût, apparaît aux chroniqueurs latins comme un sacrifice inévitable. Raymond de Poitiers et Joscelin II une fois disparus, il n'était pas possible à Baudouin III, malgré sa vaillance, d'assumer la défense de tout le pays, de l'Idumée à Antioche. C'était déjà une lourde charge que d'assurer contre les razzias périodiques de Nûr al-Dîn la protection d'Antioche où la princesse Constance—une régente de vingt ans!—devait à tout instant faire appel au roi de Jérusalem. La Jazîra perdue, puis la ligne de l'Euphrate, la Syrie franque devait se résigner à reporter ses frontières derrière l'Oronte, heureuse si Nûr al-Dîn ne les franchissait pas et désormais condamnée de ce côté à la défensive." Cahen (*La Syrie*, p. 386, n. 17, p. 388, n. 24, and p. 389, n. 25) respectively observes that "A Qal-'at-ar-Roûm le Catholicos demeura mais reçut un résident musulman ....." "I. A., At., 185 K.107 (H485), qui croit à tort que Noûr-ad-Din occupa Douloûk; ..." and "I. A., 132, place la prise de Tell-Bâchir en 549/1154, sans doute à cause du synchronisme avec le siège de Damas de cette année, au lieu de celui de 546 qu'il a omis parce qu'il a échoué." Also see in the first cited reference Cahen's discussion of the problem of the captured towns.

CHAPTER TWO

RECOVERY, RESTORATION, AND DISASTER
1151-1164

The scanty evidence, rather imprecise in chronological aspects pertaining to the House of Courtenay in general and Joscelyn III in particular during the next thirteen years from 1151 to 1164, reveals a steady improvement of their shattered fortunes. King Baldwin III made Joscelyn III his direct vassal possibly as early as the late Summer of 1150, endowing him with lands outside of Acre as well as revenue from the harbor of Acre itself.[62] These territorial and financial increments were to be augmented temporarily in the mid-1150's when he succeeded during the course of the Moslem year 551 (February 25, 1156 to February 12, 1157) in recovering Burj-ar-risas. The young count, following his demolition of the city, constructed a citadel with a leaden sheath. But his prize was only a brief one, for Nūr-ad-Dīn effected a quick recovery of the city, following which he strengthened the citadel and added to the city still more villages.[63] At some time subsequent to June 7, 1156 the former Edessan chieftain became the marshal of the Kingdom of Jerusalem as well.[64] Later on at some

---

[62] *Chronique d'Ernoul et de Bernard Le Trésorier*, ed. by M. L. de Mas Latrie (Paris, 1871), chap. iii, p. 15. (This source will henceforth be cited as *Chronique d'Ernoul*). Cf. the view of Edward Gibbon, *The Decline and Fall of the Roman Empire* (New York, 1932), II, 1147, n. 76. "His [Joscelyn III's] possessions are distinguished in the Assisses of Jerusalem.... among the feudal tenures of the kingdom, which must therefore have been collected between the years 1153 and 1187."

[63] Kamal-Ad-Dîn, *Histoire*, pp. 524-25 and n. 3, p. 525. Kamal-Ad-Dîn's statement that Nūr-ad-Dīn had captured Burj-ar-risas during the preceding Moslem year 550 (March 7, 1155 to February 24, 1156) must be rejected. See *supra*, n. 61.

[64] *Les familles d'Outre-Mer de Du Cange* in *Collection de documents inédits sur l'histoire de France*. Première Série. Histoire politique. Publiées par E.-G. Rey (Paris, 1869), p. 625. (Henceforth this book will be cited as *Les Familles d'Outre-Mer*). This book declares that Joscelyn III "... fut maréchal après Eudes [de St. Amand]....", observes that Eudes is referred to as marshal in a document issued on June 7, 1156, and supersedes the observations of the editor of *Livre de Jean d'Ibelin. Assises de la Haute Cour* (Paris, 1841), I, 414, n. a. in his listing of the marshals of the Kingdom of Jerusalem. His listing does not include Joscelyn III as the holder of this position. His listing of the marshals during the latter half of the 12th century reads as follows: "Eudes de Saint-Amand, maréchal sous le roi Baudouin III. Guillaume, 1160, 1169. Gérard de Pugy, sous le roi Amaury." [Henceforth this source will be cited as *Assises*). John L. La Monte (*Feudal Monarchy in the Latin Kingdom of Jerusalem 1100 to 1291* [Cambridge, 1932], pp. 121 and 254) observes that "Among the marshals of Jerusalem only Eudes de

unknown date in very late 1160 or, more probably, early in 1161, and prior to February 9, 1163 he assumed control of the fief of Ḥārim. This fief had been captured in January or February, 1158 by King Baldwin III, who had taken advantage of the illness of Nūr-ad-Dīn, and was successively held by Guy Fraisnel and by Reginald of Saint-Valéry.[65] The circumstances under which the transfer of this fief from Reginald of Saint-Valéry to Joscelyn III was effected are unknown. It is possible that the former's death or return to Europe was a factor responsible for the transfer. It is certain that he remained in the Holy Land until 1160.[66]

St Amand, Joscelin de Courtney, Hugh Martin, and John de Gibelet were men of any great consequence." and that Joscelyn III was a marshal from 1156 to 1159. See this same book, pp. 119-21 for a description of the powers vested in the marshal. (Henceforth this book will be differentiated from the other works of this author by the term *Feudal Monarchy*. Future references to La Monte's article, "The rise and decline of a Frankish Seigneury in the time of the Crusades," will be cited as "The rise" to differentiate them from references to the other works of this scholar).

[65] William of Tyre, Bk. XVIII, chap. xix, *op. cit.*, p. 852; Ibn al-Qalānisī, *op. cit.*, p. 344; Albert of Aachen, *Liber Christianae expeditionis pro ereptione, emundatione, restitutione Sanctae Hierosolymitanae ecclesiae*, Bk. XI, chap. xi, in *Rec. his. occ.* (Paris, 1879) IV, 683; Delaville Le Roulx, *Cartulaire*, No. 45, p. 38; Michael the Syrian, *Extrait*, pp. 351 and 353; *Chronique de Robert de Torigni*, ed. by Léopold Delisle (Rouen, 1872), I, 316. (Future references to the last-named source will be given as Robert de Torigni). Gibb ("Nūr-ad-Dīn" p. 522) and Baldwin ("The Latin States," p. 542) are respectively of the opinion that "Baldwin... recaptured Ḥārim in January or February 1158" and "Accordingly Ḥārim was besieged and taken after a siege of two months (February, 1158)." Cf. Stevenson, *op. cit.*, p. 179, n. 1 who observes that "Harim was a Christian stronghold in 1156, if therefore it was besieged and captured by the Latins in 1158 it must have been lost by them in the interval. As this loss is not recorded possibly the name Harim as given by the sources is an error." Cahen (*La Syrie*, p. 540, n. 40) comments as follows on the history of Ḥārim in the period after its Frankish recovery in 1158. "Albert, XI, 40, appuyé par Cart., I, 38 où il s'agit de dons faits dans le district de Kafartâb par le seigneur de l'endroit, Bonable, dans celui de Delthium par Robert de Saint-Lô, qui signe, et dans celui de Hârim par Roger de Florence; ce dernier ne signe pas, mais on voit signer Guy Fraisnel; comme il ne signe pas d'autre seigneur, il est probable que Guy est le suzerain de Roger. Après 1160, on ne connaît plus de seigneur de Ḥârim de la famille des Fraisnel; nous savons que Baudouin III en nomma gouverneur Renaud de Saint-Valéry, et comme celui-ci figure dans plusieurs actes à Jérusalem en 1159 et 1160, sa désignation ne peut guère être antérieure à la fin de cette année, quoi qu'il semble résulter du texte de Robert de Torigny, 508, qu'elle datait du lendemain même de la reprise de la place en 1158." (Cahen's reference to Robert de Torigny pertains to the *Monumenta Germaniae Historica SS* VI edition). Also consult Cahen, *La Syrie*, p. 384, n. 12.

[66] Röhricht, *Regesta*, No. 360, p. 94, Robert de Torigni, *op. cit.*, p. 316, n. 4. "Le séjour de Renaud de Saint-Valeri en Terre-Sainte se prolongea jusqu'en 1160; parmi les témoins mentionnés dans une charte de Hughes d'Ibelin, en 1160, on remarque: "Rainuldus de Sancto Gallerico"; *Cartulaire du Saint-Sépulcre*, p. 134." Runciman (*History*, p. 349, n. 1) states that "Renald of Saint-Valéry was still a baron of Jerusalem in 1160 (Röhricht, *Regesta*, p. 94) but returned to the West soon afterwards." Neither

Moreover, the distant kinship of Joscelyn III to and influence upon the royal family of the Kingdom of Jerusalem were greatly enhanced when his sister Agnes, following the death of her first husband,

---

Röhricht nor any other source cited in this footnote declares that he returned to the West soon thereafter. Jean Richard (*Le royaume latin de Jérusalem* [Paris, 1953], p. 77) in a subsection entitled "Le règne d'Amaury I," which is part of Chapter V entitled "Le Pouvoir Royal," states in connection with Amalric's invasion in Egypt in 1164 that "Et si le futur sénéchal Jocelin III n'était pas parmi eux, [the invaders], c'est qu'il avait reçu d'Amaury, en 1162, le fief de Harenc dans la principauté d'Antioche." I cannot agree with this dating and am inclined to believe that it occurred in the very last days of 1160 or, more probably, in 1161. The *only* evidence pertaining to the grant of Ḥārim to Joscelyn III is in Michael the Syrian, *Extrait*, p. 353. Vague as to the precise time of the grant and the identity of the donor, it reads as follows: "Cependant le roi de Jérusalem donna Harem au fils de Josselin, qui portait le même nom que son père, et qui était l'héritier de Hr'om-gla." The reference to Joscelyn II, which immediately follows this material, is merely explanatory in nature. "Celui-ci [Joscelyn II] pour venger la mort de son père, saccageant jour et nuit le territoire d'Alep. Mais au bout de deux ans il fut pris par les troupes de cette ville, conduit dans ses murs, et il y mourut dans les fers." It does not seems likely to me that "le roi" in question was Amalric, for Amalric did not become king, as Richard himself states, (*loc. cit.*) until after the death of his childless brother Baldwin III on February 8, 1163. Baldwin ("The Latin States," p. 547) is in essential agreement with Richard, in so far as the date of the death of Baldwin III is concerned, for he states that "Having confessed his sins he [Baldwin III] died on February 10, 1163." In view of the danger of Moslem reconquest of Ḥārim following the departure of Reginald of Saint-Valery, it was essential that it be placed immediately under the control and protection of a Frankish nobleman. And this in turn meant a transfer of the control of Ḥārim at an earlier time than February 9, 1163, the earliest possible time at which Amalric could have been named rightly "le roi." Dulaurier, the editor of the *Extrait* edition of Michael the Syrian, (p. 353, n. 2) seems to me to support my position, for he criticizes the next reference to "Le roi de Jérusalem" made by Michael the Syrian and which follows immediately after the explanatory citation of Michael the Syrian about Joscelyn II which I listed above. This second reference to "Le roi de Jérusalem" in Michael the Syrian reads as follows: "Le roi de Jérusalem Baudouin s'avança sur les confins de Damas, et ayant gagné les Bédouins, qui campaient dans ces lieux par ordre de Nour-eddin, il alla avec eux en Égypte, pilla ce royaume et lui imposa un tribu de 160,000 tahegans." Dulaurier's criticism reads as follows: "Cette guerre contre l'Égypte fut faite, non point par Baudouin III, comme le prétend Michel, qui brouille ici les événements, mais par son frère et son successeur, Amaury, qui entreprit contre ce pays trois expéditions, dans les limites des années 1164 et 1169." Dulaurier's failure to criticize in any way Michael the Syrian's *first* reference to "Le roi de Jérusalem" and the inference from Dulaurier's criticism of the identity bestowed by Michael the Syrian on the *second* reference to "le roi de Jérusalem" suggest to me that he believes that the king who granted Ḥārim to Joscelyn III was Baldwin III and not Amalric. In view of all the preceding discussion I cannot and do not accept the respective views of Stevenson (*op. cit.*, p. 183) and E. J. King (*The Knights Hospitallers in the Holy Land* [London, 1931], p. 85) that Joscelyn III was "governor of Harim" and "governor of Harenc," as of the time of his capture by the Moslems, which they believed occurred in July, 1160. In view of the definitive loss of the County of Edessa, John L. La Monte ("Chronology of the Orient latin," *Bulletin of the International Committee of Historical Sciences* [Paris, 1942-1943], XII, Part 2, pp. 170 and 171) is entirely correct in his observation that Joscelyn III was only the titular count of Edessa and was the last to use the title. The

Reginald of Marash, in 1149,[67] married her third cousin, Amalric, the brother of Baldwin III, over the objections of Patriarch Fulcher in 1157.[68] Two children were born of this union in 1160 and 1161 respectively. They were Baldwin, later to be known as Baldwin IV, the sixth king of Jerusalem, and his sister Sibyl.[69] Joscelyn III's growing importance is revealed by his reception of his nephew at the sacred font. And even though Agnes' second marriage to Amalric was soon dissolved in 1162 on grounds of consanguinity by the action of Patriarch Fulcher, provision was made that their children should be considered as legitimate and should have full rights of succession to the inheritance of their father.[70] And Joscelyn III *may* have been

---

title itself "... was revived only as a title in the kingdom of Cyprus where it was given to one of the more important baronies of the island." This scholar's dating of Joscelyn III's rôle as titular count of Edessa covers the years from 1148 to 1200 and hence may suggest a belief on his part that Joscelyn II was so apprehensive over the prospects of his own continued rule of the County of Edessa in the face of the waxing Moslem power that he decided to invest his young son with the title as early as 1148. (Henceforth references to this article of La Monte's will be cited as "Chronology" to differentiate them from other works of this author). Richard (*op. cit.*, p. 135), on the other hand, implies that the status of Joscelyn III as the titular count of Edessa did not begin until 1151, for he speaks of him as "Ayant perdu le comté d'Edesse (1151)...."

[67] William of Tyre, Bk. XIV, chap. iii and Bk. XVII, chap. ix, *op. cit.*, pp. 610 and 773.

[68] *Ibid.*, Bk. XIX, chap. iv, *op. cit.*, pp. 888-89; Robert de Torigni, *op. cit.*, p. 309; Runciman, *History*, Appendix III; *Les familles d'Outre-Mer*, p. 20; *Chronique d'Ernoul*, *loc. cit.*; Herzog (*op. cit.*, p. 63), while conceding Agnes's attractiveness was an element in Amalric's desire for her hand, also observes that her wealth was a factor as well. Her mother belonged to one of the wealthiest families of Antioch, namely the house of Saone which owned "Salione," the strongest castle of Syria.

[69] William of Tyre, Bk. XIV, chap. iii and Bk. XIX, chap. iv, *op. cit.*, pp. 610 and 888, *Les familles d'Outre-Mer*, *loc. cit.*; Louis Bréhier, "Amaury I," *Dictionnaire d'histoire et de géographie ecclésiastiques* (Paris, 1914), II, 998.

[70] William of Tyre, Bk. XIX, chap. iv, *op. cit.*, pp. 888-89. Runciman (*History*, p. 362) believes that the barons of the Kingdom of Jerusalem as well as the Patriarch demanded the annulment of the marriage and that their action resulted not solely from grounds of her consanguinity, which was well known, but also from the fact that "She was considerably older than Amalric".... "and her reputation for chastity was not good." Richard (*op. cit.*, p. 77) believes that "... l'hostilité des barons visait surtout son entourage, composé de barons édesséniens dépossédés qui s'étaient "repliés" en Palestine, et dont ils ne pouvaient souffrir l'influence sur le roi." This same scholar (*op. cit.*, p. 78) observes, in connection with the annulment of this marriage, that "Aussi est-il vraisemblable qu'en éloignant Agnès d'Édesse, l'"opposition" cherchait à se débarrasser de la camarilla édessénienne qu'elle ne réussit pas à écarter." This view derives support from the extreme unlikelihood that the consanguinity of Agnes and Amalric was unknown to important persons before their marriage. Gustave Schlumberger (*Campagnes du roi Amaury Ier de Jérusalem en Égypte au XIIe siècle* [Paris, 1906], p. 13) tartly remarks "Tout ce récit de Guillaume de Tyr est d'une grande naiveté." (Henceforth this book will be cited as *Campagnes du roi* to differentiate it from his

formally recognized as titular count of the now non existent County of Edessa following the death of his father, Joscelyn II, in May, 1159.[71] And that his military prowess grew and perhaps matched the one he gained in the area of politics is indicated by the admiring observations of one of the chief 12th century Moslem historians to the effect that he was one of the most illustrious and brave of the Franks.[72]

But Joscelyn III's slowly acquired prestige and influence gained during the thirteen years following the disasters in the County of Edessa in the later 1140's were soon to suffer a nearly fatal eclipse rivaling for a time that of his late father Joscelyn II. Nūr-ad-Dīn, having suffered an ignominious defeat at the hands of the Franks around Tripoli at the close of 1163,[73] took advantage of King Amalric's absence in an expedition to Egypt and resolved to avenge this disaster by an investment of the Frankish fortress of Ḥārim with the assistance of his fellow Moslem chieftains, notably the rulers of Mosul, Ḥiṣn Kaifā, and Mardin. The ensuing siege, conducted with great fury and determination, provoked the north Frankish leaders, namely Bohemond III, prince of Antioch and son and successor to the late Prince Raymond of Antioch, the younger Raymond III, son of the late Raymond II, Count of Tripoli, Joscelyn III, Hugh of Lusignan, together with a Byzantine ally, Coloman, the governor of Cilicia and a kinsman of the Emperor Manuel, and an Armenian supporter, Prince Ṭoros, to assemble a large infantry and cavalry force for Ḥārim's relief. Nūr-ad-Dīn and the other Moslem leaders decided to raise the siege rather than risk a battle.[74] Simultaneously, however, they devised

---

Numismatique). Also see Grousset (Histoire, p. 697, n. 2) on this matter as well as an account of Agnes' later marriages.

[71] Chronique d'Ernoul (loc. cit.) simply says "Amaury, the Count of Jaffa, took for a wife the daughter of the Count of Rohais [Edessa]. This woman had a brother Jocelyn who was the Count of Rohais after the death of his father." The editors of A History of the Crusades. The Later Crusades 1189-1311 (Philadelphia, 1962), II, 829, although not stating the time of the designation of Joscelyn III as the titular count of Edessa, declare him to have been such from 1159 to 1200.

[72] Ibn al-Athīr, K.-A., p. 538 and Atabecs, p. 221.

[73] William of Tyre, Bk. XIX, chap. viii, op. cit., pp. 894-95; Kamal-Ad-Dîn, Histoire, pp. 534-35; Ibn al-Athīr, K.-A., pp. 530-31 and Atabecs, pp. 208-09; Michael the Syrian, Bk. XVIII, chap. x, Chronique, p. 324 and Extrait, p. 358. Babcock and Krey, p. 306, n. 20.

[74] William of Tyre, chap. ix, op. cit., pp. 895-96; Ibn al-Athīr, Atabecs, pp. 219-22 and K.-A., pp. 538-39; Roger of Wendover, Liber Qui Dicitur Flores Historiarum, ed. Henry G. Hewlett (London, 1886), I, 40; Anon. Syriac Chronicle, p. 303. Gustav Köhler (Die Entwickelung des Kriegswesens und die Kreuzführung in der Ritterzeit von Mitte des

a plan to entice the Frankish cavalry into a vain pursuit of their own yielding right wing and then, when the Frankish cavalry and infantry had become separated, to have the Moslem left wing turn upon the Frankish infantry and annihilate it. The Frankish cavalry, following their bootless pursuit of the Moslem right wing, would then turn back, and, finding no support from their now decimated infantry, would prove to be an easy prey. And thus the plan was executed on August 10, 1164.

The Franks, emboldened by the spectacle of the retreat, pursued the Turks in aimless fashion, whereupon the latter, putting their plan into action, rallied, turned successively on the Frankish infantry and cavalry, and entrapped them in a confined and swampy place. The result was a bloody rout and shameful surrender. And all the leaders, namely Joscelyn III, Colomon, Bohemond III, Raymond III of Tripoli, and Hugh of Lusignan were captured and led ignominiously to be cast into prison in Aleppo in August, 1164 to the derision of their captors. The only leader to escape capture was Toros, who had seen the impending victory of the Moslems and had, in consequence, withdrawn from the battle in time.[75]

XIten Jahrhunderts bis zu dem Hussitenkrieg [Breslau, 1889], III, 3e partie, p. 212, n. 1) maintains, on the other hand, that the main motive behind Nūr-ad-Dīn's attack on Ḥārim was that of causing Amalric to return from Egypt to Syria and thereby relieve pressure on the forces of Shīrkūh, Nūr-ad-Dīn's field marshal, in his contents with the Caliph, who had called on Amalric for aid. For a full discussion of the Franco-Egyptian contest for the control of Egypt, see *infra*, pp. 47-53.

[75] William of Tyre, *op. cit.*, pp. 896-97; Cinnamus, *op. cit.*, p. 216; Michael the Syrian, *Extrait*, *loc. cit.* and *Chronicle*, *loc. cit.*; *Anon. Syriac Chronicle*, pp. 303-04; *The Chronography of Bar Hebraeus*, p. 288; Roger of Wendover, *loc. cit.*; *Annales de Terre Sainte* in *Archives de l'Orient Latin* (Paris, 1884), II, 432; Röhricht, *Regesta*, Nos. 403, 404, and 405, p. 106; Delaville Le Roulx, *Cartulaire*, No. 330, p. 233; Sigeberti Gemblacensis, *Chronici Continuatio Aquicinctina* in *Monumenta Germaniae Historica* (Hanover, 1844), SS VI, 411; *Epistola Gaufredi Fulcherii, procuratoris militiae Templi, ad Ludovicum* and *Epistola Aymerici, patriarchae Antiocheni, ad Ludovicum* in *Recueil des historiens des Gaules et de la France,* ed. by M. Bouquet and others (Paris, 1878) XVI, 60-62; Robert de Torigni, *op. cit.*, p. 355. Kamal-Ad-Dîn (*Histoire*, pp. 553 and 539-40) gives contradictory accounts, declaring in the first reference that an Aleppan chieftain met Joscelyn III during the Moslem year 550 = March 7, 1155-February 24, 1156) (see observations on this date by Stevenson, *infra*, p. 34) captured him, and took him to the citadel of Aleppo. The second reference, generally paralleling that of William of Tyre under the date of 1163, states that Joscelin III was captured at the battle of Ḥārim in 1164. According to this latter version, Nūr-ad-Dīn's siege of Ḥārim led Prince Bohemond, Joscelyn III, Malîh, the son of Leo, King of Armenia, Daval, the generalissimo of the Greek forces, and the Count of Tripoli to assemble their forces in a relieving action. Nūr-ad-Dīn fell back on Artāḥ in order to draw the Franks out of their own country and to secure a better defensive position,

if the latter should attack him. The Frankish forces, following an advance on Ḥārim to Sofaif, returned to Ḥārim. Nūr-ad-Dīn followed and a battle ensued in which the Moslems were defeated. Nūr-ad-Dīn thereupon, having stationed a lieutenant in an ambuscade, attacked the Franks again in conjunction with his lieutenant, surrounded them, and captured all the leaders cited above except for Malîh. Ibn al-Athīr (K.-A., pp. 538-40 and Atabecs, pp. 221-23) gives essentially the same account as Kamal-Ad-Dîn's second account but dates the battle as occurring in August, 1164 and emphasizes the idea that the initial Moslem defeat was a planned one designed to lure the Frankish cavalry far enough from their infantry to enable the Turkish cavalry to annihilate the pursuing Frankish cavalry. Also see Abou Chamah (op. cit., pp. 108-09 and 125-26) respectively for a brief account of the capture of Raymond of Antioch, the Count of Tripoli, and Joscelyn III at the battle of Ḥārim, which is dated as occurring in the Summer of 1164, and a story which implies that news of events in Egypt was perhaps responsible for Nūr-ad-Dîn's attack on Ḥārim. "Nour ed-Dîn, qui était privé de toute information sur les événements d'Égypte, apprit enfin à Damas l'invasion des Francs [of Egypt] et la trahison de Chawar. Par son ordre, des troupes furent levées de tout côté. Dès que l'armée des provinces orientales eut fait sa concentration à Alep, Medjd ed-Dîn fils d'Ed-Dayyah, lieutenant de Nour ed-Dîn en cette ville, se mit à leur tête et marcha sur Harim..." Chronique d'Amadi, ed. René de Mas Latrie (Paris, 1891), p. 38 dates the capture of Joscelyn III in 1163 and declares that it was associated with the battle of Ḥārim. The Syrian and Armenian narratives of The Chronography of Bar Hebraeus (p. 286), Michael the Syrian (chap. vi, Chronique, p. 316), Anon. Syriac Chronicle (p. 303), and Grégoire Le Prêtre (chap. cxxix, Chronique, p. 195 and chap. cclxxix, Continuation, p. 361), on the other hand, agree that Joscelyn III was captured in the year 609 (February 10, 1160-February 8, 1161). The first two cited accounts declare that Joscelyn III continuously proceeded out of Ḥārim and raided the Aleppan country, whereupon Nūr-ad-Dīn laid an ambush for him, captured him, and then imprisoned him in the same dungeon wherein his father had been imprisoned. The third account states that "In that year [1160] Raynald (Raimun) of Antioch and Joscelyn son of Joscelyn who was captured at Ḥaram ravaged the land of Aleppo; when they had enslaved and plundered at will, they returned unmolested. Raynald went to Antioch. Joscelyn sat in a village eating and drinking when a Turk army overtook him, seized him, and took him to Aleppo. They put him in chains with his father." The fourth and fifth accounts observe respectively that "Cette même année [609 = 10 février 1160-8 février 1161] le fils du comte fut fait prisonnier et emmené à Alep." and "A la même époque [609 = 10 février 1160-8 février 1161] le fils du comte fut fait prisonnier et conduit à Alep."

The disagreement reigning among the primary sources concerning the time, place, and circumstances of the capture and imprisonment of Joscelyn III still continues among modern day scholars. Stevenson (loc. cit.), Runciman (History, p. 358), King (loc. cit.) and Cahen (La Syrie, p. 305) accept the date of 1160 provided by the Syrian and Armenian sources and declare that his capture occurred in or about July, 1160. None of the Armenian and Syrian sources has evidence, as we have seen, permitting such a close pinpointing of the exact time of the capture. Stevenson (op. cit., p. 183, n. 1) states that the Blochet edition of Kamal-Ad-Dîn's Histoire lists Rajab 550 (March 7, 1155 to February 24, 1156) as the year of the capture, but asserts 1160 is confirmed as the correct year by Bar Hebraeus, Michael the Syrian, and Gregory the Armenian. On the other hand, Marshall Baldwin (Raymond III of Tripolis and the Fall of Jerusalem [Princeton, 1936], pp. 10-11 and "The Latin States," p. 551), Joseph Marie Antoine Delaville Le Roulx (Les Hospitaliers en Terre Sainte et à Chypre (1100-1310) [Paris, 1904], pp. 66-7), Paul Deschamps (Les Chateaux des Croisés en Terre Sainte. Le Crac des Chevaliers [Paris, 1934], p. 120),Grousset (Histoire, pp. 460-64), La Monte ("The rise," pp. 305-06), the editor of Michael the Syrian's Extrait (Extrait, n. 1, p. 381), Zoé

Oldenbourg (*Les Croisades* [Paris, 1965], pp. 380 and 412), Emmanuel Guillaume Rey ("Résumé chronologique de l'histoire des princes d'Antioche. Bohémond III, prince d'Antioche, 1163-1201," *Revue de l'orient latin* [Paris, 1896], IV, 374-75), Richard (*op. cit.*, p. 135), Gustave Schlumberger (*Campagnes du roi*, pp. 84-88), (*Numismatique de l'Orient latin*, pp. 38, 69, and 97), and (*Renaud de Chatillon* [Paris, 1923], pp. 125-26), and Wilhelm F. Wilcke (*Geschichte der Tempelherrenordens* [Halle, 1850], pp. 77-8) follow the version supplied by William of Tyre and/or accept the date of 1164 for Joscelyn III's capture and imprisonment. (Henceforth references to the book of Baldwin will be referred to as *Raymond III*. The first cited work of Rey, namely *Les colonies franques de Syrie aux XIIIme et XIIIme siècles*, will be cited as *Les colonies*. References to Schlumberger's *Numismatique de l'Orient latin* will be cited henceforth as *Numismatique*). Also see the generally confirmatory views of the editor of the *Recueil* edition of Grégoire Le Prêtre (*Chronicle*, p. 195, n.1). The tone of the note made by Dulaurier, the editor of Grégoire le Prêtre's *Continuation* (pp. 483-84), indicates that he tends to support the Latin and Moslem historians' view that Joscelyn III was captured in 1164. Deschamps, Grousset, and Schlumberger date the battle and imprisonment of Joscelyn III as August 10, 1164. His capture is placed in the year 1165 by John L. La Monte ("The Lords of Sidon in the Twelfth and Thirteenth Centuries," *Byzantion* [Paris, 1944-1945], XVII, 193, n. 44), Röhricht (*Geschichte*, pp. 317-18 and "Amalrich I, König von Jerusalem (1162-1174)" in *Mittheilungen des Instituts für Oesterreichische Geschichtsforschung* [Innsbruck, 1891], XII, 442-43), and Arthur Collins (*Peerage of England* [London, 1812], VI, 227). (Henceforth references to the articles of La Monte and Röhricht will be cited as "The Lords" and "Amalrich I" to differentiate them from the other writings of these scholars). Babcock and Krey (*op. cit.* p. 308, n. 21) observes in their comments on William of Tyre's account and dating of the battle of Ḥārim and the ensuing capture of Joscelyn III and other leaders, that "The year 1165 is obviously wrong, perhaps a copyist's error. William clearly intends to correlate these events with Amaury's expedition into Egypt in 1164." I may add that this observation is also applicable to the dating of 1165 for this battle which is given in the accounts thereof by Roger of Wendover and by the *Annales de Terre Sainte*. Runciman (*History*, p. 369, n. 2) also states that William of Tyre erroneously dates the battle as happening in 1165. Therefore, I reject the dating of 1165 provided by La Monte, Röhricht, and Collins, whose accounts of Joscelyn III's capture follow, at least in part, the narrative provided by William of Tyre. My own view is that the group of scholars who hold the view that Joscelyn III was captured in 1164 at the battle of Ḥārim is right. *All* the sources designate 1160 or the opening weeks of 1161 or 1163 or 1164 or 1165 as the year of his capture. The preceding discussion in n. 66, pp. 29-31 has shown that Joscelyn III received the fief of Ḥārim at some time subsequent to an unknown date in 1160. If the grant was made shortly after the ending of the rule of Ḥārim by Reginald of Saint-Valery, which certainly continued into at least the opening days of 1160, and *after* the capture of Joscelyn III at some time during the course of the year 1160 or perhaps the opening weeks of 1161—here I use the time designation provided by Grégoire Le Prêtre—then such a grant was the very essence of unreality because the uncertainty of the time, and, indeed, the possibility of his eventual release would make the time of his actual and effective assumption of the rule of Ḥārim decidedly dubious. Military realities and necessities would certainly have prompted Baldwin III to assign the rule of Ḥārim to someone else. Although some case can be made for the views that the rule of Reginald of Saint-Valery over Ḥārim came to an end early in 1160, Joscelyn III was very shortly thereafter invested with its rule, and was captured not long thereafter in the year 1160 or the opening days of 1161, it seems to me that the actual Moslem captors of Joscelyn III who held him prisoner in Aleppo for well over a decade were in a far better position to know the time and circumstances of the capture than the Armenian and Syrian historians. And the several Moslem historians, who were certainly *au courant* of the events associated with the Aleppan political leaders, are agreed that Joscelyn III was captured in 1164 at the battle of Ḥārim. Richard (*loc. cit.*) in effect supports my view that Joscelyn III held the rule of Ḥārim before his capture and no longer had that status as of the time of his release in 1176, for in speaking of the release of Joscelyn III in 1176, he says "... Jocelin III de Courtenay-Édesse, l'oncle de Baudouin IV, *l'ancien seigneur de Harenc*, pris en 1164 par les Turcs et libéré douze ans plus tard." (Italics mine). He also corroborates his view (*loc. cit.*) with his observation that Joscelyn III lost the fief of Ḥārim in 1164. Runciman (*History*, pp. 369 and 370) contradicts himself, declaring on p. 369 that "Thoros and his brother Mleh, who had been more cautious, escaped from the battlefield" [of Ḥārim] and stating on p. 370 that "There [Antioch] he [Amalric] entered into negotiations with Nur ed-Din, who agreed to release Bohemond and Thoros for a large ransom..." Hartwig Derenbourg (*Ousâma Ibn Mounkidh. Un Émir Syrien au premier siècle des Croisades 1095-1188* [Paris, 1889], I, 309) mistakenly states in his observations on the aftermath of Nūr-ad-Dīn's victory at Ḥārim in August, 1164 that "Au nombre des prisonniers étaient.... Joscelin II, comte d'Édesse..."

CHAPTER THREE

IMPRISONMENT AND RELEASE, 1164-1176.
THE MOSLEM RENAISSANCE

The experiences of Joscelyn III during his long years of imprisonment in Aleppo from 1164 to 1176 are wholly unknown, because of the complete silence of the sources. However, it may be safely surmised that as an active young man in the very prime of his physical life these years of enforced military and political inactivity spanning his thirtieth to forty-second years were especially irksome and that the natural ennui of imprisonment and his feelings toward his relatives, vassals, and Frankish associates were heightened and embittered by his knowledge, which was probably shared by his fellow prisoners, Count Raymond III of Tripoli and Reginald of Châtillon—the latter had been captured in November, 1160 by Majd-al-Dīn, the governor of Aleppo and a true friend and ally of Nūr-ad-dīn[76] —that his fellow prisoner, Bohemond III, Prince of Antioch and successor to Reginald of Châtillon in the rule of the Principality of Antioch, succeeded in gaining his own release in less than a year. It is also a fair conclusion that the release of Raymond III at some time between September, 1173 and April, 1174 was equally irksome to the erstwhile Edessan prince, especially if the rôle of King Amalric in raising the ransom of 80,000 gold pieces was known to him. For King Amalric had been the former brother-in-law of Joscelyn III by reason of his marriage to his sister Agnes whom he divorced shortly before his assumption of the kingship in 1163.[77] Whether Joscelyn III

---

[76] William of Tyre, Bk. XVIII, chap. xxviii, *op. cit.*, pp. 868-69; Anon. Syriac Chronicle, *loc. cit.*, Grégoire Le Prêtre, chap. cclxxxi, *Continuation*, pp. 363-364 and chap. cxxi, *Chronique*, p. 198; Michael the Syrian, *Extrait*, pp. 356-57 and chap. viii, *Chronique*, p. 319; Kamal-Ad-Dîn, *Histoire*, p. 533; Stevenson, *op. cit.*, p. 183, n. 2. See Schlumberger, *Renaud de Chatillon*, p. 127 for this French scholar's views on the reactions of Reginald of Châtillon to the release of Bohemond. Runciman (*History*, pp. 357-58) observes succinctly that "Neither the Emperor nor the King of Jerusalem nor even the people of Antioch showed any haste to ransom him." (Reginald of Châtillon)

[77] William of Tyre, Bk. XIX, chap. xi and Bk. XX, chap. xxviii, *op. cit.*, pp. 900-01 and 995; Ibn al-Athīr, *K.-A.*, p. 619; Abou Chamah, *op. cit.*, pp. 167-68. Michael the Syrian, chap. xi and Bk. XX, chap. iii, *Chronique*, pp. 326 and 365 and *Extrait*, p. 381; *Extrait du voyage d'Ibn Djobeïr* in *Rec. his. or.* (Paris, 1884), III, 455; Baldwin, *Raymond III*, pp. 14-15. However, Babcock and Krey (*op. cit.*, p. 390, n. 54), in speaking of the release of Raymond, observe that "The eight years of captivity would end October 18,

was aware of the full and certain circumstances of and probabilities responsible for Bohemond's release is questionable. The circumstances were, according to William of Tyre,[78] the successful endeavors of King Amalric and the loyal followers and friends of Bohemond to raise the large ransom demanded by Nūr-ad-Dīn. William of Tyre also speculates that the following fears may well have played a part in Nūr-ad-Dīn's decision: (1) the mighty Byzantine Emperor Manuel might intervene with an irresistible demand for Bohemond's release without ransom and (2) the Antiochian folk, in the event that their imprisoned ruler were detained too long, might very well defend their own interests by choosing a stronger ruler than Bohemond, who, in turn, would prove to be a more formidable adversary.[79] And perhaps the most important of all was Toros' threat in 1165 to burn alive the four hundred Turks he captured in the course of defeating Nūr-ad-Dīn's forces in 1164 and his subsequent pillaging of the Moslem stronghold of Marash unless he, Nūr-ad-Dīn, released the Christian princes he still held captive.[80]

Meanwhile important developments in the Latin states were operating to secure the release of the still imprisoned Latin princes. Joscelyn III's sister, the Countess Agnes, now the wife of Reginald of Sidon following the death of her third husband Hugh of Ibelin,—her third marriage had been contracted about 1164—engaged in persistent efforts to secure her brother's release and at length succeeded in 1176. Reginald of Châtillon was likewise released at the same time, gaining his freedom through the payment of a large ransom paid by his friends. The ransom figures for the released Latin princes were

---

1172, though the general content seems to indicate the summer of 1173 as the year of his release." Cf. Runciman, *History*, p. 395, n. 4. "The circumstances of Raymond's release are obscure.".... "The date was between September 1173 and April 1176." with Schlumberger, *Numismatique*, p. 97. "En 1171, il [Raymond of Toulouse] parvint à se racheter enfin au prix de 80,000 besants..."

[78] William of Tyre, Bk. XIX, chap. xi, *op. cit.*, pp. 900-01; Ibn al-Athīr, *K.-A.*, p. 540.
[79] William of Tyre, *op. cit.*, p. 901.
[80] Michael the Syrian, Bk. XVIII, chap. xi, *Chronique*, p. 326 and *Extrait*, p. 360; *The Chronography of Bar Hebraeus*, p. 289. Babcock and Krey (*op. cit.*, pp. 311-12, nn. 28 and 29) observe that "Bohemond III was released in the summer of 1165, as much the result of the military success of Thoros of Armenia as of Amaury's powers of persuasion. Nureddin still held a number of important Latin princes, including Renaud de Châtillon and Raymond III of Tripoli. He had held Joscelin II captive for nine years. It was only under pressure that he released such prisoners, the threat of Manuel's invasion being the most striking instance. This was another. Ordinary offers of ransom did not tempt him. Perhaps William is justified in his speculation as to Nureddin's reason for releasing Bohemond."

respectively 50,000 and 120,000 tahegans and were accompanied by stipulations, to which the princes agreed, that they would always be allies of their erstwhile Moslem captor.[81]

But the most important factors by far in the release of the Frankish princes were the manifold changes in the power structure in the Moslem dominions since 1150, which, while immediately favorable to the imprisoned Frankish leaders in Aleppo, were to sound the knell of the Latin states. Despite the continuation of Moslem disunity during the quarter century from 1150 to 1176, the general trend successively under Nūr-ad-Dīn, Shīrkūh, and Saladin was toward the union of the Syrian and Egyptian Moslems under one leadership and with it the construction of a veritable and proverbial hammer and anvil situation with the luckless Frankish states playing the rôle of the unfortunate walnut. An account of these developments follows.[82]

Grim, indeed, was the prospect of the continuation of Frankish power in North Syria in 1151. Three major changes detrimental to the vital security of the Franks had occurred during the past scant seven years. First, the County of Edessa was no more. The supremely advantageous defense provided to the Franks by its geographical position separating the Moslem lands in Syria from those in Mesopotamia and, in conjunction with the adjoining Latin Principality of Antioch, effectively isolating Aleppo as well had been lost and had been transferred to the Moslems in general and Aleppo in particular. Aleppo had no longer to fear either for its communications with its eastern allies or attack from the Franks on its rear. Aleppo's defensive posture of former years had now been changed to one of offensive encirclement of its Frankish foes on the south and southwest.[83]

---

[81] William of Tyre, Bk. XIX, chap. iv and Bk. XXI, chap. xi, *op. cit.*, pp. 890 and 1023; *The Chronography of Bar Hebraeus*, p. 305; Michael the Syrian, *Extrait*, p. 381 and Bk. XX, chap. iii, *Chronique*, p. 365; Abou Chamah, *op. cit.*, p. 183; Kamal-Ad-Dîn. *Histoire d'Alep*, ed. and trans. by Edgar Blochet in *Revue de l'orient latin* (Paris, 1896), IV, 150. (Henceforth references to the *Histoire* in Volumes III and IV will be differentiated from one another by the addition of the Roman numeral III or IV to the page citation). Babcock and Krey, *op. cit.*, p. 414, n. 21; Grousset, *Histoire*, p. 410, n. 2; Stevenson, *op. cit.*, p. 214, n. 3, See *infra*, p. 63.

[82] Excellent discussions of the trends and developments in the Moslem world from 1150 to 1176 narrated below are provided by Stevenson, *op. cit.*, pp. 153-204, Barker, *op. cit.*, pp. 54-57, Runciman, *History*, pp. 325-400, Munro, *op. cit.*, pp. 129-52, Archer and Kingsford, *op. cit.*, pp. 222-48, and chapters XVI-XVIII in *A History of the Crusades*, I. 513-89.

[83] The significance of the possession of Edessa for the Franks is well illustrated in a vivid commentary thereupon by Ibn al-Athīr (*Atabecs*, p. 119): "Les Francs, établis dans cette ville [Edessa] étaient un fléau terrible pour les musulmans du voisinage, et le mal

Second was the continued failure of Baldwin III and the Queen Mother Melisend, following the fiasco of the Second Crusade, to see that the policy of warring on Unur of Damascus, which had already been proved fatuous in the outcome of the Second Crusade, now served only to bring about unity between Unur and Nūr-ad-Dīn, who were natural rivals for the headship of the Moslem world. All this accentuated the earlier mistaken policy of Jerusalem's failure to cooperate with Antioch and the new and even more foolish policy of Jerusalem's failure to cooperate with Antioch and Damascus against the common enemy of all three states, namely Nūr-ad-Dīn.

Third and most dangerous of all was the position of Nūr-ad-Dīn. Although his dominions were far smaller than those controlled by his father Zengi because of the latter's allotment of his Mosul and Mesopotamian holdings to another son, Saif-ad-Dīn, they were free from the constant bickerings, turbulence, and wars inherited by Saif-ad-Dīn in his own allotment and enabled Nūr-ad-Dīn to concentrate all his attention on his Frankish foes. Perhaps even more ominous was Nūr-ad-Dīn's studied policy of dropping Zengi's former program of hostility toward his Moslem neighbours and adopting in its place one of cultivating friendship with them. This new policy had already been signalized by Nūr-ad-Dīn's signature of a friendship treaty with Damascus, and, in token thereof, his marriage to Unur's daughter in the Spring of 1147.[84] Complementing this new policy was the continuation of Zengi's program of unremitting attacks on the Principality of Antioch and the County of Edessa in conjunction with Unur and Masʿūd I and of playing one Frankish leader against another. An example of this was his support of Raymond II of Tripoli against his rival Bertram. These policies, as we have noted,[85] culminated in the capture and imprisonment of Bertram and Joscelyn II, the killing of Raymond II, and finally in the wresting of the County of Edessa from its older Frankish and newer and very ephemeral Byzantine owners by the close of 1151.

However, for the moment the later months of 1149 and the early 1150's augured well for a resumption of the endemic Moslem disunity. Unur decided that, following the fiasco of the Second Crusade,

---

qu'ils leur faisaient n'avait pas de limites. Édesse était, en effet, l'oeil de la haute Mesopotamie et la place la plus forte de ce pays musulman. A la possession de cette ville l'ennemi avait ajouté celle de plusieurs cantons; aussi leur empire s'était grandement étendu, et leur domination pesait horriblement sur les habitants."

[84] Abou Chamah, *op. cit.*, p. 51.
[85] *Supra*, pp. 15, 16, 21, and 28.

Damascus was no longer imperilled by Jerusalem and hence a restoration of peaceful relationships was in order. Similar viewpoints prevailed in Jerusalem and the natural result was Damascus' granting of a peace treaty for two years to the southern Franks in May, 1149.[86] Mujīr-ad-Dīn, the new ruler of Damascus after Unur's death on August 29, 1149,[87] resolutely rejected Nūr-ad-Dīn's proposals in March, 1150 that Aleppan-Damascene cooperation be reestablished and indeed besought and gained a promise of military assistance from the Franks against Nūr-ad-Dīn.[88] Although the ensuing inclement weather by preventing Nūr-ad-Dīn from mounting an effective attack on Damascus contributed to his decision to seek and to make peace in May, 1150 with its citizenry,[89] this peace rested on a very unstable basis. Nūr-ad-Dīn returned to the attack in the Spring of 1151 and waged war on Damascus. Peace was finally concluded on July 26, 1151.[90] That the hegemony of the southern Franks and the weakness of their Damascene neighbors continued were clearly attested by Mujīr-ad-Dīn's failure to seize the opportunity afforded him by the civil war in 1152 in the Kingdom of Jerusalem resulting from the quarrel between King Baldwin III and the Queen Mother Melisend over the question of the division of power between them.[91]

That, however, Mujīr-ad-Dīn's pro-Frankish policies and Nūr-ad-Dīn's ambitions should not respectively and inevitably raise hostility among the citizenry of Damascus and thereby afford Nūr-ad-Dīn a golden opportunity for self-advancement was very unlikely. Both of these eventualities came to pass in 1153-1154. Decades of misgovernment culminating in civil war in Fāṭimid Egypt together

---

[86] Abou Chamah, op. cit., p. 61; Ibn al-Qalānisī, op. cit., pp. 289-90.

[87] Ibn al-Qalānisī, op. cit., p. 296; Ibn Khallikan's *Biographical Dictionary*, trans. from the Arabic by Bⁿ Mac Guckin de Slane (Paris, 1842), I, 275.

[88] Abou Chamah, op. cit., pp. 64-65; Ibn al-Qalānisī, op. cit., pp. 296-97.

[89] Abou Chamah, op. cit., pp. 65-67; Abū'l Maḥāsin Yūsuf, op. cit., pp. 506-07; Ibn al-Qalānisī, op. cit., pp. 297-300. Runciman (*History*, p. 336) considers the fact that agreements supplementary to the peace entailed "... a promise that his [Nūr-ad-Dīn's] name should be mentioned on the coinage and in the public prayers at Damascus after those of the Caliph and the Sultan of Persia" constituted an admission that he exercised a vague overlordship over Damascus.

[90] Ibn al-Qalānisī, op. cit., pp. 302-10; Abou Chamah, op. cit., pp. 68-74.

[91] William of Tyre, Bk. XVI, chap. iii and Bk. XVII, chaps. xiii-xiv, op. cit., pp. 707 and 779-803; *The Chronography of Bar Hebraeus*, pp. 279-80. See William Stubbs, *Historical Introductions to the Rolls Series* (New York, 1902), pp. 339-40 for illuminating observations on the unsatisfactory attempts, following the death of King Fulk of Anjou in 1143, to reconcile the elective and hereditary principles in the succession to the kingship in the Kingdom of Jerusalem, notably in the time of Baldwin III.

with a desire to signalize his recent victory over the Queen Mother Melisend induced King Baldwin III to invest the great fortress of Ascalon in January, 1153 and to capture it in the following August.[92] When Egyptian appeals for aid to Nūr-ad-Dīn elicited his support, Mujīr-ad-Dīn abandoned his suspicions of his rival for a time and joined him in an attack on the Frankish stronghold of Banyas east of Tyre in May, 1153 in a move to divert Frankish power from the Egyptian theatre.[93] But a dispute soon ensued between the rival chieftains and the undertaking was abandoned with Mujīr-ad-Dīn returning to Damascus in June, 1153 and with Nūr-ad-Dīn making no further endeavor to aid Ascalon.[94] Nūr-ad-Dīn then struck at Damascus' food supplies by intercepting the usual grain convoys from the north and thereby created great distress among the Damascenes.[95] Soon a conspiracy grew up in Damascus against Mujīr-ad-Dīn which resulted from the belief of its authors that Mujīr-ad-Dīn had been guilty of political vacillation, failure to aid Ascalon, and unseemly quarreling with Nūr-ad-Dīn. The ringleader among the conspirators was Aiyūb, the emir of Baalbek and a brother of Shīrkūh, an emir of Nūr-ad-Dīn. Nūr-ad-Dīn then quickly denounced his most dangerous foes, Mujīr-ad-Dīn's loyal supporters, by means of an agent whom he sent to Mujīr-ad-Dīn. The agent accused them of insidious proposals to Nūr-ad-Dīn. Mujīr-ad-Dīn fell into the trap and effected their ouster from power.[96] Matters soon came to a head with Shīrkūh's march upon Damascus with a considerable army early in April, 1154 and the refusal of Mujīr-ad-Dīn, alarmed by Shīrkūh's moves, to receive him. Nūr-ad-Dīn quickly seized his chance, joined Shīrkūh, and invested Damascus in later April, 1154. Mujīr-ad-Dīn appealed to his southern Frankish allies, promising them money and the surrender of

---

[92] William of Tyre, Bk. XVII, chaps. xxi-xxv and xxvii-xxx, *op. cit.*, pp. 794-802 and 804-13; Ibn al-Qalānisī, *op. cit.*, pp. 314-17; *The Chronography of Bar Hebraeus*, p. 280; Ibn al-Athīr, *Atabecs*, p. 189; Abou Chamah, *op. cit.*, pp. 76-78; Michael the Syrian, *Extraits*, p. 344 and Bk. XVIII, chap. i, *Chronique*, pp. 308-09; Kamal-Ad-Dîn, *Histoire*, III, 527,

[93] William of Tyre, chap. xxvi, *op. cit.*, p. 803; Ibn al-Qalānisī, *op. cit.*, p. 315; Abou Chamah, *op. cit.*, pp. 76-77.

[94] William of Tyre, *loc. cit.*; Ibn al-Qalānisī, *op. cit.*, pp. 315-16; Abou Chamah, *op. cit.*, p.77

[95] Ibn al-Qalānisī, *op. cit.*, p. 317. Runciman (*History*, p. 341) believes that, following Nūr-ad-Din's interception of grain convoys from the north "... Ayub's agents spread the rumor that this was Mujir's fault for refusing to co-operate with his fellow-Moslems."

[96] Ibn al-Athīr, *K.-A.*, p. 496 and *Atabecs*, pp. 190-91; *The Chronography of Bar Hebraeus*, p. 281.

Baalbek in return for aid. The Franks responded but to no avail.[97] Military ineptitude and internal disaffection led to Damascus' rapid capture. Aided by a Jewish woman who let down a rope from the top of the wall, Shīrkūh's and Nūr-ad-Dīn's soldiers climbed an unmanned section of the town wall, Mujīr-ad-Dīn's estranged citizens opened a gate, and the city fell on April 25, 1154. Mujīr-ad-Dīn and his troops received clement treatment from the new master of Damascus in the form of an amnesty and a grant of units in the district of Homs.[98] The Franco-Damascene alliance proved useless in this juncture, because of the rapidity and suddenness of the attack. And the results were disastrous for future Frankish security, because the two great Syrian Moslem bastions of Aleppo and Damascus were now in the hands of a relentless foe of the Franks, a unified Moslem state lay along the eastern Frankish frontier, and Nūr-ad-Dīn could now launch his invasions to the north and south with equal ease from Damascus which, primarily and formerly a threat to Antioch and Edessa, was now an equal menace to Jerusalem.[99]

Yet Nūr-ad-Dīn chose to keep the peace for a whole decade with the Franks. His several battles with Baldwin III in 1157, 1158, and 1160 were clearly of Frankish inspiration and were not of his volition. Internal and external conditions plainly counselled a policy of peace and consolidation of his newly won position, for his control over Moslem Syria was still far from complete. Shaizar, Baalbek, and perhaps other Moslem centers as well maintained considerable independence. This attendant fragmentation of Moslem military power was effectively opposed by the superiority of the combined resources of the Frankish states. Then, too, there was the consideration of the reviving military power of the Byzantine Empire after 1159 which

---

[97] Kamal-Ad-Dîn, *Histoire*, III, 528; Ibn al-Athīr, *K.-A.*, pp. 496-97 and *Atabecs*, p. 191; Ibn al-Qalānisī, *op. cit.*, pp. 318-19.

[98] Ibn al-Qalānisī, *op. cit.*, pp. 319-21; Kamal-Ad-Dîn, *Histoire*, III, 527-28; William of Tyre, *op. cit.*, pp. 802-03; Ibn al-Athīr, *K.-A.*, p. 497 and *Atabecs, loc. cit.*; *The Chronography of Bar Hebraeus*, pp. 281-82; Michael the Syrian, *Extrait*, p. 346 and Bk. XVIII, chap. iii, *Chronique*, p. 312.

[99] William of Tyre, *op. cit.*, p. 802. Viewing harshly the conduct of Mujīr-ad-Dīn at the time of the capture of Ascalon, Schlumberger (*Renaud de Chatillon*, p. 37) remarks "Le prince ou gouverneur de cette ville [Damascus] Modjir ed-Dîn, par son indolence pleine de duplicité, avait été pour les musulmans la cause peut-être principale de la chute d'Ascalon," and then observes that "La conquête de cette reine [Damascus] des cités syriennes avait achevé de faire de Nour ed-Dîn l'arbitre unique, incontesté, des destinées du monde arabe entre l'Euphrate et les rives de Phénicie, l'adversaire tout-puissant des principautés chrétiennes en Orient."

threatened Nūr-ad-Dīn's newly won position. Hence he chose to sate his territorial ambitions in those western areas of the former Frankish County of Edessa which were now controlled by the Sultan of Iconium, Kîlîj Arslan, to renew his truce with Baldwin III in 1156 for two years, and to continue Mujīr-ad-Dīn's policy of paying tribute to Baldwin III.[100]

Fortunately for Nūr-ad-Dīn, the southern as well as the northern Franks chose to keep the peace from 1154 to 1156. Baldwin III's pacific policies resulted partly from his recognition of his present inability to reverse Nūr-ad-Dīn's capture of Damascus, partly from his apprehensions over the new and belligerent mien of Moslem Egypt.[101] Meanwhile, Reginald of Châtillon, the new ruler of Antioch following his marriage to Constance, the widow of Raymond II, in 1153,[102] wasted and scattered his strength in fruitless wars with the Armenian prince Toros and the Byzantine emperor Manuel in 1155.[103] Hence Nūr-ad-Dīn felt free to invade Kîlîj Arslan II's domains in 1155 and to seize several cities which the latter's father, Masʿūd I, had recently taken from the northern Franks. But Kîlîj Arslan's quick retaliatory action of an alliance with the Franks coupled with the shattering effects of earthquakes in Aleppo, Kafarṭāb, Apamea, ʿArqah, Homs, and Hamah soon persuaded Nūr-ad-Dīn to effect a settlement with Kîlîj Arslan, to return to Damascus in November, 1156, and to renew his peace with Baldwin III in the following month.[104]

The tenuous truce between Baldwin III and Nūr-ad-Dīn was broken in February, 1157 when the former, inspired by financial exigencies and emboldened by fresh military assistance from Europe, seized Moslem cattle and horses in the neighborhood of Banyas.[105] Nūr-ad-Dīn quickly retaliated by an occupation of Baalbek, while his

---

[100] Abou Chamah, *op. cit.*, p. 83; Ibn al-Qalānisī, *op. cit.*, pp. 322, 324-25, and 327; *The Chronography of Bar Hebraeus*, p. 285. Cf. Runciman, *History*, pp. 341-42.

[101] Ibn al-Qalānisī, *op. cit.*, pp. 323-24; Abou Chamah, *op. cit.*, p. 82.

[102] William of Tyre, *op. cit.*, p. 802

[103] *Ibid.*, Bk. XVIII, chap. x, *op. cit.*, pp. 834-35; Michael the Syrian, chaps. iv and v, *Chronique*, pp. 314 and 315 and *Extrait*, pp. 349 and 350; *The Chronography of Bar Hebraeus*, pp. 283 and 284; Grégoire Le Prêtre, chap. cxxiii, *Chronique*, p. 187; Cinnamus *op. cit.*, pp. 178-79

[104] Ibn al-Qalānisī, *op. cit.*, pp. 324-27; Michael the Syrian, chap. v, *Chronique*, pp. 315-16; Kamal-Ad-Dîn, *Histoire*, III, 529-230; Grégoire Le Prêtre, *Chronique*, p. 182 and chap. cclxvii, *Continuation*, p. 345; Cinnamus, *op. cit.*, pp. 179-81: *Anon. Syriac Chronicle*, p. 302; Ibn al-Aṯhīr, *K.-A.*, pp. 503-04; Abou Chamah, *op. cit.*, pp. 84-85; Robert de Torigni, *op. cit.*, p. 309.

[105] William of Tyre, chap. xi, *op. cit.*, pp. 836-37; Ibn al-Qalānisī, *op. cit.*, pp. 327-28 and 338-41; Abou Chamah, *op. cit.*, pp. 83-84.

lieutenants, Shīrkūh and Shīrkūh's son, Naṣīr-ad-Dīn, respectively inflicted defeats on Frankish forces raiding the Homs and Hamah districts in the north and a band of Knights of St. John en route to Banyas in the Spring and Summer of 1157.[106] Nūr-ad-Dīn then twice invested Banyas and inflicted a serious defeat on Baldwin III's army at Safad in June, 1157.[107] Toward the end of 1157 one of Nūr-ad-Dīn's emirs occupied Shaizar and successfully repelled the Franks' attempts to capture it in December.[108] The Frankish thrusts into the Hauran in November or December, 1157 and March, 1158 were followed by counter thrusts by Nūr-ad-Dīn and Shīrkūh against the as-Sawād district and Sidon respectively from May to August, 1158 and culminated in a defeat of the Moslems in July, 1158 serious enough to cause them to seek a truce with the Franks. This quest proved unsuccessful.[109]

Other Franco-Moslem fronts awoke to activity as well in 1158. Angered by their loss of Ascalon in 1153 and inspired by Nūr-ad-Dīn's invasions of the Kingdom of Jerusalem, the Egyptian Moslems launched a whole series of attacks on the southern territories of the Kingdom independently of Nūr-ad-Dīn who rebuffed their attempts to secure an alliance.[110]

Meanwhile the clash of interests of Franks, Greeks, Moslems, and Armenians in Asia Minor was operating mightily to affect the course of development in the main theatres of Franco-Moslem conflict in the south. Reginald of Châtillon, ruler of Antioch, and Toros, the Armenian chieftain, were natural allies against the Moslem Sultan of Iconium, whereas Manuel, apprehensive over and opposed to Toros' waxing power, sided with the Sultan. Manuel's invasion of Cilicia at the close of 1158 was followed by Toros' supine surrender with a subsequent acceptance of a rôle of vassalage to Manuel, Reginald's humiliating seeking and gaining of Manuel's pardon, and a new entente between Baldwin III and Manuel. The Frankish king was a principal factor in the negotiations between Toros and Manuel, for he

---

[106] Ibn al-Qalānisī, *op. cit.*, pp. 329-32; Abou Chamah, *op. cit.*, pp. 85-86.

[107] William of Tyre, chaps. xii-xv, *op. cit.*, pp. 838-45; Ibn al-Qalānisī, *op. cit.*, pp. 333-37; Abou Chamah, *op. cit.*, pp. 87-89.

[108] William of Tyre, chap. xviii, *op. cit.*, pp. 849-51; Ibn al-Qalānisī, *op. cit.*, p. 342; Abou Chamah, *op. cit.*, p. 93.

[109] William of Tyre, chaps. xix and xxi, *op. cit.*, pp. 852-53 and 855-56; Ibn al-Qalānisī, *op. cit.*, pp. 344-47; Abou Chamah, *op. cit.*, pp. 96-97 and 97-100. Also cf. Runciman, *History*, p. 351, n.1.

[110] Ibn al-Qalānisī, *op. cit.*, p. 348; Abou Chamah, *op. cit.*, p. 97.

pointed out to the latter the importance of the Armenian alliance to the Franks. This development, coupled with Baldwin III's recent marriage to Theodora, Manuel's niece, signalized his rising importance as a statesman and signified to Nūr-ad-Dīn the distinct prospect of a broadening of his present conflict with the southern Franks to include one with the Byzantines as well. With Manuel's entrance into Antioch in the Spring of 1159 the danger presented to Nūr-ad-Dīn's hard won position became even greater, for Aleppo itself was now threatened. All these developments urged Nūr-ad-Dīn to refrain from too vigorous a war on the southern Franks and to seek peace with the Greeks. Hence he released a number of Christian captives, among them Bertram, to Manuel.[111]

Yet on balance Nūr-ad-Dīn was a winner, for the newly established peace with the Byzantines gained for him freedom from further attack and recognition of his already secured position in the north. This had been his goal ever since his arrival in power in Damascus in 1154. The only unfinished business was that of gaining peace with the southern Franks. And this followed in the winter of 1159-1160 in the form of a two year truce between Baldwin III and Nūr-ad-Dīn. Baldwin III had attacked Damascus during Nūr-ad-Dīn's absence in the northern theatre—the latter had been engaged in (1) the chastisement of his brother, whose actions during Nūr-ad-Dīn's recent illness had provoked doubts concerning his loyalty and (2) the wresting of former Edessan lands from their holder, the Sultan of Iconium[112] —and had secured from its governor, Najm-ad-Dīn-Aiyūb, the liberation of certain prisoners and a money gift. The expiration of the resulting truce of three months between Jerusalem and Damascus saw Baldwin III taking the field again, but to no avail. Nūr-ad-Dīn meanwhile returned to Damascus and he and his Frankish foemen prepared for battle during the Summer of 1159. But military stalemate ensued with neither side electing to attack and, in consequence, parleys were undertaken. And, as in the case of Greco-Moslem negotiations, so now in the case of the Franco-Moslem ones, Nūr-ad-Dīn gained his point:

---

[111] William of Tyre, chaps. xvi and xxii-xxv, *op. cit.*, pp. 846 and 857-64; Ibn al-Qalānisī, *op. cit.*, pp. 349 and 353-55; Abou Chamah, *op. cit.*, pp. 104-105; Grégoire Le Prêtre, chaps. cclxxiii and cclxxv, *Continuation*, pp. 352-53 and 355-56 and chaps. cxxiv-xxv, *Chronique*, pp. 188-90; Cinnamus, *op. cit.*, pp. 181-90.

[112] William of Tyre, chap. xxvii, *op. cit.*, p. 866; Ibn al-Qalānisī, *op. cit.*, pp. 356-57; Grégoire Le Prêtre, chap. cxxvii, *Chronique*, pp. 193-94; Manuel the Syrian, *Extrait*, p. 353 and chap. iii, *Chronique*, p. 312.

the recognition by the southern Franks of the boundaries of his southern possessions.[113]

That the policy of the *status quo* supported by the Kingdom of Jerusalem as well as by Nūr-ad-Dīn in the early 1160's and underscored by the latter's failure to resume war with the former upon the expiration of the truce between them at the end of 1162 should continue was dependent upon the maintenance in royal power in the Kingdom of Jerusalem of a man of limited ambitions and upon an absence of tempting opportunities for territorial and monarchical aggrandizement for the King of Jerusalem. Neither of these conditions conducive to the maintenance of peace between the Kingdom of Jerusalem and Nūr-ad-Dīn was present by 1163. The childless Baldwin III died in February, 1163 and was succeeded by the Count of Jaffa, his twenty-five year old brother Amalric, a man of extraordinary ambition. Dissatisfied with the condition of his own Kingdom of Jerusalem, he dreamed of extending his sway by extensive conquests. To this end he endeavored to gain support from Europe and to strengthen still further the cordial relations between Byzantium and Jerusalem by marrying in 1167 the grandniece of Emperor Manuel.[114]

Even more potent as a disturbing factor was the situation in Fāṭimid Egypt. The death of Tali ibn Ruzzik, the vizier of the Egyptian caliph,

---

[113] William of Tyre, *op. cit.*, pp. 866-67.

[114] *Ibid.* chap. xxxiv, Bk. XIX, chaps. i-ii, and Bk. XX, chap. i, *op. cit.*, pp. 879-80, 883-86, and 942; *Chronique d'Ernoul, loc. cit.* See Babcock and Krey *op. cit.*, p. 293, n. 91. The dangers inherent in the foreign policies of the new king Amalric have been well stated by Grousset (*L'empire*, pp. 230-31): "La disparition de ce prince [Baldwin III] dont la sagesse égalait l'activité, fut une perte grave pour la Terre sainte. En effet, son successeur, avec des qualités non moins brillantes, n'allait pas faire preuve de la même prudence en engageant la France du Levant dans de prestigieuses mais dangereuses aventures." Speaking in similar vein, La Monte (*Feudal Monarchy*, p. 20) observes that "The helpless condition of Egypt was a deceptive lure, and Amaury succumbed to the temptation. His campaigns in Egypt, though in themselves not unprofitable, precipitated the catastrophe which later overwhelmed Jerusalem by so weakening Egypt that she fell into the hands of the lieutenant of the atābeg and gave Saladin a base from which to extend his empire and to encircle the Christian states." Yet it is only fair to observe, as Baldwin ("The Latin States," pp. 549-50) has indicated, that this foreign policy of Amalric's was not unique. "The foreign policy of Amalric, largely a series of attempts to conquer Egypt, had been foreshadowed by Baldwin III when he captured Ascalon. And it was logical that Amalric, who had been entrusted with the government of Ascalon, should be interested in the south. The combination of circumstances which had motivated Baldwin still existed. The union of Aleppo and Damascus under Nūr-ad-Dīn made the whole matter more urgent. For if Egypt fell into the power of the Syrian Sunnite Moslems, the Latin states would be encircled. Add to these strategic considerations the immense commercial value of Egypt with its great port of Alexandria, and it is not difficult to understand why Amalric persistently pushed southward."

in September, 1161 was followed by a contest for the purple by two rival emirs, Dîrgam and Shavar. Losing the struggle in 1163, Shavar was forced into exile from Egypt in August of the same year. He then repaired to Damascus where he besought Nūr-ad-Dīn's help. Thereupon, Amalric, irked by the refusal of Dîrgam, the victorious emir, to continue the practice of his predecessors of paying tribute to the Kingdom of Jerusalem, invaded Egypt in September, 1163. The Frankish invaders, after scoring an initial victory over Dîrgam's forces near Bilbais, were soon obliged to retire as a result of the Egyptians' destruction of the dams on the Nile.[115]

Meanwhile the *status quo* between the Kingdom of Jerusalem and Nūr-ad-Dīn was being steadily undermined by the events in Egypt. The fugitive Shavar, upon his arrival in Damascus on October 23, 1163, made tempting overtures to Nūr-ad-Dīn in the form of a promise of a third of the revenues of Egypt in return for aid adequate to establish him in power in Egypt. But Nūr-ad-Dīn hesitated, fearful that the geographical location of the Kingdom of Jerusalem between a mutually friendly Damascus and Egypt would cause Amalric to fear for the future and hence would lead to hostility on his part toward himself. Also there was the consideration that Shavar, once restored to power, might break his pledge to follow Nūr-ad-Dīn's orders. At this juncture Shīrkūh persuaded his superior to accept Shavar's bid, pointing out that the Egyptian population would doubtless prefer Moslem to Frankish rule and that Nūr-ad-Dīn had no significant rival in Egypt to oppose his rule in that country. And certainly the waging of the *jihad* by Nūr-ad-Dīn would be greatly assisted by the acquisition of Egypt, for the political and military union of Moslem Syria and Moslem Egypt would place the Kingdom of Jerusalem between a veritable hammer and anvil. Furthermore, Nūr-ad-Dīn's control of the Delta would enable him to dispatch navies against the Syrian littoral and to obstruct connections between the crusading states and Europe.

---

[115] William of Tyre, chap. v, *op. cit.*, pp. 890-91; Kamal-Ad-Dîn, *Histoire*, III, 536-37; Michael the Syrian, chap. vii, *Chronique*, p. 317; Ibn al-Athīr, *K.-A.*, pp. 528 and 533 and *Atabecs*, p. 215; Abou Chamah, *op. cit.*, pp. 106-07; Ibn Khallikan's *Biographical Dictionary* trans. from the Arabic by Bⁿ Mac Guckin de Slane (Paris, 1871), IV, 485; Behâ Ed-Dîn, *Anecdotes et Beaux Traits de la Vie du Sultan Youssof* (*Salâh Ed-Dîn*) in *Rec. his. or.* (Paris, 1884), III, 42 and *Saladin*, pp. 46-47. (Henceforth the *Recueil* edition of Behâ Ed-Dîn will be differentiated from the Palestine Pilgrims Text Society by the addition of the word *Anecdotes*); *Epistolarum Regis Ludovici VII* in *Recueil des historiens des Gaules et de la France*, ed. M. Bouquet and others (Paris, 1878), XVI, No. CXCIV, 59-60.

Convinced of the cogency of Shīrkūh's arguments, Nūr-ad-Dīn placed Shīrkūh in command of a Syrian expeditionary force and sent him and, perhaps, Shīrkūh's nephew, Saladin, to Egypt in April, 1164.[116] Meanwhile Nūr-ad-Dīn himself invaded the Kingdom of Jerusalem to divert attention from Shīrkūh's program.[117] Shīrkūh easily restored Shavar to power in Egypt following a battle with Dîrgam's forces and the death of Dîrgam in this battle.[118] But Shavar, increasingly disturbed by Shīrkūh's failure to retire from Egypt and his policy of reciting to him his reckless proposals which he had made to Nūr-ad-Dīn in Damascus, recognized that his independence was largely meaningless. Rather than accept this fate, Shavar appealed to Amalric for aid. Amalric replied with a second Frankish invasion of Egypt in July, 1164. The allied forces proved too much for Shīrkūh, despite his stubborn resistance, and at length he was obliged to accept Amalric's terms in October, 1164. But Amalric had merely scored a Pyrrhic

---

[116] William of Tyre, *op. cit.*, pp. 891-92; Kamal-Ad-Dîn, *Histoire*, III, 537; *The Chronography of Bar Hebraeus*, p. 288; Ibn al-Athīr, *K.-A.*, pp. 532-33 and *Atabecs*, pp. 213 and 215-16; Abou-Chamah, *op. cit.*, pp. 107-08; Behâ Ed-Dîn, *Anecdotes*, pp. 42-43 and *Saladin*, pp. 47-48; Ibn Khallikan, *op. cit.*, IV, 485-86. See Stevenson, *op. cit.*, p. 195, n. 3 for a discussion on the moot point whether Saladin accompanied Shīrkūh on the first invasion of Egypt. Slaughter (*op. cit.* p. 27), on the other hand, declares flatly that Saladin did accompany Shīrkūh on this invasion. Behâ Ed-Dîn (*Saladin*, p. 48) states that "The latter [Saladin] went against his inclination, but his uncle [Shīrkūh] required him to command the army and assist him with advice." Barker (*op. cit.*, p. 56 and n.1) believes that "For Nureddin the fight meant the acquisition of an heretical country for the true faith of the Sunnite, and the final enveloping of the Latin Kingdom..." ... "Nureddin, unlike his father, was definitely animated by a religious motive: he fought first and foremost against the Latins (and not, like his father, against Moslem states), and he did so as a matter of religious duty." Slaughter (*op. cit.*, pp. 37-38) discerns economic and strategical considerations as well as religious ones in Nūr-ad-Dīn's decision to intervene in Egypt: "... while the Sultan's motive was a desire to convert heretical Egypt to the true faith. At the same time there were practical considerations of which Nur-al-Din was aware. A line of fortresses extending north and south separated the Kingdom of Jerusalem and the principalities of Antioch and Tripolis from Moslem territory, and, although trade was carried on across the border, all transactions were at the mercy of the Latins, who had built these mighty castles to protect their frontier. Since Moslem Syria was thus effectively cut off from the coast, their trade with Egypt was all-important. Ascalon had been a kind of buffer state between Moslems and Christians; its capture by the Latins endangered the commerce with Egypt and threatened the caravan route to Mecca. Nobody could foresee how long the extravagant rulers of Egypt would be able to purchase protection, and, if the Franks gained possession of Egypt, Moslem Syria would be ruined. Nur-al-Din might be obliged to fight the Franks on two frontiers."

[117] Kamal-Ad-Dîn, *Histoire, loc. cit.*

[118] William of Tyre, chap. vii, *op. cit.*, p. 893; Kamal-Ad-Dîn, *loc. cit.*; Ibn al-Athir, *K.-A.*, p. 534 and *Atabecs*, p. 216; Robert de Torigni, *op. cit.* p. 355; Behâ Ed-Dîn, *Anecdotes*, p. 43, and *Saladin, loc. cit.*

victory over Shīrkūh, for the terms prescribed that both the Franks and the Syrian Moslems retire from Egypt.[119]

Meanwhile, Nūr-ad-Dīn, taking advantage of Amalric's absence from the Syrian scene, resumed the offensive. An initial humiliating defeat near Tripoli by the Franks[120] so angered him that he sought and gained the assistance of the Mesopotamian emirs in his proposal of a joint attack on Ḥārim. The siege soon provoked a united effort of the northern Franks to save Ḥārim, but this ended, as we have already noted,[121] in a signal triumph of Nūr-ad-Dīn's forces with the ensuing capture of the city as well as Bohemond, Coloman, Hugh of Lusignan, Raymond III of Tripoli, and Joscelyn III.[122] Only fear of Emperor Manuel's intervention and probable subsequent occupation of Antioch dissuaded Nūr-ad-Dīn from an attack on that city. Nūr-ad-Dīn then invested Banyas in October, 1164, seeking to obtain a diversion of Frankish power from Egypt and thereby a relief of Shīrkūh's sorely pressed forces. Banyas soon fell, Shīrkūh was relieved, and Amalric, now apprehensive over the losses of Ḥārim and Banyas, retired from Egypt.[123] The fall of Banyas was a serious blow to the security of the Franks, for all of the northern areas of the Kingdom of Jerusalem now lay open to Moslem invasion. Not even Nūr-ad-Dīn's defeat in October, 1164 at the hands of Toros and his subsequent release of Armenian prisoners and Bohemond in the Summer of 1165 out of fear of Emperor Manuel's intervention and threat of reprisal by Toros[124]

---

[119] Kamal-Ad-Dîn, *Histoire*, III, 538; William of Tyre, *op. cit.*, pp. 893-94; Abou Chamah, *op. cit.*, pp. 124-15; Ibn al-Athīr, *Atabecs*, pp. 216-218 and *K.-A.*, pp. 534-36; *The Chronography of Bar Hebraeus*, p. 289. Barker (*op. cit.*, p. 56) sees in Amalric's intervention strategic and economic motives: "... for Amalric it meant the escape from Nureddin's net, and a more direct and lucrative contact with Eastern trade."

[120] William of Tyre, chap. viii, *op. cit.*, pp. 894-95; Abou-Chamah, *op. cit.*, pp. 125-26; Ibn al-Athīr, *K.-A.*, pp. 530-31; Michael the Syrian, chap x, *Chronique*, p. 324.

[121] *Supra*, pp. 32-33.

[122] Kamal-Ad-Dîn, *Histoire*, III, 539-40; *The Chronography of Bar Hebraeus*, p. 288; William of Tyre, chap. ix, *op. cit.*, pp. 896-97; Ibn al-Athīr, *K.-A.*, p. 538-40 and *Atabecs*, pp. 221-23; Abou Chamah, *op. cit.*, pp. 108-09 and 125-26; Röhricht, *Regesta, loc. cit.*, *Epistola Gaufredi Fulcherii, procuratoris militiae Templi, ad Ludovicum* and *Epistola Aymerici, patriarchae Antiocheni, ad Ludovicum, loc. cit.*; Cinnamus, *op. cit.*, p. 216; Roger of Wendover, *loc. cit.*; *Annales de Terre Sainte, loc. cit.*; Delaville Le Roulx, *Cartulaire, loc. cit.*; Sigebert, *loc. cit.*; *Anon. Syriac Chronicle*, p. 304; Michael the Syrian, *Chronique, loc. cit.* and *Extrait*, p. 358; *Chronique d'Amadi, loc. cit.*; Robert de Torigni, *loc. cit.*

[123] William of Tyre, chap. x, *op. cit.*, pp. 898-900; Michael the Syrian, chap. xi, *Chronique*, p. 326; *Anon. Syriac Chronicle*, pp. 303-04; Kamal-Ad-Dîn, *Histoire*, III, 540-41; Ibn al-Athīr, *K.-A.*, pp. 540-42 and *Atabecs*, pp. 233-34.

[124] Michael the Syrian, *Chronique, loc. cit.* and *Extrait*, p. 360; *The Chronography of Bar Hebraeus*, p. 289. Also see *supra*, p. 38.

essentially repaired the damaged fortunes of the Franks. And standing as a permanent deterrent to the reestablishment of the *status quo* between Jerusalem and Amalric, on the one hand, and Damascus and Nūr-ad-Dīn, on the other, was the will-o-the-wisp, the tantalizing lure of Egypt for Franks and Syrian Moslems alike.

An essential repetition of the Franco-Syrian clash of 1164 over the Egyptian prize soon followed in 1167 when Shīrkūh persuaded his superior, Nūr-ad-Dīn, that a new and persistently supported attack on Egypt must inevitably be successful.[125] Shīrkūh's forces, ably commanded by a supremely confident leader and enjoying some support among Shavar's enemies in Egypt, invaded Egypt in January, 1167. Amalric hastily mobilized his forces and advanced into Egypt. Shavar, after an initial dismay, joined forces with the Franks. The Egyptian Moslems agreed to renew the old agreements with the Franks. Specific increases in the annual tribute from Egypt were stipulated and the Franks promised not to depart until Shīrkūh and his entire army should be destroyed or ousted from Egypt.[126] The ensuing military maneuvres and operations between the rival forces culminated in the battle of Lamonia. Shīrkūh, victorious by reason of his superior military strategy employing the familiar Selchük tactic of yielding retreat and counter attack, occupied Alexandria in March, 1167. Amalric and his Egyptian allies, nothing daunted, elected to invest the city.[127] Since besiegers and besieged alike were unable to inflict decisive

---

[125] William of Tyre, chap. xiii, *op. cit.*, pp. 902-03; Ibn al-Athīr, *K.-A.*, p. 546.

[126] William of Tyre, chaps. xiii-xiv and xvi-xix, *op. cit.*, pp. 903-05 and 907-13; Behâ Ed-Dîn, *Anecdotes*, p. 44 and *Saladin*, pp. 49-50; Ibn al-Athīr, *Atabecs*, pp. 236-37; *The Chronography of Bar Hebraeus*, p. 290; Ibn al-Athīr, *K.-A.*, pp. 546-47.

[127] William of Tyre, chaps. xxii, xxiii, and xxv-xxvi, *op. cit.*, pp. 917-19, 921-22, and 925-30; Abou Chamah, *op. cit.*, pp. 129-32; Ibn al-Athīr, *K.-A.*, pp. 547-49 and *Atabecs*, 237-39; *The Chronography of Bar Hebraeus*, pp. 290-91. Grousset (*Histoire*, p. 493) and Röhricht (*Geschichte*, p. 327) err in their statements that Joscelyn III was present at this battle. William of Tyre's reference speaks of "Joscelinus de Samosato." It is true that Röhricht's *Regesta* refers to a Joscelyn of Samosata in documents 276, 299, 308, 324, 332, 334, 447, 496 and 514. And in view of the fact that Samosata was a town in the now defunct County of Edessa (see Runciman, *History*, p. 109), the argument may be advanced that this name was an alternative one for the now merely titular Count of Edessa. But that Joscelyn of Samosata cannot be Joscelyn III is demonstrated by the datings of documents Nos. 447, 496, and 514 which are respectively 1168, 1173, and 1174. During these years Joscelyn III was a prisoner of the Turks and was situated in Turkish held territories. Documents 447, 496, and 514 were drawn up in lands under Frankish control. Babcock and Krey (*op. cit.*, p. 539) also support these arguments by their indexing of "Joscelin of Samosata" as a person entirely separate and distinct from "Joscelin III, count of Edessa." Similarly Richard (*op. cit.*, p. 77) differentiates Joscelyn of Samosata from Joscelyn III by his reference to the former as "... autre Edessénien qui avait figuré avec un certain Baudouin de Samosate parmi les principaux vassaux du

blows on the other for three months, Shīrkūh, who had recently and secretly departed from the city leaving its defense in the hands of Saladin, entered into parleys with the Franks. The upshot of this was a treaty, which Shavar approved, providing for the surrender of the city to Amalric, an exchange of prisoners by both sides, and a retirement of both Amalric's and Shīrkūh's forces from Egypt. The treaty was then executed in September, 1167. The Frankish forces were quite ready to depart because of disturbing news of the simultaneous attacks of Nūr-ad-Dīn and the Mesopotamian emirs on the territories of Tripoli. Nūr-ad-Dīn soon retired from the northern theatre, leaving a scene of devastation and ruined castles in his wake. An uneasy truce between Jerusalem and Damascus ensued.[128]

But the prize of Egypt soon proved too much for Amalric. Angered over reports that Shavar was secretly seeking Nūr-ad-Dīn's aid and to gain that end was promising to abandon the Franks altogether, he decided to acquire the whole of Egypt and to that end besought the aid of Emperor Manuel. The latter agreed to aid him in return for a share of Egypt and of any spoils that might be gained. The time for such a move seemed auspicious on still another count, namely the recent arrival in the Holy Land of William, Count of Nevers, with his band of knights eager for military action against the Moslems. Lastly, Gerbert, the master of the Order of the Hospital, warmly supported the projected invasion. The Templars, however, opposed the plan. Since the Emperor's agreement had not actually arrived at the time of these developments, Amalric rightly hesitated, fearful that such a move would lead to a union of Shavar and Nūr-ad-Dīn and hence he indicated that he desired to wait until the Byzantines' aid was available. But majority opinion, especially that of the Hospitallers who viewed askance the prospect of a division of the spoils with the Greeks, was against him. In consequence, he reluctantly yielded and set into motion plans for an invasion of Egypt in October, 1168. And so it occurred.[129]

---

comte de Jaffa." Lastly, Ernst Strehlke (*Tabulae Ordinis Theutonici* [Berlin, 1869], p. 480, Index Rerum) establishes completely separate differentiations between "Ioceliunus, Iozcelinus, Iozelinus de Samosac," on the one hand, and "Ioscelinus III, comes Edessanus et senescalcus Hierosolymitani," on the other hand.

[128] William of Tyre, chaps. xxvii-xxxii, *op. cit.*, pp. 931-39; Abou Chamah, *op. cit.*, pp. 132-34; *The Chronography of Bar Hebraeus*, pp. 291-92; Ibn al-Athīr, *K.-A.*, p. 550 and *Atabecs*, p. 240; Behâ Ed-Dîn, *Anecdotes*, pp. 44-45 and *Saladin*, pp. 50-51.

[129] William of Tyre, Bk. XX, chaps. iii-vi, *op. cit.*, pp. 945-949; Behâ Ed-Dîn, *Anecdotes*, pp. 45-46 and *Saladin*, p. 52; Ibn al-Athīr, *K.-A.*, pp. 553-54 and *Atabecs*, pp. 246-47; Abou Chamah, *op. cit.*, p. 112; Michael the Syrian, Bk. XIX, chap. iv, *Chronique*,

Bilbais soon fell into Frankish control and shortly thereafter Cairo underwent a slow and rather lackadaisical investment. Shavar, initially reluctant to seek the aid of Shīrkūh and Nūr-ad-Dīn, negotiated with the besieging Franks, seeking to gain the lifting of the siege by promises of a large bribe to Amalric, but at length successfully appealed to the Syrian Moslem chieftains.[130] Informed of Shīrkūh's approach, Amalric raised the siege of Cairo and returned to Bilbais with the plan of meeting Shīrkūh before the latter had a chance to join his 8,000 seasoned troops with Shavar's forces. Amalric's strategy failed and hence he led his forces back to Syria on January 2, 1169. Shīrkūh, in consequence, triumphantly entered Cairo a few days later on January 8. Shavar's apprehensions were soon realized, for Shīrkūh's agents, one of whom was Saladin, assassinated him and Shīrkūh became the real master of Egypt. But the master was short-lived, for he died soon thereafter on March 23, 1169, leaving Saladin, his nephew, in the saddle of power. And Saladin was to prove to be the nemesis of Frankish power in the Holy Land.[131]

---

pp. 332-33. Runciman (*History*, p. 380) observes that "Their [the Templars'] opposition may have been due to jealousy of the Hospital, which had already decided to take Pelusium as its portion, as a counter to the Templar fortress of Gaza. But the Temple was also financially connected with the Moslems and with the Italian merchants, whose trade was now greater with Egypt than with Christian Syria." Babcock and Krey (*op. cit.*, p. 351, n.11) comments as follows: "Lundgreen, following Abu-Sama, believes that the Templars did finally take part after voicing their objections to the venture. The Templars were especially concerned because their grand master, Geoffrey Fulcher, had made the treaty with the caliph at Cairo in 1167. William had given chief credit to Hugh of Caesarea (see F. Lundgreen, *Wilhelm von Tyrus und der Templerorden*, pp. 101-6)." Stevenson (*op. cit.*, p. 193) in his observations that "The charges of faithlessness against Shawir were a mere excuse or rested on suspicion." ... "He [Shavar] knew Shirkuh's temper and the danger of alliance with Nurredin" is supported by William of Tyre's own skepticism concerning these charges. Stevenson (*op. cit.*, p. 193, n. 2) neatly handles the Moslem version of this invasion with the following comment: "I. A. i. 554 includes Amalric amongst those who disapproved personally of the undertaking and thought that the Latins should be satisfied with concessions already made to them. But Tyre xx. 5 is better evidence that Amalric was personally responsible for the policy adopted..."

[130] William of Tyre, chaps. vi-ix, *op. cit.*, pp. 949-55; Abou Chamah, *op. cit.*, pp. 113-16 and 136-39; Ibn al-Athīr, *K.-A.*, pp. 554-57 and *Atabecs*, pp. 247-49; Michael the Syrian, *Chronique*, p. 333; Behâ Ed-Dîn, *Saladin*, pp. 53-54 and *Anecdotes*, p. 46; *The Chronography of Bar Hebraeus*, pp. 293-94; *Chronique d'Ernoul*, p. 20. Cf. Baldwin. "The Latin States," p. 555 and Stevenson, *op. cit.*, p. 193.

[131] William of Tyre, chap. ix-xi, *op. cit.*, pp. 955-59; *The Chronography of Bar Hebraeus*, pp. 294-95; *Chronique d'Ernoul, loc. cit.;* Michael the Syrian, *Chronique, loc. cit.;* Ibn al-Athīr, *K.-A.*, pp. 557-60 and *Atabecs*, pp. 250-53; Behâ Ed-Dîn. *Saladin*, pp. 54-55 and *Anecdotes*, pp. 47-48; Abou Chamah, *op. cit.*, pp. 118-19 and 139-45; Abū'l-Fidā *op. cit.*, pp. 36-37 and 38; Ibn Khallikan, *op. cit.*, IV, 490-91. See Sir Hamilton A.R. Gibb, "The Rise of Saladin, 1169-1189," *A History of the Crusades. The First Hundred Years* (Philadelphia, 1955), I, 563-89, Lane-Poole, *op. cit.*, pp. 3-401, Slaughter,

The new ruler of Egypt, thirty-two years old, was well suited for the external and internal problems of his new post. Dame Fortune had presided over his family even before his birth, for his father, Aiyūb, laid the foundations of his son's future eminence by his astute granting of asylum to Zengi when the latter had suffered defeat at the hands of his enemies. This single act endeared him to Zengi, who never forgot his debt. He repaid it in the form of a governorship of Baalbek to Saladin's father, who thereupon continued his earlier realistic policies by supporting Nūr-ad-Dīn, when the latter assumed the position vacated by the death of his own father, Zengi. Again repayment was forthcoming with the award of the governorship of Damascus in 1154 following its capture by Nūr-ad-Dīn's forces. Schooled in war by reason of his participation in Shīrkūh's invasion of Egypt, Saladin easily dealt with Amalric's renewed intervention in Egypt in general and belated siege of Damietta in particular in the Autumn of 1169. Although aided by Manuel's Greek naval contingents, the combined Franco-Greek naval forces failed utterly to achieve their objective. Famine in the ranks of the besiegers and the use of a fireship by the besieged against the enemy's navy weakened the effectiveness of the Franco-Greek investment. Saladin ably used the time granted him by his sluggish foemen to create an impregnable defense. At length despair of victory set in and the siege ended on December 13, 1169.[132]

---

op. cit., pp. 13-289, and Gibb, "The Achievement of Saladin," pp. 91-107. (Henceforth the first cited work of Gibb in this footnote will be designated as "Saladin.") The last four cited references provide detailed accounts of the career of Saladin.

[132] William of Tyre, chaps. xiii-xvii, *op. cit.*, pp. 961-71; *The Chronography of Bar Hebraeus*, pp. 288-89; Ibn al-Athīr *K.-A.*, pp. 568-70 and *Atabecs*, pp. 258-60; Michael the Syrian, *Extrait*, pp. 369-70 and chap. vi, *Chronique*, p. 336; Cinnamus, *op. cit.*, pp. 278-80; Behâ Ed-Dîn, *Saladin*, pp. 56-59 and *Anecdotes*, pp. 49-51; Abou Chamah, *op. cit.*, pp. 150-53. As Munro (*op. cit.*, p. 146) points out in effect, the alliance of Amalric with the Byzantines had been of dubious value to the southern Franks, for it had served only to create new misunderstandings and suspicions in the ranks of the latter: "The alliance with the Greeks, instead of improving conditions between the Crusaders and the Greek Empire, really increased the hatred felt for the Greeks, because they had not carried on the expedition as earnestly as the Crusaders thought they ought to have done. The Greeks, as usual, had been hindered by the necessity of fighting against the Turks in Asia Minor..." Writing in the same vein, Babcock and Krey (*op. cit.*, p. 368, n. 28) observe "The Greek historians have much to say about this expedition, and, needless to add, they place the blame on the Latins. William, despite the mention of charges against the Greeks, really affords the Greek historians much support. The Latins were evidently divided in sentiment, many of them being none too anxious to divide Egypt with the Greeks. Such must have been the meaning of the embassy to seek aid in the West in 1169, though they already had an alliance for the purpose with Manuel. Such too had

With equal deftness Saladin dealt with his Moslem enemies, who resented his ousting of Egyptians from civil offices and replacing of them by Syrians. A plot was formed to which Amalric was privy. Saladin got wind of it, executed the ringleader, and forced the Caliph to assume a rôle of lowly obedience.[133]

Yet the situation, while serious for the adjacent Kingdom of Jerusalem, was not immediately hopeless. Egypt had not yet fallen under Saladin's complete control. This consideration, together with Saladin's program of complete independence of Nūr-ad-Dīn, which in turn prevented meaningful cooperation with the latter, precluded the immediate likelihood of the creation of a unified common front of the Egyptian and Syrian Moslems so ominous to the continuation of the Frankish states.

Accordingly, the early 1170's were marked by relative quiet along the Franco-Egyptian border. Saladin's domestic position in Egypt was strengthened by the presence of the Caliph, for the latter was always capable of arousing native Egyptian support for Saladin in the event

---

been the meaning of Amaury's hasty expedition to Egypt in 1168, though his own envoy was at that very moment returning from Manuel's court with the signed treaty."

[133] Ibn al-Athīr, *K.-A.*, pp. 566-68. William of Tyre (chap. xi, *op. cit.*, p. 958) states that Saladin killed the caliph of Egypt at the very beginning of his rule in Egypt. Babcock and Krey (*op. cit.*, p. 359, n. 21) declare that "This account of the death of the caliph is not confirmed by other sources. It is possible that William is confusing Saladin's part in the destruction of Shawar and his family ... with the death of the caliph. Caliph Adid seems to have died a natural death, September 13, 1171." I may add the observation that it was to the selfish interest of Saladin, a non Egyptian Moslem, not to excite additional hatred for himself among the Egyptian Moslems, some of whom undoubtedly regarded him as a foreigner and, perhaps, as a usurper as well. This feeling sprang without doubt from Saladin's ousting of native Egyptians from political jobs and replacement of them by Syrian Moslems. Slaughter (*op. cit.*, p. 57) supports my view in the following passage: "From a subordinate position in an army which lacked the authority of an army of occupation, the son of Ayyub [Saladin] was now commander in chief and the actual ruler of the wealthiest country of Islam. But he was not yet secure in his high post. He still had to win his way. He had to negotiate a working plan with subordinates and superiors of several levels. No caliph on his golden throne could give him the actual control of affairs, or save him from destruction if his enemies proved too strong for him. If he had been blinded by success, if he had been weak and self-indulgent in pride of position, if he had followed the examples around him of playing power politics in disregard of personal obligations, if he had not retained his clarity of vision, his fall would have been great." Baldwin ("The Latin States," p. 556) rightly observes that "These events [the assassination of Shavar, the brief succession of Shīrkūh, the permanent succession of Saladin, and the quashing of the Egyptian opposition to Saladin] produced a revolution in the balance of power in the Levant. The Frankish protectorate over Egypt with all its advantages, economic as well as political, was ended. To all intents and purposes Moslem Egypt and Syria were united, and there began that encirclement of the Christian states which in future years was to prove so disastrous."

that Nūr-ad-Dīn should elect to invade Egypt. This fortunate condition continued until the death of the Caliph in September, 1171. Meanwhile Saladin delayed an open rupture with Nūr-ad-Dīn, preferring the rôle rather than the title of real independence and doubtless aware that Nūr-ad-Dīn regarded him merely as one of his subordinates now in charge of Egypt.[134] The recollection and reality of Nūr-ad-Dīn's aid to Saladin against the internal conspiracy in the Summer of 1169 and the external one posed by the Franco-Greek invasion of the following Autumn[135] could not be ignored. The harmony prevailing between the two leaders continued and was exemplified in April, 1170 when Nūr-ad-Dīn, in response to Saladin's request, dispatched Saladin's father, Aiyūb, to him with an army. At this time Saladin was engaged in attacks on Krak and other Frankish strongholds in the vicinity of the Dead Sea. Nūr-ad-Dīn himself presently invested Krak.[136]

But as the months progressed, an ever more obvious coolness marked the relationships of the two Moslem chieftains. The first example of this was seen in Saladin's marked reluctance to accede to Nūr-ad-Dīn's demand that henceforth prayers in the Egyptian mosques should ignore the Shī'ite Caliph of Egypt in favor of the Sunnite Caliph of Bagdad. Saladin's refusal on the ground that such a move would incite the Egyptian population to rise against him angered Nūr-ad-Dīn to such an extent that he warned his subordinate he himself would come to Egypt unless he obeyed his order. Thereupon Saladin prepared himself for the inevitable change, but he himself allowed another person, namely a visiting divine from Mosul, to effect it in his prayer on September 10, 1171 in the Great Mosque in Cairo in behalf of the Sunnite Caliph of Bagdad. With the ice thus broken, Saladin ordered the cessation of mention of the Caliph of Cairo and required the inclusion of the name of the Caliph of Bagdad in all public prayers. Meanwhile, Saladin, having been apprised of the new turn of events, refused to tell the Fāṭimid Caliph, who lay dying, of the new religious orientation. Fearful of a plot against himself, Saladin refused to accede to the dying Caliph's request that he visit him. But Saladin soon regretted his action when it was too late and continued to manifest affection for his late superior. However, this affection did

---

[134] Behâ Ed-Dîn, *Saladin*, p. 60 and *Anecdotes*, p. 52. Barker (*op. cit.*, p. 57) believes that Saladin "... made himself, on the death of the Caliph in 1171, sole ruler in Egypt."

[135] Ibn al-Athīr, *K.-A.*, p. 568-70.

[136] Abou Chamah, *op. cit.*, pp. 153-54; Behâ Ed-Dîn, *Saladin*, pp. 59-60 and *Anecdotes*, p. 50; Ibn al-Athīr, *K.-A.*, pp. 570-71. See Fedden and Thomson, *op. cit.*, pp. 84-90 for a history and description of the formidable castle of Krak.

not include the late Caliph's relatives, for Saladin at once placed all of them in a special area of the Caliph's palace and retired from the employ of the palace all the slaves and servants.[137]

A second example of strained relations soon followed in October, 1171, when Saladin, in response to Nūr-ad-Dīn's pleas, advanced north from Egypt to besiege Krak de Montréal, but departed on his rival's approach, alleging that his serious losses together with evidence of a conspiracy against him in Egypt necessitated his departure. Still seeking to maintain a *modus vivendi* with his superior, Saladin, following a family council during which he rejected the advice of his younger male relatives that he defy Nūr-ad-Dīn and instead accepted the wise counsel of his father Aiyūb that he should continue to pursue a policy of submission to Nūr-ad-Dīn, coupled his explanation to Nūr-ad-Dīn with the most serious promise of future cooperation.[138]

Matters finally came to a head in 1173 with Saladin's second spurning of Nūr-ad-Dīn. Saladin's attack upon the fortress of Krak in the south while his nominal superior, Nūr-ad-Dīn, was engaged in war with Kîlîj Arslan during June and July, 1173[139] simultaneously provoked Amalric's and Nūr-ad-Dīn's military activity. Upon Nūr-ad-Dīn's approach to aid his subordinate, Saladin departed, alleging that his control of Egypt would be endangered if the governor of Egypt, Aiyūb, who was then ill, should die. Hence his withdrawal was necessitated.[140] Saladin's true motivation was fear that the destruction of the buffer states of the Franks would enable Nūr-ad-Dīn to seize Egypt. But Nūr-ad-Dīn was undeceived and saw the reality. Masking his true feelings by an acceptance of Saladin's gifts and by

---

[137] Kamal-Ad-Dîn, *Histoire*, III, 551; Ibn al-Athīr, *K.-A.*, pp. 578-81 and *Atabecs*, pp. 282-84; Behâ Ed-Dîn, *Anecdotes*, pp. 52-53 and *Saladin*, pp. 61-62. Runciman (*History*, p. 394) correctly sees in Saladin's non compliance with Nūr-ad-Dīn's request the calculation that "... though he might own Nur ed-Din as his master, his authority in Egypt came from the Fatimid Caliph." I may add that the import of all these moves of Saladin was not lost on Nūr-ad-Dīn and served to exacerbate their relationships.

[138] William of Tyre, chap. xxvii, *op. cit.*, pp. 992-93; Ibn al-Athīr, *K.-A.*, pp. 581-83 and *Atabecs*, pp. 286-88; Abou Chamah, *op. cit.*, pp. 155-56; *The Chronography of Bar Hebraeus*, pp. 300-01; Kamal-Ad-Dîn, *Histoire*, III, 551-53; *Histoire d'Égypte de Makrizi*, trans. and ed. by Edgar Blochet, *Revue de l'orient latin* (Paris, 1900-01), VIII, 505-07. Runciman (*History*, p. 394) states that when Saladin raised the siege of Krak "He told Nur ed-Din that his brothers' wars in upper Egypt obliged him to return to Cairo." None of the sources quoted by this scholar (*History*, p. 395, n. 1) supports such a conclusion.

[139] Ibn al-Athīr, *K.-A.*, pp. 591-92 and *Atabecs*, p. 290; Behâ Ed-Dîn, *Anecdotes*, pp. 53-54 and *Saladin*, pp. 62-63.

[140] Ibn al-Athīr, *K.-A.*, pp. 593-94 and 602; William of Tyre, chaps. xxviii and xxxi, *op. cit.*, pp. 994-95 and 1000. Cf. Stevenson, *op. cit.*, p. 201, n. 2.

an observation that the retention of Egypt was more important in his eyes than any other object, he withdrew to formulate plans for war on his refractory subject. But an open clash between the increasingly ambitious rivals never occurred, for Nūr-ad-Dīn died on May 15, 1174 at the age of 56 in Damascus.[141]

---

[141] William of Tyre, chap. xxxi, *op. cit.*, p. 1000; *The Chronography of Bar Hebraeus*, p. 302; Makrizi, *op. cit.*, p. 513; Ibn al-Athīr, *Atabecs*, pp. 292-293 and *K.-A.*, pp. 593-94; Kamal-Ad-Dîn, *Histoire*, III, 555-56; Behâ Ed-Dîn, *Anecdotes*, p. 55 and *Saladin*, *K.-A.*, p. 65. Babcock and Krey, *op. cit.*, p. 394, n. 62. Gibb ("Saladin," pp. 565-66) sees a divergence of political views as the basic causes of strain between Nūr-ad-Dīn and Saladin. "Nūr-ad-Dīn regarded Syria as the main battlefield against the crusaders, and looked to Egypt firstly as a source of revenue to meet the expenses of the jihad, and secondly as a source of additional manpower. Saladin, on the other hand, judging from the former competition for Egypt and the attempt on Damietta in 1169, and probably informed of the tenor of Amalric's negotiations with the Byzantine emperor in 1171, seems to have been convinced that for the time being, at least, the main point of danger lay in Egypt. He was more conscious also than Nūr-ad-Dīn could be of the dangers arising from the hostility of the former Fāṭimid troops and their readiness to join with the Franks. In his view, therefore, it was his first duty to build up a new army strong enough to hold Egypt in all contingencies, and to spend what resources he could command on this object." The same scholar ("The Achievement of Saladin," pp. 96-97) also observes that "To Nur ad-Din the conquest of Egypt meant only an immediate and substantial accretion of military and financial resources for the war in Syria; whereas Saladin, faced with a dangerous situation in Egypt, felt that his first responsibility was to build up the local forces to hold Egypt against the threat of collusion between pro-Fatimid elements within and Frankish attacks from without. Presumably, after the failure of the Sicilian expedition to Alexandria in 1174 the general situation in Egypt would have been sufficiently stabilized to restore full understanding between Nur ad-Din and Saladin, but even before it arrived Nur ad-Din had died."

CHAPTER FOUR

THE RISE OF SALADIN
1174-1176

The year 1174 was one of the most portentous import in the history of the Frankish states, for it marked, in terms of their internal structure and security, the end of the strong rule of Amalric with his death on July 11, 1174[142] and the accession to the vacant throne of Jerusalem of his leprous son, Baldwin IV, a young lad of barely thirteen years on July 15, 1174.[143] The event afforded golden opportunities to rival nobiliary factions to contest for the control of the Kingdom of Jerusalem to the advantage of the hostile Moslems. In respect to foreign policy and the Moslem foe, the year 1174 marked the beginning of the realization of Saladin's dream of becoming the master of all of Moslem Syria as well as Frankish Syria. The result was the setting into motion of a chain of events leading to the liberation of Joscelyn III as well as Reginald of Châtillon in 1176.

The weakness of rule in the Kingdom of Jerusalem resulting from the accession of a boy king and the ensuing nobiliary intrigue had its counterpart in Nūr-ad-Dīn's Syria as well. Nūr-ad-Dīn's heir, his son as-Ṣāliḥ, was only eleven years old at his accession to the vacant sultanate. He soon became the pawn in a gigantic political game between rival emirs, namely Sham ed-din Muhammed ibn el-mukaddem, the leader of the Damascene emirs, and the Aleppan governor, Shams ed-din ʿAli ibn ed-daya. The latter saw in the young prince a useful instrument to block the ambitious dreams of power entertained by Nūr-ad-Dīn's nephew Saif-ad-Dīn Ghāzī II, the ruler of Mosul. Since the physical possession of the young sultan, who was at Damascus at this time, was highly desirable to accomplish this objective, the Aleppan governor sent his agent Saʿd-ad-Dīn Gümüshtigin to Damascus. At length the Damascene emirs consented

---

[142] William of Tyre, op. cit., p. 1001; The Chronography of Bar Hebraeus, p. 303; Babcock and Krey, pp. 395-96, n. 63.

[143] William of Tyre, Bk. XXI, chap. ii, op. cit., p. 1006; Ibn al-Athīr, K.-A., p. 619; The Chronography of Bar Hebraeus, loc. cit. Richard (op. cit., p. 137, n. 2) after erroneously stating that "Baudouin IV et Sibylle n'avaient été légitimés" (as of the time of the dissolution of Amalric's marriage to Agnes in 1162) (supra, p. 31) speculates as follows: "... le roi voyait-il dans sa lèpre un châtiment?"

and permitted Gümüshtigin to repair to Aleppo with aṣ-Ṣāliḥ, the young sultan. But Gümüshtigin, upon his arrival in Aleppo, proceeded to doublecross his master, Shams ed-din ʿAli ibn ed-daya, by deposing him and by arrogating to himself the double rôle of ruler of Aleppo and sole guardian of the captive sultan aṣ-Ṣāliḥ on August 3, 1174. The discomfited Damascene emirs, fearful of Gümüshtigin's future plans, offered control of Damascus to Saif-ad-Dīn Ghāzī II. When the latter, fearing a ruse, failed to reply, they became fearful that an agreement between him and the young sultan was about to result and hence they turned to Saladin.[144]

Saladin, having entrusted the rule of Egypt to his brother, Saif-ad-Dīn, accepted the offer, advanced into Syria with professions of a completely selfless purpose of aiding the luckless young sultan against Saif-ad-Dīn Ghāzī II, the alleged usurper of the former's rights, emphasized his own rôle as a defender of Islam against the alien Frankish Christians, and branded all present as well as future rivals of his program in Syria as persons forgetful of the duties of the *jihad* and as supporters of the Franks.[145] Arriving at Damascus on October 28, 1174, he soon obtained the surrender of the city on the following November 27 and secured possession of the citadel. Now apprised of

---

[144] William of Tyre, chap. vi, *op. cit.*, pp. 1012-13; *The Chronography of Bar Hebraeus*, *loc. cit.*; Behâ Ed-Dîn, *Anecdotes*, pp. 57-58 and *Saladin*, pp. 65, n. 2 and 67-68, and 69; Kamal-Ad-Dîn, *Histoire*, III, 557, 558-59, and 560; Ibn al-Athīr, *K.-A.*, pp. 606-09 and 614-16 and *Atabecs*, pp. 294, 319, and 320-22; Makrizi, *loc. cit.*

[145] William of Tyre, *op. cit.*, p. 1013; Michael the Syrian, Bk. XX, chap. iii, *Chronique*, pp. 364-65; Makrizi, *op. cit.*, pp. 516-17; Behâ Ed-Dîn, *Anecdotes*, pp. 58-59 and *Saladin*, pp. 68-69; Michael the Syrian, *Extrait*, p. 380; *The Chronography of Bar Hebraeus*, *loc. cit.*; Ibn al-Athīr, *Atabecs*, p. 322. Slaughter (*op. cit.*, pp. 80-81), in assessing Saladin's moves at this time, observes that "Saladin knew that the summons, although sent by influential citizens, was due to his own suggestion. He had written to them to remind them that civil disorders would make Damascus an easy prey to the Franks and he had threatened that if they could not control the situation he would take the task of administering justice upon himself as the chief officer of Nur-al-Din." .... "Saladin's conduct at this crisis may be regarded as an ambitious seizure of power or as a conscientious assumption of responsibility. A sense of ability may be indistinguishable from ambition. Saladin certainly knew that his father would have had him accept the summons for other reasons than personal prestige. Ayyub, of course, believed that whatever favored his son was the will of Allah. But even if Saladin shared that comfortable belief, they both understood that the control of Damascus by the Lord of Mosul would mean a shifting of the center of gravity eastward. It would mean that Egypt would again be separated from Syria and both countries would be more than ever at the mercy of the Franks. It might mean that the Holy War would be lost. For although the unity of the western with the eastern provinces of Moslem was the object of years of labor and Mosul was the most difficult of all to win over, Saladin saw clearly that the leadership of the Moslem union must be in the west."

Gümüshtigin's unwillingness to surrender his guardianship of the boy sultan, Saladin accordingly declared war on Aleppo and its supporters. Baalbek, Hamah, and Shaizar soon became his prizes and he obtained the surrender of the lower city of Homs in December, 1174. The citadel of this city, however, resisted by reason of the decision of the young sultan's supporters to retire there and continue the struggle. The conquering Moslem then advanced on Aleppo itself and invested it during January, 1175. Meanwhile, the Aleppo population, bestirred by the proud defiance, despite his youth, shown by the young sultan to Saladin, resisted the latter strongly. Gümüshtigin also sought to effect Saladin's assassination. Although this project proved abortive, Gümüshtigin was not daunted and sought additional Christian support by appeals to Raymond of Tripoli in which he urged him to attack one of the provinces held by Saladin in order to oblige the latter to retire from Aleppo. He also guaranteed to Raymond numerous advantages after Saladin's departure from Aleppo.[146]

Aleppo's pleas met with the approval of the leaders of the Kingdom of Jerusalem, who, greatly fearing Saladin's aggrandizement of power, saw the possibility that aid granted to aṣ-Ṣāliḥ now might encourage him to assume a rôle of enmity to Saladin. Accordingly, Raymond, complying with the appeal of refugees from Homs who besought his aid against Saladin, invested Homs, whereupon Saladin, who was now obliged to end his own investment of Aleppo, advanced on Homs and effected its release from the besieging Franks on March 16, 1175. Meanwhile Saif-ad-Dīn Ghāzī II himself besieged Sinjar in April, 1175 and dispatched his brother to Aleppo. Saladin, still posing as the supporter of the young sultan, aṣ-Ṣāliḥ, offered to surrender Hamah and Homs in return for the city of Damascus in which, so he averred, he would act as the sultan's lieutenant. When Saladin's opponents refused and demanded that he surrender all of his Syrian conquests and return to Egypt, he countered with an advance against them culminating in a resounding military victory at the Horns of Hamah on April 23, 1175. He then resumed the siege of Aleppo. At length the

---

[146] Behâ Ed-Dîn, *Anecdotes*, p. 59 and *Saladin*, pp. 69-70; Abou Chamah, *op. cit.*, p. 167; William of Tyre, *loc. cit.* and chap. viii, pp. 1017-18; Ibn al-Athīr, *K.-A.*, pp. 616-20; Makrizi. *op. cit.*, pp. 517-18; Michael the Syrian, *Extrait, loc. cit.* and *Chronique*, p. 365; *The Chronography of Bar Hebraeus*, pp. 303-04; Kamal-Ad-Dîn, *Histoire*, III, 560-63. Groussset (*Histoire*, p. 622) sees the Moslem negotiations with Raymond as an example of balance of power politics: "L'assassinat" de Saladin avait donc échoué. Restait l'appel aux Francs, recours traditionnel des puissances musulmanes secondaires pour empêcher la constitution d'un sultanat trop puissant."

defenders offered him peace on condition that the defenders and besieged alike would retain the respective areas they then controlled. Saladin agreed and repaired to Hamah.[147]

The tide of victory, flowing swiftly in Saladin's favor, became even more obvious with the withdrawal of the Frankish antagonists in late April, 1175 in return for his release of the Frankish hostages who had been left in the fortress of Homs with Nūr-ad-Dīn by Raymond at the time of his own release. Although Baldwin IV's counter stroke in the form of a successful raid into the outskirts of Damascus shortly thereafter disconcerted Saladin enough to cause him to renew a truce before August 21 with the Kingdom of Jerusalem, the year as a whole had been highly satisfactory to him. The triumphant Moslem spent the balance of the year 1175 and the opening months of 1176 in Damascus after the discharge of his Egyptian soldiery.[148]

But the central problem separating the Syrian and Egyptian Moslems, namely who was to be the ultimate and significant heir to the purple robes of power formerly worn by Nūr-ad-Dīn, had by no means been settled.[149] This circumstance was soon to entail the freeing of the two Frankish champions, Joscelyn III and Reginald of Châtillon.

---

[147] William of Tyre, chaps. vi and viii, *op. cit.*, pp. 1013-14 and 1017-18; Ibn al-Athīr, *K.-A.*, pp. 620-22; Abou Chamah, *op. cit*, p. 168; Michael the Syrian, *Extrait*, p. 381 and *Chronique, loc. cit.*; *The Chronography of Bar Hebraeus*, p. 304; Kamal-Ad-Dîn, *Histoire*, III, 563-64 and IV, 146; Behâ Ed-Dîn, *Anecdotes*, pp. 59-60 and *Saladin*, pp. 70-71.

[148] William of Tyre, chaps. viii and xi, *op. cit.*, pp. 1018-19 and 1021-23; Michael the Syrian, *Extrait, loc. cit.* and *Chronique, loc. cit.* Grousset (*Histoire* p. 626) believes that Saladin's overtures to the Franks in the Spring of 1175 resulted from his calculations that while his enemies in Aleppo had been humiliated those in Mosul had not and might, in consequence, try to secure a Frankish alliance against him. "Cependant, si le jeune Zengide d'Alep acceptait son humiliation, son cousin de Mossoul ne pouvait manquer de méditer une revanche. Saladin, qui s'en doutait, essaya de prévenir une coalition franco-zengide. Il envoya une ambassade à Raymond III pour lui promettre paix et amitié si les Francs ne secondaient pas la prochaine contre-offensive zengide."

[149] Gibb ("Saladin," p. 569) views this problem as follows: "It was not only that a prince of the Zengid house was reduced virtually to being a vassal of one of his father's creatures. What was still more disagreeable was that the creature was a Kurd, who challenged the monopoly of sovereignty enjoyed by the Turks for a century and a half, and bestowed his conquests upon his own kinsmen. To what extent, indeed, personal motives were mingled with Saladin's genuine devotion to the cause and the ideals of Islam is a question which it may never be possible to resolve. But in the circumstances of his time, however unselfregarding his motives were, the only way in which his object could be realized was by concentrating power in his own hands, and delegating it to persons on whose loyalty he could count with absolute assurance. The attitude of the Zengids drove him in the same direction, when events showed him the futility of relying upon alliances and confederations."

Restive under Saladin's overlordship and fearing further danger from him, Saif-ad-Dīn-Ghāzī II decided to attack Aleppo and advanced upon that city in the Spring of 1176 with a large infantry and cavalry force. Saladin mobilized his Egyptian forces and moved to meet the enemy. The ensuing battle of Tall as-Sulṭān on April 22, 1176 was another victory for Saladin, but the opposition to him continued to be stubborn, thanks to the decision of the Franks of Antioch to throw in their lot with Aleppo and use the strong center of ʿAzāz as their rallying point. Consequently, Saladin was obliged to spend the late Spring of 1176 in an investment of ʿAzāz before he effected its capture on June 22, 1176. Gümüshtigin, in search of still more Frankish aid and apprehensive over Saladin's victory over Saif-ad-Dīn Ghāzī II, answered Antioch's friendly moves with one of his own, namely with presents to the lord of Antioch and the release of Joscelyn III and Reginald of Châtillon. Joscelyn III's sister Agnes had persistently endeavored to secure his release, which was now gained by a money payment of 50,000 dinars. Prince Reginald's release required a larger payment of 120,000 dinars.[150]

---

[150] Michael the Syrian, *Chronique*, p. 365 and *Extrait*, pp. 381-82; *The Chronography of Bar Hebraeus*, p. 305; Ibn al-Athīr, *K.-A.*, pp. 622-24; Behâ Ed-Dîn, *Anecdotes*, pp. 61-63 and *Saladin*, pp. 72-74; Abou Chamah, *op. cit.*, pp. 182-83; William of Tyre, chap. xi, *op. cit.*, p. 1023; Makrizi, *op. cit.*, pp. 522-24; Kamal-Ad-Dîn, *Histoire*, IV, 150; Ibn Khallikan, *op. cit.*, IV, 507; Ibn Khallikan's *Biographical Dictionary* trans. from the Arabic by Bⁿ Mac Guckin de Slane (Paris, 1843), II, 442. Stevenson, *op. cit.*, p. 214, n. 3. The dating of the release of Joscelyn III is a matter of considerable disagreement among the sources as well as modern writers. The sources, namely Abou Chamah, Michael the Syrian (*Chronique*), Bar Hebraeus, Kamal-Ad-Dîn, and William of Tyre, repectively date it in the Moslem year 572 (= 1176-1177 in western chronology), 1487 (= 1176 in western chronology), 571 (= 1175 in western chronology), 573 (= 1177-1178 in western chronology), and 1175. Modern day writers, viz. Cahen (*La Syrie, loc. cit.* and p. 416), La Monte ("The rise," p. 306), Richard (*op. cit.*, p. 135 and n. 1), Gaston Wiet (*L'Égypte Arabe de la Conquête Arabe à la Conquête Ottomane 642-1517 de l'ère Chrétienne* [Paris, 1937], IV, 332), and Schlumberger (*Renaud de Châtillon*, pp. 128-29) place it in 1176, whereas Collins (*loc. cit.*), Runciman (*History*, p. 405), and Röhricht ("Amalrich I," p. 444) date it in 1175. Babcock and Krey (*op. cit.*, p. 301, n. 12 and p. 414, n. 21) in their respective observations "Joscelyn III was made seneschal of the kingdom shortly after his release from captivity in 1176 . . ." and "Presumably the regnal year is meant [in respect to William of Tyre's account], July 15, 1175-July 15, 1176, so that the release [of Joscelyn III] probably occurred in 1176." definitely favor 1176 as the date of the release. *Les familles d'Outre-Mer*, p. 301 likewise definitely accepts 1176 as the date of the release of Joscelyn III. "Il [Joscelyn III] fut fait prisonnier en une rencontre par les Turcs, avec Renaud de Chastillon et autres, et depuis fut mis en liberté, l'an 1176." In view of the high probability that the negotiations for the release of Joscelyn III were effected simultaneously with those carried on for the release of Reginald of Châtillon, I cannot agree with the view of Grousset (*L'empire*, p. 230) that Reginald of Châtillon was released at a later time, namely in the year 1177. I accept the

Since Saladin's ensuing siege of Aleppo proved unsuccessful, Saif-ad-Dīn Ghāzī II and Gümüshtigin were able to make favorable peace terms with Saladin in July, 1176 providing for the return of ʿAzāz. Following his own military thrust with only mediocre results at the Assassins and a defeat administered to his brother, Turan-Shāh, by the Franks in the Summer of 1176, Saladin installed Turan-Shāh as governor of Damascus. Then, having agreed to the Franks' requests for a truce, he returned to Egypt in September. Although the continuing Franco-Moslem opposition could not be ignored, still, on balance, the past two years had been favorable for him, for all of Moslem Syria save for Aleppo itself was now under his control.[151] And with Egypt firmly secured, he was within sight of his goal of founding a Moslem empire strong enough to drive the Franks from their sadly truncated political establishment in the Near East.[152]

---

dating of 1176, for the well kept records known as the *Regesta* definitely refer to Joscelyn III as being seneschal in 1176. See *infra*, n. 173. It seems improbable to me that the author or authors of this reference to the time of Joscelyn III's holding of the seneschalship would not have referred, at least in passing, to his holding of this important position in a year earlier than 1176, if such had been the case. As we have seen, the year 1176 is definitely stated by Michael the Syrian as the year of his release. The Moslem authority Abou Chamah's dating of this event as occurring in 572 (= 1176-1177 in western chronology) is in general agreement with Michael the Syrian's dating of Joscelyn III's release and his holding of the seneschalship in the *Regesta* account. Lastly, we have seen that it is probable William of Tyre has the year 1176 in mind for the dating of the release. It is a truism to say that the Latin East had no better informed historian for the events of the 1170's and early 1180's than William of Tyre. The dating provided by Kamal-Ad-Dîn (573 = 1177-1178) is certainly in error, for the important post of seneschal would surely not have been conferred on a man still in the custody of the Moslems. This is especially so in the light of the Franks' uncertainty as to the time, indeed possibility, of Joscelyn III's release, and both of these highly unlikely assumptions must be made, if we accept the 1177-1178 dating provided by Kamal-Ad-Dîn. In commenting on the release of Joscelyn III and Reginald of Châtillon, Runciman (*History*, p. 408) declares that "In gratitude to the Franks Gumushtekin released Reynald of Châtillon and Joscelin of Courtenay and all the other Christian prisoners languishing in the dungeons of Aleppo." In view of the high price required for this release, it seems to me that gratitude on Gümüshtigin's part hardly entered into his consideration. Rather a keen business sense did. And in view of the direct statement of Abou Chamah—"Dans leur colère (contre Saladin) les Alépins n'hesitèrent pas à conclure une trêve avec les Francs et à leur rendre ceux de leurs rois que feu Nour ed-Din avait eu tant de difficultés à faire prisonniers"—it may equally be declared that sentiments of revenge against Saladin prompted the release of Joscelyn III and Reginald of Châtillon.

[151] Ibn al-Athīr, *K.-A.*, pp. 625-26; Behâ Ed-Dîn, *Anecdotes*, p. 63 and *Saladin*, p. 75.

[152] Wiet (*loc. cit.*) aptly sums up Saladin's program as follows: "Dominons, à notre tour, les annales musulmanes, et convenons franchement que Saladin n'eut pas l'ambition mesquine d'agrandir ses États aux dépens de ses coreligionnaires, mais qu'il se préoccupa surtout d'obtenir l'unité de commandement. Ainsi l'action de Saladin contre les places

fortes syriennes, — Damas, Hama, Alep, Baalbek, etc., — partait certainement d'une ferme volonté d'encercler les Francs et non d'une vulgaire ambition territoriale. Les contemporains, ceux du moins de l'entourage intime de Saladin, ne paraissent pas s'y être trompés. Les adversaires musulmans de Saladin s'affolent: ils font appel au prince de Mossoul, aux Ismaïliens, et même au comte de Tripoli. La situation morale de Saladin y gagna naturellement un grand prestige, et il ne dut pas manquer de proclamer que les Zenguides pactisaient avec l'ennemi."

CHAPTER FIVE

FRANKISH DEVELOPMENTS, 1143-1174;
THE OPENING OF THE REIGN OF BALDWIN IV, (1174-1185);
THE REAPPEARANCE OF RAYMOND III AND JOSCELYN III;
THE COURTENAY CHIEFTAIN'S WAXING
POLITICAL AND ECONOMIC POWER AS SENESCHAL

In the Frankish states, and, most particularly, the Kingdom of Jerusalem, the internal weaknesses so apparent in both the Moslem and Frankish states, as of 1174, had not been replaced, as had been the case of the Moslem states during the ensuing two years, by growing strength and unity. Gone was the vigorous leadership prevailing under Baldwin III and his brother Amalric, an outstanding example of which had been, in the case of the former, his hurried journey to Antioch in 1150 to succour the Principality after the death of its ruler, Prince Raymond, and his subsequent sanctioning of the rule of the Principality by Patriarch Aimery. Again, there had been his convocation in 1152 at Tripoli of a general council of the nobles of the Kingdom of Jerusalem and the Principality of Antioch in an endeavor to persuade the widowed Constance, princess of Antioch, to remarry in order to provide the Principality with efficient military protection in the face of the waxing Moslem power.[153] Moreover, later on, in 1160, he had sped north to Antioch to succour Princess Constance in her hour of need following the capture of her second husband, Raymond of Châtillon,[154] by Nūr-ad-Dīn's ally, Majd-al-Dīn, the governor of Aleppo.[155] Baldwin III had provided this aid by

---

[153] William of Tyre, Bk. XVII, chaps. x and xviii, *op. cit.*, pp. 775-76 and 789-91; *The Chronography of Bar Hebraeus*, p. 275. Yet it is necessary to point out, as Grousset (*Histoire*, pp. 317-18) has done, that Baldwin III's rôle as a strong ruler has a certain gloss on it. "Dans ce royaume [the Kingdom of Jerusalem] en état de siège, perdu en plein Islam, le maintien d'une monarchie forte—et masculine—était question de vie ou de mort. Au reste, la leçon des faits l'atteste: Lorsque Baudouin III courut sauver la principauté d'Antioche envahie par les Turcs, aucun baron des fiefs personnels de sa mère ne répondit à son appel. Carence qui, dans des circonstances aussi critiques, équivalait à une véritable trahison."

[154] William of Tyre, chap. xxvi, *op. cit.*, p. 802. This marriage, which had occurred in 1153, had led to Reginald's assumption of the rule of the Principality of Antioch.

[155] *Ibid.*, Bk. XVIII, chap. xxviii, *op. cit.*, pp. 868-69. Babcock and Krey, *op. cit.*, p. 285, n. 82.

securing a two year truce with Nūr-ad-Dīn.¹⁵⁶ Lastly, Baldwin III had lingered on in Antioch throughout 1161 to pursue successful negotiations for the marriage of Princess Maria, the daughter of Constance and the late Prince Raymond of Antioch, in December, 1161 with the Byzantine emperor Manuel.¹⁵⁷ This move was an obvious attempt to strengthen the Frankish power in the Holy Land.¹⁵⁸

The vigorous leadership of Baldwin III had its counterpart, although lesser, in the ranks of the nobiliary and clerical leadership in the Principality of Antioch. When the Queen Mother of Antioch, Constance, had sought in 1162, upon her son Bohemond's attainment of his eighteenth birthday and therefore the legal age to govern, to retain her control of the Principality and thereby deprive him of his rightful rôle as ruler and, in pursuance of this purpose, had summoned the Byzantine general Constantine Coloman to grant her military assistance, the incensed magnates and the Patriarch of Antioch had appealed to Toros, the Armenian prince, to aid them. He had done so, had driven Constance into exile, and had placed Bohemond III on the throne of Antioch.¹⁵⁹

---

¹⁵⁶ Grégoire Le Prêtre, chap. cxxviii, *Chronique*, p. 194; Stevenson, (*op. cit.*, pp. 182-83) observes, in connection with the truce agreed to by Nūr-ad-Dīn, that "More than one influence may have strengthened his [Nūr-ad-Dīn's] desire for peace. No doubt he was already resolved to perform the pilgrimage to Mekka when the next pilgrimage season came."

¹⁵⁷ William of Tyre, chap. xxxi, *op. cit.*, p. 876.

¹⁵⁸ For a comprehensive survey of the reign of Baldwin III as well as that of his brother Amalric I, see Baldwin, "The Latin States," pp. 528-61.

¹⁵⁹ Michael the Syrian, Bk. XVIII, chap. x, *Chronique*, p. 324; *The Chronography of Bar Hebraeus*, pp. 287-88; *Anon. Syriac Chronicle*, p. 303, dates the event as occurring in 1160 and states that Bohemond "... drove out his mother who went to Latakia." The chances are that his rôle in this whole affair was an ancillary one to that of Toros and confirmed the latter's action. See Runciman, *History*, p. 365, n. 1. Runciman (*History*, p. 358 and n. 2) declares that "Reginald's elimination raised a constitutional problem in Antioch, where he had reigned as the husband of the Princess Constance. She now claimed that the power reverted to her; but public opinion supported the rights of her son by her first marriage, Bohemond, surnamed the Stammerer, who was however only aged fifteen. It was a situation similar to that of Queen Melisende and Baldwin III in Jerusalem a few years previously. There was no immediate danger, because Nur-ed-Din's fear of Manuel kept him from attacking Antioch itself. But some effective government must be provided. Strictly speaking, it was for the Emperor as the accepted suzerain of Antioch to settle the question. But Manuel was far away, and the Antiochenes had not accepted him without reservations. The Norman princes of Antioch had considered themselves as sovereign princes; but the frequent minorities amongst their successors had obliged the Kings of Jerusalem to intervene, more as kinsmen than as suzerains. There had, however, grown up in Antioch a sentiment that regarded the King as suzerain; and there is little doubt that Manuel had only been accepted so easily because Baldwin was

Equally astute had been the leadership of Baldwin III's brother Amalric in respect to both internal and domestic matters, on the one hand, and, on the other hand, foreign affairs pertaining to the Byzantine Empire, the Moslems, and the several crusading states. Although he had been obliged to bow to baronial opposition to his wife, Agnes of Courtenay, and to consent to an annulment of his marriage to her, he soon showed that he was not to be trifled with. During the very first year of his reign he had succeeded in enacting legislation requiring rendering of homage to the king by all rear vassals. This crafty move had strengthened notably his own power vis-à-vis his direct vassals, for now their own vassals could petition for redress of their grievances in the king's own court. This move on Amalric's part had smacked far more of the tactics pursued by the strong Norman kings of England towards the Norman feudality than it did of those followed by Amalric's contemporary, Louis VII of France, who was still markedly less potent than his great vassals. Still other maneuvers, namely his establishment of two new courts designated for urban commercial and maritime legislation, the *Cour de la Fonde* and the *Cour de la Châine*, also appear to have sought to extend the king's authority.[160]

Similar vigor had prevailed in the foreign field. Seeking Byzantine support in his projected seizure of Egypt, Amalric openly had followed the clever policy soon invoked by Emperor Manuel in respect to the new political orientation in Antioch, namely of sanctioning the new regime in Antioch but keeping careful leadings strings on it by requiring Constance's other son Baldwin and her children by Reginald

---

present to give his approval to the arrangement. It was to Baldwin, not to Manuel, that the people of Antioch looked now for a solution."

[160] *Livre de Philippe de Navarre*, chaps. lxviii and lxx, in *Rec. His. Crois. Assises de Jérusalem* (Paris, 1841), I, 538 and 540-41; *Livre des Assises de la cour des bourgeois* in *Rec. His. Crois. Assises de Jérusalem* (Paris, 1841), II, 43, n. b. Baldwin, "The Latin States," p. 549; La Monte, *Feudal Monarchy*, pp. 21 and n. 4, 99, 108-09, and 153. Cahen (*La Syrie*, p. 528 and n. 5) points out that Amalric's moves at this time in respect to his rear vassals did not apply to the Principality of Antioch and that Joscelyn III was the vassal of both Bohemond and Baldwin IV: "A Jérusalem, une assise célèbre du roi Amaury obligea en 1162 tous les arrière-vassaux du royaume à l'hommage direct au roi; aucune mesure de ce genre ne paraît avoir été prise pour Antioche, où le besoin ne devait pas s'en faire sentir: comme en Normandie, où l'usage s'en était établi avant le reste de la France, tout serment de vassalité d'un arrière-vassal à un vassal comportait une réserve de fidélité au suzerain suprême".... "Joscelin est vassal de Bohémond et de Baudouin, IV." Barker (*op. cit.*, p. 45) observes that "Midway between the seignorial *cours de bourgeoisie* and the privileged jurisdictions of the Italian quarters, there were two kinds of courts of a commercial character—the *cours de la fonde* in towns where trade was busy, and the *cours de la chaîne* in the seaports."

of Châtillon to live in Constantinople virtually as hostages. But that Amalric had been quite willing to play a balance of power game is seen in his epistle to Louis VII of France on April 10, 1162 and again in 1162 or 1163 inquiring whether he could send aid to the Franks in Syria lest Antioch fall into the hands of the Turks or Greeks.[161] And equally revealing had been Amalric's successful endeavor in 1165 to secure the release of Bohemond III from Moslem captivity which had been his fate during the preceding year following his capture at the battle of Hārim.[162] Since Amalric had been apprehensive several years before concerning the danger of the Byzantine threat to Antioch's independence, it is entirely possible that the speculation of William of Tyre[163] that "Nureddin's fears that Emperor Manuel might intervene with an irresistible demand for Bohemond's release without ransom and that the Antiochian folk, in the event that their imprisoned ruler were detained too long, might very well defend their own interests by choosing a stronger ruler than Bohemond, who, in turn, would prove to be a more formidable adversary, may well have played a part in Nureddin's decision to release Bohemond III" may be applied with only a slight change of emphasis to Amalric as well. Amalric, considerably older than Bohemond III, could easily handle him and count on his playing a balance of power game vis-à-vis the Byzantines identical with or very similar to his own. Another ruler, as an unknown quantity, might very well choose to follow an independent or, worse still, openly hostile policy in respect to the Byzantine problem. It is not without interest to note that Amalric had made no move during the remainder of his rule to seek the release of the independent minded Reginald of Châtillon, the stepfather of Bohemond III, from Moslem captivity. Meanwhile Amalric had administered the Principality of Antioch until Bohemond III's release from Moslem captivity in 1165. The latter upon his release had journeyed to Constantinople to seek and obtain from his brother-in-law, the Greek emperor, subsidies which had enabled him to pay the ransom demanded by Nūr-ad-Dīn. However, that Amalric's rôle, while devious in respect to the Byzantines, had continued to be a cautious one, which reflected his greater fear of the power of Nūr-ad-Dīn, is seen shortly after his second and, on the whole, unsuccessful invasion of Egypt in 1167 in his dispatch of envoys to Constantinople with proposals for an alliance

---

[161] *Epistolarum Regis Ludovici VII*, Nos. CXXI and CXXVI, 36-37 and 39-40.
[162] *Supra*, p. 37.
[163] William of Tyre, Bk. XIX, chap. xi, *op. cit.*, p. 901.

for the conquest of Egypt, in his marriage in Tyre on August 29, 1167 to Maria Comnena, the grand-niece of Emperor Manuel, and in his renewed recognition of the rights of Manuel over Antioch.[164] Lastly, Amalric had safeguarded the interests of the County of Tripoli by assuming the regency or procuratorship of that state during the imprisonment of its lord, Raymond III of Tripoli, from 1164 to the period of time elapsing from September, 1173 to April, 1174.[165]

The perils inherent in the presence of the boy king Baldwin IV on the throne became ever greater with every passing month after his accession on July 15, 1174. Although he was not appointed or styled as a regent, Miles of Plancy, lord of Montréal and seneschal of the late King Amalric, took over large control of the government. Partly because he was a newcomer to the Kingdom — he was a nobleman hailing from the Champagne district of France — he soon found himself an object of suspicion on the part of the native born Syrian Franks who disdained the newcomers as upstarts and questioned their political and military policies and methods. Enmity toward him arose also because he possessed a proud, arrogant, presumptuous, and indiscreet manner and bearing and because he followed the policy of ignoring and never summoning the leading barons for advice and counsel. Hence he speedily earned for himself the profound dislike of important circles and groups in the Kingdom of Jerusalem.[166]

---

[164] *Ibid.*, Bk. XX, chap. i, *op. cit.*, pp. 942-43; Cinnamus, *op. cit.*, pp. 237-38; *Chronique d'Ernoul*, pp. 17-18.

[165] William of Tyre, chap. xxviii, *op. cit.*, p. 995. Runciman (*History*, pp. 399-400) accurately summarizes the career of Amalric as follows: "Amalric was the last king of Christian Jerusalem worthy of his throne. He had made mistakes. He had been swayed by the enthusiasm of the nobles in 1168 and by their hesitations in 1169. He had been too ready to accept gifts of money, which his government needed for the moment, rather than carry out a policy far-sightedly. But his energy and his enterprise had been boundless. He had shown that neither his vassals nor the Orders could defy him unscathed. Had he lived longer he might have challenged the inevitability of the triumph of Islam." See Baldwin, *Raymond III*, p. 14. Cf. Babcock and Krey, *op. cit*, p. 390, n. 54. "The eight years of captivity [of Raymond] would end October 18, 1172, though the general context seems to indicate the summer of 1173 as the year of his release." Cf. Wiet, *loc. cit.*

[166] William of Tyre, Bk. XXI, chaps. iii-iv, *op. cit.*, pp. 1007 and 1008-09. See Baldwin, *Raymond III*, pp. 21-22 and "The Decline and Fall of Jerusalem, 1174-1189," *A History of the Crusades. The First Hundred Years* (Philadelphia, 1955), I, 592 and Munro, *op. cit.*, pp. 127-28 for discussions of the differences separating the native Frankish nobility in Syria from the newcomers hailing from Europe. (Henceforth this third cited work of Baldwin will be listed as "The Decline"). Grousset (*Histoire*, p. 611) believes that "Milon de Plancy, investi, d'ailleurs de sa propre autorité, d'une sorte de régence au nom du jeune Baudouin IV, semble avoir voulu continuer le gouvernement et l'oeuvre du grand

At this juncture, the Autumn of 1174, Raymond III, Count of Tripoli, having recently been released from his Moslem prison, reappeared in the Kingdom of Jerusalem, presented himself before the *Haute Cour,* and demanded the regency for the boy king. He based his claim for the legal guardianship of the king on the following four reasons: (1) he bore the closest blood relationship to the king, being his second cousin; (2) he was the richest and most powerful of all the loyal subjects of the king; (3) he himself had ordered, while he was still in a Moslem prison, his own Tripolitan subjects to surrender all their castles, strongholds, and lands to King Amalric and to put everything under his control and supervision; and (4) he had provided that, in the event that he should die in prison, the king should be regarded as his sole heir, being next of kin. An immediate response to these demands was not immediately forthcoming, because only a few members of the baronage were then available for consultation with the king. Upon being assured that the total baronage would be assembled as soon as possible for a discussion of this matter and that a reply would then be given, Count Raymond repaired to his own County of Tripoli.[167] Shortly thereafter Miles of Plancy fell victim to an assassin's dagger in Acre.[168] Upon Count Raymond's return to Jerusalem to receive the answer to the petition which he had presented in regard to the regency, the boy king deliberated on the problem for two days and then consented with general approval of his act. Count Raymond, the new regent (*bailli*), was presently invested with the entire government and powers of the realm.[169]

---

monarque défunt.".... "Sa fermeté tendait, semble-t-il, à maintenir intacte, sous ce règne d'un enfant malade, l'autorité monarchique."

[167] William of Tyre, chap. iii, *op. cit.*, pp. 1007-08; La Monte, *Feudal Monarchy*, p. 27, n. 2.

[168] William of Tyre, chap. iv, *op. cit.*, pp. 1009-10. Grousset (*Histoire*, p. 165) observes in appraising the significance of the assassination of Miles of Plancy that "L'assassinat du dur sénéchal dut en effet sur le moment apparaître comme un recul de l'autorité monarchique, comme le premier pas vers cette "république des barons" qui sera un jour fatale à la Syrie franque. Dans la réalité il devait en aller autrement. Si le comte de Tripoli n'avait pu faire triompher ses droits à la régence de Jérusalem que par l'assassinat de l'homme de confiance du feu roi, si son accession à la baylie avait pris de la sorte l'allure d'une victoire des féodaux sur le pouvoir royal, il n'en est pas moins vrai que d'une part Raymond III avait tous les titres juridiques pour revendiquer la régence et que d'autre part il était personnellement le seul homme capable de maintenir, pendant la pénible épreuve que constituait le règne d'un enfant lépreux, l'autorité monarchique."

[169] William of Tyre, chap. v, *op. cit.*, p. 1010; Abou Chamah, *op. cit.*, p. 168. As early as 1174, according to Baldwin (*Raymond III*, p. 28) there had begun to appear a pronounced rivalry between the two parties composed of the native barons and the

But the new regent, despite his strength deriving from his office, his close family ties with the ruling dynasty in the Kingdom of Jerusalem, his own considerable native talents including a keen mind, a vigorous physique, and a good education, and his very considerable wealth resulting from his marriage in 1174 to Eschiva, the widow of Walter, prince of Galilee,[170] was not to hold this position long, for his rôle, as well as that of his contemporary and future rival, Joscelyn III, was to be overshadowed by the problem of the growing illness of the king, the waxing ascendancy of the baronial party representing the newcomer element, and, perhaps as a result of this latter development, the increasing appearance in the Jerusalem scene of foreign adventurers intent on making personal capital out of this situation. And perhaps not the least element in Count Raymond's eclipse was the jealousy entertained by the young king toward him because of the popularity which he had gained as regent. This feeling, abetted by Agnes, who sought to control her son's policies, soon manifested itself in the king's studied exclusion of Count Raymond from the affairs of the Kingdom

---

newcomer barons from Europe. The former group supported the candidacy of Raymond of Tripoli for the procuratorship. For further discussion of the nature and reasons for this rivalry, see Runciman, *The Families*, pp. 22-5 and *History*, pp. 405-06. Baldwin ("The Decline," pp. 592-93) also observes that "... Raymond held office until Baldwin IV came of age, presumably in the fall of 1176. Not only did Raymond possess the proper legal title to the *bailliage* as the king's closest male relative, but he was highly esteemed by the native barons, now evidently in the ascendant, as one of themselves." Also see La Monte, *Feudal Monarchy*, pp. 49-54 for a discussion of the powers exercised by the *bailli* in the Kingdom of Jerusalem and Stubbs, *op. cit.*, p. 340 for an analysis of the compromise of the principle of appointment and kinship utilized by the nobles of the Kingdom of Jerusalem in their selection of Raymond as regent. Schlumberger (*Numismatique*, p. 97), on the other hand, dates these events as occurring in 1173. "En 1173, à l'époque de la minorité de Baudouin IV, le comte de Tripoli vint réclamer à Jérusalem la bailie du royaume... la cour des barons, réunie à Jérusalem, confia au comte de Tripoli, qui était dévenu populaire, "la garde et la défense du roi et du règne," c'est-à-dire les deux hautes dignités de baile du royaume et du tuteur du roi."

[170] William of Tyre, *op. cit.*, pp. 1011-12; Ibn al-Athīr, *K.-A.*, p. 674. Cf. Schlumberger, *Numismatique, loc. cit.* This scholar dates the marriage as occurring in 1173. Perhaps the best estimates of Count Raymond are supplied by Moslem historians who by that very fact cannot be charged with pro-Frankish sympathies. Ibn Djobeïr (*loc. cit.*) observes as follows: "C'est ce maudit comte, seigneur de Tripoli et de Tibériade, qui est le personnage le plus considérable chez les Francs, auprès de qui il jouit d'un grand pouvoir et d'un haut rang; il est digne du trône, pour lequel il semble né, et a une intelligence et une astuce remarquable. Pendant douze ans environ, peut-être même davantage, il resta prisonnier auprès de Nour ed-Dîn, et finit, au commencement du règne de Salâh ed-Dîn, par acheter sa liberté au prix d'une rançon considérable." Ibn al-Athīr (*K.-A., loc. cit.*) comments similarly: "... les Francs ne possédaient pas alors un homme plus élevé que lui [Count Raymond] en dignité, ni plus brave ni plus prudent." Behâ Ed-Dîn (*Saladin*, p. 112) speaks likewise: "The Count (Raymond of Tripoli), the most intelligent man of that race, and famous for his keenness of perception..."

of Jerusalem and his equally studied favoring of Joscelyn III as a counter force to Count Raymond.[171] This policy also resulted from his bonds of family relationship to the Courtenays.[172]

The other factor and eventual veritable catalyst in the interplay of the rival forces represented in the hostile parties of native and foreign nobles was Joscelyn III himself, who soon made his reappearance in the Frankish scene. Shortly after his release from a Moslem prison in 1176, he gained for himself in the same year the major office of the seneschalship of the Kingdom of Jerusalem, a position which he retained until 1193.[173] His new political prominence was complemented

---

[171] La Monte, "The rise," p. 312; Runciman, *History*, p. 407. Cf. the varying judgments of Runciman, *History*, p. 477 and Oldenbourg, *op. cit.*, pp. 404-05 in respect to Agnes of Courtenay.

[172] Runciman, *History*, p. 407.

[173] William of Tyre, Bk. XIX, chap. iv, *op. cit.*, p. 890; Röhricht, *Regesta*, No. 537, p. 143; Delaville Le Roulx, *Cartulaire*, No. 496, pp. 341-42; Baldwin, "The Decline," p. 597. Runciman (*History*, p. 407, n. l) observes that "Joscelin is attested as Seneschal from 1177 onward (Röhricht, *Regesta*, p. 147)." But that Joscelyn III held the seneschalship in 1176 is attested by Röhricht himself in his reference to Joscelyn III as "regius senescalcus" in a document issued in 1176. (Röhricht, *Regesta*, No. 537, p. 143). La Monte ("Chronology," p. 170 and "The rise," p. 306) also believes that the seneschalship of Joscelyn III began in 1176. Babcock and Krey (*op. cit.*, p. 301, n. 12) state that Joscelyn III's sister Agnes was responsible for his new start in life. La Monte ("The rise," pp. 304, 306, and 305) perceives the continuing influence of Joscelyn III's mother, Beatrice, as well as that of Agnes, in her son's new rôle in the feudal hierarchy of the time. "One is tempted to say that the inheritance which Joscelyn III lost through the sins of his father (if we are to accept the judgment of Archbishop William) he regained through the influence of his mother, for there can be little doubt that it was due to Beatrice's influence that Agnes de Courtenay had for her young brother Joscelyn that ambitious affection which caused her to push his interests at every occasion and to secure for him his great position in Jerusalem".... "Agnes had high plans for her brother when he came back after his long imprisonment" .... " ... and the high office of seneschal was the prize which Agnes desired for Joscelyn. Her persuasion was effective and Joscelyn appears with the title of seneschal of the kingdom in an act of 1176." .... "As mother of the reigning king, and Baldwin ascended the throne at the age of only thirteen, Agnes exercized a very real political power in Jerusalem in the eleven-seventies, and she devoted much of her energy and influence to securing favors and honors for her brother Joscelyn." In the light of these observations I cannot accept the statement by the editors of *A History of the Crusades*, II, 805 to the effect that Beatrice was dead after 1152. In dealing with the question of the seneschalship La Monte ("The rise," p. 306, n. 3) also observes that "Miles de Plancy was killed in the fall of 1174 (Wm. Tyre 1008-1010). He was apparently succeeded by one Ranulph who appears on a charter of Baldwin's in 1176 as a *dapifer*, but of whom we know nothing beyond this single appearance. (Röhricht, *Regesta*, 538, Delaborde, *Chartes de la Terre Sainte* [Paris, 1880], doc. 38). I am not entirely convinced that Ranulph was royal seneschal and the office may have been vacant until Joscelyn was appointed. Röhricht places the appearance of Joscelyn as seneschal in the act just previous to that in which Ranulph is mentioned but both are merely dated 1176 and Ranulph may have been Joscelyn's predecessor in the office." See La Monte, *Feudal Monarchy*, pp. 116-18, Runciman, *History*, p. 303, and Dimitri Hayek, *Le droit franc en*

about the same time by the acquisition of landed possessions deriving from his marriage to Agnes, the third and youngest daughter of Henry de Milly more commonly referred to as Henry Le Buffle. This marriage, which resulted in the birth of two daughters, Beatrice and Agnes, also brought to the new Seneschal as dowry the succession to the fief of Château du Roi and Montfort (modern Mulya and Qalaat Qurein) northeast of Acre.[174] This grant was to be the nucleus of the

---

Syrie pendant les croisades (Paris, 1925), p. 23 for analyses and detailing of the powers of the seneschalship. La Monte considers Joscelyn III as worthy of inclusion in the list of seneschals possessing outstanding ability. This same scholar (*Feudal Monarchy*, pp. 115-16) states that "Further, the grand offices of Jerusalem were normally filled from among the lords of the *principality* of Jerusalem and never from the counts of the great semi-independent states. No prince of Antioch or count of Edessa or Tripoli ever held any grand office in the kingdom. Joscelin III de Courtney was seneschal, but it was under Baldwin IV and only after his loss of the county of Edessa when his lands were confined to Jerusalem."

[174] *Les lignages d'Outremer*, chaps. xii, xvi, xix, and xxviii, *op. cit.*, pp. 452, 454, 457, 462, and 464; *Livre de Philippe de Navarre*, chap. lxxii, p. 343 and n. d.; Rey, *Les colonies*, pp. 478-79 and 488-89; Joseph Marie Antoine Delaville Le Roulx, *Cartulaire général de l'ordre des Hospitaliers de S. Jean de Jérusalem (1100-1310)* (Paris, 1897), II, Nos. 1313 and 1526, pp. 94 and 206-07; *Les familles d'Outre-Mer*, p. 408; Strehlke, *op. cit*, Nos. 53, 58, 59 and 98, pp. 43-44, 47-49, and 75-76; La Monte, "The Lords," p. 190 and "The rise," p. 306; J. Delaville Le Roulx, "Inventaire de pièces de Terre Sainte de l'Ordre de l'Hopital," *Revue de l'orient latin* (Paris, 1895), III, 74, No. 188; J. Delaville Le Roulx, *Mélanges sur l'ordre de S. Jean de Jérusalem* (Paris, 1910), No. 188, p. 49. (Henceforth citations from Delaville Le Roulx's *Cartulaire* will have Roman numerals I and II to differentiate between the two volumes of this work. The last two works of Delaville Le Roulx cited above will be referred to respectively as "Inventaire" and *Mélanges* to differentiate them from other works of this scholar). Richard (*op. cit.*, p. 135), speaking of Joscelyn III's territorial holdings, states that before his marriage to Agnes he had been granted the castle of St. Elias: "On ne lui avait inféodé à l'origine que le château de Saint Élie..." The seneschal did not gain this holding until the opening days of 1182. See *infra*, p. 100. See L. de Mas Latrie, "De quelques seigneuries de Terre Sainte oubliées dans les *Familles d'Outremer* de Du Cange," *Revue Historique* (Paris, 1878), VIII, 112-16 for a discussion on Henry Le Buffle, his family, and his property holdings. (Henceforth references to this article will be cited as "Quelques seigneuries"). The probability is that Joscelyn III was absolutely landless at the time of his release from the Moslem prison in 1176. It seems highly unlikely that King Amalric did not reassign Joscelyn III's fiefs and revenues to another feudatory after the capture of the Courtenay chieftain in 1164. It will be recalled that Joscelyn III was made a direct vassal of Baldwin III and in that capacity had been granted land outside Acre as well as revenues from the harbor of Acre. See *supra*, p. 28. The uncertainty of the time, costs, and circumstances of his eventual release coupled with the necessity of military protection of these fiefs against possible Moslem forays made it imperative that reassignment of them be made quickly. La Monte ("The rise," p. 306, n. 4) places the marriage of Joscelyn III after his "... release from prison rather than before his capture, largely because his daughters were not yet of an age to marry in 1186..." I may add that the *argumentum ex silentio* has some merit here as well. Certainly there would have been at least one move on the part of Joscelyn III's wife to secure his release during the 1164-1176 period, if they had been married. The sources are totally silent in this regard.

so-called Seigneury of Count Joscelyn which was to be characterized in part by its scattered holdings. Not long thereafter Joscelyn III resumed his earlier northern orientation by becoming the vassal of Bohemond III of Antioch on February 5, 1178 for a fief requiring the military service of five knights. The fief consisted of lands and revenues in Antioch including the abbey of Granacherie, the towns of Livonia, Baqfala, and Gaigon, the fief of William de Croisi which comprised the towns of Ṣaffūrīyah, Bequoqua, Vaquer, and Cafra, 3,000 besants a year from the revenues of three other towns of Bohemond's lands, 3,000 liters of wine from Saint Simeon and certain water rights. But, looking to the future, Bohemond III granted this fief to Joscelyn III on the distinct provision that he would be obliged to return it, if he should reconquer his lost Edessan lands.[175]

Because of these several considerations, I cannot agree with the view of Runciman (*The Families*, p. 9, n. l) that the marriage of Joscelyn III with Agnes de Milly occurred about 1155. Nor can I support the strong implication that Joscelyn III's marriage to Agnes de Milly occurred in the 1150's which is contained in the editor's observation in n. l, p. 166 of Gregory the Priest's *Chronique*: "Après que son père [Joscelyn II] fut tombé entre les mains de Nour-eddin, et que celui eut achevé de lui enlever ses États, il [Joscelyn III] se retira auprès du roi de Jérusalem Baudouin et épousa Agnes, troisième fille de Henri de Milly, dit le Buffle..." Equally can I not agree with the observation, in so far as it applies to the wife of Joscelyn III, which the editor of *Livre de Philippe de Navarre* makes (p. 543, n. b): "On peut conjecturer que le mariage de trois filles de Henri le Buffle eut lieu vers le milieu du XIIe siècle..." In respect to Joscelyn III's later acquisitions and their initial relationship to his initial gain of Chateau du Roi, Mas Latrie ("Quelques seigneuries," p. 110) observes as follows: "... nous remarquerons d'abord que ces trois fiefs [Saint-Georges, Bouquiau, et Saor] semblent avoir été dans une certaine dépendance de la seigneurie de Château-du-Roi, centre de grand fief créé pour Jocelin III, après la perte du comté d'Édesse. Le château et la seigneurie de Château-du-Roi... avaient une cour des bourgeois et un tribunal de justice." La Monte ("The rise," pp. 301-02) observes, in speaking about Joscelyn's seigneury, that "... it had no capital city like Tiberias, Jaffa, Naplouse, Rama, Caesarea, or Sidon; it had no great fortress like Toron or Montreal which dominated the entire fief; it had no natural limits or focal point—only the shrewd and ambitious policy of Joscelyn himself gave it unity." "... lasting as it did through the lifetime of its founder it was essentially the personal fief of Count Joscelyn and so most appropriately bears his name." Prutz (*loc. cit.*) points out that the so-called seigneury of Joscelyn had princely rights, particularly that of jurisdiction, the rights of the so-called Haute Cour, and the right of minting coins.

[175] Röhricht, *Regesta*, No. 555, pp. 147-48; Strehlke, *op. cit.*, No. 9, p. 10. C. R. Conder (*The Latin Kingdom of Jerusalem 1099 to 1291 A. D.* [London, 1897], p. 138) states that "A year after the victory of Gezer, [Ramla, *infra*, pp. 83-84] Bohemond III of Antioch gave to the son of Jocelyn II of Edessa lands to the value of three thousand bezants, in fief; and many other documents attest the general mistrust in presence of the power of Saladin." He cites in support of these statements Röhricht's *Regesta*, Nos. 335, 409, 416, 420, 425, 426, and 555. Only the last cited document has any relevance to Conder's views and, more particularly, to those relating to Joscelyn III. None of the other documents has any bearing on Joscelyn III or Saladin. Lastly, since the battle of Ramla was fought on November 25, 1177 and since the land grant of Bohemond III to Joscelyn III

The Seneschal's initial acquisitions in the Acre area were still further rounded out in the following year of 1179 by three grants in April, October, and November, which resulted in his gaining of most of the fief of Henry de Milly, his deceased father-in-law. The first of these consisted of the fief of John de Belleme, then the Chamberlain, which was situated to the east and south of his original holdings in Acre. Comprising houses in Acre and the villages of Lanahia, Casale Album, Clil, and Ambelie, it cost 7,500 besants and obligated its owner to furnish two knights to the king, Baldwin IV. The transaction took place at Jacob's Ford on April 2, 1179. The Chamberlain, John de Belleme, being unable to meet its financial obligations, sold this fief with the consent of his wife Isabella, Robard de Cabor, and his brothers to Joscelyn III.[176]

The second grant, which was gained some time before October, 1179 and was confirmed by King Baldwin IV on October 22, 1179 by purchase from Petromilla, the viscountess of Acre, included the villages of Sameth and Sophia and a house in Chastel-Neuf. The sale price was 4500 besants.[177]

The third one, which Joscelyn III gained by purchase from his brother-in-law, Hugh de Gibelet, the husband of Stephanie, the second daughter of Henry de Milly, on November 24, 1179, comprised the territory of St. George de Labanea and entailed the guardianship on his part for seven years of the children of the late Adam de Bethsan and Helvis de Milly. The purchase price consisted of payments of 600 besants a year with a down payment of 1300 besants. There was also a proviso stipulating that if Hugh de Gibelet wished to return to the

---

occurred on February 5, 1178, Conder's view that a year elapsed between these events cannot be substantiated.

[176] Röhricht, *Regesta*, No. 579, p. 154; Strehlke, *op. cit.*, No. 10, pp. 10-11; Rey, *Les colonies*, p. 472; L. de Mas Latrie ("Le fief de la Chamberlaine et les Chambellans de Jérusalem," *Bibliothèque de l'école des Chartes* [Paris, 1882], xliii, 648) believes that the sum of 7,500 besants was "... (vraisemblablement des besants d'or, car les besants blancs sont, je crois, postérieurs à cette époque)...." and observes that "Nous ne savons pas dans quelles conditions se fit le service de chambellan depuis la vente de 1179. Jean, s'il fut rétabli dans sa charge, l'exerca-t-il comme délégué du sénéchal? La couronne racheta-t-elle, alors ou plus tard, quelques-uns des villages vendu pour reconstituer un fief en faveur des successeurs de Jean? Nous ignorons tout ce qui eut lieu à cet égard," See La Monte, *Feudal Monarchy*, pp. 121-22 and Runciman, *History*, pp. 303-04 for an analysis and description of the powers held by the chamberlain.

[177] Röhricht, *Regesta*, No. 587, p. 156; Strehlke, *op. cit.*, No. 11, pp. 11-12; Rey, *Les colonies*, p. 497. La Monte ("The rise," p. 307) notes that "All of these places [the villages of Lanahia, Casale Album, Ancre, Clil, and Ambelie] are to be found in the district between Chateau du Roi and Acre, and apparently it gave Joscelyn an extension of his holdings to the south and west."

territory of St. George de Labanea with his wife Stephanie, Joscelyn III would be obligated to return the territory to him with the understanding that he, Joscelyn III, would be permitted to indemnify himself for the advances made by him to the peasants.[178] However, this proviso was never executed and, even before the expiration of the seven years of holding of the fief stipulated in the grant, the situation changed in Joscelyn III's favor. Baldwin IV surrendered to him in an agreement dated February 24, 1182 all suzerainty over the territory of St. George de Labanea and its dependencies.[179]

From 1176 to the later Spring of 1180 Joscelyn III's rôle was entirely secondary and, apart from military activity at the battle of Ramla in November, 1177,[180] the sources are largely silent on his activities during these years. He appeared briefly in nine charters in the capacity of a witness to sales of property, grants to religious groups, and settlements of property and other disputes. In 1176 he witnessed the confirmation by Baldwin, lord of Ramla, of the sale of the village of Bethduras to Constance, the countess of St. Gilles, by a certain Johannus Arrabitus.[181] He appeared again in the same capacity when King Baldwin IV confirmed the donation to the Hospital of Jerusalem made by his father Amalric in Egypt and to which he himself added an annual rent of 30,000 besants from the territory of Pelusium.[182] In 1177 he witnessed the grant of a sum of money and certain properties in the city of Ascalon to a religious order by Sibyl, the daughter of

---

[178] Röhricht, *Regesta*, No. 588, pp. 156-57; Strehlke, *op. cit.*, No. 12, p. 12; Rey, *Les colonies*, pp. 494-95. The legal procedures of the Kingdom of Jerusalem sanctioned the King's confirmation of sales and grants of property by one feudatory to another. Hence Richard (*op. cit.*, p. 87) observes that "Un véritable commerce des héritages existait: en 1179 Baudouin IV confirmait à son oncle Jocelin III la baylie des enfants d'Adam III de Bethsan, jusqu'alors tenue par Hugues de Gibelet qui la lui avait vendue." John L. La Monte and Norton Downs III ("The Lords of Bethsan in the Kingdoms of Jerusalem and Cyprus," *Medievalia et Humanistica* [Boulder, Colorado], VI, 66) point out that "Gremont the second lord of Bethsan of that name appears in August 1198 witnessing an act of the king with his uncle Baldwin. His father, Adam, had died before 1179, and as a minor had been under the baillage of his uncles Hugh of Gibelet and Joscelyn, count of Edessa."

[179] Strehlke, *op. cit.*, No. 14, p. 14. "Dono eciam tibi [Joscelyn III] et heredibus tuis ... hominium eciam sancti Georgii et tocius terre pertinentis ad sanctam Georgium." Cahen (*La Syrie*, n. 5, p. 528) declares that Joscelyn III was a vassal of both Bohemond III of Antioch and King Baldwin IV.

[180] *Infra*, pp. 83-84.

[181] Röhricht, *Regesta*, No. 539, pp. 143-44; Delaville Le Roulx, *Cartulaire*, I, No. 495, p. 341.

[182] Röhricht, *Regesta*, No. 537, p. 143; Delaville Le Roulx, *Cartulaire*, I, No. 496, pp. 341-42.

Amalric I.[183] The Seneschal also appeared at Jacob's Ford on November 17, 1178 to witness Baldwin IV's confirmation of the sale of the town of Seleth on the territory of Nablus and one hundred and three Bedouin tents to Roger of Les Moulins, the Grand Master of the Hospital, by his father Amalric, viscount of Nablus.[184] Shortly thereafter, in February, 1179, Odo of St. Amand, the Grand Master of the Temple, and Roger of Les Moulins settled all the outstanding disputes between their respective orders. Joscelyn III was a witness to these agreements.[185] Jacob's Ford was again the scene on April 1, 1179 of an appearance by Baldwin IV. On this occasion he granted and confirmed the ownership by a certain Alelmus of Garrenflos of three units of land near the town of Album and a house in that town. And, as before, the Seneschal was a witness.[186] A month later, on May 1, 1179, the Courtenay chieftain was again a witness at the confirmation by King Baldwin of the grant of a hundred weight of sugar at Lanahia in the territory of Acre as annual rent to Roger of Les Moulins.[187] In 1180 he again performed as a witness on two occasions. The first one occurred on January 21, when King Baldwin confirmed the ownership by the Order of the Hospital and its master, Roger of Les Moulins, of a certain territory situated between Beroea and the *tolonum* of Robard of Chabor which the latter, having unjustly tried to appropriate for himself, now formally renounced.[188] The second one fell on April 28,

---

[183] Röhricht, *Regesta*, No. 553, p. 147.

[184] *Ibid*, No. 562, pp. 149-50; Delaville Le Roulx, *Cartulaire*, I, No. 550, pp. 372-73; John L. La Monte ("The Viscounts of Naplouse in the Twelfth Century," *Syria* [Paris, 1938], XIX, 277 and n. 5) believes that this sale resulted from "... financial difficulties whether due to some unrecorded foray in which he was captured and in need of ransom or due to the equally chivalrous prodigality which was so characteristic of mediaeval gentlemen..." and indicates that, in as much as the amount of money received for Amalric's three sales, namely 3,500 besants for the Bedouins' tents, 2,800 besants for Seleth, and an unstipulated sum for the land between his castle of Lathara (Tare), is not consonant with the statement that Baldwin IV confirmed the sales for 5,500 besants, the latter figure is therefore incorrect.

[185] Röhricht, *Regesta*, No. 572, p. 152; Delaville Le Roulx, *Cartulaire*, I, No. 558, pp. 378-79.

[186] Röhricht, *Regesta*, No. 577, p. 154.

[187] *Ibid.*, No. 582, p. 155; Delaville Le Roulx, *Cartulaire*, I, No. 564, pp. 383-84; Joseph Marie Antoine Delaville Le Roulx, *Les Archives, la bibliothèque et le trésor de l'ordre de Saint-Jean de Jérusalem à Malte* (Paris, 1883), Document LI, pp. 141-42. (Henceforth this work of Delaville Le Roulx will be differentiated from his other works by the designation of *Les Archives*).

[188] Röhricht, *Regesta*, No. 591, p. 157; Delaville Le Roulx, *Les Archives*, Document LIV, pp. 145-47. Du Cange (*Glossarium Mediae et Infimae Latinitatis*, ed. Leopold Favre [Niort, 1887], VIII, 46) defines a *tolonum* as "tributum de mercibus marinis circa littus acceptum."

1180 when the Seneschal witnessed in Jerusalem the grant by King Baldwin to the same order and its master of a hundred Bedouin tents at the fortress of Belvoir. His growing political importance may perhaps be seen in his second position immediately after that of Reginald of Châtillon himself in the list of the several witnesses.[189] And it may be presumed that the Seneschal's two daughters, Beatrice and Agnes, were born during this time.[190]

---

[189] Röhricht, *Regesta*, No. 593, p. 158; Delaville Le Roulx, *Cartulaire*, I, No. 582, pp. 395-96 and *Les Archives*, Document LV, pp. 147-48. Dana C. Munro ("The Establishment of the Latin Kingdom of Jerusalem," *The Sewanee Review* [Sewanee, Tennessee, 1924], XXXII, 260) observes that "... it was the general rule in the Middle Ages that in letters the names of those who were of superior should precede those of lesser rank." Probably the same procedure was followed in listing the names of witnesses in legal documents as well. Cf. La Monte, *Feudal Monarchy*, pp. 134-35. *Infra*, n. 224. (Henceforth Munro's book *The Kingdom of the Crusaders* will be cited as *The Kingdom* to differentiate it from his article in *The Sewanee Review*).

[190] *Les Lignages d'Outremer*, chap. xxviii, *op. cit.*, p. 464.

CHAPTER SIX

THE APPEARANCE OF FOREIGN PRINCES AND ADVENTURERS IN THE KINGDOM OF JERUSALEM; SALADIN'S CHALLENGE

The center of the historical stage now came to be occupied by foreign princes and by the elder sister of the leper king. Since Baldwin's illness precluded any possibility of marriage and parenthood, it was deemed necessary to provide for the future kingship through the female line. Accordingly, William Longsword, son of William, marquis of Montferrat, was invited by the King and the baronage to take his sister Sibyl in marriage in accordance with an arrangement drawn up in 1175 when William had visited the Kingdom of Jerusalem. William Longsword arrived in Jerusalem in October, 1176 and forty days later married Sibyl, receiving as a dowry the maritime cities of Jaffa and Ascalon as well as the entire county. Unfortunately for the future stability of the kingship as well as the safety of the Kingdom of Jerusalem itself, the groom was soon seized by a mortal illness and died the following June, leaving a posthumous son, Baldwin V.[191]

William Longsword's untimely death coupled with the continued illness of the leper king required a resumption of the regency (*bailliage*). Consequently, Philip, Count of Flanders, was invited to repair

---

[191] William of Tyre, Bk. XXI, chap. xiii, *op. cit.*, pp. 1025-26; Benedictus Abbas (Benedict of Peterborough) *Gesta Regis Henrici Secundi*, ed. William Stubbs (London, 1867), I, 342; Babcock and Krey, *op. cit.*, p. 415, n. 23. Baldwin ("The Decline," p. 593) believes that at the time of his marriage to Sibyl William Longsword was "... given what apparently amounted to the procuratorship or regency." Stubbs (*loc. cit.*) sees in the marriage of Sibyl and William Longsword a move on the part of Baldwin IV to checkmate the ultimate political goals of Raymond of Tripoli. "Raymond, in claiming the wardship, [of Baldwin IV] set aside altogether the rights of the mother, and alleged himself as the nearest relation on both sides, a connexion which by itself would cancel his legal claims. He was, however, chosen by the vassals, and filled the place not only during the minority but during several occasions of Baldwin's illness. This unhappy prince could not escape the conviction that his death would be a signal for the disruption of the kingdom. If Raymond were suffered to engross the supreme power during his life, the rights of his sisters Sibylla and Isabel would be defeated. He therefore married Sibylla to William Longaspata, marquis of Montferrat, and intrusted his brother-in-law with the administration of the kingdom." See Archer and Kingsford, *op. cit.*, p. 453 for a genealogical chart.

to the Kingdom. He consented and, shortly after his arrival on August 2, 1177, he was offered the general administration of the Kingdom of Jerusalem on a *carte blanche* basis. Philip declined the honor on the ground that his motive in coming to the Holy Land was that of a pilgrim rather than that of an aspirant to political office and that he desired freedom to return to France if the need arose. He likewise declined the appeal of the king and the barons that he assume command of the Frankish forces in the forthcoming campaign against Egypt which was the result of joint Franco-Byzantine planning. The upshot of all this was the development of a divided command of the Kingdom, for Baldwin IV now appointed Reginald of Châtillon, the former prince of Antioch, as regent and commander in chief of the army with the proviso, however, that Philip be his assistant.[192]

As events were soon to demonstrate, the division was to be double in character, the first between Philip, on the one hand, and the *Haute Cour* and Baldwin IV, on the other, the second between Count Raymond and Reginald of Châtillon, on the one hand, and the *Haute Cour* and the King, on the other. Philip soon demonstrated his duplicity and engendered the suspicion of the *Haute Cour* by endeavoring to secure the betrothal of the widowed and still pregnant Sibyl without even the disclosure of the name of the prospective groom to that august body. Upon encountering solid opposition to his project, he dropped it. Not at all abashed, he then listened coldly to the *Haute Cour's* proposal that he carry into execution the plans for a joint Franco-Byzantine invasion of Egypt, a project which had been engineered and secured by a treaty between the late King Amalric and Emperor Manuel and renewed by King Baldwin IV. After initial excuses designed to permit him to avoid acceptance of the command, Philip at length admitted that his sole purpose in coming to Palestine was to effect the marriage of the two sons of his close friend, the advocate of Bethune, with his (Philip's) cousins, the two daughters of King Amalric. This admission provoked an explosion in the ranks of the baronage. Balian of Ibelin commented bitterly on the impropriety of such conduct with the acid observation: "We thought you had come to fight for the Cross and you merely talk of marriages!" Thereupon, the baronage conferred with the Greek envoys in Jerusalem. The result was a counter strategy aimed at securing from Philip iron clad agreements

---

[192] William of Tyre, chap. xiv, *op. cit.*, pp. 1027-28; Abou Chamah, *op. cit.*, p. 191. Reginald of Châtillon had never returned to Antioch, since his wife, the Princess Constance, was dead and his stepson, Bohemond III, had succeeded to the Principality.

to carry out the treaty. But it was all to no avail, for Philip's envoys refused to say that he would commit himself in this manner. The result was the rupture of the negotiations and the departure of the Byzantine imperial legates. At length the *Haute Cour* decided, in response to the question raised by Philip's representatives concerning the military theatre where his troops could be used in the defense of the Kingdom of Jerusalem, that it should be that of Antioch or Tripoli. But suspicions were openly raised that Reginald of Châtillon and Count Raymond had been in collusion with Philip, that they had actually desired to divert his forces to their own territories to aid them in gaining new lands for themselves, and that, in consequence, they had been partly responsible for the failure of the Egyptian expedition to materialize.[193]

---

[193] William of Tyre, chaps. xiv-xviii, *op. cit.*, pp. 1023-35; *Chronique d'Ernoul*, chap. iv, p. 33. William of Tyre's account of Philip's marriage maneuvres in behalf of the advocate of Bethune provided that if they were successful, Philip would be rewarded with the advocate's extensive hereditary estates. Grousset (*Histoire*, p. 639 and n. 2) believes that Philip's original plan was to become the eventual heir of the leper king and to do so by the claim that he, Philip, was the son of Sibyl of Anjou, the daughter of Fulk I, 1131-1143. This claim was decidedly faulty. "Quels étaient les mobiles du comte de Flandre? Visait-il, en effet, la couronne de Jérusalem? Il semble bien qu'en se croisant, il avait pensé à se présenter aux barons de Jérusalem comme l'héritier éventuel du roi lépreux. Par sa mère Sibylle, fille du roi Foulque, pensait-il avoir un jour des titres à faire valoir? Mais en arrivant en Palestine, il dut se rendre compte qu'il ne pouvait rien contre les droits de ses cousines, les princesses Sibylle et Isabelle, soeurs et héritières éventuelles du roi Baudouin IV." .... "En ce qui concerne les soi-disant titres de Philippe d'Alsace à la couronne de Jérusalem, remarquons que, si sa mère, Sibylle d'Anjou, était fille du roi Foulque, elle n'était pas née de Mélisende de Jérusalem, mais d'Aremburge du Maine. Toute revendication à cet égard était donc mal fondée." The resumption of warfare between the Franks and the Moslems was sanctioned in the truce recently made between them. Abou Chamah, *loc. cit.*; "Or une des clauses de la trêve conclue avec les Francs portait que s'il leur arrivait un roi ou un grand personnage dont ils ne pouvaient décliner l'autorité, ils lui prêteraient main forte, ne l'abandonneraient pas et deviendraient ses auxiliaires soumis" .... "En vertu de cette clause, les Francs levèrent des troupes et leur bataillons se présentèrent le 20 de Djomada Ier (14 novembre 1177) devant Hamah..." Grousset (*Histoire*, p. 644) notes accurately the total significance of the failure of the Franco-Byzantine program in respect to Egypt. "La gravité de cet abandon ne doit pas être sous-estimée. A l'époque où nous sommes arrivés, l'empire de Saladin, à peine constitué, aurait sans doute encore pu être ébranlé si Francs et Byzantins coalisés l'avaient attaqué à sa base, l'Égypte. Cette attaque était abandonnée. Malgré la clairvoyance politique du roi de Jérusalem, par la rancune mesquine d'un croisé nouveau-venu, la grande opération franco-byzantine contre l'Égypte, qui eût pu étouffer au berceau la puissance aiyûbide, se trouva contremandée," .... "Trois ans encore et l'empereur Manuel Comnène mourra, remplacé par des héritiers incapables ou tyranniques, qui, loin de considérer les Francs comme des alliés, les traiteront en ennemis. Le grand empire des Comnènes, protecteur de la Syrie franque, s'affaissera brusquement, emportant avec lui jusqu'au souvenir des sages constructions diplomatiques d'Amaury Ier, de Baudouin IV et de Guillaume de Tyr."

In accordance with this military plan, Raymond of Tripoli and Philip, together with their own forces and a number of Knights Templars, repaired to the County of Tripoli about October 1, 1177.[194] The united forces made initial strikes at Homs and Hamah which proved to be of no avail because of the sufficiency of these cities in respect to provisions, soldiers, and arms. The Franks, having attacked the latter city on November 14 and having invested it for only four days, were soon joined by Reginald of Châtillon. The three leaders then decided to besiege the tempting prize of Ḥārim which was then under aṣ-Ṣāliḥ's control. The garrison, however, was loyal to its former ruler Gümüshtigin who had been removed from office by aṣ-Ṣāliḥ. Hence political division and therefore weakness characterized this Moslem bastion. The promise of a quick and easy Frankish victory inherent in this situation was augmented by other considerations, namely that aṣ-Ṣāliḥ was still only a boy, his army was small, and Saladin was far away in Egypt.[195]

The ensuing investment roused Saladin to action. Apprehensive over Ḥārim's fate, he resolved upon an invasion of the Kingdom of Jerusalem itself. This plan seemed entirely feasible, for the paucity of soldiery in the Kingdom of Jerusalem resulting from the Franks' preoccupation with the siege of Ḥārim—the entire defense of the Kingdom of Jerusalem now comprised only 500 horsemen identified with the garrisons of the Orders of the Templars and Hospitallers—promised an easy victory in that theatre, or, equally satisfactory, an abandonment by the Franks of their siege of Ḥārim. Having assembled a large army, he advanced through the Desert of Sinai, bypassed the Frankish fortresses of Darum and Gaza, and suddenly appeared before Ascalon. Despite the small number of his own soldiery, the King proceeded from Jerusalem toward Ascalon, but, having learned of the enemy's great numerical superiority, prudently refrained from full military contact and retired to Ascalon itself at nightfall. Saladin and his commanders then proceeded to devastate the adjoining areas and effected the capture and burning of the deserted city of Ramla. These acts evoked a quick response from Baldwin IV. Accompanied by a force including Joscelyn III, his Seneschal, Reginald

---

[194] William of Tyre, chap. xix, *op. cit.*, p. 1036; Michael the Syrian, Bk. XX, chap. vii, *Chronique*, p. 376; *Chronique d'Ernoul*, pp. 33-34.

[195] William of Tyre, *op. cit.*, pp. 1036-37; Abou Chamah, *op. cit.*, pp. 191-92; Behâ Ed-Dîn, *Anecdotes*, p. 64 and *Saladin*, p. 76; Ibn al-Athīr, *K.-A.*, pp. 630-32; Kamal-Ad-Dîn, *Histoire*, IV, 149 and 150-51; Michael the Syrian, *Chronique, loc. cit.*, *Chronique d'Ernoul*, p. 34; Makrizi, *op. cit.*, p. 527.

of Châtillon, and other Frankish barons as well as eighty Knights Templars, he advanced out of Ascalon and inflicted the stunning military defeat of Ramla on Saladin on November 25, 1177, capturing and killing great numbers of the enemy. The victorious Franks then returned to Ascalon and thence to Jerusalem.[196]

Meanwhile the siege of Ḥārim proceeded in a lackadaisical fashion thanks to the practice of the besieging Franks of visiting nearby Antioch in search of the pleasures of the flesh and the slack and idle military posture and indifference of those who remained at their posts. The defenders, on the other hand, put up a bold defense. Four fruitless months dragged by. When reinforcements arrived from Aleppo in March, 1178, the Franks saw the futility of further investment and, having accepted aṣ-Ṣāliḥ's offer of a sum of money, raised the siege.[197]

---

[196] *Chronique d'Ernoul*, p. 34 and chap vi, pp. 41-45; William of Tyre, chaps. xx-xxiv, *op. cit.*, pp. 1037-46; Makrizi, *op. cit.*, pp. 526-27; Behâ Ed-Dîn, *Anecdotes, loc. cit.* and *Saladin*, pp. 75-76; Ibn al-Athīr, *K.—A.* pp. 627-29; Michael the Syrian, *Chronique*, pp. 374-75 and *Extrait*, pp. 386-87 and n. 1; *The Chronography of Bar Hebraeus*, pp. 307-08; Sicardus Cremonensis Episcopus, *Chronicon Patrologia Latina* ed. J.-P. Migne (Paris, 1855), CCXIII, 515; *Chronica Magistri Rogeri De Houedene*, ed. William Stubbs (London, 1869), II, 132-33 (Future references to this source will be cited as Roger of Hoveden); *Annales de Terre Sainte, loc. cit.*; Gervasii Monachi Cantuariensis Monachi (Gervase of Canterbury), *Opera Historica*, ed. William Stubbs (London, 1879), I, 274; Radulfi De Diceto (Ralph of Diceto), *Ymagines Historiarum*, ed. William Stubbs (London, 1876), I, 422-24; William of Newburgh, *op. cit.*, pp. 242-43; *Chronique de Robert de Torigni*, ed. Léopold Delisle (Rouen, 1872), II, 72-73; Röhricht, *Regesta*, No. 564, p. 150; *Ex Chronico S. Petri Catalaunensis* in *Recueil des historiens des Gaules et de la France*, ed. M. Bouquet and others (Paris, 1877), XII, 277; Sigebert, *Chronici*, p. 417; *Extrait de la Chronographie de Samuel d'Ani*, in *Rec. his. arm.* (Paris, 1869), I, 455; Vartan Le Grand, *op. cit.*, p. 436 and n. 2. William of Tyre indicates a Saracen force of 26,000 light cavalry and a Frankish force of 375 knights. The Franks' losses consisted of only four or five knights and some footsoldiers. Schlumberger (*Renaud de Chatillon*, p. 185, n. 1) more sagely observes "La vérité est que les Francs eurent environ deux mille tués ou blessés." Röhricht (*Geschichte*, p. 376) likewise considers the number of knights listed by William of Tyre as obviously too low. Also see Stevenson, *op. cit*, pp. 217-18 for confirmatory views on this battle. See Lane-Poole, *op. cit.*, pp. 154-55 for a criticism of Saladin's defective strategy and mistakes at this battle and Gibb, "The Achievement of Saladin," p. 98 for a general appraisal of his shortcomings as a general. Collins (*loc. cit.*) declares that "Josceline de Courtenay... contributed much by his bravery and conduct to the memorable victory..." Collins' view perhaps reflects the listing by William of Tyre (Bk. XXII, chap. xxvii, *op. cit.*, p. 1122) of the Frankish chieftains including Joscelyn III who assembled for the Ṣaffūrīyah campaign (*infra*, pp. 114-15) and his designation of them as "Praeterea magni et admirabiles praeerant exercitui duces, illustres genere, et armorum experientia praeclari." But the fact of the matter is that the sources are entirely silent concerning the Seneschal's rôle in the battle of *Ramla*. They merely state that he was a participant.

[197] William of Tyre, Bk. XXI, chap. xxv, *op. cit.*, pp. 1047-48; Michael the Syrian, *Chronique*, p. 376; Behâ Ed-Dîn, *Anecdotes, loc. cit.* and *Saladin*, p. 77; Ibn al-Athīr,

But the triumph of Ramla was short-lived and the temporary interruption resulting therefrom of the evil days prevailing since 1174 proved to be very transitory in both domestic and military matters for the Kingdom of Jerusalem. The problem of the regency was still unsolved, for Philip left the Kingdom of Jerusalem after the Easter season in 1178 and returned to France in the following Autumn.[198] Hope was held, at the time of the visit of an ecclesiastical delegation to Rome in October, 1178 to attend a general synod, that one of the delegates, Joscius, the bishop of Acre, would succeed in his additional rôle as an envoy entrusted with the duty of inviting Henry, Duke of Burgundy, to repair to the Kingdom of Jerusalem and become the husband of the widowed Sibyl under the same arrangements as those effected at the time of her marriage to the late William Longsword. Henry received the proposal graciously and promised solemnly that he would come. Later, however, he broke his agreement[199] and, upon being urged in the following year, 1179, to reconsider his earlier refusal, still declined to come.[200]

The failure of the diplomatic mission to Henry was soon followed by three in the military theatre. In an effort to safeguard the Kingdom of Jerusalem more efficiently, King Baldwin IV followed the suggestion of the Templars and began the construction in the Autumn of 1178 of a fortress on a well chosen site on the Jordan River known as Jacob's Ford located about ten miles from Banyas. Saladin, apparently apprehensive lest the Franks thereby become too strong, requested its demolition. The Franks replied that they would do so only if Saladin paid them the cost entailed in its construction. Saladin countered with an offer of 60,000 dinars and, upon meeting with a refusal, raised his bid to 100,000 dinars. But nothing came of these

---

K.–A., p. 632; Abou Chamah, *op. cit.*, p. 193; Kamal-Ad-Dîn, *Histoire*, IV, 151-53; *Chronique d'Ernoul*, pp. 45-46. Baldwin (*Raymond III*, p. 33), speaking adversely on the crusaders' strategy of attacking Hārim rather than Egypt, comments pertinently: "Although it is possible that a spirited attack in the north while Saladin was in Egypt may have been sound strategy, it seems more plausible to interpret the diversion as a tactical error. A concerted attack against Saladin at his base might have halted the expansion of the Aiyubid empire at its source. Moreover the last opportunity to profit by Byzantine cooperation was allowed to pass. Three years later Manuel Comnenus died and was succeeded by men disposed rather to treat the Latins as enemies." Archer and Kingsford (*op. cit.*, p. 254) put the case even more strongly: "... the Eastern Christians [as a result of their failure to attack Egypt] lost their last opportunity of striking what might have been a fatal blow at the power of Saladin."

[198] William of Tyre, *op. cit.*, p. 1048.
[199] *Ibid.*, chap. xxvi, *op. cit.*, pp. 1049-50.
[200] *Ibid.*, chap. xxx, *op. cit.*, p. 1059.

negotiations, for a military subordinate of Saladin's urged him to spend the money on the building of an army strong enough to capture the fortress. This advice he followed with success.[201]

While construction was still proceeding on the fortress, Castle Jacob by name, news reached the King in April, 1179 that the Moslems had appeared in the forest near Banyas with their herds and flocks. Since they were without military protection, the Franks believed that the success of an attack on their part was assured. Accordingly, they advanced on the enemy under cover of darkness. But the Moslems, having been apprised of the approach of the Franks and having elected to hide among the rocks to avoid enemy attack, soon saw the carelessness of their foemen's military dispositions and safeguards and hence decided to attack. The ensuing onslaught and defeat cost the Franks the lives of the valiant Constable of the Kingdom, Humphrey II, lord of Toron, as well as several other feudatories and nearly resulted in the capture of the King himself.[202]

This defeat was soon followed by another and far greater one. Saladin invaded the Banyas districts in June, 1179, whereupon King Baldwin IV advanced upon Tiberias and proceeded thence to Toron with his forces, where he learned that Saladin's infantry was still posted at Banyas but that his cavalry was now devastating the area of Sidon. Accordingly, the King advanced upon Banyas with both his infantry and cavalry. After an initial skirmish on June 10, which resulted in a Frankish victory, Saladin's numerically superior cavalry closed with that of the Franks, inflicted a great defeat, and caused

---

[201] *Ibid.*, chap. xxvi, *op. cit.*, p. 1050; *The Chronography of Bar Hebraeus*, p. 308; Makrizi, *op. cit.*, pp. 530 and 533; Abou Chamah, *op. cit.*, pp. 194, 197, and 205-06; Ibn al-Athīr, *K. —A.*, pp. 638-39; Michael the Syrian, chap. viii, *Chronique*, p. 378; *Chronique d'Ernoul*, pp. 52 and 53-54. Runciman (*History*, pp. 417-18) sees in the recent but essentially meaningless Frankish victory of Ramla and the loss of Banyas in 1164 key factors in the Franks' decision to construct a fortress at Jacob's Ford. "It [the battle of Ramla] had been a great victory and it had saved the kingdom for the moment. But it had not in the long run changed the situation. The resources of Egypt are limitless; whereas the Franks were still short of men. Had it been possible for King Baldwin to pursue the enemy into Egypt or to make a swift attack upon Damascus, he might have crushed Saladin's power, but without help from outside he could not risk his own small army on an offensive. Instead, he decided to erect strong fortifications along the Damascene frontier, where the loss of Banyas had upset the defensive system of the kingdom."

[202] William of Tyre, chap. xxvii, *op. cit.*, pp. 1052-53; Abou Chamah, *op. cit.*, pp. 195-96; Makrizi, *op. cit.*, pp. 530-31; Ibn al-Athīr, *K. —A.*, p. 635; *Chronicon Guillelmi de Nangiaco* in *Recueil des historiens des Gaules et de la France*, ed. M. Bouquet and others (Paris, 1894), XX, 739.

most of the remnants to retreat to the fortress of Belfort. Meanwhile, Reginald, the lord of Sidon, and his forces were hastening to relieve their fellows, but, upon learning of the disaster, unwisely returned to Sidon. Deprived of this badly needed military succour, the fugitives hiding in the adjacent caves were helpless to escape Saladin's search parties on the following morning. Although Baldwin IV and Count Raymond of Tripoli escaped capture, severe losses were sustained by the Franks in the capture of the stalwart champion Odo of St. Amand, the master of the Temple, Baldwin of Ramla, and Hugh of Tiberias, the stepson of the Count of Tripoli.[203]

Still another reversal followed. The arrival of a considerable number of French nobles at Acre raised the hopes of the dispirited Latins, but Saladin soon destroyed them. His investment of the newly built Frankish fortress at Jacob's Ford, which began late in May, 1179, before his invasion of the Banyas-Sidon area,[204] continued and was climaxed with its capture on August 30, 1179 largely by means of successful mining operations, the slaying and capturing of its garrison, and its ensuing razing to the ground.[205]

---

[203] William of Tyre, chaps. xxviii-xxix, op. cit., pp. 1054-57; Abou Chamah, op. cit., pp. 198-203; Makrizi, op. cit., pp. 531-32; Ibn al-Athīr, K.—A., pp. 636-37; The Chronography of Bar Hebraeus, pp. 308-09; Michael the Syrian, Chronique, p. 379; Stevenson, op. cit., p. 221.

[204] William of Tyre, chap. xxvii, op. cit., p. 1053.

[205] Ibid., chap. xxx, op. cit., pp. 1058-59; Abou Chamah, op. cit., pp. 203-08; Chronique d'Ernoul, p. 54; Roger of Hoveden, op. cit., p. 133; Makrizi, op. cit., p. 533; Ibn al-Athīr, K.—A., p. 638; Babcock and Krey, op. cit., p. 444, n. 67.

CHAPTER SEVEN

THE RISE OF RIVAL POLITICAL PARTIES IN THE KINGDOM OF JERUSALEM: NORTHERN NOBLES VS. THE COURT PARTY; SALADIN'S WAXING POWER, 1180-1182

But the four failures, one domestic and three military, plaguing the Kingdom of Jerusalem from October, 1178 to August, 1179 were as nothing compared to those of 1180, for the latter were to divide the Kingdom into bitterly opposed political factions whose quarrels and intrigues were to sound its death knell. The problem of the succession to the throne, second only to and closely interlocked with that posed by the plans of Saladin, now took a sudden and unexpected development. The news that the great feudatories, Bohemond, the Prince of Antioch, and Raymond, the Count of Tripoli, had arrived in the Kingdom with a cavalry escort caused much apprehension in the now very ill leper king. Fearful that they were contemplating a revolution to the end of dethroning him and seizing the Kingdom for themselves, he suddenly married his widowed sister Sibyl to Guy of Lusignan, a French born nobleman, passing over far more eligible native and foreign nobles and flouting well-established custom by his celebration of the marriage during Easter week before April 20, 1180 with the obvious support of Archbishop Heraclius and the Order of the Templars.[206] By reason of his gaining of his wife's dowry of the

---

[206] William of Tyre, Bk. XXII, chap. i, *op. cit.*, pp. 1062-63; *Chronique d'Ernoul*, pp. 59-60; Benedict of Peterborough, *op. cit.*, p. 343; Ottonis Episcopi Frisingensis (Otto of Freising) *Chronicon Continuatio Sanblasiana* ed. by Georg Pertz in *Monumenta Germaniae Historica Scriptores* (Hanover, 1868), XX, 318. Baldwin (*Raymond III*, p. 36) believes that "... the king's haste to have the marriage performed was, rightly or wrongly, the result of the fear that Bohemond and Raymond had come to prevent it." Oldenbourg (*op. cit.*, p. 409) has much the same emphasis. "Il [Baldwin IV] défendait âprement—non plus contre Saladin, avec lequel il espérait maintenir la trêve aussi longtemps que possible; contre ceux qu'il soupçonnait, à tort ou à raison, de vouloir l'écarter du pouvoir. Un jour, le comte de Tripoli et le prince d'Antioche décidèrent d'aller faire leurs dévotions à Jérusalem—le roi, en apprenant la chose, crut qu'ils venaient dans l'intention de le détrôner et voulut leur interdire l'accès du royaume—quels que fussent les arguments que les deux princes purent trouver pour le rassurer, il ne cessa de les soupçonner, et entreprit de remarier au plus vite sa soeur Sibylle, non pour avoir un héritier (car la jeune femme avait mis au monde en 1178 un fils, baptisé Baudouin) mais pour avoir à ses côtés un défenseur." The same author (*op. cit.*, pp. 411-12) sees in

Baldwin IV's tactics toward Count Raymond not solely the influence of Agnes of Courtenay and Joscelyn III but also his determination to retain his rôle as a king. "Il [Baldwin IV] n'eut pas la sagesse de remettre, de son vivant, le pouvoir aux mains du comte de Tripoli, qui, quels que fussent ses défauts, était encore le seul homme capable de faire respecter un ordre du moins relatif. (Il est vrai que Raymond III avait beaucoup d'ennemis—mais le roi, quand il le voulait, était capable d'imposer sa volonté; or, au lieu de chercher l'appui du comte, il faisait tout pour l'écarter des affaires.) Ici on peut deviner l'influence d'Agnès de Courtenay et de son frère Jocelin III; mais il y avait, surtout, le tenace désir du jeune roi de ne pas abandonner son poste. Il avait impatiemment subi la régence de Raymond au cours des premières années de son règne et ne voulait pas retomber sous la tutelle de cet homme que pourtant (on le verra par la suite) il estimait." Munro (*The Kingdom*, p. 154) in an analysis of the motives of Baldwin's consent to this marriage and his selection of Easter week for its performance, observes that "... the king gave his consent to it and was induced to hasten the ceremony because of the imminent arrival of many of the barons in Jerusalem for the Easter festivities. It was a foregone conclusion that they would object to the princess' marrying a newcomer from the West, and if the marriage had the king's approval it would be better to confront the barons with a *fait accompli* than to allow time for their opposition to crystallize." Baldwin (*Raymond III*, p. 39-40) observes, in the case of Raymond's opposition to the marriage that "Guy's marriage put him [Guy] in line for the procuratorship or the crown itself, both of which he ultimately acquired. In addition, Raymond especially must have realized very keenly the possible consequences to himself. Having once possessed the procuratorship, he had seen it pass to two others, neither of whom had as good a right as he. He was now determined to do all in his power to prevent its going to a third." In respect to Bohemond, the same author observes, "As for Bohemond, since as prince of Antioch he rarely concerned himself with the affairs of Jerusalem, it is the more significant that he should have stood by Raymond here. He was perhaps his closest friend and a man of similar interests. They had worked together before in 1177; and in the very next year (1181) Raymond was asked "as a very good friend" of Bohemond to accompany a delegation to Antioch to settle a scandal created by the prince. These two fast friends evidently regarded the marriage of no small import to the kingdom, as indeed it turned out. They showed greater foresight than the king." This same scholar, reaffirming these views in his later work ("The Decline," p. 597) goes even further in his belief that the marriage was opposed by the majority of the baronage of the Kingdom of Jerusalem. "Apparently Agnes and Baldwin IV were also persuaded by the Lusignans to agree to the match. Guy's suit for Sibyl's hand, carrying with it the presumption of regency, possibly even of succession to the throne, was apparently not favored by most of the barons. It was particularly abhorrent to Raymond of Tripoli who, presumably on hearing of the projected match, entered the kingdom in force along with his friend, Bohemond III of Antioch." In his earlier work Baldwin (*Raymond III*, p. 42) was of the opinion that "It now seems even more probable that Queen Agnes had been instrumental in arranging the marriage of her daughter Sibyl to Guy of Lusignan." La Monte ("The rise," pp. 312-13) sees in the king's granting of the hand of Sibyl to Guy of Lusignan an attempt to raise a counter force to Raymond. "In so doing however the king made a serious error for not only did he bring to the fore that rather incompetent and inexperienced though pleasant appearing knight, but he gravely offended the house of Ibelin which had supported the candidacy of Baldwin of Rama for the hand of the princess." Marian Louise Castle (*The Career of Guy of Lusignan to 1187. A Study of Politics in the Kingdom of Jerusalem on the Eve of Its Conquest by Saladin*, University of Chicago Master's Thesis, [Chicago, 1936], p. 13) observes correctly that "The mention by William of Tyre that there were men available of higher station and greater wealth and of more intelligence makes clear why the patriarch and the master of the Templars approved of Guy as a desirable husband for Sibylle: they did not want to jeopardize cities of Jaffa and Ascalon Guy thereupon assumed the status of the count of both cities.[207]

But this triumph over the northern nobles representing the rival faction was not enough for the court party. Seizing the opportunity provided by the death of Amalric, the Patriarch of Jerusalem, on October 6, 1180,[208] they interposed their influence to secure the election of Heraclius, Archbishop of Caesarea, to the vacant post. Obeying the request of the leper king that they repair to Jerusalem to elect a successor to Amalric, the archbishops and bishops of the Holy Land met in full assembly in Jerusalem in April, 1181, whereupon William, Archbishop of Tyre, urged them not to elect Heraclius. Such an elevation, he warned them, would lead to his acceptance by the young king and ultimately to the loss of the Kingdom of Jerusalem. Therefore, they should elect another in his place even if, in the absence of a suitable local cleric, they should have to seek one in France itself. But, since Agnes, the Queen Mother, had already signified a desire that the assemblage elect Heraclius, they refused to comply with William's plea and instead elected Heraclius and William. The king, in accordance with his mother's instructions, selected the former as the new Patriarch. The victorious Heraclius thereupon commanded the clergy to render him obedience and to forsake the Archbishop of Tyre. William then appealed to Rome, urging the deposition of his rival, and at length repaired to that city to exert greater pressure on the pope and the cardinals. There William died before Heraclius could come to take action against him.[209]

---

their influence over the king by favoring a more powerful person." This same author (*op. cit.*, p. 14) sees in the marriage of Guy of Lusignan and Sibyl the achievement of King Baldwin's plans in respect to Bohemond and Raymond "The marriage seems to have served its immediate purpose. For, as Baldwin hoped, Bohemond and Raymond when they saw that their arrival was looked upon with suspicion, returned to their homes after partaking in the Easter festival in Jerusalem." Also see Baldwin, *Raymond III*, pp. 36-38 and Grousset, *Histoire*, pp. 688-89 for respective discussions on (1) the reasons for Baldwin IV's selection of Guy of Lusignan rather than some other feudal chieftain as the second husband for his sister Sibyl and (2) the motivations of the constable Amalric of Lusignan in promoting the marriage of his brother, Guy of Lusignan, with Sibyl.

[207] *Chronique d'Ernoul*, p. 60; Röhricht, *Regesta*, No. 601, p. 160.

[208] William of Tyre, chap. iv, *op. cit.*, p. 1068; *Chronique d'Ernoul*, chap. viii. p. 82; *L'Estoire de Eracles Empereur* in *Rec. His. Crois. Occ.* (Paris, 1859), II, 57 (This third-named reference henceforth will be cited as *Eracles*.).

[209] William of Tyre, *loc. cit.*; *Chronique d'Ernoul*, pp. 82-86; *Eracles*, pp. 57-59. Babcock and Krey (*op. cit.*, p. 451, n. 7) point out that "... it was customary for the clergy to submit two names to the king for his final choice." See Baldwin, *Raymond III*, p. 42. for an apprisal of Agnes' political policies and rôle at this time as well as on earlier occasions. Runciman (*History*, p. 425) sees in Agnes' action to secure the election

This second bold move of the court party in general and the Courtenay division thereof in particular met with a quick response on the part of their opponents in September and October, 1180. Humphrey IV, the bearer of an illustrious name by reason of his descent from his maternal grandfather, Philip, the lord of Nablus in the trans-Jordanian country, and his paternal grandfather, Humphrey II, the lord of Toron and the Constable of the Kingdom of Jerusalem, now became the center of a new struggle for power. Having gained the status of stepfather of Humphrey IV as a result of his marriage to his mother Stephanie about 1177—this was her third matrimonial venture—Reginald of Châtillon undertook with great enthusiasm the task of espousing his stepson to King Baldwin IV's younger half sister, Isabel, a mere child scarcely eight years old. The betrothal agreement, which was presumably drawn up in September, 1180, provided an exchange of Humphrey IV's patrimony which he had received from his paternal grandfather, namely certain domains in the territory of Tyre: Toron, Chastel-Neuf, and the city of Banyas with their appurtenances.[210] Even though the document providing for the exchange has not survived,[211] it is a fair presumption that the grants made by King Baldwin IV to Humphrey IV for his surrender of his handsome patrimony were of equal value in terms of their political privileges and/or territorial importance. In any event, Humphrey IV had already reached man's estate and the combination of his political, territorial,

---

of Heraclius, which was exerted through her increasingly helpless son, a plan to end William's rôle as the royal tutor, a rôle which was dangerous to the Courtenays, the Lusignans, and their allies. And Grousset (*Histoire*, p. 697) believes that Agnes was markedly supported by her brother, Joscelyn III. "Le frère d'Agnès, Jocelin III de Courtenay, comte titulaire d'Édesse et sénéchal du royaume de Jérusalem, l'appuyait de tout son pouvoir, ainsi que plusieurs autres barons qui formaient autour d'eux une véritable camarilla pour exploiter cyniquement la pitoyable situation du roi et du royaume." See Herzog, *op. cit.*, pp. 64-66 and 71 for illuminating concepts on the dynamics of the characters of mother and daughter Agnes and Sibyl, and Agnes' rôle in the marriage of Sibyl to Guy.

[210] William of Tyre, chap. v, *op. cit.*, pp. 1068-69; *Chronique d'Ernoul*, pp. 81-82; Henri François Delaborde, *Chartes de Terre Sainte provenant de l'Abbaye de N.-D. de Josaphat* (Paris, 1880), No. XLI, pp. 88-89. Also see Runciman, *History*, Appendix III: Genealogical Trees; Runciman (*History*, p. 424) believes that King Baldwin IV favored the marriage of his half sister Isabel to Humphrey IV as a means of healing the factional splits of the time. "For political as well as for personal reasons the Ibelins were disgusted [over Guy's marriage to Sibyl], and the breach between them and the Courtenays, supported by Raynald of Châtillon, grew greater. In October 1180 the King tried to bring them together by betrothing his half-sister Isabella to Humphrey IV of Toron." Babcock and Krey, *op. cit.*, p. 451, n. 8.

[211] Babcock and Krey, *op. cit.*, p. 452, n. 10.

military, and financial statuses joined with those of his redoubtable stepfather would at least equal those of his rivals, namely his half sister-in-law Sibyl and her new husband, Guy of Lusignan, whose reputation prior to his arrival in the Holy Land had been stained by an heinous deed. Henry II of England had banished him for his treacherous murder of the Earl of Salisbury. Guy had assumed the cross, the usual procedure for malefactors, and had come to seek his fortune in Palestine. His own kindred had held him in contempt and continued to do so. When later in 1185 Guy obtained the kingship, his own brother ironically observed, "If he is now king, he will ere long be God."[212] And it certainly seemed that a child bride could be as easily manipulated by Humphrey, Reginald of Châtillon, and the party of the native nobles as the leper king could be controlled by his sister Sibyl, her husband Guy, and the court nobles inclusive of Joscelyn III. But these calculations were to prove baseless, for more than three years of precious time were allowed to slip away before the marriage was actually performed in the castle of Krak on November 22, 1183[213] and the rival court party made excellent use of this tactical mistake. Moreover, Humphrey IV was to prove in the coming years to be a spineless, effeminate coward.[214]

---

[212] *Chronique d'Ernoul*, chap. vii, p. 60.

[213] William of Tyre, chap. xxviii, *op. cit.*, p. 1124. Runciman's view (*History*, pp. 424-25) that "Owing to the youth of the Princess, who was only eight, the actual ceremony was postponed for three years." overlooks the fact that, in view of the fairly common medieval practice of the marriage of girls as young as Isabel, the marriage date could have been easily advanced by a year or two. The value of the political stakes in such a maneuver was obvious. William of Tyre (Bk. XXII, chap. iv, *op. cit.*, pp. 1066-67) observes that the Byzantine emperor Manuel effected a marriage between his son Alexius and "Agnes, daughter of Louis, the illustrious king of the Franks. Alexius was not yet of age, in fact hardly thirteen years old, while Agnes was scarcely eight years old."

[214] *Itinerarium Peregrinorum et Gesta Regis Ricardi*, ed. William Stubbs (London, 1864), I, 120. "... vir foeminae quam viro propior, gestu mollis, sermone fractus..." (Future references to this source will be cited as *Itinerarium*). Cf. John L. La Monte, *The Crusade of Richard Lion-Heart by Ambroise*, trans. from the Old French by Merton Jerome Hubert with notes and documentation by John L. La Monte (New York, 1941), pp. 120-21, n. 5. (Henceforth this work of La Monte's will be cited as *The Crusade* to differentiate it from his other works). An explanation, at least in part, of the troubles of the Kingdom of Jerusalem at this time may be found in the observations of Baldwin ("The Decline," p. 596) that "It is evident from what has already been described of the first six years of Baldwin IV's reign that the instability of the executive power had seriously handicapped policy. So long as it was uncertain whether the young king's health would permit him personally to govern or would force him to shift the burden of responsibility to another, there was bound to be a certain feeling of tension within the high court.'

Meanwhile, the total effect of the military disasters suffered by the Franks from the Autumn of 1178 up to August 30, 1179 had given Saladin a free hand for military operations against the southern Franks. After a brief thrust at Tiberias he withdrew again into the Banyas area to await the arrival of a fleet of fifty galleys. Apprehensive for the future, King Baldwin IV dispatched envoys in the Spring of 1180 in quest of a truce. The Moslem leader agreed, for, despite his proved military prowess exhibited in his recent triumphs over the Franks, all was not well on the home front, which had been seriously weakened by five successive years of drought in the Damascus area. Accordingly, both parties agreed in May, 1180 to a two year truce applicable to both sea and land operations, binding upon foreigners and natives alike, and relevant only to the Kingdom of Jerusalem. The failure of the northern Franks to obtain any reservations or concessions was an eloquent testimonial to their marked weakness.[215]

Now freed from the prospect of Frankish intervention on the south, Saladin turned his triumphant arms to the north and raided the County of Tripoli. Although Count Raymond was prepared to engage the enemy, the Hospitallers and Templars were of another mind and preferred to remain behind the stout walls of their respective strongholds. Saladin's forces separated those of the Count from those of the crusading orders. Although the commanders of Saladin's naval forces, which soon appeared in the area of Beirut in June, observed their master's truce with the Kingdom of Jerusalem and hence refrained from attack on the Kingdom's harbors, confining their activities solely to a futile assault upon Tripolitan territories, which resulted in the seizure of the island of Arados near the city of Tortosa, the psychological effect on the dispirited northern Franks was profound and, coupled with Saladin's unimpeded devastations with his army, probably contributed to Count Raymond's decision to sue for peace. Saladin agreed, concluded a treaty with his Tripolitan foeman in June, 1180, and retired.[216] Count Raymond had no other choice, for with the Kingdom of Jerusalem remaining neutral and with the adjacent Principality of Antioch paralyzed by Prince Bohemond's triple policies of (1) obdurately refusing to assent to the demand of

---

[215] William of Tyre, chap. i, *op. cit.*, p. 1063; Abou Chamah, *op. cit.*, p. 211; Ibn al-Athīr, *K.—A.*, p. 642.

[216] William of Tyre, chaps. ii-iii, *op. cit.*, pp. 1064-66. Cf. Stevenson, *op. cit.*, p. 223, n. 2.

Count Raymond as well as the lay and clerical leaders of the Kingdom of Jerusalem that he abandon his adulterous life with a certain Sibyl, who was a spy in the service of Saladin, (2) seizing of church properties, and (3) ousting from the Principality of Antioch of all those nobles who were opposed to his policies, military and political weakness was everywhere the order of the day in the northern Frankish domains.[217]

The failure of the party of the native nobles to translate the engagement of Humphrey IV to Isabel into an actual marriage with all the political opportunities resulting therefrom may possibly account in part for the failure of the court party to attempt to consolidate its power during the following eighteen months. This state of affairs ended abruptly in the Spring of 1182, when Count Raymond of Tripoli, who had absented himself from the affairs of the Kingdom of Jerusalem for two successive years by reason of a plethora of business which required his attention in the County of Tripoli itself, now decided to visit the Kingdom of Jerusalem to the end of attending to the interests of his wife's patrimony, namely the city of Tiberias. But Raymond did not reach his goal, for he received, upon his arrival at Jubail *en route* to the Kingdom of Jerusalem, a peremptory order from the King not to enter the Kingdom. This order was the direct result of the action of the court party, consisting of the Queen-Mother, Agnes of Courtenay, her brother, Joscelyn III, the Seneschal, and their partisan supporters. They had persuaded the King that Raymond's visit to the Kingdom was animated by a desire to supplant the King. Their plan was to handle the affairs of the Kingdom to their own liking, to use for their own ends the King's sickness, and to accomplish these objectives by barring Raymond from the Kingdom. Raymond, confused and indignant over the whole episode, returned to Tripoli. This very dangerous situation fraught with the probability of Raymond's adoption of a policy of neutralism toward the Kingdom with an ensuing great peril for it, coupled with the growing illness of the leper king which made it increasingly impossible for him to attend to his royal duties, caused such apprehension among the more

---

[217] William of Tyre, chaps. v-vii, *op. cit.*, pp. 1069 and 1071-74; Michael the Syrian, Bk. XXI, chap. ii, *Chronique*, pp. 388-89; *The Chronography of Bar Hebraeus*, pp. 310-11. Runciman (*History*), p. 429) implies that Bohemond's repudiation of his Greek wife, which followed shortly after the death of the Byzantine emperor in September, 1180, resulted, at least in part, from the calculation that such a move was now safe in view of the decline of Byzantine power subsequent to Manuel's demise.

important barons that they tried mightily to recall Raymond and soften his anger. At length the King, following a period of negotiation and advancement of various proposals, was compelled to submit to their demand that they bring the Count into the Kingdom. Count Raymond agreed, and, ignoring the insults which he had received, reestablished peace with Baldwin IV.[218]

---

[218] William of Tyre, chap. ix, *op. cit.*, pp. 1077-79. Runciman (*History*, p. 426) believes that Raymond convinced Baldwin IV of his innocence of wrong-doing. Babcock and Krey (*op. cit.*, pp. 460-61, n. 29) observe that "Perhaps this reconciliation was accomplished as early as April 27, 1182. There is extant at Jerusalem an intensely interesting document of that date in which Baldwin IV makes a grant of certain tithes at Toron to William, archbishop of Tyre. The document is witnessed by Raymond of Tripoli as well as by other great nobles and is sealed by William himself as chancellor. The transaction, a generous favor to William, may imply not only that cordiality was reëstablished between Raymond and the king, but also that William was an important factor in that happy solution (R. Röhricht, *Regesta regni Hierosolymitani*, no. 615)." A. C. Krey ("William of Tyre. The Making of an Historian in the Middle Ages," *Speculum* [Cambridge, 1941], XVI, 157) sees in the growing illness of the King the central reason for the growth of the nobiliary factions in the court of King Baldwin IV to which I have already referred. "Discussion of the question [of that of the regency and ultimate succession to Baldwin IV] had led to the formation of two definite factions. One, composed chiefly of the 'native' nobles, those whose position had been hereditary for two or three generations, looked upon Raymond of Tripoli as the best choice for regent. The other, composed chiefly of adventurous newcomers to the realm, were opposed to Raymond and turned to the new husband of the king's sister, Guy of Lusignan, as their choice. This faction had a powerful friend in Agnes de Courtenay, the king's mother, whose influence with the king was greatly enhanced by his increasing illness. The Courtenays, though an old family in Edessa, were relative newcomers in Jerusalem and therefore had much in common with the other ambitious adventurers. It was chiefly through the influence of Agnes that this faction had now gained the ascendancy at Court." It would seem that this faction saw in the impending visit of Raymond of Tripoli to the Kingdom of Jerusalem a threat to their own ascendancy and hence they moved swiftly to forestall this visit. See Baldwin, *Raymond III*, pp. 43-44 for an analysis of the motivation of the party of the native nobles in their support of Raymond at this time and their rôle in his acquisition of the procuratorship eight years before in 1174. Baldwin (*Raymond III*, pp. 42-43) also finds in the lesser degree of Joscelyn III's, on the one hand, and greater degree of Raymond's, on the other hand, kinship with the royal family a central reason for Joscelyn III's decision to align himself with the party of opposition to Raymond. "Though, like Raymond, related to the royal family, his [Joscelyn III's] relationship on the mother's side of the house was not in the royal line. Since advantages of that connection, such as, for example, the regency, would ordinarily fall to Raymond first, it was not strange that he should identify himself with the party of the opposition to Raymond." The same scholar ("The Decline," p. 598) observes that "... although William of Tyre mentions no names, it seems clear that among the supporters of Raymond were those native barons, Baldwin of Ramla, Balian of Ibelin, Reginald of Sidon, and others, who had helped him secure the procuratorship in 1174. Therefore, by 1182 two mutually antagonistic parties had appeared within the kingdom of Jerusalem. One, which might well be called the "court party," was composed of the relatives and favorites of Agnes and the Lusignans. Bound together by blood relationship, marriage, and the pursuit of power, they sought to establish their

ascendancy over the helpless Baldwin IV. The other party consisted of the native barons who increasingly looked to Raymond of Tripoli for leadership. Each group attempted to control policy, either through the high court, presumably the normal constitutional procedure, or, as the court party seems to have done, by gaining power over the king and acting quickly. The latter method worked in 1180 and the remaining barons were faced with a *fait accompli*. It failed in 1182 as the native barons reorganized their ranks." René Grousset (*L'épopée des croisades* [Paris, 1939], p. 255) well sums up the situation as follows: "Un homme pouvait seul sauver le royaume, le comte de Tripoli Raymond III. Mais c'était précisément la bête noire de la camarilla." (Henceforth references to this work will be cited as *L'épopée* to differentiate it from Grousset's other works.) Röhricht (*Geschichte*, p. 395) observes in similar vein. Grousset (*Histoire*, p. 698) sees in the enmity of the camarilla toward Count Raymond the following calculations: "Le comte de Tripoli, Raymond III, cousin du roi, représentait, semble-t-il, le seul facteur capable de sauver les institutions monarchiques. C'est précisément ce qui indisposait contre lui la camarilla et les égoïsmes féodaux." And this same scholar (*Histoire*, p. 699) sees in the baronial pressure upon Baldwin IV to come to terms with Raymond two considerations. The first was the reason that "... dans l'état de maladie où se trouvait le roi lépreux, Raymond III, en cas de décès de Baudouin IV, se trouvait le seul espoir du royaume." The second was the goal "... de détruire chez Baudouin IV l'effet des calomnies du parti Courtenay." King (*op. cit.*, p. 114) finds the differences separating the two rival groups of nobles to be rooted in differing concepts of the appropriate military and foreign policies to be followed in the Kingdom of Jerusalem. "For there were now two distinct parties in the kingdom, the European born aristocracy, and the native born, each with an entirely different policy. The former led by Guy de Lusignan and Reginald de Chatillon, supported by the Masters of the Hospital and the Temple, believed that the Holy Land could be held only by the sword. They were as a rule bitter fanatics, and considered that the Holy War should never cease so long as there was an infidel still left to slay. The national party on the other hand, led by Count Raymond of Tripolis, wished above all things to preserve their property and estates. They realized only too clearly that the Latin kingdom was helpless in face of the vast resources in men and money commanded by Saladin, and desired nothing better than to live at peace with their Moslem neighbours, until at least such time as Europe should again be prepared to pour its strength upon Asia, as it had done in the First and Second Crusades." Röhricht (*Geschichte*, p. 396) doubts that Count Raymond, despite his reestablishment of peace with the King, was able to quench the wrath in his heart against the court party who had made Baldwin IV their puppet. Richard (*op. cit.*, p. 136) strongly implies that Joscelyn III's fears for his continued retention of the many properties he had gained since 1176 (*supra*, pp. 74-77) made him a moving force behind the rebuff accorded to Raymond III. "Devant de pareils accaparements, [Joscelyn III's territorial gains] en grande partie réalisés aux dépens du domaine royal par un seul des grands officiers du royaume, on comprend que la clique groupée autour d'Agnès d'Édesse ait été effrayée par l'annonce de l'arrivée du comte Raymond III de Tripoli à Jérusalem, en 1182..."

CHAPTER EIGHT

THE FURTHER BURGEONING AND CONSOLIDATION OF JOSCELYN III'S RÔLE AS A POLITICAL AND TERRITORIAL MAGNATE, 1180-1183

Can it be said that only the factors of the growing illness of the King, the absence from the Kingdom of Jerusalem of the leader of the rival party of nobles, namely Count Raymond of Tripoli, and the failure of the native nobles to effect the marriage of Humphrey IV and Isabel afforded the Courtenays, Agnes and Joscelyn III, the opportunity and inspired in them the desire to act in such a high-handed fashion? And anticipating the still bolder moves of the court party in the early Autumn of 1183 which almost succeeded in displacing the King in fact, although not in name, by the elevation of the court party's favorite, Guy of Lusignan,[219] can we say that these three factors were the ones solely responsible for their almost successful machinations? Hardly, for the years 1180-1183 were ones of ever growing importance for the Seneschal Joscelyn III. He appeared in Constantinople in 1180, having been sent there by King Baldwin IV to attend to state business.[220] This mission, essentially of an

---

[219] *Infra*, p. 118.

[220] William of Tyre, chap. v, *op. cit.*, p. 1069; Röhricht, *Geschichte*, p. 390, n. 3; La Monte, "The rise," p. 309. Scholars differ in their views relative to the circumstances, dating, and motivations behind the journey of the Seneschal to Constantinople. Since the Byzantine Emperor Manuel was friendly to the Franks in the closing years of his life prior to his death on September 24, 1180—see Charles Brand, *Byzantium Confronts the West 1180-1204* (Cambridge, 1968), pp. 14-30—the views of Cahen (*La Syrie*, p. 422) indicate that Joscelyn III's appearance in Constantinople was at a date subsequent to Manuel's death and ascribes the Seneschal's journey to Constantinople to an effort to dissuade the Byzantine Greeks from adopting anti-Frankish policies. "En 1180, Manuel Comnène était mort. Sa veuve, Marie d'Antioche, régente pour son jeune fils Alexis II, en butte à de multiples difficultés et à un violent mouvement anti-latin, abandonna, malgré un voyage de Joscelin de Courtenay, ce qui restait de la politique entreprenante de Manuel, et en 1181 envoya conclure la paix avec Saladin." Collins (*loc. cit.*) views the situation somewhat differently in his declaration that "... and in the seventh year of Baldwin IV. [Joscelyn III] was sent on an embassy to Constantinople, to solicit assistance against the enemies of Christianity." Brand (*op. cit.*, pp. 25 and 26), on the other hand, believes that there was a connection between the diplomatic activities of William of Tyre and Joscelyn III's trip to Constantinople. This scholar, using the source material provided by William of Tyre (Bk. XXII, chap. iv, *op. cit.*, pp. 1067-68), points out that William of Tyre, following a sojourn in Constantinople, was granted permission to leave that city on April 23, 1180. He did so with instructions from the emperor to carry out

ambassadorial nature, was complemented by his ever waxing power in internal and domestic policies within the Kingdom of Jerusalem itself. An indication of this is implied in his first position in the list of the several witnesses to the concessions of free anchorage for his ships, freedom from all tolls for the right of entrance to and exit from harbors of the Kingdom of Jerusalem, and relief from all tolls made for the rights of buying and selling which were made to Benincase, the abbot of the cloister of Cava, by Baldwin IV on November 8, 1181.[221] Again, on April 27, 1182 his dominant rôle in the affairs of the Kingdom of Jerusalem is seen in his third position immediately following the names of Bishop Odo and Count Raymond of Tripoli and preceding that of Reginald of Châtillon in the list of the several witnesses to the grant by Baldwin IV of a tenth of all the revenues derived from the territory of Toron to William, the Archbishop of Tyre.[222] Still later in the year, on August 25, he appeared as a third

---

the several commands of the latter in respect to the incumbent ruler of Antioch Bohemond III and the Patriarch Aimery. Upon William's arrival in Antioch on May 12, 1180, he carried out the emperor's request and then "... went on to Beirut, where he found Baldwin IV, king of Jerusalem, with whom he and the Byzantine envoys evidently had business. William merely states that he returned to Tyre, which he reached on 6 July. Some important request was conveyed, however, for Baldwin sent an envoy of his own to Constantinople—his uncle Joscelin de Courtenay, seneschal of the realm." This same scholar (*op. cit.*, p. 26), while first observing that "Nothing is known of his [Joscelyn III] mission save that he went on the king's business," then proceeds (*op. cit.*, pp. 27 and 28) to suggest that his mission was involved in problems relating to the thrones of Byzantium and Jerusalem and which were of mutual interest to Emperor Manuel and King Baldwin IV. "Manuel, aware of his coming death, made a final diplomatic effort to protect his son; but exactly what he offered the ... crusading princes in return for their guarantees remains a mystery ... The king of Jerusalem faced the same problem Manuel did; he could not live long, and his heir was a child. Palestine also needed assistance against Saladin, whose rising power was apparent to every observer... Manuel must have made offers based on his allies' needs. The fact that Joscelin de Courtenay did not conclude his mission before Manuel's death suggests an agreement with the king of Jerusalem remained incomplete. Later refugees from Constantinople, however, believed it to be binding, so that some commitment apparently existed." Since King Baldwin IV became king on July 11, 1174, it follows that the seventh year of his kingship was identified with the July 11, 1180-July 11, 1181 period. Hence Collins and Brand are not in disagreement on the time of the mission and agree on one of the motivations for Joscelyn III's visit to Constantinople. La Monte (*loc. cit.*) also believes that the mission occurred in 1180. I am of the opinion that Brand, Collins, and La Monte are right in their earlier dating of the Seneschal's trip. My own view is that he arrived in Constantinople during the later Summer in 1180. See Baldwin, *Raymond III*, p. 37, n. 28 on the problem of the dating of Joscelyn III's mission to Constantinople and Runciman, *History*, p. 427 for an analysis of the new anti-Frankish orientation of Byzantium following Manuel's death.

[221] Röhricht, *Regesta*, No. 606, p. 161.
[222] *Ibid.*, No. 615, p. 163; Strehlke, *op. cit.*, No. 15, pp. 14-15.

witness preceded only by Count Raymond of Tripoli and Guy, the count of Ascalon and Jaffa, to a grant of a street in Acre to the Pisans which was made by Baldwin IV.[223] Toward the close of 1182 he witnessed on November 14 the confirmation by Baldwin IV of the sale of the town of Galilee which was made to the Order of the Hospitallers by Walter of Caesarea. And, as the case before, his name appears prominently in the list of witnesses with only the name of Monachus, the Archbishop of Caesarea, and Guy, the Count of Ascalon and Jaffa, preceding his.[224]

Complementing Joscelyn III's waxing political power and influence was his new rôle as a patron of the Church. No less a figure than Baldwin IV recognized this in his confirmation on February 6, 1182 of the Seneschal's grant of the annual revenue of a hundredweight of sugar to the Order of the Hospitallers.[225]

As in most of the cases in the social orders in the western tradition, Joscelyn III's waxing rôle as a political leader and ecclesiastical patron reflected his growing economic power as well. This is seen in the granting of various revenues to him by King Baldwin IV. The first of these, carefully detailed in respect to its provisions, was bestowed on the Seneschal on November 13, 1181 with the grant of a rental of 1,000 besants from the revenues of Acre which Philip le Roux had owned for life. Pending the time when Philip le Roux shall pay Joscelyn III the 2,000 besants which he had borrowed from him on the understanding that the rental will be used as security, the Seneschal shall hold and enjoy this revenue. The King, in order to safeguard his own interests, is promised in this agreement that as long as Joscelyn III shall have the rental he will be obligated to render the service of two knights which Philip le Roux had given to the King for this rental.

---

[223] Röhricht, *Regesta*, No. 617, p. 163.

[224] Delaville Le Roulx, *Cartulaire*, I, No. 645, p. 435; Röhricht, *Regesta*, No. 618, pp. 163-64. La Monte (*Feudal Monarchy, loc. cit.*), in commenting on the fact that there was no semblance of order in the names listed in the charters issued during the kingship of Baldwin IV, observes that "This shows a marked difference from the western practice where a definite order of signature among the grand officers was the rule. In France after Louis VII the order was always seneschal, butler, chamberlain, and constable. The failure of Jerusalem to develop any definite order of precedence among the grand officers can largely be explained by the lack of importance of any ceremonial in a court as loosely organized as was that of most of the Latin kings. *Further the offices were always connected with the individuals and the stronger men took precedence even though they held lesser offices.*" (Italics mine)

[225] Delaville Le Roulx, *Cartulaire*, I, No. 625, p. 424; Röhricht, *Regesta*, No. 613 , p. 162.

If the death of Philip le Roux should occur before his repayment of the money to Joscelyn III, the latter will be empowered to collect the unpaid 2,000 besants from the king. However, Joscelyn III will have to surrender to him the rental of Acre, because Philip le Roux had received this rental only as a life fief. Lastly, as long as Philip le Roux shall live and Joscelyn III shall receive this rental, he will be obligated to render the service of two knights for it.[226] Still another grant was received by the Seneschal from the King shortly thereafter and prior to February 24, 1182 when the latter gave him the fief of St. Elias located near Haifa.[227]

Soon thereafter in an apparent plan and effort to bolster his power by a policy of trading lands far removed from his main fief for those closer by and thereby securing the allegiance of his near neighbours, Joscelyn III exchanged with the King his recently acquired fief of St. Elias with the consent of the King's sister Sibyl and Guy of Lusignan for the important fief of Chastel-Neuf (with the exception of the town

---

[226] Strehlke, *op. cit.*, No. 13, p. 13; Röhricht, *Regesta*, No. 608, p. 161. La Monte ("The rise," pp. 309-10 and n. 1, p. 310) concludes that Rey and Mas Latrie are wrong in their belief that the arrangements drawn up on November 13, 1181 brought with them to Joscelyn III the lordships of Araibe and Zekanin. "Now this Philip Le Roux, who is termed in this act of Baldwin IV's *consanguinus meus*, was lord of Araibe and Zekanin, which he had received in 1174 in exchange with King Amaury for a revenue of 1000 besants which the king had previously granted him at Acre. Philip apparently had had a revenue of 1000 besants for which he owed one knight's service; this was traded for the fiefs of Araibe and Zekanin for which Philip paid still the one knight's service. But in addition at the same time the king made him a new grant of 800 besants at Acre for which he rendered two knights' service. This complicated arrangement was, I believe, a matter of the king desiring to get more service out of his cash investment and being willing to exchange land for the lower service but demanding more for any new grant in money. At any rate, some time between 1174 and 1181, Philip must have received an extra grant of 200 besants at Acre, for when he sold the revenue to Joscelyn it was a revenue of 1000 besants for which he owed two knights. There is nowhere any mention of Joscelyn's purchasing from Philip any part of his fief of Araibe and Zekanin or indeed any land at all. I am convinced that the two knights which Joscelyn owed according to Ibelin's list for the lands of Philip le Roux were actually those owed for this money fief and that the term lands is merely an error for fief. Araibe and Zekanin passed into the possession of Philip's heiress and were sold by her to the Teutonic Knights in 1234, and I am inclined to believe that both Rey and Mas Latrie were quite wrong in including Araibe and Zekanin among the holdings of Count Joscelyn."[1] ...[1] E.G. Rey, in the *Bulletin de la Société nationale des Antiquaires de France*, 1880, pp. 73-74; Mas Latrie, in *Revue Historique*, VII (1878) 110-120. Both Araibe and Zakenin (modern Arraba and Sakhnin) are in Galilee and are quite a bit south of Joscelyn's other lands, being nearer the parallel of Haifa than that of Acre. La Monte (*Feudal Monarchy*, p. 145 and "The Rise," p. 309) misdates this transaction, stating that it occurred in November, 1183.

[227] Strehlke, *op. cit.*, No. 14, pp. 13-14; Röhricht, *Regesta*, No. 614, pp. 162-63.

THE FURTHER BURGEONING AND CONSOLIDATION 101

of Iazun) commanding the valley of the Upper Jordan River, five hundred besants a year from the revenues of Tyre and a equal amount from Acre, and the fief of John Baner comprising a revenue of one hundred besants from Acre and four carrucates of land in Caimont. The Seneschal thereupon subinfeudated this last named fief to Garnier de Paris, John Baner's son-in-law, for the service of two horses and one knight. Also included in this grant were the fief of Maron and suzerainty over St. George and over Geoffrey Le Tor, lord of Manuet. In return for these several grants Joscelyn III also exchanged with King Baldwin IV the towns of Lubanie and Carrubie with the homage of John de Lumbres. This last-named exchange provided for Joscelyn III's recovery of it following the death of the dowager queen Marie. The terms of this grant required of Joscelyn III the services of ten knights and six knights for St. George and Geoffrey Le Tor respectively. The result of this exchange was the gaining for the Seneschal of a considerable area to the west and south of his former possessions and the renewal of his suzerainty over St. George which otherwise would have ended in 1186.[228]

The year 1183 was marked by still greater evidence of the Seneschal's growing opulence, for a charter dated March 19, 1183 reveals that King Baldwin IV himself confirmed Joscelyn III's purchase of fourteen towns, namely Accabara, Bellum, Camsara, Carsilia, Cassie, Deirbasta, Dere, Elgabacie, Feenix, Hourfex, Sauroefoca, Sorove, Terrabresca, and Terretrame for six thousand besants from Geoffrey Le Tor, his wife, and his son. The transaction provided for an arrangement under which the purchaser owed the service of two knights and the seller, Geoffrey Le Tor, provided the remainder of the service required from the fief, namely six knights. The Seneschal also held suzerainty over Geoffrey Le Tor's unsold areas.[229]

---

[228] Strehlke, *loc. cit.*; Röhricht, *Regesta, loc. cit.* and No. 341, p. 89 n. 2; Rey, *Les colonies*, pp. 478 and 488-89; La Monte, "The rise," pp. 310-11; Emmanuel Guillaume Rey, *Sommaire du Supplément aux Familles d'Outre-Mer* (Chartres, 1881), pp. 14-15. *Assises*, p. 422, states that the Seigneury of Count Joscelyn required the services of 24 knights, four for the fief of Chateau du Roi, ten for the fief of Saint George, six for the fief of Geoffrey Le Tor, two for the fief of Philip Le Roux, and two for the fief of the Chamberlain. L. de Mas Latrie ("Les Seigneurs du Crac de Montreal," *Archivio Veneto* [Venice, 1883], Vol. 25, p. 482, n. 2) refers to the Seigneury of Count Joscelyn as one of "Les cinq grands fiefs..." and as ... seigneurie anonyme, formée de l'aggrégation de diverses terres en faveur de Jocelin, après la perte du comté d'Édesse." Grousset (*Histoire*, p. 753, n. 2) observes that "Le Maron dont il s'agit ici est Marûn al-Râs, au sud de Tibnîn, près de Bint Umm Jubail, bien distinct du Maron tyrien, qui est Qal'at Marûn, au nord de Tibnîn (Dussaud, *Topographie*, 30 et Rey, *Colonies*, 478 et 488-489)."

[229] Röhricht, *Regesta*, No. 624, p. 165; Strehlke, *op. cit.*, No. 16, pp. 15-16; Rey, *Les*

Still another trade and an acquisition occurred on the same day. The trade involved the return of the fief of Maron to the King in exchange for the sum of one thousand besants derived from the revenues of Acre and the town of Jeth. However, the lands held by a certain Alamanna as her dower were excluded from this arrangement with the understanding that only after her death were they to go to Joscelyn III. The acquisition, which was the last grant Joscelyn III was to receive from King Baldwin IV, resulted from the grant to the Seneschal of the dragomanage of Chastel-Neuf formerly held by a certain John. The King also confirmed Joscelyn III's purchase in Chastel-Neuf of the house which John Bogalet had sold him for 150 besants. In return for all this Joscelyn III agreed to render to the King the identical service he had formerly given for Maron, namely three knights.[230]

Finally, as a sign of the Seneschal's continued importance in the political life of the Kingdom of Jerusalem, we may note his third position immediately after the Archbishop of Petra and Reginald of Châtillon in the list of witnesses attesting on April 21, 1183 to the grant made by Humphrey IV with the consent of his stepfather Reginald of Châtillon and his mother Stephanie of a gift of twenty besants a year to the colony of lepers at Saint-Lazare. This gift was derived from the customs duties of Acre which had been assigned to him, Humphrey IV, by King Baldwin IV.[231]

---

colonies, pp. 476, 477, 478, 479-80, 482, 485, 496, and 498. La Monte ("The rise," p. 311, n.1) observes that the French scholar Rey identified many of these towns as in the district near the Chateau du Roi. Here again we have an indication of the Seneschal's policy of consolidation of his holdings into units characterized by marked propinquity.

[230] Röhricht, *Regesta*, No. 625, pp. 165-66; Strehlke, *op. cit.*, No. 17, p. 16; Rey, *Les colonies*, p. 485. La Monte ("The rise," p. 312) believes that if Guy of Lusignan, who had already received the administration of the Kingdom of Jerusalem from Baldwin IV at the time of the King's last grant to Joscelyn III, had not "... overstepped his authority Joscelyn would have received further concessions from the invalided monarch."

[231] Röhricht, *Regesta*, No. 628, p. 166; Comte de Marsy, "Fragment d'un Cartulaire de l'Ordre de Saint-Lazare, en Terre-Sainte," *Archives de l'Orient latin* [Paris, 1884], II, No. XXIX, 146-47.

CHAPTER NINE

THE CONSOLIDATION OF SALADIN'S MOSLEM EMPIRE, 1180-1183

Meanwhile most of the two years of truce gained by the southern Franks in the Spring of 1180 from Saladin[232] had passed without friction serious enough to cause a premature ending of the truce. This happy circumstance resulted, at least in part, from the Moslem leader's preoccupation with more immediate and pressing problems. His relations with the Syrian emirs were still far from harmonious, for the great centers of power, namely Mosul and Aleppo, held by his Moslem rivals still eluded his grasp. 'Izz-ad-Dīn quickly filled the vacuum created by the death of his brother Saif-ad-Dīn Ghāzī II, the ruler of Mosul, on June 29, 1180[233] while the boy ruler of Aleppo, aṣ-Ṣāliḥ, continued to cling to his precarious perch. Moreover, Saladin's own possession of Raban was menaced by the growing strength of Kîlîj Arslan of Rūm. And this threat was not to be removed until October 2, 1180 when negotiations with him following his defeat at the hands of Saladin's lieutenant during October of the preceding year[234] at length secured a peace.[235] Finally the danger to Saladin provided by the aggressive tactics of Roupen III, the Armenian magnate, required a military expedition followed by a peace in November, 1180.[236] Following Saladin's return to Egypt in January, 1181 an even greater menace presented itself, namely the threat of an invasion of Egypt by sea by European invaders. To forestall this, he shortly thereafter undertook a series of defensive moves. These consisted of the development of a ring of strong forts around Alexandria to meet the expected invasion. Lady Luck also extended her favors at this time with the decision of Alexius Comnenus the Protosebastos, the chief political figure associated with Alexius II, the young eleven year old

---

[232] *Supra*, p. 93.
[233] Behâ Ed-Dîn, *Anecdotes*, p. 65 and *Saladin, loc. cit.*; Ibn al-Athīr, *Atabecs*, pp. 327-28.
[234] Ibn al-Athīr, *K.—A.*, pp. 639-40; Michael the Syrian, chap. i, *Chronique*, p. 382.
[235] Behâ Ed-Dîn, *Anecdotes*, p. 66 and *Saladin*, pp. 77-79; *The Chronography of Bar Hebraeus*, p. 310.
[236] Ibn al-Athīr, *K.—A.*, pp. 644-45; Abou Chamah, *op. cit.*, pp. 211-12; *The Chronography of Bar Hebraeus, loc. cit.*

successor to his late father Emperor Manuel—the latter had died on September 24, 1180—to dispatch an ambassador to Cairo. This envoy proceeded to offer and to make peace with Saladin and to release one hundred and eighty Moslem prisoners in May-June, 1181. A treaty between Cairo and Byzantium resulted in the Autumn of 1181.[237]

The truce with the southern Franks, which had been observed faithfully by its Latin and Moslem signatories, as of the close of June, 1181, over one-half of the two years allotted to it, might have continued to its termination date, which was set for the Spring of 1182, had it not been for the rash acts of lesser leaders in the Frankish camp which greatly contributed to the sundering of the fragile peace. The first of these was the Franks' seizure of a Moslem merchant ship near the Egyptian coast in July, 1181.[238] The second was provided by Reginald of Châtillon, who, taking advantage of his rôle of the lord of the fortress of Krak lying athwart the caravan route between Egypt and Syria, attacked a Damascus caravan in the Summer of 1181[239] seized Arabs,[240] and even laid plans, which proved to be abortive, to invade Arabia in December, 1181.[241] And the lord of Krak boldly

---

[237] Makrizi, op. cit., p. 539; Brand, op. cit., pp. 29-34.

[238] Makrizi, loc. cit.

[239] Chronique d'Ernoul, chap. vii, pp. 54-55. Although Latin and Moslem historians charge that the respective enemy side was the first to break the truce, the well known respect of Saladin for his pledged word together with the impetuosity of Reginald of Châtillon render probable the proposition that the Franks first broke the truce. Also consult Lane-Poole, op. cit., p. 166 and Runciman, History, p. 431 for the sequence of events. Cf. Stevenson, op. cit., pp. 224-25.

[240] William of Tyre, chap. xiv, op. cit., p. 1088.

[241] Abou Chamah, op. cit., pp. 214-15; Ibn al-Athīr, K.—A., p. 647. The mad folly of the deeds of Reginald of Châtillon is indicated in a penetrating fashion by Grousset (Histoire, pp. 700-01). "A cet égard l'installation de Renaud dans la terre d'Outre-Jourdain constituait déjà une invite aux aventures. Les forteresses de Transjordanie et de l'Arabie Pétrée, le Krak de Moab et Montréal-Shawbak, contrôlaient ou interceptaient à leur gré non seulement la route du Hajj, la voie sacrée du pèlerinage de La Mecque, mais, aussi les communications entre les deux moitiés de l'empire de Saladin, la Damascène et l'Égypte. Du jour où cet empire avait été fondé, à cheval sur les deux pays, avec comme seul lien la route de l'Arabie-Pétrée - puisque le Sahel palestinien, possédé par les Francs, restait hors de cause - , il était inévitable qu'il supportât avec impatience l'occupation franque de la Transjordanie et du Wâdi al-'Araba. On a vu qu'à peine en possession de l'Égypte, du vivant même de Nûr al-Dîn, Saladin, comme obsédé par ces nécessités géographiques, était venu à diverses reprises, assiéger les deux kraks. Il suffit de parcourir les historiens arabes pour se rendre compte que la seule politique qui eût pu, à ce point névralgique, endormir son hostilité était une politique de collaboration commerciale, l'imbrication des intérêts favorisant l'exploitation commune des caravanes qui, d'Aïla à Alexandrie d'une part, à Saint-Jean d'Acre d'autre part, drainaient, par les pistes du désert, les richesses de l'Inde et de l'Extrême-Orient. Politique fort nettement entrevue par les princes du temps, qu'ils

informed King Baldwin IV's envoys, upon receiving their master's plea for restitution of booty to Saladin and release of all prisoners, that he would do nothing of the kind and that he desired to be free in his movements henceforth. The frustrated King was obliged to confess his helplessness to Saladin.[242]

In retaliation, Saladin took advantage of the plight of 1500 Christian pilgrims who had been shipwrecked at Damietta in northern Egypt before Easter, 1182 and, ignoring his agreement under the truce to allow them to depart from the land unmolested, imprisoned them and seized their property. He then sent a messenger to Baldwin IV with a set of severe demands accompanied by an ultimatum to the effect that failure on the part of the Franks to meet these demands would result in his retention of the pilgrims' ship and his sundering of the truce with the Franks. When the messengers' quest proved unsuccessful, Saladin ended the truce and laid plans for invasion of the Kingdom of Jerusalem.[243]

Saladin, having mustered a large infantry and cavalry force including large contingents of Damascus men who had repaired to Egypt in former years to escape famine, set his goal on Damascus with

---

fussent musulmans ou chrétiens, car le commerce de la mer Rouge enrichissait aussi bien les douanes du royaume de Jérusalem que celles de l'Égypte aiyûbide. Nous verrons à ce propos l'exaspération du roi Baudouin IV, quand il apprendra que les brigandages de Renaud de Châtillon ont intercepté la route des caravanes. En résumé, la réunion de la Syrie Damascène et de l'Égypte en un même sultanat conférait du double point de vue commercial et politique une importance capitale au fief franc de Transjordanie, au moment précis où on inféodait ce fief à Renaud de Châtillon. En même temps, la carence générale de chefs chrétiens, l'espèce de dégénérescence qui frappait la quatrième génération de Francs créoles, l'éclipse de la royauté sous un roi moribond, tout concourait à mettre en relief le nouveau sire d'Outre-Jourdain, l'homme fort qu'était Renaud. Brusquement placé dans cette situation hors de pair, libre d'engager tous les Francs par ses initiatives personelles, sans contrepoids et sans frein, le vieil aventurier allait entraîner le royaume dans l'aventure." And this same scholar (*Histoire*, p. 703) sees in Reginald of Châtillon's ensuing defiance of Baldwin IV an announcement of the end of the royal power in the Kingdom of Jerusalem. "Remarquons que, indépendamment de ses irréparables conséquences à l'extérieur, ce refus annonçait la révolte de la féodalité franque contre les institutions monarchiques. Le sire d'Outre-Jourdain profitait de la déchéance physique du roi lépreux pour proclamer la déchéance de la royauté. Bafouant l'autorité royale, il engageait sans leur aveu, malgré eux, le roi et le royaume dans la plus redoutable des aventures. Pour qui va au fond des choses, le brigandage de 1181 annonce la fin de la royauté hiérosolymitaine avant même d'entraîner comme conséquence la chute prochaine du royaume."

[242] *Chronique d'Ernoul*, pp. 55-56.
[243] William of Tyre, *op. cit.*, p. 1087; Abou Chamah, *op. cit.*, pp. 216-17; *The Chronography of Bar Hebraeus*, p. 312; Ibn al-Athīr, *K. – A.*, p. 653; Stevenson, *op. cit.*, p. 225, n. 2.

the plan of wreaking havoc on the Frankish territories *en route*.[244] He left Cairo on May 11, 1182 and, proceeding into Syria, reached Damascus on June 22 without encountering enemy opposition.[245]

Meanwhile, the Frankish leadership mismanaged everything. Following a general council in Jerusalem, King Baldwin IV gave heed to the advice of some of the barons and Reginald of Châtillon in particular, and, over the objections of Count Raymond, stripped much of the Kingdom of Jerusalem of all its soldiery and then advanced with his army to Petra, a city about thirty-six miles distant from Saladin's camp. Thereupon, the Moslem rulers in the vicinity of Damascus, Bostrum, Baalbek, and Homs, seeing the Franks' error, proceeded to overrun part of Galilee and advanced as far as Tiberias and Acre. The Christian inhabitants, not knowing of the breaking of the truce, were taken by surprise by the invaders under cover of nightfall and soon their central defense, the town of Buria, fell under Moslem control. Worse still was the fall of the Frankish fortress of Ḥabīs Jaldak, which dominated the surrounding countryside. The fundamental and triple blunder of this defective military strategy which underlay all these specific defeats was (1) the Franks' failure to meet Saladin at the frontiers of the Kingdom of Jerusalem and thereby prevent his entrance, (2) their failure to stop his advance to Gerba with its abundance of water badly needed by Saladin's thirsty troops and (3) their failure to attack that division of his forces which now were engaged in plundering operations around Montréal.[246]

But better luck soon attended the military fortunes of the Franks. Learning that Saladin had departed from Damascus, had appeared near the city of Tiberias on July 20, and was now dispatching his forces from that city to engage in plundering operations in the environs of Baisan, Jinin, and Acre, the Franks now moved to meet the enemy. An inconclusive battle ensued in the area between the village of Forbelet and the fortress of Belvoir.[247] Saladin thereupon instructed his brother, al-ʿĀdil, whom he had left in charge of Egypt, to assemble and dispatch a fleet to Beirut and to lead his armies into the southern areas of the Kingdom of Jerusalem around Gaza, Ascalon, and Darum.

---

[244] William of Tyre, *op. cit.*, pp. 1087-88

[245] Ibn al-Athīr, *K.—A.*, p. 651; Abou Chamah, *op. cit.*, pp. 217-18; Makrizi, *op. cit.*, pp. 547-48; Behâ Ed-Dîn, *Anecdotes*, p. 68 and *Saladin*, p. 81.

[246] William of Tyre, *op. cit.*, pp. 1088-89 and chap. xv, pp. 1090-92; Abou Chamah, *op. cit.*, p. 218; Ibn al-Athīr, *K.—A.*, pp. 651-52.

[247] William of Tyre, chap. xvi, *op. cit.*, pp. 1092-95; Ibn al-Athīr, *K.-A.*, pp. 652-53; Makrizi, *op. cit.*, p. 549; Abou Chamah, *op. cit.*, pp. 218-22.

THE CONSOLIDATION OF SALADIN'S MOSLEM EMPIRE

This operation had as its aim the division of the Frankish forces between the defense of Beirut, on the one hand, and that of the Franco-Egyptian frontier, on the other, to enable him, Saladin, to assault Beirut more effectively. And so the plan was carried out. Saladin's land forces, operating in conjunction with the Egyptian fleet, invested Beirut in early August, 1182, whereupon the Franks, who had retired to Saffūrīyah after their inconclusive battle with Saladin, mustered their forces and advanced on Tyre by land, where orders were issued to the Frankish fleet lying at Tyre and Acre to aid the besieged at Beirut. But Saladin withdrew both his land and naval units from Beirut after a vigorous assault of three days and retired across the Euphrates, whereupon the Franks returned to Saffūrīyah. That he did not seriously intend to capture the seaport is indicated by his lack of siege equipment.[248]

The first eight months of the year 1182 had been, on balance, a period of victory for Saladin. Important Frankish bastions had been captured, Frankish man power had suffered considerable attrition, and last, but by no means least, Saladin had reappeared in the Syrian scene with fresh prestige, powers, and influence. Moreover, all his earlier victories over the Franks were soon to be overshadowed by far by those he scored against his Moslem rivals. His scorn for the military strength of his Frankish foemen was seen in his refusal to enter into either a truce or treaty with them.[249] His overweening self-confidence vis-à-vis his northeastern Moslem opponents was now reflected in a new campaign against them during the September, 1182-August, 1183 period which resulted in the capture of the great north Mesopotamian towns of Edessa, Nisibin, and Harran in September and October, 1182 which had been formerly owned by his rival, the prince of Mosul. Still other cities and their dependent towns constituting in their totality almost the entire region once held by that prince fell into his power through bribery or the use of armed force. And that increasingly

---

[248] William of Tyre, chaps. xvii-xviii, *op. cit.*, pp. 1096-1101; Kamal-Ad-Dîn, *Histoire* IV, 159-60; Ibn al-Athīr, *K.—A.*, p. 653; Abou Chamah, *op. cit.*, p. 223. The respective claims of the first two cited historians that (1) Saladin had raised the siege of Beirut because of receipt of news that the Frankish armies were fully prepared and would arrive in three days and that (2) Saladin raised the siege because the mustering of the Frankish forces obliged him to lift the siege are ruled out not only by the consideration of lack of siege equipment but also by the apt observation of Abou Chamah: "... il [Saladin] vit que les opérations devant Beyrout demanderaient du temps, et que d'ailleurs la flotte avait ravagé la côte, fait des prisonniers et enlevé autant de butin qu'elle en voulait."

[249] William of Tyre, chaps. xix and xx, *op. cit.*, pp. 1101 and 1102.

luckless prince almost died of a poisoned draught administered by one of Saladin's agents.[250]

For the moment Saladin's hope of gaining Aleppo as well seemed doomed to disappointment. The death of the young Aleppan prince aṣ-Ṣāliḥ on December 4, 1181 and his successful prior delegation of his now vacated post to his cousin ʿIzz-ad-Dīn of Mosul[251] augured ill for his ambitious plans. To meet this unexpected turn of events, Saladin, who was in Egypt at this time, wrote to his nephew, the prince of Hamah, as well as other Moslem leaders and instructed them to prepare for all eventualities. At the same time he wrote to the caliph to request the sovereignty of the Aleppan land.[252] These moves on Saladin's part proved to be forehanded in effect, for ʿIzz-ad-Dīn, fearing hostilities with Saladin, had entered into an agreement on February 27, 1182 with his brother ʿImād-ad-Dīn, the ruler of Sinjar, providing that he, ʿIzz-ad-Dīn, should take over the city of Sinjar, while his brother took possession of Aleppo. The agreement was soon executed with an agent of each brother taking over the respective city. ʿImād-ad-Dīn entered the citadel of Aleppo on May 19, 1182.[253] And as events were soon to show, ʿImād-ad-Dīn counted less as an enemy in Saladin's eyes than did his brother.

Saladin now learned that agents under the direction of the authorities in Mosul were in communication with the Franks and were

---

[250] *Ibid.*, chap. xix, pp. 1101-02; Kamal-Ad-Dîn, *Histoire*, IV, 161-62; Ibn al-Athīr, *K.–A.*, p. 655; Babcock and Krey, *op. cit.*, p. 481, n. 44; Grousset, *Histoire*, p. 713

[251] Makrizi, *op. cit.*, p. 545; *The Chronography of Bar Hebraeus*, p. 311; Behâ Ed-Dîn, *Anecdotes*, pp. 66-67 and *Saladin*, pp. 79-80; Ibn al-Athīr, *K.-A.*, pp. 647-48; Kamal-Ad-Dîn, *Histoire*, IV, 154-55; William of Tyre, *op. cit.*, p. 1101; Michael the Syrian, chap. ii, *Chronique*, p. 389; Babcock and Krey, *op. cit.*, pp. 457-58, n. 24. Lane-Poole (*op. cit.*, p. 165) sees in aṣ-Ṣāliḥ's transfer of his power to ʿIzz-ad-Dīn the calculation that he was "... the only prince of the house of Zengy powerful enough to cross swords with its great supplanter. The dying youth could not forgive Saladin his trespass against the sovereign rights of the dynasty."

[252] Makrizi, *op. cit.*, pp. 545-46.

[253] Behâ Ed-Dîn, *Anecdotes*, pp. 67-68 and *Saladin*, pp. 80-81; *The Chronography of Bar Hebraeus*, pp. 311-12; Michael the Syrian, *Chronique, loc. cit.* Makrizi (*op. cit.*, p. 545) observes that Saladin made a truce with an ambassador of Count Raymond. Stevenson (*op. cit.*, p. 223, n. 2) states that "Possibly this agreement was a direct result of the quarrel spoken of above." [the rebuff made to Count Raymond in his proposed visit to Jerusalem in the Spring of 1182 (*supra*, pp. 94-95)]. I think that it can be equally argued that Saladin wanted peaceful relations with the Franks to forestall during his absence in the Damascus-Aleppo theatre a flanking operation on their part to cut his line of communications with Egypt, for the language of Makrizi —"Le sultan conclut une trêve avec l'ambassadeur du comte, roi des Francs à Tarābolos (Tripoli de Syrie)"— gives no clue as to which side initiated the negotiations which culminated in the truce.

endeavoring to bring them to war on himself. This development afforded Saladin an opportunity to unite the Moslems in a *jihad*. ʿImād-ad-Dīn's ensuing attempt to obtain help from Mosul gave Saladin the excuse to depart from Damascus and to advance on Aleppo, his alleged objective. At the same time he negotiated with other Moslem leaders, notably those in Bagdad and Harran, to create an anti-Frankish, anti-Mosul coalition. After a short pause before Aleppo in late September, 1182, he crossed the Euphrates and successively captured Edessa and Nisibin, which had meanwhile passed once more into the hands of his Moslem antagonists, and then ʿAzāz, Buzāʿah, Kafarlāthā, Sarūj, Raqqa, Sinjar, and Amida. Only Mosul succeeded in escaping capture. He also received acknowledgment from the several Moslem emirs of their vassalage to him during the course of the ensuing winter of 1182-1183 and the spring of 1183.[254]

With the gaining of the several emirates and cities sympathethic to ʿImād-ad-Dīn's views now an accomplished fact, Saladin turned on Aleppo and subjected it to a vigorous siege on May 21, 1183, which continued to the following June 11. ʿImād-ad-Dīn, recognizing the futility of further resistance, surrendered the city on June 12, 1183 in exchange for Saladin's prizes of the cities of Sinjar, Sarūj, Nisibin, and Raqqa, and the district of Khabur.[255] Saladin rounded out and completed his sweep of the north Syrian emirates and the defeat of his Moslem foemen a few days later with the capture of Ḥārim on June 24 from its recalcitrant commander, who had earlier spurned Saladin's overtures to surrender in return for handsome prizes and even negotiated with the Franks to gain their aid against Saladin.[256] The two horns of the Moslem crescent, Egypt and North Syria, were now firmly in the Sultan's grasp, Moslem unity after nearly a century of disunity was now at hand, and the prospects for the Franks boded ill. And,

---

[254] Kamal-Ad-Dîn, *Histoire*, IV, 160-63; Ibn al-Athīr, *K. — A.*, 654-57; Makrizi, *op. cit.*, pp. 549-50; Behâ Ed-Dîn, *Anecdotes*, pp. 68-70 and *Saladin*, pp. 81-86; Abou Chamah, *op. cit.*, pp. 222-30; *The Chronography of Bar Hebraeus*, p. 313.

[255] Kamal-Ad-Dîn, *Histoire*, IV, 164-67; *The Chronography of Bar Hebraeus*, pp. 315-16; William of Tyre, chap. xxiv, *op. cit.*, pp. 1113-14; Ibn al-Athīr, *K. — A.*, pp. 661-62 and *Atabecs*, pp. 333-34; Behâ Ed-Dîn, *Anecdotes*, pp. 71-73 and *Saladin*, pp. 86-87; Makrizi, *Histoire d'Égypte*, trans. and ed. by Edgar Blochet, *Revue de l'orient latin* (Paris, 1902), IX, 7. (Henceforth references to this source will pertain to Volume IX in the *Revue de l'orient latin* except in two citations wherein references will pertain to Volume VIII. In these citations the Roman numeral VIII will be used).

[256] Abou Chamah, *op. cit.*, pp. 235-38; Behâ Ed-Dîn, *Anecdotes*, p. 73 and *Saladin*, p. 88; Ibn al-Athīr, *K. — A.*, p. 662; *The Chronography of Bar Hebraeus*, p. 316; William of Tyre, chap. xix, *op. cit.*, pp. 1101-02; Babcock and Krey, *op. cit.*, p. 481, n. 44.

worst of all, the leader of this new and hard won unity, Saladin, was far superior to any of his predecessors such as Zengi and Nūr-ad-Dīn in his implacable resolves, programs, and superior competence to reap abundant harvest from the errors and disunity of his Frankish opponents.[257]

---

[257] See Stevenson, *op. cit.*, pp. 230-31 for an appraisal of the problems facing the Franks on the morrow of Saladin's triumph over his Moslem opponents and Lane-Poole, *op. cit.*, pp. 173-74 for an analysis of the reasons why this triumph necessitated still further military actions on Saladin's part against the Franks. Archer and Kingsford (*op. cit.*, p. 260) and Grousset (*Histoire*, p. 721) respectively well summarize the significance of Saladin's conquest of Aleppo: "This conquest (June 12, 1183) marks the consolidation of Saladin's power; he was now beyond all dispute the head power in the Mohammedan world, and might bend his undivided energies towards the great work of his life—the expulsion of the Franks from the Holy City." "De fait la conquête d'Alep par Saladin, en supprimant le dernier État musulman rival, consommait l'unité égypto-syrienne depuis les confins de l'Abyssinie jusqu'au Taurus et au Diyârbékir. Les colonies franques encerclées se trouvaient, selon la formule de *l'Eracles*, désormais en état de siège."

CHAPTER TEN

THE FRANKISH RESPONSE
TO SALADIN'S CHALLENGE: THE DAMASCUS, RED SEA,
AND ṢAFFŪRĪYAH CAMPAIGNS AND LIMITED ECONOMIC
AND MILITARY DEFENSE MEASURES

Meanwhile (August, 1182-June, 1183) the Franks had retaliated but in an ineffective and uncoordinated fashion. The earlier attack of al-ʿAdīl in August, 1182 on Darum was followed by a second inconclusive Franco-Egyptian engagement in the same theatre during the following Spring.[258] The central area was rather the main theatre, for triple circumstances urged the Franks to strike at Damascus. These were (1) Saladin's open contempt for the Franks, (2) his preoccupation with trans-Euphratean areas and problems, which were seemingly accentuated by reports of anti-Saladin activities on the part of his enemies, resulting in a dearth of defenders, and (3) the death of his highly trusted representative in Damascus, ʿIzz-ad-Dīn, in September, 1182 and his ensuing replacement by Shams ad-Din ibn al-mukaddem.[259] Accordingly, they entered the district of Syria Minor, of which Damascus was the capital, and destroyed many of the satellite towns around Damascus. The dearth of water coupled with the Moslems' successful salvaging of some of their already harvested grain precluded much further military activity. The small Moslem defending force elected not to come to grips with the invaders and confined itself largely to observation.[260] Although only modest results attended this invasion, a greater prize was soon to be made with the recovery of the fortress of Ḥabīs Jaldak in October, 1182 after an investment of three weeks during their return through the as-Sawād district.[261] A second blow at Damascus followed in December, 1182 with a combined infantry and cavalry force crossing the Jordan River at Jacob's Ford and striking at Dāraiyā and outlying villages while *en route* to

---

[258] Abou Chamah, *op. cit.*, p. 239; Makrizi, *op. cit.*, pp. 6-7.

[259] Ibn al-Athīr, *K. — A.*, pp. 659-60; Behâ Ed-Dîn, *Anecdotes*, p. 68 and *Saladin*, p. 82; William of Tyre, chaps. xix-xx, *op. cit.*, pp. 1101-02.

[260] William of Tyre, chap. xx, *op. cit.*, pp. 1103-04.

[261] *Ibid.*, chap. xxi, *op. cit.*, pp. 1104-07. See Fedden and Thomson, *op. cit.*, pp. 59-60 for discerning observations on the "castle mentality" afflicting both the Franks and the Moslems and contributing to the Frankish loss and later recovery of Ḥabīs Jaldak.

Damascus. But the blow at Damascus itself proved abortive, for Turkish forces issuing forth from Damascus itself and stationing themselves before the surrounding orchards proved themselves, despite their failure to attack the invaders, formidable enough to deter effectively a Frankish attack. Meanwhile, Turkish cavalrymen cut down incautious Frankish foragers and stragglers. The result of this second invasion was entirely negative, for the Franks returned home empty handed. Damascus still stood as a Moslem bastion.[262]

Likewise ineffective proved to be the single example of a new strategy evolved toward the end of 1182 in a heretofore unexploited theatre of warfare, namely the Red Sea, by Reginald of Châtillon. Irked by the harassments of the Moslem forces stationed at Ailah who were protected by their location at the head of the Gulf of Akabah, an arm of the Red Sea, he evolved a daring scheme of transporting parts of ships on camels to the Red Sea, assembling them, and attacking Ailah and other Moslem cities nearby. Two of these ships were detailed to blockade Ailah, while the remainder of his fleet set sail to the region of Hejaz and the several holy cities in Arabia, attacking and burning sixteen Moslem ships and capturing a caravan. Aroused by this menace, al-ʿĀdil met it by assembling a fleet of his own in the Red Sea and by launching a counter stroke. A naval engagement ending in a Moslem victory soon followed. Frankish sea power was swept from the Red Sea and the Franks fleeing inland from the Red Sea were captured in February, 1183.[263]

The indifferent successes of the Franks in the Damascus theatre and their outright failure in that of the Red Sea had their counterpart in

---

[262] William of Tyre, chap. xxii, op. cit., pp. 1108-09; Ibn al-Athīr, K.—A., p. 655. Grousset (Histoire, p. 719) cogently observes that "Il est impossible de ne pas considérer ces expéditions répétées en terre damasquine comme une diversion pour dégager Mossoul et Alep. Au témoignage d'Ibn al-Athîr lorsque Saladin, qui assiégeait alors Nisîbîn au fond de la Jazîra, apprit l'arrivée des Francs devant Damas, plusieurs de ses émirs lui conseillèrent de rentrer séance tenante en Syrie. Il répondit en substance que les ravages des Francs resteraient assez limités, tandis que, s'il arrivait à absorber les possessions zengides, il aurait ensuite plus de force pour se retourner contre eux. Cependant il n'est pas douteux que la diversion franque avait joué son rôle, à côté de l'intervention du Shâh-Armen et des Ortoqides de Mârdîn et de la médiation du khalife de Baghdâd, dans la résolution que prit Saladin d'abandonner ou d'ajourner la conquête de Mossoul et d'Alep. En intervenant ainsi pour sauver la dynastie zengide, Baudouin IV et son cousin Raymond III de Tripoli s'étaient une fois de plus montrés fidèles aux traditions de la dynastie hiérosolymitaine, à la grande politique indigène de leurs prédécesseurs: protection des émirats musulmans secondaires contre les sultanats hégémoniques."

[263] Abou Chamah, op. cit., pp. 230-35; Abū'l-Fidā, op. cit., pp. 51-52; Chronique d'Ernoul, pp. 69-70; Ibn al-Athīr, K.-A., pp. 658-59; Makrizi, op. cit., VIII, 550-52.

the north as well. The burgeoning power and prestige of Saladin were reflected in the decision of Bohemond III, the ruler of Antioch, even after a conference with King Baldwin IV in quest of aid against Saladin resulted in the grant to him of a force of three hunderd knights, to surrender his Moslem prisoners to Saladin and to seek a temporary truce with him.[264] And apprehension over his future relations with Saladin with all the attendant possibilities of an expensive war certainly figured in Bohemond III's decision shortly thereafter to exchange the city of Tarsus, the capital of Cilicia, with Roupen III, the Armenian prince, for a large sum of money.[265]

In a manner strangely paralleling in many ways that of the beleaguered democracies seven and one-half centuries later, the Latins viewed with growing dismay the waxing power of Saladin, fearful that he would employ it against them. Accordingly, a general assembly of all the barons in the realm was held in Jerusalem in February, 1183 to discuss the problem and devise methods of resistance. The result of their several deliberations and discussions was a decision to take a census of all the lands of the realm to the end of obtaining the requisite infantry and cavalry forces to meet a renewed Moslem invasion. Furthermore, it was agreed that four men of discretion should be charged with the task of laying a graduated tax ranging from a raboin up to two besants on every hundred besants of wealth based upon or derived from land, rent, and wages on all classes, male and female, lay and clerical alike. The moneys thus collected from the cities in the Haifa-Jerusalem district were to be brought to Jerusalem and to be placed in a chest guarded by three locks and three keys in the respective possession of the Patriarch of Jerusalem, the prior of the canons of the Sepulchre of the Lord, the four citizens named above, and the castellan. In like manner the Archbishop of Tyre, the Seneschal Joscelyn III, and the four assessors of Acre were to be the respective key holders of the three locks of the chest placed in Acre and into which contributions from citizens in the cities from Haifa to Beirut were to flow. All such taxes were earmarked solely for the defense of the land, should be levied only once, and were not to be regarded as a precedent for the future.[266] These preparations together with a

---

[264] Abou Chamah, *op. cit.*, p. 239; William of Tyre, chap. xxiv, *op. cit.*, p. 1114; Michael the Syrian, *Extrait*, p. 393.

[265] William of Tyre, *op. cit.*, pp. 1114-15; Michael the Syrian, *Extrait*, pp. 393-94 and n. 1, p. 394.

[266] William of Tyre, chap. xxiii, *op. cit.*, pp. 1109-12; Röhricht, *Regesta*, No. 622, p.

strengthening of the fortifications of the cities and towns of the Kingdom of Jerusalem, especially those situated along the enemy's borders during the Spring of 1183 constituted the Franks' total economic and military preparations to, and response and understanding of, the awesome and ominous meaning of the addition of Aleppo to Saladin's empire.[267] And as was to be the case during the 1930's when half hearted measures of defense were similarly undertaken, so in the 1180's the total magnitude of the problem was not comprehended.[268]

The Moslems' blow fell soon. Advancing out of Aleppo on August 10, 1183, Saladin reached Damascus ten days later where he paused for a time to gather his forces. Then at the close of September he crossed the Jordan, captured and burned the deserted city of Baisan, and encamped at ʿAin Jālūt. A clash with the Franks soon followed, for a contingent of Moslem scouts dispatched to spy on the Franks met Frankish forces from Krak and ash-Shaubak moving up to reenforce the main army. The ensuing battle ended with many Franks killed and captured on September 30, 1183.[269]

Meanwhile a very large Frankish army comprising the forces of the Kingdom of Jerusalem as well as those of the prince of Antioch and the count of Tripoli and totaling 1,300 cavalry and over 15,000 infantry and commanded by notable soldiers such as Count Raymond of Tripoli, Godfrey III, Duke of Brabant, Ralph de Mauleon, an Aquitanian warrior of great renown, as well as the several barons of the Kingdom of Jerusalem, namely the Seneschal Joscelyn III, Guy of Lusignan, the Count of Jaffa, Reginald of Châtillon, Reginald of Sidon, Baldwin of Ramla, his brother Balian of Ibelin, and Walter of Caesarea had concentrated at Ṣaffūrīyah to meet the enemy. This

---

165. La Monte (*Feudal Monarchy*, p. 181, n. 1) declares that "... the besants meant are gold besants as the raboin was worth a third or a fourth of a gold besant."

[267] William of Tyre, chap. xxiv, *op. cit.*, p. 1114.

[268] Cf. the illuminating analysis of Stevenson (*loc. cit.*) with the changing positions of power of the victors and the vanquished in World War I in the 1920's, on the one hand, and the 1930's, on the other. La Monte (*Feudal Monarchy*, p. 38) draws a striking analogy between the Kingdom of Jerusalem in this hour of crisis with Russia on the eve of the Mongol conquest. "Russia on the eve of the Mongol conquest is not more pathetic than the little Latin kingdom, cowering in the shadow of great Saladin's advance, yet unable to put a stop to the petty rivalries and constant internal bickerings which divided the councils and prevented all coöperation among the lords whose every effort should have been directed towards holding in check the Moslem power."

[269] Kamal-Ad-Dîn, *Histoire*, IV, 169; William of Tyre, chap. xxvi, *op. cit.*, pp. 1118-19; Ibn al-Athîr, *K. – A.*, p. 663; Abou Chamah, *op. cit.*, pp. 242-48; Makrizi, *op. cit.*, pp. 8-9; Behâ Ed-Dîn, *Saladin*, pp. 88-90 and *Anecdotes*, pp. 73-75.

force, the largest ever assembled thus far in the history of the crusading states, was further augmented by north Italian sailors, namely Pisans, Genoese, Venetians, and Lombards, and the pilgrims whom they had brought to the Holy Land. The Franks now abandoned Saffūrīyah and encamped at al-Fūlah. The opposing forces were now within a mile of each other. But despite their imposing strength, the Franks did not attack and decided to entrench themselves on the hills. The Moslems sought to entice the enemy into offensive actions by repeated archery assaults, but the Franks refused to budge. After a week of extensive pillaging and plundering of the surrounding villages and failure to draw their entrenched opponents into battle, the Moslems, pressed by their growing shortage of food, decided to withdraw after eight days on October 6, 1183. The Franks then returned to Saffūrīyah.[270]

[270] William of Tyre, pp. 1119-20 and chaps. xxiv, xxvi, and xxvii, *op. cit.*, pp. 1115 and 1121-24; Ibn al-Athīr, *K.–A*, pp. 663-64; Behâ Ed-Dîn, *Anecdotes*, p. 75 and *Saladin*, pp. 90-91; Abou Chamah, *op. cit.*, pp. 243-48; Kamal-Ad-Dîn, *Histoire*, IV, 169-70; *Chronique d'Ernoul*, chap. ix, pp. 97-102; Grousset, *Histoire*, p. 725, n. 1. The Latin and Moslem accounts give varying accounts and explanations for the Franks' inactions. William of Tyre ascribes them to dissension among the Frankish leaders arising, at least in part, over a feeling of hostility towards Guy of Lusignan, the Count of Jaffa, who had recently been given charge of the Kingdom of Jerusalem by King Baldwin IV. See *infra*, p. 118. Many felt that such an important post should not be given to an obscure personage. If a battle should be fought and won by the Franks, the victory would be ascribed to the Count of Jaffa. It is clear from William of Tyre's account that he believes this is the reason, although he does offer an alternate explanation to the effect that no attack was made because Saladin's forces were so firmly entrenched as to make an attack on his lines extremely dangerous. William clearly shows his lack of sympathy for this explanation in his observation. Behâ Ed-Dîn and Ibn al-Athīr explain the Franks' inactivity on the ground that the Moslems were too numerous, whereas Abou Chamah views it somewhat differently: "... mais ils [the Franks] s'y refusèrent, effrayés qu'ils étaient par le nombre considérable des troupes musulmans." Kamal-Ad-Dîn offers no explanation for the Franks' inaction, contenting himself merely with the observation that "... mais les Francs ne firent aucun mouvement pour se dégager des Musulmans..." But all accounts agree that dearth of supplies prompted Saladin's decision to withdraw. *Chronique d'Ernoul* (pp. 97-98) gives a varying account to the effect that when King Baldwin IV heard reports that Saladin was preparing to invade the Kingdom of Jerusalem, he assembled all his forces and encamped at Saffūrīyah as the spot enabling them best to meet the enemy upon his entrance. The Franks remained at Saffūrīyah for three months. This version is seriously defective in respect to the bickering in the Frankish camp and the supply situation. It seems highly unlikely that proponents of an activist offensive military program such as Reginald of Châtillon, Balian of Ramlah, and Balian of Nablus would have tolerated such a long defensive posture. Secondly, in view of the limited output of food, services, and supplies in a medieval economy, it seems unlikely that a force as large as that described by William of Tyre and, while not specifically enumerated by Ernoul still stated implicitly to be a very large force indeed—"A ces fontaines sejournoit li rois les estés quant il n'avoit les trives as Sarrasin, et il et si chevalier et Templier et Hospitalier, et tout li baron de le

However petty or ignoble or, conversely, strategically sound the motives for the Franks' policy of not attacking Saladin may have been, the end result was a salutary one, for it had obliged Saladin to retreat. But not for long was the Kingdom of Jerusalem spared his attentions. Very possibly aware of the political dissensions in the Franks' ranks, he paused only briefly at Damascus to which he had repaired on October 13 after his recent withdrawal[271] and nine days later he struck southward at the great fortress of Krak on the Dead Sea.[272] The attack

---

tiere"—could have been maintained for a period as long as three months in one spot. Babcock and Krey (*op. cit.*, p. 497, n. 53), in commenting on William's account of the dissension within the ranks of the Franks, observe "It must be noted that William is here criticizing his own friends. Apparently he considers the needs of the nation as transcending the interest of faction, even his own." Collins (*op. cit.*, p. 228) believes that Saladin "... might have ... been greatly harassed, if not totally routed, had the Christians behaved with unanimity and common resolution." Baldwin ("The Decline," p. 600), while pointing out that William of Tyre did not accept the first of the two following explanations concerning the campaign of 1183, does believe that this explanation, as well as the other one advanced by William, merits support. "There are two possible explanations of the campaign of 1183. One, which has been developed at some length, approves the crusaders' strategy and further insists that they did precisely what they should have done four years later at Hattin. The campaign was, in this view, a success. The limited Christian forces had not been depleted; yet Saladin had been forced to withdraw. No such interpretation was accepted by the contemporary historian, William of Tyre. Although he cautiously disclaims more than hearsay information and admits that a difficult military situation existed, he strongly intimates that personal quarrels immobilized this great Christian army. A number of barons, he suggests, were unwilling to have Guy, whose *bailliage* they opposed, receive the credit for a victory. Hence a glorious opportunity was wasted. Probably there is truth in both explanations. The waiting strategy had succeeded in frustrating a possible attack. Moreover, it must be remembered that Saladin's control over the disparate elements of the Moslem Levant was recently won and depended on constant vigilance and continued success. Armies could not be kept in the field indefinitely. Soldiers were also farmers and merchants and had to return to their fields and shops. On the other hand, it is possible that Saladin could better afford to be patient than the crusaders. Certainly his strength remained undiminished during the subsequent critical years." Castle (*op. cit.*, pp. 21-22) has appraised Guy's rôle as a general as follows: "... the course of the [Ṣaffūrīah] campaign itself is evidence of Guy's failure as a commander. In the first place Guy did not adequately attend to the material needs of his army. His want of foresight in this respect, to which may be ascribed the near-famine at Tubania, was later to destroy the power of the army at Hittin. Secondly, he lacked the moral force to abide by a decision regardless of the fluctuating opinions of his advisers; on this account he lost his opportunity for attack on October 5 ..." ...."Finally, we may be justified in saying that Guy was presented with a challenge and an opportunity which an abler man faced by a similar situation might have utilized to good purpose, but which Guy let slip from his hands."

[271] Kamal-Ad-Dîn, *Histoire*, IV, 170; Behâ Ed-Dîn, *Anecdotes*, p. 76 and *Saladin*, p. 91; *The Chronography of Bar Hebraeus*, *loc. cit.*

[272] Kamal-Ad-Dîn, *Histoire*, *loc. cit.*; Makrizi, *op. cit.*; p. 9; Ibn al-Athīr, *K.–A.*, p. 664; Abou Chamah, *op. cit.*, p. 248; *The Chronography of Bar Hebraeus*, *loc. cit.*

was made in conjunction with the forces of al-ʿĀdil, Saladin's brother; the latter's support had been enlisted by the sultan. The investment, which was begun around November 1 under Saladin, became ever more pressing and grievous for the hard pressed Frankish defenders, partly because of the new strength added to the besiegers' power with the arrival of al-ʿĀdil's forces on November 22, partly because of the intensity of the fire of Saladin's siege machinery consisting of eight siege engines. The defenders, despite their strongly fortified castle walls, were handicapped by the presence of great numbers of non-combatants of both sexes, notably actors and performers who had repaired to the castle in preparation for the forthcoming wedding of Humphrey IV, the stepson of Reginald, to Isabel, the half sister of King Baldwin IV. Still other noncombatants were Syrian refugees who had fled to Krak for protection on Saladin's approach. All these groups were a marked hindrance and obstruction to the defense force. Only the intervention of a Frankish relief force could save the day and such a force could be assembled only if the factional strife in the Kingdom of Jerusalem could be abated. Finally this desideratum was achieved and a relieving force under the command of Count Raymond arrived on December 4, 1183. Convinced of the strength and power of this force, Saladin raised the siege and returned to Damascus with his brother al-ʿĀdil on December 12, 1183.[273]

Chronique d'Ernoul, p. 103; William of Tyre, chap. xxviii, *op. cit.*, p. 1124; Behâ Ed-Dîn, *Anecdotes, loc. cit.* and *Saladin*, pp. 91-92.

[273] William of Tyre, pp. 1124-26 and chap. xx, *op. cit.*, pp. 1129-30; Ibn al-Athīr, *K.–A., loc. cit.*; Behâ Ed-Dîn, *Anecdotes*, pp. 76-77 and *Saladin*, p. 92; Abou Chamah, *loc. cit.*; Kamal-Ad-Dîn, *Histoire, loc. cit.*; Makrizi, *loc. cit.*; *The Chronography of Bar Hebraeus, loc. cit.*; *Chronique d'Ernoul*, pp. 103-06.

CHAPTER ELEVEN

THE TRIUMPH OF THE NATIVE NOBLES: THE FALL OF GUY OF LUSIGNAN AND THE RISE OF RAYMOND OF TRIPOLI

Meanwhile, the internal weaknesses of the Kingdom of Jerusalem had contributed in the most major way to Saladin's growing list of triumphs during 1183. On the eve of the military stalemate in October of that year the King's leprosy, which was now so acute as to deprive him of sight as well as the use of his limbs, became accentuated by fever. Despairing of his life, Baldwin IV summoned the nobles of the Kingdom together and, in their presence and that of his mother, Agnes, and the Patriarch, appointed his brother-in-law, Guy, the Count of Jaffa and Ascalon, as regent. But the ailing king retained his title as well as the city of Jerusalem together with an annual revenue of 10,000 gold pieces. The barons as well as others of the King's subjects obeyed his command that they acknowledge themselves as vassals of Guy and swear fealty to him. Guy, to whom Baldwin IV now committed the general administration of the entire Kingdom, is said to have pledged, in accordance with the King's command, that during the remainder of the King's life he would not seek the crown himself and would not grant to others or alienate from the treasury any of the castles and cities then possessed by the King. Furthermore, as the report ran, Guy was obliged to take this oath before all the barons that he would execute these agreements.[274]

---

[274] William of Tyre, chap. xxv, *op. cit.*, pp. 1116-17. This Latin historian presents a revealing commentary on the political trends and atmosphere of the time in his observations on this episode. "It is believed that this [the promise that as long as King Baldwin IV lived, he, Guy, would not aspire to the crown and would not transfer to others or alienate from the treasury any of the cities and castles at that time in the possession of the king] was enjoined upon Guy with the most careful forethought and purpose and that he was obliged to bind himself by an oath in the presence of all the barons that he would faithfully observe that stipulation. For he had promised almost all the most important lords of the realm individually no slight portions of the kingdom in order to secure their votes and interest in obtaining his end. It was even rumored that he had taken a similar oath to these lords that he would carry out his promises. This can not be stated as a fact, for we have no definite information on the matter, but constant rumors to this effect were in circulation among the people." As Castle (*op. cit.*, p. 18, n. 1) correctly observes, "If the rumor that Guy had made previous bids for support could be proven true, the later hostility toward Guy might in some measure be

These developments, which were so manifestly to the interest of and advantage to the court party, stirred up considerable controversy. Some objected because of their own private reasons and personal interests, whereas others doubted Guy's competence to shoulder such great responsibility involving the affairs of the Kingdom. Those who hoped and believed that Guy would measure up effectively to the challenge were speedily to be undeceived, for the post to which he had aspired soon proved to be one to which he was unequal.[275] And as we have already noted,[276] the military stalemate itself may very well have resulted, at least in part, from jealousy of Guy.[277]

But the dissatisfaction with Guy during the military stalemate of October, 1183 was as nothing compared to that which followed. Believing that Guy's military leadership was unsatisfactory and that

---

accounted for." Babcock and Krey, *op. cit.*, p. 493, n. 50. Baldwin (*Raymond III*, p. 51) summarizes succintly and effectively the significance of these developments as follows: "The nomination of Guy [for the regency] together with the fact that the chronicler takes pains to mention the king's mother and the patriarch as witnesses, is evidence that the "court party," or at least three members of it, still exercised control over the king. It is not unlikely that others helped to bring pressure to bear on the king in his weakness. In any case the members of this group had now achieved what we may suppose to have been their great ambition. Guy, their own candidate, was now procurator and in line for the succession to the throne. The very fact that he was required to take an oath not to aspire to the crown as long as Baldwin lived may be interpreted as indicating that such aspirations might be expected afterward. All this had been accomplished in the face of the opposition of a great many of the barons and despite the growing popularity of Raymond of Tripolis. Thus, if our conclusions are correct, we can trace the steadily increasing influence of this "court party" from 1180, when Guy and Sibyl were married, through 1182, when the attempt was made to exclude Raymond from the kingdom, to this occasion in 1183 when Guy was made regent." See Baldwin, *Raymond III*, p. 65 and Herzog, *op. cit.*, pp. 69-70 for scholarly estimates of Guy of Lusignan's character and rôle.

[275] William of Tyre, *op. cit.*, p. 1117. Grousset (*Histoire*, p. 723) judges the situation as follows: "De fait Guy de Lusignan devait se montrer constamment capitaine malheureux et politique médiocre. Mais surtout c'était un nouveau venu, "uns estranges hom," et un homme nouveau, "homo incognitus," qui ne réussit jamais à se faire agréer de la noblesse franque. En dépit de son mariage avec Sibylle de Jérusalem, la continuité dynastique fut, avec lui, brisée. On peut dire sans exagération qu'à partir de 1183 les institutions monarchiques du royaume de Jérusalem cessent pratiquement de fonctionner." Speaking in somewhat similar vein, Schlumberger (*Numismatique*, p. 73) observes that "Grâce peut-être à son manque de capacités administratives et surtout à la haine que lui portait la noblesse, le nouveau régent ne tarda pas à se créer une situation presque impossible, entre le roi, qui ne l'aimait guère, et les barons qui l'exécraient."

[276] *Supra*, n. 270.

[277] Stevenson (*op. cit.*, p. 237) believes that King Baldwin IV "In fact... almost abdicated in Guy's favour and this mortified Raymond and estranged his friends. But Guy was not strong enough to assert his position and this seems to have been the principal cause of the inaction which the Latins displayed on that occasion."

the general conditions of the Kingdom of Jerusalem were now in a lamentable situation because of his poor judgment and inefficiency, the leper King followed the proposal of his wiser counsellors to the effect that he should recover for himself the controls over the Kingdom of Jerusalem which he had granted to Guy. The King's action also sprang from Guy's manifest unwillingness to assent to his recent proposal that he exchange Tyre for Jerusalem on the same revenue basis because Tyre was the best fortified city in the Kingdom of Jerusalem and better suited to his requirements. Furthermore, Guy was now deprived of all hopes of succeeding the King. This was accomplished by the selection on November 20, 1183 of King Baldwin IV's nephew, Baldwin V, the posthumous son of his sister Sibyl and William Longsword and a mere child scarcely five years old, as the new king and by his immediate crowning. The barons, especially Bohemond, prince of Antioch, Raymond, Count of Tripoli, Reginald of Sidon, Baldwin of Ramla, and Balian, his brother, unanimously supported this move. With such support as well as that supplied by the general population and the clergy, Guy, although present at all these developments, did not dare to raise his voice in protest.[278] Here clearly

---

[278] William of Tyre, chap. xxix, *op. cit.*, pp. 1127-28; Michael the Syrian, chap. iii, *Chronique*, p. 394; Ibn al-Athīr, *K. – A.*, p. 674. Richard (*loc. cit.*) considers Guy's refusal to exchange Tyre for Jerusalem as one tantamount to an arrogation of the rôle of the King to himself: "... il [Guy] commit la faute très grave de se comporter en roi malgré son simple titre de bayle..." He also sees (*op. cit.*, pp. 136-37) in King Baldwin IV's tactics towards his royal successor, Baldwin V, a confession of weakness. "Par une innovation aux coutumes du royaume – mesure qui montre combien Baudouin IV sentait le trône peu assuré puisqu'elle rappelle ce que faisaient les premiers Capétiens – il fit associer à la couronne le petit Baudouin V, enfant du premier mariage de Sibylle." Equally calculated as a measure to defeat Guy's policies, Richard (*op. cit.*, p. 137) believes was his immediate celebration of his half sister's marriage to Humphrey IV after a long engagement of three years: "En outre, pour empêcher Guy d'accéder au trône, le roi fit célébrer immédiatement le mariage de son autre soeur Isabelle avec Onfroi IV de Toron, bien que celle-ci n'eût que onze ans (novembre 1183)." Baldwin (*Raymond III*, pp. 54-55), in his assessment of these events, points out the major rôle of the native barons. "The particular mention of Bohemond, Reginald of Sidon, Baldwin of Rama and his brother Balian among those who along with Raymond himself approved the deposition of Guy and the coronation of Baldwin V, is especially significant. With the exception of Humphrey of Toron, now dead, and with the addition of Bohemond, the same native barons had supported Raymond's candidacy for the procuratorship in 1174. Now nine years later, led by Raymond, they had regained the ascendancy lost after 1175, while Baldwin IV had made a definite break with Guy and the "court party" which had supported him. No reason is given for the king's change of front other than his disappointment with Guy, but we may suppose that the native barons were able to exercise their influence in some way, and that they now controlled the *Haute Cour*. As has already been pointed out, they probably were the same men who in 1182 insisted that Raymond be permitted to enter the kingdom, and had since then become

was a victory over the court party. The attitude of the victors was manifestly shown in their subsequent decision, at the time of their immediately following oath of allegiance to the new king, not to ask Guy to do likewise. Yet the new moves by no means guaranteed the defeat of the court party, the victory of its opponents, the ending of factional bickering, and the strengthening of the Kingdom of Jerusalem, for some felt that the new king, Baldwin V, by reason of his extreme youth, was no more competent to rule than the leper King. Hence no benefit to the Kingdom of Jerusalem would result. Others agreed with this view, but also argued that the selection of the boy king at least had this merit, namely that it deprived Guy of all hope of succession to the crown. Therefore, it would be best to have the administration of the royal and state affairs committed to a person

---

increasingly opposed to Guy and the baneful influence of people like Agnes, Joscelin and the patriarch over the king. Their opposition was based partly on jealousy of the power of such people, especially Guy himself, and partly on a genuine solicitude for the welfare of the kingdom. Accepting Raymond as their leader, they honestly felt that he rather than Guy was the person best suited to assume the responsibility for this welfare. At the same time it is not easy to decide whether jealousy of Guy or concern for the best interests of the kingdom was uppermost in these men's minds. Raymond himself must have been provoked especially, since Guy's advancement and claims had directly thwarted his own. And as we have suggested, Baldwin of Rama also probably bore a personal grudge. It also seems likely that the native barons took advantage of Guy's failure as procurator, a failure for which they may have been partially, if not entirely responsible, to recover their own ascendancy over the leper king. In other words they had entered the game of party politics, and by the fall of 1183, had won. Perhaps the modern historian is wiser not to probe the matter too deeply. By this time the best interests of the kingdom pretty clearly coincided with their own personal wishes." Archer and Kingsford (*op. cit.*, p. 267) see in these developments involving Baldwin V the victory of the native nobles. This victory was a revolution. "The revolution which thus transferred the crown to the infant Baldwin V. seems to have been the work of the hereditary nobles of the land, and was chiefly brought about by Baldwin of Ramleh and his brother Balian of Ibelin." Speaking in similar vein, Baldwin (*Raymond III*, pp. 57-58) observes that "... Raymond, who was entitled to the procuratorship as the nearest male relative, and the native barons now in control of the *Haute Cour* and the king took care to preserve their position and prevent the possibility that Guy might become a candidate for the throne. For at least three years and perhaps longer these men had seen the kingdom, which after all was their own, controlled by a group of court intriguers and upstart "foreigners." They were determined, now that they had the opportunity to prevent a recurrence of the same calamity by forestalling such claims as their rivals might bring up." As for Guy's rôle in all these events, Baldwin (*Raymond III*, p. 55) observes that "Nor was he [Guy] entirely to blame. With only half-hearted cooperation from the other barons during that summer [1183] he had hardly had a chance to prove his worth." Castle (*op. cit.*, p. 23) plausibly suggests that "Baldwin's anxiety to have his little nephew crowned during his own lifetime was probably due to his fear of the succession of Guy and Sibylle; for the principle of hereditary succession was by now the rule in the kingdom, and according to the usual laws of inheritance Sibylle would be next in line for the throne."

wise in counsel and strong in war. Others agreed with the proponents of the view that Baldwin V was no more competent than Baldwin IV. The latter group agreed with the former in respect to the desirability of committing the affairs of the realm to the hands of a regent able to handle them efficiently. Such a regent was especially needed in the face of the Moslems' waxing military power. And most believed that Count Raymond was the obvious choice.[279]

This desideratum soon resulted. The hostile relations between Baldwin IV and Guy became so bitter that the former sought early in 1184 to effect an annulment of his sister's marriage to Guy and to that end visited Patriarch Heraclius with a demand that a day be set for the solemn pronouncement of the annulment in the Patriarch's presence.[280] Meanwhile, however, Guy, having returned from his campaign and having been apprised of the new turn of events, took decisive action by his departure from the army, hurried trip to Ascalon, and warning to his wife, Sibyl, who was in Jerusalem at the time, to depart before the arrival of the King, lest the latter, having gained power over her, refuse her permission to return to her husband.[281] Equally decisive were his direct tactics towards the King himself. When the latter sent a messenger with a summons to appear, Guy refused to heed it and pleaded illness for his non appearance. After repeated summonses still failed to secure his obedience, the King took direct action by a journey to Ascalon attended by some of the nobles of his court. Even this did not obtain the compliance of the recalcitrant Count. Baldwin IV beat his fist in vain on the closed gates of the city in full view of the entire citizenry.[282] Pursuant to these developments, the King repaired directly from Ascalon to Jaffa and installed a governor in the latter city to manage its affairs.[283]

The waxing power of Saladin was now so menacing to the very existence of the Kingdom of Jerusalem that Baldwin IV now proceeded to Acre where he called a general assembly of the magnates of the Kingdom to consider a proposal that envoys be sent to obtain the support of foreign kings and princes in the defense of the Kingdom and the Christian faith. But before this matter could be

---

[279] William of Tyre, *op. cit.*, p. 1128.
[280] *Ibid.*, Bk. XXIII, chap. i, *op. cit.*, p. 1133. Babcock and Krey, *op. cit.*, p. 507, n. 11.
[281] William of Tyre, *loc. cit.*; *Eracles*, p. l. Baldwin (*Raymond III*, p. 56) sees in Guy's moves at this time an attempt to safeguard his already impaired position. "But Guy was too clever to submit without protest to any further diminution of his rights."
[282] William of Tyre, *loc. cit.*; *Eracles*, pp. 1-2.
[283] *Eracles*, p. 2.

considered, the secondary problem of Guy's virtually treasonable actions took precedence. Baldwin IV met with his barons and refused to assent, despite their posture of humility in an appearance on bended knees, to the petition made by Patriarch Heraclius and the masters of the Templars and Hospitallers that he abandon his resentment and restore Guy to favor. Thereupon the Patriarch and his supporters indignantly departed not only from the court but from Acre as well. Guy, still insolent, elected, upon hearing of the King's action, to exacerbate still more his relations with him by an attack upon the camp of certain Arabs who were now pasturing their cattle in the vicinity of the fortress of Darum in compliance with a promise of royal protection. Unprepared, as a result, to resist, they were unable to prevent Guy from driving off their cattle and slaves and returning with his plunder to Ascalon.[284]

This final act of defiance brought matters to a head. Baldwin IV reassembled at Acre the general assembly of the baronage, which was still in session at Acre, to secure an assent to his proposal that the general administration of the Kingdom of Jerusalem be entrusted to Count Raymond of Tripoli. A majority of the assembly agreed.[285] Count Raymond consented, but stipulated that, in view of the threatening military situation, he be given the regency for ten years. However, he would not be entrusted with the care of the child king, Baldwin V, in order, in the event that the latter should die during the

---

[284] William of Tyre, *op. cit.*, pp. 1133-34; *Eracles*, pp. 2-3. Baldwin (*Raymond III, loc. cit.*) discerns in the support of Guy by Patriarch Heraclius at this time the possibility of inspiration on the part of the Courtenay faction. "The patriarch, Heraclius, might have been expected to remain faithful to Guy. His conduct was consistent with his actions on previous occasions, and was perhaps prompted by Agnes or Joscelin." Runciman (*History*, pp. 442-43) believes that Guy's resentment over the fact that the payment of a small tax to Baldwin IV by the Bedouin shepherds in return for pasturing rights went to the King rather than himself was a source of annoyance to him and hence led to his attack upon them. See Appendix B for a discussion of disputed datings.

[285] William of Tyre, *op. cit.*, p. 1134; *Chronique d'Ernoul*, chap. x, pp. 115-16. Runciman (*History*, p. 443) believes that King Baldwin IV's selection of Count Raymond as regent resulted from his realization of "... how fatal had been the influence of his mother and her friends..." La Monte ("The rise,"p. 313 and n. 1) has similar viewpoints, believing that the reconciliation between Raymond of Tripoli and Baldwin IV, which is implicit in the appointment of the former to the post of regent, may well have depended on the death of Agnes of Courtenay in this general time period. "Shortly before this, [the death of Baldwin IV in March, 1185] probably around 1183 or 1184, Agnes de Courtenay had also died. As long as she lived she exercized a powerful and on the whole unfortunate influence over her son and her death may very well have coincided with the reconciliation of Baldwin IV with Raymond of Tripoli." .... "She was certainly deceased before February 1185..."

ensuing ten years, to prevent any charge that he, Raymond, was responsible. Furthermore, Raymond stated that all the castles save one must be placed under the supervision of the Templars and Hospitallers to forestall charges that he, Raymond, had evil designs on them; the one exception was to be assigned to him to enable him to defray his expenses. Lastly, if the new child king, Baldwin V, should die during the ensuing decade, he, Raymond, would continue to hold the regency until a committee of the pope, the Holy Roman Emperor, and the kings of France and England ruled on the question which of the two daughters of the late king Amalric should inherit the throne: Sibyl, the elder, who had been born before Amalric became king, or Isabel, the younger, who had been born after her father's assumption of the kingship. The barons agreed to all this. To implement these agreements, the barons assigned Beirut to Raymond with an authorization to garrison it and to receive reimbursements from them for his several expenses incurred as regent. Joscelyn III, the new king's great-uncle, received direct charge of Baldwin V. Finally, Baldwin IV ordered the crowning of his successor and this was now performed at the Church of the Sepulchre in Jerusalem.[286] Thereupon Baldwin IV

---

[286] *Chronique d'Ernoul*, pp. 116-18; *Eracles*, pp. 6-8. King (*op. cit.*, pp. 114-15) and Baldwin (*Raymond III*, p. 58) in their assessments of Raymond's motive in entrusting the care of the castles to the Templars and Hospitallers observe respectively, "To pacify the military Orders and at the regent's request, all royal castles and fortresses were to be placed in the hands of the Hospitallers and Templars." and "Perhaps Raymond also sought in this way to appease the anger of the two masters." Baldwin ("The Decline," p. 602) observes that "These native barons were united in opposition to Guy and his associates for personal reasons and on grounds of public policy. To them, the blooded nobility of the land secure in their ancient fiefs, Guy was an upstart and adventurer whose rise to power aroused a natural jealousy and a fear that continued success might eventually jeopardize their own vested interests. In addition there is reason to believe that these men favored a purely defensive military policy. Certainly this was true of Raymond of Tripoli in 1187. At any rate they were opposed to rash adventures which the "newcomers" with everything to gain and nothing to lose might advocate." And the support of Guy on the part of the masters of the Templars and Hospitallers may very well have resulted in part from the consideration that "... they opposed the conservative military policy of the native barons." Approaching the nature, organization, and aspirations of the rival nobiliary parties from a somewhat different angle, Archer and Kingsford (*op. cit.*, pp. 268-69) state that "Raymond and his party seem to have believed in the impossibility of active resistance to the Saracens. It may be that they were only abiding their time till the coming of a new Crusade should justify them in taking the offensive once more; but so far as the evidence of contemporary writers, both Christian and Arabic goes, they were actually in communication with Saladin, and anxious for a truce which might ensure them their own in safety." .... "The party of the aliens was possibly moved by a more genuine religious enthusiasm. Guy de Lusignan may perhaps have been influenced by merely selfish aims; but selfishness can hardly be predicated of the masters of the Temple and Hospital, and possibly not of Heraclius the Patriarch;

ordered and obtained from the baronage a pledge of homage to his successor, Baldwin V, and to Count Raymond as regent and a promise of help to Count Raymond to maintain the Kingdom of Jerusalem if he, Baldwin V, should die during the next decade.[287]

---

family affection may, however, account for the part played by Joscelin de Courtenay. The members of the two great orders had not entered on their Eastern life in search for ease or luxury; their vows bound them before all else to fight the pagan, and to extend the boundaries of the Lord's kingdom; the very thought of passing long years without striking a blow for Christ was to them insupportable; thus their constant clamour was for war..." See Runciman, *History*, pp. 443-44, n. 2 for a discussion of the legal rights of Sibyl and Isabel to the throne. La Monte (*Feudal Monarchy*, p. 33) believes that the succession arrangements indicated the full recognition by the *Haute Cour* of the principle of hereditary succession: "The delegation of the choice of a successor to the committee of western sovereigns shows that the *Haute Cour* anticipated a disputed succession and did not consider itself competent to decide the matter, which would not have been their attitude had they still maintained their rights of election." Grousset (*Histoire*, p. 743, n. 2) explains the question as to which of Amalric's two daughters should inherit the throne as follows: "Sibylle avait pour elle d'être l'aînée. Mais sa mère avait été répudiée avant l'avènement d'Amaury. Isabelle n'était que la cadette, mais sa mère était reine. D'où l'incertitude du point de droit." Runciman (*History*, p. 443) regards Baldwin IV's selection of Joscelyn III "... who now began to profess a cordial friendship toward Raymond."... as the guardian of the boy king as "... a last attempt to bring the factions together." Oldenbourg (*op. cit.*, p. 412), commenting on the rôle of the Courtenays, Agnes and her brother Joscelyn III, as well as the Lusignans in these developments, observes that "Agnès de Courtenay et sa frère faisaient la loi à la cour, grâce à la faveur du roi. Or, Jocelin III, ce prince déchu de son héritage d'Édesse, était un homme intelligent et énergique, mais terriblement aigri par dix ans de captivité, jaloux de tout et tous, haïssant la noblesse hiérosolymitaine qui n'avait rien voulu faire ni pour son père ni pour lui (il n'avait été libéré que grâce à l'influence de sa soeur), et, semble-t-il, indifférent à la ruine possible du royaume. Il occupait une des plus hautes places à la cour—il avait été nommé sénéchal—et en profitant pour piller sans vergogne le trésor, d'accord avec sa soeur; il ne désirait qu'une chose: obtenir de son neveu la régence au cours de la minorité du futur roi, le petit Baudouin, fils de Sibylle. Cette régence était également convoitée par le nouvel époux de Sibylle, Guy de Lusignan, ou plutôt—par l'entremise de Guy—par le frère de celui-ci, Amaury de Lusignan, récemment nommé connétable. Les deux hommes—Jocelin et Amaury—s'entendaient du reste assez bien dans leur commun désir de faire échec aux prétentions du comte de Tripoli."

[287] *Eracles*, pp. 9-10; *Chronique d'Ernoul*, p. 119. *Chronique d'Amadi* (pp. 50-51) affords a variant and rather suspect version of these arrangements. According to this account, the leper king declared that if his successor Baldwin V died childless, the barons, in the event that they decided to make one of their own grouping the next king, should exclude all but Raymond of Tripoli from their choice. If, on the other hand, they selected a noble from overseas, they should first seek and gain Count Raymond's approval. Such an account presupposes that the ailing king, who now showed a keen perception of the political realities of his time, was unaware, in view of the powerful enemies of Raymond, that such an arrangement might well entail an eventual civil war. Baldwin (*Raymond III*, p. 58, n. 38) rightly observes that "*Eracles*... probably approximates the truth more closely here when he states that Baldwin did not consider Guy capable of governing. Less credible, however, is his assertion that Baldwin did not recognize the claim of Sibyl on account of her illegitimacy. Both Baldwin and Sibyl were

Having disposed of these matters, the Council of Acre then turned its attention to the problems of military defense and at length sent Patriarch Heraclius and the Masters of the Templar and Hospitaller orders in the Spring of 1184 to England to implore assistance from the

---

children of Amalric and Agnes of Courtenay by a marriage later declared void, but on condition that the children be considered legitimate".... "If there had been any doubt about Sibyl, it would presumably have been mentioned before." La Monte (*Feudal Monarchy*, p. 52 and nn. 1 and 2, p. 52), in explaining the governmental procedure pertaining to the bailli and bailliage in the Kingdom of Jerusalem, also reveals why Count Raymond and Jocelyn III were given their respective rôles as bailli of the Kingdom of Jerusalem and guardian of the infant king. "Until the heir should have come of age the regent exercised the royal powers. As we have seen the bailliage was given to the closest heir on that side of the family through which the throne escheated. If there was no apparent relative who could claim the bailliage, the *Haute Cour* elected a bailli; or if there were too many relatives the court decided which was to have the charge. The custody of the heir was not given to the bailli, but to the closest relative on that side of the family through which the throne did not escheat, though there were several times when this rule was violated. The principle behind this was that the bailli was always an heir of the minor ruler and while it was proper that he should have charge of the administration of the realm, it was not safe for him to be given custody of the child whose demise might make him heir of the realm.".... "Thus when Raymond of Tripoli was given the bailliage for Baldwin V, the custody of the child was given to Joscelin de Courtney, his maternal uncle." In short, Count Raymond and Joscelyn III, as the respective relatives of the two sides of the royal family through which the throne escheated and did *not* escheat, were given their respective rôles as bailli and guardian. Also consult the genealogical chart in n. 2, p. 27 of La Monte's *Feudal Monarchy*. Baldwin (*Raymond III*, pp. 58-59), in commenting on the committee of the four western rulers as the body to determine the answer to the question as to whether Sibyl, as the elder daughter of Amalric, deserved the throne in the event of the death of Baldwin V, scores the allegation of the barons that they "... did not care to approve her succession without the action of the committee. It need hardly be said that this was clearly not the real reason for the barons' objection to Sibyl. The same impediment would have applied equally well to Baldwin IV himself, yet it had not been mentioned. It was obviously not Sibyl they objected to, but Guy. Even though the king in withdrawing his procuratorship had specifically removed all hope of succession to the throne, they evidently still feared trouble in the event of the boy king's death; and since he died within two or three years, he may have been a sickly child. Their apprehension arose from one of two things. They may have been uncertain of the competence of the *Haute Cour* in the matter of altering the legal hereditary succession, despite the fact that they had already exercised this power only a short time before when, in sanctioning the coronation of Baldwin V, they set aside Sibyl's (and therefore Guy's) rights; or, fearing again to lose control of the *Haute Cour* to the "court party," they determined if possible to prevent that group from giving the crown to Guy as husband of the legal heir, Sibyl. In either case reference to the committee of western magnates and the pope would first give them an opportunity to press the candidacy of the younger sister, Isabel, and her husband, Humphrey. Second, if this should prove successful, the committee's decision would provide a higher sanction for the invalidation of Sibyl's—and therefore Guy's—claims to the throne, than the mere fiat of the *Haute Cour*. Unfortunately the chronicles give no hint of determining reasons other than the desire of the barons not to have Sibyl crowned without action by the committee because she had been born before Amalric became king, and this, as we have just explained, was pretty obviously a fiction."

King, Henry II, who had a special relationship to the problems besetting the crusading states by reason of the fact that King Fulk had been his grandfather. Landing at Brindisi, the delegation proceeded northward by way of Rome to Verona where they petitioned the Holy Roman Emperor, Frederick Barbarossa, for aid and Archbishop Gerhard supported their pleas with an inspiring sermon. Similarly in France King Philip Augustus, upon hearing Patriarch Heraclius' plea, granted a considerable financial support to the petitioners and convoked a synod of the French church, which subsequently ordered the preaching of the Cross. And in England as well, despite the development of some personal friction between Heraclius and King Henry II, the delegation met with sympathy and financial support from the King. But neither the French nor the English monarch was willing personally to participate in the desired Crusade, the former because of fear of his adversary, Henry II, the latter because of his doubt about the still uncertain attitude of the French king. The petitioners received many promises from French knights during their homeward journey through France that they would take the Cross, but all refused an immediate execution of their pledges. And so, apart from considerable financial assistance, little tangible military aid had been gained by the mission at the time of its return to the Holy Land in the Summer of 1185.[288]

---

[288] Roger of Wendover, *op. cit.*, pp. 134-36; Benedict of Peterborough, *op. cit.*, pp. 331-33 and 338; *Ex Chronologia Roberti Altissiodorensis* in *Recueil des historiens des Gaules et de la France.* Ed. by M. Bouquet and others (Paris, 1879), XVIII, 252; *Ex Gervasii Dorobernensis Chronico De Rebus Angliae* in *Recueil des historiens des Gaules et de la France.* Ed. by M. Bouquet and others (Paris, 1878), XVII, 662; *Ex Chronico Anonymi Laudunensis Canonici* in *Recueil des historiens des Gaules et de la France.* Ed. by M. Bouquet and others (Paris, 1879), XIII, 705; *Willelmi Chronica Andrensis* in *Monumenta Germaniae Historica Scriptores* (Hanover, 1879), XXIV, 716; William of Newburgh, *op. cit.*, pp. 244-47; Roger of Hoveden, *op. cit.*, p. 304; Röhricht, *Regesta*, No. 646, pp. 70-71; Rigordus, *Gesta Philippi Augusti*, ed. H. François Delaborde (Paris, 1882), I, 46-48; Gervase of Canterbury, *op. cit.*, p. 325; Giraldus Cambrensis, *Opera. De Rebus a Se Gestis*, ed. J. S. Brewer (London, 1861), I, 60-61; Giraldus Cambrensis, *Opera. Expugnatio Hibernica*, ed. James S. Dimock (London, 1867), V, 360-364; Giraldus Cambrensis, *Opera. De Principis Instructione Liber*, ed. George F. Warner (London, 1891), VIII, 202-09; Ralph of Diceto, *op. cit.*, II, 27 and 32-34. (Henceforth references to the last named source will pertain solely to Volume II). Stubbs (*op. cit.*, pp. 340-41, n. l) implies that the negotiations with Henry II of England resulted, at least in part, from the anti-Raymond faction of the Patriarch Heraclius, Joscelyn III, and the Grand Master of the Temple: "Raymond was especially hated by the Patriarch Heraclius, Jocelin of Edessa, the king's uncle, and Gerard of Bideford, the Grand Master of the Temple. It was probably at this juncture that Heraclius and the Grand Master of the Hospital were sent to offer the sovereignty of Palestine to Henry II."

CHAPTER TWELVE

RESUMPTION OF FRANCO-MOSLEM CONFLICT AND AN ENSUING TRUCE, 1184-1185

Fortunately for the well being of the Kingdom of Jerusalem the first half of 1184 passed without a resumption of Saladin's attacks and, in consequence, Count Raymond was able to strengthen his hold on the procuratorship.[289] But Saladin was merely biding his time. The decision of his brother al-ʿĀdil to remain in northern Syria rather than return to Egypt resulted from Saladin's granting to him of the government of Aleppo and perhaps also resulted from Saladin's wish that he assemble fresh forces for the war with the Franks.[290] Meanwhile Egyptian interests were assumed by Saladin's nephew and lieutenant Taqī-ad-Dīn ʿUmar as governor. Mesopotamian matters together with the reception of and negotiations with embassies arriving in Damascus to treat with Saladin and the interviews of the two brothers, Saladin and al-ʿĀdil, in Damascus in March, 1184 also consumed time.[291]

At length, however, political and military planning was completed, and, in consequence, al-ʿĀdil and Taqī-ad-Dīn ʿUmar as well as other Moslem commanders received orders from Saladin to assemble their forces in a joint assault upon Krak. The several problems of logistics were so considerable that al-ʿĀdil's northern forces did not reach Damascus until the first week of July and Krak considerably later and the Egyptian soldiery under Taqī-ad-Dīn ʿUmar arrived at Krak on July 30. Finally a full investment was established on August 13.[292] The several Moslem commanders pressed their attack relentlessly with their siege machinery on the only center of Frankish resistance, namely the

---

[289] Castle (*op. cit.*, p. 26, n. 2) also correctly observes that "Guy now lacked strong support, because of the absence of the envoys. In this way opportunity for ascendancy was given to Raymond and his followers."

[290] Behâ Ed-Dîn, *Anecdotes*, p. 77 and *Saladin*, pp. 92-93; Kamal-Ad-Dîn, *Histoire*, loc. cit.; *The Chronography of Bar Hebraeus*, loc. cit.; Stevenson, *op. cit.*, p. 234.

[291] Behâ Ed-Dîn, *Anecdotes*, pp. 78-79 and *Saladin*, pp. 93-95; Makrizi, *op. cit.*, p. 10; Kamal-Ad-Dîn, *Histoire*, IV, 170-71. See John L. La Monte, "Taki ed Din, Prince of Hama," *The Moslem World* (Hartford, Conn., 1941), XXXI, 149-60 for a brief biography of this Mohammedan chieftain.

[292] Behâ Ed-Dîn, *Anecdotes*, pp. 80-81 and *Saladin*, p. 96; Abou Chamah, *op. cit.*, pp. 249-50; Makrizi, *op. cit.*, pp. 11-12; Kamal-Ad-Dîn, *Histoire*, IV, 171-72; *The Chronography of Bar Hebraeus*, pp. 316-17.

castle, after its chief defense, a deep depression, had been filled by Saladin. This new turn of events elicited a speedy Frankish response in the advance of a relief force from Jerusalem on Krak. Saladin thereupon decided to meet the enemy at once, and, having abandoned his siege of Krak, dispatched a force to the north. The Franks encamped at Wālā, an easily defensible spot, and the Moslems consequently assembled at the opposite town of Heshban. When several days of military inaction ensued, Saladin fell back on Maʿin, thereby affording the Franks a chance to escape. This they utilized to the full and succeeded under cover of a night march in reaching Krak on September 3. Although their initial objective, the relief of Krak, was now realized, it had been accomplished at a heavy cost, for Palestine was now largely denuded of troops. Saladin took full advantage of this tactical error by a dispatch of a Moslem force across the Jordan River with instructions to wage ruthless war. Three Frankish towns, Jinin, Nablus, and Sebastia, suffered attacks and plundering operations; the attackers soon rejoined the main Moslem forces. Thereupon, the Frankish forces, having bolstered Krak's defenses, returned to Jerusalem.[293]

Meanwhile adverse climatic conditions in the Holy Land contributed markedly to a cessation of Franco-Moslem hostilities. A prolonged drought so severe as to cause Count Raymond to fear that the Moslems, upon learning of it, would attack the Franks led him to assemble the baronage, the Templars, and the Hospitallers to seek their advice and approval of his plan to seek a truce with Saladin. This was readily granted, and, accordingly, the regent sought out the Moslem chieftain. The latter, who was now faced by ominous news of disturbances in Mesopotamia which threatened his political position therein and who was perhaps also disconsolate over the modest achievements of Moslem arms during the preceding Summer, was agreeable to the Frankish overtures and, having granted a peace treaty at the close of 1184 or the opening days of 1185 for the next four years,[294] departed from Damascus in February, 1185 and retired to his

---

[293] Behâ Ed-Dîn, *Anecdotes*, pp. 81-82 and *Saladin*, pp. 96-97; Abou Chamah, *op. cit.*, pp. 250-56; Makrizi, *op. cit.*, pp. 12-14; Kamal-Ad-Dîn, *Histoire*, IV, 172; Röhricht, *Regesta*, No. 638, p. 169; Roger of Wendover, *op. cit.*, p. 133; Ibn al-Athīr, *K.—A.*, pp. 666-67; *The Chronography of Bar Hebraeus*, p. 317; Ralph of Diceto, *op. cit.*, pp. 27-28; Michael the Syrian, *Chronique*, pp. 393-94.

[294] *Chronique d'Ernoul*, chap. xi, p. 124; *Eracles*, pp. 10 and 12-13; Kamal-Ad-Dîn, *Histoire*, IV, 173; Behâ Ed-Dîn, *Saladin*, p. 98 and *Anecdotes*, p. 82; Benedict of Peterborough, *op. cit.*, p. 359; Baldwin, *Raymond III*, p. 70, n. 3. Considerable

disagreement prevails among scholars concerning the dating of this truce. Lane-Poole (*op. cit.*, pp. 180-81) seems to favor the very late Summer or early Autumn of 1184 with his statement "After this [Saladin's return to Damascus on September 16, 1184] there was peace between Saracen and Christian for a time." Gibb ("Saladin,"pp. 579-80) gives no exact dating, but the language of the narrative shows that he believes it occurred after Saladin's assault on Krak, which this scholar believes occurred during August and September, 1184 and before or certainly not later than the opening days of May, 1185. Barker (*op. cit.*, p. 59), Grousset (*Histoire*, p. 760), Röhricht (*Kreuzzüge*, p. 124), Runciman (*History*, p. 445), and La Monte (*Feudal Monarchy*, p. 33) agree that the truce was made in 1185. Stevenson (*op. cit.*, p. 237 and n. 3) places it during the winter of 1184-1185. Archer and Kingsford (*op. cit.*, p. 270) state that the truce was signed in 1185 after the death of Baldwin IV or possibly late in 1184. Baldwin (*Raymond III*, pp. 69-70 and n. 3, p. 70 and "The Decline," p. 604) believes that it happened early in 1185. De Saulcy (*loc. cit.*) declares that it occurred before September, 1185. "Le régent [Raymond] venait de conclure une trêve de quatre ans avec Selah-eddyn, lorsque l'enfant-roi mourut à Saint-Jean d'Acre au commencement de septembre." [1185] Champdor (*op. cit.*, p. 139), without stating any exact time, observes that "L'un des premiers actes du régent [Raymond] fut de signer une nouvelle trêve de quatre ans avec Saladin." Since this statement is made *after* the observation that Baldwin IV died in March, 1185, the implication *may* be that this scholar believes the truce was drawn up *after* Baldwin IV's death. Schlumberger (*Numismatique*, p. 74), on the other hand, assigns the dating of the truce to the Summer of 1186. "Mais le pauvre petit prince [Baldwin V] mourut dans cette ville [Acre] dès l'année suivante, en septembre 1186, au moment même où le régent venait de conclure une trêve de plusieurs années avec Saladin..." Grousset (*Histoire*, pp. 759-60) discerns a deeper and additional meaning in Raymond's overtures to Saladin. "Raymond III était un politique prudent qui comprenait mieux que quiconque la nécessité de négociations avec Saladin. Le royaume, encerclé par les possessions aiyûbides, épuisé par des années de guerre quotidienne, avait besoin de paix pour se refaire. La paix seule pouvait lui permettre de reprendre haleine et aussi de laisser s'amortir le premier élan de la conquête aiyûbide. L'expérience enseignait que ces empires musulmans, nés de la valeur d'un soldat heureux, mais sans autre base juridique que le droit du cimeterre, invincibles dans le moment de leur première expansion, tombaient dès la troisième génération dans une décadence rapide. Généralement réfractaires à la notion d'État, ils ne survivaient guère au héros qui leur avait donné naissance. L'État franc au contraire, assuré de continuité par ses institutions monarchiques, pouvait attendre. Le tout était, comme Baudouin IV l'avait toujours fait, de refuser à Saladin le combat décisif. Solidement étayés sur les formidables Kraks donts ils avaient, à tous les points stratégiques, garni la montagne, les Francs, s'ils continuaient à pratiquer une politique défensive, étaient inexpugnables. Mais, mieux encore, si l'on parvenait à rétablir avec Saladin la paix qui avait régné entre les Francs et les épigones zengides, le royaume était définitivement sauvé, la tourmente aiyûbide pouvait être considérée comme passée, les liens économiques—le récit d'Ibn Jubair l'atteste—rétablissaient leur réseau entre le Sahel chrétien et l'hinterland musulman." The same scholar (*Histoire*, p. 761) believes that Saladin's effecting of this truce with the Franks is conclusive proof of a "live and let live" attitude on his part towards them. "D'autre part la conclusion de cette trêve prouve que Saladin, satisfait de la constitution de son vaste empire syro-égyptien, en arrivait, malgré ses proclamations en faveur de la guerre sainte, à tolérer pratiquement l'établissement franc du Sahel." And as for the truce itself he (*Histoire*, loc. cit.) observes "Quelle meilleure preuve que la tourmente aiyûbide était peut-être passée, que l'empire aiyûbide se stabilisait dans ses limites actuelles, respectant les forces vives de la colonie franque?" And this attitude of compromise with the Frankish enemy sprang from overriding considerations in respect to foreign affairs in general and his Moslem foes in particular as well as internal difficulties in his northern provinces for the ensuing fifteen months.²⁹⁵ With the establishment of the truce, the Moslems brought in great quantities of provisions for the Franks. The effect of these developments, which prevented mass starvation, was the gaining for Count Raymond of a vast esteem in the eyes of the general population.²⁹⁶

---

holdings. See Grousset, *Histoire*, p. 762. "En ces années 1185-1186 Saladin était d'ailleurs peut-être plus attiré par les affaires de l'Est que par celles de Syrie. En avril 1185, il partit, malgré les menaces du sultan seljûqide de Qoniya, attaquer une fois de plus Mossoul qu'il bloqua d'ailleurs vainement".... "L'empire aiyûbide d'ailleurs commençait à connaître les difficultés intérieures," Lane-Poole (*op. cit.*, p. 181) sees in this truce an enhancement of Raymond's political aspirations: "With Raymond himself it was more than a truce; it was an offensive and defensive alliance. Saladin was to support him in his designs on the crown, and Raymond in return set free all the Saracens he held captive in Tripolis, and even supplied Damascus liberally with food during the dearth of 1185."

²⁹⁵ Kamal-Ad-Dîn, *Histoire*, *loc. cit.*; Makrizi, *op. cit.*, p. 14.

²⁹⁶ *Chronique d'Ernoul*, *loc. cit.* But that the truce settled nothing in respect to the basic elements of Franco-Moslem enmity and rivalry is only too clear, for as Lane-Poole (*op. cit.*, pp. 181-82) points out, "... the truce was like the troubled sleep of a soldier, which might be broken in an instant by the call to arms. It was no real peace whilst the Patriarch Heraclius scoured Europe to beat up recruits, whilst English knights from the Cheviots to the Pyrenees took the Cross, whilst the two great Military Orders were burning to strike a blow for the faith. The Holy War was sleeping, but it was sure to awake."

CHAPTER THIRTEEN

REVOLUTION IN THE KINGDOM OF JERUSALEM: THE *COUP D'ÉTAT* OF JOSCELYN III AND THE COURT PARTY, (1185-1186)

This welcome respite served to bolster the sagging fortunes of the Kingdom of Jerusalem throughout the balance of 1185. The child king Baldwin V succeeded to the throne without incident following the death of the leper king Baldwin IV on March 16, 1185. The barons, who had repaired to Jerusalem in accordance with their dying king's request, were present at the time of his death and attended his burial. Joscelyn III and Count Raymond thereupon assumed the rôles assigned to them earlier at the baronial assembly, the former repairing to Acre with the new king and the latter continuing in his status of regent.[297]

The restoration of peace between the external enemies, namely the Franks and the Moslems, and the internal enemies, the nobiliary factions, redounded to the benefit of Joscelyn III in particular, for it permitted him to resume his program of territorial advancement and expansion. Guy and Sibyl, the recipients of the fiefs of Chabor and Coquil from the late Agnes who had purchased them before 1183, sold them to the Seneschal for the sum of 5,000 besants in February, 1185.[298] In his new rôle as guardian of the child king after March, 1185

---

[297] *Eracles*, pp. 9-10 and n. b, p. 9; Ibn al-Athīr, *K.—A.*, p. 674; *Chronique d'Ernoul*, chaps. x and xi, pp. 118-19 and 129; Abou Chamah, *op. cit.*, p. 258; Benedict of Peterborough, *op. cit.*, p. 343; Roger of Hoveden, *op. cit.*, p. 308; *The Chronography of Bar Hebraeus*, p. 320; Michael the Syrian, *Chronique*, p. 394 and n. 3; *Anonymi Continuatio Appendicis Roberti de Monte ad Sigebertum* in Recueil des historiens des Gaules et de la France. Ed. by M. Bouquet and others (Paris, 1879), XVIII, 337; *Chronique d'Amadi*, pp. 52-53; *Les gestes des Chiprois* Livre I. *Chronique de Terre Sainte 1132-1224* in *Rec. his. arm.* (Paris, 1906), II, 658; *De Expugnatione Terrae Sanctae Per Saladinum, Libellus* ed. by Joseph Stevenson (London, 1875), p. 209. (Henceforth references to the last two named sources will be cited respectively as *Les gestes des Chiprois* and *Libellus*). See *Assises* pp. 29-31 for an account of the details of the coronation of Baldwin V. See King, *op. cit.*, p. 115, La Monte, *The Crusade*, p. 120, n. 3, and Grousset, *Histoire*, pp. 609-11 for encomiums on the life, character, and kingly deeds of the leper king Baldwin IV. Röhricht (*Kreuzzüge, loc. cit.*) believes that Count Raymond ruled the Kingdom of Jerusalem with exquisite care after the death of Baldwin IV. Schlumberger (*Renaud de Chatillon*, p. 247) has similar views: "... Raymond de Tripoli... continua de gouverner le royaume avec autant d'activité que d'energie."

[298] Röhricht, *Regesta*, No. 654, p. 174; Reinhold Röhricht, *Regesta Regni*

he was the recipient of royal favors from his young charge on June 1 and November 1, 1185 in the form of charters granting him freedom of sale in Acre for the honey and sugar produced within the confines of his village of Lanahia and a yearly income of 400 besants at Acre for the ensuing four years.[299] And that his political rôle in the life of the Kingdom of Jerusalem, although still overshadowed by that held by his rival Count Raymond, remained important is indicated by his continued retention of the office of Seneschal in which capacity he witnessed on May 16, 1185 the granting of the rent of half of the gastina of Mesdedule to the abbey of Josaphat. The Seneschal is the second witness, immediately following Reginald of Châtillon.[300]

But before the healing economic and political effects of the truce between Franks and Moslems and the cessation for the moment of bickering between the nobiliary factions in the Kingdom of Jerusalem could create a solid underpinning for the threatened state, disaster intervened in the death of the child king Baldwin V at Acre toward the close of August, 1186. With the question of the succession to the throne still unsettled and with the certainty that the next legal heir to the throne would be Sibyl, the daughter of his late sister Agnes or Sibyl's half sister Isabel, Joscelyn III saw his opportunity to seize the rule of the state by being the power behind the throne. Time was of the essence, for any delay would afford the baronage the chance to assemble to effect the succession to the throne in accordance with the already stipulated procedure. Accordingly, he visited Count Raymond with proposals that he, Raymond, repair to Tiberias and not go to Jerusalem with the late king's body to bury him. Furthermore, the Count should not let any of the barons of the land journey to Jerusalem. Lastly, the Procurator should entrust the Templars with the task of carrying the late king's body to Jerusalem and burying it. Count Raymond foolishly believed the advice and repaired to Tiberias and the Templars journeyed to Jerusalem with the royal corpse to bury it.[301]

Hierosolymitani (MXCVII-MCCXCI) Additamentum (Oeniponti, 1904), No. 1110a, p. 69; Strehlke, *op. cit.*, No. 22, p. 20; Delaville Le Roulx, "Inventaire," p. 86, No. 262. See and cf. Delaville Le Roulx, *Mélanges*, No. 262, p. 63

[299] Röhricht, *Regesta*, Nos. 644 and 657, pp. 170 and 174; Strehlke, *op. cit.*, Nos. 18 and 19, pp. 17-18.

[300] Röhricht, *Regesta*, No. 643, p. 170; Delaborde, *op. cit.*, No. XLIII, pp. 91-92. The editor of *Ernoul's Account of Palestine* in *Palestine Pilgrims Text Society* (London, 1894), Vol. 6, p. 58, n. 4 defines a gastina as follows: "*Gastine*, answering to the carucate of Domesday book, a division of the casale or property, amounting to about eighty acres."

[301] *Chronique d'Ernoul*, chap. xi, pp. 129-30; *Eracles*, pp. 25-26; Ibn al-Athīr, *K.—A.*,

With the stage thus set, Joscelyn III seized the castle of Acre, and then, having garrisoned it, proceeded to Beirut and gained possession by treachery of the castle which Count Raymond held as a means of defraying his own expenses. This, too, the Courtenay chieftain soon garrisoned with knights and men-at-arms. Then he informed Sibyl, his

---

loc. cit., Ex Chronologia Roberti Altissiodorensis, p. 253; Benedict of Peterborough, *op. cit.*, pp. 358 and 361; Roger of Hoveden, *op. cit.*, p. 315; *Les gestes des Chiprois, loc. cit.*; Arnold, Abbas Lubecensis (Arnold of Lubeck) *Chronica Slavorum* in *Monumenta Germaniae Historica Scriptores* (Hanover, 1869), XXI, 164. Baldwin ("The Decline," *loc. cit.*), in commenting on these moves, aptly observes that "... the associates of Guy conspired to overthrow Raymond's regency by methods which amounted to a palace revolution." This same scholar (*Raymond III*, p. 62) contends that Joscelyn III's interest in the "court party" was that of family connections and that he had much in common with all the other members of the "court party," namely that "They were all men who had attained their present position in the kingdom neither by direct inheritance, nor by addition through marriage to family estates previously established. Each had come recently into his fortune, by marriage or intrigue: Guy, Gerard, the patriarch, Reginald of Krak, even Joscelin. None came of an old family in the kingdom like the Ibelins. Joscelin's case was in a sense an exception, but since his family inheritance of Edessa was no longer in existence, he had, as we have seen, taken advantage of his close relationship to the king to acquire a fief in the kingdom. And because that kinship was second to Raymond's, he had identified himself with the opposition, Guy and his colleagues. So each of these men, whether actually a new arrival to the Orient or not, had reached his present status during his own lifetime. In this sense they were all newcomers, "nouveaux riches." They were not the real, blooded nobility of the land, and in feudal days such things meant much." Also see Baldwin, *Raymond III*, pp. 61-62, Grousset, *L'épopée*, pp. 270-71 and *Histoire*, pp. 765-66, and Richard, *op. cit.*, p. 138 for analyses of the motivations of the persons composing the "court party" at this time. Although the sources do not say so, the fact that the Templars did support the *coup d'état* suggests that there was a prior agreement between them and Joscelyn III that they would support it. The Seneschal's selection of the Templars rather than the Hospitallers, who opposed the *coup d'état*, as the caretakers of the royal corpse could hardly have occurred through chance alone. Grousset speaks of Joscelyn III as "... un créole intrigant, sans coeur ni foi" in both of his works. Richard (*loc. cit.*) explains the success of Joscelyn III in his duping of Count Raymond as follows: "... il [Joscelyn III] dupa complètement Raymond, lui persuadant qu'il paraîtrait vouloir faire un coup d'État en accompagnant le corps du petit roi à Jérusalem pour ses funérailles et qu'il aurait l'attitude la plus correcte en se retirant dans ses terres jusqu'à la réunion du Parlement." Wilcke (*op. cit.*, p. 120) sees in Joscelyn III's policy of dissuading Raymond and the baronage from attending the funeral of Baldwin V the aim of preventing them from meeting with the Vice-Regent to make decisions regarding the succession to the throne. This same scholar (*op. cit.*, p. 121) believes that the support of the *coup d'état* by the Templars sprang from a calculation that a weak ruler was more auspicious for the future of their order than a strong one. Castle (*op. cit.*, p. 28) explains Raymond's acceptance of Joscelyn III's proposals as resulting "... (undoubtedly more from policy than any acceptance of the view that his days as leader were numbered)..." Runciman (*History* pp. 446-47) believes that Joscelyn III used the following strategy in persuading Count Raymond: "Professing himself anxious to work in with Raymond, Joscelin persuaded him to go to Tiberias and to invite the barons of the realm to meet him there, in security from the plots of the Patriarch, in order that the terms of Baldwin IV's will should be carried out. He himself would convey the little corpse to Jerusalem for burial."

niece, of the new turn of events and told her that she should repair to Jerusalem with all her knights and, following the burial of her son, the late King Baldwin V, should seize and maintain control of the citadel by a strong garrison and then have herself crowned queen.[302] Sibyl complied with her uncle's proposal and journeyed to Jerusalem with her husband Guy. Soon the royal aspirants were joined by the Masters of the Hospitallers and Templars and the Patriarch Heraclius. The latter two quickly assured Sibyl upon her request for their counsel that she need not be uneasy, for they would crown her in spite of all opposition. The Patriarch's pledge sprang from the love which he bore for her late mother Agnes, while that of the Master of the Templars emanated from his hatred of the Procurator. Thereupon the trio of Sibyl's supporters summoned Reginald of Châtillon, who was at Krak, to journey to Jerusalem. Reginald complied with the summons, whereupon the Patriarch and the Master of the Templars advised Sibyl to summon Count Raymond and the barons to Jerusalem to attend her coronation, for the rule of the Kingdom of Jerusalem had fallen to her.[303]

[302] *Chronique d'Ernoul*, p. 130; *Eracles*, p. 26. Richard (*loc. cit.*) points out that the geographical position of Joscelyn III's fiefs aided him in his *coup d'état.* "... Jocelin, dont la seigneurie de Château-du-Roi et du Toron bloquait la Galilée et Acre, mettait rapidement la main sur Acre (sans doute aussi Tyr) et enlevait Beyrouth aux gens du comte de Tripoli." Runciman (*History*, p. 447) states that "As soon as he [Count Raymond] was gone Joscelin sent troops that he could trust to occupy Tyre and Beirut and remained himself at Acre, where he proclaimed Sibylla as queen." But the first two of the four cited sources which Runciman lists in documentation of this view (*History*, p. 449, n.1) "Ernoul, pp. 129-36, the fullest and most graphic account; *Estoire d'Eracles*, II, pp. 25-31; Radulph of Diceto, II, p. 47; Arnold of Lubeck, pp. 116-17," make it quite clear that Joscelyn III personally went to Beirut. Runciman himself declares the first two cited accounts to be the more reliable. And the last two cited accounts give no information on Joscelyn III's *coup d'état*. Grousset (*Histoire*, p. 767) supports my view in his statement that "Tandis que Raymond prenait sans défiance la route de Tibériade, Jocelin s'empara du château d'Acre, entra par trahison dans Beyrouth..."

[303] *Chronique d'Ernoul*, pp. 130-31; *Eracles*, pp. 26-27. Cf. Castle, *op. cit.*, p. 30, n. 2. Baldwin (*Raymond III*, p. 72, n. 11) declares that "According to the *Continuation*, Joscelin did not come to Jerusalem at all." Neither the *Chronique d'Ernoul* nor *Eracles*, which constitute the several versions of the *Continuation*, says positively that Joscelyn III did not come to Jerusalem at all. Such a view is, however, implicit in their accounts of the seneschal's movements in his execution of the *coup d'état*. The account of these events provided by *Brevis Regni Ierosolymitani Historia* in *Monumenta Germaniae Historica Scriptores* (Hanover, 1863), XVIII, 52 differs considerably, for it avers that Joscelyn III, as well as Sibyl, Guy of Lusignan, Reginald of Châtillon, and the Marquis of Montferrat, the grandfather of the late king, took the mortal remains of Baldwin V to Jerusalem and buried them. In view of the fact that the retention of the seaports of Acre and Beirut was of prime importance and Joscelyn III's physical absence together with that of his soldiers therefrom might well lead to their recovery by Count Raymond

Meanwhile, Count Raymond, having repaired to Tiberias, was now apprised of Joscelyn III's betrayal. He at once summoned all the nobles and knights of the Kingdom of Jerusalem to Nablus in accordance with their homage and oaths. All save for the authors of the *coup d'état* and the marquis of Montferrat, the late king's grandfather, complied; Joscelyn III remained in Acre where he had retired. The wrathful procurator claimed the right to continue in his rôle until, in accordance with the stipulated plan, the western monarchs should exercise their rôles as electors to select a successor to the late Baldwin V. The nobility manifested its scorn for Sibyl's summons by an open refusal and by the dispatch of two Cistercian monks to Patriarch

---

and in view of the fact that the joint military power of Sibyl, Guy of Lusignan, and Reginald of Châtillon sufficed to seize and hold Jerusalem, this variant version may be ruled out. (Henceforth this source will be cited as *Brevis*). Richard (*loc. cit.*) attributes Reginald of Châtillon's support of Guy to the following consideration: "... le sire d'Outre-Jourdain Renaud de Châtillon... venait lui [Guy] prêter son aide, impatient de secouer la domination de Raymond qui était peu favorable à ses operations de brigandage." Baldwin (*Raymond III*, p. 73) agrees with my acceptance of the accounts of the *coup d'état* provided by *Chronique d'Ernoul* and *Eracles* and succinctly summarizes the *coup d'état* as follows: "Joscelin's move was diabolically clever. He now controlled both Acre and Beirut, and his associates were in Jerusalem. How he managed to allay all suspicion and persuade the count of Tripolis not to come to Jerusalem is impossible to understand. We only know that this move, successfully executed, placed Guy and Sibyl and their associates in the strongest position possible. Not only were they in possession of the Holy City itself, where they could close the gates to their enemies outside and proceed with their plans, but they had so chosen their time that partically all the other barons were elsewhere. Those whom they chose could be admitted at their pleasure. Others could be kept out without great difficulty, and it was soon discovered that any dissenter within was powerless." And this scholar (*Raymond III*, p. 74) regards the decision to summon the barons to attend the coronation "... as an invitation to those barons to exercise their constitutional right as members of the *Haute Cour* to signify their assent or objection to the proceedings. If they refused, as was confidently anticipated, they could be said to have forfeited that right by their absence. It was a clever move." This same scholar ("The Decline," pp 604-05) believes that "It was obviously the intention of the conspirators in Jerusalem... to proceed with the coronation of Sibyl and Guy before the complicated machinery of arbitration by the pope, the emperor, and the kings of France and England could be set in motion." Because of the positive and personal reasons animating the decision of Patriarch Heraclius to support the *coup d'état*, the belief of Slaughter (*op. cit.*, p. 117) that "... they [the engineers of the *coup d'état*] induced Heraclius, the Patriarch, to crown Sibylla..." seems far-fetched. Cf. La Monte, *Feudal Monarchy*, p. 34, n. l. Grousset (*Histoire*, pp. 766-67) comments as follows in respect to Joscelyn III's trickery of Count Raymond: "Bien qu'il dût être d'emblée suspect comme étant l'oncle de la princesse Sibylle, il sut inspirer confiance à Raymond III en se présentant à celui-ci comme un allié sûr. Feignant d'entrer dans les projets de Raymond, il lui persuada de ne pas conduire en personne le corps du petit roi défunt à Jerusalem où se trouvaient les sépultures royales, mais de confier ce soin aux Templiers et de se rendre lui-même avec les barons de son parti à Tibériade, en attendant que se ressemblât le parlement chargé de choisir un nouveau roi"

Heraclius and the Masters of the Templars and the Hospitallers to warn them against the coronation of Sibyl until they had taken counsel with those who had sworn fealty to Baldwin V. The answer of the defiant Patriarch and the Master of the Templars was their declaration that they would not be bound by any oaths and would crown Sibyl and their closing of the gates of the city of Jerusalem to the end of preventing the hostile barons encamped at Nablus from entering the city during the coronation with ensuing brawling. Only the Master of the Hospitallers refused support of the *coup d'état*, averring that it involved a deed in defiance of God and their several oaths.[304]

With the stage thus set, the other engineers of the *coup d'état*, namely the Master of the Templars, Patriarch Heraclius, and Reginald of Châtillon, entered the final act. The Templar leader readily complied with the Patriarch's request for his key to the coffer containing the royal crowns, but the Master of the Hospitallers refused to accede to the demand that he surrender his key on the ground that such an act was opposed by the baronage of the Kingdom of Jerusalem. Only after a long search was the hidden key revealed; the Master of the Hospitallers elected in disgust to toss it from his house. With the three keys requisite for the opening of the coffer at long last in their possession, the plotters secured the two royal crowns. The coronation soon followed in September, 1186. Patriarch Heraclius crowned Sibyl and then observed that, in view of her need of a royal consort to govern the state, she should bestow the other crown on a suitable candidate. Thereupon Sibyl summoned Guy to receive the honor. He complied, knelt before the new queen, received the crown from her, and thereby became king.[305] Reginald of Châtillon meantime

---

[304] *Chronique d'Ernoul*, pp. 131-32; *Eracles*, p. 27; *Les gestes des Chiprois, loc. cit.* Richard (*loc. cit.*) believes that Count Raymond at the Nablus meeting of the baronage "... leur [the barons] rappela le serment prêté à Baudouin IV, déshéritant formellement Guy..."

[305] *Chronique d'Ernoul*, pp. 133-34; *Eracles*, pp. 27-29; *The Chronography of Bar Hebraeus*, p. 322; Ibn al-Athīr, *K.—A.*, pp. 674-75; Ralph of Diceto, *op. cit.*, p. 47; Arnold of Lubeck, *op. cit.*, p. 165; *Chronique d'Amadi*, p. 53. Richard (*op. cit.*, pp. 138-39) does not consider Guy to be a real king, but rather only a prince consort for the reason that "... c'est Sibylle, et non le patriarche, qui posa la couronne sur sa tête." Helan Moonan (*Women in Politics in Latin Syria*, University of Minnesota Master's Thesis [Minneapolis, 1922], pp. 47, 49, 51, and 54-56) has accurately appraised Sibyl's career and explained the factors enabling her to exercise strong influence in the political life of the time. "In the ultimate it was probably the support of the Templars and Hospitalers that brought the Throne to Sybilla and through her to Guy. Her subtlety and cleverness secured this support and herein lies the significance of her career. The kingship of Jerusalem made very little difference to these Knights. Controlling castles

gave valuable support to the proceedings by an address to the citizens of Jerusalem in which he observed that Sibyl's close kinship to two

---

and forts on the frontier, commanding great support from the West (for they were influential all over Europe), and being powerful military forces as well—these facts made them secure and independent. Yet to Sybilla, they gave the weight of their influence, and albeit reluctantly, they concurred in her desire to retain Guy as her husband. This is an assurance of the queen's cleverness and intelligence which is perhaps greater than the actual strategy she used." ... "It is strange that she could not see Guy's inefficiencies but perhaps her strong desire to have her husband crowned king was colored by her wish to actually rule through him." ... "Her weakness, as a public woman, lay in the fact of her great affection for Guido. It clouded her vision and blinded her to his deficiencies. This emotion—her unfailing loyalty—must be commended, but Sybilla by nature of her position and the critical need of her country should have been guided by that greater loyalty. If she had possessed this truer sense of values, had accepted the judgment of Baldwin, of the powerful religious order, even of Raymond, the kingdom might at least have been spared Guy's incompetency." ... "The best explanation of it [the power and position held by Sibyl] lies in the personnel of the kingdom, the conflicting elements in its environs. Even in the First Crusade opposing interests held the stage from time to time and the best interests of the whole expedition were occasionally lost in the opposing designs of the leaders. Evidence of this is found in the deadlock after Antioch. This spirit and these factions had been contributed to the kingdom set up as a result of this expedition. Men of adventure, men with possessions, had come, all seeking definite objects, the pursuit of which brought conflict. Two strong military and religious orders grew up in the kingdom and acted as checks on each other. The direct influence of the Church, acting through the Patriarchs and bishops, was another powerful element. Constantly incoming Westerners with great wealth and following had joined the different parties among the leaders. "The balance of power" was watched as anxiously there as in Europe today. So many elements inevitably would tend to nullify and make impossible united pressure for one purpose. Women of average intelligence, perceiving this situation, could easily find opportunity of gaining control and men were too engrossed in these conflicts, too busy in wars internal and external, too divided in policy and opinion, to put a check upon such feminine desires. Cooperation, united pressure, action as a unit, were characteristics lacking in this kingdom, and women simply made use of the opportunity that the lack of these forces developed. With the growth of the kingdom these divided factions became more distinct, and the balance of power more closely watched. This is very clearly seen at Sybilla's coronation. The two religious orders, both military powers and rich, were watching the designs of each other, as well as those of the various leaders. Raymond of Tiberius and Tripoli, strong in the kingdom, pitted his strength against that shown by Guido de Lusignon. Sometimes one of the men received the king's favor, sometimes another. Renaud of Kerak threw in his influence on the side of Guido because of his hostility to Raymond. Two policies, one of attack on the Turks, the other of strategic waiting, divided the leaders and the Knights Templar and Hospitalers. Little wonder, then, that Sybilla, using very cleverly one of these forces against the other, could persist in her desire to crown Guido, could even persuade the religious orders to give her act their approval." ... "Sybilla displays little of the hardness of ambition that characterized Alice. She was simply an intelligent feudal woman, endeavoring to secure the best possible position for a hopelessly incompetent husband who lacked even the feudal man's ordinary attribute—military skill and knowledge." Also see Herzog, *op. cit.*, pp. 75-77 for views generally confirming those of Moonan. Stubbs (*op. cit.*, pp. 341-42) sums up the situation succinctly as follows: "When Sibylla bestowed the crown on her husband, she acted as a true wife, and her choice under ordinary circumstances might have been a wise former rulers of the Kingdom, namely her father Amalric and her brother Baldwin IV, made her the true and legitimate heiress to the throne.[306]

---

one. But she must have known the prejudice against him which existed in the country, and ought either to have renounced the succession or to have accepted the responsibility of making a fresh choice. The nobles of Palestine would not submit to a French adventurer; the coronation of Guy practically sealed the fate of the colony." Schlumberger (*Numismatique*, p.75) declares that Sibyl "... et son mari furent couronnés reine et roi de Jérusalem, le 19 septembre 1186." La Monte ("The rise," pp. 314-15) observes that "From the accession of Guy and Sibylle in the autumn of 1185 until the fatal day at Hattin, July 4, 1187, Guy, Renaud de Chatillon and Joscelyn had things their own way and managed to wreck the country to an unparalleled degree." Presumably the dating of the accession of Guy and Sibyl is a chronological error or misprint. However, La Monte's phraseology may suggest a belief on his part that the accession of Guy and Sibyl had become a reality in everything but name not long after the assumption of the kingship by the child king Baldwin V in 1185 and that Guy, Reginald of Châtillon, and Joscelyn III were the real power behind the throne.

[306] *Eracles*, p. 28; Schlumberger, *Renaud de Chatillon*, pp. 247-49. Several variant accounts of the coronation of Sibyl and Guy are inherently improbable because of palpable errors contained therein and/or because they imply markedly inept handling of the situation on the part of Joscelyn III, whose timing and management of the earlier stages of the conspiracy had been excellent. The first of these, that of Benedict of Peterborough (*op. cit.*, pp. 358-59), states that the barons, people, clerics, Hospitallers, and Templars solidly supported the coronation of Sibyl but with the stipulation that she first divorce Guy of Lusignan. Since Guy was not of royal lineage, it was unseemly for the daughter of King Baldwin [sic] to remain his spouse. Thereupon, Sibyl, recognizing the impossibility of gaining the crown save by a policy of submisson to these demands, agreed to these requirements with the proviso that, following the divorce, she might make her selection of a new husband by her own choice. An acceptance of this proviso was speedily forthcoming and confirmed by oath, whereupon Heraclius and the bishops crowned and consecrated her. Then Sibyl announced that Guy was her selection as her new husband, for she knew him to be honest and wise and the only possible choice granted to her by God. Because of the oath of allegiance they had just taken to her, the Templars and Hospitallers recognized their inability to prevent Sibyl's remarriage to Guy and hence they gave their consent. Guy was then crowned king, although indignation was the general mood among the membership of the two orders. Roger of Hoveden (*op. cit.*, pp. 315-16) and Roger of Wendover (*op. cit.*, pp. 138-39) give generally parallel accounts, but the first one obviously errs in its claim that the Templars and Hospitallers desired Sibyl to select the procurator Raymond as her second husband. Albert of Trium-Fontium (*Chronicon* in *Recueil des historiens des Gaules et de la France* Ed. by M. Bouquet and others [Paris, 1879], XVIII, 747) echoes the afore-mentioned accounts in his statements that the Jerusalemite nobility hated Guy on the score of his foreign birth and poverty, but asserts that Sibyl refused to divorce Guy and hence the people were obliged to crown him. Robert de Clari (*Li Estoire de Chiaus qui conquisent Constantinoble* [Paris, 1869], pp. 29-30) renders another improbable account in his declaration that all the high barons of the land inclusive of Count Raymond and the leaders of the Orders of the Templars and the Hospital assembled in Jerusalem and thereupon declared that they would divorce Guy of Lusignan from his wife Sibyl, because the Kingdom of Jerusalem had escheated to her, and would then give her another husband more competent than Guy of Lusignan. The divorce was effected. However, the barons could not agree on a new spouse for Sibyl and hence they left the

The swiftly flowing tide of events in Jerusalem soon portended a civil war in the Kingdom of Jerusalem. But when the spy who had been sent by the barons assembled at Nablus to watch the coronation in Jerusalem returned to Nablus with his report, the baronage decided to accept the opposing counsels of the Procurator, Count Raymond, after hearing the despairing observations of Baldwin of Ramla that the country was doomed in the face of the fact that the new king was a fool and a dawdler and hence would refuse all the advice of the barons in favor of the ignoramuses around him. Therefore, he, Baldwin of Ramla, preferred to leave the Kingdom of Jerusalem rather than share in the ensuing reproaches over its doom. The Tripolitan prince countered these views with the observation that all was not lost, for the baronial party still had a strong position by reason of the fact that Isabel, the younger half sister of Sibyl, and her husband, Humphrey of

---

whole matter up to her. The barons then delivered the crown to her with the understanding that she would give it to whomsoever she desired to be king. Later the barons including Count Raymond assembled on another day. Count Raymond believed that Sibyl would give him the crown. Guy was present at this assemblage. Thereupon Sibyl held up the crown and surveyed the crowd until she saw Guy. Then she proceeded to place the crown on his head. Thus did Guy become king. Finally, Arnold of Lubeck (*loc. cit.*) states that Guy's coronation received general support characterized by an all day rejoicing resulting from Count Raymond's familiarity with Saladin and aspirations to be king. Only the Hospitallers refrained from the general enthusiasm. In respect to the account of Arnold of Lubeck, it must be observed that, in view of the general dislike of Guy on the score of his obvious incompetence, it is at least dubious that the anti-Raymond groupings not identified with the Hospitallers engaged in the general enthusiasm. At best they must have regarded Guy as the lesser of two evils. All these accounts ignore the extreme probability that the scheme to crown Guy had been planned long before and was strongly supported by the patriarch and Reginald of Châtillon. Lastly, although the sources are entirely silent on the rôle of Joscelyn III in these developments, it seems to me that all these accounts imply a lack of political finesse entirely out of character with that which he had already displayed in hoodwinking Raymond in the earlier stages of the *coup d'état*. Certainly the full consummation of the *coup d'état* would make the Seneschal as one of its prime movers and as the uncle of the queen a key figure in the new political orientation if not the actual power behind the throne. I cannot believe that Joscelyn III did not participate in the planning of the last stages of the *coup d'état*. And obviously the support of the new queen and her spouse would be much less, if the trickery allegedly employed by Sibyl had actually occurred. And Joscelyn III would thereby have been the loser to that extent. It was not to his interest to have this happen. It is because of these considerations I reject the apparent acceptance of the accounts of Benedict of Peterborough, Roger of Hoveden, and Roger of Wendover by Collins, *op. cit.*, pp. 228-29. La Monte (*The Crusade*, p. 122, n. 8) does not elect to apportion the degree of responsibility for the success of the *coup d'état* among its creators and simply remarks that "... whereby Sybelle was crowned and then conferred the crown upon her husband. This stroke was the work of Joscelyn, Renaud de Châtillon, the patriarch, and the Master of the Temple." This scholar supports me in my belief that Joscelyn III participated in the planning and execution of the final stages of the *coup d'état*.

Toron, were present in Nablus and they had the support of the Master of the Hospitallers and all the baronage save for Raymond of Châtillon. Furthermore, the Kingdom of Jerusalem now had a truce with the Saracens which Count Raymond believed would not be disturbed by them. Indeed, so he argued, the Saracens could be counted on to afford aid to the Franks, if such became the need. The Procurator concluded his plea with the promise that he would maintain the truce as long as he held his present rôle. The baronage then decided to crown Humphrey of Toron. But the coronation of a rival king with the inherent risk of a civil war did not eventuate, for Humphrey, reluctant to assume the duties of the profferred office, fled with his knights under cover of night to Jerusalem. Upon his arrival he presented himself to Sibyl after an initial spurning by her. The ensuing interview, during which Humphrey shamefacedly confessed that he had rejected the plans of the barons at Nablus to make him king over his objections and had fled to Jerusalem, ended with Sibyl's granting of pardon and acceptance of homage from, Humphrey.[307]

---

[307] *Chronique d'Ernoul*, pp. 134-36; *Eracles*, pp. 30-31; *Les gestes des Chiprois*, loc. cit. Champdor (*op. cit.*, p. 141) observes that "Cependant, sur le conseil de Joscelin III de Courtenay, oncle de Baudouin IV et tuteur du défunt roi, le comte de Tripoli réunit à Naplouse ses créatures et brigua leurs suffrages pour se faire offrir la couronne." There is no support in the sources for such an interpretation, and, furthermore, it runs completely counter to the actions, proposals, and advice of Count Raymond at the assembly at Nablus. Such an action on the part of Joscelyn III was not to the interest of the Courtenay chieftain. Again, as Baldwin (*Raymond III*, p. 77, n. 21) points out,"... Raymond had no aspirations to throne himself." Champdor (*op. cit.*, pp. 141-42) declares that prior to her coronation, Sibyl sent a messenger to the dissident barons "... les instruisant que, étant fille aînée du roi Amaury, soeur et mère des deux derniers rois, elle était la légitime héritière du trône, et leur faisant part du désir de la future reine de Jérusalem qui les priait d'assister aux fêtes de son couronnement. Le comte de Tripoli fit répondre que lui et les principaux seigneurs de son parti consentiraient volontiers à reconnaître son titre de reine si elle répudiait Guy de Lusignan et épousait ensuite un homme capable de commander l'armée franque et de défendre sérieusement le royaume de Jérusalem. L'astucieuse Sibylle accepta cette condition et elle fit jurer à tous les grands féodaux de reconnaître pour souverain l'homme qu'elle choisirait pour époux. Héraclius, qui connaissait ses véritables intentions, prononça la sentence de divorce." I can find no source material supporting this allegation. An acceptance of it requires a belief that Count Raymond repudiated the agreement that a committee of the pope, the Holy Roman Emperor, and the Kings of France and England should rule on the question which of the two daughters of the late King Amalric should inherit the throne. Such a repudiation would be an insult of the first magnitude to powerful secular and ecclesiastical figures in western Europe at the very time when their material and moral support was badly needed in the face of the rising power of Saladin. I cannot believe this. I may add that Baldwin's *Raymond III*, the most thorough and exhaustive account of the life of Count Raymond, lists no such account as that narrated by Champdor in his discussion of the variant accounts relative to the coronation of Sibyl and the barons' reaction thereto. See Baldwin, *Raymond III*, p. 77, n. 21. Richard (*op. cit.*, p. 139) regards

The result of Humphrey's capitulation was the decision of the entire baronage, save for Count Raymond and Baldwin of Ramla, to repair to Jerusalem to render homage to Guy. The barons promised to endeavor to persuade Guy to compensate Count Raymond for the several expenses which he had incurred and as a surety for which the late king, Baldwin IV, had granted Beirut to Raymond. Although Baldwin of Ramla did not agree with this proposal, even he wavered somewhat, for he sent his son Thomas to Jerusalem with a request to the baronage that they entreat the new king Guy to place his son in possession of his lands and to receive him. Only Count Raymond remained adamant; that leader retired to Tiberias. Meanwhile Guy convoked an assembly of the baronage at Acre and the latter carried out the requests of Baldwin of Ramla but to no avail. Guy answered

the *Haute Cour* at this time still to be a weak body. "La Haute-Cour n'avait pas alors les pouvoirs qu'elle arrogera au XIIIe siècle. Rien ne le prouve mieux que l'incapacité où elle fut d'agir." However, this scholar thinks that the Procurator believed he could surmount this weakness. "Toutefois Raymond III pensa à le faire: fort de l'alliance des Hospitaliers et de ses excellentes relations avec Saladin (qu'il pensait même faire intervenir), il essaya de décider Onfroi à recevoir la couronne." Runciman (*History*, *loc. cit.*) implies that the support of the general population of Jerusalem was an element in Sibyl's gaining and retention of the throne. "Amongst the people of Jerusalem there was much sympathy for Sibylla. She represented hereditary right; and though the throne was still nominally elective the claims of the heir could not be easily ignored. At the time of her mother's divorce Sibylla's legitimacy had been confirmed. Her brother had been King, and her son. Her one disadvantage was that her husband was disliked and despised." Baldwin (*Raymond III*, p.79, n. 25) offers the following possible explanation for the refusal of Humphrey of Toron to accept the offer of the kingship at this time: "Humphrey had a slight connection with Reginald of Krak which may have influenced his decision to refuse the responsibility thrust upon him. He was his stepson, and had been married to Isabel at Krak in 1183. Baldwin IV had arranged the marriage, but it had been urged apparently by Reginald and his wife Stephanie. The lord of Krak had provided a fitting celebration." The same scholar (*Raymond III*, p. 79) in his comments on the actions of Baldwin of Ramla observes that he "... suddenly appears as the most irreconcilable adversary of Guy. His enmity seems more personal than that of any of the others, not even excepting Raymond, and makes even more plausible that story of his own desire to marry Sibyl." ... "Though one would hesitate to picture him in somewhat romantic fashion as a disappointed lover, yet there is an unmistakable note of personal spite and jealousy in his words and actions. His estimate of Guy ... truly expresses, though not without bitterness, the new king's great weakness. Apparent to some extent before, it became increasingly evident in the following months that Guy's policies were in a large measure dictated by his friends, especially Gerard." I reject, as Baldwin (*Raymond III*, p. 72, n. 9) apparently does as well, the statement in *Brevis*, *loc. cit.*, that Count Raymond declared that he would repair to Jerusalem to prevent it, if Sibyl attempted to take the crown as it belonged to him by right. The author of the *Brevis* account was not as close to the events physically and chronologically as the authors of the two primary accounts, *Chronique d'Ernoul* and *Eracles.* Furthermore, such a declaration was not in accordance with Count Raymond's lack of a desire to hold the kingship in his own name.

shortly that he would accede to neither of the requests until Baldwin of Ramla himself came and rendered homage. If that leader did not obey, he, the king, would seize his lands. Thereupon Baldwin of Ramla reluctantly repaired to Acre and asserted to Guy that he had come to render homage to him, but that he did so as a man unwilling to hold lands from the king. The ensuing act of homage was not accompanied by the usual fraternal kiss. When his son had been formally invested with his lands and had rendered homage to Guy, Baldwin of Ramla entrusted his son to the care of his brother, Balian of Ibelin, and departed for Antioch with his forces. The prince of Antioch, Bohemond III, received him joyfully and granted him lands equal to those which he had lost. Recognizing the new trends, Guy had meantime proclaimed that Beirut was to be taken from the former regent, Count Raymond, and had demanded of him an accounting of all state funds he had expended during his regency. The net effect of these developments was the substantial military and political weakening of the Kingdom of Jerusalem, for the Moslems widely admired the political sagacity of Count Raymond, deeming him worthy of the kingship of the Kingdom of Jerusalem, and feared the military prowess of the brothers Baldwin of Ramla and Balian of Ibelin more than that of any other baron of the country.[308] The court party had won an immense triumph! But at what a cost!

With the political revolution thus consummated by the Autumn of 1186, Joscelyn III, its prime mover and author, now sought and gained his reward for his help to Guy. The new king reciprocated with economic and political favors. The former ones are illustrated by his grant on October 21, 1186 of the three fiefs of Banyas, Chastel-Neuf,

---

[308] *Chronique d'Ernoul*, pp. 136-39; *Brevis*, p. 53; Arnold of Lubeck, *op. cit.*, pp. 165-66; *Les Gestes des Chiprois*, pp. 658-59; Ibn al-Athīr, *K.-A.*, p. 674; *Eracles*, pp. 32-34; *Extrait du voyage d'Ibn Djobeïr, loc. cit.* Cahen (*La Syrie*, p. 427) sees in the territorial grants made to Baldwin of Ramla by Bohemond III an evidence of his attachment to Raymond of Tripoli. This attachment had existed ever since 1179. "Bohemond témoignait de son attachement persistant à Raymond en recevant et fieffant à Antioche Baudouin d'Ibelin et d'autres chevaliers, qui avaient refusé de prêter hommage à Guy." Baldwin (*Raymond III*, p. 80) discerns in the submisson to Guy at this time very practical considerations. "Humphrey's defection was the last straw for the barons at Neapolis. Unable to prevent the coronation of Guy and Sibyl, they had been equally unsuccessful in setting up an opposition candidate of their own. Though bitterly disappointed, they saw no further reason to keep their oath to Raymond. Guy was king *de facto*, and the best interests of the kingdom now demanded cooperation with him in preparation for the inevitable struggle with Saladin at the expiration of the truce. Since they had suffered no personal loss as had Raymond, they swallowed their pride and returned to the Holy City."

and Toron, which had been granted to Humphrey of Toron and were now occupied by the Moslem enemy. Upon their recovery they were to be held for the identical service given by Humphrey of Toron prior to his exchange of them with Baldwin IV in 1180. Furthermore, the Seneschal was to hold again the fief of Maron comprising the towns of Mees, Lahare, Cades, Quabriqembelide, and the two Megaras, which then required the service of four knights. If, on a later occasion, the *Haute Cour* should decide to return his former fiefs to the younger Humphrey, then Joscelyn III was to be compensated with the revenues and lands Humphrey of Toron had traded for them. Guy completed his grants to Joscelyn III with the cession of a house in Tyre formerly belonging to a certain Dame Vive.[309] Furthermore, the new king validated on the same day, October 21, 1186, the several grants made to the Seneschal by Guy and Sibyl, namely the fiefs of Chabor and Coquil and confirmed by the late king, Baldwin IV, in February, 1185. And lastly, Guy, having renewed Joscelyn III's right of freedom of sale in Acre of the sugar produced in his holding in Lanahia,[310] looked to the future in another document drawn up on the same day. The political overtones are obvious in the statement that he, Guy, could designate anyone he chose as guardian for the daughters of Joscelyn III, if the Courtenay chieftain should die before they reached their majority. Even more obvious political implications were discernible in the careful provision for the marriage of the Seneschal's two daughters. This was tantamount to a political and military alliance between Guy and Joscelyn III, for it provided that the latter's elder daughter was to marry William of Valence, Guy's younger brother, and to acquire as her dowry Chabor, Toron, Chastel-Neuf, and Le Chambrelaine. The document also stipulated that the younger daughter was to marry one of Guy's nephews and to acquire the balance of her father's land. William of Valence would marry the younger daughter in the event that her elder sister died before reaching the age of marriage. If he did not choose either of the Seneschal's daughters, then both of them were to marry nephews of Guy. Lastly, Joscelyn III agreed to pay William of Valence 4,000 besants a year beginning with the time of his arrival in the East until the daughter he eventually married reached marriageable age. The bridegroom would receive the promised dowry

---

[309] Röhricht, *Regesta*, Nos. 653 and 1003, pp. 173-74 and 263-64; Strehlke, *op. cit.*, Nos. 21 and 66, pp. 19 and 54.
[310] Röhricht, *Regesta*, No. 654, p. 174; Strehlke, *op. cit.*, No. 22, p. 20; Rey, *Les colonies*, pp. 475-76 and 487.

or would continue to receive 4,000 besants a year at the time of the marriage.[311]

As a result of these several grants, the total holdings of the Seneschal, as La Monte[312] has pointed out, "... formed one of the greatest seignories in the East, and much of his wealth came from the many money fiefs which he held." This was true, even if one makes due allowance for the fact that the Moslems held some of his seignory. It gave him control of all the mountain country behind Tyre and Acre.[313] The Courtenay chieftain had come a long way economically and politically since the disaster consequent upon the loss of his patrimony, the County of Edessa, in the early 1150's and the even greater disaster of his long imprisonment of twelve years from 1164 to 1176!

But the Seneschal's present and proud position was indeed precarious, for two of the native nobles, Count Raymond and Baldwin of Ramla together with their supporters, continued their schism and threatened the hegemony of King Guy and his supporters, the court nobles and their spokesman, Joscelyn III. Guy besought the advice of his supporter in the *coup d'état*, the Master of the Templars, against his defiant vassal, Count Raymond, and was soon urged to invest him

---

[311] Röhricht, *Regesta*, No. 655, p. 174; Strehlke, *op. cit.*, No. 23, p. 21.

[312] La Monte, *Feudal Monarchy*, p. 147.

[313] La Monte, "The rise," p. 315. This scholar (*Feudal Monarchy*, p. 149) goes on to say that "The feudal service of Outremer was far more French than Norman and there never developed in the crusading states any definite knight's fee."... "It is impossible to find in this [the great seignory built up by Joscelyn III] or in any other of the great fiefs any system of knight's fees, or even any consistent value in cash against which the service of a knight was charged. Several elements entered into this, and the law of supply and demand can be seen in operation. When the supply of knights was low and when the Saracens invaded the country reducing the value of landed fiefs and rendering less secure the receipt of rentals levied against the revenues of the towns, the price of a single knight was comparatively high. On the other hand in times of comparative security, or when a new crusade from the West had brought a large number of knights to the East, the value of the knight's fief was appreciable lower." He also observes ("The rise," pp. 301-02) that "For the seigneury of Joscelyn, known then as now only by that rather indefinite title, was never an homogeneous unit but was always an agglomeration of separate entities welded together by the man who acquired them and dispersed almost immediately after his death. But although this seigneury was short lived and never became an important state, it has a unique interest among all the great lordships in crusading Palestine for concerning it we are better informed than any of the other seigneuries. The seigneury of Count Joscelyn is rightly so called. In the first place it had no capital city like Tiberias, Jaffa, Naplouse, Rama, Caesarea or Sidon; it had no great fortress like Toron or Montreal which dominated the entire fief; it had no natural limits or focal point, -only the shrewd and ambitious policy of Joscelyn himself gave it unity. In the second place lasting as it did through the life time of its founder it was essentially the personal fief of Count Joscelyn and so most appropriately bears his name."

in his stronghold of Tiberias and thus oblige him to surrender.[314] Count Raymond's reply was a truce with Saladin applicable not only to his own County of Tripoli but to his spouse's principality of Galilee as well. The terms of the truce bound Count Raymond to pursue a policy of military inaction even if his overlord should become involved in a war with the Moslems.[315] Saladin soon gave substance to his pledge by a dispatch of infantrymen, archers, and armaments to Count Raymond, a promise of immediate military assistance, and the release of a number of prisoners who were knights under Raymond's command. Thereupon the Moslem leader mustered his army at Banyas. This move evoked a counter move by King Guy in his assembling an army at Nazareth.[316]

---

[314] *Chronique d'Ernoul*, chap. xii, p. 141; *Eracles*, pp. 34-35.

[315] Ibn al-Athīr, *K.-A.*, p. 675; *Eracles*, p. 35; Abou Chamah, *op. cit.*, pp. 257-58; *Brevis*, loc. cit.; Arnold of Lubeck, *op. cit.*, p. 166; Albert of Trium-Fontium, *op. cit.*, pp. 747-48; *Historia Peregrinorum* ed. by A. Chroust in *Monumenta Germaniae Historica* New Series (Berlin, 1928), V, 119. See Appendix C on the problems of the exact time of the creation of the truce between Count Raymond and Saladin, the initiative of the signing of the truce, and the circumstances of the truce.

[316] *Chronique d'Ernoul, loc. cit.*; *Eracles, loc. cit.*; Ibn al-Athīr, *K.—A.*, *loc. cit.*

CHAPTER FOURTEEN

FRANCO-MOSLEM DEVELOPMENTS, 1185-1187:
THE FINAL CONSOLIDATION OF SALADIN'S POWER;
THE SUNDERING OF THE FRANCO-MOSLEM TRUCE;
RECONCILIATION OF THE WARRING PARTIES IN THE
KINGDOM OF JERUSALEM; THE CAMPAIGN OF HATTIN

The total connotation of these developments can be understood only against the background of the steady growth of Saladin's military and political power at the expense of his Moslem rivals during the past several years. He had faced marked unrest in his northern districts on the eve of his signature of his peace treaty with the Franks at the close of 1184 or the opening days of 1185 and he had hence occupied himself in quelling it. Proceeding northward in April, 1185, he moved against the center of this discontent, 'Izz-ad-Dīn, the ruler of Mosul. Open conflict soon threatened when 'Izz-ad-Dīn's vassals, the rulers of Irbil and Jazira, sent envoys to Saladin. Kukburi of Harran openly joined Saladin and 'Izz-ad-Dīn, not at all abashed, dispatched embassies to the Moslem rulers of Persarmenia and Konya to seek their assistance. They respectively responded with the sending of some forces to 'Izz-ad-Dīn and the dispatch of a menacing letter to Saladin, which, however, was not backed up by military aid. With this new turn of events 'Izz-ad-Dīn decided to seek peace when Saladin appeared before Mosul. But it was to no avail, for Saladin spurned all his overtures as well as those made by 'Izz-ad-Dīn's old mother. However, the summer's heat and the accompanying disease which began to decimate Saladin's troops together with the strong defenses of Mosul served to save 'Izz-ad-Dīn at this time. These factors along with the alluring attraction of the conquest of cities provided by the death of the ruler of Persarmenia in August, 1185 induced Saladin to depart from Mosul with the double aim of capturing Amida and Maiyafariqin, the vassal cities of his deceased enemy, and obtaining the advantage of better climatic conditions for his troops in the highlands. Both aims were realized, but Saladin himself fell almost mortally ill soon thereafter in October. He managed to reach the friendly haven of the castle of his ally Kukburi in Harran and to obtain the services of skilled physicians who were sent by his brother al-ʿĀdil, the ruler of Aleppo. But nothing availed. Since his death seemed to be imminent and his ambitious kinsmen were already scheming to gain his properties, Saladin obliged his emirs to swear their loyalty to his sons. Then the unexpected happened with Saladin's gradual recovery of his health during February, 1186. ʿIzz-ad-Dīn of Mosul, perhaps aware of his foeman's recovery by the opening weeks of 1186, made peace overtures to Saladin at the end of February. The latter accepted them and shortly thereafter ʿIzz-ad-Dīn's and Saladin's ambassadors signed treaties on March 3, 1186 which reduced the former chieftain to the status of a mere henchman of Saladin. Although he was confirmed in his own lands, he lost all control over the trans-Tigris areas south of Mosul. These were placed under the jurisdiction of emirs selected by Saladin himself.[317] This factor obliged ʿIzz-ad-Dīn to remain loyal.

Only one element of weakness threatened Saladin's expanding panoply of power and that was soon remedied. The ruler of Homs, his cousin, a certain Naṣīr-ad-Dīn, had dared to plot during the course of Saladin's recent illness to seize the Syrian throne. Retribution soon followed from Saladin's camp: the plotter died in bed on March 5, 1186. His young son and successor on the throne of Homs, Shīrkūh II, soon faced a grim future as a result of Saladin's confiscation of the bulk of his money, but he succeeded in effecting its restoration by a quotation of an appropriate passage from the Koran which promised torture to the despoilers of orphans. By April, 1186 all hostility had vanished, Saladin had returned to Damascus, and his empire, now much augmented in size, reached to the borders of Persia itself.[318] The

---

[317] Ibn al-Athīr, *Atabecs*, pp. 335-36; Behâ Ed-Dîn, *Saladin*, pp. 100-04 and *Anecdotes*, pp. 82-87; Abū'l-Fidā, *op. cit.*, p. 54; Makrizi, *op. cit.*, pp. 15-17; Kamal-Ad-Dîn, *Histoire*, IV, 173-76; *The Chronography of Bar Hebraeus*, pp. 317-19 and 320; Michael the Syrian, p. 394 and chap. iv, *Chronique*, p. 397 and *Extrait*, p. 393. Lane-Poole (*op. cit.*, p. 193) believes that personal factors prompted Saladin's decision to make a treaty with ʿIzz-ad-Dīn. "Too weak as yet to dream of a campaign, and softened perhaps by suffering and danger, Saladin consented to a treaty..."

[318] Makrizi, *op. cit.*, p. 18; Kamal-Ad-Dîn, *Histoire*, IV, 175-76; Abū'l-Fidā, *op. cit.*, pp. 54-55; *The Chronography of Bar Hebraeus*, p. 319. Lane-Poole (*op. cit.*, pp. 197-98) aptly appraises the significance of these developments as follows: "The great crisis was at hand. Saladin was at last in a position to attack the Franks. The object of his campaigns on the Tigris and Euphrates had been attained. He had now allies instead of enemies on his northern flank. Before this no invasion of the Christian territory could safely be undertaken without posting an army of observation to guard against an attack from the north; but now he could advance with confidence. He had also more troops at his back, and could not only command the full strength of his Syrian and Egyptian levies, but also count upon large contingents from the Mesopotamian provinces."...

danger to the Frankish states had become immeasurably greater.

Perhaps aware of the new developments and the connotations thereof in Saladin's empire, Balian of Ibelin, the brother of the second of the major Frankish malcontents, Baldwin of Ramla, was probably

---

"This was indeed the most important result of his northern campaigns. He had opened up new recruiting grounds; and without this added strength he could never have met and resisted the fresh forces from Europe brought against him in the Third Crusade." Cf. Baldwin, "The Decline," pp. 609-10: "It has often been assumed that Saladin's progressive unification of a large and important section of the Moslem world rendered an ultimate victory over the Christian states inevitable. It is true that his brilliant chain of successes in Egypt and Syria seemed to point inexorably to that greatest success, the recovery of the coast lands. Nevertheless, Saladin's position in 1187, far from making his victory inevitable, still left the crusaders two possible courses of action. First, they could delay, as they had done in 1183, avoiding an open battle in the hope that Saladin would not be able to maintain his army intact for long. The intense summer heat in the arid Galilaean hill country would be an added factor in their favor. The success of such a policy depended on the sultan's decision not to risk a battle under unfavorable circumstances, and the expected disintegration of his army and consequently of his political power if he failed to win a decisive victory. In many respects Saladin's control of the Moslem hinterland from the Euphrates to the Nile was more apparent than real. It is significant, for example, that when he discussed the plan of campaign with his subordinates on the eve of the invasion of Jerusalem, he rejected the suggestion that the Christians be opposed only by small raids, sieges, and devastation of the countryside and insisted strongly on a major engagement. Apparently he realized that he was not popular at the caliph's court and that he was thought by many to be more eager to fight Moslems than Christians." Slaughter (*op. cit.*, p. 121), in discussing the motivations of the rebellions of Saladin's Moslem opponents and in explaining the speed with which he met these rebellions, plausibly observes that "Since the recovery of Edessa had removed their fear of aggression on the part of the Latin Kingdom, the Holy War seemed an insufficient reason for losing their sovereignty. Appeals from the Caliph might move the devout, but the wordly-wise suspected that to Saladin the religious motive was secondary to his imperial ambitions. They could not see that their welfare depended upon the unity of Islam. For many reasons, the Oriental Peace was not renewed. Yet it was imperative to Saladin to secure the allegiance of these provinces as a preparation for a decisive contest with the enemy on his western border. Enough of them to insure success must be ready to obey the summons when the hour struck. Whether or not he fully understood the strength of the war party in Jerusalem, he must have known that their winning of Raymond to their cause, however unwillingly he joined them, only made the menace greater. Therefore he must lose no time." Lane-Poole (*op. cit.*, p. 194) either contradicts himself or quibbles over the meaning of the word "retribution" in the following passage: "Nevertheless, during his cousin's [Saladin] illness, Nasir-ed-din had intrigued for the throne of Syria. Retribution followed swiftly; for retiring, full of wine and good cheer, on the Feast of the Victims (4 March, 1186), the pretender was found dead in his bed next morning."* *"The improbable suggestion of Ibn-el-Athir that he was poisoned by Saladin's orders hardly deserves notice." I have been unable to find such a statement in Ibn-al-Athīr's *K.-A* or *Atabecs*. Abū'l-Fidā (*op. cit.*, p. 55) does mention this as follows: "On dit que le sultan, après avoir appris ses [Naṣīr-ad-Dīn] démarches auprès des notables de Damas, avait aposté une personne qui lui administra du poison." I can see nothing improbable in this charge of Abū'l-Fidā, in view of an identical procedure of Saladin in 1182. *Supra*, pp. 107-08.

alarmed by King Guy's recent moves and certainly so by the King's mustering of his forces in the winter of 1186-1187, a season not ordinarily identified with military operations, preparatory to an investment of Tiberias, the stronghold of his rival, Count Raymond. Hence Balian made inquiry about the new developments. Upon learning of the royal intention, he indicated the stupidity of this move. The combination of the military strength of Saladin and Count Raymond was greater than the King's. Therefore, the army should be disbanded and a policy of reconciliation and unity with the dissident vassal was in order. He, Balian, accompanied by other barons, would visit Count Raymond in an effort to restore peace between the recalcitrant vassal and the king. Balian's plea won the king's support and Guy, in consequence, disbanded the army and dispatched the requested embassy to Count Raymond. But the effort came to naught, because Count Raymond demanded the return of Beirut as his condition of submission to Guy. The latter, in turn, regarded this demand as exorbitant. A stalemate ensued until the conclusion of the Easter season of 1187.[319]

The danger presented to the Frankish states by the very recent augmentation of Saladin's power was not immediate as long as that Moslem chieftain chose to abide by the terms of the truce with the Franks and they, in turn, should not elect to give him a plausible pretext to break it. He so chose and the Franks initially refrained from actions affording their doughty foeman such an excuse. But this was provided early in March, 1187 by the decision of Reginald of Châtillon to seize a Moslem caravan legally moving through Frankish territories from Cairo to Damascus in accordance with the terms of the truce. Reginald's slaying of the military escort, seizure of the rich booty of the caravan itself, and imprisonment of the merchants and their families in his castle of Krak evoked an immediate response from Saladin in the form of a demand upon Reginald that he release the prisoners and compensate them for their losses. The Frankish chieftain stonily declined to admit Saladin's messengers, whereupon they repaired to Jerusalem to complain to Guy. The King proved more obliging than Reginald, for he ordered the lord of Krak to make reparations to the aggrieved Moslems. But it was to no avail. Reginald, secure in his knowledge that King Guy had gained and continued to

---

[319] *Chronique d'Ernoul*, pp. 141-42; Arnold of Lubeck, *loc. cit.*; *Eracles*, pp. 35-36; *Brevis, loc. cit.*

hold his throne through his support, ignored the order. Guy was helpless, unable, and probably unwilling as well to bring his powerful vassal to obedience. Saladin, now incensed, swore to kill Reginald of Châtillon with his own hands, if he should capture him.[320] And the

---

[320] Abou Chamah, *op. cit.*, p. 259; *Itinerarium*, p. 12; *Eracles*, p. 34; Makrizi, *op. cit.*, p. 21; *The Chronography of Bar Hebraeus*, p. 322; Ibn al-Athīr, *K.—A.*, p. 676; Abū'l-Fidā, *op. cit.*, p. 55; Behâ Ed-Dîn, *Anecdotes*, pp. 39 and 96 and *Saladin*, p. 114; Kamal-ad-Dîn, *Histoire*, IV, 180-81; *Brevis, loc. cit.*; Baldwin, *Raymond III*, p. 86 and n. 41. Stevenson (*op. cit.*, pp. 240-41) dissents from the view that Reginald of Châtillon's attack was primarily the rash action of one man and holds that the episode was the practical result of a party opposed to the existing foreign policy of the leaders of the Kingdom of Jerusalem. "When Guy became king after the death of Baldwin V the peace with Saladin was still in force. It was an important safeguard to the kingdom for it alone restrained the sultan from seeking to deal his adversaries a crushing blow. Yet powerful influences were at work against it in the ranks of the ruling party. The peace had been concluded by Raymond, who now was an enemy of the king. In the quarrel between Raymond and Guy the Moslems had taken a side and that against the established government. Thus the peace assumed the character of something personal to Raymond, and Guy stood already in an attitude hostile to the sultan. It is easy to understand the growing feeling of a party that war with the Moslems was natural and inevitable and that the peace was the act of a suspect and almost a traitor. Under these circumstances it was scarcely to be expected that the Latins would wait for the expiry of the four years' truce before resuming hostilities. It was Reginald of Kerak in the Spring of 1187 who finally ignored the treaty obligations by which he was bound. But the responsibility of this breach of faith has been too exclusively apportioned to Reginald himself. He may have been extreme in his views and just the man likely to precipitate the conflict. But he did not stand alone and his action may reasonably be viewed as the practical outcome of the feeling of a party. Reginald struck the first blow chiefly because he occupied the most favourable position for so doing." Cf. Baldwin, *Raymond III*, p. 86; "This [the above cited observation of Stevenson] is a plausible interpretation, but, I think, omits consideration of the fact that these men who had so recently usurped the throne were not entirely certain of their position and perhaps not in complete agreement as to the wisdom of renewing the war with Saladin. It is noticeable that Guy's first move after Raymond's precipitate action—in which he was influenced, it is true, by Raymond's friends—was another attempt to win the support of the count, then an undoubted need. He also, as will be seen, tried unsuccessfully to order Reginald to make restitution. It is more than likely that he would have preferred to have the absolute assurance of Raymond's support before any actual move against the sultan. In any case, we can be certain that Reginald's impetuosity precipitated the break." Grousset (*Histoire*, p. 778) sees in Reginald of Châtillon's defiance of King Guy the triumph of feudal anarchy: "C'était surtout la fin du royaume parce que le refus de Renaud proclamait la chute de l'institution monarchique. Jamais au temps des quatre premiers Baudouin, du roi Foulque ou du roi Amaury un baron n'eût osé, devant les remontrances royales, répondre qu'il était aussi maître en son fief que le monarque à Jérusalem. Cette révolte du principal des vassaux directs, et dans une circonstance où il y allait de la paix ou de la guerre générale, montre, plus encore que la sécession du comte de Tripoli, la disparition de l'autorité royale entre les mains débiles de Guy de Lusignan. Souverain sans prestige, ne devant sa couronne qu'à la protection de Renaud de Châtillon, il se trouvait dans l'impossibilité de faire céder celui-ci. Il devait supporter à l'interieur ses insolences, à l'extérieur se laisser précipiter par lui dans la guerre inexpiable que les razzias du chevalier-brigand avaient rendue fatale. Pris entre Renaud qui entraînait tout le royaume

virtual certainty of an all-out united Moslem attack was made all the more terrifying by reason of a continuation and final crystallization of the trends towards a Moslem—Byzantine rapprochement which had their inception as far back as the Spring of 1181.[321] A massacre of Franks in Constantinople in 1182 naturally exacerbated the already increasingly hostile tone of Italians who were already alienated by the efforts of the late Emperor Manuel to recover Byzantine territories in Italy. The Italian response to all these developments was an invasion of the Greek peninsula in 1185 by a Norman army commanded by William II of Sicily and the threat of a deposition of the then ruling Byzantine Emperor Andronicus I (1182-1185), who had gained his throne by the ousting and blinding in 1182 of the increasingly unpopular Alexius Comnenus the Protosebastos associated with the boy emperor Alexius II, and, after a brief regency of his own with Alexius II, by the murder of the latter in September, 1183. Aware of his own growing unpopularity arising from his tyrannical tactics towards his opponents, dismayed by William II's capture of Thessalonica and ensuing advance on Constantinople itself, and facing the distinct prospect of a restoration of the House of Comnenus by reason of the raising of the standard of revolt by a Comnenan prince closely related to the last of the Comnenan rulers, Alexius II, Andronicus I turned to Saladin in June, 1185 with a proposal of an alliance. Saladin, understandably apprehensive over the revival of Selchük power resulting from their victory over the Byzantines at the battle of Myriokephalon in central Asia Minor in 1176, which in turn gave to the Selchüks a splendid opportunity to threaten Byzantine holdings in the Aegean as well as Saladin's in northern Syria, proved to be receptive to the Byzantine embassy's recollections of the recently established (1181) amicable relationships between Moslems and Byzantines. The upshot of all this was the tendering by the Byzantine envoys of a proposal of an alliance providing for the swearing of homage by Saladin to Andronicus, the rendering of aid by the former to the latter whenever such aid was requested, and an ensuing conquest and division of Palestine between Moslems and Byzantines; the latter

---

dans la plus insensé des aventures et Raymond III qui poussait la politique de paix jusqu'aux confins de la trahison, la situation de Guy devenait— reconnaissons-le—intenable. A la vérité l'État n'avait plus de chef. L'anarchie féodale ayant annihilé la royauté hiérosolymitaine, la Syrie franque allait délibérément au suicide."

[321] *Supra*, pp. 103-04.

were to be awarded Jerusalem and all the coastal cities save for Ascalon. If Asia Minor should be recovered, all of it up to Antioch and Armenia would be Byzantine in ownership. Although this treaty with its probable accompanying promises on Andronicus' part to aid Saladin in his struggle with the Latin Franks proved to be abortive because of the deposition of Andronicus on September 12, 1185 resulting from his failure to deal effectively with the Norman invasion under William II of Sicily, the relations between Byzantium and Saladin continued to be cordial. The new Byzantine emperor Isaac II (1185-1195), still beset by Norman military power which threatened Constantinople itself, quickly confirmed the treaty which Saladin's emissaries now presented to the new emperor. This treaty, freeing Saladin from fear of Byzantine attack on him, enhanced still more his military and political opportunities.[322]

The outraged Moslem leader soon gave an earnest of his intentions by a plan to assemble his armies in the Hauran. This he presently executed by his departure from Damascus at the close of March, 1187 to Ra's al-Mā' and his mustering of his forces in his far-flung empire to join the *jihad.* Meanwhile his defiant enemy, Reginald of Châtillon, threw down the gauntlet with his bold threat to attack Moslem pilgrims *en route* from Mecca. Saladin, nothing daunted, advanced on Krak to defend them. His ensuing encampment at Kaṣr es-salama near Bosra with a force of élite soldiery afforded ample protection to the pilgrims during their passage in the opening days of May. Reginald of Châtillon did not move, thoroughly cognizant of his foeman's power which manifested itself in Saladin's ravaging of the farms in the vicinity of Krak. The strength of the Syrian Moslems was soon augmented by the union of the Egyptian armies with those of Saladin at Karyetain.[323]

Meanwhile, these military moves of Saladin apparently sobered the warring Frankish factions in the Kingdom of Jerusalem, for King Guy,

---

[322] A full discussion of these developments is provided in the article by Charles M. Brand, "The Byzantines and Saladin, 1185-1192: Opponents of the Third Crusade," *Speculum* (Cambridge, 1962), XXXVII, 167-181.

[323] Behâ Ed-Dîn, *Anecdotes*, pp. 91 and 96 and *Saladin*, p. 108; Abou Chamah, *op. cit.*, p. 261 and 280-81; *The Chronography of Bar Hebraeus, loc. cit.*; Ibn al-Athīr, *K.—A.*, pp. 677-78; Makrizi, *op. cit.*, pp. 21-22; Kamal-Ad-Dîn, *Histoire*, IV, 176-77; Roger of Wendover, *op. cit.*, pp. 139-40; Michael the Syrian, Bk. XXI, chap. vi, *Chronique*, p. 403; *Libellus*, pp. 210-11; Benedict of Peterborough, *op. cit.*, II, 21. (Henceforth most references to the last cited source will pertain to Volume II. References to Volume I will be cited as I).

with the urging of the now apprehensive Balian of Ibelin, convoked his vassals, both ecclesiastical and secular, for a meeting with him soon after Easter (March 29, 1187) in Jerusalem. The ensuing colloquy over the present dilemma elicited from the barons the advice that the King should make his peace with the dissident Count Raymond. Baldwin of Ramla, the foremost knight of the Kingdom of Jerusalem, had already been lost to the King's service. If Guy should also lose the aid of Count Raymond, who now had a truce with Saladin, the King's cause would surely be lost. Reconciliation with Count Raymond at this juncture would remove the threat of Saladin's invasion of the Kingdom of Jerusalem through Tiberias and would secure the counsel of the foremost soldier of the land. Guy agreed with this view and accordingly appointed a committee comprising Reginald of Sidon, Joscius, the Archbishop of Tyre, Balian of Ibelin, and the Masters of the Hospitallers and Templars, Roger of Les Moulins and Gerard of Ridefort, to repair to Tiberias and secure a peace with Count Raymond.[324]

Shortly thereafter all the committee members, save for Balian of Ibelin, who was detained at Nablus on personal business, proceeded northward on April 29, 1187 with a retinue of attendants. The entire assemblage totaled one hundred and ten persons. When they neared the town of Caco, a messenger of Count Raymond met them on April 30 with the warning that the next day would see the entrance of the Moslems into Christian territory.[325] A recent agreement arranged between Count Raymond and Saladin provided for the crossing of the Jordan River and entrance into the Kingdom of Jerusalem by Moslem forces for one day. There was, however, the stipulation that these forces must do no harm to any town or village and must return to their own territory at nightfall.[326] But to no avail was the precaution! The

---

[324] *Chronique d'Ernoul*, pp. 142-43; *Eracles*, pp. 36-37; Ibn al-Athīr, *K.*—*A.*, p. 680. Charles Oman, *A History of the Art of War in the Middle Ages, A. D. 378-1278* (London, 1923), I, 325.

[325] *Chronique d'Ernoul*, p. 148; *Eracles*, p. 39; Giraldus Cambrensis, *Opera. De Principis Instructione Liber*, VIII, 201-02.

[326] *Eracles*, p. 38; *Chronique d'Ernoul*, pp. 144-45; Baldwin, *Raymond III*, pp. 88-90 and n. 46, p. 89. Oman (*op. cit.*, p. 324) implies that Saladin's invasion of the Tiberias district at this time was part of a larger and master plan of attack on the Frankish power. "In 1187 Saladin, after having cut short the borders of the Christians in many quarters, resolved to risk an attack on the centre of their strength, by a direct invasion of the kingdom of Jerusalem. He first despatched a considerable force to execute a raid into its northern parts: it was put in charge of Modhaffer-ed-din, Prince of Edessa and Haran, who crossed the Jordan, harried the hill-country of Galilee, and cut to pieces at

committee members along with their attendants and a fresh force of forty knights from Tiberias met disaster on May 1, 1187 when they came into direct confrontation with the Moslem invaders. Only a handful escaped, the remainder comprising most of the knights of the Temple and the Hospital being captured or perishing. Archbishop Joscius and Roger of Les Moulins, the Master of the Hospital, were among the slain.[327] The survivors, namely Gerard of Ridefort, the Master of the Templars, and a few of his knights escaped. Soon joined by Balian of Ibelin at Nazareth, they proceeded to Tiberias with the protective escort of some knights dispatched by Count Raymond.[328]

The Tripolitan leader proved himself amenable to the committee's quest, for he reconciled himself with King Guy, presumably after receiving a promise from the committee that the city of Beirut would be returned to him,[329] and agreed to discharge from his service at Tiberias the Moslem soldiery sent to him by Saladin.[330] King Guy, upon receipt of information about the new turn of events from a messenger sent to him by the committee, departed from Jerusalem to meet Count Raymond and the committee, who were now in the course of return to Jerusalem. The now reconciled parties met near Dotaym and the two leaders thereof, namely Count Raymond and King Guy, hailed the new day by their respective kneeling and embracing and ensuing departure to Jerusalem. There Count Raymond paid homage to King Guy and Queen Sibyl.[331] In consonance with the new harmony and in recognition of the peril posed by Saladin, all parties showed their good faith by mustering their contingents at Ṣaffūrīyah; this site was selected by Count Raymond. Bohemond of Antioch, in response to the joint appeal from King Guy and Count Raymond, buried the hatchet,

---

the bloody encounter of Saffaria (May 1) the knights of the Temple and the Hospital, who had come forth against him with more zeal than discretion, before any succours could reach them. His safe return emboldened the Sultan to ride forth in person."

[327] *Eracles*, p. 40; *Les gestes des Chiprois*, p. 659; *Libellus*, pp. 211-15; Ibn al-Athīr, *K.—A.*, pp. 678-79; *The Chronography of Bar Hebraeus, loc. cit.*; Roger of Hoveden, *op. cit.*, p. 319; Roger of Wendover, *op. cit.*, p. 140; Abou Chamah, *op. cit.*, p. 262; Benedict of Peterborough, *op. cit.*, pp. 10 and 21; Arnold of Lubeck, *op. cit.*, pp. 166-67; Kamal-Ad-Dîn, *Histoire*, IV, 177; *Annales de Terre Sainte*, p. 433; Ambroise, *L'Estoire de la guerre sainte*, ed. Gaston Paris (Paris, 1897), Col. 67. (Henceforth this source will be cited as *L'Estoire*). Röhricht (*Regesta*, No. 653, p. 173) indicates that Joscius had been made the Archbishop of Tyre by October 21, 1186.

[328] *Chronique d'Ernoul*, pp. 148-51; *Eracles, loc. cit.* and p. 43.

[329] *Eracles*, p. 44; *Libellus*, p. 217; Ibn al-Athīr, *K.—A.*, p. 680.

[330] *Chronique d'Ernoul*, p. 152.

[331] *Ibid.*, p. 153; *Libellus, loc. cit.*; *Eracles*, p. 45. This last named source indicates that Guy excused himself for his unwarranted coronation and other acts.

promised armed aid, and sent his son Raymond to aid the Tripolitan prince. The Orders of the Temple and Hospital summoned most of their membership to the colors and the former Order turned over to King Guy their part of the money which King Henry II of England had sent to both Orders in preparation for a projected crusade on the part of that monarch. The total Frankish assembly of forces at length numbered no less than 1200 knights, almost 10,000 foot soldiers, and considerable numbers of native cavalrymen. The general reconciliation between the several factions was, however, far from complete because of the lingering suspicion that Count Raymond was still secretly an ally of the Moslems. Although baseless, this view entailed disaster.[332]

Meanwhile, the united Moslem forces, now flushed with reports of the recent victory scored over the Franks on May 1 and led by Saladin, proceeded to Tall al 'Ashtarā east of the Sea of Galilee on May 27, 1187. The forces advancing from Mosul and Aleppo arrived last because of their prior military activities against the Franks in Antioch and the Armenians in Cilicia in compliance with Saladin's two fold strategy of forestalling aid on the part of the northern Franks to those

---

[332] Ibn al-Athīr, *K.—A.*, pp. 679-80; *Brevis, loc. cit.*; *The Chronography of Bar Hebraeus*, p. 323; Kamal-Ad-Dîn, *Histoire*, IV, 178; *Eracles*, pp. 45-46; *Libellus*, p. 218. Baldwin, *Raymond III*, p. 95 and p. 102, n. 18. This scholar aptly observes that "His [Count Raymond's] final repentance and reconciliation were unquestionably sincere, as later events proved, and were so accepted and interpreted by all but his bitterest enemies, Gerard and Reginald. But it was just these men who were Guy's closest associates, on whom he relied most, and who had done so much to secure the throne for him. He was deeply in obligation to them. Thus on the eve of the battle of Hattin, the court clique was again in power, and Raymond of Tripolis, though outwardly restored to favor, stood outside, distrusted and misunderstood." Although the sources are entirely silent in respect to the rôle of Joscelyn III in the creation of this new harmony between King Guy and Count Raymond, it is a fair presumption that he, as a member of the court clique, still held views towards Raymond which were identical with or very similar to those entertained by Gerard and Reginald of Châtillon toward Count Raymond. Oman (*op. cit.*, p. 325) believes that the Frankish armed forces at this time were "... the largest force that they [the Franks] had ever put into the field save that which had been mustered for the abortive campaign of 1184." [sic] Stevenson (*op. cit.*, p. 245, n. 2) estimates the Frankish forces as "... at least 20,000 strong." Dana C. Munro ("Christian and Infidel in the Holy Land," *Essays on the Crusades* [Burlington, Vermont, 1903], p. 38) declares in reference to the assemblage of the Frankish nobility on the eve of the battle of Hattin that "Count Joscelyn [III] restored all the booty which he had captured from a caravan, when he found that it belonged to the Arabs with whom he had formerly been on friendly relations." The sources do not provide any evidence for such a restoration on the part of Joscelyn III. Perhaps this is a case of confusion with Joscelyn I, who, following a raid in Moslem territory and subsequent capture of prisoners and supplies, restored them to the Moslem chieftain Najm-al-Dawlah. See Usāmah Ibn Munqidh (Kitāb Al-I'Tibār). *An Arab-Syrian Gentleman and Warrior in the Period of the Crusades*. Translated with annotations by Philip K. Hitti (New York, 1929), pp. 119-20.

in the south and of capitalizing on the present weakness of Armenia arising out of the recent death of its ruler, Roupen III. With the arrival of these forces in the third week of June an accomplished fact, the several emirs met in council on June 24, and, having laid plans to invade the Kingdom of Jerusalem, proceeded to review their forces of perhaps 25,000 men. The Moslem holy day, Friday, saw Saladin's forces breaking camp and on the following day, June 27, they crossed the Jordan River near the southern end of Lake Tiberias and established a new base close to the river banks. Since the Franks did not move from Ṣaffūrīyah, Saladin tried to lure them into taking action by deploying his own skirmishers against them for several days. Failing in this maneuver, he resorted to another one on July 2 by a division of his forces. He stationed the bulk of them west of Tiberias on a plateau, the site he had already selected for the impending battle, and proceeded to assault strongly Tiberias with choice forces for an hour. The town soon fell into his control with only the citadel into which the small garrison and Raymond's wife withdrew still holding out.³³³

Saladin's maneuvers, together with the message from the besieged countess that she would have to surrender Tiberias unless help arrived promptly, led to a council of war in the Frankish camp at Ṣaffūrīyah on the night of July 2. To the arguments of Reginald of Châtillon and

---

³³³ Behâ Ed-Dîn, *Saladin*, pp. 109-11 and nn. 1 and 2, p. 111 and *Anecdotes*, pp. 91-93; Benedict of Peterborough, *op. cit.*, p. 11; Ibn al-Athīr, *K.—A.*, pp. 679, 680-81, and 682; Kamal-Ad-Dîn, *Histoire*, IV, 177-78; Michael the Syrian, *Chronique*, p. 404 and *Extrait*, p. 396; *Ex Chronologia Roberti Altissiodorensis, loc. cit.*; *Brevis, loc. cit.*; *Chronique d'Ernoul*, chap. xiii, pp. 157-58; Abou Chamah, *op. cit.*, pp. 262-63, 264-65, 281-82, and 286-87; *Libellus*, p. 220; Makrizi, *op. cit.*, p. 22; *The Chronography of Bar Hebraeus*, pp. 322-23; Baldwin, *Raymond III*, p. 100, nn. 9 and 10. Baldwin ("The Decline," p. 611) sees in Saladin's attack on Tiberias the following calculations and strategy: "This maneuver meant that Saladin had risked everything on a gamble. Defeat would have meant disaster since orderly retirement through the narrow passes would have been impossible. To advance would have meant crossing the arid plateau to meet a Christian army well based. But he calculated that the news of his attack on Tiberias and the consequent danger to the lady of Tiberias would arouse the chivalrous ardor of the more impulsive crusaders, and possibly in this instance of the more conservative count of Tripoli. Then, he hoped, they would move out across the arid and difficult ground now lying directly between the two armies and fight under conditions dictated by himself." Consult Baldwin, *Raymond III*, pp. 96-135, Runciman, *History*, Appendix II, pp. 486-91, King, *op. cit.*, pp. 124-29, and Oman, *op. cit.*, pp. 324-33 for exhaustive discussions of the battle of Hattin. Cf. Jean Richard, "An Account of the Battle of Hattin Referring to the Frankish Mercenaries in Oriental Moslem States," *Speculum* (Cambridge, 1952), XXVII, 168-77. (Henceforth references to this scholar's other work, *Le royaume latin de Jérusalem*, will be cited as *Royaume* to differentiate them from the *Speculum* article).

the Master of the Templars that a policy of attack was the only sound strategy, Count Raymond offered a program of defense. The soundest procedure for the Franks, if they really desired to meet Saladin, was to meet him in front of Acre. Then, if defeat should follow for them, they could retreat into Acre as well as other cities nearby. This was an amplification of the one he had recently urged at the baronial assembly at Acre which King Guy had convoked on the initial news of Saladin's penetration of the cis-Jordanian country. The Moslems, so he argued, were incapable of inflicting permanent injury on their Frankish foes and, as before, would retire. Secondly, logistics were in favor of the Franks, for a Moslem attack would operate under the double disadvantage of long distance from their supply base and an inadequate supply of water. Thirdly, as for the loss of Tiberias, that was his own affair and he would willingly suffer it for the common cause. Furthermore, the loss was not permanent. Fourthly, the aforesaid scarcity of water in the Ṣaffūrīyah-Tiberias district together with the enemy's numerical superiority made an offensive strategy on the part of the Franks not only inadvisable but positively dangerous. Count Raymond's cogent arguments met with the solid support of the Frankish barons and the ensuing supposition in the late evening was that King Guy had accepted Count Raymond's strategy. But the Master of the Templars, who was still suspicious of Count Raymond's loyalty and who still believed that the Frankish army was now stronger than it had been for a number of years, told Guy that the strategy urged by a traitor was bad and hence soon prevailed on the weak-willed King to accept his counter offensive strategy, which aimed at the lifting of the Moslem investment of Tiberias. He stressed the shame entailed in the loss of a city near to the Frankish forces. On the following morning Guy without prior consultation with anyone proceeded to issue the orders necessary to implement the new strategy. These provided for the departure of the army at dawn for Tiberias. The Frankish knights, dismayed by the change in plans, protested and sought to ascertain its authorship. But Guy stubbornly refused to disclose it and so they reluctantly obeyed.[334]

---

[334] *Chronique d'Ernoul*, pp. 158-62; *Brevis, loc. cit.*; Benedict of Peterborough, *loc. cit.*; Ibn al-Athīr, *K.—A.*, pp. 681-82; *Libellus, loc. cit.* and pp. 221-22; *The Chronography of Bar Hebraeus*, p. 322; *Eracles*, pp. 47-48 and 52-53. Abou Chamah (*op. cit.*, p. 265) narrates a markedly different account of the advice given by Raymond of Tripoli. According to this, the Count, upon receipt of news of the Moslem invasion of the Tiberias area, surrendered to his fellow Franks all his possessions and urged the relief of Tiberias at once, for the loss of that area, which was now in the enemy's power,

Proceeding along the northern road from Ṣaffūrīyah to Tiberias, the Frankish forces were soon met by Saladin's hosts. Perhaps apprised by traitors from the Frankish camp, that Moslem chieftain quickly reacted by a decision to advance upon the village of Hattin, which was well endowed with watering and pasturing facilities, with the bulk of his forces and to leave behind at Tiberias only enough soldiers to maintain the investment of that city. The total absence of water along the northern road together with the galling Moslem archery fire on the vanguard and rearguard of the army, which were respectively commanded by Count Raymond, on the one hand, and Reginald of Châtillon, Balian of Ibelin, and the Templar and Hospitaller orders, on the other hand, proved to be increasingly disastrous as the hot day of Friday, July 3 wore on. When the Franks approached the plateau overlooking the village of Hattin, King Guy yielded to the plea of the Templars that they were unable to proceed farther that day and rejected the view of other barons that he order the army to continue on to the lake regardless of enemy opposition. Guy's decision to stop for the night evoked an initial cry of despair from Count Raymond, but, following his discovery that the Moslems had blocked a pass on the Frankish line of march, he advised that the camp be pitched near Lubieh in the vicinity of the Horns of Hattin, a rock strewn hill with two summits. He did not view such a procedure as a wise one but rather as the only alternate still left to the Franks. The ensuing night was a grim prelude to the disaster of the following day. Aware of their foemen's plight, Saladin's forces ruthlessly cut down every Frankish soldier departing from the camp in search of water and fired the dry grass on the hill of the Frankish encampment. The resulting blinding smoke together with nighttime conditions enabled Saladin to post his men in a tight noose around the enemy by dawn on Saturday, July 4.[335]

---

marked the end of resistance. A parallel account is contained in a letter of the Genoese to Pope Urban III in Benedict of Peterborough, *op. cit.*, p. 11. Both of these accounts are highly suspect on the ground that Count Raymond's sharp awareness that the difficulties of the terrain around Tiberias entailed almost certain destruction of a relief force precluded advice of this sort on his part. Cf. Baldwin, *Raymond III*, p. 104, n. 25 and pp. 101-02, n. 15. See Baldwin, *Raymond III*, p. 112 and Grousset, *Histoire*, p. 790 for an appraisal of the strategy advocated by Count Raymond.

[335] Roger of Wendover, *loc. cit.*; *Libellus*, pp. 222-24; *Eracles*, pp. 63-64; Ibn al-Athīr, *K.–A.*, p. 683; *Chronique d'Ernoul*, chap. xiv, pp. 167-68; *Brevis, loc. cit.*; *Ex Chronologia Roberti Altissiodorensis, loc. cit.*; Abou Chamah, *op. cit.*, pp. 265-66 and 282; Behâ Ed-Dîn, *Anecdotes*, pp. 93-94 and *Saladin*, p. 111; Ralph of Coggeshall, *Chronicon Anglicanum*, ed. Joseph Stevenson (London, 1875), p. 21; *The Chronography*

The disasters of the preceding day were as nothing compared to those in the subsequent slaughter. The thirst-maddened Frankish infantry sought to pierce the lines of the Moslem foe blockading the pass situated to the north of the Horns of Hattin and thereby reach the water of Lake Tiberias below. But it was useless, for the determined Moslems, aided by fire, obliged them to draw back. Many were slain, while the remainder were wounded and captured. Meanwhile the Frankish knights bravely hurled back attack after attack of the Moslem cavalry with heavy losses. But since their own losses together with the weakening effects of their raging thirsts foreshadowed eventual defeat, Guy conferred with Reginald of Châtillon and the Master of the Templars. They answered with a plea for a full cavalry charge. The King agreed and ordered his brother Amalric, the Constable, to prepare the battalions. This was done. Raymond of Tripoli headed the first squadron comprising among others Raymond, the son of Bohemond III of Antioch, and the four stepsons of Count Raymond, namely Hugh, William, Ralph, and Otto. Balian of Ibelin and Joscelyn III made up the rear guard. Apprised of the enemy's movements by five knights attached to Count Raymond's squadron, Saladin advanced upon the Frankish enemy, whereupon Guy ordered Count Raymond to charge. The Moslems opened their own ranks to allow the enemy to pass through and then proceeded to encircle the hapless Franks. All but a handful were captured. Count Raymond, his four stepsons, Joscelyn III, Balian of Ibelin, Reginald of Sidon, and Raymond of Antioch escaped, but all the other important leaders, namely King Guy, Reginald of Châtillon, Amalric the Constable, Marquis Boniface, the father of Conrad of Montferrat, Humphrey of Toron, Hugh of Gibeleth, Plivain, the lord of Boutron, as well as many other barons and knights were captured.[336]

---

of *Bar Hebraeus*, p. 323. Oman (*op. cit.*, p. 328) effectively points out the error in the Franks' decision to halt for the night. "The command was a fatal mistake; it would have been wise to push on at all costs to Tiberias: if this was not done, a lateral movement of only three miles northward would have brought the host to the perennial stream in the Wady-el-Hammam, where the whole army could easily slake its thirst, and four miles more would take them to the lake." Also consult Plate XI in Oman, *op. cit.*

[336] Behâ Ed-Dîn, *Anecdotes*, pp. 94-96 and *Saladin*, pp. 42-43 and 111-14; Ibn al-Athīr, *K. – A.*, pp. 683-86; Abou Chamah, *op. cit.*, pp. 266-71; *Chronique d'Ernoul*, chaps. xiv-xv, pp. 168-70 and 183; *Brevis, loc. cit.*; *Libellus*, pp. 224-27; *Eracles*, pp. 64-66; Kamal-Ad-Dîn, *Histoire*, IV, 178-79; *Ex Chronologia Roberti Altissiodorensis*, pp. 253-54; Roger of Wendover, *op. cit.*, pp. 140-41; Roger of Hoveden, *op. cit.*, p. 320; Ralph of Coggeshall, *loc. cit.*; William of Newburgh, *op. cit.*, pp. 258-59; Makrizi, *op. cit.*, pp. 22-23; *Itinerarium*, pp. 14-16; Abū'l-Fidā, *op. cit.*, p. 56; Benedict of

The triumphant Saladin thereupon left the battlefield and ordered that all the Christian prisoners be brought to him at his encampment

---

Peterborough, *op. cit.*, pp. 11-12 and 22; *Annales de Terre Sainte, loc. cit.*; *The Chronography of Bar Hebraeus*, pp. 323-24; Röhricht, *Regesta*, Nos. 660 and 661, p. 176; *L'Estoire*, cols. 68-69; *Les gestes des Chiprois, loc. cit.*; *Chronique d'Amadi*, p. 58; Michael the Syrian, *Chronique, loc. cit.* and *Extrait*, p. 398. The sources are in disagreement concerning the fate of Joscelyn III at the battle of Hattin. *Chronique d'Ernoul* and Variant C of *Eracles* declare that the Seneschal was captured and was among the prisoners brought before the triumphant Saladin after the battle. Variant D of *Eracles*, on the other hand, states that he escaped with Balian of Ibelin and repaired to Acre. Since the several accounts describing the surrender of the Frankish fortress of Acre and indicating the Frankish leadership in Acre at this time agree that Joscelyn III was in charge of the city as of July 7, it is necessary to assume, if one accepts the story that Joscelyn III was captured at Hattin, that (1) the Scheneschal escaped from Saladin's custody or that (2) he succeeded in ransoming himself at once. Neither explanation is probable, for the first assumes that Saladin, who had shown marked attention to such vital matters as servicing his army at the Battle of Hattin with ample supplies of weapons, would have been careless about maintaining effective security arrangements for his distinguished prisoners, whose individual and collective ransoms, furthermore, would enormously enrich him. The second assumes that Joscelyn III could have raised in the mere three days or seventy-two hours at the extreme limit elapsing between his capture at Hattin and his appearance at Acre the obviously large sum of money—his ransom in 1176 had entailed the raising of 50,000 dinars—required for his ransom. This is equally improbable. Furthermore, in view of the high probability that the special sums of money already collected since 1183 for the defense of the crusading states had markedly diminished the financial resources and reserves of the Franks and had already been expended for their military activities culminating in the battle of Hattin, it is unlikely that a large sum of ransom money could have been quickly accumulated. Richard (*Royaume*, pp. 141 and 142, n. 1) supports my position in the following observations: "Le 9 juillet, Saladin se faisait rendre Acre par Jocelin III, échappé au désastre..." and "*L'Eracles*, p. 66, indique sans doute par erreur le capture de Jocelin à Hattin." This same scholar (*Royaume*, p. 145) emphasizes in still another way his disbelief in the view that Joscelyn III was captured at Hattin in the following passage: "Après la bataille de Hattin, tandis que Balian d'Ibelin courait mettre Naplouse et Jérusalem à l'abri d'une surprise et que Jocelin faisait de même à Acre..." Likewise Grousset (*Histoire*, p. 802) supports my view. "Le bayle d'Acre était... le comte Jocelin III de Courtenay..."... "Il avait pu s'enfuir avec ce dernier [Count Raymond] et avec Balian d'Ibelin du champ de carnage de Hattîn." Although Röhricht (*Geschichte*, p. 438) does not declare that he disbelieves those sources affirming Joscelyn III's capture at Hattin, he implies that he does not believe them. La Monte ("The rise," p. 316 and n. 3, p. 316) accepts the version that Joscelyn III was captured at the battle of Hattin, but also admits that Variant D of *Eracles* "... says he escaped [capture at the battle of Hattin] and returned to Acre which he surrendered on terms to Saladin's general." For the reasons cited above I cannot accept the views of *Les familles d'Outre-Mer*, p. 301, Louis Bréhier, *L'église et l'Orient au Moyen Age. Les Croisades* (Paris, 1921), pp. 115-16, Castle, *op. cit.*, pp. 48-49, Lane-Poole, *op. cit.*, p. 214, Oman, *op. cit.*, pp. 331-32, and Schlumberger, *Renaud de Chatillon*, pp. 291-92 and 297-98 which state that Joscelyn III was captured at Hattin. Nor can I accept the positive statements of Bréhier and Wiet, *op. cit.*, pp. 325-26, that Joscelyn III, following his capture at Hattin, was sent to Damascus or the strong implication that this was his fate in Lane-Poole's observation (*op. cit.*, p. 215) that "... the King and the chief nobles were well used and sent to Damascus." Although the following observation on my part is purely speculative and has spot. This was done. Upon their arrival Saladin rejoiced over his victory and stated that his possession of so many notable prisoners was a cause of great honor to himself. Then he tendered a golden cup of sweetened water to the thirsty King and bade him to drink freely. Guy complied and then offered the cup to Reginald of Châtillon, who refused it. Saladin, who followed the Arabian custom of sparing the lives of captives partaking of the food or drink of their captors, was annoyed by these developments and hence quickly observed that he had not sanctioned this act of Guy's. He then questioned Reginald of Châtillon as to what he would do with him, if their respective positions of prisoner and captor were reversed. He replied that he would behead his jailor. Enraged by his prisoner's truculence, Saladin beheaded him on the spot, rubbed some of his fallen foe's blood on his face in token of his accomplished vengeance, and ordered that his head be taken to Damascus and be dragged on the ground to show the Saracens the retribution he had wreaked on the lord of Antioch. After assuring the

---

no evidence whatsoever to support it, the fact of the matter is that almost all of the membership of the group of prominent escapees from the battlefield of Hattin was made up of bitterly hostile factions in the political struggles of the Kingdom of Jerusalem: Count Raymond, his four stepsons, Reginald of Sidon, and Raymond of Antioch composed one group opposed to the policies of Joscelyn III and Joscelyn III, in turn, equally opposed the policies of the other faction. Only Balian of Ibelin played the rôle of a peacemaker. In view of the large probability that Saladin was well informed about the feud between the Courtenay-Lusignan faction and Raymond's faction, was it not a good policy to allow Joscelyn III to escape? The value to Saladin of a reawakening of the old feuds in the weakening of the military and political power of the Franks was certainly far greater than any ransom for Joscelyn III, however large it might be. Such a policy on Saladin's part was certainly consonant with his ensuing astute policies towards the conquered Franks. I agree with Baldwin and other scholars who repudiate the view that Count Raymond was guilty of treachery at the battle of Hattin. Oman (*op. cit.*, p. 333) aptly summarizes the battle of Hattin as follows: "Such were the consequences of the overhaste of King Guy, and of his determination to cut his way to the relief of Tiberias without having taken account of the character of the countryside in which he was to fight. We may safely say that if he had taken more care about supplies, and especially about his provision of water, and had carefully planned out his itinerary, he might have reached his goal. The Saracens were in a very uncomfortable position, with the lake at their backs and no place of refuge near; one more such push as the Count of Tripoli had advised on the evening of the first day would probably have led to their withdrawal. But a much more easy alternative would have been to have encamped in some well-watered spot, such as Saffaria, and awaited the retreat of Saladin. The Sultan must have soon retired for want of provender (and especially of fodder) in the wasted country about Tiberias, and he could not have dared to disperse his army for foraging purposes in the face of the Christian host, while it remained intact and concentrated in front of him. The whole battle, therefore, was unnecessary, and the details of Guy's bad generalship are comparatively small blunders when compared with the enormous initial mistake of fighting at all."

terrified King that because of his royal status he would not suffer the fate of Reginald of Châtillon, who had deserved it because of his transgression of all bounds, Saladin ordered that Guy, the Grand Master of the Templars, and the other prisoners be taken to Damascus. This was done.[337] Some two hundred of the membership of the Templar and Hospitaller Orders suffered death by decapitation.[338] Upon his appearance before Tiberias on the morrow of Hattin, July 5, Eschiva, the Countess of Tripoli, having heard of the capture of King Guy and believing that her husband and children had suffered the same fate, informed Saladin of her intention to surrender Tiberias and requested an assurance of safe passage on her part to Tripoli. The Moslem chieftain agreed, sent an agent to take over the city, and then granted the government to Kaïmaz En-Nedjmi. Then he conducted the Countess and the remaining citizens of the County of Tripoli to safety.[339]

---

[337] Behâ Ed-Dîn, *Saladin*, pp. 114-15 and *Anecdotes*, pp. 39-40 and 96-97; Abou Chamah, *op. cit.*, pp. 275-76 and 278; *Chronique d'Ernoul*, pp. 172-74; Kamal-Ad-Dîn, *Histoire*, IV, 180-81; Benedict of Peterborough, *op. cit.*, pp. 12 and 22; *The Chronography of Bar Hebraeus*, p. 324; Abū'l-Fidā, *loc. cit.*; *Itinerarium*, p. 16; Ibn al-Athīr, *K.—A.*, pp. 687-88; Roger of Hoveden, *loc. cit.*; Michael the Syrian, *Chronique, loc. cit.* and *Extrait, loc. cit.*; *Eracles*, pp. 67-69, Variant D and pp. 67-69, Variant C; *Chronique d'Amadi*, p. 59; Makrizi, *op. cit.*, p. 23; Albert of Trium-Fontium, *op. cit.*, p. 747.

[338] Abou Chamah, *op. cit.*, pp. 277-78; Ibn al-Athīr, *K.—A.*, p. 688; Albert of Trium-Fontium, *loc. cit.* Slaughter (*op. cit.*, p. 137) offers the following explanation for Saladin's execution of the Templars and Hospitallers: "Saladin's religion had taught him that there were times when revenge was justified, and that clemency was no virtue in one who was not capable of taking vengeance when vengeance was due. The Knights Templar and the Knights of the Hospital were not only the stoutest fighters in battle; they were also the most heated and outspoken in their scorn of the "true religion." Their jaunts and jibes at the Prophet were among the deepest stains from which he was determined to purify the land."

[339] *Chronique d'Ernoul*, p. 174; *Eracles*, p. 69; Kamal-Ad-Dîn, *Histoire*, IV, 181; Roger of Wendover, *op. cit.*, p. 141; Behâ Ed-Dîn, *Anecdotes*, p. 97 and *Saladin*, p. 116; *The Chronography of Bar Hebraeus*, *loc. cit.*, Makrizi, *op. cit.*, p. 22; Abū'l-Fidā, *loc. cit.*; Abou Chamah, *op. cit.*, pp. 276-77, 303, 304, and 306; Ibn al-Athīr, *K.—A.*, p. 687. Champdor (*op. cit.*, pp. 165-66) explains Saladin's chivalric provision of a cavalry escort for the Countess Eschiva as follows: ". . . par crainte qu'elle ne fût insultée au cours de son voyage par des parties bédouins qui couraient la campagne."

CHAPTER FIFTEEN

JOSCELYN III SURRENDERS ACRE AND LOSES HIS SEIGNEURY; THE ENSUING VIRTUAL LIQUIDATION OF THE FRANKISH POWER IN THE HOLY LAND

With the remaining Christian bastions now permanently bereft of their defenders by reason of the earlier muster of most of the Frankish soldiery thereof and their ensuing slaughter and capture at the disaster of Hattin, Saladin moved swiftly and easily to capture them. Acre was the first object of his attention. On July 7 he ordered one of his emirs, his nephew Taqī-ad-Dīn, to invest that city. As the latter approached Acre and reached Saffran, a hamlet located three leagues from Acre, Joscelyn III reached Acre. Apprised of the approach of Taqī-ad-Dīn, the Seneschal convoked a group of the burghers, and, in compliance with their counsel, speedily capitulated, dispatching one of the citizens named Peter Brice with the keys to the city and an offer to surrender in return for a guarantee of the properties and persons of the residents of the city. Taqī-ad-Dīn thereupon accepted the surrender of Acre from Joscelyn III on July 9, 1187, receiving as his division of the booty a sugar-factory, warehouse, and other properties. The Seneschal's abject behavior provoked many of the citizenry to threaten a riot and to start fires in the city. These, however, were speedily suppressed and extinguished and order prevailed before the formal surrender of the city to Saladin on July 10. A general migration of the Christian merchants of Acre with all of their portable properties ensued because of their misgivings concerning the veracity of Saladin's promises which included statements to the effect that the Christians would pay only the tribute which was customary between Christians and Saracens and that safe conduct would be granted to all those who did not wish to stay in Acre. Even so, they were obliged to abandon immense quantities of arms, jewels, metals, and silks and these in turn became the booty of the soldiers and comrades of the conquering lieutenants of Saladin, chief of whom was Saladin's son al-Afḍal who now became the new master of Acre.[340]

---

[340] *Eracles*, pp. 69-70; Benedict of Peterborough, *op. cit.*, p. 22; Kamal-Ad-Dîn, *Histoire, loc. cit.*; *Chronique d'Ernoul, loc. cit.*; Abou Chamah, *op. cit.*, pp. 293-97, 303,

With the capture of two of the most powerful centers of the Frankish establishment in Galilee, namely Tiberias and Acre, now an

---

and 305; Behâ Ed-Dîn, *Anecdotes*, pp. 97-98 and *Saladin, loc. cit.*; *The Chronography of Bar Hebraeus*, p. 325; Arnold of Lubeck, *op. cit.*, p. 168; *Annales de Terre Sainte, loc. cit.*; Ibn al-Athīr, *K. – A.*, pp. 688-90; Abū'l-Fidā, *loc. cit.*; *Itinerarium*, pp. 17-18; Makrizi, *op. cit.*, pp. 23-25; *Libellus*, pp. 234-36; William of Newburgh, *op. cit.*, pp. 259-60; *Les gestes des Chiprois*, pp. 659-60. Grousset (*Histoire, loc. cit.*) and Runciman (*History*, pp. 460-61) pithily and respectively estimate Joscelyn III's action at this time as follows: "Pas plus que son père Jocelin II, ce dernier des Courtenay ne paraît avoir brillé par le courage." and "The Seneschal Joscelin of Courtenay, who commanded the city [Acre], thought only of his own safety." Oman (*op. cit.*, pp. 332-33) seems to condone by implication Joscelyn III's cowardly behavior at this time on the score of the lack of military defenders in Acre at this time in the following passage: "Few victories have brought in their train more important results than that of Tiberias: within a few months the whole of the kingdom of Jerusalem save a few coast-fortresses was in the hands of Saladin. The realm had been drained dry of men to supply the army which perished on the hillside of Hattin, and its towns and castles fell helplessly before the Moslem for sheer lack of defenders. Places that had braved the assaults of the Infidel for eighty years opened their gates at the first summons, because there were none but clerks and women left within them. Jerusalem itself surrendered after a siege of only twelve days." To all this I rejoin with the observation that (1) Acre was one of the best fortified cities in the entire Frankish East and hence a very small defending force could have made at least a token of resistance with its defensive catapults and the like (2) Ascalon, perhaps equal to Acre in defensive capacities and no better supplied with military men than Acre, could and did reject the joint appeal of Gerard and King Guy to surrender and proceeded to put up a spirited defense for thirteen days (3) the defenders of the far less defensible Jerusalem could and did put up a defense which lasted for twelve days. At least Jerusalem's honor was not besmirched in its ultimate surrender and Balian of Ibelin, the prime mover in the defense of Jerusalem, performed in an honorable and manful fashion. Sidney Painter ("The Third Crusade: Richard the Lionhearted and Philip Augustus," *A History of the Crusades. The Later Crusades 1189-1311* [Philadelphia, 1962] II, 46) supports my position in his observation that "The towns of the kingdom were leaderless and had almost no soldiers, but they were strongly fortified." Richard (*Royaume*, p. 146) declares that "... Jocelin III avait capitulé à Acre, malgré les bourgeois et les habitants ..." *Eracles* shows that this capitulation occurred *after* the Seneschal had conferred with a group of burghers and in compliance with their counsel. A fair criticism of Joscelyn III is that as a military leader he ought to have led and to have resisted the advice of simple citizens unschooled in the arts of war. Certainly his conduct was markedly less resourceful and brave than that of Balian of Ibelin. That Frankish leader, who had only two knights to aid him in the defense of Jerusalem, proceeded at once to knight fifty sons of the bourgeois population to augment the number of defenders. Furthermore, he engaged in financial and foraging operations to bolster the city's defenses. Slaughter (*op. cit.*, p. 142) appraises Saladin's tactics at Acre as follows: "He [Saladin] made them a proposition which seems to prove that he cherished the hope of preserving commerce with the West and amicable relations with the Westerners under his sovereignty. His previous concessions to European merchants and the terms he offered at Jerusalem confirm the belief that his plan of dominion without extermination would have preserved the prosperity of the Holy Land. He would have preferred that Moslems and Christians should live together and work together, although it must be, of course, under his sovereignty, since the land belonged to Islam and the Christians were intruders."

accomplished fact, the remaining phases of the Moslems' "mopping up" operations in Galilee and Samaria soon ensued. Upon their completion, all of Joscelyn III's fiefs in Galilee as well as virtually all other Frankish holdings in Galilee had passed once more into the hands of their former Moslem lords. Lieutenants of Saladin advanced in several directions from their new military headquarters at Acre and overran the Seneschal's holdings, capturing his Chateau du Roi with no resistance being afforded. Such was the fate of the territorial holdings of the Courtenay chieftain! Such was the eclipse of his aspirations of recovering in time from their Moslem overlords Toron, Banyas, and Chastel Neuf which had been assigned to him for ultimate ownership by King Guy as a reward for his services in the *coup d'état*! In similar fashion Nazareth, Caesarea, Haifa, Ṣaffūrīyah, Tibnīn, Tyron, al-Fūlah, and other places near Acre fell into Moslem hands and suffered pillage. Their inhabitants irrespective of age and sex were enslaved. Some resistance was offered for a few days by the garrison force of Balian of Ibelin at Nablus, but it soon capitulated in return for honorable terms. Likewise was the fate of the castle of Toron whose garrison withstood the Moslem assaults for two weeks. Only did the great seaport of Jaffa resist strongly the investment set up by al-ʿĀdil, Saladin's brother, who advanced up from Egypt in response to his kinsman's request. But the Saracens' attack was unrelenting and eventually they carried it by storm. The luckless defenders irrespective of age and sex suffered enslavement and in time disposition in the harems and slave-markets of Aleppo.[341]

Still eluding the triumphal sweep of the Moslems were the seacoast towns of Ascalon, Beirut, Sidon, Jubail, Tyre, and Gaza. Accordingly, Saladin quickly turned his attention to these bastions. Tyre proved to be impregnable at least for the moment, because of its mighty walls and its strong garrison which had been augmented by the survivors, including Balian, from the disastrous field of Hattin. Moreover, the defenses of this city had been further strengthened by the arrival of Conrad of Montferrat, the paternal uncle of the late king Baldwin V, and his naval forces from Constantinople. The relief expedition had

---

[341] Ibn al-Athīr, *K. — A.*, pp. 690-92; Behâ Ed-Dîn, *Saladin, loc. cit.* and *Anecdotes*, p. 98; *The Chronography of Bar Hebraeus, loc. cit.*; Kamal-Ad-Dîn, *Histoire*, IV, 181-82; *Libellus*, pp. 229 and 231; *Chronique d'Ernoul*, chap. xvi, pp. 183-84; Abū'l-Fidā, *op. cit.*, pp. 56-57; Abou Chamah, *op. cit.*, pp. 300-03, 306-07, and 315; Michael the Syrian, *Chronique, loc. cit.* and p. 405 and *Extrait, loc. cit.* and p. 400; *Chronique d'Amadi*, p. 65; Makrizi, *op. cit.*, pp. 25-28 and p. 27, n. 1; Benedict of Peterborough, *op. cit.*, pp. 22-23.

paused briefly at Acre, but had retired upon being apprised of its capture by Saladin and had rejected all assurances of one of Saladin's emissaries that they could safely land. Upon his arrival in Tyre Conrad quickly accepted the request of its citizens that he be their leader, cast into the moat the two banners sent into the city by Saladin along with a demand that they be hoisted on the castle walls as a sign of surrender, and spurned the Moslem chieftain's proposal that, in exchange for his release of Conrad's captured father, he, Conrad, should surrender the city of Tyre. Conrad's arrival had occurred in the proverbial nick of time, for at the time of his arrival the disheartened defenders seem to have been considering the surrender of the city. Hence, after an initial and fruitless assault on Tyre, Saladin proceeded northward to Sidon which meekly surrendered on July 29 with its lord, Raymond Garnier, electing to retire to the greater safety of his formidable inland castle of Belfort some five miles away. Beirut and Jubail proved to be easy conquests, the former capitulating on August 6 after her initial and unsuccessful attempt at self defense, the latter surrendering shortly thereafter in compliance with the orders of Hugh Embriaco, her ruler, in return for Saladin's agreement for his release. The net effect of Saladin's post-Hattin military activities was to reduce by the end of August, 1187 the Frankish power in the Kingdom of Jerusalem to mere bobtail remnants of its once proud expanses: Gaza, Ascalon, Tyre, Jerusalem, Krak, Safad, and a few scattered and separated castles.[342]

[342] Ibn al-Athīr, *K. – A.*, pp. 692-96 and 707; Abū'l-Fidā, *op. cit.*, p. 57; Behâ Ed-Dîn, *Saladin*, pp. 116-17 and *Anecdotes*, pp. 98-99; *The Chronography of Bar Hebraeus, loc. cit.*; Kamal-Ad-Dîn, *Histoire*, IV, 182; *Itinerarium*, pp. 18-20 and 23-24; *Chronique d'Ernoul*, chaps. xv, xvi and xx, pp. 174, 178, 179-83, and 236-37; Benedict of Peterborough, *op. cit.*, I, 261; *Eracles*, pp. 73-78 and 104-05; *Libellus*, p. 236; William of Newburgh, *op. cit.*, pp. 261-63; Roger of Hoveden, *op. cit.*, pp. 320-21; Abou Chamah, *op. cit.*, pp. 303, 307-08, 309-10, and 312; Makrizi, *op. cit.*, p. 28; Arnold of Lubeck, *loc. cit.*; Michael the Syrian, *Chronique*, p. 405 and *Extrait*, p. 400; *Les gestes des Chiprois*, p. 660; *Ex Chronologia Roberti Altissiodorensis*, pp. 254-55; *Chronique d'Amadi*, p. 64. Stevenson (*op. cit.*, p. 251) believes that Saladin's decision not to besiege Tyre at this time resulted from "... his policy to make such conquests as were plainly within his grasp. Delay, and still more failure at any point, might lead to reaction." Röhricht (*Geschichte*, p. 448) labels as a myth the report of *L'Eracles* that Conrad of Montferrat had thrown into a ditch Saladin's flags which Reginald of Sidon held in readiness and the report of William of Newburgh that Conrad of Monferrat ordered the hanging of several accomplices of Reginald of Sidon. Runciman (*History*, p. 472), on the other hand, accepts the story concerning the casting down of Saladin's banners by Conrad of Montferrat. I see nothing improbable in either of the two accounts rejected by Röhricht, for the historical record of the ages inclusive of World War II shows similar accounts of the terror felt by individuals besieged or about to be besieged by an enemy and their ensuing

Far to the southwest from the theatre of his most recent military captures and triumphs still stood unconquered the great Frankish fortresses of Ascalon and Gaza. The former city, which had been the last significant Frankish conquest thirty-four years before in 1153, drew Saladin's attention soon thereafter in late August, 1187. Marching thither with two of his chief captives, Gerard of Ridefort, the Grand Master of the Templars, and King Guy, Saladin, who had informed the King that his freedom would be granted to him in exchange for the surrender of the city, allowed his royal captive to address the citizens with a plea for their surrender on August 23. Gerard also offered his oral support to Guy. But their urgings fell on deaf ears and the outraged citizens responded with jeers and a vigorous and brave defense of their city. However, Saladin pressed his attacks unrelentingly and hence on September 4 the garrison was obliged to surrender. As was his treatment of the citizens of Acre, so now Saladin treated the defeated Ascalonites, permitting them to depart with all their movable possessions, using his soldiers as escorts for them during their journey to Alexandria, and, upon their arrival, affording to them suitable housing pending their repatriation to Christian territories. Meanwhile, the Templar garrison of Gaza had surrendered quickly in response to the order of the Grand Master Gerard that it do so. In exchange for the surrender Saladin granted Gerard his liberty. King Guy, however, remained a prisoner for some months, first at Nablus and then at Latakia. Sibyl repaired from Jerusalem to join her captive husband.[343] Lastly, Saladin's army seized

---

policy of dickering with an enemy. Equally true has been the pattern of retaliation against such persons once the immediate danger of capture has passed. Röhricht himself states that the citizenry of Tyre, prior to the appearance of Conrad of Montferrat, were paralyzed by the terror of defeat and no one cared to take on the responsibility for the defense of the city.

[343] Behâ Ed-Dîn, *Saladin*, p. 117 and *Anecdotes*, p. 99; Ibn al-Athīr, *K. — A.*, pp. 696-97 and 703; *The Chronography of Bar Hebraeus, loc. cit.*; Kamal-Ad-Dîn, *Histoire, loc. cit*; *Les gestes des Chiprois*, p. 660: *Chronique d'Amadi*, p. 65; *L'Estoire*, col. 70; Michael the Syrian, *Chronique*, p. 404 and *Extrait*, pp. 398-99; Roger of Hoveden, *op. cit.*, p. 321; *Annales de Terre Sainte, loc. cit.*; *Itinerarium*, p. 20; William of Newburgh, *op. cit.*, p. 261; Makrizi, *loc. cit.*; Abū'l-Fidā, *loc. cit.*; Abou Chamah, *op. cit.*, pp. 312-13, 314 and 315; *Chronique d'Ernoul*, chap. xvi, pp. 184-85; *Eracles*, pp. 78-79; *Libellus*, pp. 236-38; Stevenson, *op. cit.*, p. 252, n. 2. Although none of the sources ascribes any of the following motivations to Saladin in his attacks on Ascalon, Tyre, Beirut, Sidon, and Jubail, it is a fair presumption that he recognized the Franks' continued retention of these seacoast towns precluded a definitive Moslem conquest of the Holy Land. The excellent port facilities of Tyre and Ascalon were standing invitations to western Europeans to use them as staging points for an ultimate Frankish recovery of the territorial losses sustained after and as a result of the disaster of Hattin. Stevenson (*op.*

JOSCELYN III SURRENDERS ACRE AND LOSES HIS SEIGNEURY

Bait Jibrīn, al-Natroun, Bethlehem, Ramla, Darum, and Hebron.[344]

cit., p. 249) supports my view in his observation that "Clearly he [Saladin] judged that the towns on the coast should be the first objects of his attack. They were the most important, for Jerusalem alone of the inland towns was of equal size; they were besides most accessible to help from Europe and most valuable for securing communication with Egypt." Slaughter (op. cit., p. 141) affirms my position completely in her observation that "Although the Battle of Hattin had destroyed the military strength of the native barons, there was always the danger of a new crusading army from Europe, and there was no safety for Islam so long as the Christians held the seaports and the mountain passes." This same scholar (op. cit., p. 162) also declares that Saladin's decision to take the coast cities first involved his apprehension concerning the other Moslem war lords. "He [Saladin] understood that after Jerusalem was taken they [the Moslem war lords] would assume that the war was over and they would be more difficult to control; that was the reason why he made sure of the coast cities first." Continuing in the same vein, the afore-mentioned scholar (op. cit., p. 146-47) observes that "He [Saladin] has been blamed for his mistake and praised for his wisdom in abandoning Tyre and proceeding at once to Ascalon. By postponing the siege, he allowed Conrad to strengthen the defenses, which were already the strongest on the coast, and to take advantage of the increasing number of refugees gathering from all quarters. On the other hand, the army was restless and impatient, and Saladin knew that a long siege would demoralize them. At all costs he must keep up their courage for the final triumph at Jerusalem. It was far more important to secure Ascalon, which connected Syria with Egypt and guarded the approaches to Jerusalem. With the remainder of the Kingdom in his control, he could afford to leave the Christians bottled up in Tyre; that was better than the risk of a long siege. He left troops to guard the neck of the bottle and hastened." Slaughter (op. cit., p. 147), in commenting on Saladin's decision to release Gerard and Guy, observes that "He [Saladin] had more to lose than gain by letting these two men go free, since there was small chance that they would keep their oaths. But if, by such bargains, he could "mow down infidelity and convert altars into pulpits and churches into mosques," he had saved many lives, as well as the cost of a siege. With a clear conscience, he had given back life and liberty to an "infidel.'" Richard (Royaume, p. 141) sees the situation in a rather similar light and regards Saladin's clement policies towards the Franks in the captured cities as astute calculations: "... partout où les garnisons se montraient disposées à résister, il [Saladin] accordait aux aussiégés le libre sortie des personnes et des biens. Si cette conduite eut pour résultat d'accumuler dans les villes de la côte les éléments d'une prochaine reconquête, elle favorisa la reddition des places fortes et évita au "sultan" de perdre son temps en sièges pendant que l'Occident enverrait des renforts." Painter (op. cit., pp. 46-47) similarly discerns shrewd considerations in Saladin's policies towards the Franks after the battle of Hattin. "Although Saladin was fully capable of savage cruelty, he preferred to be merciful—especially when mercy paid. The towns of the kingdom were leaderless and had almost no soldiers, but they were strongly fortified. The inhabitants were discouraged by the loss of the leaders and troops, and were willing to surrender in exchange for their lives. Saladin's troops were horsemen who felt at home only in the open field and had no taste for attacking fortifications. Hence it was good policy for the sultan to buy the towns by allowing the inhabitants to go free. Every such displaced person made the food problem more serious in the remaining Christian strongholds."

[344] Kamel-Ad-Dîn, Histoire, IV, 182-83; Ibn al-Athīr, K. – A., p. 697; Libellus, p. 239; Abou Chamah, op. cit., p. 314; Behâ Ed-Dîn, Saladin, loc. cit. and Anecdotes, p. 99; Abū'l-Fidā, loc. cit.; Makrizi, loc. cit.; Benedict of Peterborough, op. cit., p. 24.

CHAPTER SIXTEEN

THE FALL OF JERUSALEM

Meanwhile, Dame Fortune had raised up a champion and defender of the still uncaptured capital of the Kingdom of Jerusalem, a delegation of whose citizens had, despite his declaration that he would capture it by storm, rejected Saladin's recent proposal of the surrender of Jerusalem on the same basis as that granted to Ascalon. Balian of Ibelin, one of the survivors of the disaster of Hattin, who was now residing in Tyre, requested a safeconduct from Saladin while the latter was still investing Ascalon to repair to Jerusalem to allow him to remove his wife and children to Tripoli. Saladin agreed on condition that he remain only one night in Jerusalem and not bear arms against him. Upon Balian's arrival he was urged by the population to assume the military defense and civil rule of the city. He initially spurned the proposal on the ground that it would constitute a violation of his agreement with Saladin, but at length accepted it after the Patriarch Heraclius absolved him of his agreement and observed that the honoring of it would constitute a greater sin and would entail a great reproach for him and his heirs. Since the city, which was now overflowing with women and child refugees from other parts of the Holy Land, was nearly defenseless with only two knights as survivors of the battle of Hattin, Balian quickly knighted fifty sons of the bourgeois population and, together with the Patriarch, effected the stripping of the roof of the Holy Sepulchre of its silver to provide money for the armed forces. Lastly, the armed forces repaired each day to the surrounding countryside to secure food supplies in preparation for the expected investment.[345]

These measures were none too soon, for Saladin and his forces presently encamped before Jerusalem along the north and northwest walls on Thursday evening, September 20. On the following day the Moslems attacked the Frankish forces before the city, but soon retired

---

[345] *Chronique d'Ernoul*, chaps. xv and xvi, pp. 174-76 and 185-86; Ibn al-Athīr, *K.–A.*, p. 698; Abou Chamah, *op. cit.*, p. 320; *Eracles*, p. 81. See John L. La Monte, "John d'Ibelin, the Old Lord of Beirut, 1177-1236," *Byzantion* (Paris, 1937), XII, 419-22 for an extensive discussion on the history of the Ibelin family, its connections with the royal family of the Kingdom of Jerusalem, and, in consequence, the ability of Balian to play the commanding rôle he now assumed.

because of the military disadvantage of having to fight with the sun in their eyes. Nevertheless, they returned to the attack the following night and continued to assail the enemy for the next eight days without, however, substantial success. This circumstance led the Moslems to shift their investment lines on the following Friday to another section of the city wall which had no gate, apart from the postern of the Magdalene, whereby the defenders could issue forth to meet the enemy. The new site enabled the Moslems to set up a dozen mangonels and to bring up their archers close enough to the city walls to enable them to cover them with an archery fire so formidable that the defenders dared not appear. Thus protected, Moslem sappers steadily undermined the walls during the next two days without fear of countermining on the part of the defenders who were deterred by the murderous fire of the archers and artillerymen. At length all was ready and fire was applied to the wooden supports in the sap. A section of the city wall overlooking the Kidron Valley fell and Jerusalem was doomed.[346]

At this juncture the Frankish defenders, who were now aware of their inability to keep the city out of enemy control, declared to Balian of Ibelin and Patriarch Heraclius that they wished to carry the attack to the enemy and die honorably in battle rather than be captured and be slain shamefully in the city itself. But the Patriarch vetoed this proposal on the ground that it would lead to the loss of life of all the male defenders and the ensuing capture and conversion to Mohammedanism of the numerous women and children in Jerusalem. It would be far better to effect an arrangement with the enemy whereby the Franks could leave and repair to Christian territory. A general assent to these proposals followed and Balian of Ibelin received a request that he obtain a treaty with Saladin. Balian agreed and sought out the Moslem chieftain with a proposal of the surrender of the city in exchange for the sparing of the lives of its inhabitants. The latter was initially reluctant to enter into any kind of negotiations because his forces were at that very moment planting their standards on the city walls and entering the city. Furthermore, he had offered

---

[346] *Chronique d'Ernoul*, chap. xviii, pp. 211-14; Behâ Ed-Dîn, *Saladin*, p. 118 and *Anecdotes*, pp. 99-100; *The Chronography of Bar Hebraeus, loc. cit.*; *Eracles*, pp. 82-85; Ibn al-Athīr, *K. – A.*, pp. 699-700; *Libellus*, pp. 241-46; Abou Chamah, *op. cit.*, pp. 317, 319-20, and 326-27; Abū'l-Fidā, *loc. cit.*; Kamal-Ad-Dîn, *Histoire*, IV, 183; Makrizi, *op. cit.*, p. 29; *Itinerarium*, pp. 20-21; Roger of Wendover, *op. cit.*, pp. 141-42; Michael the Syrian, *Chronique, loc. cit.*; *Chronique d'Amadi*, pp. 66-68.

these very conditions to the enemy before and they had been rejected. Lastly, he had vowed to take the city by force. Parley was useless in view of his impending capture of the city. But his opinion changed when an unexpected Frankish rally pushed back his forces. Perhaps aware of the new turn of events, Balian warned his foeman that unless honorable terms were granted to the beleaguered population, the male Franks would retaliate by the execution of their Moslem prisoners, by the burning of the Great Mosque and other buildings and possessions of the Moslems, by the slaying of their own wives and children to deprive the enemy of their carnal use, and, finally, by their own individual self-immolation after the slaying of one or two of their enemies. Accordingly, Saladin accepted Balian's renewed plea for mercy with the stipulation that the entire population be considered as his prisoners. Only those capable of meeting his ransom terms of ten dinars, five dinars, and one dinar for each man, woman, and child respectively would be granted their freedom. Balian's response to the effect that, apart from the bourgeoisie, few could meet such terms because of the presence of great numbers of poor refugees from the surrounding countryside and hence more moderate terms were in order won from Saladin a promise that he would consider the matter and would see his beaten enemy on the following day. Thereupon Balian returned to the city with a report to the barons and the Patriarch.[347]

The ensuing colloquy between Balian, Patriarch Heraclius, and King Guy, on the one hand, and the lay and ecclesiastical leaders of the beleaguered city, on the other, resulted in agreements with the Masters of the Templars and the Hospitallers, who recognized the impossibility of retaining their possessions after Saladin's entrance into Jerusalem, that they should donate their respective contributions from the King of England for the ransoming of the poor of the city. Upon Balian's return to Saladin's headquarters, the latter finally agreed after considerable discussion to accept a ransom of 30,000 besants for the release of 7,000 persons on the understanding that two women and ten children should be respectively equated with one man for ransoming

---

[347] *Chronique d'Ernoul*, pp. 214-18; Behâ Ed-Dîn, *Saladin*, pp. 119 and 120 and *Anecdotes*, pp. 100-01; *The Chronography of Bar Hebraeus*, pp. 325-36; *Eracles*, pp. 85-89; Ibn al-Athīr, *K.—A.*, pp. 700-02; *Libellus*, pp. 246-47; Abou Chamah, *op. cit.*, pp. 317-18, 319, and 327-29; Abū'l-Fidā, *loc. cit.*; Kamal-Ad-Dîn, *Histoire, loc. cit.*; Makrizi, *op. cit.*; pp. 29-32; Michael the Syrian, *Chronique, loc. cit.* and *Extrait*, p. 399; *Chronique d'Amadi*, pp. 68-71. Roger of Wendover, *op. cit.*, p. 142. Runciman (*History*, p. 464) ascribes Patriarch Heraclius' maneuvres at this time to the calculation that he "... had no mind to be a martyr."

purposes. The Moslem chieftain allowed the vanquished fifty days in which to raise the required sum. All persons still remaining in Jerusalem after that time together with their properties would be regarded as Saladin's property. Lastly, the agreement stipulated for the protection of the released persons by Moslem soldiery against thieves until their arrival in Christian territories. Tyre was selected as the place of refuge for the ransomed Franks.[348]

With the terms of surrender thus defined and confirmed, the vanquished surrendered the keys of the several gates of the city and Saladin and his forces took possession on Friday, October 2, 1187. In sharp distinction to the veritable blood bath characterizing the capture of Jerusalem in 1099, the Moslem conquerors maintained public order in the streets and protected in the camp set up for them outside the city walls the several Franks who were ransomed. Saladin's brother, al-ʿĀdil, requested that a thousand of the unransomed Franks be given to him as a reward for his aid in the conquest of the land and the capture of the city of Jerusalem. Saladin complied, whereupon al-ʿĀdil freed them. Perhaps not to be outdone by his brother's generosity, Saladin released all old persons still in Jerusalem, but rejected the proposal of Balian and Patriarch Heraclius that he release the 11,000 still remaining in Jerusalem in return for the surrender of themselves as hostages as a guarantee until such time as would be required for the raising of the stipulated sum by their fellow Christians. Still another example of his clemency was provided by his decision, following a request by the ransomed women who had suffered the loss of their husbands and fathers by capture and death at Hattin that he release his Frankish prisoners, to comply with their plea. He also granted gifts to each of them in accordance with her respective estate.[349] Such conduct was in sharp contrast to that of the Patriarch Heraclius, who left the city with all the furniture of the Church of the Resurrection and of the other churches together with lamps of gold and silver.[350]

---

[348] *Chronique d'Ernoul*, pp. 218-20 and chap. xix, pp. 222-24; *Eracles*, pp. 89-93; *Chronique d'Amadi*, pp. 71-73; *Libellus*, pp. 247-48; *The Chronography of Bar Hebraeus*, p. 326; Ibn al-Athīr, *K.—A.*, p. 702; Behâ Ed-Dîn, *Saladin*, p. 120 and *Anecdotes*, p. 101; Makrizi, *op. cit.*, p. 32; Roger of Wendover, *loc. cit.*

[349] *Chronique d'Ernoul*, chap. xix, pp. 224-30; Behâ Ed-Dîn, *Saladin*, p. 119 and *Anecdotes, loc. cit.; Itinerarium*, pp. 21-22; Abū'l-Fidā, *loc. cit.*; Abou Chamah, *op. cit.*, pp. 318, 330-31, and 332-33; Kamal-Ad-Dîn, *Histoire*, IV, 184; William of Newburgh, *op. cit.*, pp. 260-61; *Libellus*, pp. 249-51; Michael the Syrian, *Chronique, loc. cit.* and *Extrait, loc. cit.*; *Eracles*, pp. 94-99.

[350] *The Chronography of Bar Hebraeus*, p. 327; Ibn al-Athīr, *K.—A.*, pp. 703-04; Abou Chamah, *op. cit.*, pp. 338-39.

Moreover, Saladin honored his pledged word respecting the safety of the ransomed Franks by ordering that they be divided into three columns and be led respectively by the Templars, Hospitallers, and Balian of Ibelin together with the Patriarch; each column was also accompanied by a bodyguard of fifty cavalrymen.[351] Furthermore, the victorious Moslem chieftain tolerantly allowed a prominent Greek nun to depart with her servants, eunuchs, and possessions with armed guards to Frankish territories, offered the Patriarch of the Greeks the administration of his church in Jerusalem, and even allowed four Frankish monks to remain in the Church of the Resurrection to minister to the Holy Sepulchre.[352] Equally revealing was Saladin's refusal to accede to the pleas of his friends that he destroy the Church of the Holy Sepulchre. He answered that he had no desire to discourage visits of Christian pilgrims to the site, which was the object of their veneration rather than the building itself. Hence he closed the Church for only three days and then permitted entrance on the part of Frankish pilgrims on payment of a fee.[353] The only visible signs of his rejection of the principles of the Christian faith and his devotion of those of Islam were his cleansing by rose-water brought from Damascus of the Dome of the Rock and the mosque of al-Aqsa, which had been the sites of Christian worship, and his participation on Friday, October 9, 1187 in prayers of thanks to Allah in the latter building.[354]

Meanwhile, the aftermath of the fall of Jerusalem afforded glaring contrasts between the tactics of the victors and those of the

---

[351] *Chronique d'Ernoul*, pp. 230-31; *Eracles*, pp. 99-100.

[352] *The Chronography of Bar Hebraeus*, pp. 326-27; Ibn al-Athīr, *K.—A.*, p. 703; Abou Chamah, *op. cit.*, pp. 331-32.

[353] Makrizi, *op. cit.*, p. 33; Abou Chamah, *op. cit.*, p. 340. Slaughter (*op. cit.*, p. 155) believes in respect to the fate of the Christian population of Jerusalem that "Probably the orthodox Christians had been chosen to go out first and those who remained were for the most part members of eastern sects."

[354] *Chronique d'Ernoul*, pp. 234-35; Makrizi, *loc. cit.*; Michael the Syrian, *Chronique*, p. 405 and *Extrait*, pp. 399-400; Ibn al-Athīr, *K.—A.*, pp. 704-05; Behâ Ed-Dîn, *Saladin*, p. 120 and *Anecdotes*, p. 101; *Libellus*, pp. 250-51; Ibn Khallikan, *op. cit.*, II, 634-41; *Eracles*, p. 104; Roger of Wendover, *loc. cit. Chronique d'Ernoul*, *Libellus*, Ibn al-Athīr, *K.-A.*, and Behâ Ed-Dîn all declare that the Cross over the Dome of the Rock was thrown down, but the first two named sources state that they do not attribute this act to any command of Saladin's. Herzog (*op. cit.*, p. 74) disagrees with the views of the contemporaries of King Guy who contended that the loss of the city of Jerusalem could be attributed solely to the king's inability and inconstancy. Such a turn of events cannot be attributed to one person. Rather it was the result of the principle of feudalism and its emphasis on the power of the magnates which made it impossible for the king to take decisive measures even in imminent danger.

vanquished. The refugees from Jerusalem, who were protected by Saladin's guards until their arrival in the County of Tripoli, met with a series of rebuffs from the Tripolitan Christians. Most of the less affluent refugees repaired to Antiochian and Armenian territories and later succeeded in gaining an entrance into Antioch. The remainder of the refugees, fleeing from Ascalon to Alexandria, fared better, receiving hospitable treatment and protection from the city officials until the following March. Upon hearing of the refusal of the Pisan, Genoese, and Venetian sea captains in the harbor of Alexandria to accept as passengers the thousand poor Christian refugees, the city officials required the Italian mariners to accept them free before granting sailing permits and secured promises of decent treatment and safe delivery under threats of future retaliation against their fellow citizens upon their arrival in Egypt.[355]

---

[355] *Chronique d'Ernoul*, pp. 231-34; *Eracles*, pp. 100-03. Runciman (*History*, p. 467) declares "They [the refugees] moved on to Tripoli. There, too, earlier refugees filled the city, and the authorities, short of food, would admit no more and closed the gates against them." Neither of the two sources dealing with this episode affords any evidence whatsoever for the advancement of this extenuating explanation. The sources cited by Runciman are Ernoul, pp. 320-4 [sic] (actually, pp. 231-34) and *Eracles*, II, pp. 100-3.

CHAPTER SEVENTEEN

THE TURNING OF THE TIDE: THE FRANKS RETAIN TYRE

With the fall of the city of Jerusalem now an accomplished fact, the scattered remnants of the Frankish military establishment of the Holy Land hurriedly repaired to Tyre as a haven and staging point for a possible military recovery. The several barons, namely Joscelyn III, Balian of Ibelin, Count Raymond and his four stepsons, Reginald of Sidon, the sons of the prince of Antioch, and Conrad of Montferrat, recognized the need for the creation of a real defence of this nearly impregnable city before any implementation of plans for the recovery of Tripoli and Antioch. Hence they entered into a treaty with the Genoese and Pisans to obtain their aid in the defense of Tyre. Donations of such magnitude were made to them in July and October, 1187 and May, 1188 as to place them on a level of equality with the Venetians who had formerly occupied the favored position in Tyre. These gifts comprised confirmations to the Pisans already made to them by King Baldwin III and Count Raymond of Tripoli, a district removed from the royal domain, exemptions from taxes of all varieties, as well as villages in the outskirts of the city. In addition, the Pisans received promises of properties in Jaffa and Acre together with lands belonging to Joscelyn III. Genoese support was besought with a grant of the title of castellan to a Genoese named Ansaldo Bonvicini, a grant of the freedom of Tyre, the casal of St. George, a third part "in Cathena," and many other rights after the Frankish leadership had urged upon the Genoese twin policies of aid to save the land from Moslem subjugation and abandonment of memories of injuries inflicted upon them by rulers in former times. Joscelyn III was a witness and signatory of the agreement with the Genoese in July, 1187. Lastly, the baronial group granted the Green Palace, a village, a bakery, and exemptions for their commerce to the Barcelonian group in Tyre and Acre and favors to the southern French residents in Tyre, namely citizens of Marseilles, Saint-Gilles-du-Gard, and Montpellier. Conrad of Montferrat, who now behaved as the "lieutenant of the kings of Outre-Mer" perhaps because of his knowledge that the Frankish leaders had unanimously indicated to him that he was to have the custody of the city until the arrival of one of the four great European monarchs, namely Emperor Frederick, the king of England, the king of France, or the king of Sicily, also effected the deepening of the moat defending Tyre, restored the city's walls, and summoned to the city's defenses the remaining garrisons of the cities to which Saladin had granted capitulation and which had meanwhile repaired to Tyre.[356]

---

[356] Röhricht, *Regesta*, Nos. 659, 665, 666, 667, 668 and 675, pp. 175, 177, 178 and 180; Abou Chamah, *op. cit.*, pp. 341-42 and 400; *Chronique d'Ernoul*, chap. xiv, p. 170; *Historia Peregrinorum*, p. 120; *Eracles*, pp. 64-65, 71-76, and 106-10; *Brevis*, pp. 53-55; *Ex Chronologia Roberti Altissiodorensis*, p. 255; William of Newburgh, *op. cit.*, pp. 264-65; Louis Méry and F. Guindon, *Histoire analytique et chronologique des actes et des délibérations du corps et du conseil de la municipalité de Marseille, depuis le Xme siècle jusqu'à nos jours* (Marseille, 1841), I, 190-92; Ibn al-Athīr, *K.-A.*, pp. 687, 694, 707, and 710 and Ibn al-Athīr, *Extrait de la chronique intitulée Kamel-Altevarykh* in *Rec. his. or.* (Paris, 1887), II, 3. (Henceforth all references to this last named source will be cited as I and II to differentiate the two volumes. References to Volume II will also be cited as *K.-A.*). The sources are entirely silent about the reaction, if any, of Joscelyn III to Conrad of Montferrat's grants of his properties to the Pisans. However, it is a logical surmise that such tactics on the part of Conrad created at the very least a growing coolness between him and the Seneschal, who presumably, as a native Syrian noble and an old time military antagonist of the Moslems, regarded Conrad, who was in last analysis a newcomer to the Holy Land, as an upstart and interloper with decidedly dubious political credentials. Although Steven Runciman (*A History of the Crusades* [Cambridge, 1954], III, 20) does not designate Joscelyn III by name as one of the dissident elements in Tyre during Saladin's siege of that city in the Autumn and early Winter of 1187, he does so by inference in his reference to the "Courtenay supporters." It is difficult to see how the "Courtenay supporters," who are considered by Runciman as being in the ranks of the dissidents, did not reflect the views of the only living Courtenay who was now in Tyre. (Henceforth references to this last cited work of Runciman will be cited as *History* and all references to it, apart from an occasional reference to Volume II, will pertain solely to Volume III. References to Volume II of Runciman's *History* will be cited as II). The nature of that dissidence is well summed up by Runciman (*History, loc. cit.*) as follows; "The party quarrels that had rent the latter years of the kingdom of Jerusalem had been healed by the tact of Balian of Ibelin only a few weeks before the battle of Hattin, and they had broken out again on the very eve of the battle. The disaster embittered them. The Lusignan and Courtenay supporters blamed it on Raymond of Tripoli and Raymond's friends, the Ibelins and Garniers and most of the local nobility, blamed it, with better reason, on King Guy's weakness and the influence of the Templars and Reynald of Châtillon." ... "Cooped up behind the walls of Tyre, the dispossessed nobles had little else to do but to hurl recriminations at each other. Balian and his friends who had eluded captivity now accepted Conrad of Montferrat as their leader. They had seen that it was he alone who had saved Tyre. But Guy's supporters, emerging from prison after the worst of the crisis was over, merely saw him as an interloper, a potential rival to their King. Guy's release, so far from strengthening the Franks, brought the quarrel to a head." Richard (*Royaume*, p. 147) observes in his discussion of the actions of Conrad at this time that "Il [Conrad] se comportait en "lieutenant des rois d'Outre mer," sans égards pour les droits antérieurs; on pourrait peut-être remarquer qu'il s'en prenait surtout aux biens des partisans des Lusignan (comme l'avait déjà fait Raymond III?), le Temple et Jocelin, pour enrichir les

These vigorous preparations on the part of the Frankish defenders of Tyre soon proved their worth, for Saladin's renewed investment of the city shortly thereafter on November 25, 1187 ended in flat failure. Unable to deploy effectively their artillery on the narrow Tyrian

---

Italiens, ses compatriotes." Runciman (*History*, p. 21) points out quite accurately that the arrangement providing for the control of Tyre by Conrad of Montferrat until the arrival of one of the four great European monarchs" ... suited Conrad. Richard of England, as overlord of the Lusignans in Guienne, might favour Guy's cause; but the Emperor and Philip of France were Conrad's cousins and friends." Commenting on the Tyrian episode in Saladin's military career, Stevenson (*op. cit.*, pp. 255-56) writes as follows: "There need not be any hesitation in saying that Saladin's own policy and plan of campaign were largely responsible for his failure to capture Tyre. He had consistently released his prisoners and allowed the garrisons and inhabitants of the captured towns to go free. For the most part they simply reassembled in Tyre. In this way the Latin power was concentrated in one of the most advantageous positions it could occupy. The policy which so resulted has been sharply criticised by modern and by older historians. Saladin's error, if he erred at all, did not consist simply in the postponement of the attack on Tyre. Granting that an earlier attack would have had more chance of success, and supposing Tyre could have been captured, some other city, such as Ascalon, would still have played the part of Tyre. The essential matter to be considered, therefore, is the policy of releasing captives in exchange for the surrender of towns and castles. What this accomplished must not be forgotten. Practically the whole country except Tyre was gained within a few months. Would any other policy have gained as much? Military operations would certainly have prolonged the struggle and the risk of a check and a turn of the tide long before the end was considerable. Saladin deliberately persisted in his policy long after it was clear what the result must be. That in itself forbids any rash condemnation of it. Besides we may easily exaggerate the influence which the failure to capture Tyre exercised on the course of events. The determining factor in the contest was the intervention of the west. The issue of the struggle between Saladin and the third crusade was little affected by the fact that Tyre was a Latin stronghold when the crusaders landed. It was of vital consequence that almost the whole country was in Saladin's possession and this result was largely due to the policy which he adopted." Cf. Runciman, *History*, p. 18 and II, 471. Richard (*Royaume*, p. 145) declares that "Raymond III ... fit d'importantes donations aux Gênois et aux Pisans, les plaçant sur un pied d'égalité avec les Vénitiens qui avaient jusque là tenu à Tyr le premier rang." This scholar (*Royaume*, p. 145, n. 2) cites Röhricht's *Regesta*, Nos. 659 and 665 to document this view. But Röhricht's first document makes quite clear that the concessions to the Genoese were made by the several barons rather than by one of them, namely Raymond of Tripoli. "Barones regni Hierosolymitani post cladem apud Manescalciam Tyberiadis acceptam Tyri congressi Januensibus, quos ad defensionem urbis paratos viderint, Tyri libertatem commercii et curiam liberam concedunt curtemque deputant videlicet macellum cum III domibus vicinis, platea et II domorum insulis, quae sunt ante ipsum macellum, deinde domos ei vicinas, quae ex una parte viae publicae, ex altera semitae adjacentes porriguntur ex una parte ad domum Theobaldi Aurificis, ex altera usque ad domum quondam magistri Perri (Petri) Januensis.—Joccius, Tirensis (sigillans), Let(ardus), Nazarenus, Monachus, Caesariensis, archiepiscopi; de baronibus: comes Tripolitanus, comes Joppe, regni senescalcus, Raginus, dominus Sydonensis, Balianus, Galterius Caesareae; Terricus, Templi, Borr(ellus), Hospitalis, praeceptores; Guillielmus Piperata, consul et vicecomes Januensium Tyri, Raimundus Biblii, dominus Guillielmus (de) Tyberiade, Robertus de Pincerebneo."

isthmus, the Moslem land besiegers suffered an overwhelming fire from Conrad's batteries. Equal disaster met the Egyptian sea force on December 30, for, having enticed five of the twelve galleys into the port of Tyre, Conrad thereupon raised the harbor chain, separated them from their fellows, and then seized them. The remaining seven Moslem vessels were no match for Conrad's force of equal number, five being thrown up on the coast and the remaining two being obliged to flee to Beirut. Hence Saladin, following a council of war with his emirs which resulted in their urging that he abandon the siege, raised the investment on the night of January 1, 1188. Saladin now concluded a peace treaty with Conrad, granting to the latter a large sum of money in return for his agreement to abstain from attacks on Moslem areas. Thereupon, the Moslem chieftain, having dismissed the several contingents composing his army, proceeded with his own particular troops to Acre where he remained until the beginning of March, 1188. The ensuing military contacts between the Tyrian defenders and the Moslems were mere skirmishes.[357]

---

[357] Arnold of Lubeck, *op. cit.*, p. 176; Abou Chamah, *op. cit.*, pp. 342-44; Behâ Ed-Dîn, *Saladin*, pp. 120-22; *Chronique d'Ernoul*, chap. xxi, pp. 241-44; Ibn al-Athīr, *K.—A.*, I, 707-12; *Itinerarium*, pp. 24-25; Behâ Ed-Dîn, *Anecdotes*, pp. 102-03; Kamāl Ad-Dîn, *Histoire*, IV, 184; *Eracles*, pp. 104-10; Delaville Le Roulx, *Cartulaire*, I, No. 847, p. 527. Richard (*Royaume*, p. 147, n. 4) in commenting on the treaty between Conrad of Montferrat and Saladin observes as follows; "Très favorable, comme tous les Allemands, à Conrad (cousin germain de Frédéric Barberousse comme fils de Guillaume IV de Montferrat et de la tante du grand empereur, soeur de Conrad III), Arnold essaie de l'excuser de ce pacte — qui, de fait, laissait les mains libres à Saladin pour la conquête de l'intérieur — en disant que bien des gens avaient blâmé le marquis ("unde quidam eum infidelitatis arguere conati sunt quod munera infidelium acciperet"), mais que celui-ci n'avait pu agir que pour le bien de la Chrétienté. Ces trêves étaient-elles celles que Renaud de Sidon concluait pour Beaufort?"

CHAPTER EIGHTEEN

THE INCEPTION OF THE CONTEST BETWEEN CONRAD OF MONTFERRAT AND GUY OF LUSIGNAN

The total effect of this sudden upsurge of Frankish fortunes, albeit a small one compared with the crowning disaster of the rout of Hattin, was to make Tyre the potential center of a new Frankish state in the Holy Land. Indeed, even before the repulse of Saladin's forces the Archbishops of Caesarea and Nazareth, the Bishop of Sidon, and the leaders of the crusading orders of the Temple and the Hospital had come to Tyre in October. These developments and the attempt, although unsuccessful because of adverse weather conditions, of Count Raymond to aid the beleaguered Tyrians with a rescue force of ten galleys bearing knights and provisions[358] — this effort had shown the feeling on the part of an important Frankish leader that he regarded Conrad's defense merited his loyal support — gave Conrad, who already enjoyed the support of other Frankish barons, the kernel of a new state by the opening days of 1188. Still unresolved, however, were the twin problems, namely whether Conrad, a usurper, would submit to King Guy, if and when he should restore his shattered fortunes, and whether a new crusading effort emanating from Europe would regard the new Tyrian leadership as unworthy of support because of its dubious claim to power and instead would prefer the inalienable rights which the Frankish barons of Syria had gained for themselves because of their constant struggle against Islam. Perhaps equally portentous and redolent of future friction in the new crusading state, if and when such an eventuality should come to pass, was the question as to whether Joscelyn III would willingly allow the territories formerly part of his seigneury and recently assigned to the Pisans to remain in that state.[359]

---

[358] *Chronique d'Ernoul*, p. 240.

[359] Richard (*Royaume*, p. 148) well summarizes Conrad's position as follows: "Mais sa situation restait fausse. Le "seigneur de Tyr", usurpateur par force du domaine royal, allait-il se soumettre au roi Guy quand celui-ci recouvrerait sa liberté, ou affecterait-il de ne pas reconnaître l'état de choses antérieur à Hattin? Une fois de plus, la Croisade devrait-elle s'intégrer dans les cadres de la colonie latine d'Orient ou bien ne considérer ceux-ci que comme l'armature d'une armée d'occupation dont les droits étaient douteux; ferait-elle table rase du passé pour reconstruire le "royaume latin" ou accepterait-elle de

The first of these problems, namely a contest for the purple robes of power between Conrad of Montferrat and King Guy, soon eventuated. The latter, who had gained his release from Saladin in the late Winter or Summer of 1188,[360] quickly joined Sibyl and repudiated his promise, perhaps after his absolution therefrom, never again to wage war on Saladin which he had made at the time of his release. Then he paused at Antioch where Prince Bohemond held in trust for his own son the County of Tripoli which had been bequeathed to him by the late Raymond III of Tripoli at the time of his death in October, 1187. Bohemond vaguely promised aid to King Guy. The latter, supported by his adherents, thereupon advanced from Tripoli upon Tyre with the plan of assuming the rule of the remnant of his former state. Conrad answered with a blunt closing of the gates of Tyre to his adversary and a declaration that King Guy was entitled to nothing because of his forfeiture of the Kingdom of Jerusalem at the battle of Hattin and during his ensuing imprisonment. Furthermore, he had left it without administration. Only Conrad's action had saved it from Moslem capture. Lastly, he, Conrad, intended to hold Tyre until the arrival of the Western monarchs for an arbitration of the question as to whether he or King Guy should be the ultimate ruler. Guy had no alternative but to return with his supporters to Tripoli. Conrad continued adamant in his position, rebuffing Guy again in April, 1189 when he returned with Sibyl with a renewed demand for the control of the city. Guy thereupon posted his forces before the city's walls.[361]

Meanwhile, the fact that the appeals to Western Europe from the Syrian Franks were reaping a harvest of responses in the form of arrivals of fresh Pisan naval contingents of fifty-two ships and the subsequent arrival of Sicilian ships[362] served to bolster Tyre's defenses

---

reconnaître pour droits imprescriptibles ceux qu'une longue possession, et la lutte constante contre l'Islam, malgré l'échec terminal, avaient acquis aux barons de Syrie?"

[360] Behâ Ed-Dîn, *Saladin*, p. 143 and *Anecdotes*, pp. 122-23; *Chronique d'Ernoul*, chaps. xvi and xxi, pp. 185 and 252-53; *Itinerarium*, pp. 25-26; *L'Estoire, loc. cit.* and col. 71; *Eracles*, pp. 79, 121, and 131. See Runciman, *History*, II, 462-63, n. 4, La Monte, *The Crusade*, p. 93, n. 29, and Stevenson, *op. cit.*, p. 252, n. 2 for discussions of the problem of the time, place, and circumstances of Guy's release.

[361] *Chronique d'Ernoul*, chap. xxii, pp. 256-57; Behâ Ed-Dîn, *Saladin*, pp. 143-44 and *Anecdotes*, p. 123; *Itinerarium*, pp. 27 and 59-60; *Eracles*, pp. 123-24; *L'Estoire*, cols. 72-73; William of Newburgh, *op. cit.*, p. 265. Schlumberger (*Numismatique*, p. 98) obviously errs in his contention that "De retour à Tripoli ... le comte [Count Raymond] mourut subitement, quinze jours à peine après la bataille de Tibériade, [Hattin] c'est-à-dire vers le 20 avril 1187."

[362] *Itinerarium*, p. 27.

and, presumably, Conrad's determination not to yield to Guy's demands. The stalemate between the rivals, now eighteen months in length, was made possible, moreover, at least in part because of Saladin's preoccupation in the tasks of capturing Chastel-Neuf in December, 1187, his unsuccessful storming of Tortosa and capturing the enemy castles of Sarmīn, Jabala, Latakia, Saone, Bekǎs, Burzia, Darbsāk, and Baghrās in north Syria as well as Krak de Montréal, Safad, and Belvoir in Palestine throughout 1188, in his detachment of additional army units from his command in January, 1189, in his preoccupation with affairs in Jerusalem and Acre in the Winter of 1189, in his return to Damascus in March, 1189, and in his decision to grant additional rest to his armies.[363]

The deadlock unexpectedly ended in late August, 1189 with Guy's departure with his forces and march southward to Acre and the effected decision of the Pisan and Sicilian ship commanders and crews to join him.[364] Apprised of the new turn of events, Saladin, who had meantime been engaged in the siege of the castle of Belfort,[365] at first believed that this action was a Frankish feint designed to make him withdraw from Belfort. When he learned the facts, however, from a Moslem courier on August 26, 1189, he immediately convoked a council of his emirs and councillors to devise a strategy to meet the new situation. His own view that he should attack the Franks before they consolidated their position before Acre met with the opposition of his advisors, who believed that the enemy once collected could be

---

[363] Behâ Ed-Dîn, *Saladin*, pp. 121, 122-23, and 127-43 and n. 1, p. 127, n. 1, p. 130, n. 2, p. 132, n. 2, p. 133, n. 2, p. 135, and n. 1, p. 136 and *Anecdotes*, pp. 102, 104, and 108-22; Abou Chamah, *op. cit.*, pp. 355-400; Abū'l-Fidā, *op. cit.*, p. 59; *Chronique d'Ernoul*, chap. xxi, p. 251; *Eracles*, p. 122; Kamal-Ad-Dîn, *Histoire*, IV, 187-93; Ibn al-Athīr, *K.-A.*, I, 717-32.

[364] *Chronique d'Ernoul*, chap. xxii, p. 257; Ralph of Diceto, *op. cit.*, p. 70; Behâ Ed-Dîn, *Saladin*, pp. 153 and 154 and n. 1, p. 154 and *Anecdotes*, p. 132; *Eracles*, pp. 124-25; *Itinerarium*, pp. 61-62; *L'Estoire*, col. 74; Ibn al-Athīr, *K. – A.*, II, 5-6. Runciman (*History*, p. 22) appraises Guy's action at this time as follows: "It was a move of desperate foolhardiness, the decision of a brave but very unwise man. Thwarted of his wish to reign in Tyre, Guy urgently needed a city from which to reconstitute his kingdom. Conrad was seriously ill at the time; and it seemed to Guy a fine opportunity to show that he was the active leader of the Franks. But the risk was enormous. The size of the Moslem garrison of Acre was more than twice that of Guy's whole army; and Saladin's regular forces were in the offing. No one could have foreseen that the adventure would succeed. But history has its surprises. If Conrad's restless energy had saved the remnant of Palestine for Christendom, it was Guy's gallant folly that turned the tide and began an era of reconquest."

[365] Behâ Ed-Dîn, *Saladin*, pp. 142-43 and 150-53 and *Anecdotes*, pp. 121-22 and 129-32; *L'Estoire*, col. 75.

cut to pieces by the Moslems in one day. Saladin finally agreed. Hence the Franks were already in position at the time of Saladin's arrival.[366]

---

[366] Behâ Ed-Dîn, *Saladin*, pp. 154 and 175 and *Anecdotes*, pp. 132 and 152; *Chronique d'Ernoul*, chap. xxiii, p. 259; Makrizi, *op. cit.*, p. 43; Ibn al-Athīr, *K.—A.*, II, 6-7; *L'Estoire*, cols. 75-76. Slaughter (*op. cit.*, p. 196) attributes Saladin's decision to accept the advice of his advisors to the following considerations: "It was impossible to set out against the will of his followers. The danger threatening from across the sea made it imperative that he preserve unity and good feeling. The feudal bond was again proved weak, and he could expect no special effort when the morale of the troops was somewhat low, after fighting for two years to win a country not yet conquered. They had been showing plenty of spirit. They had braced themselves to meet the new emergency that awaited them; they were keen to prove that they feared no new Crusaders. But to be obliged to pursue the King whom they had already defeated was a task that aroused little enthusiasm. Surely the garrison of Acre was able to finish with that remnant of beaten foes!"

CHAPTER NINETEEN

THE FURTHER TURNING OF THE TIDE: THE FRANKISH INVESTMENT AND CAPTURE OF ACRE

The ensuing siege of Acre[367] by King Guy and his forces proved to be a lengthy one. Unsuccessful in their endeavor to carry the city by storm, they proceeded to construct an embankment of turf around Acre with deep ditches from sea to sea despite incessant Moslem harassment. Meanwhile, reinforcements summoned by the Syrian Franks in the months after the battle of Hattin arrived from the West in the form of a big Frisian and Danish fleet in September, which now proceeded to blockade Acre by sea. Additional support ensued in the arrival of Joscelyn III as well as warriors and churchmen from England, France, Denmark, Flanders, Italy, Germany, and Hungary by the close of September. These included the redoubtable Fleming, James of Avesnes, Erard II, Count of Brienne and his brother Andrew de Brienne, Lord of Ramerupt, Helin de Wavrin, the Seneschal of Flanders, Louis II, Landgrave of Thuringia, Philip de Dreux, Bishop of Beauvais, Robert II, Count of Dreux, Henry I, Count of Bar-Le-Duc, the Count of Ferrers, Narjot de Toucy, Ancelin de Montreal, Geoffrey de Grenville, Otho de Fosse, William Goez, the Viscount of Château Erald, the Viscount of Turenne, the Castellan of Bruges, the Archbishop of Pisa, Count Bertulf, Count Nicholas of Hungary, Count Bernard, Count Richard of Apulia, Count Aldebrandus, Ingelremmus de Vienne, Herve de Gien, Thibaut de Bar, Count John of Leogria, Count John of Seis, Guy de Dampierre, the Bishop of Verona, and the nephew of the King of Denmark. The net effect of all these developments, despite the withdrawal of the Sicilian squadron because of the death of King William of Sicily in November, 1189, was to cause increasing apprehension for Saladin.[368] Hence that Moslem chieftain

---

[367] Detailed and extensive discussions of this siege are provided by Runciman, *History*, pp. 23-33 and 47-51, Archer and Kingsford, *op. cit.*, pp. 316-26, Stevenson, *op. cit.*, pp. 261-72, Champdor, *op. cit.*, pp. 224-30, Painter, *op. cit.*, pp. 50-53 and 64-69, Röhricht, *Geschichte*, pp. 502-43, Oman, *op. cit.*, pp. 333-40, King, *op. cit.*, pp. 136-47, and René Grousset, *Histoire des croisades et du royaume franc de Jérusalem* (Paris, 1936), III, 18-56.

[368] *Chronique d'Ernoul*, pp. 258-59 and chap. xxi, p. 247; *Eracles*, pp. 125-28; *Itinerarium*, pp. 63-68 and 73-74; Ralph of Diceto, *op. cit.*, pp. 73 and 79-80; *L'Estoire*,

THE FURTHER TURNING OF THE TIDE 185

believed that the problem posed by Acre was greater than that provided by the still continuing siege of Belfort and accordingly he summoned to Acre his vassals and detached a substantial part of his forces investing Belfort. His ensuing attack on King Guy's camp on September 15 proved abortive, but his nephew Taqī-ad-Dīn succeeded in getting around the Franks' line, in reaching Acre's north gate, and in establishing his own camp somewhat to the east of that of the Franks. The latter, now encouraged by the arrival of Conrad of Montferrat and his agreement to aid his fellow Franks with the stipulation that he not be obliged to serve under Guy's command, fortified their camp and placed it under the command of Geoffrey of Lusignan, Guy's brother. Then they struck the Moslem lines with great force on October 4. Misunderstanding the retirement of Taqī-ad-Dīn, who sought thereby to lure on the Templars, Saladin weakened his center to save him. The result was the flight of Saladin's center and right wing with major losses. Saladin's own tent was reached by the Franks. However, the Moslem left wing remained firm and under Saladin's guidance took advantage of the Frankish breaking of their own ranks to chase the Moslem fugitives and countercharged, driving them in confusion into their own camp. Simultaneously the Moslem garrison in Acre aided their fellow Moslems by an attack on the Frankish camp. The camp itself remained under Frankish control because of Geoffrey of Lusignan's effective defenses and the result was the safe retirement of most of the Frankish forces into it. Yet the Franks' losses had been severe including the loss of many German troops, who had panicked, as well as many Templars, one of whom was the Grand Master, Gerard of Ridefort. Only the brave deeds of King Guy himself saved his opponent, Conrad of Montferrat, from capture. However, the Moslem victory was so indecisive as to lead Saladin to withdraw some dozen miles to a hill named al-Kharrūbah southeast of Acre and to take up winter quarters.[369]

Although checked in his land operations against the Franks

---

cols. 77 and 78-79; Makrizi, *op. cit.*, pp. 43-45; Arnold of Lubeck, *op. cit.*, p. 177; Benedict of Peterborough, *op. cit.*, p. 94; La Monte, *The Crusade*, pp. 137 and 139-40, nn. 34-35 and 39-45.

[369] Behâ Ed-Dî, *Saladin*, pp. 162-70 and *Anecdotes*, pp. 140-47; Ibn al-Athīr, *K.—A.*, II, 7-14; *L'Estoire*, cols. 79-82; Kamal-Ad-Dîn, *Histoire*, IV, 194-95; Makrizi, *op. cit.*, pp. 45-46; *Itinerarium*, pp. 68-72; Ralph of Diceto, *op. cit.*, pp. 70-71; *Eracles*, pp. 128-30; Abou Chamah, *op. cit.*, pp. 415-22; Benedict of Peterborough, *op. cit.*, pp. 94-95. Archer and Kingsford (*op. cit.*, p. 320, n. 1) believe that Saladin's retirement "... probably refers only to part of Saladin's army.".... "This retreat was occasioned chiefly by Saladin's ill-health..."

investing Acre, Saladin gained a measure of success against them in naval operations. Apprehensive over the arrival of news of the approach of a German army under Frederick Barbarossa, he urged his vassals and his fellow Moslems in Morocco and Spain to aid him. This plea resulted in sympathetic written responses but little tangible help. Yet enough accretions came in to enable him to develop a naval blockade around the besieging Franks effective enough for fifty of his galleys to pierce the Frankish fleet and to furnish the Moslem garrison in Acre with additional stocks of weapons and food. An even greater victory was scored on the following December 26 with the arrival of a larger fleet from Egypt which succeeded in reopening communications with Acre.[370]

The cumulative effect of these actions was to create a growing shortage of food in the Frankish camp during the Winter months of 1190 and, because of the increasing paucity of good water as the year advanced, a health problem as well with a resultant spread of disease among the Franks. Hence the rivals, Conrad of Montferrat and King Guy, decided to bury the hatchet. Their ensuing agreement provided for the holding by Conrad of the city of Tyre along with Beirut and Sidon following their recovery and the recognition of Guy as the rightful king.[371] That the latter provision was meaningful is attested to by the fact that shortly thereafter on April 10, 1190 no less figures than the Seneschal, Joscelyn III, and Hugh, the lord of Tiberias, along with lesser feudatories witnessed Guy's grant with the consent of his wife Sibyl to all the citizenry of Amalfi resident at Acre the same privileges already held by the Venetians, Pisans, and Genoese in the

---

[370] Behâ Ed-Dîn, *Saladin*, pp. 170-71 and *Anecdotes*, p. 148; Makrizi, *op. cit.*, pp. 46-47; *Itinerarium*, pp. 77-79; Abou Chamah, *op. cit.*, pp. 430-31; *L'Estoire*, cols. 84-85; Ibn al-Athīr, *K. – A.*, II, 151-16; Kamal-Ad-Dîn, *Histoire*, IV, 195.

[371] *L'Estoire*, col. 135. *Itinerarium* (pp. 235-36) declares that the agreement between Conrad of Montferrat and Guy of Lusignan was made after the surrender of Acre. *Chronica Magistri Rogeri de Houedene*, ed. William Stubbs (London, 1870), III, 125 has an identical view. (Future references to this source, which will be cited as Roger of Hoveden, will pertain solely to Volume III). La Monte (*The Crusade*, p. 210, n. 28) directly supports the dating provided by *Itinerarium* in his declaration that the dating provided by *L'Estoire* "... seems to be out of place here." Runciman (*History*, p. 27), on the other hand, supports the earlier dating supplied by *L'Estoire* and does so on the ground that "Chastened by the difficulties of their men, Guy and Conrad patched up an agreement." I support Runciman's views on this matter rather than those of La Monte, for the nature of the difficulties facing the Franks demanded an ending of the feuding between the royal rivals and this, in turn, could be best effected by concessions of territories by Guy of Lusignan to his opponent and the latter's recognition, in turn, of the continued retention of the regal title by the former.

city of Acre, namely free entrance and exit rights to the harbor, freedom of anchoring and right of anchorage of all ships as well as their free care.[372] Furthermore on the following May 4 Guy with the approval of his wife Sibyl added to and confirmed those privileges which had been held by the Genoese before the capture of Acre by the Moslems. Again the Seneschal was a witness to this act.[373]

Meanwhile Conrad of Montferrat had departed from the Frankish camp in March, 1190, had repaired to Tyre, and had returned at the close of March with boats carrying stocks of weapons and food. Saladin's fleet had tried to prevent the arrival of the enemy ships by an interceptive action which included the use of Greek fire, but had failed in its objective. Now equipped with the necessary materials, the Franks had constructed wooden siege-towers during the Winter months of 1190 and with their use now endeavored to capture Acre on May 5, 1190. But to no avail were these efforts, for the Moslem defenders succeeded in burning the siege-towers. This defeat was soon followed by the reappearance of famine and disease among the Franks. Meanwhile the Moslem defenders suffered the same plight despite the occasional successful breaching of the Frankish naval blockade by Moslem ships, the most notable example of which occurred on June 12 when a succouring Egyptian fleet met the Frankish fleet, defeated it, and effected the delivery of sorely needed supplies to the besieged. Meanwhile, strengthened by the arrival of fresh contingents of Moslems joining his army during the Spring of 1190, Saladin at length had struck the Franks' camp on May 19, but was obliged to retire after eight days of desperate fighting. The Frankish soldiery, in turn, defied the views of their leaders and unsuccessfully attacked Taqī-ad-Dīn's camp on July 25 with an ensuing high toll of more than 4,000 dead including the famous English crusader, Ralph of Alta Ripa, Archdeacon of Colchester.[374] The net effect of the clash of arms between besieged and besiegers during the first half of 1190 was one of unqualified stalemate.

The trends and developments characterizing both the Frankish and Moslem camps during the first year of the siege were essentially duplicated during the first half of the second year of the investment.

---

[372] Röhricht, *Regesta*, No. 690, p. 183.
[373] *Ibid.*, No. 693, pp. 184-85.
[374] Behâ Ed-Dîn, *Saladin*, pp. 178-82, 190-91, and 193-96 and *Anecdotes*, pp. 155-59, 165, and 167-70; *Itinerarium*, pp. 79-91; *Eracles*, p. 151; Ibn al-Athīr, *K.-A.*, II, 18-21 and 26-27; *L'Estoire*, cols. 86-94; Ralph of Diceto, *op. cit.*, p. 84; *Epistolae Cantuarienses*, No. CCCXLVI, ed. by William Stubbs (London, 1865), II, 329.

Additional forces came from Western Europe during the Summer of 1190 with the arrival of important French and Burgundian nobles such as Tibald, the Count of Blois, his brother Stephen of Sancerre, Ralph, Count of Clermont, John, Count of Fontigny, Alan of Saint-Valery, and Henry of Troyes, Count of Champagne, and important ecclesiastical leaders such as the Archbishop of Besançon and the Bishops of Blois and Toul. German and English forces arrived in October, headed respectively by Frederick of Swabia and Baldwin, Archbishop of Canterbury. And perhaps a growing confidence on the part of the Frankish leadership in an ultimate victory over the beleaguered Moslems in Acre can be seen in the same month when Guy and Sibyl conferred on the citizenry of Marseille on October 25 privileges in Acre following its recapture. Joscelyn III was a witness to this grant. Indeed, this confidence can be discerned even earlier than this, for during the preceding month of mid-September, 1190 King Guy and Queen Sibyl granted a house and four carrucates of land in Acre to the hospital of the Teutons with the provision that if the donors should be unable to grant the house they would substitute in its place a courtyard adjacent to the house. And again the Seneschal was a witness to this grant. Similar trends were duplicated in Saladin's army, for the fall of the fortress of Belfort in July permitted the transfer of the Moslem investment forces to Acre, but this new force did not make up numerically for the troops recently dispatched by Saladin to the north to meet Frederick Barbarossa. Again, savage attacks characterized the siege, with Frederick of Swabia vainly assailing with several types of siege equipment the walls of Acre shortly after his appearance and the Archbishop of Besançon similarly failing in his assault with a battering ram. Saladin was obliged to abandon his post at Tel Keisan some five miles from Acre as a result of successful Frankish attacks in November. But this Frankish gain was only a partial victory, for while it permitted them to effect a foraging expedition to Haifa with some attendant increase of their scanty food supply, Saladin managed, following his retreat, to secure a better position at al-Kharrūbah. Lastly, the hunger of the Moslems, which was only slightly relieved by the successful piercing of the Frankish blockade in November by some ships proceeding from Alexandria, had its counterpart in the Frankish camp and illness prevailed in both camps.[375]

---

[375] Behâ Ed-Dîn, *Saladin*, pp. 197, 201-05, 206, 212-18, and 224-27 and *Anecdotes*, pp. 170, 175-79, 180, 183-84, 185-92, and 196-200; *Itinerarium*, pp. 91-95 and 109-19;

The recently hard won compromise between the rivals, King Guy and Conrad of Montferrat, was a casualty of the illness in the Frankish camp, for it had among its successive victims the two small daughters of Queen Sibyl, Alice and Maria, as well as the Queen herself. Since Sibyl's half sister, Isabel, was now the heiress of the Kingdom of Jerusalem by reason of the fact that it now escheated to her, a political problem immediately resulted, namely the right of Guy to continue as king. He had gained his regal office by reason of his rôle of Sibyl's spouse, but could his royal rights continue after her demise? The answer of the barons with Balian of Ibelin as their leader was an unqualified negative. They saw in the new developments a golden opportunity to oust a weak king and substitute for him Conrad of Montferrat. If a marriage between him and Isabel could be effected, his claims to the kingship would be superior to Guy's. However, two barriers to the gaining of this desideratum had to be surmounted. One was the distinct possibility that such a marriage would be bigamous and therefore invalid in view of the prevailing rumors that Conrad still had one wife in Constantinople and perhaps another one in Italy from neither of whom he had effected a divorce or annulment of his marital bonds. But this problem, in the realm of mere rumors which might be treated as such, was a minor one compared to the solid reality that Isabel was still married and devoted to her husband, Humphrey of Toron, who was now in the Frankish camp. The barons scorned Humphrey for his present effeminacy and his former cowardice in 1186 when he had permitted Guy to obtain the throne. The barons' goal of securing a divorce of Humphrey and Isabel proved to be an easy one of attainment, insofar as Humphrey was concerned, for the responsibilities of married life and even more those of kingly office suited him in no way. But Isabel was of another mind, partly because of her attachment to Humphrey, partly because of her aversion to the prospect of marriage to a middle-aged soldier, and partly because of her lack of ambition for the throne. At this juncture Queen Maria Comnena showed her sympathy with the barons' position by imposing her will on her hesitant daughter to give up Humphrey. To meet ecclesiastical objections Queen Maria convoked an assembly of the

---

Abou Chamah, *op. cit.*, pp. 474, 480-81, and 513-14; *L'Estoire*, cols. 94 and 105-10; Ibn al-Athīr, *K. —A.*, II, 28-29; *Eracles*, pp. 159-60; Roger of Hoveden, *op. cit.*, p. 69; Méry and Guindon, *op. cit.*, pp. 194-95. Richard (*Royaume*, p. 153) sees in the grants to the citizens of Marseille as well as those made earlier to the Genoese and others (*supra*, p. 176) a plan by which Guy detached them "... ainsi tous plus ou moins du parti de Conrad..."

bishops and urged that the annulment be granted on the triple grounds that King Baldwin IV had obliged Isabel to marry Humphrey, that she was only eight years old at the time of the arrangement of the engagement, and that Humphrey was an effeminate person. Initial opposition to this proposal speedily emanated from the representative of the ailing Patriarch Heraclius, namely Baldwin, the Archbishop of Canterbury, because of his knowledge of the devotion of his secular counterpart, King Richard of England, to the cause of the Lusignans. Hence he declined to grant the annulment, declaring that in view of Conrad's previous marriage a new union between Conrad and Isabel would be doubly adulterous. However, Conrad's cause won the potent support of the papal legate, the Archbishop of Pisa, and the cousin of King Philip Augustus of France, the Bishop of Beauvais. Reginald of Sidon, Paganus de Caïphas, and Balian of Ibelin also added their support to Conrad. The upshot of all this was the gaining from the bishops of a general assent for the divorce of Isabel and her subsequent marriage to Conrad on November 24, 1190. The wrath of the Lusignan faction was extreme, for the wedding abrogated Guy's right to the kingship. In this view they were also supported by King Richard's vassals in Guienne, Normandy, and England. But their protests were unavailing, for their leader, Archbishop Baldwin, unexpectedly died on November 19. Conrad shrewdly rejected Guy's ensuing challenge to a single combat, declaring that the case could no longer be discussed. In such a move Conrad had legitimate right on his side as well as the general recognition that the continuance of the royal line required Isabel's remarriage and her bearing a child. Conrad, as an acknowledged warrior and deliverer of Tyre, was the obvious choice. The royal couple repaired to Tyre and became parents of a daughter named Maria in the following year. But the birth of an heiress to the throne by no means cleared the political air, for Guy, refusing to surrender any of his rights, declined to abdicate and to return from Tyre to the camp, and Conrad, in turn, refused to accept the title of king prior to the coronation of himself and his wife.[376]

---

[376] *Itinerarium*, pp. 95, 97, and 119-24; *Eracles*, pp. 151-54; *L'Estoire*, cols. 104-05 and 110-12; *Libellus*, p. 256; Roger of Hoveden, *op. cit.*, pp. 69-71; *Chronique d'Ernoul*, chap. xxiv, pp. 267-68; *Epistolae Cantuarienses, loc. cit.* See La Monte, *The Crusade*, pp. 177-79, nn. 18-21 and p. 100, n. 44 and *Eracles*, p. 15, n. a for discussions of Isabel's divorce from Humphrey of Toron and her ensuing marriage to Conrad of Montferrat, the date of Isabel's marriage to Conrad, the two preceding marriages of Conrad, and the rôles of Archbishop Baldwin and the Bishop of Beauvais in this affair. Also see La Monte, *Feudal Monarchy*, p. 39, n. 1 for a discussion of the date of Sibyl's death. This

Conrad's adamantine stand seemed to make the lot of the Franks besieging Acre all the more difficult during the winter months of 1190-1191, which saw the deaths through illness of such key leaders as Tibald of Blois and his brother, Stephen of Sancerre, and Frederick of Swabia. Grave indeed was the illness of Henry of Champagne who was at death's door for many weeks. The survivors, faced not only by illness but also by starvation by reason of shortages so severe as Lent approached that a silver penny bought only one egg or thirteen beans and a hundred pieces of gold purchased a sack of corn, failed in their attempt on December 31, 1190 to scale the walls of Acre and were powerless to capitalize on the collapse of part of the land wall defending Acre on January 6, 1191. Equally disheartening was the arrival of a new relief force of Moslems on February 13, 1191 as a result of Saladin's efforts. Hence the Franks censured Conrad for his refusal to depart from Tyre and come to their support.[377]

These hardships and disasters were, however, only the darkness before the dawn, for relief of several types was at hand. The first was the arrival of a grain ship in March, 1191 which presently was followed by others. Their cheering reports that Kings Philip Augustus and Richard of England were close at hand were soon substantiated with the arrival of the former on April 20 along with his cousin Conrad of Montferrat whom he had met at the time of his initial landing at Tyre. The French king at once tightened the investment of Acre by a reorganization of the Franks' artillery and the construction of towers, but decided to defer a full attack on Acre's walls until the arrival of King Richard and his forces. The English king, who had paused in Cyprus, where he had received the anti-Conrad Franks comprising King Guy, his brother Geoffrey, Count of Lusignan, Bohemond of Antioch and his son Raymond, Humphrey of Toron as well as many of the Templar leaders, arrived at Acre on June 8 after receiving, in compliance with the orders of Conrad and Philip Augustus, a rebuff from the Frankish garrison at Tyre. Richard's arrival kindled new hope in the weary besiegers, who saw in him the leader required for a final military effort. This he proved to be. The English king initially sought to use diplomacy to terminate the

---

same scholar (*The Crusade*, p. 171, n. 12) declares that "Sybelle's death occurred sometime before October 1, 1190."

[377] *Itinerarium*, pp. 124-34; Ibn al-Athīr, *K.-A.*, II, 32-33; Abou Chamah, *op. cit.*, pp. 517-22; Behâ Ed-Dîn, *Saladin*, pp. 223 and 236 and n. 1 and *Anecdotes*, pp. 195-96 and 208; *L'Estoire*, cols. 112-18; *Eracles*, p. 150; Roger of Hoveden, *op. cit.*, pp. 113-14.

fighting. Accordingly, he dispatched an envoy to Saladin's camp with a request for an interview between himself and the Moslem chieftain. But Saladin was of another mind and replied that he considered a meeting of hostile kings an unwise move prior to their signature of a truce. Nevertheless, he approved a meeting between his brother, al-ʿĀdil, and Richard. The latter agreed and hence a truce of three days' duration was arranged. Both parties fixed a meeting place on the plain between the opposing camps. Before these plans could be effected, however, Richard fell ill of fever. Full fighting was soon resumed with Richard vigorously directing operations, despite his illness, from his sick-room. In accordance with his orders, large catapults were put into position and a large wooden tower was constructed. He himself visited the Frankish lines before his full recovery.[378]

Fortunately for the Franks, the struggle for Acre during the latter half of 1191, although bearing much resemblance to the effort during the earlier stages, had marked differences which redounded to their advantage. Again, as before, Saladin received help in the arrival of the army of Sinjar on June 25 and shortly thereafter a new Egyptian army and forces commanded by the lord of Mosul. These fresh accretions of strength to the Moslems enabled the defenders of Acre to call upon them whenever the Franks, who were now better protected with earthworks and easily defensible ditches constructed during the winter lull, succeeded by the use of siege machinery in effecting small breaches in the walls of Acre. The result was the repulse of the Franks. The Frankish stalemate on land was complemented and prolonged by one in the political sphere as well. The earlier dispute between Conrad and Guy over the kingship was now widened to include English and French adherents as well as Richard the Lionhearted and Philip Augustus as a result of the decisions of the former to support Guy and

---

[378] Behâ Ed-Dîn, *Saladin*, pp. 240, 242 and n. 2, and 248-49 and *Anecdotes*, pp. 212, 214, and 220; Ibn al-Athīr, *K. – A.*, II, 41-43; William of Newburgh, *op. cit.*, pp. 347, 349, and 352-53; *Eracles*, *op. cit.*, pp. 155-57; Richard of Devizes, *De Rebus Gestis Ricardi Primi* ed. Richard Howlett (London, 1886), III, 424 and 426-27; *Chronique d'Ernoul*, pp. 269-70 and 272-73; Ralph of Diceto, *op. cit.*, pp. 92-94; *The Chronography of Bar Hebraeus*, pp. 334-35; Abou Chamah, *Le Livre des deux Jardins, ou histoire des deux règnes* in *Rec. his. or.* (Paris, 1906), V, 6 and 8; Roger of Hoveden, *op. cit.*, pp. 100 and 112-13; *L'Estoire*, cols. 46-47, 62-64, and 119-23; Benedict of Peterborough, *op. cit.*, pp. 168-70; Rigordus, *op. cit.*, p. 108 and nn. 1 and 2; *Itinerarium*, pp. 136, 138, 195, 204-05, 211-12, 214, 218-20, and 224-25; *Libellus*, p. 257; Kamal-Ad-Dîn, *Histoire, loc. cit.* and IV, 198; *Les gestes des Chiprois, loc. cit.*; La Monte, *The Crusade*, p. 196, n. 2. (Henceforth references to Abou Chamah will pertain solely to Volume V).

the latter to support Conrad. The Pisan and Genoese naval contingents likewise divided their loyalties, the former supporting Richard, the latter favoring Philip Augustus. These unfortunate political divisions had their military ramifications and results, for Richard refused to aid his French royal rival when he planned a grand assault upon Acre. The absence of Richard's support led to the failure of Philip Augustus' attack and to Saladin's ensuing blow, which was repelled with difficulty. Yet, on the whole, as the Summer of 1191 advanced, the military balance slowly but surely tipped in favor of the besieging Franks, who received additional help from new groups of English and French knights coming from the West. The Anglo-French fleets now controlled the seas and prevented the arrival of food and war supplies to the beleaguered Moslem defenders of Acre, who were obliged to meet an unremitting fire from the Frankish catapults. The ensuing shortages inevitably engendered a movement on their part for surrender. This became a reality in July, 1191. Although an initial serious breach in the walls of Acre by the French on July 3 had ended only in their forced retirement, and an Anglo-Pisan attack on July 11 had also begun with success but had ended in similar failure, the defenders of Acre were ready to call it quits. This they soon did, despite Richard's earlier rebuff of their envoys on July 4. Much perturbed by these developments, Saladin promised aid to his fellow Moslems within Acre, but was unable to persuade his army to launch a major attack on the investing forces of the Franks on July 5. At length, following a fruitless battle with the Franks on July 11, the besieged sued for capitulation on July 12 and obtained it. The terms of surrender provided for the surrender of Acre in its entirety, the payment of 200,000 gold pieces to the Franks and 4,000 gold pieces to Conrad himself, the liberation of 1,500 Christian prisoners inclusive of 100 men of rank, and the restoration of the True Cross. In return, the Frankish negotiators agreed to spare the lives of all the defenders of Acre. Despite his dismay and displeasure over the surrender of Acre, which he had planned to prevent by the dispatch of a note to the Moslem garrison forbidding it to submit to such terms, Saladin chose to abide by the agreement effected by his officers.[379]

---

[379] Rigordus, *op. cit.*, pp. 108-09 and 115-16; Benedict of Peterborough, *op. cit.*, pp. 171-79; Ibn al-Athīr, *K. — A.*, pp. 44-46; *Eracles*, pp. 173-74; Abou Chamah, *op. cit.*, pp. 19-29; *Chronique d'Ernoul*, p. 274; Behâ Ed-Dîn, *Saladin*, pp. 258-69 and *Anecdotes*, pp. 229-39; *The Chronography of Bar Hebraeus*, pp. 335-36; Roger of Hoveden, *op. cit.*, pp. 114-121; Ralph of Diceto, *op. cit.*, p. 94; Richard of Devizes, *op. cit.*, p. 427; *L'Estoire*, cols. 123-35 and 136-39; *Itinerarium*, pp. 212-13, 217-18, 220-24, and 225-32; William

of Newburgh, *op. cit.*, p. 356; Kamal-Ad-Dîn, *Histoire*, IV, 199-200; La Monte, *The Crusade*, pp. 213-14 and 217, nn. 33 and 36. Painter (*op. cit.*, pp. 66-67) explains the decision of Philip Augustus to align himself with the party supporting Conrad as follows; "The reasons for this decision are obvious. Conrad was the husband of the heiress of the kingdom of Jerusalem. He was a vigorous soldier and effective ruler who had the support of the majority of the barons of the kingdom. In taking his part, Philip was clearly following the sensible course. Philip's decision explains Guy's trip to Cyprus to meet Richard. With Philip committed to one side of the controversy, even an old foe of the Plantagenet house had hopes that he might persuade Richard to take the other."

CHAPTER TWENTY

THE CLOSING YEARS AND DEATH
1191-1200?

The eclipse of Moslem fortunes associated with their loss of Acre soon had its counterpart, albeit on a far smaller scale, in the eclipse of the fortunes of Joscelyn III as well.[380] For the moment the position of the Seneschal seemed unchallenged, because the earlier agreements between Guy of Lusignan and Conrad of Montferrat concerning the kingship of Jerusalem[381] were now definitely confirmed with a corresponding and resulting continuation of the Courtenay chieftain in his royal office and equally corresponding lessening of the threat to him already posed by Conrad's earlier pledge of transfer of lands belonging to him to the Pisans.[382] Soon after the capture of Acre the several princes ruled that Guy should hold the kingship until his own death, at which time this office would be transferred to Conrad and Isabel and their heirs. Meanwhile Conrad would hold the lordships of Beirut, Sidon, and Tyre and divide the royal revenues with Guy.[383]

But that this arrangement was unstable was soon shown by the departure from Acre on July 31, 1191 of Conrad of Montferrat in the company of Philip Augustus ostensibly for the purpose of fulfilling an urgent need to inspect his holdings in Tyre but actually because of an unwillingness to collaborate with his rival who was backed by King

---

[380] La Monte ("The rise," p. 316) declares that "After that [the witnessing of various acts by Joscelyn III in 1190 during the course of the siege of Acre] nothing is known of him. [Joscelyn III] Perhaps he died at the siege as did so many others. Perhaps he lived on to see Guy's brother Aymeri begin the rebuilding of the state which Guy had ruined. Certainly he was dead before 1200 but when between 1190 and 1200 he died is not known." This statement overlooks the evidence provided by Röhricht (*Regesta*, No. 758, p. 202) that Joscelyn III was a witness to the grant of various privileges made to the Pisans by Bohemond IV, prince of Antioch, on August 26, 1199. It is true that no title is associated with the Joscelyn listed among the witnesses, but this omission is simply a reflection of his displacement in the seneschalship by Ralph, the stepson of the late Count Raymond of Tripoli. See *infra*, pp. 197-98. Röhricht (*Regesta*, p. 447) supports my position in his designation of the Joscelinus appearing in No. 758, p. 202 as the one identified with the seneschalship of the Kingdom of Jerusalem. P. 447 is an index page in the *Regesta*.

[381] *Supra*, p. 186.

[382] *Supra*, p. 176.

[383] *Itinerarium*, pp. 235-36; Benedict of Peterborough, *op. cit.*, pp. 183-84; Roger of Hoveden, *op. cit.*, pp. 124-25.

Richard of England. Any belief in the continuance of the fragile alliance between the royal rivals was soon to be destroyed not long thereafter in the Spring of 1192. Upon receipt of letters written by William, Bishop of Ely, and brought to him by the Prior of Hereford, Richard became increasingly apprehensive over the information contained therein to the effect that his brother John was engaged in a growing usurpation of Richard's powers. The letters also urged Richard to come home. Accordingly, Richard imparted this information at a convocation of all the barons and knights of the Kingdom of Jerusalem and stated his desire to return. Their response was that a new king of the Kingdom of Jerusalem must be chosen. Thereupon Richard proposed that the assemblage make a choice between Guy of Lusignan and Conrad of Montferrat. A unanimous vote for the latter ensued. Richard concurred in this decision and soon a mission led by his nephew, Henry of Champagne, repaired to Tyre to apprise Conrad of the new turn of events. The latter accepted the honor. The ensuing decision was that the coronation would soon occur at Acre. But this ceremony never eventuated, for on April 28, 1192 the new king after a reign of a mere three weeks fell victim to the knives of two assassins who were agents of the Old Man of the Mountain, the Sheik, Sinān.[384]

The threat to Joscelyn III's political status inherent in the definitive gaining of the kingship of the Kingdom of Jerusalem by Conrad now seemed to have been permanently dissipated. But only for a short time was this situation to continue. Apprised of the murder of Conrad, Henry of Champagne hastened back to Tyre to be greeted with acclamation by the Tyrian population as the obvious new spouse for

---

[384] *Itinerarium*, pp. 239, 333-41, and 444-45; Abou Chamah, *op. cit.*, p. 52; William of Newburgh, *op. cit.*, pp. 363-65; Behâ Ed-Dîn, *Saladin*, pp. 332-33 and *Anecdotes*, p. 297; *L'Estoire*, cols. 142, 228-32, and 233-48; Roger of Hoveden, *op. cit.*, pp. 126 and 181; Ibn al-Athīr, *K. – A.*, pp. 58-59; *Eracles*, pp. 192-93; *Chronique d'Ernoul*, p. 277 and chap. xxv, p.290; Ralph of Diceto, *op. cit.*, pp. 104 and 127-28; Roger of Wendover, *op. cit.*, pp. 225-26; Benedict of Peterborough, *op. cit.*, p. 192; Ralph of Coggeshall, *op. cit.*, p. 35; *The Chronography of Bar Hebraeus*, p. 339; Röhricht, *Regesta*, Nos. 705 and 715, pp. 188-89 and 191. See La Monte, *The Crusade*, p. 338, n. 12, Theodor Ilgen, *Markgraf Conrad von Montferrat* (Marburg, 1880), pp. 127-35, Stevenson, *op. cit.*, p. 281, n. 3, King, *op. cit.*, p. 153, and Slaughter, *op. cit.*, p. 240 for discussions of the question relating to the exact identity of the assassins of Conrad and the persons ultimately responsible for their deed and the motivations behind the assassination. Cf. Bernard Lewis, "The Ismāʿīlites and the Assassins," *A History of the Crusades. The First Hundred Years* (Philadelphia, 1955), I, 125-26. Also see Norgate, *op. cit.*, pp. 217-18, n. 8 for a criticism of the accounts of William of Newburgh and Roger of Wendover of the assassination of Conrad.

the widowed Isabel and as the rightful successor to the kingship. Despite initial reluctance on the part of both parties to assent to the popular demand, they at length agreed and the marriage was solemnized on May 5, 1192, a bare week after the assassination.[385] Shortly thereafter in May, 1192 the ex-king Guy of Lusignan, who conceivably could have continued to play a rôle as a buffer between Joscelyn III and the anti-Courtenay factions in the Holy Land had he remained in that area, departed for Cyprus never to return. He received the governorship of the island from King Richard of England, who, inasmuch as he, Richard, would have to return to England soon, decided that the ex-king would make a satisfactory governor in his place. Guy of Lusignan assented to the proposal and purchased the island from the Templars, who were already desiring to return the island to King Richard, who had recently sold it to them.[386] The full implications of these matrimonial and political shifts for the Courtenay chieftain soon manifested themselves in the association of Hugh, the stepson of the late Count Raymond of Tripoli, with Henry of Champagne. Hugh's name appears third in a list of witnesses to a grant of territories by Henry of Champagne to the Order of the Hospitallers at Jaffa in January, 1193.[387] The total absence of the Seneschal's name from this list and the prominent first and second positions assigned to the names of Balian of Ibelin and Reginald of Sidon, who had been in the forefront of the support of Count Raymond and the opposition to the Courtenay-Lusignan faction at the time of the *coup d'état* of 1186, bespeak eloquently the new political trends. Equally eloquent were the absence of the name of Joscelyn III and the presence of the names of Balian of Ibelin, Reginald of Sidon, and Hugh in that order in the following February, 1193 and the Autumn of 1193 when they witnessed land grants by Henry of Champagne to the Order of the Teutons at Acre.[388] The climax of these trends occurred during the following three months with the elevation and immediate succession of Ralph, Hugh's brother, to the post of

---

[385] *Itinerarium*, pp. 342-43 and 346-50; Abou Chamah, *op. cit.*, pp. 52-53; William of Newburgh, *op. cit.*, p. 374; *L'Estoire*, cols. 238-42; Ralph of Diceto, *loc. cit.*; Ibn al-Athīr, *K.—A.*, p. 59; *Eracles*, pp. 194-95; *Chronique d'Ernoul*, p. 291.

[386] *Eracles*, p. 191; *L'Estoire*, col. 244. Cahen (*La Syrie*, p. 581), Norgate (*op. cit.*, p. 261), King (*loc. cit.*), Slaughter (*op. cit.*, p. 239), and Stevenson (*op. cit.*, p. 281) believe that King Richard granted Cyprus to Guy of Lusignan to compensate him for the loss of the kingship of Jerusalem to Henry of Champagne.

[387] Röhricht, *Regesta*, No. 709, pp. 189-90.

[388] *Ibid*, Nos. 710 and 716, pp. 190 and 191-92.

Seneschal no later than January 5, 1194.[389] The exact circumstances of the loss of his office by Joscelyn III are unknown.[390]

The obscurity characterizing the life and career of Joscelyn III from late 1190 to early 1194 was even more pronounced during the ensuing six years. A single reference reflecting his fall from the purple robes of power is an observation that he was a witness on August 26, 1199 to the grant of various privileges to the Pisans by Bohemond IV, prince of Antioch. He is designated simply as Joscelyn.[391] The date of the former Seneschal's demise seems to have occurred at some time between August 26, 1199 and October, 1200, for there is a reference to his daughter Agnes as "quondam comitis Jozcelini filiae" in a document dated in October, 1200.[392]

---

[389] *Ibid.*, No. 717, p. 192. In the light of the primary source evidence, La Monte ("Chronology," *loc. cit.*) is clearly wrong in his dating of the seneschalship of Joscelyn III as covering the years 1176-1190.

[390] Pirie-Gordon (*op. cit.*, p. 459) declares that Joscelyn III "... seems to have resigned the office." This same scholar (*loc. cit.*) believes that Hugh became the trusted advisor of Henry of Champagne when the latter succeeded the late Conrad of Montferrat.

[391] Röhricht, *Regesta*, No. 758, p. 202. This scholar includes this reference to Joscelyn under the heading of Joscelyn III, Seneschal. See index pages 446-47.

[392] *Ibid*, No. 777, p. 207. The evidence provided by Röhricht's *Regesta* will not support the claim made by the editors of *A History of the Crusades*, II, 829 that Joscelyn III was titular count of Edessa from 1159 to 1200. Nor will the evidence support the respective views of La Monte ("Chronology," *loc. cit.* and "The rise," *loc. cit.*) that Joscelyn III was titular count of Edessa from 1148 to 1200 and "Certainly he [Joscelyn III] was dead before 1200..." This same scholar restates this view on page 317 of the latter of the two cited works in his statement that "... Joscelyn was dead by 1200..." Basing his view on Röhricht's *Regesta*, No. 773, p. 206, La Monte observes that "The document which shows us that Joscelyn was dead by 1200 is an act of Monachus patriarch of Jerusalem in which he came to an agreement with William de la Mandelée and Agnes over their respective rights over the casale of Jeth, which it will be remembered Joscelyn had received from the king in 1183. By this act the patriarch was to have possession of the casale for his lifetime and it was then to go to William and Agnes. As this was part of Joscelyn's seigneury it is evident that the old seneschal had died before this date and that his daughters had entered into the inheritance." The date of this document is August, 1200 and affords no evidence that the Seneschal actually died in the *year* 1200. The fact of the matter is that the Courtenay chieftain died at some unknown date after August 26, 1199 and prior to the Autumn of 1200.

EPILOGUE

The biographer of Joscelyn III faces baffling and puzzling problems arising not only from the marked paucity of evidence concerning his life and career but also from the military and political policies, postures, and outlooks characterizing his later adolescence and early manhood from 1150 to 1164 and his early middle age from 1176 to 1181 as compared with those of his later middle age from 1182 to 1190. That he was regarded by his elders, despite his stripling age of sixteen years in 1150, as worthy of the succession to the leadership of the County of Edessa following the capture of his father, Joscelyn II, is seen in their elevation of him to the headship of the County of Edessa. His ensuing brave and for a time successful defense of Tell Bashir in the face of potent Moslem military pressure in 1150 was in the best traditions of the Frankish warrior aristocracy in general and his redoubtable grandfather, Joscelyn I, in particular. His firm grasp of *realpolitik*, despite his youth, was displayed in his support of his mother's astute policies of abandoning the lost cause of vainly trying to retain the fragments of Frankish and Courtenay power in the County of Edessa and surrendering them to the Byzantine emperor Manuel and the Armenian Catholicos Gregory III with the stipulation in the case of the latter recipient that he return Qalʿat ar-Rūm to the new Count of Edessa upon his possible return to power in the now defunct County of Edessa. His political superior, Baldwin III, King of Jerusalem, showed his respect for the political and military talents of his distant kinsman by entrusting to his care shortly thereafter lands in the vicinity of Acre. That the young warrior-statesman warranted the trust reposed in him by his elders is seen in his conquest, albeit a temporary one, of the Moslem held city of Burj-ar-risas and his elevation to the important post of the marshalship of the Kingdom of Jerusalem in the middle 1150's while he was still in his early twenties. His rôle as marshal was sufficiently commendable to lead to his elevation to the leadership of the important fief of Ḥārim shortly thereafter. And that his military prowess continued to grow in the early 1160's was admitted by the famous Moslem historian Ibn al-Athīr in his observation to the effect that Joscelyn III was one of the most illustrious and brave of the Frankish enemy. Lastly, he played an important rôle in the disastrous Hattin campaign of 1164. All the available evidence known to the twentieth century biographer and historian and, perhaps, to his contemporaries as of 1164 as well indicates that, with further military and political seasoning, Joscelyn III would perform at least as well in the theatres of war and politics as his late grandfather, Joscelyn I, and perhaps as well as his close contemporaries, Kings Baldwin III and Amalric I.

The brilliant political and military future portended by his outstanding military and political record in the 1150-1164 period as a mere youth and young man seemed to be well on the way to realization in the seven years following his release from Moslem captivity at the mature age of forty-two. He still commanded enough respect in the eyes of his fellow Franks to gain for himself the very important position of the Seneschal in the Kingdom of Jerusalem and to gain control of important fiefs northeast of Acre by reason of his marriage to Agnes, the daughter of Henry Le Buffle. These initial territorial gains were steadily augmented during the ensuing seven years by additional ones which led to the creation of the increasingly important and imposing Seignory of Count Joscelyn. His rôle as Seneschal from 1176 to 1180, while perhaps not outstanding, was certainly respectable as is witnessed by his inclusion in the list of various witnesses to sales of property, grants to religious groups, and settlements of property and other disputes. His prominent position in the list of the several witnesses in the several charters bespeaks his importance as Seneschal in the Kingdom of Jerusalem and the esteem of his fellow magnates. His military prestige seems to have remained undimmed, for the sources pertinent to his rôle at the victorious Battle of Ramla in November, 1177 ascribe in no way any cowardice and/or military ineptitude on his part. Although the *argumentum ex silentio* is not the strongest one available to the biographer and historian, at least in this instance it has validity, for the anti-Frankish minded Moslem historians surely would have mentioned such cowardice and/or military ineptitude, if such had been the case. One of the most prominent of the Moslem historians had praised Joscelyn III's military valor in the pre-1164 period. The military and political disasters suffered by the Kingdom of Jerusalem during the late 1170's at the hands of Saladin seem to have left unscathed his reputation as a political leader, for he gained for himself the high post of ambassador to the Byzantine Empire in 1180. Only three clouds cast their shadows as of 1183 on his future as a territorial magnate, statesman, and military leader of the increasingly prestigious House of Courtenay now remarkably recovered from the disasters of the 1140's, 1150's, and 1160's. The first was uncertainty of the continuation of the House of Courtenay because of his lack of male progeny. And this uncertainty would be ended, if Lady Luck should bestow on him a son. The second was the increasing weakness of the Frankish political and military position in the Holy Land because of the presence of a leper king on the throne of the Kingdom of Jerusalem with all the attendant doubts about the succession and because of the waxing power of the Moslem enemy under the increasingly potent and dynamic leadership of the very able Saladin. And the third was the ever growing trend toward factional quarrels in the Kingdom of Jerusalem itself with resulting political parties intent on gaining political advantages for themselves out of the power vacuum identified with the growing helplessness of the leper king.

It is at this juncture, the post-1181 period, that the bright promise afforded by the preceding thirty years of Joscelyn III's career began rapidly to fade. Not even the barren twelve years of imprisonment from 1164 to 1176 interrupting his earlier flowering from 1150 to 1164 had checked the development of his immeasurably greater prestige in both the territorial and political arenas in his post-imprisonment years. But in the post-1181 period short sighted political policies far removed from the *politique de longue vue* of his earlier career and that of his celebrated grandfather, Joscelyn I, increasingly characterize him. Indeed, as early as April, 1181 he had perhaps begun to tread the dangerous road of political opportunism in his probable participation with his sister Agnes in the deposition of William, Archbishop of Tyre, from his position as tutor of the leper king, Baldwin IV. His full identification with the party of the court nobles with its program of marked hostility to the party of the native nobles headed by Count Raymond had clearly emerged by the Spring of 1182, for at that time the former party blocked Raymond's plans to visit the Kingdom of Jerusalem. The Seneschal continued to walk this perilous path despite the obviously ominous portents afforded by the waxing power of Saladin in the ensuing four years. Joscelyn III broke his pledged word in respect to the proposed succession to the throne in the event that the child king, Baldwin V, whose person had been entrusted to him, should die, deceived and tricked Count Raymond whose political and military talents were recognized by even the Moslem enemy, and for a time alienated that important Frankish leader. To the extenuating plea in his behalf advanced by

Oldenbourg[393] that he was a prince deprived of his heritage of the County of Edessa, embittered by twelve years of captivity and hating the Frankish nobility which had done nothing to effect the release of his father or himself, it may be observed that he had been well rewarded by that very same nobility in the seven years following his release from Moslem captivity. The head of that nobility, namely King Baldwin IV himself, had granted to him the major post of the seneschalship and important fiefs which, in turn, had restored the shattered financial base and sadly diminished prestige of the House of Courtenay of which he was now the acknowledged leader. Certainly the post of seneschalship in the largest and most powerful of the three surviving crusading states, namely the Kingdom of Jerusalem itself, compared very favorably in terms of prestige, power, and influence with the position of Count held by his late father and grandfather in their rôles as rulers of the now defunct County of Edessa. Although the sources are entirely silent on the question of the degree of consultation, if any, made by the leper king Baldwin IV with other members of the Frankish nobility respecting the wisdom and advisability of granting the seneschalship to Joscelyn III, it seems unlikely, in view of his distinguished rôle as the titular Count of Edessa in the political and military history of the Kingdom of Jerusalem from 1150 to 1164, that any such consultation on the part of Baldwin IV with the Frankish baronage evoked any meaningful opposition on their part. And certainly Count Raymond, his potent rival, by his very absence from Jerusalemite affairs during substantially all the 1176-1182 period had given Joscelyn III no cause to cherish toward him any reasonable dislike. Yet the Seneschal, oblivious to the political and military dangers posed by the waxing power of Saladin, increasingly refused to cooperate with the Tripolitan prince against the common enemy, the Moslem foe, and chose instead to support the patently incompetent Guy of Lusignan. Indeed, Joscelyn III had been a major factor in the elevation of this nonentity to the position of kingship in the revolution of 1186. And finally the Courtenay chieftain had disgraced himself in his cowardly surrender of Acre after the disaster of Hattin.

An explanation of the very different patterns of behavior of the Seneschal in his early years as compared to those in the post-1181 period is easier to suggest than to answer in the light of the marked paucity of information bearing on this problem afforded by the

---

[393] Oldenbourg, *op. cit.*, p. 412.

sources. Perhaps his long years of imprisonment were analogous in their total effect to certain diseases which, afflicting the human family, do not seriously or obviously affect adversely their victims until they have established themselves thoroughly and then manifest themselves in terrifying fashion. Certainly his twelve years of imprisonment do not seem to have affected adversely his judgments and policies during his first five years of freedom from 1176 to 1181. But in the post-1181 period his pattern of behavior reveals an increasing lack of clarity of judgment on the priority and importance of certain military and political problems as compared with other ones. Perhaps the bad influence of his sister Agnes, which had done so much to warp the judgment of her leper son, Baldwin IV, likewise warped his judgment. Perhaps his emotional involvement in the goals of the court party blinded him to the need for union with the opposing party of the native nobles against the common peril to *all* the Frankish nobility, namely the Moslem enemy. Perhaps he shared too much the shortrange, shortsighted political views of virtually all the Frankish nobility since their arrival in the Holy Land in the First Crusade down to the disaster of Hattin. But *one* thing is clear among all these uncertainties. The pathetic later career of Joscelyn III has a lesson for our own age, faced with the unspeakable horror of thermonuclear war. And that is the need for statesmanship emphasizing and embodying the *politique de longue vue* and capable of transforming the obsolete machinery of the nation state system into one capable of solving global problems. The ineffective political mechanism of the feudal principalities of the Holy Land operated by men of parochial vision inclusive of Joscelyn III himself failed to meet the Moslem challenge of ever growing unity posed by their sworn foes. And the nation state system, which eventually replaced the ineffective feudal political machinery of the earlier Middle Ages, has in turn become equally obsolete in the light of the industrial and technological revolutions of the past two centuries!

APPENDIX A

Analysis of the Several Accounts Relative to the Capture and Imprisonment of Joscelyn II

The several accounts of the capture and imprisonment of Joscelyn II vary markedly and, in the case of the Syrian accounts of Michael the Syrian's *Chronique* and Grégoire Le Prêtre, contain palpable biases and prejudices. William of Tyre's account is that Joscelyn II, having set out at night for Antioch attended by a single escort, turned aside to relieve the needs of nature and was then captured. The account of Michael the Syrian's *Chronique* states that Joscelyn II set out for Antioch with an escort of two hundred knights. Upon encountering some Turcomans during the course of the night, the escort fled. This account avers that Joscelyn II joined the fleeing men, whereupon he collided with a tree and fell. A Turcoman found him and, not recognizing the identity of his captive, prepared to sell him to the Christians. He was dissuaded from doing so by a Jew who identified the Edessan count. Joscelyn II was then taken to Aleppo where he was sold for a thousand dinars. This account also observes that some affirm there was no tree at the spot of Joscelyn II's fall and that his fall was attributable to God's anger. Lastly, this account states that, despite many blandishments as well as corporal punishments and threats on the part of his captors to persuade him to embrace Islam, the Edessan count remained a Christian and received the rites of the dying from a Christian bishop at the end of his life. Michael the Syrian's *Extrait* gives two entirely different accounts of the capture of Joscelyn II. The first states that Joscelyn II, accompanied by a party of horsemen during a hunt, became separated from his companions. His horse threw him against a tree. While still unconscious he was found by two Turks and was taken to Aleppo. Unaware of the identity of their captive, they sold him to a Jew. Later, having been identified, Joscelyn II was brought to Nūr-ad-Dīn, who proceeded to imprison him. The second account contents itself with the observation that "Celui-ci [Joscelyn II], pour venger la mort de son père, [Joscelyn I], saccageait jour et nuit le territoire d'Alep. Mais au bout de deux ans il fut pris par les troupes de cette ville, conduit dans ses murs, et il y mourut dans les fers." Grégoire Le Prêtre attributes Joscelyn II's capture to divine wrath and likens his capture to the vengeance of God on the son of the Hebrew king David for his rebellion against his father. "Pareille punition atteignit Josselin, parce qu'il s'était mis en opposition aux ordres divins." *Anon. Syriac Chronicle* states that Joscelyn II, upon receipt of information of the death of the lord of Antioch, set out for Antioch with a few men to assume the rule of the city of Antioch. When he came to the city of Cyrrhus during the course of his journey to Antioch, he was seized by Turkmen. Unaware of their captive's identity, they took him to the village of Dair ul Shaikh. The Christian citizenry recognized him and were on the point of buying him from his Moslem captors when a passing Jew recognized him and identified him to his masters, who thereupon took him to Aleppo. Nūr-ad-Dīn then ordered him to be blinded and imprisoned. The account of *The Chronography of Bar Hebraeus* states simply that during the course of his journey to Antioch Joscelyn II's escort of two hundred horsemen met a few Turcomans and soon fled. Thereupon Joscelyn II was captured by the Turks who brought him to Nūr-ad-Dīn. Thereafter this account is in essential agreement with the one provided by Michael the Syrian's *Chronique*. The several Moslem accounts, on the other hand, with the exception of those of Ibn al-Furat and Ibn al-Qalānisī, ascribe Joscelyn II's capture to Nūr-ad-Dīn's desire for revenge rising out of his defeat at the hands of the Edessan chieftain and the latter's ensuing insulting behavior. Aware that if he himself tried to seize Joscelyn II that the Courtenay leader would defend himself strongly with the aid of his fortresses and troops, Nūr-ad-Dīn resorted to craft. Calling upon Turcomans, he offered them rich gifts if they obtained Joscelyn II dead or alive. The offer was accepted and the Turcomans, having ascertained Joscelyn II's movements through spies, seized him, when he ventured forth on a hunting expedition. The latter bribed his captors with the promise of a large sum of money in return for his release. But one of his captors apprised a lieutenant of Nūr-ad-Dīn of the turn of the events, whereupon Nūr-ad-Dīn dispatched an army corps against the Turcomans. The latter were defeated and Joscelyn II was turned over to Nūr-ad-Dīn. Ibn al-Furat's account declares that, upon the receipt of information that Majd ad-Din ben ad-Daya, an Aleppan leader, had sent a detachment of Turcomans against Antioch, Joscelyn II proceeded to that city with some troops to aid the defenders. Proceeding with the rear guard, he had the misfortune to collide with a tree, fall from and lose his horse, and fall into the hands of the

Turcomans, who had meanwhile surrounded the rear guard. Joscelyn II's captors as well as his own army respectively remained ignorant of his identity and captured until the following day, when a Jewish dyer recognized and denounced him to his captors, who then brought him to Majd ad-Din ben ad-Daya. Joscelyn II was then brought to Aleppo. Ibn al-Qalānisī does not explain the circumstances of the capture of Joscelyn II. Lastly, the Armenian account entitled *Extrait de l'histoire universelle de Vartan Le Grand* in *Rec. his. arm.* (Paris, 1869), I, 434 declares that "[Josselin le Jeune,] seigneur de Hr'om Gla, étant allé à la chasse, tomba dans une embuscade et fut fait prisonnier par les musulmans, qui le traînèrent à Alep, où il mourut." (Henceforth this source will be cited as Vartan Le Grand).

APPENDIX B

Analysis and Discussion of Problems and Disputed Datings Thereof Pertinent to Guy of Lusignan, Baldwin IV, Baldwin V, Raymond III, and Joscelyn III During the 1183-1185 Period

The datings of (1) the deposition of Guy of Lusignan from the procuratorship and his specific exclusion from all rights of succession to the throne, (2) the association of Baldwin V as co-king with Baldwin IV and Baldwin IV's designation of Baldwin V as his successor together with the motivations for these developments, (3) the abdication of Baldwin IV in favor of Baldwin V, (4) the granting of the regency of the Kingdom of Jerusalem to Count Raymond until Baldwin V reached his majority, (*infra*, pp. 123-24) (5) the granting of the guardianship of Baldwin V to Joscelyn III (*infra*, p. 124) and (6) the coronation of Baldwin V are matters of considerable disagreement among scholars. The dating of October, 1183-January, 1184 provided by William of Tyre for the first of these problems is followed by Baldwin (*Raymond III*, pp. 53-54 and "The Decline," p. 600), Richard (*op. cit.*, pp. 136-37), and Schlumberger (*Numismatique*, pp. 74 and 98). Stevenson's discussion (*op. cit.*, p. 237), implies that the deposition of Guy from the regency and his replacement by Count Raymond occurred in late November, 1183. The first, third, and fourth named scholars place it in November, 1183. Baldwin in his first named work specifically dates it on November 20, 1183. Runciman (*History*, pp. 439-40), on the other hand, does not assign a specific date for the deposition of Guy, but the language of the events narrated before and after the deposition of Guy indicates that the deposition occurred *after* the Ṣaffūriyāh campaign (Autumn of 1183) and on or *before* March 23, 1183. [sic] The same scholar (*History*, p. 443) then observes "Before an assembly of the barons, early in 1185, he [Baldwin IV] announced his will. His little nephew was to succeed to the throne. At the express wish of the assembly Guy was not to have the regency, which was to go to Raymond of Tripoli . . ." Runciman's dating seems improbable, for, apart from the above-cited chronological inconsistency, there was the fact of the leper king's growing illness. Hence, it seems unlikely that any lapse of time ensued between the deposition of Guy and the elevation of Count Raymond to the procuratorship. And we must assume this lapse of time, if we accept Runciman's dating. As for the second problem, Louis Bréhier ("Baudouin V," *Dictionnaire d'histoire et de géographie ecclésiastiques* [Paris, 1932], VI, 1391) observes that "Baudouin V ... associé au trone par son oncle Baudouin IV (novembre 1183) ..." La Monte ("The rise," p. 313) and Richard (*op. cit.*, p. 137) respectively date it in the Autumn of 1183 and November, 1183. La Monte declares in his "Chronology," p. 144 and "The rise," *loc. cit.* that the co-kingship continued until March, 1185, the time of the death of Baldwin IV. The same scholar (*The Crusade*, p. 121, n. 7) also observes concerning the motivation of the creation of the co-kingship that "The barons feared that the succession might go to Sybelle and her husband Guy and so put through the coronation of the child Baldwin, who was only about six years old. In 1185, at the death of Baldwin IV, Baldwin V became sole king under a regency." Runciman (*History*, p. 439) states that Baldwin IV proclaimed Baldwin V as his heir on March 23, 1183. The closely related proposition, namely that Baldwin IV designated Baldwin V as his successor, Runciman (*History*, p. 443) places early in 1185. (The various datings indicated by Runciman on this as well as other chronological problems will be analyzed later). In respect to the third problem Major Proctor (*History of the Crusades: Their Rise, Progress and Results* [Philadelphia, 1854], pp. 235-36) alone expresses an opinion and that rather vaguely. Either 1182 or 1183 can be deduced from the language. Nine scholars agree in respect to the dating of the fourth problem as falling during the general period from October, 1183 to January, 1184. Archer and Kingsford (*op. cit.*, p. 267) imply and Louis de Saulcy (*Numismatique des croisades* [Paris, 1847], p. 64) says that it occurred at the time of or very shortly after the coronation of Baldwin V, which they date in November, 1183. Baldwin (*Raymond III*, p. 57 and "The Decline," p. 601) assigns it to December, 1183 or early in 1184. Schlumberger (*Numismatique, loc. cit.*) believes that it occurred shortly after November 20, 1183, the time of the coronation of·Baldwin V. Stevenson (*op. cit.*, p. 237, n. 2) seemingly accepts November, 1183 as the correct date. Charles H. Pirie-Gordon ("The Reigning Princes of Galilee," *English Historical Review* [New York, 1912], XXVII, 457) is of the opinion that Count Raymond was appointed as regent by Baldwin IV for himself, Baldwin IV, and his nephew Baldwin V at the Council of Acre, which he dates as occurring in January, 1184. Cahen (*La Syrie*, p. 427) and Reinhold Röhricht (*Geschichte der Kreuzzüge in Umriss* [Innsbruck, 1898], p. 122) simply say that Count Raymond was regent in 1183. (Future references to this work of Röhricht will be cited as *Kreuzzüge* to differentiate them from citations in other works by this scholar). On the other hand, M. E. Nickerson ("The Seigneury of Beirut in the Twelfth Century and the Brisebarre Family of Beirut-Blanchegarde," *Byzantion* [Paris, 1949], XIX, 177), although not specifying any particular time or place, clearly implies that it occurred at the Council of Acre in 1184. King (*loc. cit.*) also avers that the procuratorship was assigned to Count Raymond at the Council of Acre. Conder (*op. cit.*, p. 144) says that the regency was given to Count Raymond in 1184. Grousset (*Histoire*, p. 742) implies the granting of the regency to Count Raymond and assigns the time to the year 1184 in his statement "Ce fut alors qu'il [Baldwin IV] acheva confier tout le pouvoir au comte de Tripoli, l'ennemi de Guy (1184)." Bréhier ("Baudouin V," *loc. cit.*) indicates that Count Raymond's assumption of the procuratorship occurred no later than March, 1185 in his observation that Count Raymond continued to govern the Kingdom of Jerusalem following the succession to the throne of Baldwin V in March, 1185. Albert Champdor (*Saladin le plus pur Héros de l'Islam* [Paris, 1956], pp. 138-39) does not give an exact time, stating simply that Baldwin IV made Count Raymond the procurator after Guy's actions against the Bedouin shepherds and his closing of the gates of Ascalon to the King. Runciman (*History, loc. cit.*), on the other hand, believes that this event occurred early in 1185. La Monte (*Feudal Monarchy*, pp. 32-33) dates the creation of the *bailliage* and guardianship arrangements for Count Raymond and Joscelyn III *after* Baldwin IV's attempts to have Sibyl's marriage to Guy annulled and to seize Jaffa. Although this scholar does not date precisely these later moves on the part of Baldwin IV, he implies that they took place early in 1185 in his statement "The ordering of the bailliage to Raymond was the last act of Baldwin IV. Consumed by leprosy, the king finally 'answered God's summons' on March 16, 1185 . . ." In his later work, "The rise," (*loc. cit.*), however, La Monte places the several arrangements for Count Raymond and Joscelyn III in the Autumn of 1183. (The variant dating provided by La Monte will be analyzed later). As for the fifth problem, the same general group cited in respect to the fourth one are in agreement. Archer and Kingsford (*loc. cit.*), Baldwin ("The Decline," *loc. cit.*), King (*loc. cit.*), Nickerson (*loc. cit.*), Richard (*loc. cit.*), Röhricht (*Kreuzzüge, loc. cit.*), De Saulcy (*loc. cit.*), Proctor (*loc. cit.*), Runciman (*History, loc. cit.*), and Schlumberger (*Numismatique, loc. cit.*) agree in their respective time designations that the granting of the guardianship of Baldwin V to Joscelyn III occurred at the same general time of the granting of the procuratorship to Count Raymond. In respect to the sixth problem essential agreement prevails among scholars save for Runciman. Archer and Kingsford (*loc. cit.*) assign it to November 1, 1183. Baldwin ("The Decline," p. 600) places it in November, 1183, while De Saulcy (*loc. cit.*), M. L. De Mas Latrie, the editor of *Chronique d'Ernoul*, p. 117, n. 6, the editor of *Eracles*, p. 8, n. b, Pirie-Gordon (*loc. cit.*), Wilcke (*op. cit.*, p. 117), Schlumberger (*Numismatique, loc. cit.*), and Stevenson (*op. cit.*, p. 237) place it on November 20, 1183. Richard (*loc. cit.*) implies November, 1183 or shortly thereafter. Cahen (*La Syrie, loc. cit.*), La Monte (*Feudal Monarchy*, pp. 31-32 and *The Crusade*, p. 121, n. 7), Kate Norgate, *Richard the Lionheart* [London, 1925], p. 158, and Röhricht (*Kreuzzüge, loc. cit.*) give no specific dating within the year but agree that it happened in 1183. La Monte, however, does believe that the coronation occurred *before* Baldwin IV's attempts to have Sibyl's marriage annulled and to seize Jaffa. Grousset (*Histoire*, p. 743) implies that the coronation date was 1184. Chabot, the editor of Michael the Syrian (*Chronique*, p. 394, n. 3, states flatly that Baldwin V was crowned in 1184. Archer and Kingsford (*loc. cit.*, n. 1) state that "Perhaps there were two coronations, though this is not likely." Only Runciman (*History*, p. 444) believes that this event fell in 1185. See La Monte (*Feudal Monarchy, loc. cit.*) for a discussion of the question of elective vs. hereditary kingship at the time of Baldwin V's coronation. As regards the variant datings offered by various scholars and, more particularly, Runciman in respect to the datings of the second, fourth, fifth, and sixth problems and La Monte in respect to the fourth, fifth, and sixth problems, it seems to me, in the light of the double danger of his own increasing illness and the open defiance of the king's authority by Guy of Lusignan as early as the Autumn of 1183, very improbable that Baldwin IV would have delayed taking the precautionary measure of selecting a new procurator, securing the succession to the throne of Baldwin V, effecting his coronation, and securing the allegiance of the barons to him. In view of the above-cited considerations, it seems equally unlikely that Baldwin IV would have designated Baldwin V as his heir on March 23, 1183, but would have postponed the next logical and closely related step of designating him as his successor until 1185. And identical considerations certainly prompted Baldwin IV to select a successor to Guy of Lusignan in the procuratorship, to appoint Joscelyn III as the guardian of Baldwin V, and to effect the coronation of his successor in the kingship certainly no later than the first weeks of 1184 at the latest rather than wait until 1185 as Runciman and La Monte believe. It appears that these scholars accept the dating of *Eracles*, pp. 6-8 and *Chronique d'Amadi*, pp. 50 and 52 for the granting of the regency of the Kingdom of Jerusalem to Count Raymond and the crowning of Baldwin V. This date is 1185. And I have rejected this dating because of the above-mentioned considerations.

APPENDIX C

Analysis and Discussion of Problems Relative to the Time of the Truce Between Saladin and Count Raymond, the Initiative of the Signing of this Truce, and the Circumstances of this Truce

Scholars are divided on such problems as (1) the exact time of the creation of the truce between Count Raymond and Saladin (2) the initiative of the signing of this truce, and (3) the circumstances of this truce. In respect to problem one, Baldwin ("The Decline," pp. 605 and 606 and *Raymond III*, pp. 82, 83, and 86), Castle (*op. cit.*, pp. 35 and 37), Champdor (*op. cit.*, pp. 142 and 143), Grousset (*Histoire*, pp. 773-75 and *L'épopée*, pp. 274 and 275), Richard (*loc. cit.*), Schlumberger (*Renaud de Chatillon*, pp. 248 and 250-52), Slaughter (*op. cit.*, p. 129), and Stevenson (*op. cit.*, pp. 238 and 241) believe that the truce was effected before Reginald of Châtillon's attack on the Moslem caravan (*infra*, p. 150), whereas Lane-Poole (*op. cit.*, pp. 198-99 and 200) and Runciman (*History*, p. 450) believe that the truce was made after Reginald of Châtillon's attack on the Moslem caravan. Archer and Kingsford (*op. cit.*, p. 273) make no clear statement about the truce or the time thereof, contenting themselves with the following observation "... and Raymond of Tripoli, who remained on his lands, sullenly nursing his discontent, and if rumour may be trusted intriguing with Saladin. It was apparently about this time that Reginald of Châtillon, notwithstanding the truce, swooped down on a Saracen caravan on its way through the lordship of Kerak." Wiet (*op. cit.*, p. 325) is equally vague, merely stating that Count Raymond was "... en paix avec Saladin .." at the time of Reginald of Châtillon's attack on the Moslem caravan. Barker (*op. cit.*), Cahen (*La Syrie*), King (*op. cit.*), Oldenbourg (*op. cit.*), and Oman (*op. cit.*) say nothing about this problem. As for the second problem, Baldwin (*Raymond III*, p. 83 and "The Decline," p. 605), Castle (*op. cit.*, p. 35), Grousset (*Histoire, loc. cit.*, and *L'épopée, loc. cit.*), La Monte (*The Crusade, loc. cit.*), Richard (*loc. cit.*), Runciman (*History, loc. cit.*), Schlumberger (*Renaud de Chatillon*, p. 248), and Slaughter (*loc. cit.*) agree that Count Raymond initiated the negotiations resulting in the truce with Saladin. Champdor (*op. cit.*, p. 142), on the other hand, maintains that Saladin initiated the negotiations with Count Raymond. As for the third problem, Baldwin (*Raymond III*, p. 82 and "The Decline," *loc. cit.*) believes that it was Count Raymond's fear of Guy of Lusignan's attack on him that led him to his negotiations with Saladin. Cahen (*La Syrie*, p. 427), after observing that "... Guy parvint à se faire couronner" then states that "Alors Raymond se retira dans ses comtés, cherchant à assurer sa sécurité par une entente avec Saladin, qui était de saine politique, mais contraire à l'orientation belliqueuse des conseillers de Guy, parmi lesquels Renaud de Châtillon, prenait presque l'allure d'une alliance avec le prince musulman contre Guy." Castle (*op. cit.*, pp. 35 and 36) plausibly suggests that Saladin's deal with Count Raymond arose from a consideration that "... he [Saladin] undoubtedly preferred an orientalized Christian as king—one who respected the customs of the country, who was willing to make treaties with the Mohammedans and even to hold land from them and whose interests were primarily materialistic—rather than a king newly arrived from the West whose attitude towards the affairs of the kingdom was that of an intolerant crusader." .... "When Raymond learned that Guy had summoned his host to gather at Nazareth, only five leagues from Tiberias, he entered into an alliance with Saladin for mutual aid." Champdor (*loc. cit.*) ascribes the circumstances to the bickering between the Frankish leaders in the Kingdom of Jerusalem and Saladin's ensuing resolve to take full advantage of this situation. "Saladin dut manifester sa joie en apprenant cette bonne nouvelle. En politique avisé, il veilla à ce que cette rivalité soit soigneusement entretenue. Il proposa même au comte de Tripoli de s'associer avec lui, lui promettant pour prix de cette trahison le trône de Jérusalem." Grousset (*Histoire*, p. 775) includes Reginald of Châtillon in the factors leading Count Raymond to his negotiations with Saladin. "Raymond III, dépouillé de Beyrouth et craignant de se voir attaqué jusque dans sa "princée" de Tibériade ou dans son comté de Tripoli par Guy de Lusignan et par Renaud de Châtillon—menace qui, un moment, faillit se préciser—, prenait une contre-assurance du côté de Saladin." This same scholar (*L'épopée*, p. 274) further comments as follows: "Devant la menace, [of Guy's threatened attack] Raymond se rapprocha d'ailleurs de Saladin. Sans trahir la cause franque, comme le dirent ses adversaires, il amorça avec le sultan un pacte d'assurance et de garantie." La Monte (*The Crusade*, p. 122, nn. 8 and 9 p. 123, n. 10) observes that "It was through fear of an attack by Guy that Raymond drew closer to Saladin and strengthened the treaty between them, an action which gave rise to the charge that he had treasonably sold out

Christianity to the Moslems." .... "It was apparent to anyone familiar with the situation that some sort of treaty with Saladin would be imperative as long as such an incompetent as Guy remained in control in Jerusalem. Raymond tried to salvage what he could out of the wreckage he knew Guy would make of the Kingdom." .... "He [Count Raymond] stood nearest the throne in line of succession and would have inherited had Sybelle and Isabelle both died without heirs. There is nothing to indicate that Raymond actually ever aspired to the crown, however." Lane-Poole (*op. cit.*, p. 200) implies that the agreements between Count Raymond and Saladin occurred shortly after and as a result of the materialization of Guy of Lusignan's military threat to Count Raymond. "When Guy prepared to invade the Count's territory and conquer his submission by arms, it was on Saladin's promised help that Raymond relied." Richard (*loc. cit.*) sees in the inept tactics of the anti-Raymond faction in the Kingdom of Jerusalem the key reasons for the Count's negotiations with Saladin. "Au lieu de chercher à se réconcilier avec Raymond III, pour essayer de grouper derrière le nouveau souverain la noblesse d'origine hiérosolymitaine, le clan Lusignan chercha à pousser le comte de Tripoli à bout: sans doute faut-il y voir la main de Girard de Ridefort, devenu un des principaux conseillers du roi. On réclama de Raymond un compte des revenus du royaume pendant sa baylie, procédé qui dut l'irriter d'autant plus qu'on avait saisi Beyrouth sur les revenus duquel il devait se payer des frais de l'administration—et il était sans exemple qu'on adressât une demande de ce genre à celui qui avait exercé la baylie." .... "... c'est cette dernière avanie qui acheva de pousser Raymond à la révolte ... et entama avec Saladin des négociations assez dangereuses." Runciman (*History*, pp. 450-51) observes "At the same time he [Count Raymond] secured Saladin's sympathy and promise of support in his aim of making himself king. Wise though Raymond's policy may have been it was undoubtedly treasonable." Schlumberger (*Renaud de Chatillon*, *loc. cit.*) views the matter as follows: "... la fureur et la trahison de Raymond de Tripoli, la plus puissant personnage du royaume, qui certainement, avait brigué la couronne, et qui, déçu dans ses espérances, ne craignit pas d'entrer en négociations avec Saladin et de se faire envoyer par celui-ci au corps de cavalerie à Tiberiade, où il s'était réfugié." Slaughter (*loc. cit.*) and Stevenson (*op. cit.*, p. 238) afford explanations of a generally similar import: "When he [Count Raymond] observed Reginald's defiance of the treaty, he made a separate treaty with Saladin for his own protection." "Guy was preparing to attack him [Count Raymond] there [Tiberias] when he learned that his rival had asked and had been promised the assistance of Saladin." Also see Baldwin (*Raymond III*, pp. 81-85 and Appendix C, pp. 156-60 and "The Decline," p. 606 and n. 15) for extended analyses of the dilemma in which Count Raymond found himself after the decision of the baronage to support Guy of Lusignan as the rightful king, the motivations animating Count Raymond's negotiations with Saladin, and the accusations of treachery brought against Count Raymond. Barker (*op. cit.*), King (*op. cit.*, and Oman (*op. cit.*) say nothing about this third problem.

BIBLIOGRAPHY

SOURCES

ARABIC

Abou Chamah. *Le Livre des deux Jardins, ou histoire des deux règnes* in *Recueil des historiens des croisades: historiens orientaux.* Vol. IV. Paris, 1898; Vol. V, Paris, 1906.
Abū'l-Fidā. *Résumé de l'histoire des croisades* in *Recueil des historiens des croisades: historiens orientaux.* Vol. I. Paris, 1872.
Abū'l-Mahāsin Yūsuf. *Extraits de Nodjoûm Ez-Zahireh* in *Recueil des historiens des croisades: historiens orientaux.* Vol. III. Paris, 1884.
Behâ Ed-Dîn. *Anecdotes et Beaux Traits de la Vie du Sultan Youssof (Salâh Ed-Dîn)* in *Recueil des historiens des croisades: historiens orientaux.* Vol. III. Paris, 1884.
— —. *'Saladin'; Or What Befell Sultan Yûsuf (Salâh Ed-Dîn) (1137-1193 A. D.)* Palestine Pilgrims Text Society. Vol. XIII. London, 1897.
Ibn al-Athīr. *Extrait de la chronique intitulée Kamel-Altevarykh* in *Recueil des historiens des croisades: historiens orientaux.* Vol. I. Paris, 1872 and 1887.
— —. *Histoire des Atabecs de Mosul* in *Recueil des historiens des croisade: historiens orientaux.* Vol. II. Paris, 1887.
Ibn al-Furat. *Târikh ad-douwal wa'l-mouloûk.* Translations provided by Professor Claude Cahen.
Ibn al-Qalānisī. *The Damascus Chronicle of the Crusades.* Translated and edited by H. A. R. Gibb. London, 1932.
Ibn Djobeïr. *Extrait du voyage d'Ibn Djobeïr* in *Recueil des historiens des croisades: historiens orientaux.* Vol. III. Paris, 1884.
Ibn Khallikan. *Biographical Dictionary.* Translated from the Arabic by Bⁿ Mac Guckin de Slane. Vols. I, II, and IV. Paris, 1842, 1843, and 1871.
Kamal Ad-Dîn. *Histoire d'Alep.* Edited and translated by Edgar Blochet. *Revue de l'orient latin.* Vols. III and IV. Paris, 1895 and 1896.
Kamāl al-Dīn. *Extraits de la chronique d'Alep* in *Recueil des historiens des croisades: historiens orientaux.* Vol. III. Paris, 1884.
Makrizi. *Histoire d'Égypte de Makrizi.* Translated and edited by Edgar Blochet. *Revue de l'orient latin.* Vols. VIII and IX. Paris, 1900-01 and 1902.
Ousâma Ibn Mounkidh. *Un Émir Syrien au premier siècle des croisades 1095-1188.* Edited by Hartwig Derenbourg. Vol. I. Paris, 1889.
Usāmah Ibn-Munkidh (Kitāb Al-Iʿ Tibār). *An Arab-Syrian Gentleman and Warrior in the Period of the Crusades.* Translated with annotations by Philip K. Hitti. New York, 1929.
Sibṭ Ibn al-Jauzī. *Extraits du Mirât ez-Zèmân* in *Recueil des historiens des croisades, historiens orientaux.* Vol. III. Paris, 1884.

ARMENIAN

Grégoire Le Prêtre. *Chronique de Grégoire Le Prêtre* in *Recueil des historiens des croisades: documents arméniens.* Vol. I. Paris, 1869.
— —. *Chronique de Matthieu d'Édesse (962-1136) Avec La Continuation de Grégoire Le Prêtre Jusqu'en 1162.* Translated by Edouard Dulaurier. Paris, 1858.
Guiragos de Kantzag. *Extrait de l'histoire d'Arménie* in *Recueil des historiens des croisades: documents arméniens.* Vol. I. Paris, 1869.

Matthew of Edessa. *Extraits de la chronique de Matthieu d'Édesse* in *Recueil des historiens des croisades: documents arméniens.* Vol. I. Paris, 1869.
Samuel d'Ani. *Extrait de la Chronographie de Samuel d'Ani* in *Recueil des historiens des croisades: documents arméniens.* Vol. I. Paris, 1869.
Sěmpad. *Chronique du royaume de la Petite Arménie* in *Recueil des historiens des croisades: documents arméniens.* Vol. I. Paris, 1869.
Vartan Le Grand. *Extrait de l'histoire universelle de Vartan Le Grand* in *Recueil des historiens des croisades: documents arméniens.* Vol. I. Paris, 1869.

GREEK

Cinnamus. *Epitome rerum ab Ioanne et Alexio Comnenis Gestarum* in *Corpus Scriptorum Historiae Byzantinae.* Bk. XXVI. Bonn, 1836.
— —. *Historia* in *Recueil des historiens des croisades: historiens grecs.* Vol. I. Paris, 1875.

LATIN: DOCUMENTARY

Cartulaire général de l'ordre des Hospitaliers de St. Jean de Jérusalem (1100-1310). Edited by Joseph Marie Antoine Delaville Le Roulx. Paris, 1894.
Chartes de Terre Sainte provenant de l'Abbaye de N.-D. de Josaphat. Edited by Henri-François Delaborde. Paris, 1880.
Du Cange (*Glossarium Mediae et Infimae Latinitatis*). Edited by Leopold Favre. Niort, 1887.
Les archives, la bibliothèque et le trésor de l'ordre de Saint-Jean de Jérusalem à Malte. Edited by Joseph Marie Antoine Delaville Le Roulx. Paris, 1883.
Mélanges sur l'ordre de S. Jean de Jérusalem. Edited by Joseph Marie Antoine Delaville Le Roulx. Paris, 1910.
Regesta Regni Hierosolymitani (MXCVII-MCCXCI). Edited by Reinhold Röhricht. Oeniponti, 1893.
Regesta' Regni Hierosolymitani (MXCVII-MCCXCI) Additamentum. Edited by Reinhold Röhricht. Oeniponti, 1904.
Tabulae Ordinis Theutonici. Edited by Ernst Strehlke. Berlin, 1869.

LATIN: EPISTOLARY

Epistola A Dapiferi Militiae Templi in *Recueil des historiens des Gaules et de la France.* Edited by M. Bouquet and others. Vol. XV. Paris, 1878.
Epistola Aymerici, patriarchae Antiocheni, ad Ludovicum in *Recueil des historiens des Gaules et de la France.* Edited by M. Bouquet and others. Vol. XVI. Paris, 1878.
Epistola Gaufredi Fulcherii, procuratoris militiae Templi, ad Ludovicum in *Recueil des historians des Gaules et de la France.* Edited by M. Bouquet and others. Vol. XVI. Paris, 1878.
Epistolae Cantuarienses. Edited by William Stubbs. London, 1865.
Epistolarum Regis Ludovici VII in *Recueil des historiens des Gaules et de la France.* Edited by M. Bouquet and others. Vol. XVI. Paris, 1878.

LATIN: NARRATIVE

Albert of Aachen. *Liber Christianae expeditionis pro ereptione, emundatione, restitutione Sanctae Hierosolymitanae ecclesiae* in *Recueil des historiens des croisades: historiens occidentaux.* Vol. IV. Paris, 1879.
Albert of Trium-Fontium. *Chronicon* in *Recueil des historiens des Gaules et de la France.* Edited by M. Bouquet and others. Vol. XVIII. Paris, 1879.

Ex Chronico Anonymi Laudunensis Canonici in *Recueil des historiens des Gaules et de la France.* Edited by M. Bouquet and others. Vol. XVIII. Paris, 1879.

Arnold, Abbas Lubecensis (Arnold of Lubeck). *Chronica Slavorum* in *Monumenta Germaniae Historica Scriptores.* Vol. XXI. Hanover, 1869.

Benedictus Abbas (Benedict of Peterborough). *Gesta Regis Henrici Secundi.* Edited by William Stubbs. London, 1867.

Brevis Regni Ierosolymitani Historia in *Monumenta Germaniae Historica Scriptores.* Vol. XVIII. Hanover, 1863.

De Expugnatione Terrae Sanctae Per Saladinum, Libellus. Edited by Joseph Stevenson. London, 1875.

Gervasii Monachi Cantuariensis (Gervase of Canterbury). *Opera Historica.* Edited by William Stubbs. London, 1879.

Ex Gervasii Dorobernensis Chronico De Rebus Angliae in *Recueil des historiens des Gaules et de la France.* Edited by M. Bouquet and others. Vol. XVII. Paris, 1878.

Giraldus Cambrensis. *Opera. De Rebus a Se Gestis.* Edited by J. S. Brewer. London, 1861.

— —. *Opera. Expugnatio Hibernica.* Edited by James S. Dimock. London, 1867.

— —. *Opera. De Principis Instructione Liber.* Edited by George F. Warner. London, 1891.

Chronicon Guillelmi de Nangiaco in *Recueil des historiens des Gaules et de la France.* Edited by M. Bouquet and others. Vol. XX. Paris, 1894.

Historia Peregrinorum in *Monumenta Germaniae Historica.* New Series. Edited by A. Chroust. Volume V. Berlin, 1928.

Itinerarium Peregrinorum et Gesta Regis Ricardi. Edited by William Stubbs. London, 1864.

Ottonis Episcopi Frisingensis (Otto of Freising). *Chronicon Continuatio Sanblasiana* in *Monumenta Germaniae Historica Scriptores.* Edited by Georg Pertz. Vol. XX. Hanover, 1868.

Ralph of Coggeshall. *Chronicon Anglicanum.* Edited by Joseph Stevenson. London, 1875.

Radulfi De Diceto (Ralph of Diceto). *Ymagines Historiarum.* Edited by William Stubbs. London, 1876.

Richard of Devizes. *De Rebus Gestis Ricardi Primi.* Edited by Richard Howlett. London, 1886.

Rigordus. *Gesta Philippi Augusti.* Edited by H. François Delaborde. Paris, 1882.

Ex Chronologia Roberti Altissiodorensis in *Recueil des historiens des Gaules et de la France.* Edited by M. Bouquet and others. Vol. XVIII. Paris, 1879.

Chronique de Robert de Torigni. Edited by Léopold Delisle. Rouen, 1872.

Anonymi Continuatio Appendicis Roberti de Monte ad Sigebertum in *Recueil des historiens des Gaules et de la France.* Edited by M. Bouquet and others. Vol. XVIII. Paris, 1879.

Chronica Magistri Rogeri De Houedene (Roger of Hoveden). Edited by William Stubbs. London, 1869.

Roger of Wendover. *Liber Qui Dicitur Flores Historiarum.* Edited by Henry G. Hewlett. London, 1886.

Ex Chronico S. Petri Catalaunensis in *Recueil des historiens des Gaules et de la France.* Edited by M. Bouquet and others. Vol. XII. Paris, 1877.

Sicardus Cremonensis Episcopus. *Chronicon Patrologia Latina.* Edited by J.-P. Migne. Vol. CCXIII. Paris, 1855.

Sigeberti Gemblacensis. *Chronici Continuatio Aquicinctina* in *Monumenta Germaniae Historica SS.* Vol. VI. Hanover, 1844.

Willelmi Chronica Andrensis in *Monumenta Germaniae Historica Scriptores.* Vol. XXIV. Hanover, 1879.

William of Newburgh. *Historia Rerum Anglicarum.* Edited by Richard Howlett. London, 1884.
William of Tyre. *Historica rerum in partibus transmarinis gestarum* in *Recueil des historiens des croisades: historiens occidentaux.* Vol. I. Paris, 1844.
A History of Deeds Done Beyond the Sea by William Archbishop of Tyre. Translated and edited by Emily A. Babcock and A. C. Krey. Vol. II. New York, 1943.

Old French

Ambroise. *L'Estoire de la guerre sainte.* Edited by Gaston Paris. Paris, 1897.
The Crusade of Richard Lion-Heart by Ambroise. Translated from the Old French by Merton Jerome Hubert with notes and documentation by John L. La Monte. New York, 1941.
Annales de Terre Sainte in *Archives de l'Orient latin.* Vol. II. Paris, 1884.
Chronique d'Ernoul et de Bernard Le Trésorier. Edited by M. L. de Mas Latrie. Paris, 1871.
Ernoul's Account of Palestine. Palestine Pilgrims Text Society. Vol. 6. London, 1894.
L'Estoire de Eracles Empereur in *Recueil des historiens des croisades: historiens occidentaux.* Vol. II. Paris, 1859.
Les gestes des Chiprois. Livre I. *Chronique de Terre Sainte (1132-1224)* in *Recueil des historiens des croisades: documents arméniens.* Vol. II. Paris, 1906.
Les Lignages d'Outremer in *Recueil des historiens des croisades: historiens occidentaux. Lois.* Vol. II. Paris, 1843.
Livre de Jean d'Ibelin. Assises de la Haute Cour in *Recueil des Historiens des croisades.* Vol. I. Paris, 1841.
Livre de Philippe de Navarre in *Recueil des historiens des croisades. Assises de Jérusalem.* Vol. I. Paris, 1841.
Livre des assises de la cour des bourgeois in *Recueil des historiens des croisades. Assises de Jérusalem.* Paris, 1841
Robert de Clari. *Li Estoires de Chiaus qui conquisent Constantinoble.* Paris, 1869.

Old Italian

Chronique d'Amadi. Edited by René de Mas Latrie. Paris, 1891.

Syriac

"The First and Second Crusades from an Anonymous Syriac Chronicle," translated by A. S. Tritton, with notes by H. A. R. Gibb, *Journal of the Royal Asiatic Society,* London, 1933.
The Chronography of Abû'l Faraj (Bar Hebraeus). Translated by Ernest A. Wallis Budge. Vol. I. London, 1932.
Chronique de Michel Le Syrien. Translated and edited by J.-B. Chabot. Vol. III. Paris, 1905.
Extrait de la chronique de Michel Le Syrien in *Recueil des historiens des croisades: documents arméniens.* Vol. I. Paris, 1869.

SECONDARY WORKS

Books

A History of the Crusades. The First Hundred Years. Volume I. Philadelphia, 1955.
A History of the Crusades. The Later Crusades 1189-1311. Volume II. Philadelphia, 1962.

Archer, Thomas Andrew and Kingsford, Charles L. *The Crusades.* New York, 1902.
Baldwin, Marshall. *Raymond III of Tripolis and the Fall of Jerusalem.* Princeton, 1936.
Barker, Ernest. *The Crusades.* London, 1925.
Brand, Charles M. *Byzantium Confronts the West 1180-1204.* Cambridge, 1968.
Bréhier, Louis. *L'église et l'Orient au Moyen Age. Les Croisades.* Paris, 1921.
Cahen, Claude. *La Syrie du nord à l'époque des croisades et la principauté franque d'Antioche.* Paris, 1940.
Castle, Marian Louise. *The Career of Guy of Lusignan to 1187. A Study of Politics in the Kingdom of Jerusalem on the Eve of Its Conquest by Saladin.* University of Chicago Master's Thesis. Chicago, 1936.
Champdor, Albert. *Saladin le plus pur Héros de l'Islam.* Paris, 1956.
Collins, Arthur. *Peerage of England.* Volume VI. London, 1812.
Conder, C. R. *The Latin Kingdom of Jerusalem 1099 to 1291 A.D.* London, 1897.
Delaville Le Roulx, Joseph Marie Antoine. *Les Hospitaliers en Terre Sainte et à Chypre 1100-1310.* Paris, 1904.
Deschamps, Paul. *Les Chateaux des Croisés en Terre Sainte. Le Crac des Chevaliers.* Paris, 1934.
Fedden, Robin and Thomson, John. *Crusader Castles.* London, 1957.
Gibbon, Edward. *The Decline and Fall of the Roman Empire.* Volume II. New York, 1932.
Grousset, René. *Histoire des croisades et du royaume franc de Jérusalem.* Volumes II and III. Paris, 1935 and 1936.
———. *L'empire du Levant.* Paris, 1946.
———. *L'épopée des croisades.* Paris, 1939.
Hayek, Dimitri. *Le droit franc en Syrie pendant les croisades.* Paris, 1925.
Herzog, Annie. *Die Frau auf den Fürstenthronen der Kreuzfahrerstaaten.* Berlin, 1919.
Ilgen, Theodor. *Markgraf Conrad von Montferrat.* Marburg, 1880.
King, E. J. *The Knights Hospitallers in the Holy Land.* London, 1931.
Köhler, Gustav. *Die Entwickelung des Kriegswesens und die Kreuzführung in der Ritterzeit von Mitte des XIten Jahrhunderts bis zu den Hussitenkrieg.* Breslau, 1889.
Kugler, Bernhard. *Studien zur Geschichte des zweiten Kreuzzüges.* Stuttgart, 1866.
La Monte, John L. *Feudal Monarchy in the Latin Kingdom of Jerusalem 1100 to 1291.* Cambridge, 1932.
Lane-Poole, Stanley. *Saladin and the Fall of the Kingdom of Jerusalem.* London, 1926.
Les familles d'Outre-Mer de Du Cange in *Collection de documents inédits sur l'histoire de France.* Première Série. Histoire politique. Publiées par E.-G. Rey. Paris, 1869.
Méry, Louis and Guindon, F. *Histoire analytique et chronologique des actes et des délibérations du corps et du conseil de la municipalité de Marseille, depuis le Xme siècle jusqu'à nos jours.* Vol. I. Marseille, 1841.
Moonan, Helen. *Women in Politics in Latin Syria.* University of Minnesota Master's Thesis. Minneapolis, 1922.
Morison, James Cotter. *The Life and Times of Saint Bernard, Abbot of Clairvaux.* London, 1889.
Munro, Dana C. *The Kingdom of the Crusaders.* New York, 1935.
Norgate, Kate. *Richard the Lion Heart.* London, 1925.
Oldenbourg, Zoé. *Les Croisades.* Paris, 1965.
Oman, Charles. *A History of the Art of War in the Middle Ages, A. D. 378-1278.* Vol. I. London, 1923.
Proctor, Major. *History of the Crusades: Their Rise, Progress and Results.* Philadelphia, 1854.
Prutz, Hans. *Kulturgeschichte der Kreuzzüge.* Berlin, 1883.
Rey, Emmanuel Guillaume. *Les colonies franques de Syrie aux XIIme et XIIIme siècles.* Paris, 1883.

Rey, Emmanuel Guillaume. *Sommaire du Supplément aux Familles d'Outre-Mer.* Chartres, 1881.
Richard, Jean. *Le royaume latin de Jérusalem.* Paris, 1953.
Röhricht, Reinhold. *Geschichte des Königreichs Jerusalem, 1100-1291.* Innsbruck, 1898.
— —. *Geschichte der Kreuzzüge in Umriss.* Innsbruck, 1898.
Runciman, Steven. *A History of the Crusades.* Vols. II and III. Cambridge, 1952 and 1954.
— —. *The Families of Outremer.* London, 1960.
de Saulcy, Louis. *Numismatique des croisades.* Paris, 1847.
Schlumberger, Gustave. *Campagnes du roi Amaury Ier de Jérusalem en Égypte au XIIe siècle.* Paris, 1906.
— —. *Numismatique de l'Orient latin.* Graz, 1954.
— —. *Renaud de Chatillon.* Paris, 1923.
Slaughter, Gertrude. *Saladin (1138-1193).* New York, 1955.
Stevenson, William Barron. *The Crusaders in the East.* Cambridge, 1907.
Stubbs, William. *Historical Introductions to the Rolls Series.* New York, 1902.
Ter-Grigorian Iskanderian, Galust. *Die Kreuzfahrer und ihre Beziehungen zu den armenischen Nachbarfürsten bis zum Untergange der Grafschaft Edessa.* Wieda in Th., 1915.
Wiet, Gaston, *L'Égypte Arabe de la Conquête Arabe à la Conquête Ottomane 642-1517 de l'ère chrétienne.* Paris, 1937.
Wilcke, Wilhelm F. *Geschichte der Tempelherrenordens.* Halle, 1850.

ARTICLES

Baldwin, Marshall. "The Decline and Fall of Jerusalem, 1174-1189," *A History of the Crusades. The First Hundred Years* (Philadelphia, 1955), I, 590-621.
— —. "The Latin States under Baldwin III and Amalric I, 1143-1174," *A History of the Crusades. The First Hundred Years* (Philadelphia, 1955), I, 528-61.
Berry, Virginia G. "The Second Crusade," *A History of the Crusades. The First Hundred Years* (Philadelphia, 1955), I, 463-512.
Brand, Charles M. "The Byzantines and Saladin, 1185-1192: Opponents of the Third Crusade," *Speculum* (Cambridge, 1962), XXXVII, 167-81.
Bréhier, Louis. "Amaury I," *Dictionnaire d'histoire et de géographie ecclésiastiques* (Paris, 1914), Vol. II.
— —. "Baudouin V," *Dictionnaire d'histoire et de géographie ecclésiastiques* (Paris, 1932), Vol. VI.
Cahen, Claude. "Note sur les seigneurs de Saone et de Zerdana," *Syria* (Paris, 1931), XII, 154-59.
Chabot, J.-B. "Un épisode inédit de l'histoire des Croisades (le siège de Birta, 1145)," *Comptes rendus des Séances de l'Académie des Inscriptions et Belles-Lettres* (Paris, 1917), pp. 77-84.
Comte de Marsy. "Fragment d'un Cartulaire de l'Ordre de Saint-Lazare en Terre-Sainte," *Archives de l'Orient latin* (Paris, 1884), II, No. XXIX, 121-57.
Delaville Le Roulx, Joseph Marie Antoine. "Inventaire de pièces de Terre Sainte de l'Ordre de l'Hopital," *Revue de l'orient latin* (Paris, 1895), III, 36-106.
Der Nersessian, Sirarpie. "The Kingdom of Cicilian Armenia," *A History of the Crusades. The Later Crusades 1189-1311* (Philadelphia, 1962), II, 630-59.
Diehl, Charles. "The Byzantine Empire and the Crusades," *Essays on the Crusades* (Burlington, Vermont, 1903), pp. 91-118.
Gibb, Sir Hamilton A. R. "The Achievement of Saladin," *Studies on the Civilization of Islam* (Boston, 1962), pp. 91-107.
— —. "The Career of Nūr-ad-Dīn," *A History of the Crusades. The First Hundred Years* (Philadelphia, 1955), I, 513-27.

———. "The Rise of Saladin, 1169-1189," *A History of the Crusades. The First Hundred Years* (Philadelphia, 1955), I, 563-89.
———. "Zengi and the Fall of Edessa," *A History of the Crusades. The First Hundred Years* (Philadelphia, 1955), I, 449-62.
Krey, A. C. "William of Tyre. The Making of an Historian in the Middle Ages," *Speculum* (Cambridge, 1941), XVI, 149-66.
La Monte, John L. "Chronology of the Orient latin," *Bulletin of the International Committee of Historical Sciences* (Paris, 1942-1943), XII, Part 2, pp. 141-202.
———. "John d'Ibelin, the Old Lord of Beirut, 1177-1236," *Byzantion* (Paris, 1937), XII, 417-58.
———. "Taki ed Din, Prince of Hama," *The Moslem World* (Hartford, Conn., 1941), XXXI, 149-60.
———. "The Lords of Sidon in the Twelfth and Thirteenth Centuries," *Byzantion* (Paris, 1944-1945), XVII, 183-211.
———. "The rise and decline of a Frankish Seigneury in Syria in the time of the Crusades," *Revue Historique du Sud-Est Européen* (Bucarest, 1938), XV, 301-20.
———. "The Viscounts of Naplouse in the Twelfth Century," *Syria* (Paris, 1938), XIX, 272-78.
———. "To What Extent Was the Byzantine Empire the Suzerain of the Latin Crusading States?", *Byzantion* (Paris, 1932), VII, 253-64.
——— and Downs, Norton III. "The Lords of Bethsan in the Kingdoms of Jerusalem and Cyprus," *Medievalia et Humanistica* (Boulder, Colorado), VI, 57-75.
Lewis, Bernard. "The Ismāʿīlites and the Assassins," *A History of the Crusades. The First Hundred Years* (Philadelphia, 1955), I, 99-132.
de Mas Latrie, L. "De quelques seigneuries de Terre Sainte oubliées dans les *Familles d'Outremer* de Du Cange," *Revue Historique* (Paris, 1878), VIII, 107-20.
———. "Le fief de la Chamberlaine et les Chambellans de Jérusalem," *Bibliothèque de l'école des Chartes* (Paris, 1882), XLIII, 647-52.
———. "Les Seigneurs du Crac de Montréal," *Archivio Veneto* (Venice, 1883), XXV, 475-94.
Munro, Dana C. "Christian and Infidel in the Holy Land," *Essays on the Crusades* (Burlington, Vermont, 1903), pp. 1-41.
———. "The Establishment of the Latin Kingdom of Jerusalem," *The Sewanee Review* (Sewanee, Tennessee, 1924), XXXII, 258-75.
Nickerson, M. E. "The Seigneury of Beirut in the Twelfth Century and the Brisebarre Family of Beirut-Blanchegarde," *Byzantion* (Paris, 1949), XIX, 141-85.
Painter, Sidney. "The Third Crusade: Richard the Lionhearted and Philip Augustus," *A History of the Crusades. The Later Crusades 1189-1311* (Philadelphia, 1962), II, 45-85.
Pirie-Gordon, Charles H. "The Reigning Princes of Galilee," *English Historical Review* (New York, 1912), XXVII, 445-61.
Rey, Emmanuel Guillaume. "Résumé chronologique de l'histoire des princes d'Antioche. Bohémond III, prince d'Antioche 1163-1201," *Revue de l'orient latin* (Paris, 1896), 321-407.
Richard, Jean. "An Account of the Battle of Hattin Referring to the Frankish Mercenaries in Oriental Moslem States," *Speculum* (Cambridge, 1952), XXVII, 168-77.
Röhricht, Reinhold. "Amalrich I, König von Jerusalem (1162-1174)," *Mittheilungen des Instituts für Oesterreichische Geschichtsforschung* (Innsbruck, 1891), XII, 432-93.

INDEX

A

Agnes, Countess
  Daughter of Joscelyn II and wife of Reginald of Marash 15
  Receives protection of Baldwin III 24, 25-26
  Marries Amalric, her third cousin 30-31
  Dissolution of marriage to Amalric 31, 68
  Third marriage to Hugh of Ibelin 38
  Fourth marriage to Reginald of Sidon 38
  Effects release of her brother Joscelyn III 38-39
  Seeks control of policies of her son, Baldwin IV 72
  Supports Heraclius as the new patriarch 90
  Effects exclusion of Raymond III from Kingdom of Jerusalem 94
  Grants fiefs to Sibyl and Guy of Lusignan 132

Agnes, Daughter of Henry Le Buffle
  Marries Joscelyn III 74

Agnes
  Daughter of Joscelyn III 74

Aimery, Patriarch of Antioch
  Protector of Constance, widow of Raymond II 21

Aiyūb
  Emir of Baalbek and brother of Shīrkūh 42
  Aids Nūr-ad-Dīn in ouster of Mujīr ad-Dīn 42
  Father of Saladin 54

Aksungur
  Moslem leader 3

al-ᶜĀdil, Saladin's brother
  Ordered by Saladin to attack Franks by land and sea 106-07
  Defeats Reginald of Châtillon 112
  Invests Krak 116-17
  Made governor of Aleppo 128
  Invests Krak 128-29
  Captures Jaffa 166
  Rôle in conquest of Jerusalem 173

ᶜAlī Küchük
  Governor of City of Edessa 9

Amalric, King of Jerusalem and brother of Baldwin III
  Marries Countess Agnes 30-31
  Dissolution of marriage to Agnes 31, 68
  Aids in effecting release of Raymond III 37
  Succeeds to kingship 47
  Marries grandniece of Manuel 47, 70
  Unsuccessful first invasion of Egypt 48
  Second invasion of Egypt 49-50
  Third invasion of Egypt 51-52
  Fourth invasion of Egypt 52-53
  Franco-Greek investment of Damietta 54
  Dies 59
  Gains release of Bohemond III 69
  Governmental innovations 68
  Balance of power game 69-70
  Assumes regency of County of Tripoli 70

Amalric. Patriarch of Jerusalem
  Dies 90

Andronicus I, Byzantine Emperor
  Creates alliance with Saladin 152-53

B

Baldwin III, King of Jerusalem
  Saves Azāz from Moslem capture 19
  Journeys to Antioch 23
  Accepts Manuel's proposals in re County of Edessa 23
  Grants lands and revenue to Joscelyn III 28
  Captures fief of Ḥārim 29
  Quarrel with Queen Mother Melisend 41
  Captures Ascalon 42
  Makes entente with Manuel 45

Baldwin III (*continued*)
Marries Theodora, grand-niece of Manuel 46
Makes two-year truce with Nūr ad-Dīn 46, 66-67
Death 47
Succours Principality of Antioch 66
Succours Princess Constance 66-67
Negotiates marriage of Manuel and Princess Maria 67

Baldwin IV, King of Jerusalem
Son of Countess Agnes and Amalric 31
Accedes to throne 59
Grants regency to Raymond III 71
Excludes Raymond III and favors Joscelyn III 72-73
Appoints Reginald of Châtillon as regent and army chief 83-84
Participates in battle of Ramla 83-84
Effects marriage of Sibyl with Guy of Lusignan 88
Selects Heraclius as new Patriarch of Jerusalem 90
Seeks and gains truce from Saladin 93
Bars entrance of Raymond III 94
Reestablishes peace with Raymond III 95
Makes Joscelyn III ambassador to Byzantine Empire 97-98
Grants revenues and fief to Joscelyn III 99-100
Exchanges fiefs with Joscelyn III 100-02
Confirms purchase of 14 towns by Joscelyn III 101
Fails to effect restitution by Reginald of Châtillon 104-05
Receives ultimatum from Saladin 105
Grants military aid to Bohemond III 113
Appoints Guy of Lusignan as regent 118
Complete rift with Guy of Lusignan 122-23
Entrusts regency to Raymond III 123
Orders crowning of Baldwin V 124-25
Dies 132

Baldwin V, King of Jerusalem
Posthumous son of William Longsword and Sibyl 80
Selected and crowned as king 120
Placed in guardianship of Joscelyn III 124
Succeeds to throne 132
Taken to Acre by Joscelyn III 132
Grants favors to Joscelyn III 132-33
Dies 133

Baldwin, Lord of Marash
Aids Joscelyn II in recapture of city of Edessa 10-11
Attacks Nūr ad-Dīn 12
Dies 12

Baldwin of Ramla
Captured by Saladin 87
Participates in Ṣaffūrīyah campaign 114-15
Supports selection and crowning of Baldwin V as next king 120
Utters counsels of despair 140
Refuses but later renders homage to King Guy 142-43
Receives Lands from Bohemond III 143

Balian of Ibelin, brother of Baldwin of Ramla
Participates in Ṣaffūrīyah campaign 114-15
Supports selection and crowning of Baldwin V as next king 120
Seeks reconciliation between Guy and Raymond III 150
Rôle in battle of Hattin 159-60
Defends Jerusalem 170-74
Rôle in defense of Tyre 176
Opposes continued rôle as king by Guy 189
Supports Conrad of Montferrat 190
Joins Henry of Champagne 197

Basil, Armenian prince
Captured by Kara Arslan 20

Basilius Bar Soumana
Designated bishop of Edessa 5

Battles, Campaigns, Sieges, and Captures
Acre 164, 184-93; Ailah 112; Ain Jālūt 114; Aintab 26; al-ᶜArimah 15; Aleppo 109; al-Fūlah 166; al-Natroun 169; Amida 109; Antioch 16; Apamea 16; Artāḥ 16; ᶜAzāz 14, 26, 109; Baghrās 182; Baisan 114; Bait Jibrīn 169; Banyas 186; Behesni 23; Beirut 107, 167; Bekǎs 182; Belfort 182, 185, 188; Belvoir 182; Bethlehem 169; Bira 6-7,

Battles, Campaigns, Sieges and Captures
(*continued*)

26; Buria 106; Burj-ar-risas 26, 28; Burzia 182; Buzaʾah 109; Caesarea 166; Cafersoud 26; Chastel-Neuf 182; Chateau du Roi 166; Cyrrhus 26; Damascus 111-12; Darbsāk 182; Darum 111, 169; Duluk 26; Edessa (County and City) 5, 6, 10-12, 21-22, 26, 107, 109; Ḥabīs Jaldak 106, 111; Haifa 166; Ḥārim 16, 29, 32-33, 83-84, 109; Harran 107; Hattin 156-60; Hebron 169; Hisn Kerzin 26; Hisn Sînâb 14; Hisn S r. r̥. (b?) 14; Hisn Tell R. mân 14; Inab 15; Jabala 182; Jacob's Ford 87; Jaffa 166; Jerusalem 170-74; Jubail 167; Kafarlāthā 26, 109; Kesoun 23; Khourous 26; Krak 26, 116-17, 128-29, 182; Latakia 182; Marash 18; Marzban 23; Nablus 166; Nahr al-Djauz 26; Nazareth 166; Nisibin 107, 109; Qalᶜat Jaᶜbar 10; Qalᶜat ar-Rūm 26; Raban 23; Ramla 83-84, 169; Raqqa 109; Ravendan 26; Safad 182; Ṣaffūrīyah 114-15, 157, 166; Samosata 26; Saone 182; Sarmīn 182; Sarūj 6, 109; Sidon 167; Sinjar 109; Tall Khālid 26; Tell Bashir 18-19, 23, 26; Tiberias 157, 163; Tibnīn 166; Toron 166; Tortosa 182; Tyre 166-67, 178-79; Tyron 166.

Beatrice
Daughter of Count Joscelyn III 74

Beatrice of Saone
Widow of William of Saone, wife of Count Joscelyn II, and mother of Joscelyn III 1
Consents to donation of village of Cisembourg 2
Vainly tries to save remnants of County of Edessa 22
Receives protection of Baldwin III 24

Belek
Moslem leader 3

Bertram, grandson of Raymond of Toulouse
Seizes castle of al-ᶜArīmah 15

Bohemond III, Prince of Antioch
Captured and imprisoned by Nūr ad-Dīn 33, 50

Gains release 37, 50
Circumstances of his release 38
Placed on throne of Antioch 67
Grants fief to Joscelyn III 75
Arrives in Kingdom of Jerusalem 88
Engages in foolish policies 93-94
Seeks truce with Saladin 113
Negotiations with Roupen III 113
Supports selection and crowning of Baldwin V as king 120
Grants lands to Raymond III 143
Effects reconciliation with Guy 155-56
Visits King Richard in Cyprus 191

C

Colomon, Byzantine governor of Cilicia
Captured and imprisoned by Nūr ad Dīn, pp. 33, 50

Conrad of Montferrat
Defends Tyre 166-67, 176-79
Contest with Guy 180-82
Effects reconciliation with Guy 186
Rôle in siege of Acre 187-91
Marries Isabel and becomes a parent 190
Refuses title of king prior to coronation 190
Provision for his ultimate gaining of kingship 195
Elected king 196
Assassinated 196

Constance, widow of Raymond II of Antioch
Protected by Patriarch Aimery 21
Receives aid from Baldwin III 66
Intrigues against her son Bohemond III 67
Driven into exile 67

D

Daulah, Turkish ruler
Seizes convents of Zabar 17
Treats scornfully Joscelyn II 17

Dîrgam, Egyptian emir
Winner in struggle with rival emir Shavar 48
Dies in battle with Shīrkūh 49

E

Eschiva
Wife of (1) Walter, prince of Galilee and (2) Raymond III 72
Appeals for aid in Hattin campaign 157
Surrenders Tiberias to Saladin 163

F

Fulcher, Patriarch
Opposes marriage of Amalric and Countess Agnes 31

Fulk, King of Jerusalem
Military policies 3-4

G

Gerard of Ridefort, Master of the Temple
Visits Europe 126-27
Escapes death at hands of Moslems 155
Rôle in battle of Hattin 157-60
Imprisoned in Damascus 163
Urges surrender of Ascalon 168
Death 185

Gregory III, head of Armenian church
Receives Qalᶜat ar-Rūm from Countess Beatrice 24-25

Gümüshtigin, Aleppan leader
Proclaims self ruler of Aleppo and sole guardian of aṣ-Ṣāliḥ 60
Seeks support of Raymond III against Saladin 61
Makes peace with Saladin 64

Guy Fraisnel
Holder of fief of Ḥārim 29

Guy of Lusignan, French nobleman, Count of Jaffa and Ascalon, and King of Jerusalem
Marries Sibyl 88
Gains cities of Jaffa and Ascalon 88, 90
Early reputation 92
Participates in Ṣaffūrīyah campaign 114-15
Appointed regent of Kingdom of Jerusalem 118
Complete rift with Baldwin IV 122-23
Receives fiefs from Countess Agnes 132
Sells fiefs to Joscelyn III 132
Crowned king 137
Hostile attitude toward Raymond III 143
Seeks and gains reconciliation with Raymond III 154-55
Effects reconciliation with Bohemond III 155-56
Rôle in campaign and battle of Hattin 158-63
Imprisoned in Damascus 163
Urges surrender of Ascalon 168
Rôle in siege of Jerusalem 172
Released by Saladin 181
Contest with Conrad of Montferrat 180-82
Siege of Acre 184-93
Effects reconciliation with Conrad of Montferrat 186
Refuses to abdicate 190
Meets King Richard in Cyprus 191
Confirmed in kingship 195
Receives governorship of Cyprus 197

H

Ḥassān, Lieutenant of Nūr ad-Dīn
Captures Tell Bashir 26

Henry, Duke of Burgundy
Refuses to marry widowed Sibyl 85

Henry of Champagne, nephew of King Richard
Marries Isabel 196-97

Henry II, King of England
Grants financial aid 127

Heraclius, Archbishop of Caesarea
Supports marriage of Sibyl and Guy 88
Selected as new Patriarch of Jerusalem by Baldwin IV 90
Sent to Europe for aid 126-27
Helps *coup d'état* of Joscelyn III 135-37
Rôle in siege and capture of Jerusalem 171-73

Hugh of Ibelin
Third husband of Countess Agnes 38

Hugh of Lusignan
Captured and imprisoned by Nūr ad-Dīn 33, 50

Hugh of Tiberias, stepson of Raymond III
Captured by Saladin 87
Rôle in battle of Hattin 160

Hugh of Tiberias (*continued*)
   Joins Henry of Champagne 197

Humphrey II, Lord of Toron and Constable of Kingdom of Jerusalem
   Journeys to Antioch 23
   Killed 86
   Paternal grandfather of Humphrey IV 91

Humphrey IV
   Son of Stephanie 91
   Betrothed to Isabel 91
   Married to Isabel 92, 117
   Refuses office of king 141
   Captured in battle of Hattin 160
   Divorced from Isabel 189-90
   Meets King Richard in Cyprus 191

I

Il-Ghāzī
   Moslem leader 3

ᶜImād ad-Dīn, Ruler of Sinjar and brother of ᶜIzz ad-Dīn
   Receives rule of Aleppo 108
   Surrenders Aleppo to Saladin 109
   Receives Sinjar, Sarūj, Nisibin, Rakka, and the district of Khabur from Saladin 109

Isaac II, Byzantine emperor
   Confirms alliance with Saladin 153

Isabel, half sister of Baldwin IV
   Betrothed to Humphrey IV 91
   Divorced from Humphrey IV 189-90
   Marries Conrad of Montferrat and becomes a parent 190
   Marries Henry of Champagne 196-97

ᶜIzz ad-Dīn, ruler of Mosul, brother of Saif-ad-Dīn Ghāzī II, and cousin of aṣ-Ṣāliḥ
   Becomes ruler of Mosul 103
   Receives rule of Sinjar 108
   Plots against Saladin are quashed 147-48

J

Jaqar b. Yaᶜqub, emir of Zengi in Mosul
   Assassinated 6

Joscelyn I, Count of Edessa
   Grandfather of Joscelyn III 1

Joscelyn II, Count of Edessa
   Father of Joscelyn III and husband of Beatrice of Saone 1
   Opposes Raymond, prince of Antioch 4
   Leaves city of Edessa and repairs to Tell Bashir 4
   Antagonizes Syrian church circles in Edessa 4-5
   Withdraws to Antioch 5
   Agrees to aid Artukid princes 5
   Seeks aid from Raymond of Antioch and Queen Melisend 6
   Agrees to surrender Bira 7
   Recaptures most of the city of Edessa 10-11
   Attacks Nūr-ad-Dīn's forces 12
   Escapes from city of Edessa 12
   Inactive during Second Crusade 13
   Seeks and gains Nūr-ad-Dīn's clemency 14-15
   Mistreats Syrian Christians 17-18
   Attacked at Tell Bashir by Masᶜūd I and Kîlîj Arslan 18
   Concessions and surrenders to Masᶜūd I 19
   Unsuccessful aid tendered to Prince Basil 20
   Captured, imprisoned, and blinded by Nūr-ad-Dīn 21
   Dies 21

Joscelyn III, Count of Edessa
   Ancestry 1
   Birthdate 2
   Confirmation of the donation of the village of Cisembourg 2
   Raised to headship of County of Edessa 22
   Successfully defends Tell Bashir 23
   Receives protection of Baldwin III 24, 25-26
   Confirms Beatrice's grant of Qalᶜat ar-Rūm 25
   Receives lands and revenues from Baldwin III 28
   Effects temporary conquest of Burj-ar-risas 28
   Becomes marshal of the Kingdom of Jerusalem 28
   Assumes control of the fief of Ḥārim 29
   Captured and imprisoned by Nūr-ad-Dīn 33, 50

Joscelyn III (*continued*)
    Imprisonment from 1164 to 1176   37
    Gains release in 1176   38, 63
    Receives favor of Baldwin IV   72-73
    Gains seneschalship   73
    Marries Agnes, daughter of Henry Le Buffle   74
    Receives fief of Château du Roi and Montfort   74
    Becomes vassal of Bohemond III   75
    Gains additional lands   76-77
    Rôle as witness to sales of property, etc.   77-79
    Birth of daughters, Agnes and Beatrice   79
    Participates in battle of Ramla   77, 83-84
    Effects exclusion of Raymond III from Kingdom of Jerusalem   94
    Made ambassador to Byzantine Empire   97-98
    Rôle as witness to concessions, grants, and sales   98-99, 102
    Receives revenues and fief from Baldwin IV   99-100
    Exchanges fiefs with Baldwin IV   100-102
    Purchases 14 towns   101
    Made guardian of treasure chest in Acre   113
    Participates in Ṣaffūrīyah campaign   114-15
    Made guardian of Baldwin V   124
    Takes Baldwin V to Acre   132
    Purchases fiefs from Guy of Lusignan and Sibyl   132
    Receives favors from Baldwin V   132-33
    Retains office of Seneschal   133
    Effects *coup d'état*   133-35
    Receives fiefs and political favors from King Guy   143-45
    Rôle in battle of Hattin   160
    Surrenders Acre   164
    Loses his Galilean fiefs   166
    Rôle in defense of Tyre   176
    Rôle in siege of Acre   186, 188
    Loses seneschalship   197-98
    Death   198

Joscius, Archbishop of Acre
    Visits Rome   85
    Killed   155

K

Kara Arslan, Sultan of Iconium
    Foe of Zengi   6
    Treatment of Christian populations   17-18
    Captures Prince Basil   20
    Participates in total conquest of County of Edessa   26

Kîlîj Arslan I, father of Masᶜūd I
    Captures Marash   18

L

M

Manuel, Byzantine emperor
    Quarrels with Raymond II   6
    Sends aid to city of Edessa   6
    Reconciliation with Raymond II   9
    Makes offer in re County of Edessa to Countess Beatrice   23
    Takes over Edessan fortresses   24
    Invades Cilicia   45
    Secures a new entente with Baldwin III   45
    Marries Princess Maria   67
    Policies toward Principality of Antioch   168-69

Mar Bar Cauma, a convent
    Property stolen therefrom and returned thereto by Joscelyn II   4-5
    Second pillaging by Joscelyn II   17

Maria, princess and daughter of Princess Constance and Raymond of Antioch
    Marries Manuel in 1161   67

Maria Comnena, grandniece of Manuel
    Marries Amalric   47, 70

Masᶜūd I, Sultan of Rūm and son of Kîlîj Arslan I
    Invades Principality of Antioch and County of Edessa   18
    Captures Marash   18
    Invests Tell Bashir unsuccessfully   18-19
    Invades County of Edessa   21, 22
    Captures Edessan towns   23
    Fails to capture Tell Bashir   23
    Participates in total conquest of County of Edessa   26

Melisend, Queen of Jerusalem
    Supports Joscelyn II   6
    Quarrel with Baldwin III   41

Miles of Plancy, Lord of Montréal and Seneschal of King Amalric
   Governmental rôle in Kingdom of Jerusalem 70
   Assassinated 71

Mujīr-ad-Dīn, ruler of Damascus
   Pro-Frankish and anti-Nūr-ad-Dīn policies 41
   Fails to intervene in Frankish civil war 41
   Temporary reconciliation with Nūr-ad-Dīn 42

N

Naṣīr-ad-Dīn, ruler of Homs and cousin of Saladin
   Unsuccessfully plots against Saladin 148

Nūr-ad-Dīn, Moslem leader
   Second son of Zengi and latter's successor in principality of Aleppo 10
   Recaptures city of Edessa 11-12
   Attacks ᶜAzāz 14
   Grants clemency to Joscelyn II 14-15
   Besieges Inab 15
   Captures Artāḥ and Apamea 16
   Besieges Antioch 16
   Invades County of Edessa 21
   Participates in total conquest of County of Edessa 26
   Recovers Burj-ar-risas from Joscelyn III 28
   Invests fortress of Ḥārim 32
   Wins battle of Ḥārim 33, 50
   Marries Unur's daughter 40
   Wages war on Damascus 41
   Temporary reconciliation with Mujīr ad-Dīn 42
   Ousts Mujīr ad-Dīn and captures Damascus 42-43
   Chooses *status quo* policy towards Franks in 1157-1160 period but clashes with them militarily 43-45
   Releases Bertram 46
   Makes a two-year truce with Baldwin III 46
   Sends Shīrkūh with an army to Egypt 49
   Growing coolness toward Saladin 56-58
   Dies 58

O

Odo of St. Amand, Master of the Temple
   Captured by Saladin 87

P

Philip Augustus, King of France
   Grants financial aid 127
   Participates in siege of Acre 191-93

Philip, Count of Flanders
   Clashes with leaders of Kingdom of Jerusalem 80-82
   Attacks Homs, Hamah, and Ḥārim 83

Q

Qalᶜat ar-Rūm, a town
   Retained briefly by Beatrice and then given to Gregory III 24-25

R

Ralph, stepson of Raymond III
   Rôle in battle of Hattin 160
   Gains seneschalship 197-98

Raymond II, Prince of Antioch
   Opposes Joscelyn II 4
   Quarrels with Manuel 6
   Refuses aid to Joscelyn II 6
   Seeks and gains reconciliation with Manuel 9
   Inactive during Second Crusade 13
   Dies in battle 15

Raymond II, Count of Tripoli
   Seeks aid of Unur and Nūr-ad-Dīn 15

Raymond III, Count of Tripoli
   Captured by Nūr-ad-Dīn 33, 50
   Released from captivity 37, 71
   Seeks and gains regency of Kingdom of Jerusalem 71
   Marriage to Eschiva 72
   Excluded by Baldwin IV 72-73
   Arrives in Kingdom of Jerusalem 88
   Barred from Kingdom of Jerusalem 94
   Reestablishes peace with Baldwin IV 95
   Participates in Ṣaffūrīyah campaign 114-15
   Relieves Krak 117
   Supports selection and crowning of Baldwin V as next king 120
   Receives regency and support therefor 123-25

Raymond III (*continued*)
   Gains truce with Saladin 129
   Hoodwinked by Joscelyn III 133-34
   Defies leaders of *coup d'état* 136
   Opposes counsels of despair of Baldwin of Ramla 140-41
   Refuses to pay homage to Guy 142
   Makes truce with Saladin 146
   Refuses reconciliation with Guy 150
   Effects reconciliation with Guy and Sibyl 155
   Rôle in battle of Hattin 158-60
   Rôle in defense of Tyre 176, 180
   Death 181

Reginald of Châtillon
   Capture and imprisonment 37, 66
   Gains release in 1176 38, 63
   Seeks and gains Manuel's pardon 45
   Second husband of Princess Constance 66
   Appointed regent and army chief 81
   Participates in battle of Ramla 83-84
   Marries Stephanie and becomes stepfather of Humphrey IV 91
   Espouses betrothal of Humphrey IV to Isabel 91
   Anti-Moslem activities 104-05
   Unsuccessful naval attack in Red Sea 112
   Participates in Ṣaffūrīyah campaign 114-15
   Helps *coup d'état* of Joscelyn III 135-39
   Attacks Moslem caravan 150
   Rôle in battle of Hattin 157-60
   Dies 162

Reginald, lord of Marash, husband of Countess Agnes, and son-in-law of Joscelyn II
   Perishes in battle 15

Reginald of Saint-Valéry
   Holder of fief of Ḥārim 29

Reginald of Sidon
   Fourth husband of Countess Agnes 38
   Participates in Ṣaffūrīyah campaign 114-15
   Supports selection and crowning of Baldwin V as next king 120
   Rôle in battle of Hattin 160
   Rôle in defense of Tyre 176
   Supports Conrad of Montferrat 190
   Joins Henry of Champagne 197

Richard the Lionhearted, King of England
   Receives anti-Conrad Franks in Cyprus 191
   Participates in siege of Acre 191-93
   Proposal concerning the next king 196

Robert the Fat
   Abortive rescue mission in behalf of Frankish defenders of Bira 7

Roger of Les Moulins, Master of the Hospital
   Visits Europe 126-27
   Killed 155

Ṛoupen III, Armenian magnate
   Military clash and ensuing peace with Saladin 103
   Negotiates with Bohemond III 113

S

Saif ad-Dīn, brother of Nūr-ad-Dīn and son of Zengi
   Aids Nūr-ad-Dīn in recovery of al-ᶜArīmah, 15
   Receives Mosul and Mesopotamian allotments 40

Saif-ad-Dīn Ghāzī II
   Ruler of Mosul 59
   Death 103

Saladin, son of Aiyūb
   Participates in Shīrkūh's invasion of Egypt 54
   Defeats Franco-Greek investment of Damietta 54
   Growing coolness toward Nūr-ad-Dīn 56-58
   Summoned to Damascus by discomfited Damascene emirs 60
   Declares war on Aleppo 61
   Installs Turan-Shāh as governor of Damascus 64
   Battle of Ramla 83-84
   Battle of Banyas 86-87
   Captures and destroys fortress of Jacob's Ford 87
   Grants truce to Baldwin IV 93
   Raids County of Tripoli 93
   Concludes treaty with Raymond III 93
   Gains peace with Byzantium 103-04
   Seizes and imprisons Christian pilgrims 105
   Ends truce with Baldwin IV 105

Saladin (*continued*)
   Advances on Damascus 105-06
   Invests Beirut 107
   Campaigns against Moslem opponents 107-08
   Captures Aleppo 109
   Invests Krak 116-17
   Grants government of Aleppo to al-ᶜĀdil 128
   Grants truce to Raymond III 146
   Quashes plots engineered by ᶜIzz ad-Dīn 147-48
   Creates alliance with Byzantines 152-53
   Rôle in campaign and battle of Hattin 156-60
   Post-Hattin conquests 164-69
   Siege and capture of Jerusalem 170-74
   Unsuccessful siege of Tyre 178-79
   Rôle in defense of Acre 184-193

aṣ-Ṣāliḥ, son of Nūr-ad-Dīn
   Pawn in struggle between Damascene and Aleppan leaders 59-60
   Dies 108

Sevar
   Lieutenant of Zengi 9

Shams-al-Mulūk Ismāᶜīl, atabeg of Damascus
   Opposed by Zengi and Sevar 9

Shavar, Egyptian emir
   Defeated in contest with rival emir, Dîrgam 48
   Assassinated 53

Shihāb-ad-Dīn Maḥmūd, atabeg of Damascus
   Opposed by Zengi and Sevar 9

Shīrkūh, emir of Nūr-ad-Dīn
   Marches on Damascus 42
   Urges Nūr-ad-Dīn to accept Shavar's bid 48
   First invasion of Egypt 49
   Second invasion of Egypt 51-52
   Effects Shavar's assassination 53
   Dies 53

Sibyl
   Daughter of Countess Agnes and Amalric 31
   Marries William Longsword 80
   Marries Guy of Lusignan 88
   Receives fiefs from Countess Agnes 132
   Sells fiefs to Joscelyn III 132
   Crowned queen and selects Guy of Lusignan as king 137
   Receives submission of Humphrey IV 141
   Receives homage of Raymond III 155
   Death 189

Stephanie
   Mother of Humphrey IV 91
   Wife of Reginald of Châtillon 91

T

Tāj-al-Mulūk Böri, atabeg of Damascus
   Opposed by Zengi and Sevar 9

Taqī-ad-Dīn ᶜUmar, nephew of Saladin
   Entrusted with Egypt by Saladin 128
   Invests Krak 128-29
   Receives surrender of Acre 164
   Rôle in defense of Acre 185-87

Timurtash, Artukid ruler of Mardin
   Participates in total conquest of County of Edessa 26

Ṭoros, Armenian prince
   Rôle in battle of Ḥārim 32-33
   Surrenders to Manuel 45
   Drives Constance into exile 67
   Places Bohemond III on throne of Antioch 67

Turan-Shāh, brother of Saladin
   Installed as governor of Damascus by Saladin 64

U

Unur, Moslem ruler of Damascus
   Opposed by Zengi and Sevar 9
   Aids Raymond II, Count of Tripoli 15
   Involved in war with Baldwin III and Melisend 40
   Grants peace treaty to southern Franks 40-41

V

W

Walter of Caesarea
   Participates in Ṣaffūrīyah campaign 114-15

Walter, prince of Galilee
   First husband of Eschiva 72

William, archbishop of Tyre
  Opposes selection of Heraclius as new patriarch of Jerusalem 90

X

Y

Z

Zengi, Moslem leader
  Entrusted with function of commissioner of Iraq and the principalities of Mosul and Aleppo 3
  Invades County of Edessa 5
  Captures city of Edessa and Sarūj 6
  Abandons siege of Bira 7
  Besieges Qalᶜat Jaᶜbar 10
  Assassinated 10